Europe, 2013

Barents Sea

ICELAND

Norwegian Sea

Faroe Islands (Den.)

Shetland Islands. (U.K.)

ATLANTIC OCEAN

North Sea

NORWAY

SWEDEN

FINLAND

Baltic Sea

ESTONIA

LATVIA

LITHUANIA

RUSSIA

RUSSIA

IRELAND

UNITED KINGDOM

DENMARK

NETH.

BELG.

GERMANY

LUX.

POLAND

BELARUS

UKRAINE

Channel Islands. (U.K.)

Bay of Biscay

FRANCE

SWITZ.

LI.

CZECH REP.

SLOVAKIA

AUSTRIA

HUNGARY

MOLDOVA

SLOV.

CROATIA

ROMANIA

S.M.

BOSNIA

SERBIA

PORTUGAL

SPAIN

ANDORRA

MON.

Corsica

ITALY

Adriatic Sea

M.

K.

MAC.

ALB.

BULGARIA

Black Sea

Balearic Islands

Sardinia

GREECE

TURKEY

Mediterranean

Sicily

MALTA

Crete

Rhodes

N. CYPRUS

SYRIA

CYPRUS

LEBANON

ISRAEL

MOROCCO

ALGERIA

TUNISIA

Sea

JORDAN

LIBYA

EGYPT

Country Abbreviations:
Alb. = Albania
Belg. = Belgium
K. = Kosovo
Li. = Liechtenstein
Lux. = Luxembourg
M. = Montenegro

Mac. = Macedonia
Mon. = Monaco
Neth. = Netherlands
Slov. = Slovenia
S.M. = San Marino
Switz. = Switzerland

0   500 Miles

European Union members

A Patriot's History®
of the
Modern World, Vol. II

ALSO BY LARRY SCHWEIKART

Seven Events That Made America America

48 Liberal Lies About American History

A Patriot's History of the United States (with Michael Allen)

What Would the Founders Say?

You Keep Me Hangin' On (with Mark Stein)

ALSO BY LARRY SCHWEIKART
AND DAVE DOUGHERTY

A Patriot's History of the Modern World, Vol. I

The Patriot's History Reader

A Patriot's History®
of the
Modern World, Vol. II

From the Cold War to the
Age of Entitlement: 1945–2012

Larry Schweikart and Dave Dougherty

SENTINEL

SENTINEL
Published by the Penguin Group
Penguin Group (USA) LLC
375 Hudson Street
New York, New York 10014

USA | Canada | UK | Ireland | Australia | New Zealand | India | South Africa | China
penguin.com
A Penguin Random House Company

First published by Sentinel, a member of Penguin Group (USA) LLC, 2013

Map illustrations by Philip Schwartzberg, Meridian Mapping, Minneapolis

Library of Congress Cataloging-in-Publication Data

Schweikart, Larry.
A patriot's history of the modern world / Larry Schweikart and Dave Dougherty.
v. cm.
Includes bibliographical references and index.
Contents: [v. 1.] From America's exceptional ascent to the atomic bomb : 1898–1945
ISBN 978-1-59523-089-8
Contents: [v. 2.] From the cold war to the age of entitlement: 1945–2012
ISBN 978-1-59523-104-8
1. United States—History—20th century. 2. United States—History—21st century. 3. United States—Foreign relations. 4. United States—Influence. I. Dougherty, Dave, 1939– II. Title.
E741.S247 2012
973.91—dc23

                          2012027033

Printed in the United States of America
10 9 8 7 6 5 4 3 2 1

Set in Janson Text Lt Std
Designed by Spring Hoteling

To Eunice May Schweikart Chandler (1919–2013),
who adopted me, then treated me as her own.

CONTENTS

INTRODUCTION

It could have been a postwar American town or the Farmer's Market in Los Angeles. Busy streets served as the setting for a bustling vegetable market, teeming with customers, awash in produce—a rich bounty spread out over hundreds of stands. As far as one could see, makeshift shops in the open air stretched down the street—in post–World War II Romania. Communism, in the early 1950s, still had not gained total control of the Romanian market, and farmers came from the countryside to sell their goods. A young Romanian, Gabriel Bohm, walked through the marketplace with his mother in awe of the cornucopia of fruits and vegetables, displayed under homemade tents or on crates by ordinary farmers. Bohm remembered seeing a market "full of merchandise . . . good looking, healthy stuff." Yet within twenty years, Bohm witnessed a dramatic change. The same scene in 1965 would be much different: empty streets, devoid of vendors, patrolled by police. "Those markets were deserted," he recalled years later: "not a single carrot, not a single vendor selling a carrot."

There were other changes as well, ending many of the mainstays of life. Churches were closed, political gatherings banned. What had happened in the interim to Bohm and other Romanians? Communism took full control of the economy. "We saw the country deteriorate," he noted. "Anyone who could get out would. You had to be brain dead not to get out."[1] Yet they could not get out. Nor could their neighbors in Bulgaria, Hungary, Poland, or East Germany, all of them trapped as prisoners of the Soviet Union, which since 1945 had embarked on a program of expansionism dictated by Soviet communism's godfather, Vladimir Lenin. Nor were the scenes of want and desperation in those Communist-controlled countries different in any of the other Eastern European nations that could be observed—Hungary, Bulgaria, Poland—and often they were worse.

East Germans lived in constant fear of the Stasi, the state's secret police, which recruited informants and compiled dossiers on almost every citizen to crush any potential opposition to the state. Even so much as an anti-Communist cartoon or joke was sufficient grounds for jail. One East Berliner who escaped to West Germany discovered decades later, after communism's collapse, that one of her best friends had informed on her to the Stasi. Everywhere in the Iron Curtain countries (as they were labeled by Winston Churchill in 1946), the state spied on average citizens. Even children were tricked into informing on parents. Bulgarians knew that people simply disappeared—but they did not know that a secret prison island, kept off official maps, was their ultimate destination.

An atmosphere of discontent and fear permeated the Communist bloc. After a time, the fear and depression produced a numbing absence of vitality. Western visitors to Eastern Europe at this time all came back with the same impression of the visual images that awaited them there: "gray," "it was grime, gray," "all gray," they said.[2] Millions of people were prisoners in their own countries, unable to leave and usually afraid to resist.

A stunning contrast could be seen, literally, across borders where Western European nations thrived after 1945. Even Germany, crushed into rubble, with up to 10 percent of its 1939 population killed or wounded in the war, staged an astonishing revival after VE Day.[3] The success could be attributed to the massive humanitarian and economic assistance provided by the United States, the adoption (even in quasi-socialist countries such as France, Italy, and Greece) of markets and price mechanisms, and the determination of Europeans themselves to recover from war yet again.

But Western Europe would soon drift into a lethargy of planned economies at the very time that a cold war was being waged to free Eastern Europe from those very ideas. By the time the Berlin Wall fell in 1989, the West had lost or deliberately given up many of the freedoms that the East had sought and just gained. And within another decade still, the advent of the European Union would subtly and quietly impose controls on ordinary life that, while wrapped in a velvet glove, felt to some like the iron fist they had resisted.

Worse still, Europe was not alone. From 1945 to 1970, virtually all of the then-labeled Third World, including Africa, Asia, and Latin America, embraced state planning and rejected markets. Many of the European colonies (Uganda, Congo, Rwanda), winning their freedom in the postwar division of the world, immediately put dictators in power who squelched talk of republics and democracy. By the 1970s, postwar optimism had been replaced by widespread anger and desperation, with one set of masters exchanged for another.

None of this was supposed to have happened. Just as in the post–World War I era, the end of war was to have meant a golden age of freedom and equality. Unlike after World War I, however, this time there was little doubt in non-Communist countries that the United States was in charge of the postwar world. Emerging from the war with its homeland and domestic industries not only entirely intact, but cranked up to full production, American productivity exceeded the wildest expectations of the Truman administration. Racing to shore up Europe from 1947 to 1950, the United States introduced the Marshall Plan, aiding war-torn Europe without asking for anything in return. Understanding the Soviet threat to the rest of Europe, America created a new alliance system and took virtually all of the major Western European nations under its protection.

As much as America was to be the leader and role model in this new era, all the efforts of U.S. occupation forces and all the money delivered by foreign aid could not address the fundamental weakness of postwar development efforts. The salient point of the post–World War II period was that by 1957 no nation had adopted the four pillars that made American exceptionalism successful in the first place. As developed in the first volume of this history, those pillars consisted of a Christian (mostly Protestant) religious foundation, free enterprise, common law, and private property with titles and deeds. Missing even in postwar Europe, these features were almost totally unknown throughout the rest of the world. Long-established nations such as France and Italy seemed little different from emerging states such as Uganda or Cameroon, or the reconstructed countries of Germany or Japan.

Thus, another thirty years later—by 2000—the promise of global liberty that appeared so imminent in 1946 seemed to have slipped away to a significant degree almost everywhere. Drone spy technology monitored the movements of ordinary citizens; big-city mayors banned not only guns, but also soft drinks and fats and plastic bags; European cities saw "no-go" zones of Muslims abolish Western law and replace it with Sharia; countries published lists of children's names that were permitted and not permitted; street preaching was banned, and pastors jailed for speaking the Gospel aloud in churches. That these liberty-limiting developments occurred in African or Asian nations hardly raised an eyebrow—so far had many of those countries fallen after 1945—but that they all occurred in the United States or Europe seemed a shocking and stunning reversal of the very reasons the "Good War" had been fought in the first place.

Why had this subtle but dangerous reversal occurred so rapidly and so unexpectedly (to some)? Indeed, what were "democracies" doing engaging in such practices at all? In fact, all along the promise of postwar liberty itself was illusory, constructed on the premise that most of the world would be rebuilt along the lines of American-style democracy and freedoms. Our argument is that without the four pillars of American exceptionalism, such developments were not only likely, they were inevitable. Moreover, we argue that Europeans' use of terms such as "democracy," "republic," and even "liberty" were not the same as those understood by Americans, and therefore other nations never entertained any intention of adopting the American pillars. In our previous volume of *A Patriot's History of the Modern World: From America's Exceptional Ascent to the Atomic Bomb*, we reviewed the impact of common law, a Christian (mostly Protestant) religious culture, access to private property (including ownership with easy acquisition of deeds and titles), and free-market capitalism, which brought America to the forefront of world power by the end of the war. Instead of copying American success, victorious or liberated nations more often sought only to dip their toes in the water of freedom, adopting free markets without common law or restricting capitalism, permitting Christian religion but steadily edging away from acknowledging the Christian foundations of society, paying lip service to private property without instituting the land-ownership institutions, such as titles and deeds, that are necessary to make it a reality. More often still, nations ignored all four of the pillars. Thus, the American model was only implemented piecemeal, where implemented at all (South Korea, for example). As we pointed out in volume 1, while any one of the pillars might be beneficial to a society, without all four no true American-style republic could be developed. The pillars were simply mutually dependent.

This volume continues the story of America's rise to world dominance through three themes. First, we trace the battle that began early in the twentieth century between the Progressives and the Constitutionalists. The former, grounded in the "reform" movement of the late 1800s, sought to perfect man and society by a process of government-directed and controlled change. The Progressives wanted to deemphasize the Constitution as it was written, and with it, American exceptionalism. They conducted a century-long assault on the notion that the United States had any providential founding, that its heroes and heroines were particularly wise, just, or courageous. By insisting that laws needed to be continually reassessed in light of current morality, Progressives saw the Constitution as outdated or irrelevant. Constitutionalists, on the other hand, maintained that America's founding stemmed from her Christian roots, and that the Declaration of Independence and Constitution were representative of common law doctrines in which codes of conduct, given by God to the people, bubbled up, supported and promoted by the people (as opposed to being handed to a king or ruler to be dispensed downward). Moreover, Constitutionalists maintained that the Founding Fathers were, in fact, wise and visionary, and that they established a framework of laws that addressed every eventuality. Progressives enacted a legislative campaign to regulate markets, redistribute wealth, and limit private property ownership. Constitutionalists wanted to free markets, enable all to pursue wealth, and restrain government's ability to infringe upon individuals' property rights. Finally, the Progressives—many of whom, in the early stages of the movement, were nominal Christians—fervently labored to remove Christianity from the public square, from all political discourse, and from entertainment. Indeed, Christianity stood in the way of implementing most of their reforms. Constitutionalists, of course, understood the admonitions of the Founders, who urged that the nation adhere to its Christian roots and above all pursue virtue.

Over the course of the second half of the twentieth century and the first decade of the next, American exceptionalism faced hostility abroad, but more surprisingly, antipathy by numerous groups at home. The Progressive Left endeavored through the educational system, the law, and entertainment to denigrate and ridicule the very concept that America had anything special to offer, and to insist that the United States had become just one nation among many. That a number of Western and non-Western powers arose to challenge American dominance was to be expected, particularly when the American public had so generously provided the financial and commercial means of their recovery in many cases. Germany and Japan took the best of the American industrial, manufacturing, and management practices, modified them, and implemented them with zeal, producing world-class automobiles, electronics, robotics, and a host of other products that drove American goods either fully or partially from the market. Once several nations could claim economic proximity to the United States (though none could claim parity), were not their systems, goals, practices, and cultures worthy of emulation as well? But the Progressive assault did not stop there: it insisted that undeveloped cultures were no worse than ours, only different. Americans were urged to seek out the value in what in previous generations would have been termed "backward" cultures, and to "understand" practices once deemed undesirable at best or barbaric at worse. President Barack Obama's 2009 Cairo speech, as one example, cited advances and greatness in Islamic culture that never existed, implying that Americans needed to be more like Egypt rather than Egyptians being more like Americans.[4] Absurdly saying that "Islam has always been a part of America's story," Obama claimed that Islam "pav[ed] the way for Europe's Renaissance" and gave us "cherished music," the "magnetic compass and tools of navigation," and furthered "our understanding of how disease spreads and how it can be healed."[5] Although his intention may have been to strike new chords of friendship, the act of ascribing to people accomplishments they never achieved looked phony and, according to polls in the subsequent three years, had no effect on Muslim views of America.

By 2012, the culmination of this Progressive march saw the United States elect a president with little or no understanding of free market capitalism, no appreciation of private property rights, little demonstrable Christian religious influence (to the point that by 2012 polls showed that up to half of the American public thought he was a Muslim), and an apparent disdain for American exceptionalism. Barack Obama repeatedly apologized to foreign nations for past American "mistakes" or transgressions and denigrated (or greatly mischaracterized) American exceptionalism by insisting that "the Brits believe in British exceptionalism and the Greeks believe in Greek exceptionalism." As the British magazine *The Economist* stated, Americans had put into power "a left-wing president who has regulated to death a private sector he neither likes nor understands. . . ."[6] In 2008, in his famous "Joe the Plumber" comment, Obama stated that it was government's duty to "spread the wealth around," and in 2012, referring to private businesses that had become successful, he said, "You didn't build that [business]. . . . Somebody else made that happen." That "somebody else" was, of course, government—not the private sector. Comments such as those showed Obama had no concept of what made markets work. Likewise, in his bailout of General Motors, he demonstrated that he had no regard for private property—in that case, the property of the bondholders who were saddled with an enormous loss to protect union pensions.

Obama's national health care law forced the Catholic Church to compromise on its core religious beliefs regarding conception. His Supreme Court appointments routinely interpreted the American Constitution in the light of international law. And when it came to private property, Obama continued to implement the United Nations' antigrowth/anticapitalist Agenda 21 initiatives, which were inserting themselves into all aspects of American life.

Of course, some of the erosion had already occurred. Fearing Islamic terrorists, after 9/11 Americans readily assented to substantial limitations on their freedoms, from airport body searches to cameras on stoplights. Once necessary Patriot Act precautions had grossly expanded with new computerized surveillance and monitoring technologies, including "latch-on" phone tapping, air drone camera planes, and listening devices, to the point that virtually anyone could be found by the national government. Benjamin Franklin's comment, "They who can give up essential liberty to obtain a little temporary safety, deserve neither liberty nor safety," looked more prescient all the time. Worse still, by 2012, few politicians anywhere were seeking to limit such powers, let alone roll them back.

The exceptionalism that had saved the world had not met a receptive audience, even if at first the rhetoric and spirit were wildly embraced. Quite the contrary, it seemed that to some extent, Europe insisted on revisiting post–World War I practices yet again, and certainly in the former colonies the delusion of creating new "democratic" states without at least some of the pillars of American exceptionalism proved especially vexing. Yet the record of such efforts seemed abundantly clear by 1946. Europeans, after all, had witnessed the full-blown collapse of their societies not once in the first half of the twentieth century but twice. They had likewise seen the manifest failure and folly of both variations of socialism—fascism and communism.

From 1917 to 1989, neither outright government ownership under Soviet-style communism nor ownership-by-proxy through German/Italian fascism provided material prosperity or human dignity. Indeed, both heaped unparalleled inhumanity on top of astronomical levels of state-sanctioned killing. According to R. J. Rummel, perhaps the leading authority on government murder, the top governments in terms of democide (the murder of a person or people by a government including genocide, politicide, mass murder, and deaths arising from the reckless and depraved disregard for life, but excluding abortion deaths and battle deaths in war) from 1900 through 1987 were:

Country	Deaths	Years	Type of Government
Soviet Union	61,911,000	1917–1987	Communist
Communist China (PRC)	35,236,000	1949–1987	Communist
Nazi Germany	20,946,000	1933–1945	Fascist
Nationalist China	10,214,000	1928–1949	Militaristic/ Fascist
Imperial Japan	5,964,000	1936–1945	Militaristic/ Fascist
China (Mao's Soviets)	3,466,000	1923–1949	Communist
Khmer Rouge Cambodia	2,035,000	1975–1979	Communist
Turkey (Young Turks)	1,883,000	1909–1918	Militaristic
Vietnam	1,670,000	1945–1987	Communist
North Korea	1,663,000	1948–1987	Communist
Poland	1,585,000	1945–1948	Communist
Pakistan	1,503,000	1958–1987	Authoritarian
Mexico	1,417,000	1900–1920	Authoritarian
Communist Yugoslavia	1,072,000	1944–1987	Communist
Czarist Russia	1,066,000	1900–1917	Authoritarian
China (Warlords)	910,000	1917–1949	Authoritarian

Country	Deaths	Years	Type of Government
Turkey (Atatürk)	878,000	1919–1923	Authoritarian
United Kingdom	816,000	1900–1987	Democracy
Portugal	741,000	1926–1982	Authoritarian
Indonesia	729,000	1965–1987	Authoritarian[7]

The only democracy on the list, Great Britain, attained its numbers only during the course of World War I and World War II through the economic blockade of the Central Powers and bombing of German cities. Even Rummel's chart is somewhat misleading, however, in that if one looks at democide as a percentage of a country's total population, still other non-democratic regimes top the list, including Cambodia under Pol Pot, Turkey under Kemal Atatürk, Yugoslavia, Czechoslovakia, Mexico, Uganda, Romania, and Mongolia.

It is a mockery of honest statistics to claim that the United States by these measures is in any way a "violent nation" (6,000 deaths from intergroup or collective violence from 1900 to 1987), and its residence at nearly the bottom of Rummel's list reflected the fact that by this standard alone, America was truly exceptional. But the point stands that by far the most deadly ideological systems were the Communist, fascist, and authoritarian systems tested on multiple occasions by the Europeans and exported to their colonial cousins. A quite contrary point emerges, namely that only when the fundamental elements of the American foundation are applied can a nation routinely protect its citizens from such murder.

Europe's global failure to maintain peace, stability, and human rights over the course of over one hundred years—even with relatively free markets and democratic governments—points out the essential symbiosis of the American pillars. The United States of America had largely avoided anything approaching such carnage by government. She did so not because of any one of the four legs of exceptionalism, but because all four worked together. That began to change in the postwar era as Progressives accelerated their attacks on these pillars.

Their central target was America's Christian roots, and the Progressives had help from intellectuals, elites, and even the Supreme Court. After the war, pressure from humanism, statism, and communism pushed religion further into disfavor—especially among elites. John Dewey, the so-called father of American progressive education, had already penetrated the schools with a covert war on faith. His goal was nothing less than full secularization and humanization of American education. Then in 1947 the groundbreaking Supreme Court ruling in *Everson v. Board of Education of the Township of Ewing* seemed to separate religion from all government in all cases, effectively changing the First Amendment's intent from protecting religion from the government to protecting government from religion. Despite massive revival appeal by preachers such as Billy Graham in the 1950s and 1960s, media elites instituted a guerrilla campaign against religion, highlighted by the infamous 1966 *Time* magazine cover announcing "God Is Dead." Sheer numbers of people disproved such a silly assertion, of course, as evangelical church rolls continued to grow, but Christianity was already being successfully branded as a "crutch" for the uneducated, the rubes, and the slow-witted. Increasingly, Christians were made to feel out of touch and isolated, when in fact their faith remained the majority view. Depending on how one asked the question in a poll, between 60 and 90 percent of Americans still considered themselves Christian by 1970.

Television, although more slowly, soon added to the assault on religion. At first, television shows depicted generic ministers (with their collars) as genial problem solvers—as opposed to serious moral teachers—but by the mid-1970s clergy were increasingly portrayed as crooks or buffoons, or, even worse, as hypocrites. For the media, the church, ministers, and Christianity had ceased to exist except when a plot line needed a convenient villain or comedic foil. For example, a 2012 ABC show originally called *Good Christian Bitches* provoked such an uproar that ABC had to change the title to *Good Christian Belles*—but still advertised it with a blonde in a miniskirt choir robe. Movies such as *Monsignor* (1982), *Agnes of God* (1985), and any number of horror films portrayed clerics and nuns as depraved, conniving, or utterly powerless. (Hollywood did begin to change slightly after 2000, when a market for Christian and/or Christian-friendly films was demonstrated to be a sure money maker by Mel Gibson's *The Passion of the Christ* (2004) and by *Facing the Giants*, an extremely low-budget movie made essentially by amateurs from Sherwood Baptist Church in Albany, Georgia, and earning ten times its budget.)

But the ridicule had its effect on church attendance. By the late 1990s, in a desperate effort to recapture members and prove themselves relevant, American mainline Protestant churches underwent a revolution that saw them open coffee bars, establish date nights, provide sports leagues, and introduce modern music, all to little or no effect in raising total numbers. Quite the contrary; as the mainline Protestant denominations liberalized and adopted moral relativism, their believers fled to other churches, including the Catholic Church, that professed stricter doctrines and adherence to God's law and absolute moral teachings. Megachurches rose rapidly, their converts generally consisting of "churched" people who had stopped going to their original mainline denominational gathering. In 1900 Christians represented fully 96.4 percent of all Americans, and 46.1 percent were members of Protestant churches. In 2000, the numbers had fallen to 84.7 and 23.2 percent respectively. By 2025, it is expected to drop further to 80.3 and 21.2 percent.[8] However, evangelicals increased to 14.6 percent of the church membership by 2000, or 50 percent more than the mainline churches.

Of all the pillars of American exceptionalism, none would erode more during the time covered by this volume than the moral foundation provided by Christianity, and especially Protestant Christianity. But the steady debasement of American Christian morality and the underpinning of American democracy were not by-products of the Progressive agenda. They *were* the Progressive agenda. Moral relativism, as taught in American schools, universities, and recently, mainline Protestant churches, asserts that morality is not based on any absolute standard but depends on variables such as individual feelings, backgrounds, culture, specific situations, polls, and various opinions. "Truth" itself is relative depending on one's viewpoint. This can best be seen in generational attitudes toward marriage between homosexuals. In a Pew Research poll in 2012, only 36 percent of Americans born before 1946 favored same-sex marriage, but those born after 1980 favored it by 63 percent.[9] Similarly, most churches have all but given up on the issue of divorce, and quietly seek to manage it rather than prevent it. And the Catholic Church, despite remaining firm in its opposition to artificial birth control, seems to have fought a losing battle. By 2011, almost 70 percent of Catholic women used some form of birth control.[10]

While much of Europe (and the rest of the world) was not Protestant, the Catholic Church might have substituted as one of the pillars outside America. But Catholicism suffered from other problems than its positions on social issues. Worldwide it had been late coming to the table of republicanism and the Church had been on the wrong side in the Dreyfus affair in

France. Not until the 1920s did the Vatican finally permit Italian Catholics to form a political party and take an active part in the pseudo-democratic government. The Vatican had supported the Nationalist/anti-Republican forces in the Spanish Civil War, then the Third Reich because of its opposition to communism, losing substantial credibility as a bastion against evil. By the end of World War II, then, the Catholic Church—along with many of the German Protestant churches—had ceded any moral authority it had when the century began.

By 1946, most emerging nations had absorbed the ideological structures and religious attitudes that had failed their former colonial masters simply because that's what they had been taught. India, for example, warmly embraced Keynesian state planning; Egypt adopted a variant of state socialism; and one African nation after another imposed high levels of government regulation on top of considerable degrees of outright state ownership of the "commanding heights" of industry. Virtually none—not even prostrate Japan—tried to recreate the American experience or erect the four pillars of exceptionalism. Where adopting Protestant Christianity might have proved impossible, a religion that could not be easily manipulated by the state, as Shinto was by the Japanese in the 1930s, proved the second best option. Nevertheless, when evaluating their situation at the end of World War II, Japan and most newly decolonized states did not even consider examining Christian principles as possibly being an important element in their future recovery. Christian missionaries had made little headway in Japan, with its strongly Shinto and Buddhist population, and after 1932, Shintoism was melded with the state and any other religion discouraged by the government. Japan and other (at the time) Third World nations thereby also cavalierly ignored common law in that they had no history of government emanating from the people and, without Christianity, no religious structure that would encourage democracy. Likewise, outside of Europe, private property ownership tied to deeds and legal documents was rare, mainly due to the long-standing traditions of personal honor that obviated the (apparent) need for such paperwork. While Japan managed a miraculous recovery and implemented a democratic political system, weaknesses stemming from the missing exceptional elements soon brought Japan's rapid rise to a halt, cresting in the late 1980s. Japan's decline started immediately thereafter, producing two decades of stagnation and the onset of a national malaise.

Indeed, Christianity worked hand-in-glove with free markets, and while capitalism and commerce certainly were not impossible without

Christianity, the absence of the religion tended to result in commerce that was heavily regulated by government, as government picked and chose industries and corporations to receive support. Europeans, of course, still worked and innovated, but from about 1970 through 2000, excluding the Communist states, the European continent did not add a single net new job while the United States added more than 20 million net new jobs.[11] Even after a short setback with the dot-com bust, then after suffering through the economic impact of the 9/11 terrorist attacks, the American economy revived to produce an additional 6 million jobs under George W. Bush before the 2007 mortgage industry collapse. Meanwhile, the average workweek in Europe continued to decline and deficits mounted; by 2010, many members of the European Union teetered on bankruptcy, relying solely on the strength of Germany and its loans to keep them afloat. All Europe seemed to assume that German war guilt for World War II would provide for the citizens of the victimized nations what they could not provide for themselves. But sixty-five years was a long time, and by 2010, Germans were clamoring for France and the other nations to assume some responsibility for their own welfare. Greece, Spain, Ireland, Portugal, and Italy all faced unsustainable debt levels due to their social welfare policies. France was little better off, and the 2012 elections in France even installed a socialist prime minister who lowered the retirement age. All of this reduced the incentive for individuals to care for themselves and their families, and replaced both God and the family with the state. Virtually every aspect of life—from child-care subsidies to education grants to housing vouchers to retirement—were all provided (poorly) by government.

Without common law—which was lost by the few European states that ever had it—and without limits on what private property governments could seize, the European free market became increasingly more restricted between 1945 and 2012. China, in contrast, moved in the other direction. She saw her weaknesses under communism exposed by tiny Hong Kong, to the point that even before the Cultural Revolution, Deng Xiaoping pragmatically had tried to meld capitalism and a Marxist political system, noting, "It doesn't matter whether a cat is white or black, as long as it catches mice." With this admission that China would permit a price system to operate "as long as it caught mice," communism in its pure state was doomed in China. Instead of fully adopting all the American pillars, however, China floundered with a mixed economy moving in the direction of state capitalism, lacking common law and a free political system.

Yet China had one advantage that even Japan and Europe lacked: her

Protestant Christian population was rapidly growing, providing a basis for a movement that could, conceivably, transform China from the inside in the decades to come. Indeed, in sheer numbers China had become one of the larger Christian countries, with more than 89 million Christians in 2000.[12] That number represented an increase from 1.7 million in 1900, and is expected to reach more than 135 million by 2025 (though as a percentage of its population, Christianity remains a minority). Did that mean that China was the world's next superpower? Not at all, for the absence of common law and private ownership of property meant that China—like Europe—would struggle with the political aspects of liberty and be fundamentally unable to hear the voice of the people when they spoke.

Liberty continued to be advanced in China and everywhere else by the continued application of some of the American pillars, despite Europe's slow retreat from them. The pressure from the productive power of the American economy opened otherwise closed societies to a willingness to examine American values. For forty-five years after World War II, the American invention/innovation machine had produced a level of wealth and prosperity unseen before in human history. This technological stampede culminated in the early twenty-first century with a communications revolution exceeding that of Gutenberg's printing press. Much more than the effect of the printing press in the 1400s, the new telecommunications explosion mitigated the ability of any society to restrict freedoms. While still not powerful enough to entirely prevent such abuses, the communications technology often transmitted the news (and video) of government oppression instantaneously. At worst, this could embarrass the violator, and at best, so publicize abuses that restrictions were lifted or individuals permitted to leave their abusive country. Footage of Tiananmen Square, with its lone protester standing defiantly in front of a tank, did not bring about instantaneous change, but over time was a contributory factor in China's (still wanting) liberalization.

But technology and the rise of electronic entertainment also had other, less desirable effects on the modern world, fracturing the social fabric by, ironically, reducing genuine communication between people. Cell phones, personal computers, and the rise of social network Web sites such as Facebook and Myspace dramatically reduced the membership not only in churches, but in virtually all social organizations. In America, this meant a dwindling membership in such organizations as the Elks, Kiwanis, Rotary, Eastern Star, Masons, and Shriners, as well as dealing a severe blow to group activities such as bowling, picnics, and parades.

Elsewhere, in Japan and Korea, for example, young adults either fully embraced the communication and entertainment revolutions—with their demand for products literally driving much of the new market—or, in some cases, completely withdrew from society in unique and troubling new ways. But whether in an American shopping mall or a Tokyo street or a Dutch coffeehouse, particularly after the advent of cellular telephones and texting, it was not unusual to see a gathering of several teens or even adults where not one but all would be engaged in some communication with someone elsewhere, and none talking with those immediately present. For American nuclear and extended families, this shattered their cohesion. For Asians, with their strong (but weakening) structures of familial honor, the youth retreated inward, convinced that their futures were dim. Such trends were not true of all, of course, but were increasingly common as the fracturing of social bonds gained momentum and the realities of decaying economies set in. A somewhat odder circumstance developed in Europe, where parents reported spending more time with their children, but not always for positive reasons. Studies of European teens—whose family divorce rate had doubled since the 1970s—found anxiety and depression had increased 100 percent from thirty years earlier, although that rate hit a plateau in 2004. Those same European teens shifted heavily from work to education, with work levels falling by half since the 1980s and the number of youth in education more than doubling. Essentially, European young people quit working and began to mill about colleges and universities.[13] But, like Americans, European young people seldom participated in organizations (only 20 percent according to one study), and movie attendance was more popular in Europe than in America (82 percent of European young people routinely went to movies).[14] Families saw their cohesion shattered as conversation in households disappeared and family members each went their own ways as ready access to the outside world and its influences opened up.

This atomization became readily seen in not only communications but also television viewing (with its hundreds of channels), music listening (with *USA Today* compiling no fewer than a half dozen different "top 40s"), and publishing (with *The New York Times* featuring a dozen bestseller lists, by genre). In short, the wealth and prosperity of the United States in the postwar years had resulted in the shattering of community—sometimes for the good (no one doubts that social nosiness was a problem in previous decades), but usually for the worse. This was especially true with the American white middle class, where American sociologist Charles Murray noted that the number one television show in 1963–64 was *The Beverly Hillbillies* with a Nielsen share of 39.1 percent, meaning that almost 40 percent of all American TV viewers watched the show. (In contrast, the number one show in the United States in 2004 was *American Idol*, whose Nielsen share was less than one third that!) The demise of such shared cultural touchstones could not be underestimated.

A similar diversification occurred with news, which at one time had played a role of uniting people around a few daily event narratives, usually nonpoliticized. By the 1970s, however, the major networks and large city newspapers, plus major magazines such as *Time* and *Newsweek*, had tilted decidedly to the left and had politicized everything from proper diets to the weather. Their tilt would continue steadily, until they were virtually horizontal, and little more than mouthpieces for Progressive politicians by the turn of the century. In response, numerous alternative media began to arise, and became exceedingly popular—talk radio, alternative newspapers, then later, Internet sources such as the Drudge Report and the new television network Fox News. Once the major media conglomerates lost their monopoly power as alternative news media and other news sources became widely available to everyone, a new competition for news arose that hadn't been seen in the United States since before the Civil War.

Variety was a good thing, but it came at a steep price, for the youth—now hearing from both sides that the other was always wrong—reverted to cynicism and detachment from the political process. In addition, much of the information available on the Internet was simply incorrect, whether by design or ignorance, but it often masqueraded as "news." Given the blurring of traditional news into political opinion, it became increasingly difficult to rely on either as an ultimate source of facts. Misinformation was rampant and spread rapidly. (For example, in an analysis made by one of the authors in 2010, more than sixty sites, including blogs, stated that Thomas Jefferson had used the phrase "wall of separation" between church and state twice. In fact, only three debunked the second citation—showing Jefferson's letter to Virginia Baptists in 1808 having the phrase added later by editor Eyler Coates in a lead-in paragraph to his discussion of Jefferson and freedom of religion.[15]) At the same time, however, the penetration of Western, and especially American, news and media into virtually all of the world became a force for opening closed societies to an alternative view that oppressive governments found nearly impossible to stop.

Yet instead of spreading American exceptionalism—and a road map for nations still struggling to succeed materially and culturally—the new message of unfettered freedom and sexual liberation was the one often seen and heard by other countries. They failed to appreciate the three hundred years of training and discipline in individual liberty that came through property ownership and common law, which (like religion) stood as barriers to tyranny and constrained individual excesses. In the United States, state and local governments, each of which had delineated powers and as late as 2012 still retained considerable autonomy (U.S. states actually retained more sovereignty that nations in the European Union), frequently prevented abuses by the national government. Intervening cultural, social, religious, and political barriers to tyranny (including states' rights and federalism) served as a powerful—but increasingly diminishing—buffer to the highly centralized state. Where were such barriers in other societies? Some of Africa, still dominated by tribalism, found that the tribes merely grafted themselves onto the state and manipulated it. Otherwise, where were any intermediary or intervening institutions in China? Iran? Or even most states within the European Union? Instead of observing American success and letting it serve as a beacon, most states had steadily moved toward greater centralization, observing fewer individual rights and eroding the power of nongovernmental institutions such as family and church.

It was the American pillar of common law that had manifested the other three pillars in the political world. Through the evolution of common law, American politics had developed over more than two centuries a unique electoral system that mitigated against tyranny and extremism—but which no one else adopted. First, the electoral college itself demands that every four years presidential candidates must address the issues of the heartland with some degree of seriousness. No candidate can write off the swath of states that runs from Ohio through Missouri to Nevada. In the 2000 election, these were called "red" states (for Republicans, versus "blue" states for Democrats, which hugged the coasts). Europe has no such electoral protection for the large majority of its nonelites. Second, the common law that undergirds the entire U.S. structure assumes that all the people are imbued with a sense of political understanding and are the source of all power, as exemplified by the Arkansas state motto, "The People Rule." The U.S. Constitution begins with "We the People" whereas, for example, the Treaty of Lisbon, looked upon as the constitution of the European Union, begins, "His Majesty the King of the Belgians, The President of the Republic of Bulgaria . . ." Of course, the rise of the so-called low-information voter and citizen apathy challenges this notion that the population as a whole features a solid sense of political understanding.

Third, American politics since the 1820s has accepted the "winner-

take-all/single-member-district" system, whereby the majority vote winner
in a district carries the entire district. There is no proportional representation.[16] Fringe groups must be absorbed into one of the two mainstream
parties, or risk being as irrelevant as the Libertarian Party or the Communist Party of the United States. While sometimes large numbers of a splin-
ter group, such as the Populists in the late 1800s or the Tea Party movement
in 2010, can have a significant impact on a major party's platform and
agenda, standing on its own, a third party has little chance of surviving.
Europe, and virtually the rest of the world's democracies (including Israel),
has embraced proportional representation with its concomitant demand of
appeasing each subgroup through coalitions. It was the requirement to
form coalitions that doomed Spain to civil war in 1936 (there were twenty-
one political parties represented in the Spanish Cortes) and enabled the rise
of Adolf Hitler in Germany. Instead of providing a more honest representation of the people, proportional representation has allowed governments
to duck and dodge difficult political issues even more than the U.S. Senate
and House, for one can always blame "the other guy" in another minority
party who will not unite. French coalitions fractured so instantaneously in
the 1950s that the nation went through twelve governments in ten years. In
the place of functioning legislatures, established and terrifically powerful
entrenched bureaucracies arose. Germany had long featured government
by bureaucracy (*Beamtentum*). The full extent of its ossification is perhaps
best exemplified by the bureaucrats hard at work in the Economic Ministry
in Berlin in April 1945. While they calculated the year's coal and steel production from Silesia (a province almost entirely occupied by the Red Army
the preceding month), the bureaucrats were interrupted by Soviet tanks on
the street below. So buried were they in red tape that they literally ignored
the real situation on the ground.

By 2000, all Europe had followed suit. Armies of faceless "public servants," often unionized, churned out regulations, dealt with appeals, saw
that garbage and taxes were collected, and delivered mail. Most of all, the
bureaucratic structure ensured that virtually no rapid change could occur
and that the public's role in any policies would be drastically minimized.
The assurance of uninterrupted daily services came at a price, sapping European will and energy by creating the illusion that government could meet
all needs. With the exception (at times) of Germany and Britain (under
Margaret Thatcher), Europe on the whole began to resemble the Ottoman
Empire in its death throes with its inability to act, and its utter incapacity
to act decisively.

From 1945 to 1989, the Soviet Union and its allies remained apart from these changes. If anything, the Communist bloc intensified the bureaucratization with its infamous nomenklatura that administered every element of life. There was even a Soviet "Ministry of Rock" to supervise rock and roll music. But during that forty-four year period, class divisions reasserted themselves as the nomenklatura began to look like Western-style CEOs with nicer homes, cars, and better privileges. Nikita Khrushchev, Stalin's successor, had liberalized the USSR only to a point, ending most of the genocide but replacing it with systematic institutionalization of political opponents in asylums. Well into the 1970s, the Soviet leadership believed it could not only fight, but win, a nuclear war with the United States—especially if the American president was weak enough to be bullied.

What forced the change at first was the free market: communism simply didn't work, and its structures began to disintegrate. Despite the appraisal by many Westerners that the Soviet economy was sound—and even accelerating—the truth was much different. Communism was failing to provide even the most basic goods, including food and toilet paper (much less cars), to average citizens. The "commanding heights" that Lenin sought to hold were themselves crumbling. What pushed the USSR over the edge was an alliance of Westerners—Margaret Thatcher, Ronald Reagan, and Pope John Paul II—who actively sought to bring an end to the "Evil Empire." Once it became official policy not to tolerate a Communist Russia, but to defeat it, the end came quickly.

Still, this did not result in the complete victory of American exceptionalism worldwide. Instead, by the last part of the twentieth century, the simultaneous deemphasis on American culture and power and the new emphasis on the "equality" of other nations resulted in horrific inaction. The Europeans (like American Progressives) stood aside meekly as Rwanda was wracked by murder and war in the 1990s, and barely lifted themselves off life support to resist Serbia in that decade. Even then, the Serbian intervention was primarily to placate the Muslim Middle East to ensure an uninterrupted supply of oil. While Britain and even France participated in the UN-sanctioned eviction of Saddam Hussein's Iraqi forces out of Kuwait in 1990–91, neither they nor any other Europeans would take the additional necessary steps of deposing him and searching the country for weapons of mass destruction. Meanwhile, Libya, under its dictator Muammar Gaddafi, quietly conducted its own WMD programs. Throughout the Middle East, Africa, and parts of Asia, ruthless "elected" thug-presidents, prime ministers, and monarchs crushed popular dissent, oppressed minority populations and women, pillaged natural resources, and defiantly ignored the international community whenever criticism was raised. While in the latter half of the twentieth century the United States would resist the Soviet Union aggressively, threats judged less immediate survived and metastasized. In one of the last instances of Westerners exerting power in their own interests without UN sanctions, votes, tribunals, committees, or support, the United States removed Manuel Noriega of Panama from power in 1989. No one offered assistance, despite the fact that France would convict him in absentia for murder and money laundering and confine him for fourteen months before extraditing him back to Panama in 2011.

Between the eviction of Noriega and the terror attacks on 9/11, one is hard pressed to find any instances of Westerners using old-fashioned power projection for national interests. Quite the contrary, the only nondomestic efforts of the European Union have been to reduce and restrain American military and political power worldwide; to use propaganda to denounce the notion of a superpower existing at all; and—with the help of China—to stage a relentless assault on the dollar as the world's reserve currency. This strategy, particularly the attack on the dollar, seemed successful in the 1980s when, briefly, Tokyo replaced New York as the world's leading financial center. China next mounted a challenge—still ongoing as of this writing—but already the Chinese economy has begun to founder, and financial experts question whether the "Chinese miracle" will be as illusory as the "Irish miracle" or the "Japanese miracle" of previous years.

China's current trend seems to again reaffirm our contention that no democratic system can succeed in modern times for long on both political and economic grounds without the four pillars of exceptionalism. It is no overblown claim to say that as of 2012 not one other nation in the world possessed the four pillars, and that the absence of common law—dictated to much of the world through the European civil law system—was as much to blame for the world's problems as trade fluctuations, energy prices, or terrorist threats. Indeed, a more appropriate way to view the twentieth and twenty-first centuries would be that it was because of the American ascendance, dominance, and influence, and its extension of significant elements of its four pillars to the rest of the world, that progress took place at all! This "Americocentric" view has been ridiculed and demagogued, but seldom seriously examined, let alone disproved. By 2012, the world's weaknesses stemmed substantially from the weakness and decline of the United States of America and the lack of faith by Progressives in its founding principles and pillars.

Making this campaign against American preeminence all the more perplexing is the fact that Europeans and free nations around the world since 1945 had enthusiastically welcomed an American military presence, willingly invited in American culture, and greedily pocketed American Marshall Plan funds when the Soviet Union constituted a genuine threat. During most of that time, criticisms were muted and usually accompanied by a "but-we're-glad-you're-here" sentiment. Once the Soviet threat evaporated, however, the Europeans—having profited for decades from extremely low defense budgets that allowed them to spend extravagantly on domestic programs—criticized Americans as too warlike, and insufficiently concerned with social welfare. Europe, having imposed on the world two of the most horrific wars in human history, now lectured the United States about human rights.

None of this posed a danger so long as American political and intellectual leadership remained, well, pro-American. But by the late twentieth century, the entertainment and music industry (to a large extent) and at least half of the political culture had come to see the United States as the source of the world's problems, not the solution. Of course, there never was such a thing as "Greek exceptionalism" or (for at least one hundred years) "British exceptionalism" as defined by the four pillars that characterize the American experiment. But the fact that a left-wing politician would fail to understand American exceptionalism shouldn't be surprising: historian Gordon Wood missed the target as well, writing that "our beliefs in liberty, equality, constitutionalism, and the well-being of ordinary people" gave Americans a special sense of destiny.[17] As usual, however, it was Alexis de Tocqueville in *Democracy in America* who came closer:

> Thus the Americans are in an exceptional situation, and it is unlikely that any other democratic people will be similarly placed. Their strictly Puritan origin; their exclusively commercial habits; even the country they inhabit, which seems to divert their minds from the study of science, literature, and the arts; the accessibility of Europe, which allows them to neglect these things without relapsing into barbarism . . . His desires, needs, education, and circumstances all seem united to draw the American's mind earthward. Only religion from time to time makes him turn a transient and distracted glance toward heaven. We should therefore give up looking at all democratic people through American spectacles and try at least to see them as they actually are.[18]

Tocqueville revealed his understanding of the American political system's unique structure and the free market that he saw everywhere. He also warned of the dangers to liberty that arose from the radical egalitarianism he sensed in the American character.

In a sense, then, the cold war provided the perfect object lesson in the value of America's ascent—pitting Christianity, law coming from the people, private property, and free markets against an enemy who accepted none of those principles. And, in a sense, it has been the demise of Soviet Russia that has loosed the shackles of self-restraint on the part of Progressives and other statists both at home and abroad. With no visible, obvious foreign threat (al-Qaeda, when it is mentioned at all, is dismissed as a group of religious radicals, not the spear point of a competing worldview), self-restraint has been replaced by self-loathing. Guilt and lack of conviction were natural results. American leadership no longer championed American exceptionalism, because by 2012 American leaders no longer believed in it. The mission that killed Osama bin Laden was heralded as essentially the end of the war on terror, with the West having never come to grips with the persistent threat of radical Islam.

This is the story, then, of the world from 1945 to 2012 as it celebrated, then abandoned, the four essential elements of the American character. It is also the story of the abandonment of the very concept of virtue, for virtue is not relative. In the American past it was learned, to paraphrase Lincoln, in every act of being an American. And it can be taught, though the education of virtue in America (let alone the world) is as obsolete as a black-and-white television set. Above all, virtue must be practiced. Any society unwilling or unable to support virtue is a society adrift. The world's immediate quest for the advantages derived from American-like qualities of liberty, justice, and equality was laudable and timely, but the steady—and often deliberate—deterioration of the principles that underlay those qualities has been inversely pathological and sudden.

This, then, stands as the question of the hour. Can enough Americans find their founding principles again to save themselves? And if they do, is it too late to save the rest of the passengers on the sinking world ship? One thing is certain: we remain the "last, best hope" for mankind, for a world without an exceptional America will not long tolerate even a France or a Belgium, or any Western democratic power with free markets. It is entirely possible that without American exceptionalism and its pillars, there would be no free markets, for the impetus toward wealth and power redistribution is utterly unstoppable in their absence. Once private property, citizen virtue, and free markets are gone, democide, violence, and murder will take their place, for in such a world without liberty, the horrors of Nazi Germany or the gulag archipelago will not only become common—they will cease to be horrors at all.

CHAPTER ONE

Hot Spots, Cold War

TIME LINE

1945: Yalta, Potsdam agreements; Franklin Roosevelt dies; Germany surrenders; atomic bomb dropped; Japan surrenders; Germany divided into occupation zones; Japan pulls out of China and other territories; high inflation in United States

1946: CIA established; ENIAC, first digital computer, produced; Churchill gives "Iron Curtain" speech; Nuremberg trial verdicts; decoding of Venona intercepts reveals names of Soviet spies in United States

1947: Canadian independence granted; Communists seize power in Poland; Marshall Plan instituted; Communists seize power in Hungary

1948: Communists seize control of Czechoslovakia; Berlin airlift begins; first trial of Alger Hiss; Harry Truman reelected

1949: NATO formed; USSR tests first atomic bomb

1950: Rosenberg spies indicted; McCarthy's Wheeling speech; Truman orders development of hydrogen bomb; Korean War begins; second trial of Hiss

1951: UNIVAC, first commercial computer, delivered

1952: Elizabeth II becomes queen of England; Truman attempts nationalization of American steel industry; Eisenhower elected president

1953:   Korean War ends; Khrushchev becomes secretary of So-
        viet Communist Party; rebellion in East Germany
        crushed; Rosenbergs executed for espionage

1954:   *Brown v. Board of Education*; Army-McCarthy hearings

1955:   Soviets and Allies withdraw from Austria; Eisenhower
        suffers heart attack; Montgomery, Alabama, bus boycott

1956:   Hungarian Revolution suppressed; Eisenhower reelected;
        Sudanese independence

1957:   *Sputnik* launched by USSR; Civil Rights Commission es-
        tablished; Governor Orval Faubus blocks black students
        from attending Little Rock (Arkansas) Central High
        School

1958:   NASA formed; Hewlett-Packard creates first micropro-
        cessor

1959:   Castro seizes power in Cuba; Titan intercontinental bal-
        listic missile (ICBM) fired; Alaska and Hawaii admitted
        as states

Ghosts Walking in Procession

The flattened landscape could have been Mars, at least what people knew
of the planet. No one had been there, and no man-made robotic cameras
had yet photographed it. But the charred scene, interrupted occasionally
by a shell that only upon close inspection could be identified as a building,
had been entirely created—and destroyed—by humans. This was Hiroshima, only hours after the atomic blast that leveled buildings as though
they were cardboard and incinerated Japanese citizens like kindling. Partial structures that had only minutes earlier been multistory buildings
stood atop mountains of rubble and burned bodies. Akihiro Takahashi,
then a student at a junior high school, watched from a playground as the
silver plane flew over. It was the last thing he remembered before he was
blown backward thirty feet from where he stood, his ears "nearly melted
off." He was badly burned everywhere—his back, arms, legs. When he
regained awareness (somehow, he had instinctively walked to the river to
cool himself), he saw horrific images. Years later, he told an interviewer the
people "looked like ghosts walking in procession."[1] In the river, corpses

bobbed in the water. And beyond, the city was flattened, turned to rubble, devoid of life.

The scene in Berlin just a few months earlier was scarcely different. Spared an atomic attack, the German capital nevertheless had been pulverized, buildings hollowed out from Soviet artillery and bombing, brick and stone piles blocking streets, vegetation scarce. Berlin's residents cowered in the basements of their apartment buildings, many structures blasted apart on one or two sides. There may have been no radiation, but the extent of the devastation was much the same as in the Japanese cities ravaged by atomic bombs, and in the case of cities such as Dresden and Hamburg, perhaps worse.

An unexpected, even shocking, change occurred within a short time (by historical standards). By 2000, both Berlin and Hiroshima not only had come back, restored to vitality and health, but were rebuilt anew, making them both in many ways more "modern" than some American industrial centers such as Detroit. Indeed, a popular Internet mail item compared pictures of Detroit in 2012 with Hiroshima, and concluded by asking, "Who won the war?"

Both the decisive victory by the Allies and the subsequent "hard peace," as John Kennedy called it, occurred during a time when America had emerged as the primary world power. Although the Soviet Union—by 1949 in control of large swaths of eastern Europe—had used its manpower advantage to overwhelm the Nazis on the Eastern Front, there was no doubt that the United States was years ahead of the USSR in science, technology, medicine, and the material condition of its most ordinary citizens. Determined to close this gap and eventually overtake the United States, the Soviets committed themselves domestically and in their foreign policy to expansionism in the purest sense of Lenin's doctrine. Communist "greatness" had to be spread to the world, by force if necessary. And, for a short time, only the USA stood between the Communists and their goal.

This came at a tremendous (and at the time, often hidden) cost. The United States—as late as the mid-1970s—doggedly shouldered the burden of protecting Europe with high defense spending, allowing America's own heavy industries to wither under the weight of regulation and taxation, compounded by rising inflation. Calls to remove American military bases from the Far East and Europe were met with legitimate concern by hawks at home who feared Soviet expansionism, but also by foreign calls for the United States (and its money!) to remain right where it was. Isolationist voices of the prewar period had been silenced by Nazi aggression and Pearl

Harbor. At home, by the 1960s the economic reengineering implemented during the New Deal had lost its association with World War II necessities and was finally being questioned, both by conservatives fearing the growing power of the federal government, and by liberals fearing the rise of corporate power, especially when Democrat John F. Kennedy implemented Mellonesque tax cuts to stimulate investment.

Europe, 1961

NATO members

Neutral non-Communist nations

Warsaw Pact members

Nonaligned Communist nations

Country Abbreviations:
BELG. = Belgium
Li. = Liechtenstein
LUX. = Luxembourg
MON. = Monaco
NETH. = Netherlands
S.M. = San Marino
SWITZ. = Switzerland

0   500 Miles

Nevertheless, the detrimental impact of New Deal policies in all sectors of American productivity became increasingly apparent for all to see. The transformation toward a more planned economy was accompanied by the rise of various social pathologies of Progressivism, which gained new momentum in the 1960s. As these three tributaries converged in a single river, the current was accelerated by Progressive animosity to American exceptionalism, made manifest in public schools and slowly integrating itself into popular culture. This was seen in the ridicule of American traditions and religion starting to take root, the ongoing assault against the free market (especially through environmentalism), and the revisionist teaching of American history by the so-called New Left historians that deplored America's place in the world. The cold war, a necessary and noble expenditure of blood and treasure (ultimately ending in victory for the United States), provided the canvas upon which these other strokes appeared. By 2012, one could hardly recognize the portrait of America, so greatly had it changed from 1945.

Well before the defeat of Nazi Germany, Allied leaders Franklin Roosevelt, Winston Churchill, and Joseph Stalin had met at Yalta in the Crimea

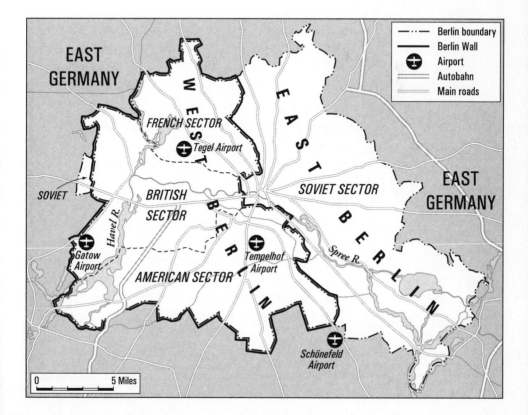

in February 1945. By that time, the Red Army was sweeping German forces before it in the East and would reach Berlin in two months, while the British and American forces would cross the Rhine on March 24. All but the most delusional Nazis understood that not only had Germany lost, but it stood a good chance of being eradicated. Indeed, at Yalta, the Allies agreed to unconditional surrender on the part of all Axis powers, and Germany would undergo demilitarization and denazification. Stalin promised free elections in Poland and the clear implication was that aside from Germany herself, all occupied nations would soon be handed back to their citizens.

Germany was split eventually into four sectors, one each under the control of the Americans, British, French, and Russians; and Berlin—inside the Soviet sector (soon called East Germany)—was similarly divided into four sectors. In Eastern Europe, the Soviets disregarded their Yalta agreements. Instead of withdrawing from the other countries it occupied, the Soviet Union set them on a path to Communist control, and in Poland, installed a Communist government immediately. At Yalta, however, Roosevelt—who always thought he could handle Stalin—came away thinking the world was "on the road to a world of peace." But his own aides, including ambassador to the USSR Averell Harriman, warned him that the Soviets had no intention of allowing democracy in the eastern European states.

At Potsdam, in July and August 1945, President Harry Truman (who succeeded Roosevelt after his death), Clement Attlee (who took over as prime minister from Churchill), and Stalin discussed the postwar disposition of Japan under what became the Potsdam Declaration. Truman alerted Stalin to a "powerful new weapon" without specifically telling him the United States had an atomic bomb—but the Soviets already knew all about its development through their extensive spy network inside the U.S. government and the Manhattan Project. Soon thereafter, Poland, Bulgaria, Hungary, Romania, Czechoslovakia, and Albania were designated as Soviet satellite states with Communist governments.[2] Japan fell to American occupation forces headed by General Douglas MacArthur, who ignored the Soviets, reconstructed Japan along American lines, gave women the vote and developed a democratic constitution. But in Europe, the reconstruction process was different for it directly involved the two former allies now politically and philosophically opposed to each other.

An American diplomat, George Kennan, in February 1946 had sent an analysis of the situation to the U.S. Treasury Department—the so-called Long Telegram—responding to a query as to why the Soviets had not supported the new World Bank or International Monetary Fund. He described a paranoid, insecure, and "neurotic" expansionist Soviet Union.[3] He declared there could be no permanent modus vivendi between the West and the USSR, but Kennan thought military force would not be necessary (and the reality of the day was that short of using atomic bombs, the West did not have enough ground strength or air power to force the Soviets to do anything). Only the nonmilitary option remained, and he urged a "vigilant containment of Russian expansive tendencies."[4]

At the same time, the USSR was going out of its way to shut down all travel and communications between the West and Communist territories, imposing what Winston Churchill in a 1946 speech called the Iron Curtain. Therefore, to forestall the outbreak of another European war, this time caused by Soviet expansionism, the United States was forced to become the leader of a group of European states, something it had never done before and which was expressly contrary to its entire political history. Kennan's strategy came to be known as "containment," which, at its core, inverted Leninism. In a 1917 book, *Imperialism: The Highest Stage of Capitalism*, Lenin insisted capitalism could not survive without taking over other countries for new markets. But now Kennan had shown that communism was the ideology that could not survive without expansion, and if trapped within a closed system, it would rot from the inside out. Putting containment into practice, however, first required that the "Old" Europe be rebuilt sufficiently to stand on its own politically and economically, and to resist Soviet expansion . . . when it came.

Rotting in the Train Station

The material damage in 1945 Europe as seen by arriving English and American troops was sobering. First, the most photogenic aspect of ruin—the cities—was evident to all. Rubble covered the streets, and the landscape was pockmarked with craters and shell holes. Three quarters of Germany's houses were uninhabitable, yielding a homeless population of 20 million in Germany (with 500,000 in Hamburg alone). In Berlin, 75 percent of the buildings were uninhabitable, and 40 percent of all German homes throughout the country had been destroyed. Much of Europe's transportation system had been destroyed. Railroads, power stations, and communications centers were flattened, not just in Germany but in all other European nations once occupied by the Nazis. France, for example, could only put a little over 20 percent of its locomotives on the tracks, and her entire merchant fleet lay at the bottom of the Atlantic or Mediterranean.[5] Holland had seen much of her land flooded. All of this came on top of a staggering human cost. Between 1939 and 1945, more than 36 million people had died from war or direct genocide by the Nazis and Communists, and almost half that number were noncombatants. Germany lost 5.5 million soldiers in the war; the USSR, 10 million. The United States lost an astonishingly low 2.5 percent of its armed forces in all the services (just under 417,000). Britain—not counting the colonies—lost nearly as many as America (384,000) even though almost twice as many Americans served.

At times it looked like the whole continent had shut down. European industry had been eradicated by bombing, and cities often consisted of little more than rubble with streets. Displaced persons wandered about looking for family, relatives, food, and shelter, and with males of military age in very short supply, the burden of survival fell on the women. More than 10 million people had fled before the Russians.[6] Many refugees were housed under wretched conditions, and more than 7 million Germans were in POW camps, over 2.6 million in American camps alone.[7] In one American camp, Bretzenheim, German prisoners received only 600 to 850 calories per day.[8] In the summer of 1946, 100 million Europeans consumed fewer than 1,500 calories per day. In 1945, the average German consumer lived on a mere 850 calories a day.[9] Over the summer in 1945, rotting corpses in Berlin posed a risk of disease, dysentery was widespread, and one American adviser said that in October of that year ten people a day were dying in the Lehrter railway station from malnutrition and illness.[10] The situation grew even worse in 1947 due to a devastating snowstorm that stopped food production, and in Berlin 19,000 Berliners suffered frostbite. Inflation soared: a carton of cigarettes costing fifty cents in the United States sold for 1,800 Reichsmarks in Germany. Europe could not buy goods abroad, and Europe's balance-of-payments debt to the United States was $5 billion and growing. Once only leftist intellectuals blamed capitalism for the dislocations; by 1947 that opinion was becoming widely shared by people of all walks of life due to the slowness of economic recovery. The criticism was misplaced, of course; the primary problem in Western Europe was that the governments were socialist with large Communist minorities, and the Communists were actively working against recovery.

As the Soviets moved in toward the end of the war and afterward, the horrors grew worse not only for Germans, but everywhere the Red Army seized control. In Vienna alone in April 1945, an estimated 37,000 women were raped by the Red Army.[11] In Berlin, an ocean of children disappeared—some 53,000—most dead, some kidnapped and sent east, but a tragic fate awaited children everywhere. Czechoslovakia had 49,000 orphans, Holland, 60,000, and Poland as many as 300,000. Aid flowed in through the Allies and the new United Nations Relief and Rehabilitation Administration (UNRRA), but not nearly enough. Just as after World War I, millions of people were forcibly relocated once again—many to the Soviet-controlled zone of Germany as Poland and the Soviet Union emptied their territories, along with those of East Prussia, West Prussia, Silesia, Pomerania, and New Brandenberg, of their former German inhabitants. Likewise, Romania, Yugoslavia, Hungary, and Czechoslovakia also expelled everyone of even partial German ethnicity, with most of the refugees ending up in the three zones of occupation under American, French, and British administrations.

A very real chance existed of the entire German nation disintegrating, and with it, the likelihood that the Soviets would move in on "humanitarian" grounds to strip West Germany of its remaining industry, as it had in the East. Only the United States, and, to a lesser degree, Britain and France, both of which relocated hundreds of thousands of German POWs to their countries to work as slave labor, prevented this scenario.

President Truman, after the report of his economic mission to Germany and Austria, wisely repudiated the then-popular Morgenthau plan, which would have deindustrialized Germany permanently and turned the country into an agrarian nation. A separate report from General Lucius D. Clay, the military governor of the U.S. zone, through industrialist Lewis Brown, reached similar conclusions. A policy of pastoralization not only would fail to feed postwar Germany, but would push the nation toward communism. Quickly, Clay announced a new policy oriented toward the "complete revival of German industry, primarily coal mining."[12] It all meant restoring Germany to be a partial economic counterweight to the Russians, who increasingly appeared untrustworthy in the extreme.

Holding a hard line against the Soviets did not come easy for Truman, who at one point in late 1945 described Stalin as "a fine man who wanted to do the right thing," an "honest man who is easy to get along with—who arrives at sound decisions."[13] Even as Churchill delivered his Iron Curtain speech at Westminster College in Missouri, Truman continued to refer to the Soviets as "friends" and offered Stalin the opportunity for rebuttal at the school. After his first meeting with Stalin at Potsdam, Truman likened the dictator to his old Missouri political boss Tom Pendergast and felt he could deal with him. These statements were eerily similar to Roosevelt's comments about the Soviet dictator, made to Winston Churchill just a few months earlier: "I think I can personally handle Stalin better than either your Foreign Office or my State Department," and presaged President George W. Bush's assessment of Russian leader Vladimir Putin in June 2001 when he said, "I looked the man in the eye. I was able to get a sense of his soul."[14] At Tehran, FDR thought his teasing and disparaging of Churchill would soften up the Soviet dictator: "I kept it up until Stalin was laughing with me . . . The ice was broken and we talked like men and brothers."[15] The "brothers" then discussed Stalin's demand that fifty thousand German officers be shot after the war, to which Roosevelt quipped, "I have a compromise to propose. Not 50 thousand, but only 49 thousand should be shot."[16] The dictator, although claiming it was a joke, had in fact been deadly serious.

Roosevelt, with his penchant for personal negotiations, like so many American presidents before and after (Wilson, Obama), had made many of the same mistakes Woodrow Wilson made twenty-six years before, agreeing to a series of demands (this time from a potential enemy instead of allies, as Wilson did with France and Britain), making secret concessions, and snobbishly negotiating apart from Britain (while, of course, Churchill negotiated with Stalin apart from FDR). Emerging from the Tehran and Yalta conferences with platitudes, declarations, signatures, and above all "assurances," a deluded FDR handed over Eastern Europe to the Soviets as meekly as Wilson had surrendered on point after point to the Allied powers at Versailles. Each president then proceeded to congratulate himself on his shrewd and skillful negotiating powers. While the British certainly had their own interests to guard, they nevertheless saw the road map more clearly than the Americans, observing that "Stalin has got the President in his pocket."[17] Yet the British were in no position to do much about it, and Roosevelt deliberately kept Churchill at arm's length so as not to "feed Soviet suspicions that the British and Americans were operating in concert."[18] Since the president was unaware that the NKVD (predecessor to the KGB) had penetrated high levels of both the American State Department and British Foreign Office and other government offices—and therefore knew exactly what the level of cooperation (or lack thereof) was—the point was moot. Even more so since the man with whom FDR was dealing was a maniacal mass murderer who could laugh at Hollywood films one minute and sign execution orders the next without the slightest break in mood.

Most of all, Stalin was a man who had internalized Lenin's dictum to "probe with the bayonet," searching for Western weaknesses. Even when it became abundantly clear in the last months of Roosevelt's life that Stalin had betrayed him and violated virtually every agreement he had signed, the president took it as a personal wound, not as the disastrous foreign policy misjudgment it genuinely was. Rosy reports from the U.S. ambassador to the USSR, Joseph Davies, a man in thrall to communism and Joseph Stalin himself, further amplified Truman's initial positive assessments of the Communists. Davies insisted that to "distrust Stalin was 'bad Christianity, bad sportsmanship, bad sense.'"[19] Within a few months Truman recovered from his initial misperceptions of Stalin and laid down the law in one of his first meetings with Soviet foreign minister Vyacheslav Molotov (an assumed name meaning "the Hammer"). "I gave it to him straight," Truman said. "I let him have it. It was a straight one-two to the jaw." Molotov blustered, "I have never been talked to like that in my life," when, of course, he frequently suffered far worse from his bloodthirsty boss. Truman dispatched him by replying, "Carry out your agreements and you won't get talked to like that."[20] Undeterred, Stalin kept a step ahead of Truman thanks to his spy networks and his steely-eyed focus on gobbling up as much territory as possible.[21] Few in the West wanted to contemplate the possibility of yet another malevolent dictator equal to Hitler at work, this time in the USSR. Surely, went the typical thinking, having evicted one demon from the world stage, another had not taken his place? It was cognitive dissonance in its most virulent form.

Truman, however, only slowly acknowledged the threat that the Soviet Union posed to the American way of life. Following George Kennan's Long Telegram in February 1946, Truman received another blunt note: "I think it is now time for [the president] to get tough with someone."[22] It was from his mother. The Clifford-Elsey Report, produced by Truman's special counsel Clark Clifford and aide George Elsey, told Truman that all of his top staff considered the Soviet Union "expansionist," and the United States must be prepared to take military action if necessary to counter Soviet threats. The morning after he read the report, Truman met with Clifford and ordered him to bring all copies of the report to him immediately for destruction: if he allowed the report to be made public, Truman said, it would ruin any possibility of Soviet-U.S. rapprochement.[23]

Indeed, Truman reacted cautiously to Stalin's steady encroachments, and the fait accompli of a divided postwar Europe might have been far worse if not for the Lone Ranger antics of Truman's secretary of state, James F. "Jimmy" Byrnes. Byrnes no doubt felt he was much better qualified to be president than Truman, and tended to act as if he was. An Irish Catholic from South Carolina who converted to Episcopalianism, Byrnes could boast he had been in all three branches of government, as a congressman for fourteen years, senator for ten, a Supreme Court justice appointed by FDR in 1941, resigning in 1942 to head Roosevelt's Economic Stabilization Office (controlling wages and prices), and in 1943 the Office of War Mobilization. Byrnes was totally bereft of any formal education, but was the consummate political fixer, and thought he had Roosevelt's backing for vice president in 1944. But FDR had settled on Truman for reasons unknown, and Byrnes left the Chicago convention distressed and humiliated. FDR took Byrnes with him to Yalta, possibly as a consolation prize, and later Truman chose Byrnes for secretary of state to patch things up, but also to co-opt his acumen. Distrustful of "those little bastards at the State Department," Byrnes often negotiated directly with Soviet officials without Truman's instructions, and even without informing the president, who complained, "I have to read the newspaper to find out about American foreign policy."[24] Yet the president also distrusted the State Department, and with good cause. The department was riddled with individuals like Joe Davies, who took the Soviet side at Potsdam in almost every instance. After one of Byrnes's communiqués in January 1946, Truman finally concluded, "I do not think we should play compromise any longer . . . I am tired of babying the Soviets."[25] But Byrnes also made mistakes. It was Byrnes who resolved the reparations issue by giving Stalin recognition of the western Neisse as Poland's western border (thus giving Silesia to Poland), as well as recognizing the Soviet puppet governments in Bulgaria, Hungary, and Romania. For him, the settlement was just another political "fix."

Between the Kennan containment doctrine and Truman's new sober approach to dealing with the USSR, the Marshall Plan was born in 1947. As Army chief of staff (1939–47), General George C. Marshall had become a powerful and respected force in the United States and was widely credited for wartime efficiency. He could be petty—officers whom he deemed unsuitable were shunned for promotion, including one whose name Marshall mistakenly and unfairly took for someone else. But he was also a no-nonsense organizer.

Secretary of State Byrnes had shared Truman's views, but increasingly was seen by the president as competition. Byrnes resigned in 1947, and Marshall was named secretary of state, to lend credibility and moral force to the administration. Determined to save Europe, Marshall instructed Kennan and others to develop a plan to do exactly that. Under the Marshall Plan, the United States would give $6 to $7 billion per year in aid to Europe for three years. Outlining his blueprint on June 4 at Harvard, Marshall announced his objective as "the revival of a working economy in the world so as to permit the emergence of political and social conditions in which free institutions can exist. . . . Our policy is directed not against any country or doctrine but against hunger, poverty, desperation and chaos."[26] Over time, more than $13 billion poured into eighteen countries, with Britain and France receiving over 44 percent of the funds while nonbelligerent countries such as Ireland, Iceland, Portugal, and Turkey—none of whom suffered war damage—took substantial bites of the Marshall Plan apple. In the end, although the Marshall Plan contributed much less than expected to the rebuilding of Europe, it stabilized European governments and prevented communism from dominating Western politics.

Like Truman, Marshall originally misjudged the potential to work with Stalin, feeling that Byrnes and Truman had taken too hard a line with the Soviets. Until his March 1947 meeting with the dictator in Moscow, Marshall felt confident he could influence Stalin with humanitarian points and reach an agreement with him on collaborative efforts to rebuild Europe. The meeting was long and difficult, but noting Stalin's lack of concern for any meaningful actions to ease the postwar suffering, Marshall finally came to understand what Stalin had in store for Europe. Germany was to have a strong central government, which Stalin could nudge into communism and make into another Soviet satellite state. France and Italy were on the verge of becoming Communist, and even Great Britain was moving rapidly left. Charles de Gaulle had resigned in frustration in France, and had been replaced with a socialist government under Léon Blum that was shaky at best. The Fourth Republic, founded in December 1946, appeared doomed, and suffering from substantial Communist gains, was expected to succumb to Stalin's wishes. At stake was nothing less than the future of a free Europe.

At the Moscow meeting, Marshall talked with his counterpart from England, Ernst Bevin, a trade-union sympathizer who had often used his position as minister of labor to secure higher wages for workers during the war, and had been named foreign secretary in 1945, in the Attlee government. Also involved was the French foreign minister, Georges Bidault. Both committed themselves to working with Marshall for a free Europe and an economically restored Germany. Nonetheless, Europe continued to deteriorate before their eyes, and communism was on the rise everywhere, but particularly in Italy and France. Although the United Nations Relief and Rehabilitation Administration had distributed $4 billion in relief aid, mostly food and medicine, that had merely kept Western Europeans alive and partially clothed.[27]

Virtually all of Europe became eligible for the Marshall Plan, except Spain (deemed "not only a bad credit risk [but] a moral risk" as well).[28] The Soviets pressured their Eastern European allies to reject all Marshall Plan assistance, and Finland declined to participate to avoid antagonizing its next-door neighbor. Officially, the Soviets claimed Marshall's program would interfere in the domestic affairs of countries accepting the aid. Nonetheless, as Truman insisted in 1949, the United States intended to "assist the people of economically underdeveloped areas to raise their standard of living."[29] Implementing the plan was more difficult than one might think. The devil was in the details, and after bringing together the sixteen countries that were the intended recipients into the Committee of European Economic Cooperation, national interests often proved difficult obstacles to overcome. Marshall's design, voted into law as the Economic Cooperation Act (ECA) on April 3, 1948, was sometimes opposed by the British where it tended to reduce their status, and sometimes by France, which wanted to demonstrate her independence from the United States. With American money, Europe seemed to rise like a phoenix from the ashes to reject communism, although many Europeans embraced a softer version of socialism.

American goods accompanied American aid, rushing into devastated European countries desperate for employment and relief from wartime scarcity and squalor. Encompassed in FDR's Four Freedoms, the principle of a rising standard of living for all seemed no longer just an American goal but an international one. The United Nations Charter in Article 55 affirmed its objective of promoting "higher standards of living" worldwide. This in itself was remarkable, as it meant the UN explicitly dedicated itself to a capitalist end instead of mere subsistence.

The Communists, of course, feared the Marshall Plan and attempted to stop it, but their efforts failed. At an Italian Communist Party rally in 1948, twenty thousand people heard Communist leader Palmiro Togliatti denounce American aid. He was booed for more than five minutes before the Communist crowd began chanting "Long live the United States."[30] When the first ship bearing Marshall Plan aid arrived in Bordeaux, it was greeted with wild cheers of dockworkers who only months before had protested "American imperialism."[31] And it was the Soviets' own actions, such as their harsh response to the Czech crisis of March 1948, that sharpened support for the Marshall Plan: fully 73 percent of Americans then polled thought U.S. policy toward the Russians was "too soft."[32] Communists' fears were well grounded. The first reports of the Marshall Plan's results in 1948 showed that industrial production in Europe had risen above prewar levels, exports were 13 percent above the 1938 levels, and electrical and steel output had risen to postwar highs. By 1950, Europe's industrial production was 24 percent higher than before the war and its agriculture reached an all-time high.[33]

Although not part of the Marshall Plan, the Bretton Woods Agreement, secured in 1944 at a small resort hotel in New Hampshire out of a desire to avoid the economic chaos that had followed World War II, addressed another support plank for rebuilding Europe. Finance ministers and economists from Europe and the United States, featuring the last major appearance and policy influence by John Maynard Keynes, established the World Bank, the International Monetary Fund (IMF), and an international money structure tied to the U.S. dollar. For Bretton Woods to work, the dollar had to remain strong—but for the developing nations to benefit from the system (and, in theory, not become breeding grounds for communism), the World Bank and IMF had to lend generously, largely at the urging of Harry Dexter White, a Soviet agent in place as assistant secretary of the treasury. Since the United States was (and would always be) the leading source of funds for those institutions, it meant that tremendous pressure existed for the United States to lend and the temptation was built in to run deficits . . . which would weaken the dollar. In short, Bretton Woods embodied diametrically opposing objectives. Economist Robert Triffin would describe this in a theory that was named for him, "Triffin's dilemma." Of most immediate importance after the war, however, was that the fragile economies of Greece, Italy, and France needed stabilizing before the voters elected Communist governments, but soon the objectives were broadened to include most of the European countries and Great Britain. The United States ended the immediate postwar period by almost single-handedly saving free markets (and free peoples) in Europe and by committing herself to future outlays for development of the Third World. Virtually no other nation in history had approached the end of a conflict with such magnanimity.

Theft of the Century

When it became clear that a free Western Europe would not topple internally after the Marshall Plan took effect and NATO was formed, the Cold War accelerated on both sides. Soviet-occupied Eastern Europe was stripped, its factories dismantled and shipped east. News of executions of repatriated POWs reached the West. Soviet forces did not withdraw from Iran, prompting Truman to threaten the USSR at the United Nations. Yugoslavia shot down two U.S. transport aircraft. And all this was just what the Americans could actually *see*. Worse was the hidden and effective penetration of Western governments at almost every level by Communist agents while the United States curtailed its intelligence operations. Truman had abolished the Office of Strategic Services over OSS Chief William J. Donovan's strenuous objections and, according to historian Burton Hersh, had told Donovan, "I am completely opposed to international spying on the part of the United States. It is un-American." Fortunately, British intelligence came to the rescue under UKUSA, a 1946 agreement made between the United Kingdom and the United States to share information and pursue joint operations.

But in many ways the horse was out of the barn: Soviet agents operated at high levels—and in critical posts—in the State Department and Treasury. Harry Dexter White, Treasury's number two man, whose influence over policy was extremely substantial, was on the NKVD's payroll.[34] Senator Joe McCarthy had just arrived in Washington, and would not focus on communism in government as a political issue until 1950. Thus, Soviet agents not only penetrated the American and British governments, but operated nearly unchecked for many years, and while it is possibly overstated to say they "cost us China," or "gave the Reds the A-bomb," in every respect the actions of Communist cells greased the wheels of Soviet actions.

The Soviet effort in espionage was so widespread and devastating, it is difficult even sixty years later to comprehend and accept the enormity of the crimes of so many people—all but a few escaping all punishment. The McCarthyism so loved as an issue by the American Left failed to scratch the surface of the Soviet penetration of the U.S. government, and the tally of identified spies clearly exceeds the numbers bandied about by Tail Gunner Joe. Unrecognized by the American public to this day, the USSR had mounted an unprecedented espionage effort that literally stripped the United States of the vast majority of its secrets, including how to make an atomic bomb. Malmstrom Air Force Base near Great Falls, Montana, became perhaps the most significant port of exit for information and technology the world has ever seen. Planeloads of classified documents and espionage reports moved through Malmstrom on their way to Moscow, and largely because of them the Soviet Union was able to maintain a rough parity with American military technology for another fifteen years. This fact made the American victory in the Cold War in the 1990s all the more impressive.

A combination of Byrnes's consistent nudging, Churchill's blunt warnings, and Kennan's Long Telegram combined to convince Truman that cooperation with Stalin was impossible. He reinforced the U.S.-British alliance while Stalin blundered badly, uniting the fractious Western powers with an act of aggression. At Molotov's instigation, Stalin began throwing up obstacles to travel between the Soviet-controlled sector of Berlin and the American/British sectors in January 1948. Truman, of course, could not tolerate this, nor could he send tanks and ground forces into a situation where they would be hopelessly outnumbered, even with European allies. General Clay insisted that the United States could not give up such a substantial enclave in the East, calling it a "symbol of American intent." His counterpart in the Army Air Force, General Curtis LeMay (who wanted a much more aggressive stance against the Soviets), was asked, "Can you haul coal?" He reportedly answered, "We can haul anything." Clay and Truman enlisted LeMay in developing a strategy that relied on an airlift to supply all of the city's needs, while at the same time shifting the onus to the Soviets to fire the first shot, and assume the war guilt of any subsequent fight. Although Clay still was not sure it would work, he saw it as the only option, and one that permitted the British Royal Air Force to play a role (France, lacking any air power, was necessarily excused from duty). By mid-July 1948, Western planes were depositing thirteen thousand tons of food, clothing, and medicine *a day* for the two million people trapped behind the blockade—an amount ten times that supplied to the trapped German Sixth Army at Stalingrad.[35] The airlift lasted a year, ultimately bringing in more goods than the preblockade rail lines had provided. With the "Easter Parade" of April 15–16, 1949, the Americans and British inundated the city and humiliated the Soviets, who lifted the blockade under the cover of negotiations. Victorious General Clay, who had administered Berlin, returned home to a massive ticker-tape parade.[36]

Latin American Revival

Amid the uncertainty surrounding a divided and rebuilding Europe, the United States was gratified that, at least for the moment, its southern neighbors in Latin America were relatively amiable diplomatically and stable economically. But the trajectory for growth in the region remained low. Despite having gained their independence over a century before the African states, the nations of Latin America had nevertheless made only marginal progress shortly before and after World War II. United States markets for South American goods had dried up during the Depression, then rebounded during the war as the Allies needed raw materials. Although Americans continued to purchase heavily after the war, the Latin American nations had lost the entire European and Japanese market and, for all intents, Britain's too, with her shrinking treasury. Intercontinental trade made up some of the difference; Paraguay exported timber and extracts to its neighbors, and the southern tier of countries had by 1941 developed a plan to create a customs union to promote multilateral trade, led by Argentina's finance minister, Federico Pinedo. This increased the share of exports going from one South American country to another, and helped buffer the collapse of intercontinental exports after 1945. Had Latin America used the respite to diversify and modernize, it might have maintained a more positive development trajectory, but most countries remained extraordinarily dominated by single products. In ten different nations, one exported commodity claimed 50 percent of the total shipment of goods.

In other ways, however, the war benefited South America. Immigrants fleeing Europe brought new skills as Germans and Italians streamed into Argentina and Brazil, Germans moved to Chile and Uruguay, and Spaniards fled to Mexico. But lacking capital and facing state competition in many cases, immigrant companies had limited impact. Worse, the war brought inflation. Argentina saw wholesale prices rise 12.3 percent from 1939 to 1945; Brazil, 17 percent; Chile and the Dominican Republic, over 19 percent, provoking governments such as Argentina's to nationalize foreign-owned properties. Under such chaotic circumstances, the ascension of dictators such as Colonel Juan Perón in Argentina was predictable. Perón led a coup in 1943, accelerating the state's role in the economy and (like Anastasio Somoza in Nicaragua) using the excuse of war to boost defense spending to keep himself in power.

Many South American countries turned to military dictators after the war, including Venezuela, Cuba, and Nicaragua. By 1954, only four democracies remained on the continent "even by generous standards of classification: Uruguay, Costa Rica, Chile, and Brazil."[37] Dictators were acceptable, but Communists were not, due to the Catholic Church's strong resistance to Marxism. Despite a collectivist bent, the Vatican remained vehemently opposed to "godless" communism and aligned with any Latin American group that stood against Marxists. At least that was true at the top levels of Catholicism—at the village priest level, communism and "solidarity with the poor" were already starting to take root.

American policy sought to battle red influence on the continent less through religion—which it thought the Vatican entirely capable of handling—and more through trade, increasing exports from one fourth to one third between 1946 and 1950. Seeking to please their new sponsor, several Latin American countries cracked down on pro-Communist labor unions and some nations completely outlawed Communist parties (Brazil in 1947, Chile and Costa Rica in 1948), while in other countries, including Mexico, the Communist Party was legal, but could not get on a ballot or register for elections. These measures had an impact: Communist Party membership fell by half in South America, and by 1954, all Latin American nations except Argentina had banned Communists.

But the inverse was not true, and the *norteamericano* was not welcomed with open arms (the famous Mexican saying "so far from God, so close to America" characterizing the general attitude that sovereignty demanded freedom from American influence). The wake-up call that these attitudes existed came with Vice President Richard Nixon's trip to Caracas, Venezuela, in 1958, when his car was pelted by rocks and a crowd rocked it back and forth. Nixon later said the "spit was flying so fast the driver turned on his windshield wipers."[38] He attributed the hooliganism to Communist agitators, but the tour "prompted an immediate (but incomplete) reassessment of U.S. policy toward LA." Nixon suggested the United States distance itself from authoritarian rulers, recommending a "formal handshake for dictators; an *embraso* for leaders in freedom."[39] That this constituted political, and not cultural, opposition to the United States could be seen when American jazz groups toured South America. At the very time Nixon's car was pelted with eggs, jazz greats such as Louis Armstrong—on U.S. State Department–sponsored tours—were playing venues in Latin America to packed houses of receptive audiences.

Whether the U.S. was guilty of neglecting its southern neighbors, with minor and infrequent exceptions the United States did not have to fear Soviet incursions from the south for more than a decade. Such assurances allowed America to focus much-needed resources elsewhere, such as in Asia, where new Communist aggression was afoot.

Chinese Dragons, Korean Tigers

Marshall's economic aid program may have saved Europe, but no amount of money could save China and much of the Far East from the red menace. There the stage was set for forty years of Communist aggression that would not cease until after the fall of the USSR.

In July 1947, General Albert Wedemeyer, who had replaced General Joseph Stilwell in China, submitted a memo known as the Wedemeyer Report to President Truman, recommending the United States send aid and advisers in various military and economic fields to the Nationalist Chinese.[40] He later placed the blame for the loss of China on the Truman administration and, in particular, the State Department, for its failure to sufficiently support the Nationalists. In reality, however, the Kuomintang under Chiang Kai-shek (Jiang Jieshi) was probably too corrupt to withstand the Communist pressure even if the United States had donated all its World War II military equipment as aid to his Nationalist armies. Marshall, Truman, and the American public recoiled at the thought of getting involved in a large-scale Asian land war—wresting isolated islands from fanatical Japanese had proved difficult enough, and a Communist China was simply not seen in the United States as a substantial threat. After all, China, with its population of 500 million people, had been unable to defeat or even hold back Japan, a nation only one seventh its size, during World War II. Since the middle of the nineteenth century, Anglo-Europeans had tended to dismiss China as irrelevant. Even up to May 1945, Japanese armies carried out offensive operations in China, seizing substantial territory while the seaward approaches to their home islands fell like dominoes to U.S. forces. In China, the Japanese had made extensive use of poison gas, as well as chemical and biological weapons, even dropping fleas infected with bubonic plague. Like Germany marching against Russia, theirs was a war of annihilation.

China's civil war between the Communists under Mao Zedong and Chiang's Nationalists (Kuomintang) shifted into high gear following Japan's defeat. Although the Kuomintang held two thirds of the population and three quarters of China's area, the Communists received the Japanese arms captured by the Soviets as well as much additional Soviet aid. Marshall, heavily influenced by Dean Acheson, who tended to believe Soviet propaganda, refused to believe the Soviets were backing their fellow Communists. But more important, the Chinese Communists were a cohesive force, while there was bitter in-fighting among the Nationalists and their various supporting warlords. In addition, the Communist promise of land reform, wherein the peasants would receive plots of land in the breakup of large land holdings, was irresistible to huge numbers of starving and landless peasants. That those plots would later be collectivized was left unsaid.

Truman initially supported Chiang, sending $2.8 billion in aid and credits by August 1949 (a third of the allotment of the Marshall Plan), but rapidly soured on continuing any involvement in China. Following the Japanese surrender, fifty thousand Marines in two divisions were sent to China to supervise the Japanese withdrawal. American troops were not to fight alongside the Nationalists, only to look out for American interests. Even so, they took casualties (ten killed and thirty-three wounded), one of whom, Captain John Birch, was killed by Communists and became enshrined by American conservatives as the first battle death in World War III. Truman reduced the force to less than half its original size by June of 1946, and a year later, only small units remained to protect American citizens. By the time Marshall resigned as secretary of state in January of 1949, the Nationalists had suffered heavy defeats. In October, Chiang, his command fractured and riddled with corruption, fled the mainland with remnants of his army to Taiwan (Formosa), from which he continued to represent China in the UN.

The next shoe to fall in Asia was Korea. Unfortunately, the United States had dismantled its armed forces, with total numbers of men in uniform falling by about 10.5 million between 1945 and 1947.[41] This demobilization occurred not just to fulfill the national sentiment to "bring the boys home," but to give vent to Truman's great distrust of the professional officer corps and their lack of (in his eyes) fiscal management. Although Truman possessed many noble attributes, his background in the National Guard had made him contemptuous of military brass. He had been turned down in his applications to West Point and Annapolis due to poor eyesight, and never seemed to get over that rejection.[42] He insulted the military with his appointments; a political fixer, Harry Vaughan, became his senior army aide and adviser; Louis Johnson, another political hack, was named secretary of defense; and Francis "Rowboat" Matthews secretary of the navy.

Convinced that military expenditures contained a great deal of waste and fraud, Truman slashed the military budget to $12 billion, supporting an Air Force of 450 bombers and 2,475 fighter planes and a 238-ship Navy. The Marines were reduced to 86,000 men, and the Army to ten divisions with all its combat battalions reduced by a third. Only one division in the entire U.S. military—the 82nd Airborne—stood even remotely ready for combat. Clearly this had a beneficial effect on the American economy, where "government spending fell like a stone," and government's share of GDP plummeted from 44 percent to a mere 8.9 percent.[43] But military preparedness suffered badly. The peacetime draft failed to fill the Army's quotas, and with deferments accepted for almost any reason, supplied the military with indifferent, unwilling, and disgruntled troops. Training was perfunctory and troops were rushed overseas to maintain some semblance of military presence. Even the stockpile of atomic bombs was in woeful shape, and the United States possessed no bombers capable of delivering atomic bombs to Russia from the U.S. mainland and returning. By early 1949, the United States still had fewer than seventy-five atomic bombs (and even some of those were being retired), and included no tactical atomic bombs at all. In August 1949, intelligence detected an atomic explosion in the Soviet Union. Truman brushed it off, expressing doubt that the Soviets possessed the technological know-how to build an atomic bomb. Having emerged from the Second World War as a lion, Truman rapidly transformed himself into a lamb due to his continued desire to see Stalin as reasonable—at the very time that Asian Communists decided to test America's resolve.

The crisis in Korea (the "Hermit Kingdom" of Choson) was long in coming. The Soviets had wanted all of Korea and more for their last-minute entry into the war against Japan. FDR had agreed at Yalta that Korea would become an Allied trusteeship administered by all four powers, including China. But with Russians pouring into northern Korea, two U.S. Army colonels at the Pentagon, one being Dean Rusk, later secretary of state, after consulting a National Geographic Society map during the night of August 10–11, 1945, suggested the thirty-eighth parallel as a convenient dividing line for the Japanese to surrender to Soviet forces above the parallel, and American below.[44] Although the United States had wanted the dividing line to be as far north as possible, the Soviets had reached well into Korea, and the United States would not have troops in Korea until September 4. The Soviets accepted the line immediately, since the USSR was separated from Korea by only the Tumen River, while the U.S. mainland was an ocean away. The formal division took place on August 15 per General Order #1 when the Soviets were already south of the thirty-eighth parallel, but they withdrew northward and began establishing the parallel as a national border, with "People's Committees" for governing.

In 1946–47, the US-USSR Joint Commission meetings failed to reach positive agreements, and in 1947, the United States managed to obtain UN agreement to establish a UN Temporary Commission on Korea. The Soviets refused to cooperate, and in 1948, elections were held in South Korea and the Republic of Korea was born. The formation of the Democratic People's Republic of Korea followed in September 1948, with Kim Il Sung as its premier. In South Korea, an independent democratic government arose under Syngman Rhee, although the structure hardly was indicative of stability, as at one time South Korea featured 113 political parties.[45] The U.S. State Department handled the transition of transferring power to the South Korean government, and John J. Muccio, a career diplomat and U.S.

ambassador to South Korea, assumed the command of all U.S. military advisers. Muccio was a forty-eight-year-old bachelor, ruggedly handsome and reputed to be "a chronic womanizer," who got along well with American military personnel and liked to play soldier. MacArthur, the "American Caesar" who had liberated the Philippines and polished his reputation as the hero of the Pacific Theater in World War II, ignored Korea since he had no command responsibility there, and even maintaining a combat-ready force in Japan was far beyond his resources.

To the north, however, more than 100,000 native Koreans who had fought in Chinese Communist armies were returned to their homeland. They became the nucleus of the North Korean People's Army under the command of Kim Il Sung. Soviets provided T-34 tanks and modernized North Korea's army, while the United States created a South Korean constabulary of 20,000 men to help combat frequent Communist guerrilla activities, rebellions, and disruptions of political activities in the South. This force grew to 50,000 men by 1948. With the American withdrawal in June 1949 of its last combat troops, the Republic of Korea (ROK) increased its forces further to about 65,000 men, mostly equipped by the United States but denied tanks, mobile artillery, and aircraft—supposedly to prevent the South Korean government from invading its neighbor. The bumbling expansion was overseen by Muccio, who did little when North Korea began flexing its muscles with border incidents. Throughout the remainder of 1949 and until the invasion on Sunday, June 25, 1950, the North Koreans regularly attacked southern outposts and border installations. In the last six months of 1949, more than four hundred such attacks occurred.[46] Probing with a bayonet in classic Communist style, Kim Il Sung was developing his plans thorough combat intelligence, keeping his troops sharp, and weakening the morale of ROK troops by frequently annihilating outposts and small units.

Into this arena of heightening tension stepped Secretary of State Dean Acheson. A liberal's liberal, considered by the U.S. Progressive establishment as one of its most brilliant spokesmen, Acheson gave a speech on January 10, 1950, in which he described the United States' position in Asia by saying, "This defensive perimeter runs along the Aleutians to Japan and then goes to the Ryukyus [the island chain that includes Okinawa]." He went on to note that "so far as the military security of other areas of the Pacific is concerned, it must be clear that no person can guarantee these areas against military attack. . . . Should such an attack occur . . . the initial reliance must be on the people to resist it and then upon the commitments of the entire civilized world under the . . . United Nations. . . ."[47] If the United States had wanted to tell Stalin it was permissible for the North Koreans to attack South Korea, the message could not have been more explicit. In April 1950, Stalin approved Kim Il Sung's plan to invade the South; in May Kim received Mao's blessing and promise of support.[48]

A week after Acheson's remarks, Congress voted down an aid appropriation of $10 million for South Korea. Then Democratic senator Tom Connally, chairman of the Senate Committee on Foreign Relations, responded to a reporter's question as to whether the United States would seriously consider abandoning South Korea. Connally answered, "I am afraid it is going to be seriously considered because I'm afraid it's going to happen whether we want it or not."[49] Border incidents had reached almost three a night, but suddenly in May they stopped and North Korean civilians were evacuated from the border zone.

These signals went unheeded by Muccio and everyone else on the U.S. side. The ROK army was put on emergency alert that lasted from June 11 to June 23, and ROK intelligence was on record as stating an attack was inevitable, but the time was unknown. The CIA, just in its infancy, paid no attention to Korea, and MacArthur's intelligence chief, Major General Charles Willoughby, simply disregarded all indications of a North Korean attack. He considered none of the intelligence reports strong enough to issue a warning of an invasion. On June 20, Assistant Secretary of State for Far Eastern Affairs Dean Rusk testified before a congressional committee that "we see no present intention that the people across the border [North Koreans] have any intention of fighting a major war for that purpose [to seize the South]." Two days earlier Kim Il Sung had given the order to invade the South, and five days later the attack began.

Even then, the United States responded slowly, partly due to the glowing and false reports regularly coming out of South Korea as to the status of its army and training—information readily believed by the cost cutters in Washington as proving the case for their policies. The reality was enormously different. Although ROK units performed well at times, in general the North Korean army, the Inmin Gun, went through the South Koreans like a hot knife through butter.

When news of the attack reached Washington in the evening of June 24, Truman directed Acheson to request the United Nations Security Council to convene an emergency session the following day, condemning North Korea and demanding a cease-fire. However, the Army chief of staff was not notified of Truman's actions until nine hours later. Acheson, under public fire for defending Soviet spy Alger Hiss, became the most hawkish of Truman's advisers, possibly to divert attention from his earlier blunder. The UN Security Council passed a resolution (with the Soviets absent, having boycotted meetings since January) calling upon all members to assist South Korea in repelling the attack. After a late dinner with the Joint Chiefs of Staff and Acheson, Truman assessed the situation. The Air Force and Navy argued that air and sea action alone might suffice as a response, but the Army's General J. Lawton Collins thought otherwise.[50] Later that evening, Truman and the Joint Chiefs held a teleconference with General MacArthur, during which he was ordered to send a survey party to Korea and report back on the military situation. Almost a full three days after the invasion started, MacArthur finally was placed in command of military operations in Korea. But with only a single division even remotely combat ready, but unavailable for Korea, it would be a photo-finish race to keep from losing all of South Korea before significant U.S. forces (or anyone else, for that matter) could intervene.

The initial relief force, Task Force Smith with 440 men, of whom only about 75 had combat experience, was easily overrun by the North Koreans. Poorly trained and out-of-shape occupation troops from Japan were thrown into battle; U.S. bazookas were too light to penetrate the armor of the T-34s; and no one had prepared for the Korean climate or terrain. Americans encountered one rugged hill after another with scant cover, and the physical demands rendered some hapless units ineffective before they ever fired a shot. Two American understrength regiments crumbled in the first week of fighting as the North Korean troops advanced fifty miles.

A full 10 percent of the active U.S. Army units were not in Korea but holding bases in Europe; and the army that did arrive in Korea met defeat in every engagement. Troops pushing papers in a plush billet in Japan two weeks earlier suddenly found themselves defending a rocky road junction with an M1 Garand, eighty rounds of ammunition, and an understrength company against T-34 tanks and merciless battalions of hardened North Koreans. In scenes reminiscent of the early stages of World War II, American troops surrendered or died in shocking numbers as whole companies were annihilated. Not only was the North Korean Army effective, they were also barbaric. Many Americans thought that, having defeated the Japanese, they would never encounter such cruelty in an enemy again. They were wrong. Captured and wounded Americans were tied with barbed wire and murdered in foxholes they dug themselves. Some of the troops that died had only received eight weeks of basic training before facing the North

Koreans. It is perhaps needless and redundant to look for someone to blame for the massacres the troops were sent into: such military unpreparedness had always been a feature of an American democracy steeped in a suspicion of standing armies and wedded to the Western Way of War principle that peace was the norm and conflict the exception. But certainly the situation in Korea was worsened by Progressive politicians, who had deliberately and uniformly viewed the Soviets as partners or allies as opposed to opponents or even enemies.

On July 18, a third understrength division began landing in Korea (the combat strength of the first three divisions was slightly less than 50 percent), but by then it was clear the best the U.S. forces could do would be to retain a small toehold on the southeast corner of the Korean Peninsula. Savage and costly fighting in August and September maintained that precarious position, known as the Pusan Perimeter because it controlled the approaches to the port of Pusan. Then came MacArthur's legendary strategy of using his reinforcements, not to fight northward from Pusan up the entire peninsula, but to land behind the North Korean army and cut it off using his superior sea power. The plan involved an amphibious landing at Seoul's port, Inchon, and was fraught with extreme risks. Tidal mud flats and high tides at Inchon severely limited the windows in which an invasion could occur, and narrowed the approaches in which it had to land, making any assault highly vulnerable. Most generals of lesser status, not to mention audacity, would not have considered the scheme. Compared with Inchon, Normandy in 1944 was, in betting parlance, a "lock."

Success at Inchon came in no small degree because of its boldness and surprise. American intelligence also played one of the most decisive roles yet in the war. The North Koreans, assuming the United States was too sclerotic to respond quickly, did not even bother to encode their military transmissions of battle plans and troop movements. American analysts, working in Japan, quickly discovered this and worked backward with that information to break all of the North Korean codes within thirty days after the war began—"one of the most important code-breaking accomplishments of the twentieth century."[51] Intercepting and translating one third of all of the North Koreans' enciphered messages, by August 1950 the Armed Forces Security Agency (AFSA) provided "near complete . . . real-time access to the plans and intentions of the enemy forces" faced by Lieutenant General Walton Walker.[52]

General Douglas MacArthur's daring deserves most of the credit for the Inchon landing in September 1950, but it would not have been possible without the signal intelligence coming from AFSA, which tracked the location of virtually every North Korean unit. One young field commander, James Woolnough, later recalled that "they knew exactly where each platoon of North Koreans were going, and they'd move to meet it. . . ."[53] Indeed, the U.S. intercepts revealed that the North Koreans anticipated such a landing, but *south* of Inchon, much as Hitler had bet his chips on the D-Day landings coming at Calais. MacArthur's forces came ashore behind the North Korean positions, sending the North Koreans reeling in retreat hundreds of miles up the peninsula. MacArthur drove hard for the Yalu River, the boundary separating Korea from China. As in 1944, Americans expected to push back the enemy and have their troops home by Christmas. But the enemy found new resources, this time in the form of more than a million Communist Chinese soldiers.

Late in October 1950, Chinese troops began making their presence known. An ROK division was attacked by two Chinese divisions, then two others ran headlong into ambushes by separate Chinese armies. Chinese prisoners captured by Americans on October 29 could have yielded valuable intelligence, but division and higher headquarters refused to believe the men were Chinese. First and foremost among the doubters was Major General Charles Willoughby (again), MacArthur's G-2 (Intelligence Section). His presence on MacArthur's staff had nearly always been a negative factor, since the opening days of World War II, as he always expected the enemy to do what he personally would do, rather than understanding the full range of potential actions. Willoughby argued that if the Chinese had planned to intervene, they would have done so earlier and certainly before most of the North Korean forces were destroyed. (In fact, it did not bother Mao at all that Korea lost much of its fighting force—one less enemy on the border.) But Willoughby went far beyond offering his opinion, actually falsifying intelligence reports to feed MacArthur what he thought MacArthur would want to hear.[54]

By November, Chinese troops assaulted forward units of the U.S. Eighth Army, only to suddenly disappear. Lieutenant General Edward "Ned" Almond's X Corps pushed to the Yalu River, unwisely separating his units in his zeal to reach the river first. Now, finally, MacArthur accepted the likelihood that he was in a war with the Chinese, and feared he might soon see large numbers of the enemy crossing the Yalu. He ordered the Yalu bridges to be attacked by the Air Force—an order immediately countermanded by the Joint Chiefs, who directed him not to bomb within five miles of the Yalu for fear of provoking the Chinese. For the first time,

American wartime restraint gave the enemy a substantial military advantage: the Chinese could now cross the river in absolute safety. Although the order was rescinded three days later, the attacks failed to destroy the bridges, and once the river froze, the bridges became unimportant.

On the evening of November 25, the Chinese army, which lay in wait, struck with hurricane force, overwhelming the American troops. Instantly, Eighth Army on the western side of the peninsula raced south to escape. They would not stop until Seoul had fallen again. The X Corps on the east, separated from the Eighth Army by rugged mountains, was isolated at the Chosin Reservoir, where Task Force MacLean-Faith, a temporary unit made up of 2,300 men, lost more than 1,000 in killed and missing on its eastern shore. The weather went from cold to colder, and to stop moving often meant frostbite or death. The 1st Marine Division produced an epic tale of hardship, heroism, and success under the most adverse conditions. They did not retreat, but attacked from a different direction. Staying together in units large enough to produce sufficient firepower to turn back battalion-sized assaults, they showed the world how to defeat massed bodies of infantry. Finally, carrying their wounded and many of their dead, they reached the port of Hungnam in safety. Notable in the fighting was a lieutenant, Chew-Een Lee, leader of a weapons platoon and a Chinese-American (he would simply say "an American"). Wounded, his arm useless, Lee led a nighttime attack on Chinese who were blocking the withdrawal of two Marine regiments from Yudam-ni. Described as "hard as steel, tough as nails, cold as ice—all the clichés apply. . . . [Lee] was a natural-born battle leader."[55] With such men, the vastly outnumbered Marines fought the Chinese to a standstill. The Chinese went into battle against the Marines with twelve divisions and 120,000 men, lost 72,500, and did not seriously contest the embarkation of the 1st Marines from Hungnam. Three Chinese armies disappeared from the Chinese order of battle until reconstituted in the spring of 1951. After lines were stabilized just above the thirty-eighth parallel, the war dragged on for more than two years, until a cease-fire enacted in July 1953 under the newly elected president, Dwight Eisenhower.

America's ability to survive in the Korean War, while deliberately refraining from using atomic weapons, constituted the first occurrence in modern history where a nation with superior military technology voluntarily refused to use it out of moral concerns. Of course, MacArthur had appealed for the use of such weapons. He also wanted to broaden the war by attacking China from the outset. Truman skillfully outmaneuvered him among the officer corps, all of whom were outranked by MacArthur, and many of whom resented his imperial demeanor. The resentment ran both ways—the American Caesar had only disdain for Truman as a wartime leader, routinely slighting him in almost every conceivable manner. MacArthur lumped the president in with "those who advocate appeasement and defeatism in Asia," as he called it in his planned speech to the Veterans of Foreign Wars (which was withdrawn upon Truman's review and order).[56]

For Truman's part, he harbored similar disdain toward MacArthur, calling the general "Mr. Prima Donna, Brass Hat, and Five Star MacArthur." Truman already had predicted that MacArthur would seek to run against him as a Republican in 1952 and would try to go over his head to the voters. Another serious breach of protocol followed when MacArthur sent a letter to the House of Representatives that contained the phrase "There is no substitute for victory." Truman gave the general the boot on April 11, 1951, bringing MacArthur back from the Far East into retirement, and unleashing a firestorm. Polling showed Truman with a 26 percent popularity rating contrasted with MacArthur's 69 percent, and the general's televised address to Congress upon his return garnered an audience of 30 million. Walking through the streets of New York City—without an organized parade—MacArthur drew a crowd of 7 million.

But MacArthur began to lose support almost as soon as he specified what his version of victory entailed, not the least of which was his promise to drop fifty atomic bombs on Chinese cities. Senior officers lined up against him: General Omar Bradley, in hearings before the joint Senate Foreign Relations and Armed Services Committees, predicted that a conflict such as MacArthur desired in Asia would denude Europe of troops and would be the "wrong war at the wrong place and with the wrong enemy."[57] Bradley, a press favorite, seemed the antithesis to "fighting generals" such as MacArthur or the now-deceased George S. Patton. Reporters had carefully cultivated an image for Bradley as "the GI's General" (largely to minimize the aggressive actions of commanders such as Patton). In reality, Bradley was ruthless in sacking other officers and, concealing his intense ambition, had risen faster and higher than anyone other than Eisenhower in the European theater during the Second World War. In Korea, however, Bradley applied a global strategic context to the conflict that MacArthur's theater approach lacked and recognized the importance of avoiding a war with the Chinese while the USSR stood poised to overrun Europe. As General Matthew Ridgway, MacArthur's successor, stabilized the situation at the front, MacArthur's poll numbers dropped by half. Following an uninspired speaking tour in Texas, the general's political star dimmed, and he

declined to run for the Republican nomination. He was replaced in the
presidential race by another general-turned-politician, Dwight D. Eisenhower, who, as supreme commander of Allied forces in Europe, resigned
his position in May 1952 to run as a Republican. Ike had much of what
MacArthur lacked—the reputation as a conciliator, deal maker, and team
player. He certainly had not ruffled feathers in the Truman administration
as MacArthur had. Yet by aggressively countering the isolationist positions of Ohio senator Robert A. Taft, and by promising to fight "communism, Korea, and corruption," he deftly made the transition from soldier
to politician.

MacArthur's arguments lived on, however, so much so that by January
1952 the Joint Chiefs and Truman began to seriously contemplate the use
of atomic bombs and pondered the necessity of more radical actions against
China. General Mark Clark, whose slow plod up the Italian boot in World
War II had frustrated the Allied command, succeeded Ridgway and sent an
audacious plan to Washington that involved dropping atomic bombs on
selected Chinese targets. In 1953, President Dwight Eisenhower also studied the use of atomic bombs "on a sufficiently large scale" to end the war.[58]
Public opinion likewise favored employing atomic artillery shells if "truce
talks break down."[59]

Standard misinterpretations of the Korean War as a "draw" have become so common among liberal American historians, the media, and the
public that all perspective has been lost. Even though the USSR itself had
not provoked the war, or conducted it, the conflict was every bit as much a
test of American willpower as Berlin had been in 1948. Despite Mao's independence from Moscow, the North Koreans were proxies once removed
and would not have lasted without help from both major Communist powers. Not only did the Chinese contribute substantial land forces and provide
the bulk of the manpower at war's end, but Soviet MiG-15 pilots fought in
the skies against the U.S. Air Force from March 1951 until the end of the
war. The Soviets furnished two Guards Fighter Aviation Divisions and
thirteen squadrons, decorated sixteen aces, and claimed to have outscored
American F-86 Sabre pilots by two to one. On the other hand, Americans
may have knocked down Chinese and North Korean MiGs at a rate of thirteen to one.[60] The Soviets also regularly attacked American B-29 bombers,
and on Black Tuesday, October 23, 1951, sent up eighty-four MiG-15s
against nine B-29s, and shot down five, for an American loss of 56 percent
in the greatest jet engagement in the history of aerial warfare. America accepted such losses in the air, and often heavy casualties during bloody en-

gagements on the ground, yet persevered to the end. If anything, the war constituted an Antietam on a larger scale—a tactical stalemate and a strategic gain. Communist forces had been repelled, kept again from expanding their empire. North Korea did not give up, however, and went back to its prewar strategy of subverting South Korea, and from the cease-fire on July 27, 1953, to 2012, has breached the armistice agreement more than four thousand times. More than 1,200 American personnel have died during that time, with hundreds wounded, and 87 captured, along with more than 3,000 ROK casualties.[61]

Korea was a microcosm of two monumental realities of the modern world. First, it reflected a much deeper philosophy about the nature of communism than even Kennan or Truman vocalized (if they understood it at all), and one that stood Lenin on his head. When Lenin published *Imperialism: The Highest Stage of Capitalism* in 1917, he had argued that to survive, capitalism had to conquer and exploit colonies. Confined to existing borders, capitalist nations would fail due to the inherent contradictions stemming from the business cycle. In fact, the postwar world was proving just the opposite. Lacking a war to justify totalitarian control and maintain production, Communist states experienced an economic slowdown eventually leading to their collapse, but not those in the West. As long as "colonies," in the form of conquered territories acquired during war, could be pillaged, the inevitable could be delayed. Korea accelerated that collapse by consuming resources to no good effect, as North Korea was unable to attain a military victory. The capitalist United States could absorb unprofitable wars, but Communist powers could not.

Contrary to notions that Korea represented a demonstration of the "remarkable self-limiting character of the American Republic," the entanglement reflected something more significant: a deep understanding of the nature of the long-term struggle in which Americans were engaged. A military victory in a peninsula in which American territory was not directly threatened, and in which our ally only saw the restoration of his original borders, was neither necessary nor worth the cost of a full-scale war with China. Certainly the Chinese gained nothing from the Korean War. On their doorstep, and even when vastly outnumbering their American foes, the best they could achieve was a stalemate. And the South Koreans bulked up their military, reducing the necessary permanent troop levels from the United States and committing Seoul to acquiring and maintaining state-of-the-art equipment. The Soviets were unimpressed with the Chinese effort, while China's southern neighbor, India, which had begun to look warily across her border, decided the Sino threat was not as formidable as formerly supposed.

The second significant development of the war involved the global role of the United States as the world's policeman. This proved critical because on one level, the United States had *abrogated* this role, or, at the very least, compromised it by bringing in the feeble United Nations. Allowing the war to unfold as a UN action, as opposed to strictly a defense of American interests, planted a weed in the garden that soon threatened to choke off all legitimate U.S. overseas actions. Nevertheless, the conflict showed that on another level Americans had the stomach for the rugged, long-term struggle against militaristic communism that was demanded.

Such a commitment involved remarkable staying power, for while American politics were (and are) short-sighted and generally confined to time frames going no further than the next election, the worldwide Communist/Marxist movement was multigenerational in its planning. Communism placed a *dictatorship* at the helm of every Communist state—an imperial monarch unrestricted by any laws or rules, and one depending on terror and violence to maintain his position. There have been no exceptions to this mode of government. As demonstrated in the introduction, mass murder has always been the order of the day, whether the country is North Korea, Spain, China, the USSR, Venezuela, Cuba, Poland, Cambodia, Vietnam, or any other country where Communists seized power and fundamentally transformed the political form of government and the country's society. The butcher's bill by 2010 would reach well over a hundred million deaths, not even including those in war.

Penetration at the Highest Levels

Modern histories of the cold war era, particularly of the first decade after the war's end, have been written in the most remarkable of vacuums. While many—though not all—acknowledge the presence of Soviet spies in American government and the diplomatic corps, the impact of these agents is treated as little more than an inconvenience. One gets the sense that these works toss in "Oh, then there were a few spies . . ." for balance, as if a doctor examining a patient in critical condition is told, "Oh, then there is the cancer. . . ." In reality, Soviet espionage worked beyond the Kremlin's wildest dreams, and the USSR's stunning success made America's eventual victory in the cold war seem miraculous in hindsight.

Among all the nations in existence in 1945, the United States was probably the slowest in public acceptance of an intelligence apparatus. Russia under the czars had the Okhrana, transformed and eventually enhanced under the Communists as the KGB. European states, including France and England, had well-established secret services; during World War II, the British had more than thirty thousand people working on cryptanalysis alone. But after World War I, peacetime America possessed a few (although highly efficient) code breakers housed in the Army Signal Corps, with both the Army and Navy having a smattering of officers and analysts assigned to intelligence slots within the service branches. At the time of the Japanese attack on Pearl Harbor, only about three hundred analysts labored in the American cryptologic effort. The Army's Office of Strategic Services, formed in 1942, served the country admirably until disbanded by Truman in 1945. Truman harbored suspicions about its Republican, New York socialite head, "Wild Bill" Donovan (who appeared to operate outside the chain of command), and even feared the agency might work against American interests. He therefore broke up the thirteen-thousand-strong OSS within a month after the Japanese surrender and with only ten days' notice, transferring its functions and research to the State Department. The War Department retained only a small secret intelligence group named the Strategic Services Unit.

Besides the demise of the OSS, 1945 saw the nearly complete collapse of American communications intelligence efforts. During the war, there had been two separate and independent intelligence organizations: the Army's Signal Security Agency and the Navy's Naval Communications Intelligence Organization. In September 1945, the former was redesignated as the Army Security Agency (ASA), and the Navy's group was deactivated entirely. By the end of 1945, the organizations had lost 80 percent of their personnel, the military's listening posts were occupied by caretakers, and the ability to intercept radio traffic had all but disappeared. Code-breaking work nearly ceased, and going into 1946, there was essentially no intelligence on foreign countries and their military establishments other than that collected by State Department personnel operating out of embassies.

Through the March 1946 UKUSA Agreement, the British and Americans shared their intelligence efforts. The Anglo-American alliance had been strained during the war by the constant sniping and insubordination of British top-level officers to General Dwight D. Eisenhower's command. What neither Ike, nor Roosevelt, nor Truman knew was that the British had spied on the United States extensively prior to the war, and had penetrated the State Department with agents designed to support the continuation of the British imperial possessions. (We discussed in the previous volume how British agents also penetrated the major polling organizations, trying to swing public opinion toward a war with Germany prior to 1941.) On the other hand, when times got desperate, the British shipped all their top atomic scientists and major military secrets, including their radar designs, to the United States.

UKUSA's code-breaking operations scored a success almost immediately. By 1947, three Soviet cipher systems had been broken, but almost as quickly Soviet penetration of the Arlington Hall group (the Army's equivalent intelligence operation to England's Bletchley Park) soon brought all that to a halt. After receiving information on Arlington Hall's successes from Soviet agent William Weisband, who also informed them of the Venona project, the Soviets, on October 29, 1948 (Black Friday), the single worst day in American intelligence history up to that point, changed essentially all their cipher systems, machines, call signs, and frequencies. Soviet radio communications went utterly dark, and would remain so for the next thirty years. With signal intelligence gone, it would be up to human intelligence to close the gap.

Truman belatedly formed the Central Intelligence Group in 1946 to fill the vacuum left by the dissolution of the OSS and provide early warning of hostile intentions from whatever origin. This organization was replaced by the Central Intelligence Agency (CIA) under the National Security Act of 1947, but it hardly got a running start. Its powers and budget were limited, and although increased in 1949, it was not until 1953 that the Agency took on substantial importance, even then still severely lacking in effectiveness.

In the meantime, an organization almost unknown today picked up the slack in American intelligence work. The Army's Counterintelligence Corps (CIC) assumed extensive intelligence-gathering duties in Europe and Japan as a natural outgrowth of its occupation operations. In Europe, the CIC handled the interrogation centers for refugees coming from the East, as well as all military personnel processing and de-Nazification. Here again, an unthinkable blunder severely and negatively impacted American intelligence capabilities. Truman agreed to return all Soviet citizens to Soviet control, and this proceeded at an alarming rate, often before the CIC could even think about using some of these individuals as agents. Displaced people from other Eastern European countries offered some potential, but there was little money and almost no time to make assessments. Black market operations were widespread, and chaos seemed to reign supreme. The only bright spot was that the CIC did not suffer a severe reduction in force like the remainder of the American military establishment. By 1947, the

Army had shrunk to 550,000 men, but the CIC's personnel dropped only 24 percent, from 5,000 to 3,800.[62] The CIC was merged with the 285 military attaché and consulate personnel around the world, plus the Signal Corps group of SIGINT personnel called the Army Security Agency, to make up the Army's Intelligence Division. With such a tiny intelligence establishment, the United States ventured forth to fight the Soviet Union's vast intelligence services.

In Europe, anti-Communist and anti-Soviet activities rapidly collapsed in Ukraine and satellite countries. Any such movements were immediately branded by the Soviets as fascist or reactionary and brutally suppressed. Even defectors from before the war and refugees had been liquidated in the West, which seemed unable to protect them. First, Stalin's old rival Leon Trotsky had an ice pick plunged into his skull while living in exile in Mexico in 1940. The following year, Walter Krivitsky, a Soviet general in the Red Army intelligence service, died in Washington of a gunshot to the head, almost certainly assassinated by a Soviet agent. Krivitsky, who had been repeatedly and savagely attacked by American Progressives for exposing the true nature of the Soviet regime, was nevertheless at the top of the NKVD (the predecessor of the KGB) assassination list. Others, like Ukrainian leader Stepan Bandera and Bulgarians Georgi Markov and Vladimir Kostov, succumbed to induced "heart attacks" (actually poison gas) in public after being touched with the point of an umbrella by an unknown passerby.

Nonetheless, the 1,400-man CIC in West Germany staffed the refugee reception centers and sorted out those Soviet agents, Nazi war criminals, and individuals who might prove useful in performing covert missions in Soviet-occupied territories and the Soviet Union itself. Mostly staffed by reserve officers, the CIC units provided a wealth of human intelligence, and their widespread activities gave hope to Western Europeans, perhaps even more so than the Marshall Plan, that the United States would not abandon them. The CIC's most pressing problem was determining Soviet intentions, and with radio communications impenetrable, telephone operators, truckers, railroad personnel, and anyone who could report on military communications and movements were prime sources of information. By the late 1950s, nothing could move in East Germany by road, rail, or canal without being reported through Army intelligence channels. With technical and signal intelligence unable to penetrate Soviet organizations, a small army of low-level informants who hated the Communists spread out across Eastern Europe and told the Army what it needed to know.

One key breakthrough occurred in 1946, when General Edwin Sibert, assistant chief of staff for the European theater, brought General Reinhard Gehlen, former head of Wehrmacht intelligence on the Eastern Front, back from captivity in the United States to an American intelligence center located in Oberursel, Germany. Recovering Gehlen's files, the United States gained a list of agents exceeding 3,500 names. The subsequent Gehlen Organization not only provided the United States with cold war intelligence, but eventually formed the nucleus of Germany's CIA, the Bundesnachrichtendienst (BND) or Federal Intelligence Service.[63]

Nothing, however, compared to the intelligence breakthrough that came from the so-called Venona project. Initiated in 1943 by Brigadier General Carter Clarke of the Army's Special Branch, Venona was the decryption operation targeting Soviet cable traffic to and from the United States by the Army's Signal Intelligence Service at Arlington Hall. According to Venona researchers Herbert Romerstein and Eric Breindel, Eleanor Roosevelt got wind of Clarke's initiative through her government contacts, and ordered him to cease and desist. Nonetheless, he ignored her interference and persisted.

With great effort, and after receiving critical information from intercepted and decoded Japanese messages, message traffic from Soviet "one-time pads" was deciphered. Finnish cryptographic personnel had developed some understanding of Soviet codes and been able to identify certain features, and their sharing of this information with the Japanese gave American analysts a head start. As the name implied, one-time pads were single-date, single-code pads for use only once. Amazingly, some of them were reused as a Soviet cost-cutting measure, permitting code breakers to track patterns.

Arlington Hall discovered that the Soviets had reused pages over a four-year period, 1942–45, and code breakers were able to solve cipher keys and read significant strings of NKVD code by December 1945. Using the Venona intercepts, cryptanalysts were able to determine the code names and real identities of Soviet agents in the United States, and to some degree, Great Britain.

But Army intelligence and the CIC focused narrowly on military subjects, and what neither Britain's MI5 (counterintelligence) nor the FBI could do before the late 1940s was catch Communists within the British government or the Roosevelt administration. Their ineptitude in rounding up spies was all the more remarkable because it was, as the saying goes, a target-rich environment. One agent in England, the harmless-looking

Harold "Kim" Philby, was a Soviet operative for years (1934–51), in 1944 actually being the head of MI6's (foreign intelligence) unit targeted at the Soviet Union. He became the British liaison officer to the CIA, and after betraying nearly every important British and American secret to the Soviet Union, was awarded the position of officer of the Order of the British Empire (Britain was spared the embarrassment of having made him one of the higher ranks that required him to be called "sir"). He worked throughout the British possessions, and in Turkey and Washington, where he housed another spy, Guy Burgess. Described as "unstable, dangerously alcoholic, and flamboyantly homosexual," Burgess lived in Philby's home and proved a source of perpetual embarrassment.[64] Apparently even a spy had "family values," and Philby disliked Burgess—his wife despised him even more so—but he could not boot him into the street, for Philby needed to supervise him. Burgess's actions brought constant surveillance by J. Edgar Hoover's FBI for espionage. Cited with three speeding tickets in a single day, Burgess pleaded diplomatic immunity, and Hoover fumed that Burgess routinely used British diplomatic vehicles while cruising for homosexual encounters.[65] Finally, Burgess, attempting to place another spy on a ship to France, ended up boarding the vessel with him and eventually arrived in London. The single serious British investigation into Philby during this time cleared him, and Foreign Secretary (later prime minister) Harold Macmillan told the House of Commons, "I have no reason to conclude that Mr. Philby has at any time betrayed the interests of this country. . . ."[66] Philby survived the investigation, but was briefly out at MI6 before being re-recruited to conduct espionage in Lebanon for the British. In his role as double agent, Philby seemed once again secure, until Anatoliy Golitsyn, a major in the KGB, defected in 1961 and confirmed Philby's spy activities.[67]

Philby demonstrated how easily spies who penetrated one Western government could expose others. Had the United States not been subjected to a single agent who came from another country, however, it still would have housed a virtual rats' nest of spies, most of them within the Roosevelt administration and most of them ultimately exposed by Venona. Among the most poisonous of the domestic agents was Harry Dexter White (code name JURIST), the assistant secretary of the treasury in the Roosevelt administration, and a man who had extensive influence over American monetary policy. White, though not a member of the Communist Party of the USA, nevertheless was evaluated by another Soviet agent inside the treasury, Harold Glasser, who had begun his work at a low level in the Monetary Research Division and saw substantial promotions after that. Glasser informed his Soviet superiors that as of 1937 White was providing all the information of importance that they needed.[68] Working for the NKVD, White facilitated the hiring at treasury of eleven Soviet sources, and shielded some when they came under scrutiny. White also successfully labored to get Ji Chaoding, a member of the American Communist Party, a key spot in the Chinese Nationalist Treasury Department, in which capacity he advised the Nationalist government in its financial policy toward Mao Zedong. When the Communist Chinese took over in 1949, Ji, having openly announced his Communist affiliation, remained as a senior official of the new Communist government.

Treasury's influence was significant when it came to policy debates about the reconstruction of Europe, and Venona decrypts specifically referenced White advising the Soviets on how far they could push on certain European issues, such as the annexation of Estonia, Latvia, and Lithuania. He met covertly with the Soviet delegation at the UN founding conference in 1945 and supplied them with information on American negotiating strategies.[69] Presented with a questionnaire by an NKVD agent outlining numerous issues about which the Soviets needed information, White wrote down all the answers. When White considered leaving the diplomatic corps to make more money in private business, the NKVD offered to pay for his daughter's education. When it came to direct involvement, White's hands were bloody there as well: the Soviets had asked for a $6 billion loan in 1945, but White persuaded his boss, Henry Morgenthau, to increase it to $10 billion, with better terms and a lower interest rate. White earlier had successfully stalled a loan of gold to Chiang's Nationalist government, badly damaging Nationalist attempts to battle inflation.[70] Working in tandem with another Soviet agent, Frank Coe (code name PEAK), at the State Department, White delayed the gold loan.

White was abetted in his work by Alger Hiss, a State Department official, and Lauchlin Currie, a senior administrative assistant to the president. Hiss had been a member of the Yalta delegation, where it was argued that FDR "gave away the farm," was the secretary general of the conference establishing the United Nations, and had already come up on the government's radar during the House Un-American Activities Committee (HUAC) hearings in 1948. Lying his way through the hearings, Hiss was eventually outed as a Soviet spy by Whittaker Chambers, a fellow Communist agent before the war whom Hiss claimed not to know. Once again, Venona produced solid evidence that Hiss was the agent code named ALES, and that he had been taking orders from the Kremlin while at Yalta.[71] The evidence was there; as John Earl Haynes and Harvey Klehr, two of the foremost scholars on Venona, concluded (and as they said in the title of their 2007 article): "Alger Hiss Was Guilty."[72]

Nonetheless, Hiss, a Harvard Law School graduate and member of the eastern American liberal elite, was readmitted to the Massachusetts bar in 1975. Tall, spare, and looking every bit the patrician he was, Alger Hiss managed to bifurcate his two personas so successfully that one might think he possessed multiple personalities. When exposed by Whittaker Chambers, he so outclassed his accuser—an overweight, rumpled character with bad teeth—that Hiss's attorneys successfully used a reputational defense, contrasting the smooth, erudite, educated Hiss with the disheveled Chambers. From 1932 until 1937, Chambers had actively conducted espionage for the USSR. He came to lose his faith, and in 1938 broke with communism altogether. After storing crucial documents, as well as microfilm of other papers, to serve as a bargaining chip, Chambers hoped to just drop out. But as so many mobsters discovered, leaving the "family" was never a realistic option. Nevertheless, as Stalin allied with Hitler in the 1939 nonaggression pact, Chambers decided to inform on other agents provided he received immunity from prosecution. Among those he named as spies were Alger Hiss and Lauchlin Currie.

In August 1948, Chambers was summoned to testify before HUAC, where he revealed the members of the Ware group, which included Hiss, although he did not name Hiss as a spy, only a Communist. The committee tended to side with Hiss—despite his shifting testimony and inconsistent statements—and only Richard Nixon supported Chambers. Armed with information from the FBI, Nixon pursued Hiss and began to turn the committee. Harry Truman, who had inherited FDR's viper's nest of Communist agents, dismissed the allegations as a "red herring." But privately Truman knew that Hiss and other Soviet agents could easily bring down his administration if fully exposed, and in 1947 he issued Executive Order 9835, establishing a loyalty screening for federal employees. Astonishingly, however, the willingness to support Hiss extended to Dean Acheson, who obtained a post for him at the Carnegie Endowment after Hiss was called upon to resign from the State Department. Acheson even reviewed Hiss's statement before HUAC and consulted with Hiss's attorney during the subsequent trials.

Regardless of the evidence and what people thought, the statute of limitations on espionage was up and Hiss could not be prosecuted. Chambers had stated that Hiss had engaged in espionage, and true to his patrician sense of effrontery, Hiss filed a $75,000 libel suit against Chambers in October 1948. It was his greatest mistake: Chambers produced a set of damning documents, called the "Pumpkin Papers" because he had kept them hidden in a hollowed-out pumpkin, and which contained various documents with Hiss's name on them that had been stolen from the State Department and given to the Soviets. While Chambers was suddenly more believable, Hiss had foolishly exposed himself to new charges of perjury, and he was indicted again in 1949. During the trial, Hiss's testimony shifted as one lie after another was revealed as being inconsistent with hard evidence and multiple witnesses, and Chambers was speaking verifiable truths. Quite possibly, the only reason Hiss was able to swing four jurors to his side in his first trial was that the jury foreman was the brother-in-law of Austin MacCormick, the noted leftist criminologist who opposed the death penalty and helped prepare Hiss to cope with his time in prison. Evidence was introduced by the prosecution at Hiss's first trial that the foreman favored Hiss, but the judge refused to disqualify him.[73] At a second trial in 1950, however, Hiss was convicted largely due to evidence that his wife Priscilla had used a Woodstock typewriter to type the espionage documents—a typewriter Hiss himself went out of his way to produce. Although the charge was perjury, the issue was espionage and all the jurors knew it.[74]

Perhaps because of his conviction, Hiss remade himself in the ensuing years, successfully convincing a large number of American liberals of his innocence, ceaselessly (and shamelessly) portraying himself as a victim of McCarthy-style persecution. In effect, he set himself up as the American Dreyfus to discredit the U.S. government and anticommunism in general. For this tactic to work, his supporters had to already be committed to destroying most of the pillars of American exceptionalism. When the Russian general Dmitri Volkogonov said in 1992 that he had been unable to find anything on Hiss in the KGB archives, the major television networks in the United States reported it immediately; but when he retracted his statement, all were silent.[75] Volkogonov later admitted he had spent only two days in the Foreign Intelligence Archive, had not examined any archives, and instead asked the former head of the KGB to provide him with information. Yevgeny Primakov, who by then oversaw the SRV—the replacement to the KGB's foreign intelligence section—told his researchers to give Volkogonov only "selected files." After multiple references to Hiss's service *were* uncovered in the Soviet archives during glasnost, one would think the Left would quietly drop their assertions. But the ideology is never wrong, just slightly in error on a few details. A number of Progressives continued to work tirelessly for Hiss's exoneration. Their voices were only muted after the 1995 release of the Venona documents, but even then the Progressive Nation Institute in 2007 held a conference proclaiming Hiss's innocence, against all logic and evidence, even from the former USSR officials themselves.

Plenty of other Soviet agents busily toiled in the U.S. government. White's Treasury Department also produced Lauchlin Currie (code name PAGE). Although Currie did not cooperate as often as did some other spies, he handed over critical documents to the NKVD, such as those in 1945 indicating FDR's bargaining position regarding the postwar Polish government. In July 1941, immediately after the Nazi invasion of Russia, Roosevelt and Treasury Secretary Morgenthau instructed Currie and White to develop measures for dealing with the Japanese. They proposed an economic blockade of Japan, but FDR adopted a much less confrontational oil embargo on July 26.[76] Ultimately, the oil issue would accelerate the Japanese attack on the United States, and then subsequently with Germany—all to the benefit of the Soviet Union. It takes little imagination to see Stalin's hands at work through Currie and White. During the war, the FBI lacked enough evidence to prosecute Currie, given that Venona was classified and could not be brought up in court proceedings. But Currie felt the investigators closing in, and in 1950 he gave up his U.S. citizenship and left for Colombia.[77]

Less subtle and even more damaging were the efforts of the husband-wife tag team of Julius and Ethel Rosenberg. Liberal historians insist to this day—in spite of Venona identifying them in a number of NKVD messages—that the Rosenbergs were not guilty of espionage.[78] When the U.S. and British governments, in 1950, unearthed a Communist spy ring involving Klaus Fuchs, a German physicist who had worked on atomic bomb research, the investigators soon were led to Harry Gold (his courier), then to David Greenglass (Julius's brother-in-law, who worked on the Manhattan Project), then to the Rosenbergs themselves. At his trial, Greenglass testified that Julius Rosenberg passed to the Soviets schematics of the "lens" device that activated the atomic bomb. It was one of the most heavily guarded secrets of the war, and after Rosenberg's action it was in the hands of the Soviet Union.

Julius Rosenberg, a disheveled, bespectacled son of Jewish immigrants, had worked in the U.S. Army Signal Corps, then as an engineer-inspector through the war, where he had access to high-level electronics, communications, and radar information. He was recruited by the Soviets, appropriately, on Labor Day 1942 and became a part of an "engineers' cell," which he soon headed (under code name LIBERAL). In 2001, Alexander Feklisov, his former handler at the NKVD, wrote that Rosenberg provided thousands of classified documents to the USSR, including the design for a proximity fuse that in 1960 was used to shoot down Francis Gary Powers's U-2 spy plane.[79]

Like Hiss and Currie, Julius Rosenberg recruited many others to his cause, including Joel Barr, Alfred Sarant, Morton Sobell, and William Perl. Through Perl, Rosenberg passed along design and production documents for the USAF P-80 Shooting Star interceptor aircraft. Greenglass also implicated both Rosenbergs deeply in the reproduction and transmission of a variety of documents of the "Fat Man" atomic bomb. Their actions advanced the Soviet development of the bomb by an estimated five years. At their 1951 trial under Judge Irving Kaufman, the Rosenbergs were convicted and sentenced to death under the Espionage Act of 1917. Kaufman was devastating in his comments to the couple during his sentencing on April 5, 1951:

> I consider your crime worse than murder . . . I believe your conduct in putting into the hands of the Russians the A-Bomb years before our best scientists predicted Russia would perfect the bomb has already caused, in my opinion, the Communist aggression in Korea, with the resultant casualties exceeding 50,000 and who knows but that millions more of innocent people may pay the price of your treason. Indeed, by your betrayal you undoubtedly have altered the course of history to the disadvantage of our country. No one can say that we do not live in a constant state of tension. We have evidence of your treachery all around us every day for the civilian defense activities throughout the nation are aimed at preparing us for an atom bomb attack.[80]

Despite the efforts of countless writers, and reams of paper dedicated to arguing the couple's innocence, history has proven the verdict correct and vindicated Kaufman's rhetoric. Not only did Venona identify Julius as a spy, but subsequent evidence has shown Ethel's complicity as well. The coup de grâce came in 2008 when their coconspirator, Morton Sobell, admitted that both he and Julius were Soviet agents. Confronted with that admission, even one of the Rosenbergs' sons, Michael Meeropol, glumly concluded, "I don't have any reason to doubt Morty."[81] And, as if a higher confirmation was needed, Soviet premier Nikita Khrushchev said in his memoirs that both Rosenbergs "provided very significant help in accelerating the production of our atomic bomb."[82]

Hysteria or Sobriety?

Understanding the so-called Red Scare of the 1950s is difficult in the modern age, where terms such as "McCarthyism" and "hysteria" are commonplace. But hysteria is an ungrounded, irrational reaction—a child shrieking when someone tosses him a pencil, as opposed to a person recoiling when someone throws a cobra on the table. Concerns about communism in the early 1950s were grounded in abundant evidence:

- The USSR had gained, then still occupied, Eastern Europe and, despite its promises, there was no indication the Soviets would ever permit free elections there

- The Soviets had blockaded Berlin

- China had fallen to the Communists

- Communist North Korea invaded South Korea, with air support from the USSR and ground intervention from the Chinese Communists

- The USSR obtained the atomic bomb five years before Western intelligence thought it would be able to do so

- Extensive spy networks were discovered in the U.S. government and defense establishment

- The Communist Party of the United States of America was public, vocal, and active in its intention to make the United States into a Communist state

- Labor unions and Hollywood were populated with CPUSA members and/or sympathizers

Thus, when Senator Joseph McCarthy, a Republican from Wisconsin, made his famous Lincoln Day speech at Wheeling, West Virginia, on February 9, 1950, there was ample evidence for even his "wildest" allegations. Debate continues to the present day over what he actually said, because there was no audio recording of the event, although a version of it was reprinted in the *Congressional Record* of the Senate on February 20, in which McCarthy said, "I have in my hand 57 cases of individuals who would appear to be either card carrying members or certainly loyal to the Communist Party, but who nevertheless are still helping to shape our foreign policy. . . ."[83] But these remarks were edited, and McCarthy may have ad-libbed, as witnesses later said he produced two numbers that day, for one witness wrote down both, and recalled that he said there were 205 individuals under investigation, of which already 57 were known Communists. But the difference between the two numbers became a central point for critics wishing to undermine the broader point McCarthy raised: that despite his having alerted the government to dozens of members of the Communist Party working in the State Department, few had been fired.[84]

McCarthy instantly became both the icon of the Right, who considered him a watchman sounding a clarion call, and the nemesis of the Left, who saw him as the focal point of unreasonable suspicion and fear. McCarthy was an Irish Catholic who had switched parties, who counted as two of his closest friends John Kennedy and Richard Nixon, and who employed Robert F. Kennedy as one of his investigators. He was a hard drinker and tough, a friend of farmers, and a champion of civil rights. Using his Permanent Subcommittee on Investigations, McCarthy tended to operate on the fringes as often as he could, holding hearings, challenging witnesses. Although it would later be claimed that he tarred innocent people with his accusations, in reality McCarthy refused to name names in public from his list, instead insisting that he would reveal all those on his list in a Senate secret session.[85] McCarthy insisted that he did not want to wrongfully implicate anyone as a Communist before an investigation, and repeatedly stated in public, "I do not have all the information about [them]," which is why he wanted the FBI to follow up.[86] Democrats seeking to shield Truman, and Roosevelt's legacy, refused to allow a secret session. They knew such a session would reveal the extent of Soviet penetration into the administration. Years later, most of those McCarthy named, including Mary Jane Keeney, Lauchlin Currie, Solomon Adler, Harold Glasser, and Virginius Frank Coe, turned out to be . . . Communists! McCarthy actually had only led with his list of known agents: the list of "suspected" agents that he identified added *dozens* of additional names, including a roster of State Department employees, some in the Commerce Department, a judge, and the head of Truman's Council of Economic Advisers.[87]

McCarthy overstepped in the hearings on the U.S. Army, eventually calling into question the integrity of former Army chief of staff George Marshall, although actually he may have had grounds, particularly over China. But Marshall enjoyed immense popularity, and that was too much. Washington supporters deserted McCarthy, and the press, which often worked with him to generate headlines, turned against him. "McCarthyism" became a code word for crazed abuse of power—only on the Right, however—and Eisenhower disavowed the senator.[88] Yet he had not only been correct in his claims, but, if anything, they had been understated and *late*. By the time McCarthy began investigating the State Department, the FBI had already purged several people and was investigating many more. That was, after all, how McCarthy knew that a number were under scrutiny. More important to the modern historical debate was the notion that McCarthy led a "movement" (let alone, as Dean Acheson claimed, "a mob"). One third of Americans didn't even know who he was and as of 1953—the height of his power—two thirds had no opinion of him at all.[89]

One of the more interesting lines of speculation to explain McCarthy's allegations, advanced after the Venona documents were published, was that someone leaked to McCarthy information on Venona itself. The Soviets, of course, had been informed of Venona's existence and the penetration of their messages using a one-time pad for communications as early as 1946 from at least three sources. Lauchin Currie also apparently became aware of Venona in 1944. Using his White House position, Currie sent instructions to the Army's Special Branch to stop all work on Soviet cipher communications, which would have effectively killed the Venona project. Fortunately, the Army ignored the White House order. Currie also sent a White House order to the OSS, instructing it to stop collecting information on Soviet intelligence operations. When that failed, Currie employed his State Department contacts to muscle the OSS, and that worked. In an act of sheer naïveté, or because it was influenced by Currie's minions, the State Department ordered the OSS to cease all operations concerned with Soviet influence, and furthermore, in the spirit of "Allied cooperation," to give all its material on Soviet codes, including the code book the OSS had obtained from Finnish sources that allowed it to read Soviet dispatches, to the USSR. Obediently, the OSS complied and did not even keep a copy of the code book.

A second individual compromised Venona—William Weisband, an NKVD agent (code named LINK) assigned as a Russian linguist to the Arlington Hall group working on the Venona intercepts in 1945. Shortly after Weisband saw code breaker Meredith Gardner extract a number of names of American scientists from a Soviet intercept in 1945—indicating the scientists were "dirty"—all Soviet use of the one-time pads stopped, and America's ability to read current Soviet mail ceased. Weisband had successfully blinded the United States at a critical time during the cold war.

Venona was also disclosed to the Soviets by Kim Philby, but somewhat later. By 1950 at the latest, then, the Soviets were fully informed, although the American public had to wait until forty-five years later to receive an inkling of the damage done by Soviet spies. It took a major effort by researchers and the influence of Senator Daniel Patrick Moynihan, who thought the records would reveal little that wasn't already known, to persuade NSA to publicly release the Venona information. Eventually, these revelations showed that McCarthy's numbers, even while varying, were low but still not far off the mark set by Venona. According to Venona, 349 individuals provided information to Soviet intelligence operatives as actual vetted Soviet agents, and several hundred more have been identified as occasional but sometimes valuable sources.[90] Curiously, many of these agents were Jewish, rather ungenerously referred to by the Soviets as "rats." Most of these individuals escaped all prosecution, and firmly supported by the American Left, many lived long and fulfilling lives. Forty-five years later, the picture was crystal clear: of the 218 proven to be Soviet spies identified to the FBI, 101 (including 61 Soviet officials) left the United States before the statute of limitations ran out, 11 had died, 14 cooperated with the FBI, 77 were not prosecuted for various and sometimes incomprehensible reasons, and 15 were prosecuted.[91]

Nationally, J. Edgar Hoover, sensing an opportunity to fill McCarthy's void, "turned anticommunism at the Bureau nearly into a personal vendetta."[92] His investigations uncovered Communists, but more important, had a dampening effect on recruitment efforts into the CPUSA. From its 1944 high of eighty thousand members, the CPUSA's membership fell below ten thousand in 1956, and by 1971 counted fewer than three thousand.[93] Many Americans at all levels feared and loathed communism, to the extent that even Harvard University in 1953 banned known Communists and rightly called the ideology "beyond the scope of academic freedom."[94] A handful of anti-Communist films emerged as well, such as I Married a Communist and The Red Menace, public schools instituted democracy classes, and insider exposé books appeared, relating the writers' hidden lives as Communists.

While certainly excesses occurred, and occasionally an innocent person was wrongfully persecuted, or fired from a job, the overwhelming reality of America during the Red Scare was that no one acted scared enough to take any serious action against the American Communist Party. It continued to function legally throughout the McCarthy era, its spokesmen publicly advocated its doctrines, recruiters openly solicited new members, and its press daily published a variety of tracts, newspapers, pamphlets, and books totaling millions of copies.[95] College purges rarely occurred: out of 400,000 college faculty in the 1950s, only 126 cases of dismissal or threatened dismissal due to Communist views were recorded. Yet without any official sanctions or repression, the movement shriveled, becoming as irrelevant after a decade as the Ku Klux Klan in the twenty-first century.

There were several reasons the FBI chose not to publicize the hunt for Communists or to prosecute Soviet spies at this time: embarrassment, fear of Soviet retaliation, and the desire to keep Venona a secret. Nonetheless, the opening of the Soviet archive (the Russian Center for the Preservation and Study of Documents of Recent History) since 1991 has provided much verification of known spies and also added new leads on Soviet sources. With regard to the atomic spies, the Rosenbergs were the tip of the iceberg; Klaus Fuchs, Theodore Hall, and J. Robert Oppenheimer all performed valuable work for the Soviet Union, and Hall, whose treason was extensive and well documented, was one of those never prosecuted. The highest-ranking official in the FDR administration working for Soviet intelligence was Roosevelt's close friend and special adviser Harry Hopkins.[96] What is so shocking about this disclosure is that Hopkins on several occasions negotiated on FDR's behalf alone with Stalin.

Even journalists were recruited to help spread Soviet propaganda, one of the most loyal being writer and reporter for the left-leaning *Nation* I. F. Stone, who became the guiding light and mentor to many well-known media figures still active as of this writing. Progressive commentator and journalist Walter Lippmann regularly met with Vladimir Pravdin, an assassin and agent in the NKVD stationed in the United States until 1945, and shared inside information from highly placed sources in the Roosevelt administration.[97] The Soviets also planted an agent in Lippmann's office—his secretary, Mary Price (code named ARENA), who spied for the USSR and performed courier duties from 1941 to 1945.[98] An example of a Soviet spy who lived large with impunity in the public eye after supposedly terminating her Soviet connections, Price moved to North Carolina, organized a Progressive group, the Southern Conference for Human Welfare, ran for governor on the Progressive Party's ticket in 1947, moved back to Washington and worked at the Czechoslovakian embassy when it was a Soviet satellite, and finally worked for the National Council for Churches. Her career is also worth noting because of the affinity outright Communists had with subsequent so-called human rights groups, some of which proved mere fronts for leftover, out-of-work Communist agents.

What makes this period so particularly troubling is that the American Left backed these spies and traitors to the hilt, acclaiming them as heroes of American liberalism. And this has continued to the present day, as even Hiss's case is still considered in many modern textbooks "controversial."[99] Stone, Hopkins, the Rosenbergs, Hall, Oppenheimer, and others are still defended by the Left, and the blacklisting of Communists in Hollywood is still portrayed as having been unfair, unwarranted, un-American, and seemingly in all cases, visited on innocents. Presenting blacklisted writers at Hollywood award presentations drew enormous applause when such individuals returned to work, and many "Red Diaper Babies" are carrying on the tradition in Hollywood. And more disconcerting still, Venona only constituted a small fraction of the penetration of America's government. Even in terms of Soviet communications from the United States, Venona only accessed a tiny number, 1.5 percent of the NKVD traffic in 1945, 49 percent in 1944, 15 percent in 1943, and 1.8 percent in 1942. Of the Soviet military traffic, 50 percent was read in 1943, but nothing from any other year.[100] Of the three thousand messages that were decoded, most were only partially decoded, and most of the agents identified in the traffic were never linked to a particular individual. There are probably hundreds or even thousands of Americans, some of whom may be still alive, who could be exposed from Russian archives.

On the American side, few, if any, attempts were made before 1946 to recruit agents in the NKVD or its successors by military intelligence. The Soviets had laid their groundwork in the 1920s and '30s, whereas the United States first recognized the need to penetrate high levels in the Soviet Union only following World War II. Forced to play catch-up, the United States recruited few Soviet spies—almost all were "walk-ins" who contacted American intelligence voluntarily before being approached. One of the few KGB officers to provide intelligence information to the CIA while remaining in Soviet service was Colonel Vladimir Vetrov, code named FAREWELL, who would literally enable Ronald Reagan to win the cold war. Colonel Oleg Penkovsky, code named HERO, was a Red Army officer in the Chief Intelligence Directorship of the General Staff rather than a KGB officer, but the two, both volunteers, one for the CIA in 1961 and 1962, and one for the French from 1980 to 1982, made enormous contributions. Both were executed by the KGB, Penkovsky after being betrayed by a Soviet agent in the CIA—one that has not been found to this day. All in all, the CIA probably earned a grade of C- in human intelligence from 1947 to the fall of the Soviet Union, and an F in recruitment. Most Soviet sources were defectors, who betrayed personnel and operations. A typical agent in place was Soviet major Petr Popov, who worked for the CIA from 1952 to 1955 in Austria, and furnished the United States with the Field Service Regulations of the Red Army. But more typical were walk-ins like KBG major Peter Deriabin, who defected in 1954, and KGB major Yuri Nosenko, who defected in 1964. The United States played catch-up rather poorly until the fall of the Soviet Union.

The United States, however, was not alone in being penetrated to its very core by Soviet agents. It was perhaps to be expected that the West German government would be heavily infiltrated by Soviet agents, and France and Italy possessed large Communist parties that at times were part of their governments and could send secrets wholesale to their masters in the Kremlin. But Great Britain, Canada, and Australia were shot through and through with Soviet agents, so much so that in the late 1940s the American intelligence community, itself riddled with Soviet spies, refused to share information with Canada and Australia.[101] When Igor Gouzenko, a Soviet cipher clerk in the Ottawa embassy, attempted to defect, he was turned away from various Canadian agencies, including the Royal Canadian Mounted Police, for two days until it became apparent the Soviets were aggressively attempting to find him. Prime Minister Mackenzie King didn't want to give Gouzenko asylum because he feared becoming embroiled in "an unpleasant diplomatic incident" with the Soviets.[102]

But the case with the greatest impact on the United States occurred in Great Britain. The Cambridge Five, a ring of Soviet spies who had become Communists while attending Cambridge University in the 1930s, not only affected the workings of the British government and submitted huge numbers of British secrets to the Soviets, but also revealed American security secrets. Guy Burgess, Kim Philby, Donald Maclean, Anthony Blunt, and John Cairncross—Soviet code names HICKS, STANLEY, HOMER, JOHNSON, and LISZT, respectively—were extremely well placed due to their social standing and their being in the British old boy network. But the jewel in the Soviet espionage crown was probably Roger Hollis, director-general of England's MI5 (counterintelligence service) from 1956 to 1965.

In addition to the contentions of various officials in the British intelligence services that Hollis was on the Soviet payroll based on evidence that convinced some, but not others, Robert Lamphere of the FBI also thought Hollis was a Soviet spy, and had betrayed the Venona project to the Soviets. Lamphere wrote, "To me, there now remains little doubt that it was Hollis who provided the earliest information to the KGB that the FBI was reading their 1944–45 cables."[103] Given these exceptional penetrations of the highest levels of Western governments, and especially the government of the United States, the victory in the cold war now seems outside the bounds of probability and an even greater testament to the exceptional core elements of America.

Aware of the stigma (not to mention genuine threat) of an association with communism, many U.S. labor unions began to purge their rolls as the cold war began. Walter Reuther's United Auto Workers (UAW) and Philip Murray's Congress of Industrial Organizations (CIO) both booted out Communists before McCarthy's speeches. Equally important, an emerging Hollywood leading man, Ronald Reagan, waged a war against the "Stalinist machine" in the film industry.[104] Reagan, with the help of a tough Hollywood labor leader who mentored and trained him, Roy Brewer, built a bipartisan base to work against avowed Communists. They kept the Screen Actors Guild a group run by the anti-Communist majority, not the Stalinist minority. Reagan had joined HICCASP (the Hollywood Independent Citizens Committee of the Arts, Sciences, and Professions), which had originated as an FDR support group, but found that meetings were dominated by pro-Communist rhetoric. A group of ten met in secret, including Reagan and actress Olivia de Havilland. Reagan whispered, "You know, Olivia, I always thought you were one of 'them.'" She laughed and said, "That's funny, I thought *you* were one of them."[105] When it became obvious to Reagan and eleven others that HICCASP had become little more than a Communist front organization, they all resigned. In 1947, Reagan won the first of seven elections to be president of the Screen Actors Guild, where he fought a two-front battle to purge Communists while at the same time protecting innocent industry people from the House Un-American Activities Committee. He succeeded in doing both, cleansing Hollywood of any overt Stalinist influences (though, over time, the film industry and television would drift steadily to the left) and saving many wrongfully accused of being Communists.

America's firsthand brush with communism showed that the pillars of American exceptionalism were stronger than the promise of utopia, and that in America's free marketplace of ideas, radical, imposed egalitarianism did not stand a chance. But the Soviets quickly trained their sights on another target, one possessing few of the American institutions, cultural ideas, or attitudes about work and property—the Third World. That proved a target-rich environment indeed.

CHAPTER TWO

Dark Continents

Time Line

1945:   Indonesia declares independence; Ho Chi Minh seizes power in Hanoi; United Nations founded; Nag Hammadi Gnostic gospels discovered in Egypt; Gandhi and Nehru order British forces to leave India

1946:   King David Hotel bombing in Israel

1947:   *Exodus* incident off Palestine; India partitioned into India and Pakistan; Dead Sea Scrolls found

1948:   Burmese independence; Gandhi assassinated; Organization of American States founded; Arab-Israeli War begins; Republic of Korea established; Truman reelected president

1949:   Chinese Communists defeat Nationalists

1950:   Chiang Kai-shek moves Nationalist government to Taiwan (Formosa); Korean War begins; French-Indochina war begins

1951:   China seizes Tibet; Libyan independence

1952:   Mau Mau Uprising in Kenya

1954:   Nasser becomes premier of Egypt; Viet Minh defeat French at Dien Bien Phu; Algerian civil war

1955:   U.S. advisers sent to South Vietnam

1956:   Britain, France, and Israel attack Egypt (Suez Crisis); Moroccan and Tunisian independence

1957:   China's Mao Zedong states that 800,000 "class enemies" have been liquidated; Ghanaian independence

1958:   Eisenhower sends troops to Lebanon to protect government; Guinean independence

1959:   Madagascar independence; Castro seizes power in Cuba; North Vietnam invades Laos

De-Europeanizing the World

America had fought the last year of World War II with one eye on the USSR as a major, possibly antagonistic, power. "Atomic diplomacy," the leftist historical argument that President Harry Truman dropped the atomic bombs more to intimidate the Soviets than to defeat the Japanese, has been proven a myth by both American and—more recently—Japanese sources. But even before Soviet premier Joseph Stalin made it clear he intended to greatly expand Soviet influence, if not boundaries, U.S. leaders calculated communism's influence and potential for mayhem when assessing the postwar realities in the Far East and Europe.

The United States' other major ally, Great Britain, kept her eye on something quite different: her empire. British wartime decisions, particularly in India and Asia, were made based on whether the empire would be strengthened or weakened. Decolonization, supposedly begun in the 1920s with long periods of "preparation," became a sudden reality for Britain and other European countries immediately after the war, when the attrition of their military forces and the diminution of their treasuries prevented them from continuing to sustain a global effort.

Britain and other colonial powers faced a spectrum of poor choices to make up for their past sins, and a painless decolonization proved impossible. Throughout the world, the imperial powers would be castigated for building their colonial empires, then savaged even more when they left the colonies to govern themselves. Critics of imperialism, even those who admitted some benefits of occupation, complained about Britain's feeble attempts to establish self-government (however far in the future that lay), and complained louder when nations such as Belgium made virtually no effort to ensure native autonomy. Centuries of human sacrifice, cannibalism, slavery, oppression of every conceivable stripe, tribal divisiveness, and lack of successful self-government by natives were glossed over, excused, forgotten, or wished away in the literature in order to pin the Third World's problems on the Europeans. (The term "Third World" itself is of mixed origins, first used in print by French dissident writer Alfred Sauvy in 1952.) These criticisms completely ignored the fact that it was *only* in the context of European ideas that these *were even contextualized as problems!* Barrels of ink have been spilled lambasting the European decolonization process in the twentieth century, with the bulk of it spent describing the end of the British empire as a preamble to the rise of the "American Empire" and corollary cautionary tales about employing American power in a dangerous world.

As matters turned out, much of the fretting was for naught. Britain's empire unraveled with shocking speed, though not nearly as fast as the Soviet bloc would collapse just forty years later. It ostensibly began to crumble with the Battle of Britain, when a German invasion of England loomed and revealed to the colonies not the empire's strength, but its weakness. Despite controlling territories that stretched from Latin America to the Far East, by 1940 Britain was reduced to begging for aged American destroyers and seeing her treasury emptied. The very levers Britain had pulled to govern the masses in India and Africa had prevented those regions from developing their own industry and invention—the lifeblood of a nation at war. Although England could call on the colonies to provide troops, most of whom dutifully served and courageously fought, they had been denied the elements of autonomy and innovation that had made England and the United States great. It was akin to expecting the practice team to walk onto the field and take over from the all-pros.

During the last months of World War II, General George Marshall had stoutly supported his Supreme Allied Commander, General Dwight D. Eisenhower, in his struggle with British antagonist-counterparts Field Marshal Alan Brooke and Field Marshal Bernard Montgomery over control of the Allied forces. Winston Churchill's demand that Eisenhower designate a deputy supreme commander of all ground forces was not finally defeated until after Yalta. As incomprehensible as it might seem to historians writing in the twenty-first century, the top British command wanted British personnel placed in all large American formations, supposedly for liaison. But their duties would actually be twofold: spy on the Americans for the British (Montgomery automatically did this in American units under his command) and advise them on military strategy.

Marshall's stance was that since the United States was supplying three fourths of the manpower fighting in Western Europe, 45 percent of the world's armaments, half of the world's goods, and two thirds of all the ships—an American should indeed be in charge.[1] The British may have had an inferiority complex that manifested itself in arrogance and disdain for their allies, but with good cause—they *were* inferior. Field Marshal Harold Alexander (later governor general of Canada), speaking with Marshall at Yalta, was as patronizing as ever concerning American failures in the Battle of the Bulge and intimated that it was the British who saved them. Marshall shot back, "Yes, American troops start out and make every possible mistake. But after the first time, they do not repeat their mistakes. The British troops start in the same way, and continue making the same mistakes over and over."[2]

At its core, the struggle over British or American command was not about how to defeat Germany—it was to establish who would be dominant in postwar European affairs, and, secondarily, to ensure that Britain could retain effective control over her colonies. In Marshall's eyes, never again was the United States to be called upon to pull Europe's chestnuts out of the fire. If the children weren't going to play nicely together, then the United States would have to oversee the playground. The Americans had to become the keepers of the peace in Europe, and if the British complained, they, as well as the French, had proven themselves unable or unwilling to do what was necessary. Especially in the context of retaining their empires, the Europeans had been helpless to prevent their fragmentation or, conversely, to properly prepare their subjects for independence. Nowhere did this prove more troublesome and bloody than in India, the Crown Jewel of the Empire.

India, Gandhi, and Nehru

Britain's continued presumption that the colonies would remain intact was based on the flawed notion that their colonial people loved the mother country and would help her in time of war. Many did not, or did so only out of an expectation that independence would be granted out of gratitude. This attitude, of course, was entirely wishful thinking on the part of colonies, dosed heavily with hints, winks, and nods from dishonest British officials and MPs who alluded to murky plans for independence without ever developing clear policies for such an eventuality. For the colonies, war presented the opportunity to bolt from a weakened empire once and for all.

Unfortunately, the war also convinced colonial nationalists of the illusion that Soviet-style command or planned economies could succeed, especially for a poorer country seeking to climb out of want. Invisible to those colonies and the outside world was the Soviet Union's human cost—the archipelago with its gulags, thousands of political prisoners, and the unmarked graves of "wreckers." Also largely unseen in the Soviet "miracle" had been the role of Americans and other Westerners in propping up Lenin and Stalin, either through loans and transfers of necessary goods or as the largest customer for bargain-basement sales of priceless artwork. Andrew Mellon alone acquired some $6 million worth of art from the Soviets, providing hard currency the dictatorship badly needed.

Given the steady stream of horror stories emanating from collectivist states even in the 1930s, it was somewhat surprising that the spiritual leader of Indian independence, Mohandas Gandhi (1869–1948), was so impervious to the realities of the Soviet Union, as well as to Hitler's national socialism. A grocer's son who was educated in law by the British, Gandhi was born into the business caste. He wanted to be a doctor, but his older brother sternly rebuked him about a career in medicine: "[W]e Vaishnavas [followers of Vishnu] should have nothing to do with the dissection of dead bodies." Gandhi's father instead demanded he go into law. The legal profession required him to go to London, at the age of eighteen. It attracted the young Mohandas, and he relented.[3]

Gandhi wanted to become English. His school-age letters to his father often complained about the presence of too many Indians at school. His dress was (like Nehru's later) thoroughly British and professional. Nevertheless, Gandhi observed the vow he made to his mother to follow Hindu dietary practices, avoiding meat and alcohol, even to the point that he joined the Vegetarian Society. Married (at age thirteen) with a child (at age fifteen), Gandhi avoided any mention of his family to those in his social circles, embarrassed at having married so young. Combining the vows to his mother with the absence of his wife, and her marital temptations, Gandhi "was in many ways more nearly like . . . a Christian monk than the Hindu husband and father he was."[4] His life was a sea of contradictions and of pressures from both East and West: he attacked Western medicine, but when he had appendicitis, only a Western-trained surgeon was acceptable. He preached against the consumption of milk, while drinking it himself.[5]

In studying Christianity on the advice of a friend, Gandhi sought to meld it with Hindu teachings. Hindu teachings included a personal, daily morality driven by karma, a cause-and-effect cycle in which one's actions would produce a reaction in the spiritual world. Instead of Christian-style natural law given by God, Hinduism operated on the basis of *dhamma*, or

dharma, an abstract sense of duty that drove correct behavior and established caste rules. Gandhi did not see Hinduism and Christianity as mutually exclusive and often drew influence from both. Later in his life, he would
repeatedly use the term "crucify" when referring to his self-imposed hunger strikes. He read the Bhagavad Gita, reinterpreting "Hinduism's most
famous philosophic justification for murder into a paean of Christian pas-
sivity."[6] Paradoxically, Gandhi simultaneously became "more Hindu" while
increasingly absorbing British culture, wearing winged collars, spending
ten minutes a day arranging his bow tie, and taking private lessons in dancing, French, and even violin.

After a brief homecoming, Gandhi had a humiliating encounter with a
British political agent on a train, where despite having a first-class ticket, he
was tossed off after a white passenger protested his presence. That incident
convinced Gandhi he had to again leave India. His brother informed him
that South Africa was in need of lawyers and in 1893, Gandhi left for the
dark continent. There he founded the Natal Indian Congress in 1894. Life
for a colonial in Africa was little different from India. He saw the legal system as a means to fight for the franchise for Indians working in the colony,
but after only a year, he returned to India to organize farmers against taxation and discrimination. Formulating his tactics, Gandhi concluded that
pacifism would work best. But his pacifism was idiosyncratic and spotty.
When the Second Boer War broke out, Gandhi—then back in Natal—
urged Indians to organize the Indian Ambulance Corps to support Britain.
(While recruiting for the British, he once said, "We are regarded as a cowardly people. If we want to become free from that reproach, we should learn
to use arms. . . .")[7]

After the Boer War, he yet again journeyed back to India, where he led
a village-by-village cleanup of the rural countryside. All the while, he fomented protests and resistance to the British and to British businesses, adding to his reputation as a lightning rod of local anti-British sentiment.
Evolving a philosophy of *satyagraha*, or devotion to the truth, Gandhi came
to be addressed as *Mahatma*, or "Great Soul." "A satyagrahi gives no thought
to his body," Gandhi explained. "Fear cannot touch him at all. That is why
he does not arm himself with any material weapons."[8] Yet control did not
extend to his sexuality, and his appetites fostered guilt within him over his
own "carnal lust" that had produced his children. After the war, Gandhi
increasingly slept with his young female followers as a test of his control,
determined not to be aroused, fortified by repeated baths and massages.
Throughout these trials, he berated himself, writing in his diary, "I can see

there is some grave defect in me. . . . All around me is utter darkness," and was overheard to mutter, "There must be some serious flaw deep down in me which I am unable to discover. . . ."[9]

Under satyagraha, suffering became the new weapon, and, without Gandhi's fully understanding how this worked, the tactic depended fully upon the humanity and mercy of his British masters to be effective. As historian Carroll Quigley wrote,

> Gandhi never seemed to recognize that his fasting and nonviolent civil disobedience were effective against the British in India and South Africa only to the degree that the British had the qualities of humanity, decency, generosity, and fair play which he most admired, but that by attacking [them] through these virtues he was weakening Britain and the class which possessed these [traits] and making it more likely that they would be replaced by nations and leaders who did not have these virtues.[10]

Gandhi conveniently ignored the fact that the truly cruel and totalitarian regimes cared little if political opponents suffered. Quite the contrary, they reveled in it. Throughout his career as a voice of opposition, Gandhi never grasped why no equivalent to him ever emerged in Nazi Germany or Stalinist Russia. (Still later, one looks in vain for a Cambodian Gandhi, or a North Korean Gandhi, because such individuals, if they ever existed, were dispatched posthaste.) Likewise, the entire Gandhi-led protest movement produced plenty of symbolic acts "where thousands gave up their medals or burned foreign clothing [but which] did not give Indians training in government."[11]

Gandhi's speeches and writings abounded with biblical metaphors, references, and phrases—Samson, Jesus, innocence, sin, blessings, disciples, saints, Satan, "fear and trembling," and, above all, sacrifice. "[N]o nation has ever been made without sacrifice," he observed. "It is arrest and imprisonment we seek."[12] Yet he lacked no sense of law enforcement when it came to his own family. His instruction to followers to refrain from sex alienated his son Harilal, whom he regarded as "mean and faithless" for marrying and having a child of his own, to the point that Harilal became a Muslim. Yet Gandhi carried on an all-but-consummated love affair with a Danish missionary.[13] Indeed, the Mahatma seemed to attract a strange collection of female European admirers, including Helene Haussding, a German singer he called "Sparrow," and Madeleine Slade, the daughter of a British admiral, whom he renamed "Mirabehn." Gandhi's obsession with constipation, his Koran-like view of women and sex, and the phenomenal expense required to "keep Gandhi living in poverty" would in other people have been amusing traits had not Gandhi taken them so seriously.[14]

The Mahatma's public authority rose, irrespective of the fact that violence accompanied Gandhi everywhere, and not always by his opponents. At Chauri Chaura, marching peasants burned a police station to the ground, and then the mob hacked to pieces police trying to escape the blaze, killing twenty-one. The episode disgusted Nehru, then a representative of the Indian National Congress, who began to question Gandhi's leadership.

Nehru also had been deeply affected by the April 1919 killing of unarmed Indians by British troops at Amritsar—more than 350. With this event, Nehru came to appreciate the power of the Western newspapers, all of which covered Amritsar and exposed British brutality. Gandhi perceived that this was a one-way street. Soon after Amritsar, the slaughter of three times as many unarmed Sikhs by Hindu guards in February 1921 was ignored by the Western press. Gandhi's answer was peace-by-spinning-wheel: literally, a return to hand weaving and the rejection of industry. To one visitor from the United States, he said, "My message to America is simply the hum of this spinning-wheel. It is . . . [the] substitute for gunpowder."[15]

Violence built between Muslims and Hindus. In 1947, of the 350 million persons living in India, about one quarter were Muslims. Increasingly conflicts tore at the two groups; at Kohat in 1924, for example, with more than one hundred Hindu and Muslim bodies lying in the streets, every survivor slept next to his rifle. During the Salt March of 1930 (in which Gandhi led Indians on a coastal march where they stopped to make salt without paying the British tax), Calcutta and Karachi descended into violent riots; at Chittagong, a few days later, two men were shot. Gandhi condescendingly congratulated the parents for the "sacrifices of their sons."[16] A massive charge by satyagrahis against a barbed-wire-enclosed salt depot resulted in police counterattacking the "nonviolent" marchers. This was, in fact, a new type of aggression—nonviolent aggression, playing on the humanity and emotion of the opponent to dull his reactions.

The more Gandhi preached nonviolence, the more it was obvious to leaders of all factions that utopian pacifism was unrealistic at best and dangerous at worst. For Gandhi, however, it became a test of universals. If India could gain independence through nonviolence, he claimed, "she would have made the largest contribution yet known to world peace."[17] Summoned by Viceroy Lord Irwin (later Lord Halifax) to New Delhi to discuss the deteriorating situation in 1931, Gandhi spent most of their time together trying to convert him to hand-spinning. It was, Irwin said, "rather like talking to someone who had stepped off another planet."[18]

When disasters struck in the form of massive floods, however, Gandhi suddenly returned to earth, particularly England, to beg assistance. The simple self-sufficiency Gandhi preached proved utterly incapable of rendering aid. Actually helping the Indian people required massive, immediate food transfers, with crops grown with the latest technology, which depended on highly industrialized train and shipping networks—all made possible only by capitalism. It began to dawn on many Indians that no one could spin a railroad, an airport, or overnight cultivation and delivery of foodstuffs.

Yet the Mahatma was neither parliamentary fish nor anarchist fowl. Unwilling to dirty his hands with necessary political compromises (allowing the Muslims to have their own state) or to preach violent revolution, Gandhi turned to the spirit world to alleviate India's physical ills. Nehru, on the other hand, decided that salvation lay in the state. The fact that Gandhi did not sully himself with practical matters merely enhanced his mystique, which then benefited further from outsiders' later projecting their own ideological positions onto the Mahatma. His image was exaggerated further by Richard Attenborough's 1982 film, *Gandhi*, winning a best actor Oscar for Ben Kingsley.[19]

Similar to some late-twentieth-century activists, Gandhi seemed incapable of discerning between essentially moral regimes that behaved badly (the British) and inherently oppressive, totalitarian governments with mass murder inherent in their character. Japan, which had expressed minimal interest in India until formulating the Greater East Asia Co-Prosperity Sphere in the 1930s—the program to envelop all of Asia beneath the Japanese economic and political umbrella—began by mid-1940 to consider the value of the subcontinent. At first Gandhi worried that a Japanese thrust toward India would solidify the British position even further. Then, true to his double standards for Britain and colonial people, when Japan *did* invade Burma in 1942, Gandhi excoriated the British for evacuating *too* rapidly. He claimed, "The whole civil administration collapsed and those in charge sought their own safety. . . . Private motor cars were commandeered for the evacuation of [Europeans]. The police force was discharged or withdrawn."[20]

What was Gandhi's solution for India's security? What plan for defense? As the guiding force in the Indian National Congress, he proposed to "defend" India nonviolently against the Japanese—an obvious contradiction in terms. His pacifism was received with incredulity in England, where he recommended to the British that they "let Hitler and Mussolini take possession of your beautiful island, your homes, and allow yourselves to be slaughtered, but refuse to owe allegiance to them."[21] The Indian people, he asserted, "make no distinction between Nazism and the double autocracy that rules India."[22] Of course, the Indian people had never been subjected to a brutal totalitarian regime such as the Nazis or Japanese had planned for them, nor had Indian people been polled about their allegiance. It was all Gandhi's imagination.

The Pandit

While Gandhi built a messiah-like reputation but did almost nothing to improve daily life in India, Nehru, elected president of the Indian National Congress (INC) in 1936 and 1937, actually translated some of Gandhi's beliefs into practical political action. Because of the European attitudes he inherited, Nehru's actions, predictably, were socialist or Progressive.

Jawaharlal Nehru (1889–1964) was by temperament a socialist—he had accompanied his family in 1926 to Europe, where he first became attracted to socialism—and saw state planning as the appropriate economic model. A decade later, as president of the INC, he led its members to proclaim socialism as the right model for an independent India, largely because he knew no other model.

Hatred for the British experience only accelerated Nehru's views that a top-down structure was necessary for India's struggling masses. Nehru had lived a privileged life; his father, an attorney from Allahabad in the north, "lived in a house with fifty or more servants, a swimming pool, and the latest European cars."[23] Like Gandhi, Nehru studied law in London and traveled through Europe; he became urbane and sophisticated, and increasingly dissatisfied with India's humiliating servile position. He was particularly intrigued by the story of the Indian Mutiny of 1857, in which both Hindus and Muslims in the British Indian army rebelled over new rifles that purportedly had either beef fat or pork fat grease for the cartridges (they had neither, but vegetable oil). The British seemed unable to understand Indian culture or the power of rumors. Mahatma Gandhi's legend energized Nehru by showing him changes were possible, and that independence was near.

In 1920, following the upheavals surrounding the Amritsar massacre of

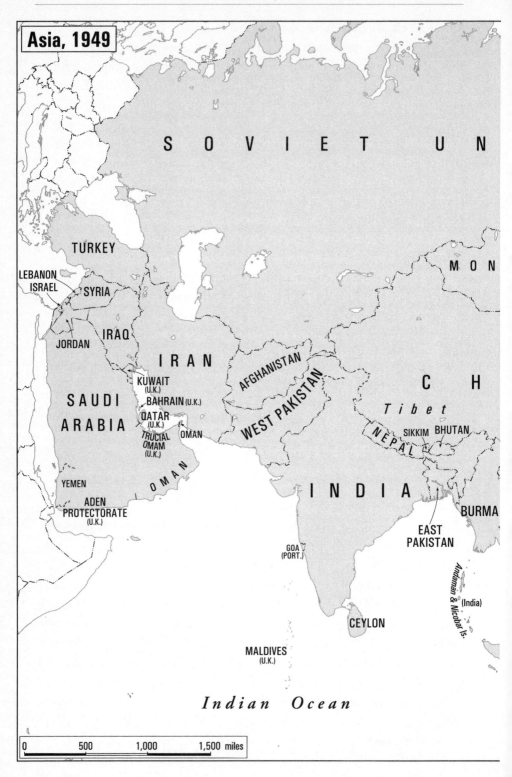

Asia, 1949

SOVIET UN

TURKEY

LEBANON
ISRAEL

SYRIA

JORDAN

IRAQ

IRAN

SAUDI
ARABIA

KUWAIT
(U.K.)

BAHRAIN (U.K.)

QATAR
(U.K.)

TRUCIAL
OMAM
(U.K.)

OMAN

OMAN

YEMEN

ADEN
PROTECTORATE
(U.K.)

AFGHANISTAN

WEST PAKISTAN

MON

CH

Tibet

NEPAL SIKKIM BHUTAN

INDIA

BURMA

EAST
PAKISTAN

GOA
(PORT.)

Andaman & Nicobar Is.

(India)

CEYLON

MALDIVES
(U.K.)

Indian Ocean

0   500   1,000   1,500 miles

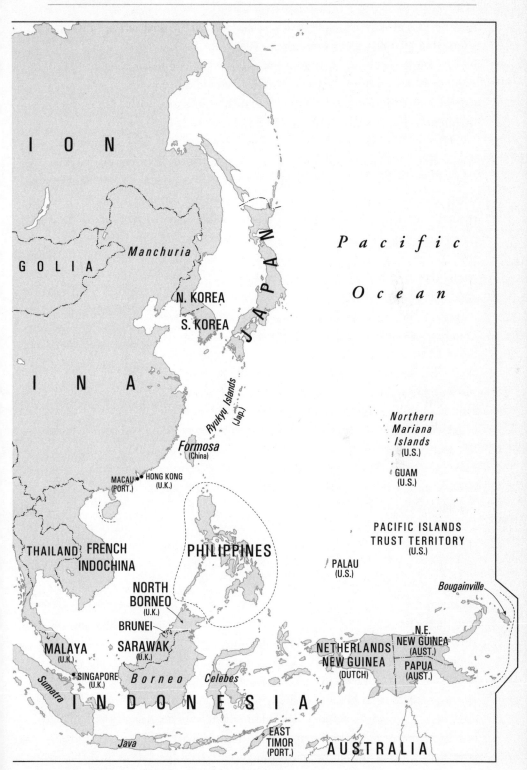

the previous year, in which British soldiers opened fire with massed rifles on a crowd of 15,000, killing more than 350 people, peasants descended on the Nehru family compound in hopes of finding the Mahatma. Disappointed that Gandhi was not there, the crowd persuaded Nehru to lead a new investigation into the massacre, and so began his mission in life. He traveled throughout India, seeking to view India's problems firsthand.

During his journey, Nehru's life was transformed, as was his name, from "Joe" (his public school name in England) to "Pandit," or teacher. Nehru—"still an Indian sahib in a hat and silk underwear"—was overwhelmed by the faith the masses now had in him.[24] Although Gandhi motivated the people to resist the British, Nehru gave direction to their frustrations. Peasants constructed roads so his car could move deeper inside the country, and physically carried his car over mud bogs. (Here was high irony, that the man who would liberate India was, on a grander scale, recreating the portrait of the Westernized elite literally being borne in shaded litters on the backs of the masses.) His intention was neither to replace Gandhi nor to use him, but to channel and augment his sway with the people of India.

"That visit [to the countryside] was a revelation to me," Nehru wrote in his autobiography. "We found the whole countryside afire with enthusiasm. . . . Looking at them and their misery and overflowing gratitude, I was filled with shame and sorrow, shame at my own easy-going and comfortable life and our petty politics . . . which ignored this vast multitude of semi-naked sons and daughters of India. . . ."[25] Filled simultaneously with a new passion for the suffering throngs and with an ambition for political action, Nehru wrote to his father, "Greatness is being thrust on me."[26]

Nehru felt he had much in common with Colonel T. E. Lawrence (Lawrence of Arabia), the champion of Arab liberation from English control. In prison in 1930 for violation of the Salt Law tax, Nehru read and reread Lawrence's *Seven Pillars of Wisdom* (1922), telling the woman who arranged his library, "I suppose I am very different from Lawrence—still sometimes we touched."[27] Nehru's psychological attraction to Lawrence involved more than politics; the Pandit's most recent, and famous, biographer, Stanley Wolpert, referred to "homosexual encounters" as a youth, and suggested that the Lawrence passages detailed Nehru's "hidden" but long-running battle with homosexuality. Referring to *The Seven Pillars of Wisdom*, Nehru wrote, "The book has held me, not only because of the writing but also because of his problems and difficulties with himself . . . [a] problem [that] was not unlike mine in some ways."[28] Wolpert described this as

Nehru's "deepest secret self whose continued existence terrified him."[29] If his "deepest secret self" caused any long-term trauma, Nehru managed to suppress it.

Nehru approached India's participation in World War II somewhat differently from Gandhi, with his full-throated surrender to the Japanese. Whereas Gandhi had sought "to deliver the so-called weaker races of the earth from the crushing heels of Western exploitation," the Western exploiters did not look so bad to Nehru in the face of an expansionist Japan.[30] As the lead writer and redrafter of India's war resolution, Nehru stated, "The Congress has repeatedly declared its entire disapproval of the ideology and practice of fascism and Nazism," and condemned the aggression against Poland.[31] Implying that a free India would join the Allies, Nehru's resolution made it clear that "a free, democratic India will gladly associate herself with other free nations," but could not "offer any cooperation in a war which is conducted in imperialist lines."[32] Aware that "the international situation is by no means clear," and Indians needed to "be prepared for everything," Nehru added, "I do not see how we can ward off an armed attack by nonviolence."[33]

Raging like a tropical storm across Asia, Japan's string of victories in 1941–42 forced the British to reassess their India policy. Pressure mounted to find a "just and final solution" to Indian independence. Churchill knew the inevitable outcome of such an exchange: "When you lose India, don't blame me!" he muttered to his war cabinet.[34] Franklin Roosevelt, who needed a stable Indian buffer to restrain the Japanese to the southwest, squeezed Churchill to support the mission of diplomat Sir Stafford Cripps, in March 1942, whose real job was to persuade the Muslims not to secede. Gandhi met with Cripps and advised him to give Quaid-i-Azam Muhammad Ali Jinnah, the leader of the Indian Muslims, the position of running a united, independent India, which the British rejected. Nehru, meanwhile, expressed a desire to attach India to America, if only the United States would declare the necessity of Indian independence. Writing Roosevelt directly, Nehru reiterated India's willingness to "fight [the Japanese] with all the strength and vitality we possess. . . . We are a disarmed people. But our potential is very great. . . ."[35] A month later, he concluded that the Indian Congress was "ready to hitch 'India's wagon to America's Star.'"[36]

Roosevelt was sympathetic to Indian independence, but he saw matters entirely in the context of an expanding Japanese empire, warning Churchill via special assistant Harry Hopkins that if India was "subsequently invaded successfully by Japan with attendant serious defeats," American public

opinion would turn against the British government.[37] When confronted
with the reality that a British withdrawal from India would spark anarchy
and bloodletting, Gandhi replied coldly to the British, "Leave India to
God. If that is too much, then leave her to anarchy."[38] Mayhem surely would
have ensued. Churchill summed up the situation in his typical blunt fashion, telling Roosevelt that the Muslims, who formed the main fighting elements of the army, "will not allow themselves to be governed by . . . the
Congress Caucus and the Hindu priesthood."[39] There was no nonviolent
solution.

Having spent much of World War II in a British jail for opposing the
salt tax, Nehru thought violence inevitable when the British pulled out,
with or without Gandhi. "What will happen if [Gandhi] dies?" he asked.
"An end of an era . . . and bitterness that will eat into the very soul of India.
It will be war in every way, war continuously. . . ." The stage was already set:
the cancer-ridden Muslim leader Jinnah, later the founder of Pakistan, refused to even meet with antipartition Muslim leaders. (The viceroy, Lord
Mountbatten, found his considerable charm wasted on Jinnah, whom he
called an "evil genius," a "psychopathic case," a "lunatic," and a "bastard.")[40]
Jinnah knew the new Viceroy's Council—the cabinet—would always see
the Sikhs and untouchables voting with the Hindus, putting Muslims in a
permanent minority.[41] Whereas the British had their suspicions about
Nehru, he seemed infinitely better than Gandhi.[42] Nehru, of course, did
nothing to dispel such thinking, calling Gandhi "out of touch," a "spent
force," and irrelevant to the goal of independence.[43]

India came off its moorings even before the British Parliament began
action on the Indian Independence Bill in 1947. Hindu-Muslim violence
had rocked the major cities since 1945. Then came Direct Action Day, on
August 16, 1946, when Jinnah announced the Muslim delegation had "said
good-bye to constitutions and constitutional methods," and soon blood
ran in Calcutta, beginning in Maniktolla, where Muslim mobs assassinated Hindus. The following day, Hindu mobs butchered Muslims. Although Nehru knew he could no longer "manage" India, Gandhi still
believed "he could manage Nehru," and more: as late as 1947, he still
thought he could persuade the Congress to invest in Jinnah the leadership
of all India.[44] At any rate, it was Gandhi, not Nehru, who was delusional
about India's future.

Britain still clung to the notion that India might remain in the empire under dominion status—a relationship Indians wanted no part of.
When independence finally came in 1947, the Indian Independence Bill

partitioned British India into two dominions, India and Pakistan (in which modern-day Pakistan then comprised West Pakistan and Bangladesh, which was called East Pakistan). But the unstated reality was that more than 14 million people caught on the wrong side of the India-Pakistan border would face irresistible pressure to relocate. As one side effect of this massive shift in humanity, Indians and Pakistanis came to endow paper passports and other documents with quasi-religious status, and to "have paper" (even for programs that did not have the slightest relation to the holder) was viewed as desirable. Although partition was not the origin of paper passports, which dated back to Queen Elizabeth I in England, it permanently entrenched them in the psyche of the peoples of the subcontinent.[45]

Back in England, British ministers tried to soften the blow for Churchill (by then no longer prime minister), who was stunned by the news of the act's passage. India's last British viceroy, Lord Louis "Dickie" Mountbatten, returned home from India to a fierce scolding from Churchill: "Dickie . . . what you did to us in India was like whipping your riding crop across my face."[46] In fact, Churchill's delusion of a "free" India choosing dominion status was as grand as Gandhi's vision of a peaceful Hindu-Muslim state.[47]

With the passage of independence, Hindus and Muslims quickly engaged in open combat. In October 1947, bowing to the inevitable, Nehru sent a Sikh battalion into Kashmir, formally marking the first Indian-Pakistani War. The Kashmir expedition saved some of India's territorial integrity, at the cost of a hollowed-out interior, as Nehru stripped services from other areas, including famine relief. A cease-fire was arranged in August 1948, and a United Nations resolution adopted the following January. Under the terms of the resolution, Pakistan retained about two fifths of Kashmir, while India held the populated and more fertile regions.[48] Nor were the Muslim areas cohesive, or even similar. Bengali Muslims looked and acted like Bengali Hindus except for their religion, and spoke Urdu; Pathans (or Pashtuns) in the northwest had more in common with Afghans, and wanted their own state. Large northern provinces containing Muslims were separated by vast distances and large non-Muslim populations, making them ungovernable as a single state. Predictably, more wars would ensue over the region in the future. But for the moment, the two-state solution seemed practical.

The Crown Jewel, Independent

Gandhi was assassinated in January 1948 by a Hindu nationalist angry at Gandhi's apparent favoritism toward Muslims. In death, Gandhi left a smaller but unified India, led by Nehru, that he had not been able to produce while alive. This result was achieved only by moving millions of people around. Partition had occurred on religious grounds, not racial or ethnic, but was the only sensible approach. Like Turkey, India had become another example of states with markedly dissimilar population groups unable to survive as a harmonious whole. But the separation, when it came, was neither peaceful nor orderly. One "procession of terrified Hindus and Sikhs . . . stretched for fifty-seven miles from the West Punjab."[49] Nehru described partition as the "cutting up of a living structure" of India, "far worse than even we had anticipated."[50] What partition was not was unexpected. Despite criticisms of Mountbatten for his "impatience," and even taking into account his own admission about the Indian independence process that he had "fucked it up," Mountbatten had no more power to restrain Jinnah or any of his successors from splitting from the Hindus than he had in preventing independence in the first place.[51]

With millions of people now relocated according to religion, and the large Muslim minority now gone, India set about to crawl out of poverty. Gandhi had advocated *swadeshi*, or self-sufficiency, a concept that industrialized societies had left behind half a millennium earlier, and which would undoubtedly condemn India's masses to crushing poverty. Nehru's solution was only slightly better—Lenin-style top-down economic controls. Nehru gushed in his book *The Discovery of India*, written while he was in jail, "the Soviet Revolution had advanced human society by a great leap and it lit a bright flame. . . ."[52] Nero's torches had also "lit a bright flame," and at a lot lower human cost.

Although as president, Nehru stated that India was inspired by America, she had absorbed *none* of the four pillars of American exceptionalism. India practiced Hinduism, and had a creeping civil law with only some elements of common law, a state-dominated market, and controlled access to land. Nehru was even more "fascinated by the advance of the Soviet Union in education [!] and culture and medical care and physical fitness . . . and by the amazing and prodigious effort to create a new world out of the dregs of the old."[53] Nehru tolerated private property as Lenin had ("free enterprise is not ruled out as such"), but only at the lowest ends of the economic order. On the "commanding heights" of heavy industry—steel, coal, transportation, and communications—the state would remain in charge. "I'm all for tractors and big machinery," he announced, and he soundly dismissed Gandhi's *swadeshi*.[54] State ownership was not necessarily required, but control of the industries "had to be rigid."[55] Speaking to the U.S. House of Representatives in 1949, Nehru praised the Declaration of Independence and claimed India had been "greatly influenced by your own constitution."[56] India "may speak to you with a voice that you may not immediately recognize or that may perhaps appear somewhat alien to you," he assured Americans, "yet in a voice there is a strong resemblance to what you have often heard before."[57]

Americans would not perceive the voices they heard coming from India as anything remotely familiar. Nehru's criticisms of America's efforts to stop communism would also have seemed alien. When North Koreans surged into South Korea and the United States responded, Nehru called Americans "more hysterical as a people than almost any others. . . ."[58] Presumably his own "hysteria" was not to blame for subduing the Naga tribesmen in 1952, or for sending forty thousand Indian troops to subjugate Portuguese Goa in 1960 (an action condemned by the United Nations, but whose condemnation was vetoed by the Soviet Union). Nehru was dead by the time of the second Indo-Pakistani War in 1965, the Bangladesh Liberation War in 1971, and the Kargil War in 1999, but the Indian state continued his aggressive and violent foreign policy.

Speaking at Columbia University in 1949, Nehru assessed the causes of war as imperialism, race relations, and poverty, a mantra echoed repeatedly by Progressives in the United States over the century.[59] Yet a poverty-stricken India under British rule was a far more peaceful country than a free, modernizing India. Nehru pontificated about imperialism at every turn to attentive audiences in the Western press and among Third World dictators, except when it came to the Chinese invasion of Tibet in 1950, which he did not oppose. Assuming the moral high ground over the United States, he blustered, "We have not got an atom bomb. . . . We rejoice in not having the atom bomb."[60] Yet the year he died, India commissioned a reprocessing facility to turn Eisenhower's "Atoms for Peace" nuclear technology into weapons-grade plutonium, and the first Indian nuclear test occurred just ten years later in 1974, described by the government as a "peaceful nuclear explosion."

Of more immediate geographic concern, China saw an opportunity to use Nehru's naïveté against him, putting up a friendly front long enough to secure provinces in the Aksai Chin and Arunachal Pradesh regions. Although in 1956 Chinese premier Zhou Enlai promised that his nation had no claims on Indian territory—and Nehru believed him—when the opportunity arose, China moved. Much like Stalin denying the reality of Germany's invasion plans in 1941, Nehru refused to accept intelligence provided by Burmese premier Ba Swe suggesting that Zhou was deceiving him.[61] In a review of the war, recently released CIA documents labeled the Chinese diplomatic effort "a five year masterpiece of guile."[62]

Maneuvering cautiously, China anticipated war with India throughout the 1950s, but feared American intervention, especially considering the security of the nuclear test site at Lop Nor.[63] Nehru's flirtation with the Communist Chinese ended abruptly in 1959 when, acting out of humanitarianism, India gave asylum to the Tibetan Dalai Lama after the abortive Tibetan uprising. Mao Zedong ordered the Chinese news agency to report that Indian expansionists were operating in Tibet, and that all future Indian news should take a hostile position toward Nehru.[64] In what had to be a cruel irony, Nehru and the Indians were now branded "imperialists," and Zhou referred to Nehru's "class nature."

Despite continued provocations on both sides, Indian military unpreparedness was shocking. As late as early 1962, the Indian air force was instructed *not* to prepare for war with a nation whose air force the CIA had assessed to be the fourth best in the world.[65] For a country steeped in nonviolence and whose military lacked combat experience against a foreign foe, India's overconfidence was stunning: there were a grand total of two army divisions in the region, and Indian chief of the general staff Major General Joginder Singh Dhillon assured his troops that "a few rounds fired at the Chinese would cause them to run away."[66]

Right up to the week before the war, Zhou Enlai promised peace. Then in late October 1962, at the same time as the United States was absorbed with the Cuban missile crisis, Chinese troops launched attacks in both the western (Askai Chin) and eastern (Northeast Frontier Agency, east of Bhutan) theaters. Suffering heavy casualties, the Chinese nevertheless reached their "claim line" in Aksai Chin and Indian forces fell back. When the People's Liberation Army (PLA) closed in on Tezpur near the Brahmaputra River, Nehru knew he needed help and begged for American air strikes. A U.S. carrier was ordered to the Bay of Bengal, but the Chinese had already overstretched their supply capacities, and India agreed to a cease-fire before American help arrived.

Prisoners were exchanged and the PLA returned heavy artillery, unable to transport it back to central China. Mao's pronouncement that "the way to world conquest lies through Havana, Accra, and Calcutta" was taken more seriously by India's government, although predictably other non-aligned nations in the UN Security Council sided with the Chinese.[67] Defeat brought India several benefits, not the least of which was the realization that a modern power had to be able to militarily defend her borders. This, in turn, only further concerned the Pakistanis. The Communist Party in India lost influence, while the threat posed by a Chinese Communist giant again was taken seriously by many seeking to forget the Korean War.

The Intellectual Journey of Western Capitalism

India's willingness to embrace top-down central planning and a soft socialism reflected the intellectual state of the modern world at that time. Britain's struggle to remain an international power had hinged on retaining her empire, and her failure to do so began when the intellectual underpinnings of the concept of empire were eroded even before the war, due in part to the influence of the Bloomsbury Group.[68] A group of elite English writers, artists, and philosophers, whose number included Virginia Woolf, Lytton Strachey, E. M. Forster, and John Maynard Keynes, the Bloomsbury Group had begun meeting in 1906 and soon became well known for its support of women's suffrage and then for its opposition to the First World War.

The group was not all of one opinion, however. Keynes, who published his *Economic Consequences of the Peace* after the war, stood on one end with those espousing a slow creep of socialism through government control of the economy, while some of the others, including Leonard Woolf, argued for a faster pace toward socialism. All denounced imperialism, patriotism, and traditional family structure. When challenged about his war views at a town hall in 1916, and asked, "Tell me, Mr. Strachey . . . what would you do if you saw a German soldier attempting to rape your sisters?" Lytton Strachey cleverly replied, "I should try to come between them."[69] Oddly, Bloomsbury's members produced little—few books, fewer pieces of art or literature—and this trait seemed to describe the energy of the group as a whole, although Forster and Keynes proved especially prolific. But their impact on British culture and identity was significant in a number of ways (including that Bloomsbury produced three known Soviet agents, including Guy Burgess)—most notably, however, by influencing British public opinion after the 1920s, among whom their anti-Christian and anti-imperialist views germinated and became prevailing wisdom by 1945. More specifically, Bloomsbury's anti-imperialist/antigovernment ideas shaped England's appeasement policies throughout the 1930s, and continued to do so after the Second World War. It was at this time that Forster's book *A Passage to India* (1924) saw a revival and sparked resistance to maintaining England's hold over the Crown Jewel of the Empire.

Many of the Bloomsbury members suffered from a range of vices and pathologies. Virginia Woolf, who had come from a family of self-absorbed female models, was thoroughly unstable mentally and was institutionalized for a time. According to allusions in her essay "A Sketch of the Past," her depression stemmed from sexual abuse at the hands of her half-brothers.[70] Forster and Keynes were both homosexuals, Keynes the more arrogant and thoroughly elitist (and ultimately more famous) of the two and director of the British Eugenics Society for seven years.

The group's pacifism led some to argue in the 1930s that there was little difference between Britain and Nazi Germany—although Keynes finally came to see war as a necessity. Keynes's role at Bretton Woods in creating the postwar world monetary structures further advanced the Bloomsburyian nostrums of internationalism and the erosion of national sovereignty—particularly the sovereignty of Great Britain. The internationalism of the Bloomsburys in both diplomatic influence and economic policy undercut Britain's unity at home concerning the empire. Thus at the very time Britain more desperately grasped her empire with one hand, the monetary and financial policies she supported loosened its grip with the other.

The Bloomsburys had been the heralds of an age when Keynesianism and Marxism were advancing steadily, while at the same time free markets contracted. Many of these advances by advocates of controlled economies came because of the perceived "success" of the Soviets during the war and the belief that the quasi-socialist New Deal had "saved capitalism" in the 1930s. India and the rest of the Third World paid a steep price for the inability of free-market champions to better state their case to the world.

Opponents of capitalism had begun their attacks not long after the printer's ink dried on *The Wealth of Nations* in 1776 and, with few exceptions, encountered only a handful of defenders in the 1800s. Most thought the obvious success of capitalism's wealth creation and the broad prosperity it had brought to the West spoke for itself. In fact, the proponents of capitalism had neglected to explain it, diffuse it, and champion it for almost 150 years.

On the other hand, a long and recognizable string of critics, running from Francois Charles Fourier and Pierre-Joseph Proudhon to Robert Owen and Karl Marx, then finally to Vladimir Lenin, had, in some sense, surprised free marketeers, who believed the common sense of their views to be so obvious as to need no defense. Modifications by political economists throughout the nineteenth century had nibbled around the edges of the morality of capitalism and the fundamental immorality of socialism/communism. Some, such as England's Herbert Spencer, had been led down the path of social Darwinism, a concept driven by Malthusian constructs of want and scarcity in which the state needed to allow the weak to die in order to preserve the rest of society. Others, such as America's William Graham Sumner, with his tract *What Social Classes Owe to Each Other* (1883), had argued:

> We shall find that all the schemes for producing equality and obliterating the organization of society produce a new differentiation based on the worst possible distinction—the right to claim and the duty to give one man's effort for another man's satisfaction. We shall find that every effort to realize equality necessitates a sacrifice of liberty.[71]

More often, however, arguments about the morality of free markets descended into epic tomes about tariff rates or the gold standard instead of confronting the alternative Progressive-state views for what they were: dangerous and perverted. It often fell to industrialists such as Andrew Carnegie to offer a defense of capitalism, as Carnegie did in *The Gospel of Wealth*.[72] Not until William Graham Sumner's essay "The Forgotten Man" (which today would be America's middle class) in *What Social Classes Owe to Each Other* did an academic challenge the fundamental immorality of socialism.[73] Sumner asked how any individual or group had a moral right to burden any other. He foresaw the modern society in which different groups would vie with one another for state benefits—always at someone else's expense. When "A" wishes to help "C," he forges a coalition that taxes "B" to give to "C," hence "B" becomes the "forgotten man." Or, when the rich politician "A" wishes to gain power through the votes of poor people "C," he taxes the middle class "B."

Voices such as Sumner's were nearly drowned out during the American Progressive era by vote-buying politicians. In Europe, French socialists and Communists already wielded powerful political influence between the wars. One European academic, however, was able to stand against the prevailing winds. Ludwig von Mises (1881–1973) was an economist from the University of Vienna. His primary emphasis was on money and business cycles, but in 1922 he published probably the best comprehensive criticisms of socialism written to date, *Socialism: An Economic and Sociological Analysis*.[74] According to von Mises, prices were merely pieces of information, and no government had enough knowledge to determine where to put resources or what prices should be—only markets could do that, because only markets automatically and efficiently collated all the information. Information theorists would later point out that having perfect information rendered a single decision superior to all others, while a lack of information produced a variety of solutions, all appearing relatively equal in credibility. The catchphrase was "variety (of information) destroys variety (of valid decisions.)"[75] And again, only free markets could do that. Government attempts to "plan" economies would inevitably fail, and the more governments insisted on trying to control the market, the higher the human cost. Von Mises argued from a strictly scientific methodology: "If we were to regard the Soviet regime as an experiment, we would have to say that the experiment has clearly demonstrated the superiority of capitalism and the inferiority of socialism."[76]

A young former lieutenant in the Austrian army, Friedrich von Hayek, attended the University of Vienna after World War I intent on making socialism (which he considered the only just economic system) work. Instead, he walked into a seminar led by von Mises. The ideas he encountered transformed him. "*Socialism* [von Mises's 1922 book] shocked our generation. . . . [It] told us we had been looking for improvement in the wrong direction."[77] Hayek worked first as von Mises's research assistant, then, upon graduation, as a professor at the London School of Economics. A social democrat before converting under von Mises's influence, Hayek understood the pull of socialism: it was "almost inevitable," he observed, that any "warm-hearted person, as soon as he becomes conscious of the existing misery, should become a socialist."[78] Nonetheless, he believed that capitalism, entrepreneurship, and risk taking needed to be fostered and rewarded to enable charity to help alleviate misery. Attempting to take from the engine of an economy, private-sector business, and transfer resources to unproductive elements through government action (redistribution of the wealth) meant that all would suffer, leveling all nonelite humanity in hopeless poverty.

Of course, even that moderate view would be challenged in the 1980s by George Gilder, who would make the first argument that capitalism was not only efficient, but the only moral economic system because it was based on giving, not taking. A much different defense of capitalism—cultural as much as economic—emerged from the pen of Russian-born novelist and philosopher Ayn Rand (1905–82). Born Alisa Rosenbaum, she changed her name to Ayn Rand while at Petrograd State University, then emigrated to the United States in 1925. She became an extra in the Cecil B. DeMille film *The King of Kings* and subsequently a screenwriter. By the 1930s, she had produced her first novel, *We the Living*, followed by *Anthem*, both dealing with the struggles between the individual and a totalitarian government. Through an acquaintance, economist Henry Hazlitt, she immersed herself in von Mises's Austrian School theories, which influenced her first big hit, *The Fountainhead*, in 1943. The book's hero, Howard Roark, is an architect who refuses to compromise his innovative and brilliant designs to fit the wishes of corrupt city planners, ultimately blowing up his work rather than allow it to be degraded by politicians. Roark is the fountainhead—the spirit of creation in man incarnate to some, and the spirit of entrepreneurship which triumphed over the slavery of the collective to others.

But it was *Atlas Shrugged* (1957), with its seemingly endless monologues and the creative strength of Rand's heroine, Dagney Taggart, and hero, John Galt, that outlined in fictional form her worldview called "objectivism." Returning to her theme of man against the state, Rand describes a capitalist strike, in which the creators, engineers, and generators of wealth simply withdraw from the world. Atlas, as it were, shrugs and puts down his globe. Without these captains of industry, virtually all progress stops and society collapses. The book made Rand an international celebrity, and more than almost any other single work, encapsulated the strengths of a free market. Rand essentially popularized the ideas of Hayek and von Mises, who mostly spoke to academics.

Hayek, teaching in England, had much more immediate impact on economic thought than his mentor von Mises. In 1944, with his book *Omnipotent Government*, von Mises correctly placed Nazi economics alongside communism as bedfellows of a totalitarian state, an alignment that ran contrary not only to the popular notion that "communism was on the left and fascism on the right," but to the depiction of these ideologies in typical economics textbooks.[79] It was Hayek, however, and not von Mises who contested these ideas with the cream of England's economic minds, particularly John Maynard Keynes. Hayek became "not only the most consistent but indeed the most vocal critic of Keynes' work," while, predictably, the haughty Keynes dismissed Hayek's ideas as "rubbish."[80]

Not content to debate on a stratospheric intellectual plane as von Mises seemed to prefer, Hayek reached for the popular imagination. The same year as von Mises published *Omnipotent Government*, Hayek released *The Road to Serfdom*. While he had to take care not to offend Britain's wartime ally, the Soviet Union, he nevertheless blasted the Keynesian interventionism that dominated Western economic thinking. Keynes said *The Road to Serfdom* was a "grand book," and he was in "deeply moved agreement," yet typically called for even greater planning, not less.[81]

Hayek succeeded in reaching the common man when *Reader's Digest* printed a condensed version of *The Road to Serfdom* in April 1945. Among the readers of his tome was Margaret Roberts, an Oxford undergraduate who read it and was deeply influenced by its message. As Margaret Thatcher, later the prime minister of England, she would attempt to follow the blueprint Hayek laid out.

Oddly, though, in the world of academic economics, having a popular book was the kiss of death. It implied that the writer lacked sufficient substance, as only things that could not withstand peer review were published for a wide audience. (The reverse—that academic writings had become so esoteric and narrowly focused as to be irrelevant to expanding the understanding of large numbers of people—was never considered in the ivory towers.) Hayek took a position at the University of Chicago as a professor of social and moral sciences, but remained disappointed that the university did not recognize his contributions to economics. He never became comfortable in America, even though at Chicago he produced his other seminal work, *The Constitution of Liberty* (1960).[82] In that book, he argued additionally that laissez-faire alone could not produce fair or efficient outcomes without government generally playing the role of a restricted referee. In short, he echoed Adam Smith. In 1947, Hayek invited nearly forty economists, historians, and philosophers to a spa on Mont Pelerin, Switzerland, to discuss the statism and Keynesianism that was sweeping the globe. This group became the Mont Pelerin Society. Returning to Europe in 1962, Hayek and other intellectuals (including a young economist from the University of Chicago, Milton Friedman) continued to meet on a biannual basis. Becoming the world's defender of free-market capitalism, the society produced a steady drumbeat of criticism of collectivism.

Even with Hayek gone, Chicago became a bastion of free-market ideas, attracting a stable of economists and public policy theorists that included future Nobel Prize winners Milton Friedman, Robert Fogel, George Stigler, Ronald Coase, and Gary Becker. (By 2007, nineteen other University of Chicago economists would go on to win Nobel Prizes.) In the 1950s, however, it remained a midwestern school with a number of renegade thinkers, looked down upon by Harvard, MIT, and even Stanford. Chicago students lived and died in the workshops, where they presented papers and endured ruthless criticism. Only the thickest of skins—and the strongest of ideas—could survive in that climate. Moreover, the faculty, as Gary Becker observed, "saw economic analysis as a powerful way to understand behavior. . . . [A]t most places economics was taught as a game; it was not clear that teachers elsewhere thought economics was a powerful tool. Chicago did."[83]

Aside from these few enclaves of freedom, most academic thought in the West limped leftward to the embrace of planning and collectivism in the postwar years. Keynes died in 1946, but his disciple at Princeton, John Kenneth Galbraith, had learned from Hayek's success that to influence policy, one had to write in English—not Swahili or Cherokee, to paraphrase Keynes, as it seemed many of the economists did. Galbraith's trilogy—*American Capitalism* (1952), *The Affluent Society* (1958), and *The New Industrial State* (1967)—made the Keynesian case for government interference in the market. Arguing that America had become wealthy in the private sector but still lacked "infrastructure," and thereby perpetuated "inequities," Galbraith provided an economic excuse for public spending, particularly what would be called *directed* public spending that benefited some groups over others. Echoing Vance Packard's *The Hidden Persuaders* (1957), which argued that advertising had permanently distorted markets, Galbraith played the funeral dirge of small business and the private entrepreneur. From that point on, all power was in the hands of large combinations of labor, capital, and government. This was premature at best; government regulations were still few compared with what they would become in the twenty-first century, labor unions in the private sector would decline precipitously from 1970 to 2012, and small businesses continued to be the prime creator of jobs.

The Funeral March of Planned Economies

In the developing Third World, from which aspiring technocrats went to school in the United States and Britain, the Keynesian orthodoxy remained powerful and loud Marxist voices seemed reasonable. Less fortunate, however, were those students who received "educations" in the Soviet Union. Yet when they all returned to their native countries, the fusion of the two was government and more government, and a sense that the market could provide trinkets for tourists and perhaps a tomato patch for villagers, but was not the stuff on which solid economic growth was based. Instead of absorbing von Mises, Hayek, or even Rand, the majority of the new, desperately poor countries struggling to gain independence (just under one hundred between 1947 and 1980) turned to state activism or statism. India was their test tube; statistician P. C. Mahalanobis "became the prophet . . . of the development economists . . . and Calcutta became their Mecca."[84] Mahalanobis developed a neo-Marxist input-output model (the Mahalanobis model) that played a crucial role in India's second five-year plan.

Many of these thinkers reflected the influence of Alexander Gerschenkron's *Economic Backwardness in Historical Perspective* (1951), which argued that nations who were latecomers to economic development, such as Germany, France, and Russia, needed a way to speed up their growth through government intervention. Gerschenkron, like Marx, focused extensively on capital, as they claimed developing countries had plenty of land. The analysis never explained why such land remained in the hands of government or elites, or how the absence of title deeds affected landholding. Land was, of course, capital, but without deeds it could not be leveraged to raise money. Likewise, they struggled to explain how essentially landless states, such as Hong Kong, Japan, and later, Taiwan, leapfrogged vast nations such as Chad and China. Government needed to step in to supply capital because, the argument went, the risk for private investors was too great.[85] The American economist Walt Rostow and Cambridge-trained P. T. Bauer joined the chorus, reinforcing collectivist nostrums by claiming such a "take-off" would bring prosperity to backward nations.[86]

Though none of the 1950s writers who pioneered what is today called developmental economics subscribed to Communist doctrine as they understood it, the notion that the Third World required massive inflows of capital to civilize it was taken for granted. Lenin had first broached this view in *Imperialism: The Highest Stage of Capitalism* (1917), an extreme but logical extension of David Ricardo's "Iron Law of Wages," wherein surplus capital—which was not used for wages, as the leeching owners refused to pay "fair" salaries—had to go somewhere. For Lenin, that somewhere was Africa and Asia. Like Marx, Lenin had few original ideas, absorbing and expanding J. A. Hobson's 1902 book, *Imperialism*, whose thesis was that the Boer War was a wicked conspiracy of "finance capitalists," a term universally acknowledged to be code for Jews; not surprisingly, most of the totalitarian governments that arose were anti-Semitic. Quest for empire, Lenin and others argued, would ensure war in the colonies between imperialist nations. In fact, war came to the colonies only after—and because of—the combat that had already started in Europe. Despite incidents such as the confrontation between French and British forces at Fashoda in Sudan (1898), no sensible European monarch or democratically elected leader contemplated going to war over African boundaries.

Colonialism had, on the whole, resulted in substantial investments in the emerging countries, many of them narrowly focused toward extraction and export, not internal development. Upon assuming independence, the Third World governments found an astonishing absence of water and sewage facilities, working roads, and electricity. "The typical electricity network," wrote Daniel Yergin and Joseph Stanislaw, "consisted of erratic diesel turbines that supplied the villas and offices of the colonial administration."[87] Some working railroads remained since the pre–World War II fit of colonial spending, providing many countries with their only reliable mass transit. Other than that, how would the emerging nations obtain infrastructure?

One possible solution for the new governments was to throw out a welcome mat to investors and businessmen. Certainly an examination of early American development was in order. Take the example of John Fitch, who developed the first steamboat (then failed to make it profitable). Fitch was followed by Robert Fulton, who made money, but abhorred competition, and then finally by Cornelius Vanderbilt, whose lines challenged Fulton's and drove prices down for all travelers and shippers. All of the gains came without government aid—or in spite of it. Likewise, early American canals were heavily financed by, and mostly built by, the private sector, taking advantage only of government bond guarantees. Alexander Graham Bell and Thomas Edison received little government support to construct their national networks of telephones and electricity, only occasionally benefiting from monopoly rights to do business in certain areas. In short, it not only could be done, it was. American oil tycoon John D. Rockefeller, pilloried for establishing cartels and otherwise shutting out competition, did so not by breaking existing laws but by consistently leaping ahead of laws to form networks not yet subject to state control.[88]

Policy makers in the Third World countries ignored the early record of the American frontier, especially that of land law and property rights, often enforced at the end of a gun. There, the private sector built all the roads, invented a rapid mail delivery system in the form of the Pony Express, and even built a transcontinental railroad, James J. Hill's Great Northern, without a dime of public support. American cities in the nineteenth century sprang up along river routes, completely devoid of central planning or government expenditure; the entire landholding system of titles evolved from the reality that no government could survey and parcel out land nearly as fast as free people could settle it.[89] Vanderbilt again and again defeated publicly subsidized rivals in packet steamer transport, then transatlantic shipping. Half a century before that, John Jacob Astor had driven government fur trading posts out of business with his superior efficiency. In 2010, when President Barack Obama would tell entrepreneurs "you didn't build that" (meaning their businesses) but that somebody else did, because government had provided the infrastructure, it was an entirely false history of the critical decades in America's development. While later, in the twentieth century, it was common for governments to build roads and bridges, the *mode* of transportation—always created by private individuals—always preceded government investment. Ford's car came before the demand for paved roads; the Wrights' airplane came before the first airports; Fulton's and Vanderbilt's steamboats preceded the canal era; and Jobs and Wozniak's personal computer came before the Internet.

Entrepreneurs demonstrated business acumen that is taken for granted in free societies. In the late 1800s, Albert Fink introduced a new accounting system to allocate funds for depreciation, a basic market concept that James J. Hill, for example, invoked relentlessly when insisting that his railroad pay for itself in the future, not just the present.[90] Hill gave away farmland so that growers would later pay for his services and experimented with new crops and breeding of cattle—even though he was a railroader—because farmers were his customers. Money was routinely set aside for repair and replacement. Yet in Tanzania, from 1978 to 1998, some $2 billion poured in to build roads that never improved because a lack of maintenance on existing roads led them to deteriorate as fast as new ones were built.[91] This was not surprising. Not enough people owned cars to demand a decent road system, and if they did, the political structure was usually so dictatorial the citizens were ignored.

After Bretton Woods, it was common to find the World Bank hurling money at grandiose projects in the Third World, providing vehicles (but never spare parts, gasoline, money for repair), schools (but not teacher salaries or materials), and clinics (without medicine). It made little sense to provide vehicles for undeveloped nations where most of the rural roads required chronic rehabilitation.[92] The answer for improving the condition of the people was clearly not capital or investment, nor was the failure of emerging societies to build infrastructure due to the lack of money. It was in producing entrepreneurs who could create a demand so that *consumers* forced (and even paid for) the construction and maintenance of infrastructure.

Underneath the American business principles lay a Western/Enlightenment/European agreement on basic principles of human dignity, civil and property rights, free expression, a tradition or experience of common law, and Christian restraint, virtually none of which had taken root in the former colonies of Asia and Africa. Or, put differently, both the critics and defenders of the free market took as their starting point a Western bourgeois society under civil law (even in former British colonies) in which certain fundamental principles were already deeply entrenched, and in which clanism and tribalism had been substantially banished more than three centuries earlier. Imposing *either* capitalism or top-down managed socialism on cultures that still sacrificed chickens to determine whom one should marry, or in which cliterodectomies, dowry death, and suttee were still widely accepted, was doomed to failure on a countrywide basis. But that was not to say that free markets could not produce improvements over state planning. They did. On the margins, as economists like to say, top-down controlled economies performed demonstrably worse in the Third World, although either was preferable to internal strife or chaos.[93]

Decolonizing Amid Chaos

Leaving aside anticolonialism as a motivation, then, what possessed the emerging nations to cling to such demonstrably poor economic structures? One explanation is that it was what they learned from Western educators in school. Many Third World dictators received some of their education in England, France, or the United States (including Julius Nyerere of Tanzania, Kwame Nkrumah of Ghana, Nnamdi Azikiwe of Nigeria, and Léopold Senghor of Senegal), or from Catholic and Protestant missionary schools in their native lands. Statism was viewed in the European and American educational institutions as the political system of the future. The high road went through government and many of the anticolonialists began as teachers; virtually none were businessmen or entrepreneurs. Infected with the notion that governments led by charismatic personalities could impose modernization on premarket economies, leaders such as Kwame Nkrumah predicted of the Gold Coast (later Ghana), "If we get self-government, we'll transform the Gold Coast into a paradise in ten years."[94] Top-down control also evolved out of an unhealthy faith in the power of science and technology to solve all problems, a faulty concept still evident in politicians (though not engineers) posturing in contemporary times on alternate sources of energy. "Nkrumahism," as the Kwame Nkrumah Ideological Institute announced, "draw[s] its strength from modern science and technology."[95]

Planning, whether of the scientific or business variety, took on a religious quality. Marketing boards were set up. In Ghana, the Cocoa Marketing Board was the first, followed by agencies for timber, diamonds, foodstuffs, fish, and virtually everything else. (Eisenhower was not fooled, knowing Nkrumah's Communist sympathies, but when John Kennedy heard the Ghanaian president cite Thomas Jefferson at a United Nations speech, Kennedy naively exclaimed, "The disease of liberty is catching.")[96]

As with any government-directed activity, the marketing boards neither produced goods nor managed them very well, a weakness made fatal by the fact that their decisions were entirely constrained by Nkrumah's support for public companies that were ludicrously inept. Having already demonized "careerism" or "self-seeking" in his April 1961 "Dawn Broadcast," Nkrumah shifted money from cocoa incomes to the failing public companies. Farmers smuggled cocoa out of Ghana seeking higher prices or switched crops entirely. Once the world's largest cocoa producer, and awash in bauxite, Ghana stumbled backward into massive loans and barter trade, importing its bauxite from Jamaica. With each step backward, Nkrumah grew more irrational and delusional, taking for himself the title *Osagyefo*, or "the Redeemer." He was stopped only when the army staged a coup in 1964 while he was out of the country.[97]

For more than a century, the Europeans' territories had been little more than siphons for raw materials (even though, it is true, England poured millions of pounds of investment in infrastructure into India and Africa, mainly to facilitate exports). Influxes of raw materials lent some credence to the Leninist extraction hypothesis, for once established, colonial supply lines enabled advanced processing of finished products and elevated manufacturing levels in the mother countries. For purposes of the decolonization debate, however, once Europeans were out, the infrastructure they built remained—until the natives failed to maintain it and it decayed.

In spite of the schools Europeans had built and the flowery ruminations about self-government recited to pupils, there was precious little effort to either move the colonies to independence or prepare them for self-government. The mother countries fostered colonial dependency to the last second, and none of the European possessions were prepared for independence when it came. As Herbert Morrison of the Labour Party put it, independence for the Africans was akin to "giving a child of ten a latch-key, a bank account and a shotgun."[98] The only real example of a possession being prepared and groomed for independence was the Philippines, and that was by the United States.

Attitudes toward empire in Britain and France were poles apart, making for much different—though no less painful—transitions to indepen-

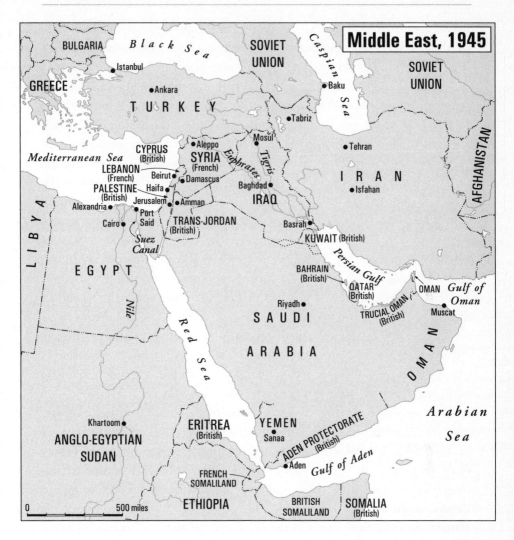

dence. England believed her colonies loved her because, well, they were *her* colonies. Conflating attitudes toward Britain in the largely white dominions of Canada, Australia, and New Zealand with those of India or Africa, the assumption arose that England and the empire were the same. Schoolchildren were heavily indoctrinated with the existence of the empire through cinema, comic books, and even processed foods such as biscuit tins covered in artwork of the world painted with the proper imperial colors. To English youngsters, "the names of colonial and dominion cities, rivers and political figures [i.e., virtually all white and British] were as familiar as those of Great Britain herself," wrote one raised during that era.[99] The French, on the other hand, treated the colonies as "administrative extensions of France itself," and sought to inculcate in natives from Algiers to Saigon the aspiration to become French, going so far as to teach Arab and Asian schoolchildren about *"nos ancêtres les Gaulois"* ("our ancestors the Gauls").[100]

None of the Europeans embraced true assimilation accompanied by political, let alone social, equality. France spoke of it more than England, Holland, or Spain, but as noted before, only the United States ever willingly and deliberately handed conquered territories back to native peoples (Cuba and the Philippines). At the same time, the Europeans were destined to be damned for making a "smaller white footprint" in Africa, where the "colonial imprint was barely noticeable."[101] Northern Nigeria's 10 million were governed by nine administrators and a regiment of 3,000 black troops commanded by Europeans; and even after the merger of Southern Nigeria to create a territory of 20 million, fewer than 400 administrators ran the colony. British Sudan saw 140 political appointees governing 9 million; French Equatorial Africa, which comprised eight separate territories and 15 million people, was run by only 385 administrators.[102] These statistics alone reveal why the Europeans ruled indirectly as much as possible, through village chieftains and convenient alliances with local thugs, notwithstanding the stunning disregard the Europeans had for erecting territorial boundaries around, over, and through tribes and villages.

Not only did this have the effect of delegitimizing European puppets, but it de facto embroiled the Belgians, Dutch, French, British, and Spanish in tribal politics, ensuring future score settling on a genocidal scale. Hutus were pitted against Tutsis, Xhosa against Zulus, Muslims against Christians, Hindus against Muslims, and everyone against the Sikhs, forcing the Europeans to back minorities who, in turn, used their elevated status to brutally oppress longtime enemies. Commonly, the tiny European presence maintained itself by playing off one group against another.

Europe—small by comparison—had to control vast amounts of territory on other continents. In Africa alone, France sought to control nearly four million square miles; England, two million. Late-nineteenth-century agreements between the Europeans had rent apart some ethnic groups and tribes while artificially joining others, some of them bitter enemies, into neatly drawn provinces. Britain's Lord Salisbury admitted, "We have been giving away mountains and rivers and lakes to each other, only hindered by the small impediment that we never knew exactly where they were."[103] Lands and peoples had been traded like deeds in the game of Monopoly, with Britain handing Heligoland in the North Sea to Germany for Zanzibar, or sections of Nigeria exchanged by the French for fishing rights off

Newfoundland. The result was a continent of "nations" that had no national characteristics, save their names. Nigeria's first prime minister, Abubakar Balewa, admitted in 1957, "Nigerian unity is only a British invention."[104] Another Nigerian politician, Obafemi Awolowo, wrote, "Nigeria is not a nation. It is a mere geographical expression."[105] Liberia, created by the American Colonization Society as a refuge for freed slaves out of part of the old Mali and Songhai empires, formally declared itself the Republic of Liberia in 1847, even though the new black American settlers did not integrate into African society. Indeed, they continued referring to themselves as Americans, electing a Virginian, Joseph Jenkins Roberts (1809–76), as their first president in 1848.

One can see the futility of European territorial boundaries even after the decolonization of Africa and the independence of the new states that emerged. In 1955, there was French West Africa, which fifty years later had broken apart into Mauritania, Niger, Burkina Faso, Côte d'Ivoire (Ivory Coast), Senegal, Guinea, Togo, Ghana, and Benin (partly created by taking some of Nigeria). French Equatorial Africa remained essentially unchanged geographically during that period, as did Libya and Egypt. A few other states merely renamed themselves: Anglo-Egyptian Sudan became Sudan; Togoland became Togo; Portuguese Guinea became Guinea Bissau; Rio de Oro became Western Sahara; Bechuanaland became Botswana; and so on. The process of decolonization never involved deliberate policy—except for the British, who "intended to intend" to develop such a policy. Hundreds of conferences, including almost a dozen over Rhodesia/South Africa alone, resulted in the colonies' stumbling toward independence and European withdrawal. It is therefore misleading to suggest, as Paul Johnson does, that "all territories were to be prepared for independence, and given it when ready."[106] The wording of the 1948 white paper stating "The central purpose of British colonial policy . . . is to guide the colonial territories to responsible self-government within the Commonwealth in conditions that ensure to the people concerned both a fair standard of living and freedom from oppression in any quarter" incorporated three separate problems.[107]

First, British colonial policy had not shown itself eager to ever part with territories, especially nonwhite ones. The United States won independence in 1783 after a seven-year-long rebellion; in 1867, Canada was given a measure of home rule on internal matters; and the Statute of Westminster (1931) created the British Commonwealth and recognized New Zealand, Australia, the Union of South Africa, Canada, Newfoundland, and the Irish Free State as independent with various reservations. The Australia Act of

1986 signaled final, full independence for that nation, while Canada gained the right to issue passports in 1949 and finally obtained full independence in the 1960s. Newfoundland and Labrador remained under British rule until 1949, when they became a province of Canada as Newfoundland. Grudgingly, Ireland received its sovereign status after several home rule bills and a bloody civil war. Aside from these, Britain never quickly (if it could be argued that these were quick) handed independence to any colony. Second, many of the colonies did not wish to remain within the Commonwealth, no matter how beneficial the British thought it was for them to do so. Finally, determining when conditions could ensure that colonial populations would have a "fair standard of living and freedom from oppression in any quarter" was, as history proved, impossible. Since gaining independence after World War II, the British (and all other Europeans') colonies have been a maelstrom of civil wars, genocide, assassinations, coups, and dictatorships. It was, then, a mush-phrase to permit the British to dawdle on independence as long as they desired, or, conversely, to avoid what Colonial Secretary Iain Macleod called a "resounding decision" and instead embark on preserving the formalities of negotiations culminating in a "grandiose orgy of constitution-making."[108]

Another factor complicating independence for the colonies—and one largely ignored in the West—was that there were large numbers of Muslims who wished to establish fundamentalist Islamic states under Sharia law. Clerics in Iran, Saudi Arabia, and Egypt especially saw the removal of the Europeans as the beginning of the new caliphates, where nonbelievers would be an underclass, called *dhimmi*, and their rights would be substantially less than those of Muslims. No better statement to understand their attitude toward Western institutions was made than that on February 27, 2011, by Anjem Choudary, a Muslim cleric born a generation after decolonization in Britain. In other words, this was a cleric who should have been fully "Western." Instead, Choudary took a decidedly fundamentalist stance saying, "Muslims don't want democracy and freedom. Democracy and freedom are anathema to Islam and the *Shariah*."[109] Even well-intentioned Western governments failed to appreciate the often fatal resistance many Muslims had to "preparing" them for democracy and Western-style self-government.

Each of the British-governed African territories was run independently of the others, and as far as practicable, a black, professional elite was groomed for power—doctors, attorneys, educators, businessmen—all of which ultimately crashed up against the demands of the local white populations, particularly in Rhodesia and South Africa. Universities were established, but predictably based on what the natives learned from British teachers, the most ambitious students went into government and law, not business, engineering, or science. This was a common response from subject peoples: the Irish, who came to America in large numbers, gravitated to fire departments and police work, seeing their salvation as plying the levers of government.[110] They thereby deprived themselves of a vibrant business community, and of the entrepreneurs needed to lift the common man out of poverty. Well into the twentieth century, Irish-Americans lagged behind more business-oriented immigrants, such as Jews, Italians, Asians, and even black West Africans.

Like India, Africa's decolonization occurred in part because the West was exhausted and natives were imbued with ideas of liberty. Agitators from Nigeria to Madagascar held meetings, published pamphlets, boycotted, and at times even engaged in strikes because Western influences promoted such activities. American black separationist Marcus Garvey had said in 1920, "We believe in the inherent right of the Negro to possess himself of Africa, and that his possession of same shall not be regarded as an infringement on any claim or purchase made by any race or nation."[111] Garvey, like most Westerners of any color, failed to appreciate the fact that Africans did not see themselves as a "Negro people," but rather as tribes, and that only detribalizing Africa would achieve the material prosperity that the agitators thought decolonizing the continent would bring.

Israel's Miraculous Creation

Stirred into this decolonization soup was another ingredient: the rebirth of the state of Israel, prophesied in the Bible and promised by the Balfour Declaration of 1917. After World War I, Britain governed the area of Palestine (as Judea was renamed by the Romans after the fall of Jerusalem in A.D. 70) and had to determine whether to honor the Balfour Declaration. Matters were complicated by the antics of Colonel T. E. Lawrence, who had helped organize Arab resistance to the Turks and zealously promoted a national state for Arabs. Muslims inferred from Lawrence that the British would support Muslim states throughout the Middle East, and the British in 1921 seemed to validate that perception by authorizing a Supreme Muslim Council to direct religious affairs in Palestine. Muhammad Amin al-Husseini, a "dedicated killer who had devoted his entire adult life to race murder," had been sentenced to ten years in prison for his role in anti-Jewish riots, then was inexplicably released, became the grand mufti of Je-

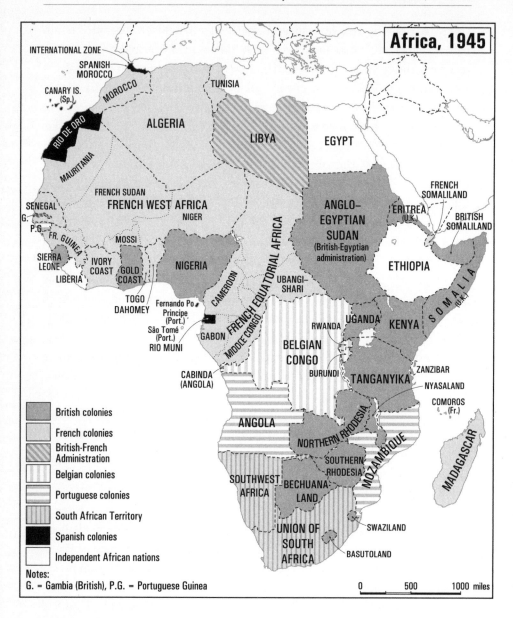

Africa, 1945

INTERNATIONAL ZONE

SPANISH MOROCCO

CANARY IS. (Sp.)

MOROCCO

TUNISIA

RIO DE ORO

ALGERIA

LIBYA

EGYPT

MAURITANIA

FRENCH SUDAN

FRENCH WEST AFRICA

NIGER

SENEGAL

G.

P.G.

FR. GUINEA

MOSSI

SIERRA LEONE

IVORY COAST

GOLD COAST

NIGERIA

LIBERIA

TOGO

DAHOMEY

Fernando Po Principe (Port.)

São Tomé (Port.)

RIO MUNI

CAMEROON

FRENCH EQUATORIAL AFRICA

MIDDLE CONGO

GABON

UBANGI-SHARI

ANGLO-EGYPTIAN SUDAN (British-Egyptian administration)

FRENCH SOMALILAND

ERITREA (U.K.)

BRITISH SOMALILAND

ETHIOPIA

SOMALIA (U.K.)

CABINDA (ANGOLA)

BELGIAN CONGO

RWANDA

BURUNDI

UGANDA

KENYA

TANGANYIKA

ZANZIBAR

NYASALAND

COMOROS (Fr.)

ANGOLA

NORTHERN RHODESIA

MOZAMBIQUE

MADAGASCAR

SOUTHWEST AFRICA

SOUTHERN RHODESIA

BECHUANA-LAND

SWAZILAND

UNION OF SOUTH AFRICA

BASUTOLAND

British colonies

French colonies

British-French Administration

Belgian colonies

Portuguese colonies

South African Territory

Spanish colonies

Independent African nations

Notes:

G. = Gambia (British), P.G. = Portuguese Guinea

0   500   1000 miles

rusalem, and was named head of the Council. Thus, the British ensured there would be no peaceful resettlement of the Jews in the region.[112] Al-Husseini so hated Jews that in World War II he organized a Muslim division from the Balkans for the Wehrmacht, inspecting them and giving the Nazi salute. He personally met with Hitler, where he was told that the goal of the Third Reich was to destroy the Jews. Hitler told him to "lock this secret in your heart."[113]

At al-Husseini's direction, not only were Jews targeted but so were Arab moderates who just sought to run businesses and raise families. Employing terrorist Emile Ghori to assassinate Arabs who cooperated with Jews, he attempted to drive out all the Arabs who could have forged a joint, peaceful state. Al-Husseini's efforts notwithstanding, Jewish immigration continued through 1939, when British colonial secretary Malcolm MacDonald issued the so-called White Paper recommending partitioning Palestine based on proportional population numbers of Arabs and Jews. However, it shut off all new Jewish immigration after five years, and elicited a bitter reaction from Jews. As war with Germany engulfed Britain, David Ben-Gurion, head of the Jewish Agency for Palestine, responded, "We will fight Hitler as if there were no White Paper; we will fight the White Paper as if there were no Hitler."[114]

Over the next six years, news began to leak about the Holocaust—although even when most nations intuitively knew what the Final Solution entailed, none liberalized their immigration policies; indeed, the United States tightened its visa regulations. Somehow the British envisioned a partition between Jews and Arabs but provided no details as to how that would actually occur and certainly did not want to accept more Jews in Palestine. As late as 1944, Churchill told Chaim Weizmann of the World Zionist Organization that England would permit only another 1.5 million Jews into Palestine over a ten-year period. But matters quickly spun out of British control.

A Jewish military organization had existed since 1921, and had materially aided the British during their suppression of the Arab Revolt of 1936–39. During that time they evolved from a home defense militia to a tactical army, and in World War II provided soldiers for the British army, which organized the Jews into their own regiments. In 1946, facing an intransigent British anti-Zionism ensconced as official policy, the Jewish army (called the Haganah) began an open struggle against British rule. Two Jewish groups, Lehi (or, as the British labeled them, the Stern Gang) and a Haganah breakaway organization, the Irgun (headed by Menachem Begin from 1943 to 1948), had worked for years to move Jewish immigrants into Palestine surreptitiously. Since the 1930s, they had engaged in an eye-for-eye retaliation killing of Arab terrorists. Working from the ideas of Ze'ev Jabotinsky and his Revisionist Zionism, "The policy of the [Irgun] was based squarely on Jabotinsky's teachings: every Jew had the right to enter Palestine; only active retaliation would deter the Arabs; only Jewish armed force would ensure the Jewish state."[115] The Irgun staged a public attack on four Arab police stations in 1944. But the British were as much the targets of Irgun attacks as were Arabs, on the premise that the "regime" would break if they could destroy the prestige of the British in Palestine.

It was the Irgun's assassination of the British deputy resident minister of state, Lord Moyne, in November 1944 that started the "Hunting Season" by the British working in concert with the Haganah. Virtually all Irgun-associated people were removed from public offices, schools, and workplaces, and more than a thousand were arrested. Then came the King David Hotel bombing in July 1946—for which the Irgun claimed it had given sufficient warning to evacuate—which killed forty-one Arabs, twenty-eight British, seventeen Jews, and five others. Britain banned further emigration to Palestine, and, already weary of trying to police the mandate, in February 1947 British foreign secretary Ernest Bevin admitted that the Jews and Arabs could not peacefully partition the land. Before Britain could hand the problem over to the United Nations, however, Irgun operatives staged the Acre prison break, in which forty-one members of the underground were freed, but in the process three Irgun attackers were captured. In retaliation, the Irgun took as hostages a pair of British sergeants. When the prison attackers were executed, the two hostages were hanged, strung up from trees, and their bodies booby-trapped. More than the King David bombing, this incident convinced Britain to leave Palestine.

At the same time, the United Nations Special Committee on Palestine witnessed the voyage of the *Exodus 1947*, which contained 4,500 Holocaust survivors. When it arrived at the port of Haifa, it was not permitted to disembark its passengers. World opinion recoiled at the image of those who had survived Hitler's camps enduring horrendous conditions in another type of gulag because they were not allowed to leave the ship. On November 29, 1947, the United Nations ended the British mandate and divided Palestine into a Jewish state and an Arab state. Of the thirty-three votes in favor, the United States was joined by nearly all Latin American countries, all European nations (including, surprisingly, the Soviet Union and its satellites), Liberia, South Africa, and the Philippines. Thirteen countries, all Islamic except Cuba, India, and Greece, voted against the creation of Israel. Many, including India's Nehru, complained about heavy lobbying by the "Zionists," including outright bribes. Ten nations, including several Latin American nations and Britain, abstained from the vote.

Fighting immediately broke out, as Jordan's Arab Legion (the best trained and equipped of the Arab armies) seized Old Jerusalem. Other Arab forces struggled badly against the outmanned and outgunned Jews.

Whereas the Jews had promised that Arab residents would remain full citizens and their property would remain inviolate, thousands of Arabs in the area moved to Muslim-controlled areas in response to threats from the Islamic states that there would be retribution against turncoats. Likewise, Jews in Islamic-controlled areas fled to the new Israel.

That Roosevelt's death had brought Harry Truman to power at the instant of Israel's creation was viewed by Jews as a miracle. The chief rabbi of Israel, Isaac Halevi Herzog, meeting with Truman at the White House, told the president, "God put you in your mother's womb so that you would be the instrument to bring about the rebirth of Israel after two thousand years."[116] Truman's administrative assistant David Niles observed that when Herzog said those words, "I looked over at the President [and] tears were running down his cheeks."[117] Indeed, Truman read through the foreign policy records and statements of his predecessor, noting that the State Department had described the "question of Palestine" as "a highly complex one."[118] Truman, however, while writing in his memoirs that he "was in agreement" with Roosevelt's position, intended to "do everything possible to carry out that policy," and had "carefully read the Balfour Declaration," decided the Jews were owed a national homeland.[119] Expressing skepticism about the "striped-pants boys" in the State Department, Truman, in a remarkable and courageous feat of rationalization, reinterpreted FDR's policies in line with the establishment of a state of Israel.

Israel's reappearance constituted a nearly unprecedented historical event. Of course there was a natural affinity between Zionist leaders and the West, particularly among Western leaders from the Judeo-Christian tradition. Americans especially saw much of their own exceptional story in the special status afforded in the Bible to the Chosen People. Even with that self-evident relationship, however, the reappearance of Israel after centuries was nevertheless a miraculous development. After all, no signs existed, anywhere, in the modern world that mentioned the ancient neighbors of the Jews. As one Christian evangelist asked, "Have you ever met a Moabite? Do you know any Hittites? Are there any tours to visit the Ammonites? Can you find a postal code of a single Edomite?"[120] Egyptians and Syrians were restored artificially by Western powers, but except for the Christian Copts of Egypt, neither maintained a national identity by any stretch of the definition; and even the Babylonians and Persians (modern-day Iraqis and Iranians) had undergone massive changes. Israel alone had made a transition to a modern nation-state, separating religion from government and yet retaining its unique character.

Second, powerful forces were aligned against the Zionists. Virtually the entire U.S. State Department and British Foreign Ministry opposed a Jewish state. It was only the ascension of Harry Truman to the presidency that overrode the elite American diplomats. The British, of course, never overcame their Foreign Ministry, hence their abstention in the final vote. Beyond that, under normal circumstances the USSR would have opposed as a general practice any position the United States advocated. But precisely because the *British* opposed the creation of Israel, the Soviets concluded that it must be something to be desired and would further the breakup of British interests in the region.

Of course, the entirety of the Islamic states opposed Israel and had never agreed to the concept of a Jewish state since the brief discussions in which British officials had negotiated a protocol between Chaim Weizmann, the head of the World Zionist Organization, and the Hashemite prince Faisal in 1919.[121] But the British (and Weizmann) had backed the wrong horse, and Ibn Saud, head of the Saud family that had adopted Muhammad Wahhab and become the main proponent of his Wahhabi Islamic movement, had emerged the monarch of the new Saudi Arabia. With Saud's acquisition of the throne, possibly all chances for a reasonable settlement with the Zionists vanished. But in the interim, the British had guaranteed there would be no reconciliation by appointing al-Husseini to be the wolf in charge of the sheep. By the time Arab "nations"—"tribes with flags" as one observer called them—began to take shape, an unrelenting campaign against Israel was inevitable.

Pharaoh in Uniform and Fez

Nationalism, which was an insanely absurd concept in most tribal-dominated territories of the Middle East, had taken on another distinct characteristic in which it became entirely personality oriented. There was Nkrumahism, Nasserism, and endless other isms. Nelson Mandela spoke of "undiluted African nationalism."[122] Nkrumah proclaimed that "the flowing tide of African nationalism sweeps everything before it."[123] Usually, it was political opposition and inconvenient tribal leaders who were swept. Gamal Abdel Nasser, the driving force behind the Egyptian revolution of 1952, melded all powers into his person in 1956 as Egypt's president and dictator. His control extended to the media, trade unions, churches, mosques, and even youth organizations. Almost every aspect of business life was absorbed by Nasser's government, including industry, trade, banking, department stores, and retail vendors.

Politically, Nasser and his Third World doppelgängers were thoroughly corrupted by the heady froth of power. Nasser rounded up political prisoners by the thousands, keeping them in line through kangaroo courts and, when necessary, police torture. One of them, the future spiritual founder of al-Qaeda and member of the Muslim Brotherhood, Sayyid Qutb, spent three years in jail and experienced Nasser's torture methods firsthand. Egypt was growing at stupendous rates, reaching 40 million in the 1970s, nearly 60 million by the mid-1990s, and numbering more than 84 million by 2010. Having come to power with Major General Muhammad Naguib in a coup that overthrew King Farouk (after securing British and American assurances of noninterference), Nasser rode the wave of anti-British anger, particularly by mobilizing the city's students at the slightest urging to take to the streets.

As with other members of the Bandung Generation of leaders (so named for the group influenced by the Asian-African Conference in Bandung, Indonesia, in April 1955), Nasser came from the middle class and was educated at good Egyptian schools. He was wounded participating in a demonstration and from that point he became an Egyptian Abbie Hoffman, agitating and leading student protest groups. Then, abruptly, he was admitted to the military academy and joined the army. While stationed in Sudan, Nasser and future Egyptian president Anwar Sadat plotted a rebellion with the assistance of the Italians. It never came off. Transferred to Palestine, Nasser fought the Jews in the 1948 war before he and his Free Officers movement launched their revolution. Although Naguib was installed as president in 1952, within two years, Nasser had deposed the general and purged his supporters from the army. Nasser survived his own assassination attempt in 1954 at the hands of a member of the Muslim Brotherhood—an early incarnation of al-Qaeda that, at the time, was still targeting Muslim leaders who were insufficiently pious. At just thirty-six, Nasser was the first native-born Egyptian leader since the pharaohs. He hated England from a young age, recalling that during World War II he prayed for Allah to deliver "a calamity to overtake the English."[124]

Egypt, like most of the newly independent states, adopted a constitution to serve the purpose of the new ruler. In June 1956, 99.95 percent of Egyptian voters voted to elect Nassar president of Egypt, and 99.8 percent voted to approve the Egyptian constitution that made Egypt into a single-party socialist state with Islam its official religion. (This changed somewhat in 1971, when Anwar Sadat introduced a new constitution that supposedly provided for free and democratic elections, rule of law, political parties, and free speech, although all of these words were meaningless to a public that had been subject to autocratic rule all their lives.) As in so many of the other Bandung states, the constitution was ignored when it became inconvenient. Worse, the constitution proclaimed the "destruction of capitalistic influence." Predictably, an economic decline followed, proving the principle that any system that excludes capitalists is doomed to fail. Neither the education system nor the social incentives rewarded or encouraged anything that would build wealth. Certainly Nasser wasn't concerned with entrepreneurial-driven growth, only with joining the rising chorus of anti-American, anti-British, and anti-Zionist radicals that included Indonesia's Sukarno and India's Nehru.

The Soviets saw their opportunity early with Nasser. He was the first Arab-world leader courted by Moscow, with overtures beginning six months after he took office.[125] After nationalizing the Suez Canal in the summer of 1956, a desperate Nasser begged the Kremlin for advice on how to hold it, and the Soviets were only too happy to respond. KGB agents met with the president and instructed him on how best to avoid assassination attempts (keep a caged bird on the premises at all times, he was told, as an early warning sign of poison gas). Nikita Khrushchev even summoned Nasser to the May Day Parade in 1958, escorting his guest to the Bolshoi Ballet to watch *Swan Lake*. When the black swan appeared on stage, Khrushchev said, "That's [John Foster] Dulles!" referring to the U.S. secretary of state as the figure of evil in the ballet. "Don't worry, Comrade Nasser," the pudgy premier assured the Egyptian, "at the end of the act we'll break his wings!"[126]

Although it engaged in a full-court press to enlist all Middle East leaders, the KGB in the short term hoped to create a Communist client state in the United Arab Republic, a short-lived union of Syria and Egypt from 1958 to 1961 that was actually formed to prevent a Communist takeover in Syria. When that fell apart, Moscow hitched its star solely to the Egyptian strongman.[127] Together, Nasser and his Soviet sponsors crafted slogans— and Nasser was a master sloganeer—such as the "noncapitalist path"—to conceal Egypt's socialism. More than 40 percent of all Soviet aid given to the Third World between 1954 and 1961 went to Egypt, and at one point, the Egyptian Communist Party disbanded itself to merge with the ruling Arab Socialist Union. Kim Philby, the disgraced British spy who defected to the USSR in 1963, wrote an ode to Nasser in 1962 called "Nasser's Pride and Glory," while Soviet advisers in Egypt exceeded twenty thousand. In 1964, Nasser was made a Hero of the Soviet Union, the Communists' highest award. As Christopher Andrew, who processed Soviet KGB defector Vasili Mitrokhin's vast archives, noted, "Throughout the 1960s more Soviet hopes were pinned on Nasser than on any other Third World leader outside Latin America."[128]

It was too late: the Egyptian economy unraveled under Nasser's rule, and only foreign aid, mostly from the Soviets, sustained the regime. "The people can't eat socialism," Nasser said. "If they weren't Egyptian they'd beat me with their shoes."[129] His greatest accomplishments, the Aswan Dam and the Helwan steel works, were both bankrolled by the Soviets, and both dislocated local economies. The Aswan High Dam raised the water table in the lower Nile valley, increasing salinity and ultimately ruining agriculture by suppressing the annual floods that refertilized the land. Nasser did nothing to improve conditions in Cairo, with its nine million people in a city built to hold three million, on its way to becoming one of the dirtiest and noisiest urban areas on earth.

The Soviet-backed Aswan Dam project ultimately led to the Suez Crisis of 1956–57. Seeking World Bank funds of $200 million, largely coming from the United States, Egypt sought to construct the dam to increase agricultural output and employment. American experts determined it would do neither, and Eisenhower refused the loan request in July 1956 in what Nasser portrayed as a national rebuke. He seized control of the Suez, touching off a ridiculous (and damaging) plot hatched by the British and French to unseat him.

Neither Sir Anthony Eden, the British prime minister, nor the leadership of the Fourth French Republic had legal grounds on which to act; Egypt had not violated the 1888 agreement, which permitted the nationalization of foreign assets with proper compensation. Worse, neither Britain nor France had Eisenhower's support, nor did either have the military power to mount a serious invasion in less than six weeks. Instead of acting on their own and standing on what minimal principle they had, the two former great powers roped the Israelis into the scheme on the grounds that they had been denied passage through the Suez. If the plot was transparent and pitifully obvious, the more destructive by-product was that it cemented in the Arab mind that the West was controlled and directed by Jews.[130] Ike, in the middle of an election, was outraged—a trait he rarely displayed in public (but that was well known to his officers in World War II)—but the U.S. president had no intention of allowing the United States to get sucked into a Middle East war. During the crisis, most of the president's ire was directed at Anthony Eden, largely because the prime minister did not take the old general's advice to leave Nasser alone: "Nasser thrives on drama," Ike had warned him.[131]

By September, Eisenhower had strongly warned the British and French not to expect American support in the event of adventurism. He had, in part, made a reputation as a man of peace, having cobbled together an exit from Korea. Earlier, in Indochina, Ike had refused to send troops to rescue French soldiers under siege by the Viet Minh at Dien Bien Phu, limiting aid mostly to a modicum of airlifted supplies. He did permit sorties by U.S. B-26 bombers—but not the commitment of ground forces or B-52s, with the heavy suppressive bombing that the surrounded French expected and needed. By 1954, when the French lost Indochina, Eisenhower had already written them off as a world power. This shocked the French, who, as they had in the two world wars, expected that the Americans would cheerfully save them. When the United States refused, France held America accountable for its loss in power, prestige, and honor. Almost immediately after Dien Bien Phu, the situation in Laos became an open sore, one that Ike failed to close during his administration.

Little question existed about the morality of the comedic Anglo-French-Israeli operation in the Suez. It was a fraud from the get-go, undertaken with little conviction on the part of any of the participants, and lacking authority of law, precedent, or even absolute necessity. Once initiated, the invasion would naturally become a pissing contest between the West and the Third World, with the only possible outcome a bad one for all except Nasser, and perhaps the Soviets. If Ike hoped to win world acclaim for temperance and restraint in the Suez Crisis, he was badly mistaken. The Arab world believed the United States had a hand in provoking the affair, and already were searching for their own "man on a white horse," a position Nasser gleefully filled.

A second humiliating defeat at the hands of Israel in the Six-Day War in 1967 pushed Nasser further into the red camp, but only three years remained for him to further damage Egypt before his death. Nasser stated, "What is important for us is that we now recognize that our main enemy is the United States and that the only possible way of continuing our struggle is for us to ally ourselves with the Soviet Union. . . ."[132] Between the 1957 and 1967 defeats, Moscow had responded with more tanks, air bases, and missiles. In the dark rooms of the Kremlin, however, there was concern. During the Six-Day War, a vastly outnumbered Israel military had utterly crushed the Arabs, despite the new equipment shipped in by the USSR. Israel destroyed 286 of 340 Egyptian aircraft before they even got in the air, and displayed total armor domination over Arab tanks. By the end of two decades of Israeli independence, the Arab states had launched two wars, and the Israelis had provoked a third, and in each of the conflicts the Arab-Egyptian forces had been humiliated, requiring the United States to step in diplomatically to save them from further loss of territory.

Fifth Columns in the Third World

Even as the United States confronted communism through economic and military strength in Europe and Asia, a back door was left open. Progressive educators worked tirelessly in American schools to destroy the four pillars of American exceptionalism and to substitute for them the reliance on government for individual rights and one's well-being. Emotional, rather than substantive, appeals by teachers and professors attacked capitalism, and with Christianity declining in the United States and Europe, communism/Marxism/socialism became attractive to both the elite rulers and the bottom rung of the economic ladder. Since the end of World War II, the middle classes in all capitalist countries have been under assault by power-seeking statists and are declining. It had become partially a religious war, one in which modern, thoughtful religions of subtlety lose and stricter, more fundamentalist religions like Islam and Roman Catholicism seem best suited to win. As their own worst enemy, the Europeans always had tolerated a "soft" socialism and seemed immune to its invasiveness in their societies, not to mention their personal liberties. Lacking the American spirit of frontier independence, long denied land ownership to the same degree as was possible in North America, and devoid of common-law principles (except in England and some of Germany), it was somewhat understandable that Europeans would display such blindness to their decline. What was new was that progressives in the United States looked to Europe for leadership in their war against American exceptionalism, and against all logic, the American people were buying into European criticisms of America and socialist initiatives.

America, and often America alone, had to manage the cold war, made more difficult by the decolonization in the Third World. There, America's deepening concern about Soviet power melded with the Europeans' interest in maintaining their empires, for the KGB remained active in fomenting anti-European sentiments. Nelson Mandela, speaking at his 1964 trial, recalled, "For many decades the Communists were the only political group in South Africa who were prepared to treat Africans as human beings and their equals; who were prepared to eat with us; talk with us, live with and work with us."[133] Quite often before the Soviets could even act, Third World dictators destroyed their own economies as KGB field agents dispatched desperate cables to Moscow filled with a depressing record of African mal-feasance. After Dahomey's president "proclaimed himself a Marxist-Leninist," and asked for Soviet aid, KGB officer Nikolai Leonov recorded in his diary,

> our ambassador . . . broke into a sweat out of fear, and was incapa-
> ble of answering yes or no. . . . This action of the Dahomeyans
> looks absurd . . . 80 percent of the population of 3 million are illit-
> erate, power is in the hands of a military clique. There is neither
> industry, nor parties, nor classes.[134]

"What is communism in African conditions[?]" asked Aghostinho Neto, an exiled Angolan revolutionary and Soviet loyalist, of KGB officer Oleg Nazhestkin. "Help me to come to grips with this question. After all, you're a communist and you must understand it as well."[135] Samora Machel, who vowed to make Mozambique "Africa's first Marxist state," admitted he hadn't read Marx or Engels. His worldview came from watching his father grow cotton and sell it at the market at a lower price than the Portuguese growers.[136] In Somalia, the "Victorious Leader," Siad (also spelled Siyad) Barre, flanked himself with portraits of Marx and Lenin in public appear-ances, although he claimed his "scientific socialism" was a fusion of Marx and Islam. He produced his own blue-and-white "little book," reminiscent of Mao's, and after seizing power in 1969, abolished the legislature and banned political parties, then for good measure expelled the U.S. Peace Corps and half of the embassy personnel. This laid the groundwork for overtures to the Soviets, the admission of 3,600 Soviet advisers, and a warm welcome for the Soviet navy.

In Kenya, an unknown economist at the Ministry of Finance named Barack Hussein Obama sought to find the key to success. He converted from Islam to Christianity, then became an atheist and adopted Marxism. He dreamed of building a socialist Kenya through government planning and control, and cursed all things British. While studying in the United States, he took a second wife—a white American teenager who became pregnant at seventeen—then abandoned her after his son, also named Barack Hussein Obama, was born. One can see the seeds of Barack Junior's disdain for private entrepreneurship and capitalism in Senior's screed, which claimed to define "African socialism." Barack Obama Sr. insisted,

"Theoretically, there is nothing that can stop the government from taxing 100 per cent of income so long as people get the benefits. . . . I do not see why the government cannot tax those who have more and syphon some of these revenues into savings which can be utilized for investment. . . ."[137] The utter blindness to the question of why people would work at all if someone takes everything they make (itself the definition of slavery) and the notion that the state can "save" money when it has already been drained from private savings and investment was astonishing in Obama's article. He also noted that there was in Kenya "disguised unemployment, which, if we were to plan sensibly, could be utilized to the benefit of society," one of the earliest statements of the later concept that radicals should not "allow a good crisis to go to waste."[138] Decades later, the son sought out the elder Obama and published *Dreams from My Father*, which perfectly captured the worldview of those who embraced the premise that all issues boiled down to power/powerless, oppressed/oppressor. The younger Obama would attempt to realize his father's dreams as president of the United States, but it was a high irony: whereas America had failed to mold Africa in its own image, the younger Obama would attempt to fundamentally transform America into Africa's.

Africans proved just as uncontrollable for their Soviet supporters as they had for their former European masters. Dictators such as Mengistu Haile Mariam in Ethiopia invoked Lenin and his Red Terror to justify massacres of political opponents. Ahmed Sékou Touré, in Guinea, employed the East German Stasi and Czech secret police to construct his interrogation facilities and prison camps replete with torture chambers. Nkrumah's security apparatus was packed with KGB-trained operatives who were "placed everywhere—in factories, offices, drinking bars, political rallies and even churches, not forgetting the taxi drivers, bus drivers, shop assistants, peddlers and seemingly unemployed persons who were all acting as informants."[139] Similar penetration was achieved in the governments of Mali and Guinea, where Soviet operatives leaked word of plots and coups to play on the paranoia of Modibo Keïta and Touré. Predictably, these reports resulted in the dictators' denouncing the "imperialist conspiracy" to undermine their state.

Soviet covert operations targeted African diplomats at the UN, in one instance distributing one hundred copies of a racist pamphlet that supposedly emanated from an American extremist group. Officers of the KGB also "bombarded African diplomats at the UN with racially insulting correspondence purporting to come from US white supremacists."[140] Forgeries were a common weapon in Africa as well, being fed to dictators such as Touré to convince him of CIA plots to overthrow him. "The filthy imperialists!" he screamed, vowing to expel the Americans.[141] Fortunately, the KGB spent almost as much time contending with the perceived Chinese competition in Africa as it did seeking to undermine the West, and despite the incredible popularity of Mao Zedong's Little Red Book (four million copies in Mali alone, or one per person), the Chinese had little influence.[142] The closest any African leader came to identifying with Mao was Robert Mugabe, the revolutionary head of the Zimbabwean movement and the first prime minister of Zimbabwe (1980), who described himself as a "Marxist-Leninist of Maoist thought."[143]

Welfare for the World

With the exception of South Africa, the decolonized nations of the African continent followed statist policies because, in large part, that was what they had been taught. But they also had never even been seriously exposed to the four pillars of American exceptionalism because their colonial masters did not themselves possess them. Authoritarian mind-sets proved nearly universal in Africa, Latin America, and much of Asia, while America's relatively free markets were viewed as inapplicable. Only on the Pacific Rim and to some extent in Southeast Asia did the American model find favor, but even in those emerging states, some of the exceptional elements were always missing. Once the Europeans no longer controlled their former colonies, however, they "reinvaded" through massive humanitarian efforts.

Whether out of guilt or out of compassion, the aid missions to the developing world took on a mystical, quasi-religious quality in the West. Natives who had never seen a paved road or operated an advanced piece of machinery were lionized as the key to the future, provided enough assistance could be directed to them. Yet even the favored term "developing world" was a misnomer, for in many places there was little development at all, and within thirty years, environmental policies of the "developed" world would severely shackle what progress existed in the first place.

Within only a few decades after the aid transfer began, a sober realization began to dawn on Western do-gooders: aid often retarded development in the Third World, in a real sense, by short-circuiting the entrepreneurship necessary for growth and fertilizing an attitude of blame. A "development assistance industry" was birthed after the Second World War, in no small part due to white guilt brought on by the widespread internalizing of leftist arguments about what caused development in the first place. In the late twentieth century, certainly academics and the media did their share to foment confusion and self-loathing in the West, colored by subordinated strains of anti-Semitism amid a palette of big money.

No matter how empirically one could demonstrate the invalidity of the Lenin-imperialism thesis, the West embarked on the most massive income transfer in human history. By 2006 aid had amounted to the staggering total of $2.3 *trillion*—with almost nothing to show for it. One World Bank economist noted that despite the mind-boggling sums sent to the poor countries, foreign aid still had not managed to "get twelve-cent medicines to children to prevent half of malaria deaths . . . [or] to get four-dollar bed nets to poor families."[144] Thomas Dichter, an anthropologist intimately involved in dozens of development projects, organizations, foundations, and international bodies, "knew of no organization that really accomplished much in the way of sustained alleviation of poverty."[145] The infamous rich/poor gap, whether measured by earnings or wealth, skyrocketed. Even though the measurement was itself somewhat meaningless in a truly dynamic economy—where there will be sudden accumulations of wealth as new products are invented—the gap constituted a shocking indictment of statism and planning rather than of the inequities caused by capitalism. It had doubled since the 1960s, reaching seventy to one, whereas it had stood at only six to one richest-to-poorest countries two hundred years ago. Poverty played itself out in the world's poorest cities, which had 100 million children on the streets and a billion people in urban slums.

Indeed, while few wanted to acknowledge them, numerous studies (some done by the very organizations created to provide aid) were providing convincing evidence that aid was counterproductive. At first, scholars thought that "bad governments" might be the culprit, showing that aid recipients in countries with "bad governments" did worse than aid recipients in those with "good policies."[146] William Easterly, a research economist for the World Bank involved in countless aid programs, examining the period 1970–93, found "no evidence that aid raised growth among countries with good policies, indicating no support for the conclusion that 'aid works in a good policy environment.' "[147] Far from encouraging investment, aid had no impact at all.[148] Still others found that it did not matter if the aid was short-term or long-term; it still had no positive effect on growth.[149]

Perhaps the great humanitarians were inept at effecting any genuine change in people's lives, but they proved champions at creating bureaucracies and organizations to distribute the aid. The International Monetary Fund, the U.S. Agency for International Development, the African Development Bank, the American Development Bank, the World Health Organization, the International Labour Organization, the Food and Agriculture Organization, the United Nations Children's Fund, the United Nations Development Program, and the Asian Development Bank—all drifted nowhere. And those were only the government or public aid organizations. A maze of private philanthropies and mission societies, universities and think tanks, private foundations and solo do-gooders covered the international poverty landscape. Whereas in the nineteenth century concerned Western busybodies at least attempted to change the spiritual condition of their charges, the twentieth-century development experts—heirs to the missionaries, nuns, priests, colonial officers, and military governors—discarded sin and salvation for gold and silver, manifested in their modern incarnations of hospitals and universities.

Academia, ever obsessed with verbiage, came up with a new term to describe the aid cycle: the "Big Push," coined by a Polish-born economist, Paul Rosenstein-Rodan, but generally associated with Walt Rostow and his famous book *The Stages of Economic Growth* (1960). Every "big push" generated yet another big push. Each "takeoff" stage came and went, never taking off, always providing ample blame for capitalists, America and Britain, and Christianity, and always bringing new demands for still more money. Aid actually increased when growth fell![150] The Third World recipients became champion takers, with the average African country receiving more than 15 percent of its income from foreign sources in the 1990s.

All Western aid was not equal, though. Workers in Africa, for example, found that simply providing deworming drugs tended to keep children in school, but broader programs to educate on worms and their infections failed.[151] Beyond that, however, no model emerged of an efficient or successful method of assisting poor and undeveloped countries in climbing out of poverty. Increasingly, researchers discovered that laws and trust played a critical role in facilitating economic growth. Peruvian Hernando De Soto, writing late in the twentieth century, was mystified by the contradiction that although he observed capitalism to be the only successful economic system, several poor countries (some with nascent capitalist economies) never seemed to improve their circumstances. He discovered that undeveloped countries did not lack "wealth"—their people had property, possessions, and businesses—but rather lacked mechanisms to give legal status to those wealth instruments.[152]

De Soto observed that in Egypt, a person who had lived in his home for twenty years and could establish that it was his nevertheless had to clear more than 150 separate bureaucratic steps, over seven years, in order to acquire a right to consider it his property. De Soto found this typical of most poor countries. This had profound implications: legal title to property facilitated trade, sale, and purchases, but more important, it provided the most common means of obtaining credit through offering collateral. Thus, he noted, the Third World lacked in the most basic sense a system of law that permitted people to engage in risk taking. World Bank researchers discovered that in Mozambique it took 153 days to comply with the regulations to start a new business, as compared with only two days in Canada; and it cost 126 percent of the value of a debt to collect on a contract in Indonesia, as opposed to only 5.4 percent in Seoul. Bankruptcy laws in parts of India yielded only 13 percent of a debt after collection, while that figure was 90 percent in Japan.[153]

However, if it were as easy as merely imposing title-deed systems, the Third World would no longer be the Third World. But as William Easterly contended, non-Western countries have much different cultures concerning property rights—not socialist, but not Western. Kenyans, for example, had a traditional seasonal exchange, similar to sharecropping in the United States, that involved land patrons and clients. In order to enforce property rights, Easterly asked, "Would the government give the titles to the *weg lowo* [patron] or to the *jodak* [client]?"[154] Factor in the use of the land as collateral for a loan, and the difficulty of determining property rights increased substantially. When kinship networks are heaped on top of this fragile system, it breaks down completely. Imposed systems failed repeatedly, as in Mexico and Russia, especially where informal mechanisms of establishing trust are superseded from the outside (e.g., the World Bank) by formal structures. Put another way, two of the key pillars were lacking in African reform even when it sought to use the free market: common law and private property with title deeds. Throw in the general absence of Christianity and failure was a given.

One solution that had unfolded in North America during the conquest of the Great Plains was that non-Western property rights as understood by the Indians—which differed dramatically from those of the white settlers—were simply overruled. Only a handful of tribal rights were protected, but even those, in the capitalist twentieth century, succumbed to European concepts. A harsh reality of globalization, whether it be DVD players, patents, Internet protocols, or property rights, was that a single standard inexorably emerges, and for all intents and purposes, that standard was increasingly Western and substantially American.

Social capital, or trust, played as great a role in separating poor from wealthy countries as did legal systems, in essence serving as unofficial legal systems themselves. Studies have revealed that rich societies have more trust than poor societies.[155] Wealthy societies such as Denmark had high levels of trust, where 58 percent of the people said they could trust others, and mothers could leave babies alone in strollers on the street without fear for their safety. One experiment in Denmark, where a full wallet was dropped, found that almost all wallets were returned with no money missing. In poorer economies, distrust is rampant. African grain traders personally inspect each lot of grain because they have no trust in their employees, prompting one economist to quip that Africa had developed a "flea-market economy, not a free market economy."[156]

Early American southern banking, often conducted by private individuals lending to people they knew, experienced remarkably low levels of defaults—though levels appropriate to the interest rates charged and risk incurred.[157] When it came to establishing banks, wealthy American merchants in the Northeast routinely engaged in what is today called "insider lending," which not only was not illegal at the time, but was expected, constituting the main reason people founded such banks.[158] The key is that the United States, in a relatively short time, transformed those personal trust relationships into formal structures that provided strangers with reliable credit information, largely due to the efforts of Lewis Tappan, a Christian activist and abolitionist who had used his network of evangelists as "holy spies" to unearth immoral behavior, including prostitution and gaming houses.[159] His Mercantile Agency, founded in 1841 after a financial panic had driven Tappan to extend credit, expanded to 300 correspondents and 280 clients in three years.[160] Robert Graham Dun eventually took over the firm a year after a competitor, John M. Bradstreet, published volume I of Bradstreet's *Book of Commercial Reports* (1857), which listed 20,000 merchants. The two companies were merged into Dun and Bradstreet in 1933 and became the largest credit reporting organization in the world, yet it still relied on local knowledge as the centerpiece of its reliability. However the information was attained, discerning between "reputation" and "character" was essential ("to *seem* rather than *to be*," as the *Daily Illinois Journal* distinguished them in 1856).[161]

By 2008, such third-party institutional agencies of trust (occasionally abused, to be sure) provided instantaneous substitutes for trust. An American family could sell its existing house and purchase a new one in less than two hours by sitting around a table with a couple of real estate agents and title company officers; but African coffee planters still could not obtain legal title to their fields for years. Amazon.com, one of the world's largest booksellers, provided virtually no recourse for fraud (given the typical low value of the books bought and sold), yet merchants went to extreme lengths to encourage satisfied buyers to post favorable ratings so their online reputations would not be damaged, to accept returns, and to replace products lost in the mail. Not surprising, per capita income correlated strongly with trust, and equally unsurprising, in poorer countries, courts and legal systems elicited low levels of confidence.

Merely handing a Third World country a legal system failed to provide the necessary framework for a thriving market, usually because it was civil—not common—law and because it was not accompanied by private property ownership. Likewise, merely increasing per capita wealth did little to change the delivery of government services. Democracy, instead, proved the key to ensuring higher levels of government response—yet again, the obvious answer (more democracy) was not as simple as it seemed. Lacking established rules of fair play, and absent a heritage of common law where the people governed from the bottom up, undeveloped or decolonized countries displayed stunning levels of fraud, election rigging, and electoral mischief. When minorities suddenly gain power—even in a democracy—the result can be the bloody suppression of those minorities in a revolution or in actions of revenge after losing power. This was especially true where centuries of tribalism produced a "get even with them" mentality for the group that seized power. There were *no* truths that were self-evident, *no* real constitutional guarantees that all accepted as the foundation for political action. Rwanda's genocide of Tutsis by the Hutus in the 1990s took place in a republic with an elected president, not a military dictator. While there were attempts to blame the genocide on the vestiges of imperialism and Belgian colonialism, that argument disintegrated in an ocean of blood.

As argued in *A Patriot's History of the United States,* possibly the most important election in America's history occurred in 1800, when John Adams, leader of the incumbent Federalist Party (ostensibly, the majority in the country), peacefully and without fanfare departed the new city of Washington, D.C., to allow the newly elected Thomas Jefferson to become president. It was the first time a major nation had witnessed the peaceful exchange of power from one group to its avowed rabid rival.[162] In numerous African and Latin American nations, however, majorities have proven completely unwilling to share power—let alone surrender ruling status—because there are no accepted rules protecting minorities.[163] Without genuine American-style constitutional protections, Third World democracies have a high probability of state-sponsored political and ethnic genocide.[164]

Oligarchs in Third World countries routinely pointed to higher initial growth by supporting favored businesses—and certainly those businesses did not object to government support. Part of the tradeoff, however, soon led oligarchs to back the wrong horse, as governments inevitably do.[165] They missed the radical innovators and entrepreneurs in their midst—the African, Asian, or Latin American Cyrus McCormicks, Sam Colts, Henry Fords, and Walt Disneys—none of whom received any kind of state largesse until long after they had proven their products or services. With a handful of exceptions—New Zealand is one—an inverse relationship developed between agriculture and democracy, for agricultural societies tended to be less advanced, thus failing to produce a middle class that was conducive to invention and entrepreneurship.[166] Virtually any resource-dependent society tends to undermine or short-circuit democracy. This trend was brutally obvious in the oil-rich Arab states, to which we shall turn later.

"Dev Biz"

America's plunge into foreign aid for the Third World began with Harry Truman's 1949 inaugural address, formalized as policy a year later in the Act for International Development, and distinguished for labeling development a "program." It explicitly declared that America would provide "technical assistance so that these peoples themselves, with a very small capital investment from us, would be able to develop their own resources," thereby improving their working and living conditions.[167] Hoping to distribute knowledge rather than money, the Point Four program accelerated rapidly—as programs do—and expanded beyond all recognition. The development industry then skyrocketed in the 1960s with the United States Agency for International Development (USAID), the Peace Corps, and the United Nations Development Program (UNDP), where assistance was virtually thrown at newly born countries, which had no ability to process it or, often, to use it with any degree of effectiveness or competence.

Merely a sample of the monumental efforts by the United Nations to address poverty in the Third World since 1960 exposed the aid programs' utter ineffectiveness, as one begat another in a genealogy of biblical proportions: the 1960 Freedom from Hunger Campaign was followed by the 1960–70 UN Development Decade (resolved to increase economic growth by 5 percent by 1970), which gave way to the Declaration on the Human

Environment and a second UN Development Decade (resolved to create both a "just world order" and, having failed to increase economic growth by 5 percent in the previous ten years, now undertook to expand undeveloped economies by *6 percent*.) Next came the Universal Declaration on the Eradication of Hunger and Malnutrition, and a year later, the Lima Declaration, which resolved to ensure that the undeveloped nations' share of world production would nearly *triple* over the subsequent twenty-five years, despite the fact that after more than thirty years of independence (at a minimum), undeveloped countries' share of global production remained at only 7 percent. The International Decade for Women was announced in 1976, the Alma Ata International Conference on Primary Health Care (resolving to provide health care for all by 2000) occurred in 1978, and the Decade of International Drinking Water and Sanitation, aiming at clean water for all by 1990, was declared in 1980.[168] The fact that virtually none of these resolutions, declarations, or commitments achieved their goals (indeed, most did not come close), or that Africa was becoming an economic disaster of the first magnitude once the European powers pulled out, was explained away, excused, or simply ignored.

New, arrogant Western paternalistic aid agencies—by now referring to themselves as in the "dev biz," or development business—took on a life of their own. Many of them were the size of medieval armies and as numerous as ants. By century's end, more than 430 "nongovernmental organizations" or NGOs (the new buzz-phrase for private philanthropies) existed. These spanned a broad spectrum of interests, from World Vision, CARE, and Save the Children, to Amnesty International, Oxfam, Action Aid, and Catholic Relief Services, all of which were layered on top of existing activist groups, such as Zero Population Growth, Feed the Children, Doctors Without Borders, and even traditional agencies such as the International Red Cross. Urged on by think tanks and advocacy groups (the International Food Policy Research Institute, the Soros, Rockefeller, and Ford foundations, or the International Center for Maize and Wheat Improvement), given high profiles by entertainers and singers (Bob Geldof, Bono), and lent intellectual heft by university affiliates that included the School of International and Public Affairs at Columbia (SIPA), the Woodrow Wilson School at Princeton, and the Kennedy School at Harvard, the dev biz not only competed for resources among its members but justified its existence through ever-growing bureaucracies. By 1997, the World Bank had a staff of 5,500 sucking up annual expenditures of $810 million—more than half the annual budget of Chad. This did not include the Bank's 4,000 part-time consultants. A venture of this magnitude was typical for a midsize NGO in the dev biz, which could operate in twenty or more countries and have 3,000 to 4,000 full-time staff. Thomas Dichter, who worked in several of the NGOs, noted, as of 2003, "A conservative global estimate would be roughly half a million people whose livelihood depend[ed] on the industry."[169] He was speaking of well-off bureaucrats and administrators, *not* the starving, huddled masses.

Some Westerners and NGO administrators began to conclude that many African countries would need foreign assistance permanently. Without realizing it, they confirmed what the colonialists of a century earlier had maintained: that Africans and Latin Americans lacked the capacity for self-government or wealth production. When the verdict on foreign aid finally started to become obvious, namely that it was failing to show any meaningful improvement in development, the advocates of the dev biz started to act like the adherents of a religion being debunked.

Meanwhile, critics on the Right complained that foreign aid was "a wasteful and futile effort to buy the friendship of other nations," and those on the Left countered that it was used to support dictatorships.[170] Both were correct. Postwar Western societies, at least, after 1950, found themselves rich and getting richer, and increasingly burdened by guilt. Some of it was legitimate: there was no denying the abusive and oppressive colonial regimes of the Belgians and Spanish, but at one time or another inevitably every colonial power ran its charges with a heavy, occasionally ruthless, hand. Britain claimed to be preparing the Africans and Asians for self-government, and perhaps many British leaders believed that. After all, they passed out constitutions to their territories like they were raffle tickets to a chicken dinner. Some British colonies had more legislators per capita than any previous nation in history, and taken together, Britain's holdings produced some one hundred written constitutions—an oddity, as Paul Johnson noted, for a mother country that doesn't have one herself!

A much different type of self-loathing, though, emerged quite quickly. Deeply embedded in new Western liberalism, as influenced by Marx, was the belief that the Third World was poor *solely because* of the colonial exchange. Fanned by academics who were founding the new "isms" industry—racism, feminism, classism—this guilt went far beyond taking Europeans and Americans to task for specific policies or actions, instead imputing guilt merely for *being* European or American. Some wore the Western oppressor hair shirt as a result of social and historical theories then in vogue, many of which had been advanced long before World War II before their abrupt revival in 1946. In particular, a new brood of young historians, known as the New Left, challenged the cold war liberalism of New Deal scribes such as Arthur Schlesinger, Jr., John D. Hicks, Richard Hofstadter, and William Leuchtenburg. Whereas the Progressive historians had operated from the position that facts and values had to be separated so only "objective" history would be written—and that only by avoiding all "value judgments"—the New Left subscribed to an entirely different proposition, namely that *because* such objectivity was impossible, one's own bias demanded a conscious counterbalance in research and writing. Because one was an American historian, his view of the atomic bombing of Japan would necessarily be distorted to a pro-American position, no matter how careful he was at rooting out bias, this view held.

It did not take long for the new guilt baggage to be heaved onto American foreign policy. This took an even sharper turn after the Kennedy assassination in 1963, whereupon American liberals especially "began to argue that the purpose of national policy was more to punish the nation for its sins than to build a brighter and more secure future for all."[171] It was only a short step to then blaming the United States for almost all of the world's ills. Since the focus shifted from explaining America's place in the world and inspiring others to emulate our example to finding ways of dishing out punishments and redressing past grievances, both domestically and abroad, American liberals drifted into an emphasis on compensation for historical wrongs. Viewed through such a lens, foreign aid soon became less about helping the recipients than about punishing the givers. At the very least, virtually all aid was top-down effort that could be measured, with typical development projects including a rope factory, a biogas facility in India, or a women's legal information center in North Africa. Success was measured by whether the facilities were completed on time, and annually, the NGOs or government bureaus operated on the basis that they had to spend all of their existing money to receive new funds. William Niskanen's theory of "bureaupathic" behavior was proven over and over again.

At two levels, then, assistance was treated much like the low-quality autos made in the Soviet bloc during the cold war: it was dependent solely on what administrators decided, and it was immutably immune to market efficiencies demanded by real-world budgets. No wonder that as early as 1957 Eugene Castle wrote, "The history of foreign aid has been littered with the wreckage and rubble of incompetent and wasteful administration."[172]

If anything, foreign aid propped up the world's most vicious and undemocratic regimes, with twenty-five of the worst offenders getting some $9 billion in 2002, and the top fifteen aid recipients in 2002 (each getting at least $1 billion) ranking in the bottom 25 percent of all governments in the world.[173] Far from shunning these tyrants, aid donors gave more to them than they did well-behaved, liberal countries.[174] Frustrated aid officials fumed at the willingness by the World Bank and NGOs to look the other way when it came to malignant governments, often expressed in euphemisms such as "difficult partnerships" or described as having "governance issues." The "Docs" of Haiti—Papa Doc Duvalier and Baby Doc Duvalier— over a twenty-nine-year period received almost all of the IMF's twenty-two short-term loans, despite their record of terror and malevolence. Aid agencies helped Cameroon's thug leader, Paul Biya (who, having seized power in 1982, still remained in office more than thirty years later), promoting a "supportive environment" for development goals. Patently absurd descriptions of corrupt and tyrannical regimes in Africa as "emerging," "improving," "showing continued progress," or "displaying differences that still needed to be reconciled" concealed the simple reality that most of the nations had come nowhere close to meeting *any* of the UN's or World Bank's development goals after three decades. Yet with each new report, aid was said to be working, with officers in 1984 observing that "African leaders increasingly recognize the need to revise their . . . strategies," then in 1986 adding, "Progress is clearly under way." Three years later, despite no significant improvement, the same agencies claimed, "African countries have made great strides in improving policies and restoring growth," followed by "signs that better economic management has started to pay off" five years after that. Shooting galleries at a carnival have never seen such moving targets![175]

International poverty gurus routinely insist that IMF money comes with strings, and that developing countries must be accountable for the aid given. That accountability produced unintended consequences. Ecuador, which received sixteen standby loans between 1960 and 2000, was instructed that the latest round of aid demanded reductions in teacher salaries, which promptly produced teacher strikes and massive demonstrations. Burundi spent sixty-two years in the IMF program, with the state finally collapsing in 1995; Liberia, seventy, followed by a 1986 collapse; and Somalia and Zaire each over seventy-three years, both failing in 1991.[176] Unstable governments were sinkholes and definitely bad. But dictatorships, while stable, were often equally bad. Assuming American do-gooders could automatically solve their problems usually did not change their prospects, except (sometimes) to turn stable (but bad) governments into unstable (and horrific) situations, resulting in unstable (and bad) governments.

Dwight Eisenhower had been cautious in assuming the Third World, particularly Africa, would benefit from smug insertions of American philanthropies, especially when it came to the continent's newly emerging independent states. Referring to Africans and Asians as "dependent peoples" of the world, Ike astutely prophesied that "chaos" would ensue once the European powers departed, leaving Africa's "restless and militant population in a state of gross ignorance."[177] Assistant Secretary of State C. Burke Elbrick echoed that view when he said of Africa, "premature independence and irresponsible nationalism may represent grave dangers to dependent peoples."[178] Deeply suspicious of Nkrumah's Communist ties, Ike also distrusted Sékou Touré of Guinea—"a communist operative beyond hope of redemption" and the "Castro of Africa"—and blocked further aid to the "crowd of malcontents," as he called the Guineans.[179]

Missionaries of Americanism

A new attitude seemed to accompany John F. Kennedy and his foreign policy in 1961. Kennedy's inaugural address, in which he stated, "Let every nation know, whether it wishes us well or ill, that we shall pay any price, bear any burden, meet any hardship, support any friend, oppose any foe, in order to assure the survival and the success of liberty."[180] As is the tendency with the arrival of most new leaders, especially younger ones, outsiders anticipated that Kennedy would institute major changes in the direction of American cold war policies. At first, Kennedy appeared to meet their expectations.

He decided to hitch his African star to strategic countries, telling Peace Corps director Sargent Shriver to focus U.S. efforts on Ghana, Nigeria, Tanzania, then later, Guinea and Cameroon. Although recognizing that Africa was "going through a revolution," JFK ignored or minimized Nkrumah's and Touré's Communist links.[181] Lambasting France for Algeria, France and Britain for the Suez Crisis, and virtually all the colonial powers for their imperialism, Kennedy positioned himself sharply to the left of Eisenhower in terms of his criticism of allies, while at the same time alluding to a more activist foreign policy that appealed to the Right. It was a clever tightrope act.

As senator, Kennedy characterized the Republican era as "eight years of a drugged and fitful sleep," and promised "we are going to do better." The "theme of this campaign is . . . action abroad to meet the challenge of our adversaries." Kennedy hoped the people of Latin America and Africa would "start to look to America" and see what "the President of the United States is doing, not [what] Khrushchev or the Chinese Communists [are doing]."[182] Eisenhower, he complained, failed to staff the foreign service, especially embassies, with diplomats who could speak the local language, with some 70 percent having no foreign language skills at all. America's image in Africa suffered for having only "26 Negroes in the 6,000 of our Foreign Service officers," and Ike sent men to serve in countries who could not even pronounce the name of the head of state where they were assigned.[183] Of course, these numbers excluded ambassadors, usually political hacks or campaign contributors who put the party in office.

Kennedy's vision of creating Third World allies through more peaceful societies—and to appear "less 'ugly' and more culturally sensitive"—led him to form the Peace Corps less than two months after he took office.[184] Described by subsequent historians as a "bold experiment," "an example of American idealism," or as "making a difference," the Peace Corps was to rectify the problems of American foreign policy, which Kennedy said was "being starved on a diet of negatives."[185] In fact, the only thing new about the Peace Corps was that it originated with the government. Already there were 33,000 American missionaries working abroad under the direction of more than 400 religious bodies, and before conceiving the Peace Corps, Kennedy expressed admiration for the Latter-day Saints Church's program of having all its young men serve a two-year mission. Still, as with all "bold" moves, the Peace Corps counted among the elites and intellectuals only because government was involved; Nixon, at the time, stood nearly alone in thinking it a "juvenile experiment" and a likely haven for draft dodgers. Not surprisingly, its proponents sought to infuse it with religious overtones, calling for the volunteers to display "the zeal of hardy missionaries."[186]

As Senator Hubert Humphrey encapsulated the goals of the Peace Corps in the Senate bill, it was supposed to "develop a genuine people-to-people program in which talented and dedicated young American men teach basic agricultural and industrial techniques, literacy, the English language and . . . sanitation and health procedures" in the Third World.[187] Cloaking the Peace Corps as a crusade that would enlist a new generation to serve the cause of freedom, Kennedy appealed to youthful enthusiasm and spared its participants the often bloody side effects of military service.

In short, it had everything, which is to say the Peace Corps promulgated the delusion that "several hundred twenty-two-year-old liberal arts graduates, with no experience or particular skills, sent abroad for two years, could make a difference in a country's development."[188]

Robert F. Kennedy would later confess that the best and the brightest fooled themselves: "we thought we were succeeding because of all the stories of how hard everybody was working."[189] Little attention was paid to the fact that 95 percent of the trainees for Cameroon, for example, knew absolutely nothing about the country. Peace Corps teachers sent to Cameroon "found themselves teaching Cameroon history," and almost two thirds of the teachers handled subjects for which they had no education or training. Some 85 percent of the volunteers were assigned to teach music, despite never having taken music courses in college.[190] Having been taught surveying and basic construction, they went into the field with no knowledge of local conditions or terrain, and less actual building experience. Before a single Peace Corps volunteer stepped off an airplane, Nehru had warned not to be "too disappointed if the Punjab, when [the Americans leave] is more or less the same as before they came."[191]

Such attitudes about civilian volunteers were completely consistent with almost two hundred years' worth of assessments by foreigners of American *military* capabilities, as we have seen. The apparent tendency to underestimate the ruggedness or mental toughness of a people who had survived malarial swamps, cleared massive forests and erected towns, dug coal out of insufferable black pits, battled locusts in the western plains, settled in the scorching Arizona sand and the numbing Alaskan tundra; who had ethnic infusions of Apaches who could walk fifty miles a day through parched desert, of Irish who had escaped the potato famine, or former slaves who had overcome the lash; or immigrant stock from the most oppressed countries on earth, only to found the most shining beacon of liberty in history—this tendency was as mystifying in 1898 when applied to Roosevelt's Rough Riders or Dewey's sailors as it was in 1961 when applied to Peace Corps volunteers or as it would be in 2001 when invoked against the U.S. military about to embark on an invasion of Afghanistan. For all its faults, the Peace Corps demonstrated beyond doubt, once again, that Americans could and did overcome living conditions, the elements, and local impediments to achieve their objectives.

Unfortunately, too often sending the "best and the brightest" to the Peace Corps meant sending kids who were perfectly competent at clerking for a circuit court or analyzing advanced statistics, but who were now three or four generations removed from the frontier skills that were necessary in the bush. Too often, they lacked enough of a sense of their own history to realize that their own forefathers had already "been there, done that." One girl was awestruck when, after delivering a lecture about stopping diarrhea to Tunisian townspeople, she was informed matter-of-factly by a grand-mother, "Give the child rice," as if such wisdom were unavailable among Americans.[192] A Yalie, sent to Mauritania, where she discovered she actu-ally could process raw food, was as dumbfounded as if she had discovered DNA.

Whereas the Eisenhower foreign policy may have been characterized by the "Ugly American," the Camelot era brought a fawning, dreamy-eyed news coverage that overestimated the genuine contributions of the Peace Corps. Reports lionized New Frontiersmen such as Peace Corps director Sargent Shriver, JFK's brother-in-law—yet another appointment smacking of nepotism that was never addressed by the press—as "a man of action who finds it hard to stand still."[193] Asked to head the new Peace Corps, Shriver recruited staff as rapidly as possible, telling them by phone, "come as you are," "come quickly," "we need you in a hurry." Under other circumstances, one would be reminded of George Custer's frantic messages for more am-munition from his pack train at the Little Big Horn, "Come Quick. Big Village. Bring packs. P.S. Bring packs."[194]

Shriver saw his mission as no less than constructing a working and growing economy in the entire Third World, and to accomplish that, he planned to lure the star graduates from college campuses. Even Shriver was surprised by the response; Peace Corps phone lines lit up as operators struggled to handle the thousands of inquiries and applicants. Anxious to draft minorities who could present a more "diverse look" of America, in fact the Peace Corps found it nearly impossible to recruit blacks (about 3 per-cent of the Peace Corps volunteers between 1961 and 1986), and the overall minority composition of the Corps hovered at 6 percent. Prosperous whites made up the vast majority of volunteers (as they have for almost all reform movements in American history), and, at first, men volunteered by a margin of two to one. The Peace Corps became feminized over time, however, which itself was a problem: Iranians, for example, expressed outrage that unchaperoned, unmarried girls would be on their own. "Their conclusion is that such girls are up to no good," reported the Peace Corps director in 1965.[195] Another Peace Corps worker had to be lectured on why working bare-breasted was not a good idea.

There were some ways in which the Peace Corps involved a "paradigm shift" for the development industry, primarily in the way in which the volunteers were assigned to local operations and worked directly with poor people, as opposed to governments. Soon, much of the aid industry would copy the Peace Corps example—as indicated by the fact that Ireland, Canada, and Britain soon adopted similar programs—but all of these reinforced the illusion that this was "self-help," or that Africans and Asians were being "taught to fish." In reality, the Peace Corps underscored the ongoing reality that the West was giving away something for nothing, and that the Third Worlders remained dependent people.[196]

In Kennedy's mind, the volunteers were spreading American culture— "missionaries of Americanism," as Peace Corps historian Gerard Rice called them—and perhaps that was the case for many of the volunteers. Some served out of idealism; others, because it kept them from the draft. More than a few became activists, including Paul Theroux, who wrote *The Mosquito Coast*, and Charles Murray, whose *Losing Ground* became a clarion call against Great Society welfare programs. More than a hundred former Peace Corp volunteers had joined congressional staffs by 1985, while four were elected to the House of Representatives and two, Paul Tsongas and Christopher Dodd, became U.S. senators.[197]

Over time, the Peace Corps experiment was all the more ironic because of its predictable emphasis on physical labor. Volunteers could count on benefiting from their Peace Corps experience in their academic or political pursuits at home, but the program needed people who could do physical labor—rarely the strong point of such young intellectuals. Among older American intellectuals, however, there was deep resentment that the Eisenhower administration had made life so easy for so many people. Home and car ownership had exploded; families could afford to travel long distances, often by airplane, for the first time; and the universality of electricity and cheap oil meant that labor-saving devices of all sizes and shapes reduced work hours and effort. The *Harvard Crimson* admitted as much when describing the students of the 1950s as "the first generation . . . which is not going to school for purely economic reasons."[198]

This did not sit well with America's intellectual class, who were convinced that the United States was in decline. Many cited the absence of sacrifice, especially among the young, implying that they had not suffered sufficiently to the degree their forefathers had. Harvard president Nathan Pusey was alarmed by the "desire for diversion, personal comfort, and safety," while journalist Walter Lippmann's book *The National Purpose* complained about American lethargy.[199] Arthur Schlesinger, invoking a theory of "cyclical rhythm in our national affairs," urged Kennedy to take advantage of a forthcoming period of action and liveliness.[200] As international events would show, JFK soon had more action than he ever bargained for.

CHAPTER THREE

Freedom's Chariots

TIME LINE

1946: American auto industry begins producing civilian cars again

1948: West Berlin airlift begins

1949: Soviets explode atom bomb; China falls to Communists

1950: Korean War begins; UN forces land at Inchon

1952: Eisenhower elected president; Nixon gives "Checkers" speech

1953: East Berlin revolt crushed by Soviets; *Playboy* magazine founded; Korean War ends; Rosenbergs executed for espionage

1954: Bill Haley's "Rock Around the Clock" puts rock and roll on the charts; Elvis Presley records first hits

1956: Poznan food riots in Poland crushed by Polish troops; Eisenhower reelected; National Highway Act establishes interstate system

1957: *Sputnik* launched

1958: First Monterey Jazz Festival

1959: First Daytona 500

1960: Civil rights "sit-ins" at Woolworth Department Store, Greensboro, North Carolina; first televised presidential debates; John F. Kennedy elected president; oral contraceptive pill approved for use

1961: Eisenhower coins term "military-industrial complex"; Bay of Pigs; neutralist government established in Laos; Vienna Summit; Berlin Wall erected; refugees in West Germany from eastern provinces reach eight million; Cuban missile crisis; Alan Shepard becomes the first American in space

Another Brick in the Wall

African and Asian independence movements ended the façade that Europe, even collectively, remained a superpower. Britain, France, Belgium, and Holland all saw their overseas possessions disappear by the 1970s as the cold war cast its shadows over the entire world and former empires became the object of intense Soviet-American competition. But that was little more than a sideshow.

Europe itself remained the locus of most strategy and military planning, and with good reason: it was where the enslaved Russian empire touched the free world. Nowhere was this more apparent than in Berlin. No city in human history had become more starkly an image of the different outcomes in political and economic ideas than Berlin after the Wall went up in August 1961.

The Berlin Wall stood for oppression, subjugation of the individual, and above all, the desperation of communism in its attempt to be a practical form of government. It represented the culmination of numerous other attempts by the Soviets and their allies to expand communism. Perhaps *because* Berlin remained such a conspicuous demonstration of the stark differences between the two systems, communism's other successes had not satiated the Communists' own appetites. Therefore, impressive victories, including securing the atomic bomb, planting hundreds of spies inside the U.S. government, seizing control of the Chinese mainland, and forcing a near-disastrous confrontation in Korea, all seemed diminished by the shining star of West Berlin. And, by logic and in symbolism, Berlin continually reflected the superiority of the West as a whole.

Germany's postwar prosperity—and Europe's—had come in spite of initial postwar policies imposed by the U.S. Army, which tended toward

top-down control. Predictably, early results were, in the words of Eisenhower's deputy, General Lucius Clay, that "the Germans are close to starving."[1] Eisenhower proved indifferent to German suffering, and his antipathy
for Germans, although he himself was of German extraction, impeded recovery and reconstruction. After replacing Eisenhower as military governor of occupied Germany in 1947, Clay immediately took action and shook
things up.

Clay fired Johannes Semler as director for economic administration,
and replaced him with the rotund and cherubic-looking Ludwig Erhard, an
anti-Nazi and member of the "Ordoliberal" economic group (also known as
the Freiburg School). No one could have been more perfect for the situation.
Ordoliberal free marketeers abhorred the cartels that in their eyes had sustained Hitler, but at the same time accepted German welfare-state concepts
of providing a safety net for their citizens. They also accepted, in the words
of economist Wilhelm Röpke, "the principle of absolute, and even if necessary, one-sided free-trade."[2] Above all, however, the state was to stay out of
market mechanisms such as prices or controlling production. Erhard found
a loophole in the Allied price control regulations in that there was no clause
actually prohibiting their elimination entirely! So, in June 1948, he simply
eliminated the controls. Overnight, food, clothing, and other necessities of
life appeared in store windows in plentiful supply, somewhat to Clay's con-
sternation. He summoned Erhard and said, "My advisors tell me that what
you have done is a terrible mistake." Erhard replied, "Pay no attention to
them. My own advisors tell me the same thing."[3] The irony lay in the fact
that this ingenious stroke of revoking the price controls could never have
happened through the legislative process, and owed its success to the power
Clay had invested in Erhard and to Erhard's courage. Clay, who could have
acted like the pontificating bureaucrat who so often stifles genuine improvement, allowed Erhard the flexibility to essentially save Germany.

From Clay's and Erhard's beginnings, free trade began to spread across
Western Europe. Under German chancellor Konrad Adenauer's and Erhard's leadership, Germany buried the hatchet with France and Great Britain. From the Allied side, reconciliation took place slowly. In 1945, 54
percent of Britons said they either hated or had no sympathy for Germans.[4]
The people were forced to ignore that as much as 25 percent of Britain's
agricultural productivity was coming from the labor of unreturned German prisoners from World War II, and more than a million German prisoners had been taken, under essentially slave labor conditions, to rebuild
France.[5]

Aggravating the problem was that the Allies had three categories of prisoners: POWs, Surrendered Enemy Persons, and Disarmed Enemy Persons. The Geneva and Hague conventions did not regulate the last two classifications, and they were subject to any treatment and use their captors desired. France in particular treated the Germans in its sector unusually harshly. By the middle of 1948, at least one million POWs had not yet been returned to Germany, not counting the other two classifications, which seemed to disappear. In 1950, Adenauer announced that several hundred thousand German men, women, and children were still in Russia and Poland, and it wasn't until 1956 that the countries officially declared that all prisoners had been returned to Germany.[6]

By 1950, Germany and France were not only recovering, but speaking to each other on a civil basis, most notably regarding the origination of the European Coal and Steel Community (ECSC). The ECSC (which also involved Italy and the Benelux countries) was first proposed in 1950 by French foreign minister Robert Schuman to prevent any further European wars by eliminating the economic competition he believed drove them into conflict. By eliminating tariffs and lowering costs, the ECSC increased trade between member nations tenfold, and provided loans to industry within the member states.[7] It also expanded welfare, now on a supranational level, by financing housing for workers and paying "redeployment" costs for workers whose facilities were closed due to lack of productivity. In addition, the ECSC levied a flat tax across the members' regions of 1 percent on production.

Schuman's ideas were put into action by the president of the High Authority (the governing body of the ECSC), Jean Monnet, the "Frenchman ... Washington trusted most."[8] Monnet, a driven and energetic former deputy director of economic affairs for the League of Nations, was a latecomer to the kumbaya of postwar supranationalism. His Monnet Plan of 1945 had proposed redirecting coal production from all German areas toward France, thereby crippling Germany. But by 1950 he had a change of heart as new tensions arose, and he joined German chancellor Adenauer in urging integration instead of competition. Monnet therefore used the European Coal and Steel Community as the groundwork for the "relaunching of Europe" in 1955 with talks at Messina. This culminated in the Treaty of Rome two years later, which formally established the European Economic Community (EEC, or more commonly called the Common Market) composed of France, Germany, Belgium, the Netherlands, Luxemburg, and Italy. Britain refused to join out of well-grounded concerns about national sovereignty. The key to the revival, however, was not the cooperation per se, but the reemergence of Germany, labeled "the most spectacular feature of the postwar miracle" by economist Herbert Giersch.[9]

The new rose of cooperation had its thorns. Erhard's free-market exuberance was shackled by the presence of an internal quota system—which in the short run had the beneficial effect of increasing exports—and by additional controls from the EEC. Walter Hallstein, its first president, who looked "like an oversized doll stuffed into a bad suit, his featureless demeanor fronted by thick-rimmed black plastic glasses," had already conceived of a system in which sovereign power would be transferred to a single European authority.[10] Integration, he noted, was a *création continue* (work in progress). Inadvertently, he identified the key threat posed by government dabbling in any aspect of society: "every step we take creates new situations, new problems, new needs which in turn demand another step, another solution to be worked out on a European basis." Further, he observed, "the authority to make social and economic policy *would and should spill over into the fields of culture* and internal security" (emphasis ours).[11] The hive mentality already was abuzz with possibilities for a collective future.

Revolt Against the Reds

Lost in much current analysis is the reality that Eastern Europe fought ferociously against communism. Textbooks often portray the Soviet empire not only as tolerated by the captive people, but welcomed. It was exactly the opposite. Although Western Europe would never come to grips with American capitalism, individualism, and freedom—in spite of all its politicians' high-sounding words—the contrast of even a watered-down market system impeded by socialist controls against the full-blown Communist economic failures on the other side of the Wall was glaring. Western Europeans may have automatically expected their economies to be even more bountiful than they were, but the Eastern Europeans suffering daily under communism fully understood the reality of Western success versus Communist failure. Revolts reflecting their frustrations and deprivations were ruthlessly put down with Soviet tanks and heavy weapons, starting with the East Berlin Uprising of 1953.

In that year, Walter Ulbricht's Stalinist regime in East Germany declared that production quotas for workers were to rise by 10 percent at the end of June. Against the backdrop of pitifully low wages, East Berlin construction workers greeted such a pronouncement with a strike. Word raced throughout the entire country, inspiring workers to travel to the city to take part in the demonstrations. Strikers stormed the House of Ministries, prompting some sixteen Soviet divisions to roll into the city. Tanks and troops shot indiscriminately into crowds of demonstrators and onlookers, mowing down all those who did not disperse quickly enough. When order was restored, about a hundred lay dead and a thousand wounded. Police arrested another six thousand in round-ups of actual and suspected dissidents. In the face of such repression, the United States responded cautiously and timidly, its primary action being to initiate a food distribution program for East Berlin. East Germany, now realizing America would not come to its aid, slipped into quiescence until the Soviet Union fell in 1990.

Eastern Europe's next uprising came in Poland in the summer of 1956, when workers in the industrial city of Poznan flooded the streets on June 26 to protest higher quotas and high taxes, and demonstrate for more independence from the Soviet Union. Their appeals were met with similar results as in East Berlin, although this time the suppression was ordered by Soviet marshal Konstantin Rokossovsky, the Polish minister of national defense. After about 100,000 protesters made some headway, two Polish armored divisions with 400 tanks rumbled in, and it took two more divisions of infantry four days to quiet the city after killing 75 protesters and wounding 600. For a second time, the United States reacted with a hands-off policy. The only appreciable gain from the uprising was that the Soviets released the Polish Communist leader Władysław Gomułka—imprisoned for three years as a "reactionary"—from jail, allowing him to vie for power. Gomułka was successful in persuading Khrushchev to restore him to power over Rokossovsky's objections, and the marshal returned to the Soviet Union.

After the Polish uprising, it was the Hungarians' turn, in October 1956. Emboldened by the events in Poland, a student revolt in Budapest produced 20,000 demonstrators issuing demands. Soon their numbers were strengthened by workers from the island of Csepel (previously a Communist stronghold) and the protest grew to more than 200,000. Yet again, Soviet troops swung into action to restore order, but in contrast to Germany and Poland, units of the Hungarian army joined the rebels. Russian tanks were rendered relatively ineffective by youths throwing Molotov cocktails (gasoline-filled bottles with a burning wick) in the narrow streets of Budapest, forcing Soviet troops to organize separate cease-fires. Within a few days the Soviet forces appeared to be withdrawing from the city, or at least distancing themselves from the turmoil. Imre Nagy, then serving as the chairman of the ministers' council, was named premier, and for a moment it appeared the first ever anti-Communist revolution might succeed.

Like a wisp on the wind, the hope vanished. On October 31, the Soviet Presidium decided to put down the rebellion using whatever force was necessary, and four days later Soviet heavy units, under the command of Soviet marshal Ivan Konev (a hero of the Second World War), crushed the prodemocracy forces. Some 2,500 Hungarians lay dead, another 13,000 were wounded, and 26,000 arrested (of which 350 were executed). An additional 200,000 Hungarians fled the country. Despite televised images of heroic resistance by Hungarian Freedom Fighters, many in their teens, the United States refused to intervene, or provide any support at all. A toothless UN Security Council resolution met the predictable veto from the Soviet Union. As far as international assistance was concerned, Hungary in 1956 was no different from Ethiopia in 1932.

American action in Hungary was severely limited by the invasion of Egypt on October 29 by Britain, France, and Israel and the continuing Suez Crisis. But Eisenhower went further with a policy of "active nonintervention," ordering NATO to do nothing that could be interpreted as provocative.[12] Previous rhetoric about liberating the captive peoples of Eastern Europe proved hollow and empty: the Hungarian revolution—encouraged by what the Hungarians saw as America's support, based on the United States' declarations of commitment to freedom and echoed in major papers—collapsed. Eisenhower's administration had prepared no plans to take advantage of any such revolt, and Ike went to elaborate lengths to avoid a confrontation with the Soviets. The betrayal was potentially fatal to America's image behind the Iron Curtain, if not for the difficulties of communicating between oppressed states.

Unrest continued in the captive lands as well as in the Soviet Union itself. Food riots in Novocherkassk, USSR, erupted in June 1962, to be put down by bayonets and tanks as in the satellite countries.

Crafting a Free Europe

Rising food prices in the East Bloc translated into the most basic struggle for survival. But across the border from the Iron Curtain, in the West, capitalism produced a turnaround almost instantaneous by historical standards. American aid certainly played a central role, but could not have accomplished anything had the Europeans not grasped the necessity of reviving a spirit of trust and law that they had sacrificed to Mussolini and Hitler. In Italy, revived leadership came in the form of Prime Minister Alcide De Gasperi, a sixty-five-year-old Catholic from the northern, formerly Austrian, and primarily German-speaking region of South Tyrol (the Italians call it Alto Adige). De Gasperi held a deep suspicion of the state and urged Italians to "be Catholic first, then Italian," then democratic—and he always listed them in that order.[13] He had staunchly opposed Mussolini, viewing fascism as wholly antithetical to Christianity. Mussolini rewarded him for his views with a two-year stint in Regina Coeli prison; De Gasperi was eventually taken under protection by Pope Pius XI, who sheltered him from worse repercussions by hiding him inside the Vatican Library and employing him as a cataloguer for fourteen years. Consequently, he had escaped any association with the fascists when the war ended and was able to found the Christian Democrat Party with the approval of the Truman administration. De Gasperi typified the only viable postwar European leaders—those who had not collaborated with the Nazis or the Italian fascists.

German chancellor Konrad Adenauer had a similar story. Four years older than De Gasperi (born 1876), he too was kicked out of office and, like De Gasperi, subscribed to an American-style love of individual freedom. As mayor of Cologne in 1933, he ran afoul of Hitler and (fortunately) lost his job, enabling him to resurface as another leader untainted by the Nazis. With the Nazis in power, Adenauer hid in a Benedictine monastery for a year, then lived quietly in retirement until arrested in 1944 as an enemy of the Nazi regime, barely avoiding being transported east to certain death.[14] His primary political opponent, Kurt Schumacher, a one-armed Prussian Protestant who was infatuated with big government, sought typical big-state solutions, hearkening back not only to Hitler and the Prussian aristocracy but to Stalin's collectives across the border. Adenauer became the leader of the Christian (generally Catholic) Democratic Union following World War II and he recognized the need to repair the German psyche in a way that did not reinvent Nazism, but empowered Germans to get back to work. He insisted that "[w]e, you and I, are not guilty for this misery [of Nazism]," but that all Germans bore the burden of cleaning it up.[15] By making the Germans as much the victims of fascism as anyone else—"I learned to experience the cruelties of National Socialism, and the consequences of dictatorship"—Adenauer freed the postwar generation from a Versailles-type war guilt.[16]

Adenauer won election as the chairman of the Christian Democratic Union (CDU) in 1946, and rose to international prominence immediately with his "Basic Principles Speech" in March of that year. He reiterated, "I demand no acknowledgment of guilt from the whole German people," pointing out the strong pockets of resistance to Nazism.[17] He thrived in the postwar political scene, winning the 1949 national election with a new constitution. Partly, he did so by riding a wave that had already started among German Christians of forging a union of Catholics and Protestants and transcending doctrinal differences with an appeal to the rule of law.[18]

In that regard, Adenauer came as close as anyone to instituting latitudinarianism in Germany. Unfortunately, rather than leading to a Christian revival, latitudinarianism led to pacifism and atheism, with a large part of the German population professing neither Protestant nor Catholic church membership, if for no other reason than to avoid the state-collected taxes supporting the two religions. Adenauer fought the new secularism, criticizing the materialism of the Nazis and Germany's abandonment of Christian morality before they even came to power, labeling Berlin a "pagan city." Above all, he excoriated socialism: anyone who "strives for a centralization of political and economic power in the state or in a class and who as a result advocates the principles of class conflict, is an enemy of freedom of the individual; he necessarily prepares the way for dictatorship in the thoughts and feelings of his supporters, even if it is another who takes the prepared path."[19]

He unquestionably allied with America and Britain, and wanted Bonn established as the capital of the Federal Republic of Germany so that Germany's "windows are wide open to the west."[20] But even in his success at leading Germany back from the rubble of war, and for all his talk of liberty, Adenauer believed in a united Europe, albeit one free from socialism.

Blocking the Social Democrats and their plans for a nationalized economy, Adenauer (now known as *Der Alte*, or the old one, for being the oldest elected leader of a nation in world history), nevertheless laid the foundation for a European megastate that would destroy sovereignty. West Germany's quick recovery—made all the more obvious by East Germany's malaise—positioned Adenauer as a hero. At the same time, he reduced the influence of the Social Democrats (SPD) for more than a decade, convincing them that the only way to win elections was to abandon their more radical socialist positions. He also harbored a deep distrust of the German people, elites and commoners alike, and thought them capable of participating in a modern democracy only under a rigid set of laws. Essentially, Adenauer was Alexander Hamilton reincarnated.

Above all, Adenauer knew he had to revive the German economy. Just as Japan's resurrection infused it with sparkling new factories and a twentieth-century work ethic, Germany's recovery employed a postwar union structure in which the government (contrary to the English and

American models) held on to vast amounts of union money that minimized the unions' ability to strike. And, contrary to the other Western nations, Germany's unions needed a three-fourths vote to strike. If unions were desirable at all, at least the Germans got all the advantages of the British and American systems with none of the weaknesses. Then Adenauer worked on the owners, convincing them of the Henry Ford philosophy that high wages reaped high profits. In short, he depoliticized the unions for over a decade by copying the Samuel Gompers model of directing them to wages and hours.

Simultaneously, Adenauer, acknowledging the popularity of Bismarck's social security initiative of the late 1800s, reorganized the program and made it a part of his own political agenda, further co-opting the SPD legislators. Real income in Germany rose 300 percent under Adenauer, and Germany's currency established itself as the strongest on the Continent.[21] Adenauer's obsession with the rule of law elevated West Germany decisively over the lawlessness inherent under the Soviet puppet in East Germany, Walter Ulbricht.

Less cooperative, but no less important, France's Charles de Gaulle had managed to emerge from World War II as the savior of France, having offended all his allies, but escaping the stain of Vichy by leading the Free French after the surrender of France in 1940. Exceptionally tall and cursed by perpetually bad breath and an enormous nose, de Gaulle seldom got close to people physically. Emotionally, as well, he was isolated; "he did not accept any Frenchman as his peer," observed a correspondent from *The New York Times*.[22] In one sense of the word he was completely progressive, in that he elevated the concept of France above French people in the same manner that Communists always touted "society" above the lives of individual people who made up that society. A prisoner of war in World War I, de Gaulle rose quite slowly through the ranks, his promotions, like Eisenhower's, coming on the strength of his literary skills. Willing to champion new military ideas, he produced a number of lectures arguing that the army was an instrument of politics in 1927, which became his book *Le Fil de l'Épée* (*The Edge of the Sword*) in 1932. His next book, *Vers l'Armée de Métier* (*The Army of the Future*), in 1934, contradicted official doctrine, and according to de Gaulle's biographer Lucien Nachin, only "seven hundred copies were sold," yet in Germany, the translation "was snapped up by the thousands."[23] This work was followed in 1938 by *Le France et son Armée* (*France and Her Army*). A Cassandra from 1934 to 1940, de Gaulle was shunned by his fellow officers and certainly those above him. It was Paul

Reynaud who brought him in from the cold shortly before France's collapse, using him for liaison with Churchill, and providing him the access he needed to become legitimate.

Made a temporary general in May 1940, de Gaulle received an armored division that he led well against the German panzers. By June he reverted back to his rank of colonel under the French surrender as he gathered the bits and pieces of what became the Free French forces in England. It was a small army: a light division of alpine troops from Norway, half a brigade of the French Foreign Legion, and a handful of odd battalions pulled out at Dunkirk with the British, plus an assortment of French sailors, one hundred airmen, and volunteers from the French empire.

Though England sheltered and supported him, de Gaulle never expressed gratitude or even attempted to form amicable relations with his British patrons. Indeed, he prided himself on his prickly nature, as though it were a sign of strength. On his return to France in 1944 with the Allied forces he found a nation much different from the one he had left, even after accounting for the perversions of the Nazis. The occupation had eliminated many of the Communists, but those who remained were celebrated as heroic freedom fighters. How many there really were remains in question.[24] By 1946, the Communist Party claimed 5.5 million members, and extended its influence far beyond its membership with its own newspapers, literature, and ruthless discipline. Thus, while de Gaulle inevitably assumed the mantle of postwar French leadership, he found his administration hamstrung immediately and irrevocably. He refused to give the Communists any of the three major ministries—diplomacy, police, or the army. They compromised his government, and because of it, he resigned in January 1946 and was replaced by Paul Ramadier and the fractured Fourth French Republic. De Gaulle had no interest in coalition building or in securing a broad-based foundation of support that rested on something other than himself, or even in reform. "Regimes never reform themselves," he said in 1955. "They simply fail. They collapse. France has had 13 regimes in the last 193 years. None of these ever reformed themselves."[25]

The Communists and many of the obstructionists from the Third Republic continued to sabotage rebuilding efforts after the war—unless, of course, they were in charge. This could be seen in the flimsiness of the Fourth Republic's constitution, which was adopted in 1946 by a half-million-vote majority with 8.5 million abstentions. Its greatest flaw was that, like other European constitutions, it rested on proportional representation, ensuring that coalitions had to be constantly drawn and redrawn.

Shifting sands within the cabinets, their arrival and dismissal, and the coming and going of ministers at a rapid clip consigned the Fourth Republic to inevitable drift, especially in foreign affairs. It did not take long for the new government to find itself enmeshed in a war in Indochina as it attempted to recover its prewar empire. In such cases, the generals often made more policy than did the civilians, a reality made painfully clear in the Algerian crisis that followed the French defeat by the Viet Minh. The Fourth Republic failed both tests.

Only at home did the efforts of the persistent internationalist Jean Monnet, who was tasked with reconstructing the French economy, meet with success. Just as Adenauer looked to an eventual economic alliance with France, so too did Monnet see Germany as the natural trading partner of his nation. Along with the Netherlands, Germany and France adopted a common tariff in January 1948, and when the Common Market was created in 1957, Germany obtained access to France's large population and market, and France received German capital and expertise to revamp its sagging agricultural sector and modernize its industry.

Whether the Common Market could have been realized without de Gaulle is a topic worthy of debate. He certainly made the process easier, for several reasons. First, he remained the embodiment of the French resistance to the Nazis, and earned considerable goodwill on those grounds alone. Deliberately disappearing briefly after the end of the war, he presented himself as "pure" to the French people. Second, his view of the state was the same as that of Louis XIV: *"L'état, c'est moi." New York Times* correspondent C. L. Sulzberger, in a memo to President Kennedy, later advised that "de Gaulle tends to confuse himself with France. . . ."[26] More than Louis, however, de Gaulle viewed his connection with the nation as a spiritual obligation, and saw himself assuming the burden of France. He was a monarch in a postmonarchical age. Third, because he viewed himself as a great intellect, new and interesting processes and arrangements amused him, and he viewed the Common Market as a thought experiment. This allowed him to accept a version of France that fell below a position of world leadership. He soberly admitted that "the real trouble with France today [1954] is that Frenchmen were used to glory and prestige . . . [and] they have the habit of thinking in terms of French grandeur; and there is no French grandeur."[27] Such an attitude allowed him to deal on a somewhat equal footing with the Germans.

De Gaulle thought a great deal of himself, and referred to himself in the third person (the way so many modern sports figures do): "de Gaulle, now well-known but with no other weapon save his legitimacy, must take destiny in his hands."[28] He also occasionally introduced himself as the "great man." Sulzberger described de Gaulle as possessing "blazing areas of ignorance."[29] It conditioned in him a certain bluster, while producing an extreme sensitivity to criticism. Using a law passed in 1881, de Gaulle prosecuted 350 people for "insulting" the French head of state—writers, cartoonists, even people who shouted "Down with de Gaulle" when his car went by.[30] This trait reinforced his propensity to go it alone, and ignore the advice or feelings of others.

As we will see later, de Gaulle exploited the weaknesses of the Fourth Republic, especially during the Algerian crisis, to regain power. But prior to 1955, de Gaulle's major contribution to France was to tie her to the West, to Germany, and especially to a (more or less) capitalist system that would mesh well with Erhard's economic policies across the Franco-German border.

Ike's Industry

Overseeing this period of often radical transformation, President Dwight D. Eisenhower brought his organizational skills with him from World War II, holding down deficits, pretending to drive the bus while more skilled operators revved the engines. Armed with a seemingly perpetual smile, the chain-smoking Ike had returned from Europe a hero, though not a politician. Many didn't even know which party he belonged to until he declared himself for the Republican nomination in 1952. Eisenhower's reputation as a manager who could unify disparate groups toward a common goal melded well with his public relations image as a "get it done" general who would stand up to the Communists. Historians have long insisted that Ike did little but play golf—celebrating only his "military-industrial complex" comments. Conservatives have championed Ike as a hands-off leader who steadfastly refused to give in to warmongers at the Pentagon.

In reality, Eisenhower was far more engaged than is generally thought, and his involvement didn't always portend capitalist or small-government solutions. Ike's National Interstate and Defense Highways Act (1956) got the federal government involved in road building, and spending on the space program after *Sputnik* placed the federal government squarely in the halls of science. For all his warnings about a military-industrial complex, Ike did as much as anyone to further the intrusion of the federal government into everyday activities, especially through the hidden, less threatening areas of a domestic space policy. In the process, he created a "government-industrial complex" that posed a greater threat than anything associated with the military.

The America over which Ike presided was a dynamo, to some degree due to the "golden accident" of the postwar reality in which the United States emerged as both the world's leading producer and consumer among the free nations. This, obviously, was because America was neither touched in the continental United States by enemy bombs nor suffered foreign invasion. While the Europeans and Japan rebuilt, the United States alone could ship products and deliver expertise. Nowhere was this more apparent than in the steel industry, the most dominant in the world, led by U.S. Steel. Carnegie's old company had emerged from World War II with a 500 percent increase in revenues from 1938 and only suffered briefly during the Korean War in 1951, when its labor force sought vastly higher wages. While the issues were complex, President Truman had created an Economic Stabilization Agency in 1950 to manage wage and price controls so that supplies needed for the war would not be interrupted. In order to avoid the debacle of FDR's NIRA in 1933, Truman had established two subagencies, the Office of Price Stabilization and the Wage Stabilization Board (WSB), so there was an appearance of actions on wages and prices not being linked. Of course, a lesson of economies everywhere is that wage and price controls do not work; they only drive normal commerce underground, where prices will, in the end, have their say.

When America's inflation rose rapidly after China's entry into the war in October 1950, wages no longer kept pace, and the powerful steel unions mobilized. Truman was forced to reconstitute the WSB in 1951 with an expanded membership of academics and union representatives that effectively gave unions control of the board. As steel profits declined under federal pressure to produce low-profit steel for the war while high-profit civilian orders were sidelined, the unions threatened to strike for higher wages. Negotiations were rancorous, and in April 1952, Truman seized U.S. Steel's properties to guarantee steel production for defense purposes. The U.S. Supreme Court ruled in June that Truman's action was unconstitutional, opening the door for a strike, which shut down not only the steel industry, but also the automobile industry for lack of steel, and exhausted defense supplies. With the nation's economy and war effort approaching a crisis, the strike was settled in August on the union's terms. Industrial output had dropped to 1949 levels, and nearly 80 percent of small defense contractors had closed. It took the company four weeks to begin delivering steel again, but with the pent-up demand, the company started setting postwar productivity records. Aside from this single hiccup, from 1950 to 1955, U.S. Steel's production rose from 96 million net tons to 115 million—and exports doubled.[31]

Nevertheless, market share declined to about 30 percent, which reflected the reality of growing worldwide competition. Worse, in the decade of the 1950s, American consumption of steel per million dollars of GNP fell by one quarter, as Americans shifted to aluminum and other lighter-weight metals. But America still simultaneously accounted for the large majority of the world's production *and* consumption after the war, leaving it with almost 15 percent of all world trade and, by one estimate, an astonishing 45 percent of world industrial production.[32] This was untenable—not because the United States couldn't continue to produce, but because it resulted from Japan and Germany being thoroughly prostrated, France, Britain, and Russia badly wounded, and China chaotic. It was just a matter of time before the American share of trade and production shrank, and that was desirable, as monopoly control tends to destroy innovation and growth. Even in the fifties—though obviously because they started from such a low point—the Japanese experienced a 16.6 percent increase in raw steel production while only one new integrated steel plant was built in the United States, a U.S. Steel plant at Fairless Hills, Pennsylvania. Virtually all of America's steel capacity (83 percent) lay in states bordering the Great Lakes or the Ohio River, and all the companies were slow to implement new technology.

In addition to foreign competition, labor costs soon caught up to U.S. Steel and other American steelmakers, in large part due to the three-year contract cycles that continually boosted wages and benefits. A strike in 1959 delivered a powerful blow to the industry. Almost 530,000 strikers idled 87 percent of America's steel industry and caused layoffs of a quarter of a million workers in related fields. By that time, foreign steel was able to take advantage of American production problems, and the strike sent many American buyers to foreign steel. Still thinking the industry could recover as it had in 1952, and basking in the warmth of the "golden accident," the company gave in under federal mediation, establishing wage and benefits levels that over time would be impossible to sustain. Big Steel's profitability sank further.

New peaks of demand led to a surge in the 1960s, when the industry agreed to yet more generous wage and benefits packages. Each of those brought in more low-cost foreign steel, and consigned American steelmakers and their unions to a day of reckoning. Typically, the industry lobbied for protection from Congress and won voluntary restraints from the Japanese and Europeans (with their associated rise in import costs of 20 percent). As always, American steel did not maintain lower prices to regain its position, but kept them close and just below imports'. Nor did American steelmakers take advantage of the shelter to invest and upgrade their facilities: investment actually fell by 50 percent from 1968 to 1972.[33] This failure came on top of the $10 billion invested in the 1950s in obsolete technology.

But America's competitors—most of whom had regenerated their industries in the mid-1950s—had state-of-the-art equipment. High-quality, low-cost steel now came not only from Japan, but also from integrated mills along coastal locations in Italy (Taranto), France (Dunkirk and Fos-sur-Mer), Belgium (Ghent), the Netherlands (IJmuiden), and England (Port Talbot and Teesside).[34] The industry that, next to automobiles, was most closely identified with American greatness had signed its own death warrant with high labor costs and malinvestment. It had routinely punted the looming fatal impact of wages and benefits for more than two decades. By the mid-1970s, foreign steel in the United States was generally cheaper than that produced by domestic corporations.

As significant competition began to appear from foreign producers, the large labor unions, backed unconditionally by the Democratic Party, became increasingly militant about receiving their share of prosperity. Crippling strikes resulted in opposition to automation and new technologies, and management simply retreated from forging ahead with new technology by seeking power through government influence or escaping by moving plants to other countries with lower labor costs and less militancy. Chase Brass and Copper became the perfect example. Their Euclid, Ohio, facilities experienced lengthy strikes during the 1960s over the introduction of new technology. After the strikes, the lowest seniority on the mills' production floor was twenty-three years, meaning there were no employees left under forty years old. Harvard Business School published a case study of Chase, presenting the creation of single-purpose facilities to achieve rock-bottom costs as the solution to Chase's problems, but the company lost the manufacturing flexibility needed to survive in changing markets and shifting demand. Even in these circumstances, the unions resisted all efforts at cost reduction.

Part of the inability of corporate America—not just autos, steel, and other primary metals production and manufacturing—to deal with both new innovation and labor costs grew out of a systemic shift within the management of large corporations. The change occurred late in the 1950s when the "finance men" began taking over the major companies, wresting control from the "production men" (and engineers) who knew how to make their products. It was a transformation that climaxed the managerial revolution begun in the 1850s, when professional managers began to direct companies, but the new manifestation of the managerial revolution had taken on an entirely different nature from its nineteenth-century relative. The inherent conservatism of the managers—their avoidance of risk—led them to rely increasingly on statistics and numbers. Consequently, the intuition of the production men (for all creation of any type relies heavily on a certain amount of guesswork and gut instinct) was discarded in favor of quantifiable processes, which elevated people such as Robert McNamara to positions of power in corporate America. As the finance men seized control of the companies, the game inevitably became "what is the bottom line?" Quality products, brand names, reliability, trust—all these were secondary to showing strong stock values and paying regular dividends.

With the ascension of the money men, businesses became risk averse, seeking to avoid any costly and risky innovations in favor of safe incremental growth. It also led middle and top management to accept corrupt bargains with the unions to avoid strikes. None of those contracts could be sustainable as the baby boomers began to retire and as companies such as General Motors found themselves paying more for employee health care benefits than they did for all their raw materials combined.

Another transformation whose sprouts had just begun to poke through the cultural earth came in the demonization of business in academia and popular culture. The press had howled when Charles "Engine Charlie" Wilson, named Ike's secretary of defense, said that he could not conceive of a situation in which the Defense Department's interests would run counter to those of his former company, General Motors. For years, he said, "I thought what was good for our country was good for General Motors, and vice versa." He did *not* say "what's good for General Motors is good for the country." Yet, for the most part, he was right: when corporate America prospered in the 1950s, when industry grew, America benefited. New challenges to industry from consumer advocates such as Ralph Nader and from environmentalists would soon turn all business into the enemy of the public, inverting Wilson's maxim to read, "What's good for General Motors must be bad for the country."

The Ideology of Mobility

Leaders such as Adenauer and De Gasperi, assisted by the Marshall Plan and the American defensive umbrella, produced such prosperity among ordinary citizens that they could obtain goods and services only dreamed of a decade earlier. European prosperity came from a reapplication of American-style liberty, and no manufactured item more epitomized personal freedom than the automobile.

Although automobile ownership became democratized in America in the 1920s, it only spread to the masses in Europe after World War II. Europeans would never embrace the car culture as Americans did, but the pent-up demand for autos, which originated in the United States, soon crossed the seas on "highways" of freighter ships.

American postwar autos became more than transportation devices, gripping the public's imagination for the inherent freedom and individuality they represented. American songwriter Glenn Frey later would refer to a "yearning undefined," but in the postwar era, Americans easily identified the object of their desire—a car—for it embodied the "conception of what it means to be modern and free."[35] A young Martin Marty, later to emerge as a preeminent theologian, published his essay "The Altar of Automobility" in 1958, lamenting the "gathering symbol of our pervasive materialism," which, he insisted, was "something profoundly sexual."[36]

Liberals have consistently misunderstood the auto's appeal: it was *always* thrilling and often revolutionary, but the trick in the United States was proving that it was ordinary and mundane, affordable and accessible to everyone. Critics decried the loss of personal autonomy in the workplace, but the car extended and expanded the scope and magnitude of individual freedom, making Americans "transformed: winged, invincible. . . ."[37] Another columnist would later observe that autos were "a tangible expression of our most important values. Freedom. Choice. Privacy. Individualism. Self-reliance."[38] Whether it was the cowboy on a horse or the driver of the Model T—"a man enthroned," as E. B. White called it in 1936—movement was an essential part of the American character, and the mobile man was viewed as inherently different from his static counterpart in the Old World.[39] As early as 1939, in the Futurama exhibit at the World's Fair, industrial designer Norman Bel Geddes had insisted that "a free-flowing movement of people and goods across our nation is a requirement of modern living and prosperity."[40] It was a special freedom, an *American* freedom.

American intellectuals, however, had only contempt for the automobile, particularly after World War II. Marty wrote an article after visiting the 1958 Chicago Automobile Show in which he disdained Americans' "disproportionate reverence" for cars.[41] Car critics complained that autos represented "love objects. . . . Venerated, called friends, lovingly polished and assigned the virtues of ponies, veterans, and dogs."[42] Likewise, the independence and autonomy provided by the automobile particularly irritated Progressive collectivists, who yearned for mass transportation and "walking communities." Vance Packard's *The Hidden Persuaders* (1957) and John Keats's *The Insolent Chariots* (1958) led the way, but over time, attacks on the automobile by the chattering classes have been relentless.[43]

It was supremely ironic, then, that the Soviets had likewise become so mesmerized by the auto. As early as the 1920s, the Soviets displayed an obsession with Henry Ford and *Fordizm* for its "American efficiency"; in 1924 Stalin lectured Sverdlov University about the necessity of bringing American production techniques to bear on the "Russian Revolutionary Sweep."[44] Obediently, Soviet citizens worshiped Ford and attributed "magical powers" to his industrial efficiency (at a time, it should be noted, when he had already fallen badly behind his rival General Motors in the United States).[45] Stalin soon realized his mistake and had to backtrack. He couldn't praise Ford too much, and by 1932, a propaganda cartoon mocked Ford for "lowering the wages for workers" and concluded that Ford's "bourgeois carriage" was inappropriate to the workers' paradise.[46] Instead, in the USSR a new auto for a new man would be produced. Auto plants such as those in Nizhny Novgorod (formerly Soviet Gorky) supposedly featured green areas, parks, apartments with bathtubs and showers. (An American visitor to the city, on the other hand, recalled being overwhelmed by "an odor change caused by unwashed bodies, excrement.")[47] What they didn't have were cars: not until 1937—five years after opening—did the *entire* Soviet auto industry produce the 130,000 cars expected from the Gorky facility alone. Soviet factories proved entirely incapable of meeting the demand for autos, and Fiat, an Italian company, remained the leading automaker there for years.

The desire for cars in the USSR during the 1950s grew so intense that one was defined as a criminal for trying to jump a line to buy a car; buying a car in a secondhand store outside the state sales apparatus; speculating in cars or spare parts; registering different members of one's family to a car; or stockpiling fuel vouchers.[48] The irony was that once the Soviet state began mass-producing autos and allocating them to the population, it guaranteed that "millions of its citizens would become entangled in webs of essentially private relations that were ideologically alien and often in violation of Soviet laws."

The Pobeda, a meat-and-potatoes sedan whose simple shape was refined by Volvo, was the workhorse of the Soviet auto industry until 1960. Lacking sophistication of any kind, the Pobeda seemed as likely to see a battlefield as the second most popular car in the USSR, the American Willys Jeep. By 1957, the Soviets were installing Pobeda engines in American Jeeps, but the major engineering flaw in Soviet autos was their breakdown-prone automatic transmissions.

Soviet dictators oversaw a planned economy in which cars were targeted to be a major item of production. It was a stunning failure. By 1970, the USSR had 45 cars per kilometer of paved road; in the United States the ratio was 37.5—but the United States had fifteen times as much paved mileage. Soviet roads and autos became the butt of jokes. In 1929, when the USSR had only 10 percent as much paved road as Germany, a proverb said, "In Russia there are no roads, only directions." After the Soviet auto industry unleashed its wares on unsuspecting consumers, another proverb said that "in Russia owning a car brings joy twice—when it is bought and when it is sold."[49] Over time, road deaths soared, to 20 fatalities per 100,000 people in 1996, and as high as 41.4 in the Kyrgyzstan province.[50] In 1990, a Russian writer, R. M. Gasanov, recalled what this had implied as a cultural difference over the years:

> While over there [in America] they made automobiles and flexible production systems, we put the emphasis on organizing ministries and departments. They created work, while we tried to cultivate "the new man." . . . They bought raw materials and produced cars, we sold raw materials and bought auto factories. . . . There, people were chosen according to the task and their capabilities, over here, by questionnaire. . . . The fantasy of how smartly, quickly and in such a revolutionary manner we would bypass them has led to nothing but greater backwardness.[51]

Elsewhere in the Soviet bloc, the story was much the same. East Germany's Trabant, which started being produced in 1958, was a squat, ugly auto that made the Edsel look appealing. It was such a poor car that in 1975 *Time* magazine labeled it one of the worst cars in the world. Powered—if one could call it that—by a two-cylinder, eighteen-horsepower engine(!), the Trabant was obsolete when it was designed in the early 1950s, and actual production only made matters worse. Trabant engines "smoked like an Iraqi oil fire."[52] West Germany, with its access to American ideas and productivity enabled by its British labor union structure, witnessed a revival of the Volkswagen, Hitler's once-vaunted "people's car." The British army decided to use the heavily damaged Wolfsburg factory to produce light transportation vehicles for military use, and in late 1945 gave it a 20,000-vehicle order. In 1948, the ownership of the factory reverted to a trust controlled by the German government and veteran auto manager Heinrich Nordhoff and the plant began civilian-oriented production.[53] Immediately Nordhoff determined that Germany had to export the Beetle as well as use it domestically to generate hard cash, and his team introduced an export version with more power, a wider color range, and other improved features. The demand was stunning: by 1955, Volkswagen sold more Beetles abroad than at home.[54] Over 120,000 Beetles had come to America by 1959, meeting with good reviews in popular consumer magazines. The Beetle's low cost and round shape, easily identified against the long, sharp-contoured American cars, enabled it to capture a niche market.

At the same time, Volkswagen lost its association with the Nazis as American newspapers and television reels "helped lower the cultural roadblocks to [Volkswagen] exports," while highlighting German hard work and craftsmanship.[55] Clever ads posed seven-foot basketball star Wilt Chamberlain next to a Bug, with the caption, "They said it couldn't be done. It couldn't." Likewise, their "think small" campaign was a grand success.[56] Later, the VW played on the counterculture and its affinity for odd and alternative products, particularly the famed Volkswagen flower-power van (*Kastenwagen*). By the time it was featured in the 1969 Disney film *The Love Bug*, Volkswagen had buried its Third Reich roots once and for all.[57]

But even with the Beetle, the ratio of autos per person remained low in Germany and Italy, and was nonexistent in other continental European countries. Spain had only 89,000 private cars in 1950, or one for every 314,000 Spaniards. England had more than 2 million cars—most of them registered in London—but the auto could hardly be considered common.[58] But by 1960, 2 million Italians owned cars (a tenfold growth), and by 1970, 15 million Italians had cars, or a car for every 3.5 people, constituting a higher ratio than the United States had before the war. The vast majority of these autos were tiny, mostly coupes, or in the case of the Isetta, had only a single door. They were flimsy, underpowered, and unsafe to drive, but everywhere. The storied Italian automakers Ferrari, Maserati, Alfa Romeo, and Lamborghini had captured the essence of the Italian macho-yet-sophisticated culture, and became the objects of desire for millions of young Italian men—as did American luxury autos such as the Buick Riviera. This, too, fed cultural idiosyncrasies: wags visiting Italy noted that Italians used only two parts of a car to drive, the accelerator and the horn. Yet in spite of these cultural variations, Europe's small cars of the fifties had a common purpose: to render automobile ownership accessible and affordable for almost every West European family."[59] Europe's experience with the automobile, however, never came close to that of the American car culture.

Long-held and oft-repeated notions that the 1950s were a decade of sameness and conformity in the United States miss the revolutionary changes occurring in the decade—radical shifts that, fundamentally, may have altered America and the world far more than the superficial changes of the 1960s. For example, thanks to the explosion in automobile ownership and use, Americans for the first time became truly mobile. War had brought vast shifts in population from the Northeast and Midwest to the West and South, and now migrants visited relatives "back east," or encouraged relatives to visit them. Merely having a family car for vacations to remote places exposed millions of Americans to unfamiliar foods, ethnic groups, dialects, customs, and music. This movement imposed a new demand for lodging and food that was comfortable and reliable, giving rise to such giant franchises as Holiday Inn and McDonald's. As people experienced new tastes, clothing, and entertainments, they brought back a demand for those products to their home regions, giving rise to the first appearance of Chinese and Mexican food in the South, pizza and bagels in the West, and grits and crawfish in the Northeast.

Without question, the National Interstate and Defense Highways Act enhanced the appeal of the automobile. Justified on grounds of national defense (Eisenhower had once traveled in a convoy cross-country, finding it a distressing and painfully slow experience), the act was "the largest public works project in human history," constructing more than 42,500 miles of paved highway in the continental United States from 1956 to 1975.[60] The act distressed the critics even more, who claimed it undercut "mass transportation" (that no one wanted). Increased freedom, of course, brought out the Progressive critics: Ken Purdy, writing for *Catholic Digest*, whined that "the U.S. makes, crashes, and junks more cars than any other nation. Every 15 seconds or so, we smash a car into some unyielding surface, haul it away, mop up the blood, and hurry on."[61] In fact, while the number of vehicle deaths in America rose from 34,763 in 1950 to a high of 39,628 in 1956—before dropping by 1,700 by 1959—the number of vehicles on the road and miles driven rose by 30 percent and the number of drivers shot up from 62.2 million to 84.5 million.[62] In other words, vehicles, drivers, and miles driven outpaced accident increases more than two to one.

Far from reflecting a widespread sameness among Americans, life in the 1950s witnessed a burst of new businesses, consumer products, artistic expression, and social cross-pollination. New Yorkers and Jerseyites visited Florida, Michiganders trekked to the Gulf Coast, Texans drove to California, and Oregonians took in the national parks of Wyoming and the Dakotas. Already, American pop music and automobiles had forged a remarkable symbiotic relationship in which cars, with their radios, became mobile teenage meeting places, while the music industry (and movie industry) romanticized the automobile. James Dean, forever associated with *Rebel Without a Cause*, epitomized the equation of autos with youth, and, perhaps fittingly, Dean died in a car crash.[63] It was not just the movie industry that romanticized cars. Already there was a car culture developing in rock and roll, beginning with the first giant auto-related hit, Chuck Berry's "Maybellene" (1955). Despite the widespread presumption that whites were the majority of car owners, it was Berry, a black man singing about chasing Maybellene, who became the first African-American in the *Billboard* top ten.[64]

The drive-in theater, which was conceptually founded by Richard Hollingshead in Camden, New Jersey, in 1932, evolved into a creature of its own, producing its own culture, complete with fogged-up windows from heavy necking sessions, and security attendants who peered into autos with their flashlights to ensure limits on sexual behavior. By 1958 there were more than four thousand drive-ins in the United States.[65] While autos hardly initiated the sexual revolution, sexual relations seemed to accelerate, so to speak, in the new, mobile automobile age. Alfred Kinsey's studies had shown, among other things, that the car had grown in importance as a favorite spot for sexual liaisons.[66]

Consumers and Capitalism

Auto ownership in Europe signaled new affluence for the continent. German GDP per family head tripled between 1950 and 1973, rose faster in Italy, and even increased by one and a half times in France.[67] Per capita GDP soared threefold in Spain and almost fourfold in Austria, while Holland sported a 3.5 percent per year growth rate from 1950 to 1970. Such remarkable growth largely correlated to the production rates across Europe: output per capita in Germany (6.5 percent), Italy (5.3 percent), and

France (3.5 percent) all reflected the productivity revolution under way across the West. It also mirrored the heavy postwar investment in private industry made possible by Marshall Plan loans.

This growth also occurred during a population boom which temporarily, at least, countered claims that rising populations were a burden.[68] France saw its fastest rate of population increase ever from 1950 to 1970, much of it coming from French settlers and Algerians returning or immigrating to France.[69] Germany's population settled at 69.2 million in 1950, after war losses and the influx of Germans from eastern lands, but by 1960 reached only 72.6 million for an increase of 0.49 percent per year. In the same period, 1950–60, the United Kingdom's population rose from 50.127 million to 52.372 million, or an increase of 0.45 percent per year.

With more people who had more money, consumer spending soared and spending on necessities as a percentage of total expenditures fell in Western Europe. For example, Germans bought just under one million pairs of nylon stockings in 1950, but by 1954 they purchased 58 million. Holland had only seven supermarkets in 1961, but by 1971 counted more than five hundred. Similar expansion of supermarkets was seen in Belgium (from 19 to 456) and France (49 to 1,833).[70] By 1974, 82 percent of Belgian and British homes had a refrigerator, 88 percent of French households, and 94 percent of Italian homes, making the Italians the most refrigerated population in Europe. Italy not only used the fridge, the Italians were Europe's largest manufacturer as well, producing more than 5.2 million refrigerators per year, almost as many as the United States.[71] This kind of prosperity was shockingly different from what existed in the Soviet bloc.

Many of the Communist European states adopted nationalized health care, from which extraordinary benefits were claimed. In Czechoslovakia, for example, child mortality fell from the prewar level of 50 per 1,000 to 15 per 1,000. Free day care was provided to women so that they could enter the workforce; the numbers of primary schools and universities rose (Poland saw a fivefold increase in the number of university students between 1939 and 1960). Zdeněk Mlynář, secretary of the Czech Communist Party, optimistically opined that due to communism, "poverty as a social phenomenon had disappeared."[72] Many of these statistics merely represented the short-term gains achievable to authoritarian or closed societies before the reality of taxes and disinvestment catches up, and other gains came merely from large injections of labor during the war, not from productivity or capital growth. In reality, communism had not eliminated poverty so much as it ensured that everyone had the same portion of it.

Soon, however, even the Communist nations could see reverses, invalidating their claims of benefits from communism. Whereas Czechoslovakia and Austria had the same level of car ownership before the war, by 1960, the Western-oriented Austrians had three times as many cars as the Soviet-bloc Czechs, and Czechoslovakia was well ahead of its sister Communist states. Overall growth in the East Bloc slackened, then dropped, and in part it was this stultification of Eastern European economic decline suffered by the younger generation—the "Hero's Children," as Hungarian Paul Neuburg called them—that led them to distrust Communist ideology.[73] Nationalistic and certainly anti-Russian, these young people were also cosmopolitan, embracing much of Western culture, particularly music and consumer products.

But no nation came close to America's "attitudinal and institutional context that made the domination of American civilization inevitable."[74] Autos placed the major burden of cost on the individual (compared with expensive and often unreliable streetcars or trains), and the car strongly appealed to Americans' sense of individualism and self-reliance, while greatly expanding a person's ability to go anywhere without the preexistence of costly rail lines.[75] Not surprisingly, historians have blamed the auto for a myriad of ills, mostly centered around the decline of both small-town America and central cities and most of all for the failure to develop European-style mass transit attitudes.[76]

Agents of a World Mission

The freedom inherent in mobility spread to other elements of American social life. Historian Alan Petigny called the era the "Permissive Turn," which originated in the widespread belief in continued and permanent postwar prosperity.[77] America's blessings, it was to be expected, would be shared with all: industrial pioneers dating back to the early Republic had viewed themselves as "agents in an American world mission to raise a regenerate society in the forests of the New World."[78] This dynamic was often lost on American academics, who could not conceive why Americans would not want to be like Europeans. When Neapolitan singer Renato Carosone did a hit song, "Tu Vuò Fà l'Americano" ("You Wanna Act Like an American") in 1956, addressed to the swaggering twenty-year-old of the city streets who "loves rock 'n' roll and baseball but can't hold his whiskey and soda," he was expressing the same values as those in Milan's high society who spoke of the United States as "the only place where they would all like to live."[79] At the same time, pundits in the United States spoke of

Florida where the old people went to die, and California where the young people went to die.

The economic devastation of the war and the socialistic culture held the Continent back compared with the United States, although the Europeans nevertheless eventually succumbed to the American ideal. The gap was obvious in 1950, when Europeans only consumed 3 percent more than they had in 1938 on a 50 percent rise in industrial output, and as late as 1954, 76 percent of French households still had no running hot water, 90 percent no washing machine, 91 percent no refrigerator, and only 5 percent of men took a car to work. Fifty-seven percent had never used credit.[80] When a French polling company posed the question, "You earn 20 percent more; what are you going to do with it?" it was the first time the average European had ever been queried about discretionary income. But the answer came immediately—they'd spend it on consumer goods. When color televisions were introduced in France, 5,000 were sold; by 1965, the number had leaped to 4.2 million.[81] Indeed, another spinoff of the auto, the supermarket—while savagely resisted in parts of Europe—nevertheless took root when Supermarket Italiani, Via Milanese in Florence opened in February 1961, constituting the first large-scale profitable European supermarket. In contrast, Piggly Wiggly, the first American supermarket, appeared in 1916, and A&P supermarkets were common by the 1920s. Acceptance of the new American-style shopping model differed among countries—the Italians still spent only 2 percent of their food budgets in supermarkets by 1981, as opposed to 32 percent by the West Germans and 70 percent by Americans.[82] Consumer purchasing and sales habits also changed slowly in several areas, such as self-service, employed by only 4 percent of northern Italian retailers in the 1970s, of which only two thirds had telephones and only 11 percent had cash registers. Nearly three quarters had never run an inventory check.[83]

Elsewhere, however, the relentless march of American consumer conveniences seemed irresistible: between 1949 and 1965, the output of washing machines in France quadrupled, and by the 1980s, four fifths of all French homes had a washing machine. Françoise Giroud complained in 1953, "The great seducers of our age are no longer called Don Juan or Casanova: they bear the names of detergents, insecticides, and toothpastes."[84] Giroud had merely restated Jean-Luc Godard's comment that Europeans were "the children of Marx and Coca-Cola." There was no better indication of the restructuring of the world by American products than that found by the U.S. Marines, sent ashore in Lebanon by President Eisenhower in 1958 to support the Lebanese Maronite Christian government against threats from Nasser's Egypt and Syria. Had the troops been confronted by a hostile force as they waded ashore, they might have been in trouble. Instead they were greeted by an enterprising vendor selling bottles of Coke.

Coca-Cola excepted, perhaps the most famous and popular American product in the world was the Barbie doll—which crossed cultural lines into Japan and Europe long before Disney products—and like many Americans, she, too, had come from Europe. Ruth Handler and her husband, Elliot, had pioneered new marketing techniques at Mattel Toys during the mid-1950s with a small plastic "burp" gun, which the company virtually direct-marketed to little boys on the hugely popular *Mickey Mouse Club*. Looking for a toy for little girls, Handler found what she wanted in Europe when she spied the Lili doll—a coquettish, sexy doll figure often owned by men. Handler convinced Mattel to develop the doll, and following an initial hiccup, she produced a series of television ads and went straight to the source of doll purchases: little girls. Barbie revolutionized the way little girls saw themselves, for the first time seeing a toy that portrayed them as grown up.[85] Male toy buyers, of course, were aghast. Above all, Ruth Handler thought, the doll's breasts threatened them.

After Handler's television campaign, Barbie took off. No toy in history has ever achieved such popularity, continuing annually to sell more than $2 billion by the twenty-first century. Harold Evans observed that Handler's strategy completely overthrew the traditional method of buying toys, wherein a parent consulted with a salesperson in a toy store. Other analysts even attributed to Barbie's television sales campaign (and the later advent of children's TV channels) the transformation of American consumer culture, and the rest of the world's as well.[86]

Whether it was the Barbie doll (a toy girls could take anywhere); or the Polaroid camera that allowed people to see pictures of friends, family, or property taken in one part of the country as quickly as mail could carry them to another part; or the rise of Top 40 Radio, in which similar songs were played at stations all around the country, a universal thread was the powerful desire for the familiar. A generation of historians, in their eagerness to credit "change" and liberation to the radical movements of the 1960s—and to portray the 1950s as stodgy, dull, robotic, and conformist (epitomized by *The Man in the Gray Flannel Suit*)—have badly missed the 1950s boat. America's tumultuous shifts had already started a decade earlier than the hippie movement or the sit-ins. Cultural commentary by books such as *The Organization Man* represented *responses* to the rapid, and often radical, social changes rather than illustrations of them. The need to dissect a corporate culture in which armies of men in gray flannel suits itself constituted a major change from the industrial age with its masses of blue-collar workers. The "sameness" and "uniformity" critics saw in the 1950s were in fact superficial attempts to cling to a society that was already fraying at the seams in more important ways.

Atomic shadows and the substance of the Red Scare had many Americans genuinely concerned about fiery destruction in an exchange of bombs with the USSR. Anxiety about racial issues, especially after *Brown v. Board of Education* (1954), made clear to most white people that demands for equality by blacks were upon them. Like speculators before a market shift, the public sensed the storm that was coming, and began to look for a mast to lash itself to. That the racial tempest struck mostly in the 1960s does not mean that Americans were unaware that the weather vanes turned much earlier. After all, Eisenhower sent the 101st Airborne to Little Rock to enforce integration at Central High School in 1957. Taken together, the atomic threat and the coming racial unrest—all combined with the radical new freedom of movement provided by widespread automobile use and relocation of significant parts of the population—led people to desperately seek bastions of familiarity, buoys of the commonplace, reminders of home (wherever that was).

Liberation and Un-liberation of Women

Family life in the United States and Western Europe in the 1950s still revolved around the nuclear family, with Europeans tending to include larger extended families in the more intimate circles. Most Americans still saw the husband as the main breadwinner, despite the burst of women into the workforce in World War II, and it was not at all uncommon for suburban families to have a single car that the father drove to work while women remained at home. But even when families included grandparents, the growing influence of the automobile increased the likelihood that a man's job might be farther away, or that the family would move altogether. It was not uncommon for aspiring executives to move their families every several years to new cities and states. General Electric instituted a three-year Manufacturing Training Program for future managers, requiring a relocation move each year and six different job assignments.

Yet these were not entirely new: most changes in America and Europe had been unfolding for years, and "the undercurrents for the call for gender equality were readily evident during the late 1940s and 1950s."[87] Total

American female employment had risen from just over 20 percent in 1900 to over 35 percent in 1960, and married women's employment tripled—yet another tension in the transformative fifties, for during the decade married female employment rose by one third.[88] This in part was due to the experience women had gained in the workforce during World War II, in part due to the decline in younger women (age sixteen to twenty-four), whose percentage of the total U.S. population fell by 10 percent between 1900 and 1950, and in part due to the fact that the number of younger women attending college doubled from 1900 to 1960. All this sucked more married women into employment outside the home. But it is also important to note that relatively low taxes, and, after 1950, low inflation, meant that a male breadwinner could support a family of four on a single salary. Government-induced changes in the family's economic circumstances, therefore, gave women more purchasing power and idle time to pursue new activities and were more important than the changes in sexual practices associated with the sexual revolution. Put another way, without the Great Society's massive social spending, without the expense of the Vietnam War, and without the inflation generated by a decade of deficits beginning in 1960, the radical changes of the 1960s would have come much more slowly.

The upheaval in women's attitudes about their roles had also already changed by the 1950s. One survey done in 1947 demonstrated that women were no longer satisfied with traditional roles of wife, mother, homemaker. They wanted their own jobs, their own money, and more opportunities to express themselves.[89] Alan Petigny found that the frequency of single motherhood shot up dramatically between 1940 and 1960—hardly considered the era of Free Love.[90]

Corporations, aware of changing roles, attempted to ensure domestic tranquillity by making the wife a partner in her husband's occupation. Between 1946 and 1959, more articles addressing the "corporate wife" were published in the American business press than in all years prior to World War II, and the number would triple again in the next twenty years.[91] The president of a Chicago management consulting firm told *American Business* in 1957 that "probably the most significant trend in American industrial life in the past decade has been the emergence of the American wife as a business partner. . . . It has reached the state where many companies will not hire or promote an executive without taking a good look at his wife."[92] In the popular press, the numbers were more revealing of the significance of marriage for executives: no fewer than 136 articles appeared in major general-interest magazines such as *The Saturday Evening Post*, *Harper's*, and

American Magazine, as well as more than 50 articles in women's magazines such as *Better Homes and Gardens* and *Good Housekeeping*. Indeed, nothing spoke to the rise of the suburban housewife like the explosion in circulation of the latter magazine, which went from 300,000 readers in 1911 to 5.5 million by 1966. *Better Homes and Gardens* received the ultimate nod to its significance in 1958 when *Mad* magazine published a satire of it called "Bitter Homes and Gardens."

Another role that changed for women during the 1950s was that of "mom," particularly the variety described by Philip Wylie in his 1942 book, *Generation of Vipers*. Although journalists would always describe a woman with children in any story as "mother of 'X,'" by 1970 such a tag had lost its punch. In the twenty-first century, most Americans would be hard put to say how many children even female cabinet secretaries had, and usually the number of children was only emphasized if the woman was involved in some tragedy, such as dying at a young age. In short, motherhood ceased to define a woman.

One analysis of women's roles, ironically, came from William H. Whyte, author of *The Organization Man*, whose thesis that American society was becoming homogenized completely missed the import of his survey done for *Fortune* magazine in 1951.[93] The emphasis on wifely deportment and entertaining skills was viewed as forcing women into a cookie-cutter mold by eliminating their individuality through work outside the home. What went unnoticed by academicians was that women had quietly moved from household subordinates to coequals with their husbands on the path to success, and while men's and women's roles were different, each was absolutely critical. Women were encouraged to engage in community involvement, presumably as a source of new business contacts, and to be the leading partner in conducting entertainment, parties, and dinners for both public relations and marketing.

A tendency has arisen among historians to view America's postwar homes as a "fount of homophobia, misogyny, and conservatism," an oligarchic mini-society replete with spousal and child abuse by husbands.[94] The statistics tell a different story. Three separate studies of family decision making revealed a fairly even distribution of power between husbands and wives; even when it came to big decisions, such as large-scale purchases, marriage partners tended to play an equal role.[95] Moreover, the pattern seemed classless. For example, research on Detroit families found the "egalitarian" model twice as prevalent as the "husband-dominant" structure. "Neither the farm families, nor Catholic families, nor the older generation, nor poorly educated families adhere to a patriarchal way of life," the Detroit study concluded.[96] Perhaps more surprisingly, a survey of Brigham Young University students—members of the supposedly traditionalist Church of Jesus Christ of Latter-day Saints (Mormons)—by a 60 percent margin said they believed husbands and wives should play an equal role in disciplining children and in other family decisions, including spending money.[97]

Such evidence seemed to leave historians unfazed. Ruth Rosen's *The World Split Open* claimed that wherever women were in the 1950s, whether at home or at work, they were "treated as subordinates."[98] Steven Mintz and Nancy Kellogg insisted that marriage "did not mean equality. A wife's primary role was to be her husband's ego massager, sounding board—and housekeeper . . . the fifties' ideal of a marital partnership were based on the assumption of a wife's role as hostess and consort."[99] Predictably, with such a mind-set, historians have seen the fifties as oppressive and the sixties as liberating. A few, however, have discerned that the data do not support such a view, including Lizabeth Cohen, who studied consumer habits. She found that men increasingly played a prominent role in grocery shopping, women more so in appliances, and men overwhelmingly so in automobiles.[100] Yet when it came to the ultimate big-ticket item, buying a house, decisions were made jointly, and where one spouse played a dominant role, it was more often the wife rather than the husband. Over the long term, when couples were reinterviewed, the wife's plans were more likely fulfilled than the husband's by every category of purchase.[101] It could be said that women shopped with stuff in mind; men, with women in mind. Despite the apparent reliance on men, therefore, women were not confined to the home—rather, the home increasingly extended past a narrow geographical strip adjacent to the husband's workplace and into sprawling surrounding areas that introduced yet another cultural and geographic shift. Vast suburban communities such as Long Island's 82,000-unit Levittown development sprang up, freed by the auto from the tyranny of the big city, with its corruption and crime. The new sun belt cities of Phoenix, Albuquerque, El Paso, San Diego, and even Denver were substantially designed around the automobile.[102] Such suburban-oriented cities featured wide streets, clearly marked exits and signs, and abundant parking for shopping areas (which coincided with the rise of the enclosed shopping mall). Often laid out on a grid, these fast-growth postwar metropolitan areas spread out their new "clean" industries of electronics, defense, and communications. Central city cores, while not ignored, no longer dominated planning. A new concept for planning, "travel time quality," was developed that located bedroom communities and shopping malls based on networks of roads not defined by distance, but by time and the quality of travel.[103] For most modern cities with low densities, this model showed mass transit by rail to be unworkable. Suburbs, conducive to the automobile, also gave birth to new forms of shopping, enclosed malls. America's first true mall, in Edina, Minnesota (1956), sparked a burst of mall construction across the nation from 1961 to 1975, including Winrock Center (Albuquerque, 1961), Tacoma Mall (Tacoma, 1965), Regency Square Mall (Jacksonville, 1967), 100 Oaks Mall (Nashville, 1967), Crossroads Center (Waterloo, Iowa, 1970), and Rimrock Mall (Billings, Montana, 1975).[104] Dallas opened four major malls between 1965 and 1973—just part of over nine million square feet of prime retail mall space constructed in the city in less than seventeen years. When combined with real or perceived higher crime rates in the cities and their decaying structures, the new auto-based suburbs and their shopping venues proved overwhelmingly appealing.

Just Pill Me

Suburbanization and chain retailing was the focus of another major change involving women through an explosion in drugstores in the 1950s. Drugstores represented in a small sense the ascendance of science (and with it, medicine) as the final authority in all aspects of life. There was a significant amount of faith placed in the possibilities of science, leading to a liberalization of values as researchers—and especially the new field of behavioral researchers—"proved" that traditional values were no longer necessary or even valuable. One survey in 1957 found that an astonishing 80 percent of respondents answered the question "Overall would you say that science and technology have done more good than harm?" positively (whereas in 1985, that number had fallen to 58 percent).[105] The publicly funded growth of scientific endeavors and institutes skyrocketed after the war: between 1946 and 1950, Congress created the Atomic Energy Commission, passed the National Mental Health Act, and established the National Science Foundation.

Scientists, researchers, doctors—the American public still granted them all an unlimited amount of trust. Any television commercial featuring a doctor in a white coat guaranteed that the product was "medically proven" to work, even to the point that "doctors" could appear in *smoking advertisements* touting the safety of cigarettes. (It was never established if the people on camera were, in fact, M.D.s or not.) Organizations such as the American Heart Association (founded in 1924) or the American Cancer Society (1913) came on the scene shortly after their British and European counterparts (Cancer Research UK, for example, was founded in 1902) and predated most societies in other European countries (German societies came in the 1930s). Such organizations seemed to advocate for better public health and appeared to have no monetary agenda, and therefore they not only became the leaders in introducing scientific research to the public, but also assumed a cloak of morality because they had no financial interest in the issue. A similar group, the *Bulletin of the Atomic Scientists*, created a position for itself as the "authoritative voice on the Left with respect to issues of international peace."[106] In each case, however, the existence of such concerned organizations led to a rather disturbing realization that the organization was without a mission the minute the disease was eliminated or the problem solved. Any organization involved in solving a given problem survived intact by immediately taking up another cause, and needless to say, it behooved all of these organizations to avoid ever finding a cure or solution to a problem, for that imperiled their very existence.

Government was not inactive in promoting good health, with Germany leading the way as historically the most progressive nation (obviously, not always a good thing). In the 1880s, cooperatives were formed that collected premiums from workers to provide relief to sick individuals who couldn't work. Chancellor Otto von Bismarck issued the *Reichsversicherungsverordnung*, the Imperial Insurance Order, in 1883, mandating that all workers below a certain earnings level pay into such a sickness fund. This was the birth of government-mandated health insurance, although it was properly more of a sick pay fund. This "Bismarck Model" underwent many revisions, morphing into a true government-sponsored health insurance system that became wildly popular. Hitler installed the system in France, Belgium, and the Netherlands during World War II, and in spite of being a Nazi program, those countries kept it. Ultimately, it blended private health care delivery with universal mandated coverage. The actual sickness fund is selected by the individual, the mandate is on the individual, coverage is portable, and employers pay half of the premium.

The United States adopted many progressive initiatives under the New Deal, but not government-supplied health care or health insurance. FDR included "the right to adequate medical care" in his State of the Union Address in 1944, but did not push the issue. Truman asked Congress for national compulsory health insurance to be funded by payroll deductions in October 1945, but his initiative went nowhere. Meanwhile, the British National Health Service was established in 1948 to provide health care, primarily funded through taxation rather than insurance payments by employers and individuals. Instead of being an insurance system paying for private health care, it delivered the health services itself, most of which were free to citizens of England. In addition, European countries generally funded medical research through one or more agencies, private and governmental. All of these programs and activities tended to promote improvements in health care, in providers, hospitals, and other institutions. Even so, in the 1950s, U.S. health care was still generally considered to be the best in the world.

Although the United States did not follow Europe into a national system of health insurance or health care, advances in medicines and treatments in America during the 1950s were unparalleled. Federal support of science and research made possible new drugs, but also opened new fields of research. A vast new market for user-friendly medicines and medical products appeared, making it possible for average people to obtain some sort of pain relief or disease treatment even without a doctor's care. With the proliferation of drugstores came another unexpected development: contraceptives and prophylactics became products that ordinary Americans purchased with great frequency.

Prophylactics had come under FDA regulation in the late 1940s, thus improving their reliability, leading to still wider use. (As late as the 1990s, however, prophylactics still failed at a rate of 15 percent.) Birth control became commonplace: in 1939, Planned Parenthood contacted 1,400 doctors to provide training in contraception methods, but only 210 signed up, whereas in 1955, 2,200 doctors and 6,000 nurses received Planned Parenthood training.[107] Pre- and extramarital sex was made more attractive still by the conquest of most venereal diseases through penicillin, with its twenty-fold price decline between 1943 and 1945. By 1947, a vial of penicillin cost $.30, triggering a decrease of 75 percent in the syphilis death rate as some 650 billion units *per month* came on the market. The disease became so rare that one medical journal, *The American Journal of Syphilis*, ceased publication. Thus, the notion of the staid and boring 1950s, almost universally accepted as a truism by scholars, does not withstand the evidence.[108]

The only real difference between the so-called sexual revolution of the 1960s and the "uptight" 1950s was that "Americans were simply more willing to acknowledge the extracurricular activities of their youth [in the 1960s] than they had been during the previous decade."[109] Higher rates of sexual intercourse nevertheless were closely accompanied by a "new regime of dating [with] a stronger incentive on the part of single men to protect the reputations of their girlfriends by keeping mum about how far they had gone. . . ."[110] Far from being the trailblazers that they are commonly portrayed as, Alfred Kinsey, Masters and Johnson, Hugh Hefner, and Elvis were lagging indicators, not leading.[111] They publicly reflected what was already occurring privately, and it was sexual candor, not sexual activity, that was the true characteristic of the "free love" decade that followed. Nevertheless, individuals such as Hefner and Elvis *did* reflect reality—and change. The shift could be seen in the change in attitudes between the time of the Ingrid Bergman–Roberto Rossellini affair in 1949, which essentially banished the popular Bergman from the United States for seven years, and the Elizabeth Taylor–Eddie Fisher affair a mere nine years later, where Taylor—by then a critically acclaimed actress—received an Oscar nomination a year later and won the Academy Award in 1960. She became the first female movie star to command $1 million to appear in a film (and a box office bomb), *Cleopatra*, suggesting that her private life had much less of an impact on her career than Bergman's had. Conservatives bought into the sixties mythology (and its corollary of a tepid, uneventful 1950s) every bit as much as the leftist bards who rendered the fable in the first place. William Bennett, Mona Charen, Robert Bork, and others routinely cited the sexual revolution of the 1960s without noticing that out-of-wedlock births had increased sharply before the arrival of the hippies in 1968.[112] In fact, the rising rates of single motherhood occurred *prior* to the 1960s, particularly in the immediate postwar half decade (an almost 40 percent increase in single motherhood from 1945 to 1950). This undermines the importance placed on the Pill as an encouragement to have more sex because of reduced risk of pregnancy. Whereas the typical view of the Pill is that it was the "drug that changed the world" and "launched the sexual revolution," the Pill, like the Organization Man, rode the wave but did not start it.[113]

If indeed any one drug changed the world, it more likely was penicillin, but the appearance of the oral contraceptive seemed to reinforce the prevailing myth because of its timing, coming onto the market in 1960. Consequently, it has been standard fare for historians to ascribe the rise in premarital sexuality to the widespread availability of oral contraceptives.[114] Yet at first, the Pill wasn't cheap ($11 per month at the time), required a prescription, and could only be refilled by six-month returns to the doctor's office. Moreover, doctors themselves discouraged use of the Pill, and when Brown University physician Roswell Johnson, the director of health services, prescribed the Pill for some women, it sparked a ferocious debate.[115] That was in 1965! Thus, it becomes harder to argue that the Pill played a significant role in the sexual revolution of the 1960s when it still was not widely available on a general basis by mid-decade. Indeed, a number of factors expanded sexual experimentation, including the ease of male condom use combined with the "hassle factor" associated with the frequent renewals of birth-control pill prescriptions. These concerns were all reflected in the first serious survey of birth control in 1971, when only 10 percent of women ages fifteen to nineteen said they used the Pill (although use among older, college-age girls was undoubtedly higher).[116]

Psychology, Self, and Religion

Endowed with its new position of authority in society, science—and particularly the government-funded programs in medical science and health—began to dictate behaviors from eating to sex. This reality was particularly seen in the field of psychology, where the American Psychological Association saw its numbers rise sixfold between 1940 and 1960, when its membership topped eighteen thousand. Psychology was, indeed, democratized during the decade of the 1950s, so that by 1965, one quarter of Americans admitted to having used tranquilizing drugs. Alcoholism—formerly viewed as a moral vice— now was considered (by some) a disease capable of being combatted through treatment. Norman Vincent Peale touted the disease model for alcoholism, and became a leading proponent of psychological counseling, leading to the growth of what Philip Rieff called "Psychological Man."[117]

Psychology touched on broad issues in American society, from family life to religious activity. In the area of child raising, Dr. Benjamin Spock influenced millions of mothers with his ideas that families needed to be more permissive toward children's wants and needs.[118] Even within religious circles, psychology increasingly took on the mantle of authority: at the Louisville Southern Baptist Theological Seminary, the number of psychology courses rose from four in 1942 to eleven in the late 1950s, and at Southwestern Theological Seminary in Fort Worth, the number of psychology courses quadrupled in the same period.[119]

Major magazines and newspapers ran a steady stream of articles warning about losing one's "self," and one of the most popular psychological programs of the decade was Carl Rogers's "consciousness raising" or "self-actualization." Called the "father of humanistic psychology," Rogers introduced the notion that all values were the result of inputs over a person's life, denying any universal concepts like sin or heredity. Rogers's interpretations fit well with the new "scientification" of virtually everything, in which the latest finding always became truth.

Liberalization in psychology, religious instruction, and family life was matched by similar liberating in education. American universities lowered their standards, giving college students more free time to indulge themselves in hedonistic pursuits. Most of those taking advantage of the GI Bill had already flowed through the system, while women were just starting to appear in strong numbers. The impetus for the changes was, as with the other forces of liberalization, a concern for "fairness" and that no one be denied a college education. One engineering college lowered its four-year engineering curriculum requirement from 168 semester hours to 142, making the previous program a five-year course of study. Full-time loads were lowered from 18 to 24 semester hours to 12 to 15. Most liberal arts colleges lowered their four-year programs to 120 hours. At the same time, grade inflation infested higher education: grades in most universities went up by a half grade between 1963 and 1970. In some departments, notably education, the most frequent grade given was A; often a class of thirty students would result in twenty-three A's, five B's, and two C's. The grades of D and F simply disappeared. Dropping courses without penalty was initiated, even up to two weeks before the semester ended, soaking up most of those who previously would have failed. Often, courses taken a second time would end up with only the second (usually higher) grade being recorded and factored into a student's GPA. Taking all these changes into account, college students were liberated from the necessity of studying. But of course, this was all part and parcel of the new standards of leniency, nonjudgmentalism, and allowing everyone to "find themselves."[120]

Even religious attitudes in the decade revealed sharp disconnects that hardly conformed to the traditionalist/conservative model. Although traditional churches—many quite constrained in their worship services and music—remained the norm, a new form of personal spiritual engagement arose with the advent of nationally known traveling evangelists. William Franklin "Billy" Graham, Jr., packed massive venues with his crusades. A North Carolina boy raised in the Reformed Presbyterian Church, Graham went to Wheaton College in Illinois and earned a degree in anthropology before coming to the Lord in a California camp meeting. Before long he was speaking, then preaching sermons, then producing an evangelistic radio show. In the late 1940s, he began holding revival meetings in tents, and conducted his first officially named crusade in 1947 in Michigan. (By 2012, he had held more than four hundred crusades.) Despite what some saw as a fundamentalist, no-holds-barred approach to sin and salvation, Graham attracted saints and sinners alike, speaking to the American spiritual core of a redemption that was always possible. He avoided sophisticated theological arguments in favor of salvation sermons in which the nature of man's sin was juxtaposed with the reality of God's forgiveness and the crowds were invited to an "altar call" in which they would accept Jesus as their savior in front of the public. Graham, as St. Paul said nearly two thousand years earlier, preached "Christ, and Him crucified." It was the perfect message for a nation starting to feel the stresses of race relations, the atomic bomb, and the sexual revolution.

Likewise, Granville "Oral" Roberts energized the faith/Pentecostal movement with messages of divine healing and prosperity. Born in Oklahoma of Cherokee descent (and a member of the Choctaw Nation), Roberts began preaching earlier than Graham, but had his moment of faith at almost the same time. Associated with the Pentecostal Holiness Church, Roberts held camp meetings and crusades around the world, founded Oral Roberts University in 1963, and preached on a weekly television show. Like Graham, Roberts taught a simple—but not simplistic—message that had widespread appeal, not only of salvation but also of a life in which faith could produce real-world changes in one's health and finances.

Nevertheless, at the same time Graham and Roberts encountered some of their greatest success, studies of evangelical youth showed sharp changes in attitudes toward drinking, attending movies, studying on Sunday, or dancing, all shifting toward more permissiveness.[121] Church giving toward proselytization efforts dropped by almost 25 percent during the decade. Attitudes toward teenagers' "going steady" regularly liberalized in the 1950s, with no difference in surveys among Roman Catholics and others.[122] Perhaps more astonishingly, teenagers came to side with their parents' judgment even *more* when it came to dating decisions during the decade, again contrary to the tale told by most historians.[123] One Michigan survey taken in mid-decade found that 65 percent of teenage males thought their parents were "lenient," as opposed to only 29 percent who said "strict."[124]

In other words, the popular teen alienation story upon which most Americans grew up is largely false when it comes to the 1950s. Purdue University conducted surveys during the decade revealing that teens, by a three-to-one margin, said "religious faith is better than logic for solving life's important problems," and over half cited religious figures as the "one group of people" who could do the "most to promote peace in the world."[125] The Boy Scouts saw its ranks swell by more than 800,000 from 1945 to 1960 in another example of a search for stability and traditionalism.[126] Nevertheless, parents were admonished in the *National Parent-Teacher Magazine* to expect clashes as teens experimented and grew, and *The New York Times* prepared parents for "Adolescence: Time of the Rebel."[127]

Where teens did begin to break away was in their consumption, purchases, and tastes, especially in clothes, music, movies, and cars (to the extent teens listened to car radios and could build or acquire hot rods). There were other areas of entertainment, though, that specifically addressed the youth market's rebellion, most notoriously *Mad* magazine.

Mad as Hell

Founded by William Gaines in 1952, *Mad* was a departure from a series of horror comics (*Vault of Horror, Crypt of Terror*) Gaines had devised that premiered in 1950 under the EC Comics label.[128] One of Gaines's writers, Harvey Kurtzman, came up with the idea of a comic magazine, and while the first *Mad* wasn't earthshaking, it quickly developed a following. Gaines financed it out of his more profitable titles, some of which sold 400,000 copies each by the early 1950s. Perhaps *Mad*'s greatest boost, though, came from Fredric Wertham, a psychiatrist at Bellevue who, in 1954, published an attack on comic books' impact on youth called *Seduction of the Innocent*. Wertham and his supporters found the most perverted side of everything: Batman and Robin were homosexual partners; Wonder Woman had a bondage subtext or, conversely, was a lesbian; hidden female nudity was abundant. Immediately, the federal government leaped into the debate, holding hearings before the Senate Subcommittee on Juvenile Delinquency, and called Gaines as a witness. Under threat of censorship, Gaines and other comic book publishers established the Comics Code Authority to review materials and ban violent images, even removing "code words" such as "terror" and "zombies." Based on the motion picture code, the CCA required that criminals always be punished, drug use prohibited, only "classic" vampires depicted, and sex and horror toned down.

With his terror and horror lines nearly shut down, Gaines shifted his emphasis and resources to *Mad*, making it slicker and putting it out bimonthly—and giving it the name "magazine" instead of comic book. *Mad* spoofed every element of American life, including products, psychology, medicine, social mores, and, of course, other comics. A classic 1964 issue captured the Breck hair products' full-page ad with a painting of Beatle Ringo Starr (instead of a woman) and the caption, "Make Beautiful Hair . . . BLECCH." The magazine's trademark character was a freckle-faced, gap-toothed boy, Alfred E. Neuman, with his trademark comment, "What—me worry?" Neuman appeared on every issue since 1955, capturing the publication's approach to life. As one editorial cartoonist characterized the image, "the face, the character itself, has come to epitomize stupidity."[129] *Mad* generated widespread appeal—some 60 percent of college students reported reading the magazine—and not just among the young. Soon, as with all symbols of irreverence and youth culture, adults began reading *Mad* as well.[130]

To be sure, literature of all sorts still reflected a heavy dose of unconformity, specifically reflecting a prevailing anti-German and anti-Nazi attitude after the war. The literary decade began with *Catcher in the Rye* (1951), the essence of teen rebellion, and ended with *To Kill a Mockingbird* (1960), which saw the hero Atticus Finch defend a black man accused of rape. A half-dozen other books still cautioned against following the rules or becoming too conformist (including Theodor Adorno's *The Authoritarian Personality* and William H. Whyte's *The Organization Man*). Few, however, took up the crusade like Philip Wylie in *Generation of Vipers*, probably the most iconic "antinormal" book produced during the 1940s.

Another nonconformist strain developed through the Beat Generation, typified by Allen Ginsberg and Jack Kerouac. Ginsberg's poem *Howl* brought on an obscenity trial, and Kerouac's novel *On the Road* inspired thousands of young Americans to take to the road, working to provide gas money, and to see America from coast to coast. Universal standards were rejected altogether, Buddhism and Hinduism were favored topics of study along with Freud and Jung, politics were meaningless, and what mattered was to experience everything that could be experienced. According to the Beats, there were no causes worth fighting for, certainly not civil rights, only a casual but maximum effort to seek new vistas (see Kerouac's *The Dharma Bums*, which featured group sex). Considering themselves incredibly cool, the Beats were certainly predecessors to the hippies of the 1960s, and for some, essentially indistinguishable except in their volume of drug use and media exposure.

Of course, America's renewed greatness in the 1950s had little to do with scientification, self-actualization, or even the entertaining unconformity illustrated by *Mad* magazine and Kerouac's books. Europe had already started to import a rising standard of living associated with Americanness and to benefit from its blessings. But in some cases the transfer foundered on shoals of cultural differences—dare we say, cultural weaknesses. A British productivity team visiting the United States in 1953 discovered the "real secret of American productivity," which was that "American society is imbued through and through with the desirability, the rightness, the morality of production. Men serve God in America, in all seriousness and sincerity, through striving for economic efficiency."[131] To put it another way, Americans by 1960 had still not abandoned the religious pillar of exceptionalism.

How the Future Went

By 1960, America still possessed a sense of destiny and confidence that anything was possible. When the USSR launched *Sputnik*—a 184-pound satellite—into orbit in 1957, the United States responded with its own space program. Created in July 1958, the National Aeronautics and Space Administration (NASA) had in fact originated in 1915 with NACA, the National Committee for Aeronautics, whose mission was to promote and undertake research in aeronautics. It set up laboratories and test facilities that produced a number of breakthroughs including an engine cowl, airfoil, and wind tunnel research capabilities. But *Sputnik* sparked a transformation of the agency in 1957 into space technology, which was to be "the responsibility of a national civilian agency" working with the military.[132] Space was already beginning to capture the American imagination. Movies and television shows such as *Invaders from Mars*, *Buck Rogers*, and *Commando Cody: Sky Marshal of the Universe*, not to mention a fascination with flying saucers, drew Americans toward space. The look at the skies also exposed some questionable sightings: in June 1947, aviator Kenneth Arnold reported the first "flying disc" that was well documented. This was followed by the U.S. Air Force's secret study of UFOs (unidentified flying objects) later that year. UFO sightings, according to most analysts, strongly reflected the struggle in the cold war with aliens who, like Communists, controlled the thoughts and actions of ordinary people and who passed among us as normal. In policy terms, however, the enthusiasm for space led to the ingenious political solution of artificially separating the space program into military and civilian functions.[133]

Although *Sputnik*, which the Soviets launched into orbit in October 1957, was only 184 pounds, it might as well have been a million for all of the concern it generated. It seemed as if in an instant the Soviets had eclipsed American science. The technology, of course, meant that the Soviets had greatly reduced the flight time and distance of a rocket to the United States by going into orbit, and that, in turn, meant that the Soviets could entertain ideas of lobbing atomic warheads at America. Upon hearing the news in Huntsville, Alabama, General John Medaris recalled:

> There was a moment of stunned silence. Then [Wernher] von
> Braun started to talk as if he had been vaccinated with a Victrola

needle. . . . "We knew they were going to do it! Vanguard will never make it. We have the hardware on the shelf. For God's sake, turn us loose and let us do something. We can put a satellite up in sixty days. . . . Just give us the green light and sixty days!"[134]

Sputnik was more than a technological jump. It constituted the physical embodiment of a supremely important metaphysical question: should technology serve as the means by which humans satisfied their unique drive to explore, or was it a tool to change human nature through the introduction of globalization and the advent of an age of material prosperity? It was not a new concept to unite civilian and military experimentation and innovation: Napoleon had established civilian prizes for inventions (which he would use for military purposes) leading to, among other things, pickled and canned goods. But the scale upon which the Space Race was played out was unmatched, dwarfing the nineteenth century's colonial land grabs. Now, the USSR had completely fused civilian with military technology, obliterating any lines between the two sectors in what space historian Walter McDougall called the "centralized mobilization of science."[135]

Sputnik also challenged the seeming American (and Western) lead in all technology, and, by extension, the superiority of the Western system of science. Soviet superiority, however, was not homegrown; the Soviets' spy apparatus had stolen thousands of American technological secrets, and thus they could focus on engineering implementations rather than expending time and money in basic research. Furthermore, in the Soviet Union, the government enthusiastically embraced engineering technology while at the same time remaining ideologically opposed to freedom of thought and the exchange of ideas. Years earlier, Lenin had concluded that the message of World War I was that those who had the best technology and organization won—an erroneous inversion of Victor Davis Hanson's argument that certain states *had* the best technology and organization because of their culture. But even as resources poured into a Soviet space program, it stifled the creativity of scientists while erecting a scaffold of bureaucratic barriers. Simultaneously, Stalin's purges had wiped out thousands of engineers.

From the outset, the Soviets' ideology of inevitable technological superiority necessitated a race into space. After the war, the USSR dumped millions into improved facilities, high wages for scientists and engineers, and widespread technological investment in electronics, radar, jets, and combustion research. Heavy rocket development began in 1954, at the same time as similar programs started in the United States. Stalin's death in 1953 not only did not end the competition, but actually accelerated military and R&D spending in the USSR. Nikita Khrushchev, who inherited (or stole) Stalin's mantle, recognized that for all the advantages the Soviets possessed, they were still too weak for world domination. Hence, he proposed "peaceful coexistence" while sharpening every blade in his armory.

Only in a single aspect did the Soviets eclipse the Americans: they gave equal status to scientists and engineers, and in some cases elevated engineering personnel above scientists to shorten developmental time. In the United States, academics and scientists often had little use for or even appreciation of engineers, considering them little more than highly paid mechanics. The engineer who built the first digital general computer, J. Presper Eckert, fell afoul of John von Neumann for that reason, and even Eckert's partner, physicist John Mauchly, was similarly tainted.

The United States, utilizing the skills of captured German scientists and engineers in Huntsville, was already building its own rockets. German engineers, fresh from their work on the V-2, had always maintained an ulterior motive of making rockets that were also suitable for spaceflight. They were the most advanced rocket developers in the world, and had been swept from under the Red Army's nose—while the Soviets got the labs and equipment of Peenemünde, the Americans made off with the real treasure, the minds of its personnel.

At first, American rockets were spectacularly unsuccessful, as chronicled in Tom Wolfe's book *The Right Stuff*: they went off course, exploded on the launch pad, or could not produce sufficient power to escape their silos, and so on. The first four Vanguard multistage rockets all failed; the Army's Jupiter C had one successful test, followed by a second test in which the rocket engine took it wildly off course. A week later, another Jupiter went out of control while a Thor had to be destroyed on the pad before it blew up.[136] Although the United States was never nearly as far behind as the press made it appear (or the generals feared we were), it was once again the American propensity for pursuing multiple solutions—through the Navy's solid-fuel rockets and the Air Force's liquid-fuel rockets—that finally produced boosters that worked. Russia's *psychological* impact, however, had been real and substantial. Overnight, Americans sensed that the oceans no longer protected them from attacks on their homeland.

Looking to create a stronger base in math and science, and regain the advantage the Soviets now appeared to hold, Congress, with Ike's blessing, flooded the universities with money directed at science, math, and foreign languages under the National Defense Education Act (1958), which increased educational spending by $40 million. In higher education, however, as any student of collegiate football programs knows, money never stays where it is supposed to be placed (accounting for the remarkable lack of opposition on the part of faculty to collegiate men's sports, which generates funding for academic research). With the federal money, it was no different: though it had been targeted for science and math, universities' budgets merely were rearranged to spread their own science and math funds elsewhere. All departments benefited, and while the sciences did receive a boost, money was siphoned off across liberal arts as well. In addition, math in colleges at the time was pure mathematics, not applied math as used in engineering, and in the end, the act's effects were slight. Meanwhile, politicians' knee-jerk reaction to *Sputnik*—pour more tax money into public universities—bordered on panic, fed in no small part by the press. "Let us not pretend that Sputnik is anything but a defeat for the United States," blared *Life* magazine.[137]

Whereas Eisenhower was satisfied to let Congress follow and work through slow, institutional processes, Kennedy, by nature the nation's first celebrity president, sought out programs that made news, that were visionary and idealistic—and the space race became his new obsession. Seeing the Soviets' apparent edge in space, JFK grew almost frantic. In April 1961, when the Russians blasted Yuri Gagarin into orbit, giving the Soviets another first, Kennedy drilled his staff: "Is there any place where we can catch them? What can we do? Can we go around the Moon before them? Can we put a man on the Moon before them. . . . If somebody can just tell me how to catch up!"[138] JFK reacted by staking out a big goal. On May 25, 1961, in his message to Congress, Kennedy observed that "space is open to us now. . . . We go into space because whatever mankind must undertake, free men must fully share."[139] Therefore, he continued, "I believe that this nation should commit itself to achieving the goal, before this decade is out, of landing a man on the moon and returning him safely to the earth."[140] Four months later, in an address at Rice University, Kennedy repeatedly compared the space effort to the explorers of earlier years. Invoking William Bradford in 1630, who said that "all great and honorable actions are accompanied with great difficulties, and both must be enterprised and overcome with answerable courage," Kennedy insisted that "man, in his quest for knowledge and progress, is determined and cannot be deterred."[141] Espousing American exceptionalism in one of American history's great speeches, Kennedy soared:

We set sail on this new sea because there is new knowledge to be gained, and new rights to be won, and they must be won and used for the progress of all people. . . . [O]nly if the United States occupies a position of pre-eminence can we help decide whether this new ocean will be a sea of peace or a new terrifying theater of war. . . . We choose to go to the moon. We choose to go to the moon in this decade and do the other things, not because they are easy, but because they are hard, because that goal will serve to organize and measure the best of our energies and skills, because that challenge is one that we are willing to accept, one we are unwilling to postpone, and one which we intend to win, and the others, too. . . . And, therefore, as we set sail we ask God's blessing on the most hazardous and dangerous and greatest adventure on which man has ever embarked.[142]

JFK's Rice address captured the essence of America—a nation willing to do the difficult because no one else could, or would. He emphasized exploration for the sake of science, because true exploration can only come from a nation committed to liberty. Only through the give and take of free thought and the scientific method could such grand efforts take place, as the Soviets, who were soon to be eclipsed, would see. Freedom's chariots came in many forms, many ways. Kennedy's commitment to world preeminence, more than even the actual moon landing itself in 1969, epitomized the exceptional American commitment to liberty. Except for his Berlin speech in June 1963, in which Kennedy noted that while democracy wasn't perfect, "We have never had to put a wall up to keep our people in," his speech dedicating the United States to placing a man on the moon would be the last truly visionary American address for the next twenty years. The optimism and hope associated with exploring space would darken, then vanish as Americans—and the world—gradually lowered their eyes toward a darkened earth.

CHAPTER FOUR

Castles Made of Sand

TIME LINE

1960:   John F. Kennedy elected president; French generals' mutiny in Algeria

1961:   Bay of Pigs (Cuba); Laotian Agreement establishes neutralist government; Vienna Summit; Berlin Wall built; China's Great Leap Forward fails; cosmonaut Yuri Gagarin first man in space; JFK begins sending eighteen thousand military advisers to South Vietnam

1962:   Cuban missile crisis; John Glenn makes first U.S. orbital spaceflight; France grants Algeria independence (Evian Accords); Students for a Democratic Society (SDS) issues Port Huron Statement; Sino-Indian War; first Walmart store opens; food riots in USSR; Beatles record first album; American involvement in South Vietnam escalates

1963:   American travel to Cuba made illegal; CIA establishes domestic operations division; Beatles release first album; Buddhist riots in South Vietnam; South Vietnamese president Diem overthrown and murdered; JFK assassinated

1964:   First draft card burning; Civil Rights Act of 1964 passed, abolishing segregation; Gulf of Tonkin incident; Congress gives President Johnson war powers; Beatles arrive in America; Johnson reelected

1965:   Great Society programs announced; Malcolm X assassi-
         nated; American combat units sent to Vietnam; Johnson
         sends troops to Dominican Republic; Social Security Act
         of 1965 establishes Medicare and Medicaid; immigration
         bill abolishes quotas based on national origins; Affirma-
         tive Action made law by executive order

1966:   Cultural Revolution in China; France withdraws from
         NATO; NATO HQ moved to Brussels; Black Panther
         Party founded; Soviet Union expels all Chinese students;
         France and USSR sign nuclear research treaty

1967:   British steel industry nationalized; Six-Day War; China
         conducts successful H-bomb test; hippie culture takes
         hold in San Francisco in the Haight-Ashbury district
         during the Summer of Love

1968:   Tet Offensive; Johnson announces he will not run again;
         Czechoslovakian Prague Spring liberalization crushed by
         Warsaw Pact troops; first statewide teachers' union strike
         (Florida); Martin Luther King, Jr., assassinated; Robert F.
         Kennedy assassinated; Civil Rights Act of 1968 passed;
         hippies and Yippies disrupt Democrat National Conven-
         tion in Chicago; Richard Nixon elected president

1969:   Nixon's "Silent Majority" speech; Woodstock Music Fes-
         tival; Apollo 11 moon landing; Nixon orders first with-
         drawal of U.S. troops from Vietnam; draft lottery
         reinstated

1970:   Polish food riots suppressed by Polish troops

The Kennedy Mystique

John F. Kennedy's call for a national program to put a man on the moon
reflected the purported idealism of his administration, named "Camelot"
by the press (after the popular musical), which upheld an absurdly and artificially concocted fantasy-universe view of the White House. In reality,
construction of the Camelot myth began long before JFK ever set foot on
Pennsylvania Avenue, as virtually his entire life was staged to craft the image of a heroic president in life, then a martyr in death. Jack, as he was
known to his friends, burst on the national scene in World War II, when his

PT-109 exploits in the Pacific captured the imagination of an American public starved for heroes. No critic has doubted his resourcefulness in rescuing the survivors, but the rest of the story was a magnificently successful exercise in political myth making, largely undertaken by his father, Joseph Kennedy, Sr. Indeed, most other commanders would have been court-martialed for their malfeasance, not catapulted to the presidency. But with Kennedy, the United States had its first true media president, elected far more for his celebrity status than for any actual accomplishments. He would not be the last.

Born in 1917, not long after the United States entered World War I, John Kennedy was the second son of an Irish Catholic family whose patriarch made a fortune bootlegging rum, then, after booze became legal, added to his wealth by purchasing dirt-cheap stocks during the Great Depression. Joe Kennedy had been tapped by FDR to head the new Securities and Exchange Commission with the famous line, "It takes a thief to catch a thief." Later, in 1938, FDR made the very questionable choice of appointing Kennedy as ambassador to Great Britain, despite his well-established antipathy toward England. He showed pro-Nazi and anti-Semitic attitudes, followed Neville Chamberlain's appeasement line, became defeatist, opposed giving aid to Britain, and fled London to avoid the Blitz. Quoted in the *Boston Sunday Globe* on November 10, 1940, while temporarily back in the United States, Kennedy said, "Democracy is finished in England, it may be here."[1] FDR forced him to resign later in the month.

The Kennedy family had their sights set on power early, and Joe carefully positioned his eldest son, Joe Jr., born two years ahead of Jack, for a life in American politics, with his eyes on the Oval Office. Joe dutifully matriculated at Harvard, then the London School of Economics, and returned to Harvard for law school. World War II intervened at a time when military valor was viewed by the public at large as a sine qua non for a political career, and so Joe Jr. joined the Navy as an aviator to fly antisubmarine patrols. Stationed in England in 1944, he volunteered for the extremely dangerous Operation Aphrodite, which transformed bombers taken out of service into missiles laden with explosives aimed at heavily fortified German emplacements, such as U-boat pens or V-1 launch sites.[2] On what proved to be his final mission, the eldest Kennedy son and another crew member flew an explosive-loaded Liberator bomber, planning to bail out when the plane was in its final run. But the explosives went off early, killing both men. Joe Jr. was recommended for the Medal of Honor by his commanding officer, Commander James Smith, but the medal was disallowed and he received a posthumous Navy Cross.[3] More than a few historians have questioned whether in fact he recklessly disregarded a number of warnings about the detonators, and some argue he acted out of a desire to match Jack's heroics a year earlier, which were already well known.[4]

Jack, meanwhile, had also joined the Navy, and was assigned to Naval Intelligence in Washington, D.C. There, his womanizing (following the example of his father) quickly got him in trouble. Among his liaisons, he was linked to Inga Arvad, the Swedish beauty known to the FBI as "Inga Binga," a Nazi sympathizer whom the bureau watched closely under suspicion of being a German spy. Kennedy's compromised position forced Joe Sr., alerted by administration insiders, to intervene. He secured an assignment for Jack to the Pacific, where Lieutenant Kennedy ended up in command of PT-109 in January 1943. During a night patrol in the Blackett Strait while awaiting a return run of Japanese destroyers in the "Tokyo Express," he exhibited amazing lethargy. Standing at the wheel as his boat idled on one engine, he was suddenly warned by a crewmember that a ship was closing fast. Kennedy sounded general quarters, but only at the last second did he spin the wheel to escape. The Japanese took more effective action, and Kennedy watched as the destroyer *Amagiri* turned toward him and sliced his boat in two. Jack's boat went up in a ball of fire—the only PT boat during the war to be rammed by a larger and slower vessel. It remained partially afloat, and by morning the men clung to a large board, which they paddled toward an island. Two men had died, and of the ten survivors (plus Kennedy) two were badly hurt. Kennedy pulled an injured crewman through the water by a tether he clinched in his teeth. It took them four hours to reach the uninhabited Plum Pudding Island about three and a half miles away, in the midst of Japanese-held or -patrolled territory. After several days they were rescued, thanks in large part to the efforts of an Australian naval coast watcher, Lieutenant Arthur Evans.

With Jack safe, Joe Sr. ensured that a writer recorded the events surrounding the loss of PT-109 with the proper spin, then further guaranteed publication of the story (and national visibility for Jack) in *Reader's Digest*. Although the Kennedy family hagiographers papered over Jack's actions, evidence suggests he did not have his crew on high alert—two men were sleeping, two more lying down—and if there were lookouts, they never spotted the destroyer, no small ship, when visibility was a good 1,500 yards, according to a sailor on another PT boat in Kennedy's flotilla.[5] The radioman was not on duty; another PT boat tried to warn Kennedy, but received "No response. Nothing."[6] Yet the destroyer captain had time to spot and open fire on the tiny torpedo boat from his forward gun turret, then alter his course to ram and avoid a torpedo attack.[7] Kennedy later lied, saying he had actually *attacked* the destroyer; did nothing to disprove the bogus story that he made three swims from the wreckage to the rescue island; and completely cut out Evans's report that actually saved the crew. Evans saw the whole episode and had already sent messages calling for rescue parties before Kennedy's famous coconut message was scrawled.[8] But even JFK later admitted he didn't think the rescue operation had been botched, and that his heroism was involuntary. After all, he reasoned, "they sank my boat."

Though Kennedy originally was recommended for the Silver Star, his award was downgraded to the Navy and Marine Corps medal after cooler heads prevailed, and even then it took the intervention of Navy Secretary James Forrestal to procure that. To have lost one of the most nimble vessels in the Navy in a broad strait with good visibility was no easy feat. But the myth was already growing; *Reader's Digest* ran a condensed story by *New Yorker* writer John Hersey that repeated and enhanced Kennedy's heroics. By itself, the incident would have constituted just another mix-up in the chaotic fog of war, as when one of the flag raisers at Iwo Jima was not properly recognized at a time when the others achieved unwanted celebrity status.[9] For Kennedy, the event became an outstanding punch in his ticket to greatness—handled as it was for public consumption.

The episode reflected on Kennedy's character, which was already under some suspicion for his "book," *Why England Slept*, a 150-page college paper published in 1940 that Joe Sr. had funneled to Arthur Krock of *The New York Times*, an ally and mouthpiece. Krock helped JFK rewrite the thesis (including verbatim sections that Kennedy simply injected into the work), then Joe Kennedy's personal speechwriter was assigned to rewrite it again. He would call it a "mismash, ungrammatical, [with] sentences without subjects and verbs. It was a very sloppy job, mostly magazine and newspaper clippings stuck together."[10] Few read it, but JFK could use it as evidence that he was a writer and an intellectual.

Kennedy's writing (even ghosted by others) also enabled him to claim the status of a journalist. It was one reason the press loved JFK so much—he was, after all, "one of them"—and he briefly worked for the Hearst newspapers, covering the first United Nations meetings in San Francisco. But even then, his immediate intention was to run for office. In 1946, he was handed a safe district in Massachusetts, where he lived in a hotel room to establish residency. Kennedy won the primary, then defeated the Republican opponent for the House. In 1952, he became a senator after defeating Republican

Henry Cabot Lodge, Jr. JFK took politics seriously. He worked with a tape recorder to improve his delivery. He walked the streets and kissed babies, living on candy and ice cream, occasionally collapsing from fatigue.[11] Joe's cash, to the tune of perhaps a quarter million dollars, didn't hurt either, and Jack defeated Lodge with the ease of "an elephant squashing a peanut."[12]

In the Senate, he spent much of his time literally on his back, suffering through several spinal operations. When he could get to the Senate chambers, he supported compromise on civil rights legislation that appeased some southerners, but thanks to majority leader Lyndon Johnson's procedural maneuvering, his votes were shielded from harming him seriously. During the McCarthy censure, JFK was in the hospital and did not vote. In short, whether through physical incapacity or through the protection offered by Johnson, Kennedy emerged from the Senate never having to take a controversial stand on anything. Moreover, his experience with logrolling and compromising essentially amounted to "Let Lyndon handle it." This strategy for a potential presidential candidate to never show his ideological cards while in elected office was classic, and set the standard for later elections.

JFK's life was a tissue of fabrications and public relations. Afflicted with Addison's disease (a chronic autoimmune illness that attacks the adrenal glands and causes sluggishness or extreme weakness) and congenital back problems, as a boy and young man, he spent endless hours in hospitals, often in great pain.[13] He referred to himself as "the pet of the hospital," and his bowel problems resulted in his being subjected to several enemas a day.[14] The family was concerned: Kennedy suffered not only from the typical childhood afflictions of chicken pox and ear infections, but from a recurring set of illnesses whose symptoms included dizziness, hives, extreme fatigue, weight loss, coughs, flulike symptoms, knee and back pain, and asthma. After his death, Jack's brother Bobby would note, "At least one half of the days he spent on this earth were days of intense physical pain."[15] JFK once told his boyhood friend LeMoyne "Lem" Billings that he would trade all his wealth and political successes "just to be out of pain."[16] But even his physical ailments were spun in such a way as to boost his public image. Kennedy and the family put forth stories that his health issues were a result of football injuries, further aggravated by his Navy service.

In order to cope with the pain, Jack had to undergo a steady stream of cortisone injections from his own doctor, as well as supplementing them with visits from New York doctor Max Jacobson, known to New York elites as "Dr. Feelgood." Beginning in September 1960, just before the first presidential debate, Jacobson secretly provided Kennedy with injections that included a mix of vitamins, steroids, amphetamines, and numerous other ingredients he did not divulge. They improved Kennedy's mood and relieved his pain, making Jacobson so important that he flew with JFK to Vienna. Others, however, could detect the symptoms of such drugs on the president. The outgoing White House physician, General Howard Snyder, watched the inauguration and saw Kennedy sweating profusely despite standing in frigid weather. Snyder exclaimed, "He's all hopped up!"[17]

Reporters may not have known about Dr. Feelgood, but they did know about Kennedy's Addison's disease—because Lyndon Johnson's presidential campaign cochair, India Edwards, told them—and they kept it secret.[18] How much they knew about his other health problems, and hid them, is a matter of dispute. At the very least, the news media willingly covered up medical issues that the public not only had a right to know, but which could have directly affected Kennedy's performance and judgment as president. When Dr. Snyder learned of Kennedy's cortisone shot regimen, he said, "I hate to think of what might happen to the country if Kennedy is required at three A.M. to make a decision affecting the national security."[19]

Other features of John Kennedy made for entertaining reading and bolstered the public perception that he was somehow exceptional and admirable. He had a pretty wife, Jacqueline Bouvier, whose class Joe simply could not buy. Jack, however, relentlessly cheated on her. And JFK had a winning smile, anti-Communist foreign policy credentials, married to the appropriate domestic concerns for social justice.

John Kennedy's cold warrior status was unquestioned, though he was hardly a deep strategic thinker on that issue or the economy (or much else for that matter: Kennedy's "intellectualism" was as much a creation of the family mythmakers and propagandists as his health). In 1955, JFK "wrote" *Profiles in Courage*, a collection of senatorial biographies that won a Pulitzer Prize. He claimed to be the book's sole author, but later very credible evidence surfaced that indicated his speechwriter, Ted Sorensen, actually wrote much if not most of the book. This was the subject of open discussion on television in 1957 between correspondents Drew Pearson and Mike Wallace, with Pearson saying that "Jack [needed] . . . less profile and more courage."[20]

JFK, as per Joe's grand strategy, had been positioning himself for the presidential nomination of 1960 since his early years in the Senate. Outmaneuvering Adlai Stevenson for the Democratic nomination, Kennedy had the great fortune to run in the first era of political television, which played to his physique, his hair, and his grin. While campaigning, he took a simple, tried-and-true Democrat approach to the Eisenhower years: whatever Ike did was wrong. Thus he campaigned on an infamous "missile gap" representing the lead that Eisenhower had supposedly permitted the Soviets to gain in nuclear weapons. It proved a complete fraud and another of Jack's lies when, immediately after the election, more accurate numbers of the U.S. arsenal surfaced. Candidate Kennedy had been briefed extensively on American and Soviet strengths, but Kennedy's opponent, Vice President Richard Nixon, could not provide specifics without revealing classified data, and thus had to content himself with offering generic defenses to Kennedy's charges. Nixon had astoundingly bad luck, too: a bout of phlebitis in the critical final weeks of the campaign, just before the televised debate, made the healthier of the two candidates look sickly, while Kennedy, reportedly serviced by a call girl immediately prior to his televised debate, appeared tanned, vibrant, and energetic.[21] On camera, the difference was stunning, and Nixon's makeup, horrid. "My God!" Chicago mayor Richard Daley exclaimed. "They've embalmed him before he even died."[22]

Then there was Bobby, a force Nixon could not match: Bobby "gave new meaning to the term 'hardball,'" telling state and county organizations that their survival was unimportant.[23] Stevenson called Bobby the "Black Prince," while Ike, who called JFK "Little Boy Blue," referred to Bobby as "that little shit."[24] All that mattered to Bobby was getting his brother elected. Robert had been assistant counsel on the Senate Subcommittee on Investigations, appointed by Senator Joe McCarthy, and he ferociously pursued Communists for the senator. Bobby was so loyal to McCarthy that he walked out in protest during a speech by Edward R. Murrow, who had vehemently attacked McCarthy.[25] Now Bobby became the bagman for the Kennedy campaign, rewarding loyalists with hard cash, and also the enforcer, threatening wavering Democrats with political extinction.

Jack also benefited from the ruthless big-city Democratic political machines (the Republicans in most states having forgotten bare-knuckle politics after Reconstruction). In Chicago, Mayor Daley, doing his imitation of Christ, managed to resurrect dead voters to provide the winning votes. Ultimately Kennedy won by a razor-thin margin of 118,000 votes out of 68.8 million cast, with virtually all of JFK's edge coming in Illinois and Texas, where his vice presidential candidate Lyndon Johnson—himself notorious for producing phantom voters—helped carry the Lone Star State. In Illinois, Daley held back the vote count announcements of Cook County until he determined that Nixon led by 3,000 votes, at which point Kennedy aide Dick Donahue ecstatically yelped, "He's got them! Daley made them go first! He's still holding back—watch him play his hand now!"[26] The presumption was that, knowing the number he had to beat, Daley would manufacture sufficient votes. As the saying went, "It isn't who votes that counts, but who counts the votes."

Nixon, in one of the great acts of political altruism in American history, ranking alongside John Adams's pausing to allow Thomas Jefferson the opportunity to challenge electors in the 1796 roll call, refused to employ lawyers or call for a recount. Asking for a recount was well within his rights, given the closeness of the vote, but Nixon thought it would damage the electoral system. Nixon's biographer Stephen Ambrose admitted that "no one can know . . . which of the two candidates the American people chose in 1960."[27] Eisenhower appeared ready to urge a recount, arguing he "felt he owed it to the people to assure them . . . that the federal government did not shirk its duty."[28] At the same time, a recount would have likely taken a year with the technology and voting machines of the day, and Nixon mulled over the prospect of setting a bad example for nations abroad, "who for the first time were trying to put free electoral procedures into effect, [seeing] the United States wrangling over the results of our presidential election, and even suggesting that the presidency itself could be stolen. . . ."[29] Nixon had nearly pulled off a miracle: without the enthusiastic backing of the incumbent president, facing a younger, more physically appealing, richer candidate, against a heavy disparity in the number of registered Democrats over Republicans, opposed by the national media, and saddled with a record he had not helped craft, he still got half the votes!

Doubtless the segregationist U.S. senator Harry Byrd of Virginia—just one of many Democrats whose racism was conveniently forgotten or ignored by the media in subsequent decades as reporters attempted to portray the GOP as the party of racism—would have boosted Kennedy's margin further had he not been in the race, as his Democratic votes would have gone to JFK. On the other hand, Kennedy benefited from overwhelming support among Catholics and blacks; certainly, too, the fraud in Illinois and Texas helped immensely.[30] (Even sympathetic Kennedy biographer Robert Dallek admitted that Daley "probably stole Illinois from Nixon," but hedged by saying that Texas still would have gone for Jack—a dubious assertion.)[31] *Slate* magazine, hardly a right-wing bastion, admitted that the "question [of fraud in Illinois] remains unsolved and unsolvable," and the fact that "multiple election boards saw no reason to overturn the results" was hardly surprising in that they were Illinois election boards.[32] The *Chicago Tribune* concluded that "the election of November 8 was characterized by such gross and palpable fraud as to justify the conclusion that [Nixon] was deprived of victory."[33]

Once in office, Kennedy repudiated some items in his campaign platform, such as quietly acknowledging that the missile gap did not exist. But he was obsessed with another issue, the nation of Laos, where a Communist insurgency was under way. Even though it was not in the news, Laos was viewed as the "cork in the bottle," as Ike's aides had called it when they briefed Kennedy. Its collapse, they thought, could trigger the demise of Thailand and the Philippines. Given the recent eviction of the French from (now) North Vietnam and the expansionist rhetoric of Communist China, both Ike and Kennedy had reason to be concerned with Laos. The United States had already seen evidence of the "domino effect" in Eastern Europe; as Communists gained a foothold in one country, they would begin expanding into the next until the whole line of dominoes fell. Closer to home, there was also a threat from the Communist island of Cuba, which posed an immediate concern.

Kennedy saw none of these problems as insurmountable if he could apply enough brain power and skill. He sought to seed his cabinet with the so-called best and the brightest, summoning Harvard liberals Arthur Schlesinger, John Kenneth Galbraith, and Seymour Harris for service, and tapping his family for either direct appointments (Bobby at Justice) or as key advisers in the interim (Sargent Shriver, his brother-in-law, who headed the "talent search"). He brought in the old Massachusetts mafia of Ted Sorensen, Kenny O'Donnell (the primary procurer of women for Kennedy's private trysts), Pierre Salinger as press secretary, and Lawrence O'Brien (JFK's campaign manager), along with Wall Street banker C. Douglas Dillon (Treasury) and Robert McNamara (Defense), two liberal Republicans.

More than any other, McNamara's choice would prove critical and controversial. Described as "tidy" and possessing "decisive efficiency in putting over dubious policies," McNamara was the first real finance man to ascend to the top position in any auto company.[34] Having served in the Army Air Corps's Office of Statistical Control in World War II, McNamara became obsessed with numbers. He analyzed bombing efficiency, building metrics for effectiveness, and constructed schedules to maximize resource use. His efforts were praised, and he was discharged as a lieutenant colonel with a Legion of Merit. Strictly a staff man, McNamara avoided all production and operational experience, and his worldview boiled down to a tale told by raw data.

Taking the podium at the House of Representatives on January 30, 1961, Kennedy laid out a decisive message of hard-line action, and immediately set his sights on the Soviets: "Each day, the crises multiply. . . . Each day, we draw nearer the hour of maximum danger, as weapons spread and hostile forces grow stronger . . . the tide of events has been running out—and time is not our friend."[35] Aware that his youth and inexperience could constitute a problem and cognizant of the previous decade's revelations of Communist infiltration in the government, Kennedy decided to be tough on the Soviets. His first actions not only set the tone for the next two years, but dramatically shaped the Soviet-U.S. relationship over the next decade.

The First Test: Cuba

The easiest and most obvious target of action for Kennedy was Cuba. During the campaign, Kennedy had ratcheted up the rhetoric against the new Communist dictator, Fidel Castro, in hopes of short-circuiting an invasion by Eisenhower (which would have ensured the election of Nixon). As president, though, Kennedy discovered a thornier problem; any move against Cuba—in itself, easy enough, given American forces—would be offset by a Soviet move against Berlin, where the Russians had the advantage. The United States could not risk war over the American commitment in Germany. True liberals in the administration, such as Arthur M. Schlesinger, Jr., bristled at the idea of invading Cuba. But pragmatists knew Kennedy needed to bolster his hard-line credentials and bring them in line with his rhetoric. A scaled-down operation, code-named Zapata, was hastily drafted. Almost as quickly, the plan was leaked to the press by liberals opposing it. Kennedy exploded, "All [Castro] has to do is read our papers!"[36]

More than a few within the administration thought the cleanest solution involved simply removing Castro, a task the CIA's Allen Dulles embraced. Dulles, under Eisenhower, already had established Operation 40, a band of forty officials and agents working in the Caribbean and particularly Cuba, that evolved into an assassination network. According to Frank Sturgis, one of its members, Operation 40 concentrated its hits extensively on Cuba. Bobby Kennedy found these covert activities useful, saying, "My idea is to stir things up on the island with espionage, sabotage, general disorder" using Cuban exiles.[37] What Bobby failed to include in his list of actions to stir things up was the most important item, assassinating Castro, which the Kennedy administration and CIA were bent on doing. When the first wave of attempts by the CIA itself failed, the Agency brought in the Mafia, in one instance providing poison pills to Mafia don John Roselli in Miami to use on the Cuban dictator.

No paper trail apparently exists of either a JFK assassination go order, or direct contacts between Kennedy and the mob (presumably for the purposes of orchestrating a hit on Castro), but leading historians agree the connections were real and that Kennedy was kept in the loop about the impending attempts on Castro's life.[38] In fact, the president's involvement went much deeper. By approving Operation Mongoose in November 1961 at a budget of $50 million per year, JFK put into play "four hundred American employees, two thousand Cuban agents, a small navy and air force, and more than fifty business fronts. Its headquarters in Miami became for a time the world's largest CIA station."[39] Mongoose also reactivated the Mafia hit on Castro. Questioned later by Congress about what, exactly, he was told to do, the CIA's Richard Helms said his directions were to "get rid of Castro," and he "assumed that meant by any means necessary." General Edward Lansdale, supervising Mongoose, said in 1975 that Kennedy had an intermediary deliver orders to remove Castro, including by assassination if necessary.[40]

Eliminating foreign leaders who stood in the way of Kennedy's view of progress was commonplace in Camelot, and Castro had plenty of company in Kennedy's gunsight. Under the Alliance for Progress, an economic program designed to counteract Communist influence in Latin America, a rash of new military coups ensued (six in 1962–63 alone), and military juntas were established in Bolivia and Ecuador, which were already under military control. Many of these dictators rubbed JFK the wrong way, and in some cases, the United States sought to reverse the coups. The CIA spent $5 million to destabilize Brazil's João Goulart, and JFK let the Brazilian military know that he would support a coup against Goulart's government.[41] A "country-by-country, crisis-by-crisis standard" of aid would be offered to Latin American regimes.

But it was General Rafael Trujillo of the Dominican Republic, assassinated in May 1961 by a coup backed and supplied by the CIA, who was the first real casualty of Kennedy's policies. No shrinking violet, Trujillo had attempted to bomb Venezuela's president Rómulo Betancourt; acquiesced in (or ordered) the murder of the Mirabal sisters, who had opposed his regime; and repressed black Haitians in favor of Caucasians (this policy extended to admitting Jewish refugees during the 1930s). Yet he was scarcely different from many Third World dictators, including Castro. Over subsequent years, Kennedy court hagiographers attempted to deflect blame from

Jack for links to CIA-backed "removals"—even if it meant shifting the responsibility onto Bobby. Recent evidence has revealed that Juan Almeida, the commander of Cuba's army, was in on a coup to oust Castro (code named AMWORLD) and that his participation was kept secret throughout the Warren Commission and subsequent congressional investigations due to ongoing attempts to destabilize Cuba.[42]

One major mission that undeniably had Kennedy's full support was the Bay of Pigs operation. The operation relied entirely on the removal of Castro first, and was doomed when assassination plots failed. With only 1,400 Cuban exiles arrayed against Castro's army of 250,000, and a handful of CIA-supplied B-26 bombers to confront Castro's entire air force of jet fighters, forging ahead with the dictator still in power was sheer folly. Attacks on Cuban airfields began on April 15, 1961, and two days later transport ships landed the exiles. They came under air attack immediately, and within a day, Cuban regular forces had recaptured most lost areas. Most fighting was over by April 19.

Kennedy's support for the operation had vacillated from the beginning, and to a large degree, he was carried along due to his confidence in Richard Bissell, who was heading up the effort, having been chosen by Kennedy to take over the CIA in July from Allen Dulles.[43] But there was no doubt that promises had been made to the Cuban exiles making up the Cuban Brigade. In the words of one of the exiles' leaders, former Cuban premier José Miró Cardona, "I had an understanding they would send in the troops, if necessary, and give us what was required to make this thing succeed."[44] Kennedy gave the go-ahead on the invasion, but strongly rejected any attempt to involve U.S. troops when it became clear it would not succeed. "Under no circumstances!" he yelled at his aides who recommended sending supporting troops. "The minute I land one Marine, we're in this thing up to our necks. . . . I'm not going to risk an American Hungary. And that's what it could be, a fucking slaughter."[45] UN ambassador Adlai Stevenson, irate about the invasion and obsessed with world opinion, fumed about Kennedy's "boy commandos." American embassies in Warsaw, Cairo, Tokyo, and New Delhi were stoned. Anti-American students marched in Mexico City and throughout Latin America.

Landing at the Bay of Pigs, the exiles' forces were crushed—114 killed and 1,189 captured, many to be tortured or shot. Kennedy made a nonapologetic speech to the American Society of Newspaper Editors, then, astoundingly, cut off all further questions on the invasion: "I do not believe that such a discussion would benefit us during the present difficult, uh, situation."[46] The Camelot press meekly complied. Inside Washington, meanwhile, the president continued to gently slide responsibility for the fiasco to his advisers ("How could I have been so stupid as to let them go ahead?") or to Ike ("It was Eisenhower's Plan"). In fact, Kennedy never once gathered his entire Soviet team together to analyze whether, in fact, Khrushchev would retaliate in Berlin if the United States struck in Cuba. Denials were also forthcoming from Bobby, who wrote that neither he nor the president knew "that the Cuba forces were as good as they were and would fight."[47] Moreover, the spooked Almeida, commander of Cuba's army, demanded assurances from JFK that necessary support would be forthcoming if he went ahead with his coup against Castro, and in his Miami speech of November 18, 1963, Kennedy included several lines written specifically by CIA officer Seymour Bolton to reassure Almeida.[48]

Having been stung once by the foiled invasion, and numerous times by failed assassination attempts on Castro, Kennedy expressed reluctance to leap into other foreign fields. In Laos, the well-armed and well-backed (by North Vietnam) Communist Pathet Lao, active since 1950, were successfully pushing the American-backed Royal Laotian forces from most of the country. No regular U.S. troops were stationed there, only CIA advisers, and the number of military units involved remains murky as the North Vietnamese officially were not there either. American involvement had not started until 1958, when the first five-man team of CIA personnel arrived in Laos to assist the Royal Laotian forces in dealing with the, by then, some 7,500 Pathet Lao soldiers and their advisory group of PAVN (People's Army of Vietnam) officers and political commissars. In 1959, twelve Army Special Forces training teams of eight men each were dispatched to Laos under Operation Hotfoot. By 1960, the U.S. embassy's Program Evaluation Office had grown to 175 military and civilian personnel, and Special Forces deployments under Hotfoot to 107. A coup by supposed neutralist paratrooper captain Kong Le succeeded in taking control of the Plaine des Jarres, and with Soviet equipment pouring in, the Pathet Lao and Kong Le's troops went on the offensive. Royalist forces began to crumble, and Kennedy suddenly faced new challenges. Soviet, Czech, Chinese, and PAVN transport planes, equipment, fuel, armored vehicles, and all the means for waging war were stacked on the Plaine des Jarres, exposed to air attack.[49]

Effective resistance in Laos was offered only by Hmong tribesmen under the leadership of Vang Pao.[50] At the Geneva Conference on Laos in May 1961, the United States pressed for a political settlement of the situation in Laos, one that eventually involved the Communists in a governing partnership with the other two parties, the neutralists and royalists. It was the classic case of the camel putting his nose into the tent—from the establishment of a coalition government headed by the neutralist Souvanna Phouma, it was a foregone conclusion that the Communists would eventually seize control unless the United States intervened. At that time, the royalists boasted of 51,000 troops, but with severe problems in training and support, and they were opposed by 19,500 Communist Pathet Lao and 9,000 PAVN.

Whether Kennedy accepted the premise of Ike's dominoes, he certainly acted as though he did. Yet he couldn't go on the offensive and displayed an unwillingness to take the necessary next step and depose Ho Chi Minh in North Vietnam. Eisenhower had warned Kennedy about half-measures, especially inviting Communists to participate in the government: "Any time you permit Communists to have a part in the government of such a nation, they end up in control."[51]

Convinced he had solved Laos by agreeing to a coalition government, JFK jetted off to Vienna in June of 1961 for a summit with Khrushchev. Warned by Charles de Gaulle and others that the premier would steamroll him, Kennedy found his tepid democratic ideals and limited understanding of a free-market economy instantly overwhelmed by Khrushchev's aggressive tone and unabashed Communist ideology. Prep school roommate Lem Billings recalled that Khrushchev's bellicosity "absolutely shook" the president, who had never "come face to face with such evil before." Appropriately enough, JFK likened the episode to dealing with his father. After the summit, a sobered Kennedy admitted:

> I think he thought that anyone . . . so young and inexperienced as to get into that mess [with the Bay of Pigs] could be taken. . . . So he just beat hell out of me . . . I've got a terrible problem. If he thinks I'm inexperienced and have no guts, until we remove those ideas we won't get anywhere with him. So we have to act.[52]

Kennedy's impressions were correct: Khrushchev's aide Fyodor Burlatsky said his boss thought JFK acted more like "an advisor, not a political decision-maker or President."[53] Khrushchev later observed he browbeat the young president so brutally he could not help "feeling sorry for Kennedy." Nor were other leaders whom Kennedy encountered on the European trip impressed: Germany's Konrad Adenauer called him a "cross between a junior naval person and a Roman Catholic Boy Scout," directing a gaggle of "cooks," "whiz kids," and "prima donnas."[54]

Imprisoning Half of Europe

Convinced he had the measure of his American counterpart, Premier Khrushchev returned to Moscow and gave his approval for construction of the Berlin Wall. He would push Kennedy while the pushing was good, with one provocation after another until there was a response. It was just the latest Leninist probe-with-the-bayonet experiment.

On August 13, 1961, the East Germans sealed the border with West Berlin. The East-West German border running from the Baltic to Czechoslovakia had been effectively closed in 1952 by East Germany's introduction of a "special regime on the demarcation line." It was intended to eliminate all escape from the Communist side, but Berlin had remained a well-used escape route, since West and East Berliners traveled constantly back and forth. Between 1952 and 1961, 20 percent of the East German population, 3.5 million people, had fled to West Germany through West Berlin. Now that hole was filled, initially with a wire fence, but the border subsequently underwent three substantial upgrades, finally ending with a twelve-foot-high concrete wall. As viewed initially from the West, there was a cleared area from the border about twenty yards to a double barbed-wire fence, sometimes with trip-wire mines, concrete bunkers, and watchtowers with floodlights. Behind the towers were access roads, and all civilian inhabitants were moved back from the border, thereby creating a wide area into which any intrusion was a criminal offense. It went up so quickly that literally those who went to sleep on one side or the other spent the next twenty years there. Families were ripped apart with no concern from the Communist government. Escapes still continued, however, until both the East-West German and East-West Berlin borders were strengthened under the modern border program starting in 1967. After that point, escapes from East Germany were extremely rare.

Allies and enemies alike were shocked that the United States appeared to do nothing as the Wall was built. JFK attempted to deflect blame, feigning surprise and then later implying that once again (despite being fully apprised of the likelihood of Communist action) the CIA had failed to inform him. West Berlin mayor Willy Brandt said "the Soviet Union had defied the major power in the world and effectively humiliated it."[55] Intoxicated by his schooling of the young president, Khrushchev later told Interior Secretary Stewart Udall, "War in this day and age means no Paris and no France, all in the space of an hour. It's been a long time since you could spank us like a little boy—now we can swat your ass."[56]

In fact, the administration did persuade Congress to significantly boost military spending. Western allies rallied around West Berlin and solidified, with little prodding from Kennedy. Kennedy felt that he had lost Berlin already and was determined to act with caution, thereby frustrating Khrushchev's objective of provoking the United States into action that would have allowed the Soviets to occupy West Berlin with some legitimacy. The 2,300-man American Berlin Brigade remained in West Berlin as a trip wire for World War III, and, as many troops understood their role, to resist and die in the event of an attack in order to inflame the U.S. civilian population for war. What the American and German people didn't know was that the first line of defense against a Soviet invasion of West Germany was in reality the Rhine River—which would cede the vast majority of West German territory to the Red Army while fighting only delaying actions.

It slowly began to dawn on the Camelot crew that the Soviets saw Berlin, Laos, nuclear testing, and Cuba as intertwined parts of a Stalinesque offensive, and that Berlin was a city to be "internationalized," or put under East German control. Kennedy rationalized that the original Yalta and Potsdam agreements for free elections in the two Germanys were "not serious," a view that would have shocked Harry Truman. On September 24, Kennedy gave a speech to the UN General Assembly and called for "Established rights to be respected" and that ". . . we believe a peaceful agreement is possible which protects the freedom of West Berlin and Allied presence and rights, while recognizing the historic and legitimate interests of others in assuring European security." In Moscow the speech was interpreted as another sign of weakness.[57] When the U.S. military announced it was going to reinstitute military patrols on the autobahn to West Berlin, Marshal Konev denounced the move as a provocation. Kennedy backed down again. West Berliners assumed it was merely a question of time before their sectors were taken over by the Communists.

Kennedy decided to rattle his saber. He knew the Soviets had only thirty-five operational intercontinental ballistic missiles (ICBMs) while the United States possessed hundreds of ICBMs, augmented by at least six Polaris subs, each armed with sixteen missiles, as well as hundreds of land-based bombers. The administration allowed a Defense Department deputy, Roswell Gilpatric, to publicly cite American missile levels in an October 1961 speech as part of Jack's frantic effort to dispel the illusion of Soviet superiority. Aware of Soviet resident agents (later termed "moles" by novelist John le Carré) within the defense services of allies, McNamara held a series of classified briefings for friendly nations which, the administration knew, would result in the information being transmitted immediately to Moscow. In response to Kennedy's attempts to flex his muscles, Khrushchev resumed testing of atomic bombs in October 1961 with the "Tsar Bomba," the most powerful nuclear weapon ever detonated (about fifty megatons). He simultaneously sent JFK a twenty-six-page personal letter appealing to him to resume negotiations over Laos and Berlin. He refused to let Kennedy score any points whatsoever, and responded with classic Communist deception and disinformation. Laos was exactly what the Russians wanted it to be—it had a neutralist-dominated coalition government making steady concessions to the Pathet Lao, while West Berlin hung like a ripe plum ready to fall at any time.

Laos, the Bay of Pigs, the Vienna summit, the Berlin Wall, the autobahn patrols, and the nuclear tests all constituted diplomatic losses that took a toll on Kennedy. He confided to James Reston that Khrushchev most likely had concluded that "I'm inexperienced. Probably thinks I'm stupid. Maybe most important, he thinks that I have no guts."[58] Despite high poll numbers, he increasingly fretted that everything was coming undone. Those concerns lay behind his decision to install recording systems in the Oval Office, the cabinet room, and the executive mansion's library. Sympathetic biographers portrayed the installation of the voice-activated Dictaphone system as Kennedy's wise contribution to history ("he knew how important a detailed contemporary record was to an accurate reconstruction of the past," as Robert Dallek put it).[59] It was the Bay of Pigs failure, however, that especially concerned Kennedy, although he justified installing the system by reasoning that if a nuclear war ever occurred, people would not have to ask "How did it all happen?" and have no answer.[60] Barbara Tuchman's book *The Guns of August* weighed heavily on his insistence that history understand the pressures and complexities of the president's decision-making process. At the same time, after only a year in office, Kennedy was already troubled by what he thought might already become significant stains on his legacy. The taping system could provide a buffer for the harsh glare of history. Although never as obsessed with image or appearances as his self-proclaimed protégé, Bill Clinton, some thirty years later, Kennedy nevertheless differed sharply from the present-oriented Eisenhower and Truman in always keeping one eye on the future.

By late 1961, both John and Robert Kennedy had concluded that the Communist threat in Cuba had to be removed, and accelerated Operation Mongoose efforts to kill Castro. McNamara shared their view: "The only way to get rid of Castro is to kill him . . . and I really mean it."[61] The Cuban dictator, realizing his frail position, worked assiduously to ally himself formally with the Warsaw Pact and the USSR. Khrushchev, unwilling to be drawn in, rejected both overtures, but increased Soviet trade with the island to $750 million. Castro insisted a new invasion was imminent, manipulating his own intelligence service into distorting evidence to support such a conclusion. His machinations placed Khrushchev in a box.

The pudgy Soviet dictator, while light-years away from Stalin's bloody tyranny, nevertheless knew what was expected of him. Born in Ukraine in 1894, Khrushchev had worked in factories and mines before Red October, then joined the Red Army. He had the foresight to ally himself with Stalinists and to befriend Stalin's wife after he moved to Moscow in 1929. As a result, he was propelled up the ranks of the Moscow party, then onto the Central Committee, before he became the political commissar at Stalingrad during World War II. Upon Stalin's death, only Lavrentiy Beria posed a significant threat to all the top officials, who united behind Khrushchev to execute Beria. This marked the last major power struggle in the USSR to end violently until the 1991 attempted coup.

Elevated to the top of the party in 1956, Khrushchev stunned the Soviet Congress with his "Secret Speech" denouncing Stalin's crimes. Some hoped he would usher in a more liberal Soviet regime, although he had supported all of Stalin's purges and personally approved thousands of arrests. Under Khrushchev's orders, thousands of political prisoners were released—not out of great compassion by the premier, but because he thought it would help unite the country behind his leadership. His "Virgin Lands" campaign, under which young volunteers would settle western Siberia and Kazakhstan and turn them into agricultural regions, saw early success before turning into an ecological disaster. Instead of solidifying Khrushchev's rule, many of these policies laid the groundwork for insurrections as dissidents began to speak domestically, not just against an individual party leader, but against all communism, and abroad as rebellious Poles and Hungarians saw an opportunity to break with the USSR.

Aware of the Soviet Union's serious scientific and technological disadvantages, Khrushchev hoped to project an illusion of Russian superiority with stunts such as the *Sputnik* flight. His visit to California in 1959 left him contemptuous of American life, although the information he gleaned about U.S. agriculture shook his confidence in the superiority of a "people's" production system. Crude and earthy, peasant-looking to the core, and not particularly well educated, Khrushchev often appeared out of control and erratic—precisely the characteristics that terrified the Kennedy White

House. Advisers were humiliated and insulted, internal enemies were berated and embarrassed (though, unlike in Stalin's time, not stood up before
firing squads), and world leaders at the UN were subjected to his temper,
culminating with the infamous shoe-banging incident in which, having already taken off his shoes in the General Assembly in anger over the U.S.
U-2 incursion into Soviet airspace, the premier began pounding the table
with his fist until his wristwatch fell off, at which point he grabbed his shoe
to continue hammering the surface.[62]

Minutes from Midnight

Although he had not gone to Harvard Business School, Khrushchev clearly
understood the rules of engagement in the practice of brinksmanship. Considered a cold war term, brinksmanship was (and remains) a technique of
management applied every day. Simply put, in a confrontation or negotiation between two individuals, the one who first threatens to become irrational, or clearly demonstrates exactly how far he will go, ultimately wins the
negotiation. When Khrushchev banged his shoe on the desk in the UN, he
sent a strong message to give him whatever he wanted, lest he blow up the
world. The rational person will always give in to an irrational maniac. But
Khrushchev had his own irrational maniac to deal with: Fidel Castro, whose
paranoia about pending invasions threatened to produce a conflict not of
Khrushchev's time or choosing. The crafty premier joined all the issues
together, hoping to use an established client state in Cuba to win concessions not even Stalin had been able to produce. He planned to install
medium-range ballistic missiles in Cuba, then spring the fait accompli on
Kennedy after the U.S. elections in November. His was a gamble of incredible proportions with extraordinary possibilities.

Because the so-called atomic clock marking the end of civilization
seemed to be moving close to midnight, it is worth examining the Cuban
missile crisis in some detail. Only then can one appreciate how close the
two superpowers came to extinction that October in 1962.

Khrushchev's plan was to ship medium-range R-12 missiles to Cuba in
September, along with Soviet technicians and other military units. With a
range of 1,300 miles, the missiles could possibly reach Washington and
certainly most major southern U.S. cities. The R-14s that would follow—
shipped in segments as rapidly as shipping resources permitted—possessed
a 2,300-mile range that would include Denver and North Dakota. In a single blow, Khrushchev would have overcome any Soviet deficiency in ICBMs.
At the very least, the missiles would provide a bargaining chip for the Turk-

ish Thors and Jupiters and to demand American withdrawal from West Berlin, give freedom of action to Cuba, possibly spur the repeal of the Monroe Doctrine, perhaps cause total withdrawal from Germany, and potentially even let Africa and Asia become the Soviet Union's exclusive spheres of interest. The premier only needed two months to build up his Cuban missile forces and make them operational. This would put him in an unbelievably powerful position to bully the young American president. Literally, anything Khrushchev might demand for the removal of his missiles would be an offer Kennedy couldn't refuse; the alternative would be the end of the world. Informed of the offer to deploy missiles on his island, Castro eagerly agreed. They will "serve as the salvation of the Cuban revolution," he told the Soviets. "Once more," the Maximum Leader proclaimed to the Cuban people, "I have raised the banner of rebellion."[63] The stakes, however, were far beyond Castro's comprehension.

Khrushchev didn't know that U.S. Army Intelligence had put together detailed photos and analyses of Soviet missile installations in the USSR and could tell the difference between SAMs (surface to air missiles), the medium-range ballistic missile R-12, and the intermediate-range ballistic missile R-14 from the air. In August, Soviet personnel began to arrive in Cuba, and the United States took notice. Suspicions were aroused by a number of reports in September as cargo ships arrived; CIA director John McCone and Senator Kenneth Keating of New York both received reports out of Cuba of missiles being emplaced, and Keating publicly released his information on the floor of the Senate. But Kennedy was slow to respond to the threat, and National Security Advisor McGeorge Bundy went on national television to debunk Keating's claims. After the suspension of American U-2 overflights of Cuba in September (due to a U-2 straying over Sakhalin Island and the loss of another over China), they resumed in October, and then only tardily.

America's first photographic evidence of the threat unfolded when U-2 flights revealed the presence of the R-12 medium-range missiles on October 14, at San Cristóbal, at which point the weapons had actually been in Cuba for over a month. The Soviets had started construction on nine sites with forty launchers, each supported by SAM missiles. JFK pored over the intelligence photos on October 16. "How do you know this is a . . . missile?" asked the president of an analyst. "The length of the missile, sir," came the response.[64] In the October 16 meeting of the NSC's executive committee, Kennedy, aware his options were disappearing with each passing minute, repeatedly prodded the experts as to when the missiles would be ready to fire. Above all, Kennedy blamed himself for misjudging Khrushchev yet again. "We certainly have been wrong. . . . Not many of us [in Washington] thought that [Khrushchev] was gonna put [missiles] in Cuba."[65]

Contrary to the Camelot myths perpetrated by Schlesinger and others, secret tape recordings of the NSC meetings show that only by October 1962 did Kennedy begin to appreciate his misjudgment of the Soviets. The tapes reveal extreme concern and great caution on JFK's part as his team walked through all possible outcomes of an invasion of Cuba. They also contain surprising evidence that the military was reluctant to undertake any action short of a full-scale invasion, lest it result in a Bay of Pigs II. Most of Jack's advisers agreed that in the process of such an attack, Castro had to go. McGeorge Bundy concluded "his *demon* is self-destruction, and we have to help him to that."[66] JFK was aware that Soviet influence in Cuba was rising, and General Curtis LeMay had produced a preinvasion bombing plan in September. Nonetheless, planning was proceeding slowly and deliberatively.

On Tuesday, October 16, fresh U-2 images outlined intermediate-range R-14 missiles being unloaded, these with a range to hit everything east of the Rocky Mountains. Any attack sufficient to guarantee the destruction of the missiles would certainly kill Russian technicians—and the CIA estimated there were six to eight thousand Soviets in Cuba, when in fact there were more than forty thousand.[67] Soviet deaths would prompt a Soviet response. The administration dithered the next four days, and JFK even went on a campaign trip through the Midwest. His alternatives seemed to boil down to an air strike or blockade of Cuba. A blockade would signal a willingness to negotiate, but at the same time, it might give the Soviets time to complete their installations. Kennedy worried that it brimmed with potential for accidents, which could quickly escalate into full-scale war.

Lost in the American assessment was an appreciation of the Soviet preparations. Their plan to emplace missiles in Cuba had been in operation since July, and involved eighty-five ships, 230,000 tons of supplies, and five missile regiments, three equipped with R-12s and two with R-14s, all of which possessed nuclear warheads. Other forces deployed to Cuba included four rifle regiments with tactical nuclear weapons, two cruise missile regiments with eighty nuclear warheads and sixteen launchers, a regiment of MiG-21 fighters, forty-eight attack bombers with nuclear bombs, a helicopter regiment, a missile patrol boat brigade, a submarine squadron, and two antiaircraft divisions.[68] On October 19, the Soviet 79th Regiment had declared its eight launchers combat ready with R-12s, and the "agricultural workers and students" were ready to fight in a struggle that would feature the use of nuclear weapons at every level.

The following day, Jack, chatting with his brother and Ted Sorensen, glumly admitted that even with a blockade "we are very, very close to war," then, adding a dose of Kennedy wit, quipped, "I hope you realize there's not enough room for everybody in the White House bomb shelter."[69] Two days later, Khrushchev met with his Presidium to discuss the situation. Nothing had been heard yet from the Americans, but the premier was convinced Operation Anadyr had been compromised and the missiles discovered. The next step would be up to Kennedy. Khrushchev believed an American invasion of Cuba to be a distinct possibility, and that was laden with danger to both sides. Soviet troops in Cuba possessed tactical nuclear weapons, and he was prepared to authorize the Soviet commander in Cuba to use them against American forces. Above all, Khrushchev equated the presence of Soviet medium-range R-12 missiles in Cuba with the American medium-range missiles in Turkey. To him there was no difference.

Meanwhile, Kennedy had conferred with the Senate Armed Services Committee, and they had stiffened his back. Georgia senator Richard Russell wanted an air strike followed up with an invasion, agreeing with General LeMay that war was inevitable, and sooner was better. Senator J. William Fulbright of Arkansas, normally a voice against military adventures, urged that an "all-out" invasion should be conducted as soon as possible. Kennedy, stung by the criticisms of his earlier defeats by Khrushchev, decided inaction was too dangerous both for the nation and for himself politically. He rejected air and ground action for the moment, but announced a blockade of Cuba on television in a national address on the evening of October 22. Privately he informed his advisers that if an attack was necessary, he would order that as well, but any attack would have to be kept secret even from the allies, "because otherwise we bitch it up."[70]

Khrushchev, apparently expecting some American action against Cuba, was relieved for the moment, as the Soviet forces were not yet fully deployed. The R-14 nuclear warheads were still on the Atlantic Ocean, specifically on a freighter near Kennedy's demarcation line, and without submarine or other naval protection. Khrushchev recalled most ships that had not reached Cuban waters, and redirected others to avoid a confrontation with the Americans. In Cuba, all Soviet forces were put on full combat alert. On October 23, the freighter with the twenty-four R-14 warheads docked in Cuba.

The quarantine line that stretched five hundred nautical miles from

Cuba would not go into effect until 11:00 A.M. on October 24, and that gave the Soviets time to frantically complete a number of installations. American Crusader aircraft overflew their sites at one thousand feet to record their progress, and both sides prepared for war. While the world held its breath, two Soviet cargo ships turned back from the line toward Europe, and it became clear the Soviets would respect Kennedy's quarantine. But the crisis was far from over, as both sides pondered their next actions. Kennedy allowed innocent-looking ships to pass the line, some even without inspection. The United States went ahead with its preparatory plans to invade Cuba with 120,000 troops, and the Soviets deployed their 42,000 troops for nuclear war, distributing target information to their operational missile sites.

Information that invasion plans were nearly finished—and the only thing holding Kennedy back was Khrushchev's "flexible policy"—went directly to the Kremlin. Suddenly realizing that JFK had reversed their positions by first becoming irrational instead of negotiating, Khrushchev understood that Kennedy was willing to end human civilization before giving in again. He had pushed JFK too far, and his forces in Cuba weren't sufficiently ready to force Kennedy to reconsider. Khrushchev sent a message to the president on the morning of October 26 through back-channel negotiations involving ABC correspondent John Scali and a KGB operative under diplomatic cover at the Soviet embassy, Alexander Feklisov. He proposed a solution in which the Soviets would pull the missiles out of Cuba in exchange for Kennedy's promise not to invade the island. In effect, Khrushchev didn't even try to take a strong negotiating position or attempt to get all he could with an opening offer. Scali immediately relayed this world-saving proposition to the White House and soon came back with Kennedy's response, telling Feklisov that the terms were acceptable. (Later, the Kennedy court historians would credit Kennedy with first suggesting the terms.)[71]

While this was going on through back channels, Khrushchev sent a formal message suggesting that in return for a promise not to attack Cuba, "the necessity for the presence of our military specialists would disappear."[72] The note indicated this shift in policy had "already been approved" by the Presidium, thus giving Khrushchev's overture formal support.[73] It had taken twelve hours to transmit this message. Meanwhile, the Soviets had trained three missiles with nuclear warheads on the Guantánamo Bay Naval Station, preparing to obliterate it under a mushroom cloud. Five of the six R-12 batteries had reached full combat readiness, and were aimed at targets in the United States. American B-52s stationed at Wright-Patterson Air Force Base in Ohio and elsewhere were airborne twenty-four hours a day with atomic bombs, ready to head for Russia.

While the two superpowers were apparently heading for mutual destruction, columnist Walter Lippmann opined that the United States ought to consider exchanging its missile sites in Turkey for the Soviet ones in Cuba. Khrushchev believed Lippmann was on intimate terms with the Kennedys—any such statement in the Soviet Union would have had approval from the highest levels—and assumed this was Kennedy's counterproposal for an agreement. Accordingly, Khrushchev sent another message on the October 27 that linked the removal of the Cuban missiles with the American withdrawal of the Thor-Jupiter missiles in Turkey—a new issue not previously on the table, in JFK's mind. That same day, Khrushchev met with Presidium members who "looked at me as though I was out of my mind or, what was worse, a traitor."[74] Complicating matters, a U-2 was shot down over Cuba; another U-2 was forced down in Alaska after straying over Soviet airspace; and the United States touched off a test atomic bomb at Johnston Island in the North Pacific. In addition, Castro told Khrushchev that an American invasion was imminent.

One could sense the atomic clock reaching midnight. Hastily, Bobby met with Soviet ambassador Anatoly Dobrynin, telling him the U.S. military was nearly out of the president's control—an astounding statement to a representative of a militaristic power that was planting missile sites ninety miles off the American coast like so many daffodils. But the sheer unreasonableness of the statement made it all the more believable and persuasive. Bobby informed Dobrynin that JFK would be willing to provide a guarantee not to invade Cuba if the Soviets would withdraw, and that the United States would later withdraw the Thor and Jupiter missiles in Turkey, but would not formally include them in the current settlement.

When the Soviets received word that Kennedy was about to make a major speech the following morning, the Presidium felt it had only six hours to accept the deal offered by Bobby or, as they saw it, face nuclear annihilation. Khrushchev sent his assent to the deal, after telling the Presidium they had to defuse "the danger of war and nuclear catastrophe . . . To save the human race."[75] Kennedy had no such address planned. A mistake in intelligence had ended the crisis. On October 28, a Radio Moscow message began arriving in which the Soviet government had issued instructions to "dismantle the weapons . . . and to crate and return them" to the USSR.[76]

Khrushchev had blinked, and the world had avoided a nuclear holocaust. Blame would fly in all directions from the Soviet side after the crisis was resolved. Castro claimed Khrushchev had not informed him of the USSR's military weakness and imposed the missiles on Cuba; Khrushchev would allege that Castro was a madman, bent on war. In fact, Khrushchev played on the dark fears of a paranoid dictator who at various times had sought counsel from such level heads as Che Guevara. Castro needed no encouragement to act rashly. Michael Beschloss, whose comprehensive study of the missile crisis remains the best available, identified Raúl Castro (at his brother's instructions) as the instigator of the entire crisis during a July 1962 Moscow visit.[77]

Kennedy also was subject to scrutiny by both the pacifist Left, who thought he turned a minor issue into a near war, and the conservatives, who thought he settled for too little. Both "Castro and Russia did very well out of Khrushchev's brinkmanship," the conservative historian Paul Johnson claimed. "When Kennedy called Khrushchev's bluff, he had Russia at a disadvantage [and] Russia really had no alternative but to back down completely."[78] This analysis misses that the bluff never could have been called had Army Intelligence not given the CIA the capability of verifying the presence of Soviet missiles in Cuba. Khrushchev later was reported to have said, "Cuba was 11,000 kilometers from the Soviet Union. Our sea and air communications were so precarious that an attack against the United States was unthinkable."[79] But this was reported much later by Russian linguist and *Time* magazine correspondent on Soviet-American relations Strobe Talbott, whose relationship with the Soviets was somewhat controversial, and it's more likely that Khrushchev was surprised at Kennedy's resistance in the crisis. Nonetheless, had the U-2 flights not been resumed in October, Soviet preparations in Cuba might well have been completed before Kennedy was ready to confront the issue. At that point, Khrushchev would have held the upper hand, and his bluff would have been quite possibly not callable.

America enjoyed a substantial advantage in conventional forces, but while a Cuban invasion might have achieved its objective quickly, the tactical nuclear weapons possessed by Soviet forces on Cuba were already operational and under the control and discretion of commanders on the island for use. If nuclear shells had been fired at American forces, as seems likely, escalation would surely have followed. In addition, the Soviets easily could have counterattacked in Europe, possibly with fatal consequences. In hindsight it seems almost inconceivable that a nuclear holocaust was avoided. Kennedy, however, claimed a public relations victory while the Soviets emerged with the status quo ante in Cuba and the removal of the Thor-Jupiter missiles. Worse, the United States now had a permanent thorn in its Caribbean side.[80] It was a testament to the dangers of appeasement, inaction, poor decision making, and half-hearted measures.

In other respects, Kennedy similarly came up short. Throughout the president's first year and a half, both he and McNamara had failed to appreciate the Soviet interpretation of perfectly reasonable American terms, such as "taking the initiative" and "counterforce," both of which translated in Khrushchev's mind into "surprise attack on the USSR." Thus, the Soviet premier felt fully justified in wanting the Americans to feel what it was like to taste "a little of their own medicine."[81] Kennedy, even as the missiles were being installed, failed to understand Khrushchev's perspective and consistently ignored evidence that the so-called missile gap (now favoring the Americans) could be closed rapidly by the installation of shorter-range missiles in Cuba. Invoking the "Grand Design" to shape Europe's development while increasing the United States' power, in a Fourth of July speech in 1962 to dignitaries at Independence Hall, supposedly to tout a partnership of two equals—Europe and America—Kennedy unleashed a speech that was "sweeping in scope, messianic in tone, breathtakingly arrogant in concept, and wildly irresponsible in potential consequence" in an attempt to bind Europe to American leadership.[82] Khrushchev took all this in as a provocation.

Origins of the Vietnam Quagmire

Misperceptions and communications breakdowns almost led to a hot war in Cuba. Yet intrigue in Southeast Asia revealed much more severe and even dangerous disconnects between the superpowers, and, equally disconcerting, between the administration and rogue elements in both the State Department and the Central Intelligence Agency. The CIA distrusted Kennedy as unreliable, and the State Department (as it almost always has) saw itself as the sole voice of American diplomacy. Neither had completely fallen in line under JFK's leadership. Just as Kennedy thought he had an agreement over Laos wrapped up in 1962, the *Times* of London reported that the CIA was "actively opposing US policy in Laos and working against a neutral government," causing JFK to distrust the CIA even more than after the Bay of Pigs.[83] The only person Kennedy had trusted in the CIA had been Richard Bissell, the architect of the Bay of Pigs, and when that failed badly, Bissell was sacrificed. Like George W. Bush during the war on terror thirty years later, Kennedy was constantly undercut by both the "striped-pants boys" of the State Department and the CIA, telling his cabinet, "I just see an awful lot of fellows who . . . don't seem to have *cojones*."[84]

As Laos destabilized, Kennedy was immediately confronted with the revolutionary Viet Cong in South Vietnam, backed by North Vietnamese Communist leader Ho Chi Minh. Ho sought the overthrow of the nominally democratic government of Ngo Dinh Diem, and had quietly worked for months, with the support of the Russians, beneath the administration's radar. Ho Chi Minh ("He Who Enlightens," born Nguyen Sinh Cung), had attended the Versailles Treaty negotiations in Paris as a representative of the Vietnamese people (largely based on a single petition he made to the Allies), only to find that the treaty continued to support colonialism in Asia. Briefly before and during World War I, he worked in menial jobs in New York City, but became a founding member of the French Communist Party in the 1920s before traveling to the Soviet Union. In 1941, he returned to Vietnam and led the Viet Minh Communist resistance to the Japanese, for which he received substantial support from the American OSS. Well after World War II he continued to enjoy American favor. Ho came to idolize Americans, particularly Major Archimedes Patti, an OSS officer sent to organize Vietnamese resistance to the Japanese. Patti represented the United States as the only foreign government given a place of honor when the Democratic Republic of Vietnam officially came into existence on September 2, 1945. Patti stood next to General Vo Nguyen Giap on the stage.[85] Patti armed and supported Ho's troops, while taking care not to assist the French in any way. Thus, Ho's affection for Americans increased, and after an American colonel was shot by Viet Minh soldiers who thought he was French, Ho vowed no Americans would ever be killed again by his people except over his own dead body.

Kennedy, meanwhile, had steadily drifted toward full support of Ngo Dinh Diem, the Catholic premier of South Vietnam (a nation overwhelmingly Buddhist). He approved sending U.S. military advisers via the Southeast Asia Treaty Organization (SEATO), a regional mini-NATO constructed to enforce "containment." Insisting the United States would not become involved in a war on the Asian mainland, he nevertheless simultaneously built up the Army Special Forces, giving them exclusive rights to wear a distinctive green beret. General Maxwell Taylor, who supported putting in the first seven thousand military advisers, nevertheless warned the president that it would be "difficult to resist the pressure to reinforce," and that the ultimate commitment might be open-ended.[86] But at his final press conference in 1963, Kennedy reiterated, "we are going to stay there [in Vietnam]" and "for us to withdraw . . . would mean a collapse not only of South Vietnam but Southeast Asia."[87]

By November of that year, JFK had ordered a minimum of 17,000 American forces to Vietnam. In a little-referenced speech in Billings, Montana, in September 1963, Kennedy said that there were "over 25,000 of your sons and brothers bearing arms" in Southeast Asia, although it was not clear if he was also including naval forces and troops in Thailand.[88] The Joint Chiefs—when JFK would listen to them—consistently warned that it would take many, many more to purge the Viet Cong from South Vietnam. Their estimate was that victory in Vietnam needed between 700,000 and one million American troops, and would necessitate round-the-clock bombing of the North, perhaps even an invasion to defeat the then-17,000 North Vietnamese and Viet Cong in the South. Thus, the continued efforts by "Jackobites," as Kennedy consultant John P. Roche later called the Kennedy hagiographers, to shift the blame for Vietnam off Kennedy are absurd.[89] Up to the end, JFK insisted the United States would stay in Vietnam while simultaneously ignoring his own military's estimate of what it would take to win. Yet his tantalizing 1963 withdrawal of a single engineering unit whose task was completed has been the straw to which a generation of Kennedy apologists have clung as proof that JFK was "getting us out."

Ironically, the press, at one time Kennedy's biggest supporters, may have helped expand the Vietnam War. Kennedy began to view journalists no longer as his pals but as "the most privileged group" who were hypersensitive about their right to publish information indiscriminately. In October 1962, Kennedy issued new directives to the State and Defense departments prohibiting officials from holding one-on-one meetings with reporters. Any attempt to persuade journalists to act responsibly was met with resistance—columnist Joseph Alsop called them "news-control devices," but Kennedy insisted they were "aimed at the protection of genuinely sensitive information."[90] Although the directives soon became a source of ridicule within the administration, they started to sour the once fawning press JFK received, and for the first time, he started to see what the military and embassy staff had been experiencing in Vietnam. Just one month before, an embassy official complained that journalists believed "the situation in Viet Nam is going to pieces and . . . we have been unable to convince them otherwise." General Taylor observed that reporters stationed in Saigon were "uninformed and belligerently adverse to the programs of the U.S. and [South Vietnamese] Governments," and urged the president to insist on "responsible reporting."[91]

Despite the lengths to which JFK went to make the media the most malleable in American history—with considerable success—the tail began to wag the dog when it came to Southeast Asia, and that strange and fateful relationship bears some examination. JFK had a lifestyle many journalists admired and aspired to. The young president shared most of their values, and for more than a few, this included the ability and inclination to womanize without guilt. "JFK" easily could have stood for "Journalists For Kennedy."[92] During the campaign, reporters had consistently run to Kennedy insider and historian Arthur Schlesinger, Jr., for comments about the characteristics of "great presidents," and not surprisingly, Jack always seemed to possess exactly those traits. Had Nixon pulled some of Kennedy's tricks, the press would have howled. Candidate, then president, Kennedy "attempted to 'plant' stories, required the clearance of speeches by high administration officials, sought to prevent the publication of information he deemed sensitive, and tried to induce the *New York Times* to remove David Halberstam for his unfavorable reporting of the situation in Vietnam."[93] Kennedy's closest intimates—Ted Sorensen, Pierre Salinger, and Paul Fay, among others—viewed his preoccupation with image manipulation as bordering on obsession.[94]

JFK "converted the reporters [at his press conferences] into a cast of supporting players who complemented his starring performance," a situation described by Alsop as "a kind of court."[95] Theodore H. White of *Life* was at the family's beck and call. When necessary, recalcitrant reporters could be bullied; one *Newsweek* writer commented that the administration was "intolerant of any criticism," and appointments secretary Kenny O'Donnell replied that a reporter was either for Kennedy or against him.[96] It was no contest: Hugh Sidey of *Time*, who was allowed into the Kennedy inner circle, recalled the period as "a golden time for scribes. [Kennedy] talked to us, listened to us, honored us, ridiculed us, got angry with us, played with us, laughed with us, corrected us, and all the time lifted our trade to new heights of respect and importance."[97]

Paradoxically, however, most American reporters and editors had developed a near-universal loathing for Kennedy's protégé and fellow Catholic, South Vietnam's president Ngo Dinh Diem. *The New York Times* especially was in the vanguard of anti-Diem sentiment, based on the reports of David Halberstam, despite contrary evidence appearing in the dispatches of *New York Herald Tribune* reporter Marguerite Higgins. Many other large publications had a similar anti-Diem bias; *Newsweek*'s editors "had never made any secret of their dislike for Diem and his regime," noted one historian of journalism in the war.[98] When Kennedy's personal support for Diem faltered, press coverage intensified on Diem's "abuses," most notably of the Buddhist monks who had started a massive political protest against the Catholic premier. Higgins, in the field, found that the monks were exceptionally astute at playing the American press, but her extensive work was not filed as breaking news, thus yielding the front-page stories to Halberstam and other Diem haters.

Exacerbating the journalists' own prejudices against Diem, reporters tended to get information from Americans in Saigon who themselves were critical of the premier, and who used the press as their blunt instrument. Reporters later complained that the news in Vietnam was "managed," but generally journalists did the managing. The Saigon cabal pushed aside Higgins's information that contradicted their own reports; after her death in 1966, their views on Vietnam went unchallenged entirely. A critical point came in January 1963 at the battle of Ap Bac, where a superior South Vietnamese force allowed a Viet Cong battalion to escape a trap devised by American advisers. Reporters, led by Neil Sheehan and based on the angry accounts of Colonel John Paul Vann, concluded the Army of the Republic of Vietnam (ARVN) was unwilling to fight.

That July, coup stories began to circulate, mostly from unnamed "Western officials" (i.e., reporters), although some information was traced to the newly appointed U.S. ambassador Henry Cabot Lodge. *Newsweek* and other publications ran unrelenting coup pieces. Shortly after the July stories, JFK convened a "coup group," in which the CIA steadfastly opposed removing Diem, who was described as a "mandarin" (a privileged Asian official or bureaucrat) and an authoritarian, but hardly a U.S. puppet. Diem, at one time characterized as the "Jefferson of Asia," willingly and enthusiastically listened to American advice and just as whimsically disregarded it, while gladly taking all the war matériel the United States could supply. At that point, the option, as one adviser put it, was to go home: If "Diem volunteered to be skipper of the *Titanic*," he quipped, "we didn't have to buy tickets."

One month prior to his own death, Kennedy nevertheless authorized Diem's removal, and Vietnamese generals, with U.S. financing, deposed and murdered the president. Expressing his shock and disgust at Diem's murder, Kennedy was disingenuous at best: Vietnam was a Third World country and, clients or not, the subjects of coups usually ended up dead. One administration insider, John Roche, glumly admitted that Diem's assassination nailed the U.S. flag to the pole in Saigon, while the new president, Lyndon Johnson, put a distinctly western spin on it, referring to the coup as "playing cowboys and Indians in Saigon."[99] "We were now," Roche said, *"in loco parentis* to 16 million South Vietnamese." The press, which had cheered the coup on, described the central conspirator, General Duong Van "Big" Minh, as a "deceptively gentle man" who spoke with "a discernible tone of apology in his voice" when discussing the takeover.[100] The "deceptively gentle" Minh made certain Diem and his brother were shot and stabbed several times before they reached their promised exile, and the Viet Cong celebrated, calling the assassination a "gift from Heaven for us."[101]

Roche, then a hard-leftist and on the national board for the Americans for Democratic Action, later came to rethink the events that drew the United States into Vietnam. He concluded it was anything but a civil war. General Vo Bam told a French television crew in 1983, "On May 19, 1959, I had the privilege of being designated by the Vietnamese Communist Party . . . to unleash a military attack on the South to liberate [South Vietnam]."[102] In sum, this was a deliberate invasion by a foreign power. Yet having lobbied Kennedy to oust Diem, the press's support lasted scarcely a historical nanosecond. Supporting editorials from *The Washington Post* in 1964, urging the administration to demonstrate to the North that "persistence in aggression is fruitless and possibly deadly," shifted to opposition by summer 1967, *The New York Times* having deserted Lyndon Johnson the previous year.[103]

The JFK Assassination and the End of Patriotic Liberalism

Leftists have routinely tried to portray high murder rates in the United States (and American violence in general) as interconnected with the Vietnam War. This, of course, was rationalization after the fact; the war had been instigated by one of their own, John Kennedy, and the Left worldwide had to somehow gain separation from one who was now a tragic figure. So the argument was devised linking Vietnam to American violence—but only American violence. What else could be expected of a "gun culture" than the bombing of villages and massacre of innocents? The effort to link together individual (often random) violence in the United States with government-sanctioned acts of war came about somewhat haphazardly, facilitated in large part by the misinterpretations of Kennedy's assassination. JFK's death represented to many a sense that "public life [was] out of control or subject to direction by conspiracies or crazed individuals."[104]

The assassination of John F. Kennedy has been told so often, and from so many viewpoints, that the simple facts are often forgotten. On November 22, 1963, Kennedy, traveling in an open car in a slow-moving motorcade in Dallas, was shot in the back of the head by Lee Harvey Oswald, who was situated in the Texas Book Depository. Texas governor John Connally was also wounded. Kennedy was pronounced dead at Parkland Hospital of a massive head wound. Oswald was arrested not long after in a theater, then shot and killed during a transfer from one jail to another by Texas nightclub owner Jack Ruby. Despite more than forty years of conspiracy theories and "exposés" (none of which ever have yielded any conclusive evidence), the fact remains that no one has ever found one other shell cartridge or bullet at the scene or produced any sound recording with more than three audible shots on it. Ruby, who is frequently thought to be in on the conspiracy to silence Oswald, served three years in prison before dying of cancer. His last statement from his hospital bed was "There was nothing to hide. . . . There was no one else."[105]

A virtual cottage industry of assassination books has been building since 1963.[106] If anything, the Kennedy assassination had two unexpected effects. First, it shook the fundamental tenets of prewar liberalism: that there was an essential superiority of the free market (subject to regulation for "excesses") and that communism was an ideology to be defeated. Thus, among liberals who admired JFK, there "was a tendency to view the [assassination] through the prism of loss and disappointment: How could this have happened? What if he had lived?"[107] Such a view led to the perpetuation of a thoroughgoing false Kennedy mythology of "Jack, who would have gotten us out of Vietnam," or "Jack, who embraced civil rights." Whereas liberals had, like conservatives, previously expressed pride in being Americans, rescuing millions of people from despotic regimes, and providing a brighter economic future for all through capitalistic growth, after Kennedy's assassination much of that changed. Liberals now saw an unjust, dark, violent America, and their policies shifted dramatically to expose and punish the United States for past sins. Occupied with crimes of the past, liberalism became a grim judge who took from some in order to assign to others. Dispelling American exceptionalism began to become a prominent feature in liberals' speeches and policies.

A second unexpected but related result of the Kennedy assassination was the growing body of conspiracy theories as an explanation for almost any unpleasant or "unfair" event in human experience. Surely bad things did not just happen: some evil (human) force had to be behind them. The CIA was a favorite culprit, but shadowy international groups such as the

Bilderbergs, the Illuminati, Freemasonry, Opus Dei, or the Rothschilds provided recurring foils in these conspiracy tales. In a fair or just world, Kennedy never would have been shot: someone must have been behind it. Lee Harvey Oswald, ignored or deemphasized, should have sparked a revulsion against communism, socialism, and left-wing doctrines across the board, yet radicals such as Che and Lenin "enjoyed a greater vogue in the United States than at any other time in our history."[108] Instead of a reaction against leftism, American liberals marched steadily toward the radical cliff, but in 1964 few saw the precipice on the horizon.

Continuing the Commitment

After Kennedy's assassination, Lyndon Johnson was elevated to the presidency with a level of public sympathy probably unmatched in American history. The public, in a solid majority, accepted his vision for civil rights legislation, and still accepted Kennedy's commitment to Vietnam. Little was known about the Johnson-Kennedy tensions; the Kennedys despised Johnson and tried to keep him under wraps as much as possible during Jack's three years. Even less was known about Johnson's worldview.

In short order, Johnson escalated what was already a significant American presence in Vietnam, first expanding the number of advisers, then, in August 1964, asking for a congressional resolution to deploy troops based on the August 2 attack on an American destroyer *Maddox* in the Tonkin Gulf. (The notion that the attack events did not occur, or were imagined, as some on the Left claimed, was debunked by no less than General Vo Nguyen Giap, North Vietnam's defense minister at the time, who admitted to Robert McNamara in 1995 that the attacks had taken place.)[109] While reports of a second attack on August 4 indeed proved wrong, and uncertainty remains over the motivation of the August 2 attack, there is no question that North Vietnamese patrol boats fired at the USS *Maddox*. Moreover, on August 7, when the Congress enacted a joint resolution by a 504–2 vote authorizing the president to use whatever force was necessary, it was clear this authorization was based on more than one attack:

> these attacks are part of a deliberate and systematic campaign of aggression that the communist regime in North Vietnam has been waging against its neighbors. . . . [and it authorized the president] to take all necessary measures, including the use of armed force, to assist any . . . protocol state of the Southeast Asia Collective Defense Treaty requesting assistance. . . .[110]

Johnson would have preferred packing all the nation's resources into his new Great Society welfare programs, but he wrestled with two demons. The first was the legacy of JFK, and the reality that Kennedy saw Vietnam as critical to contain communism in Southeast Asia. Johnson, therefore, could not lose "Kennedy's war." Second, Johnson barely inherited the presidency before he had to run for reelection on what would essentially be Kennedy's record. By late 1964, Johnson knew that Republican presidential candidate Arizona senator Barry Goldwater would seek to make Johnson appear soft on communism. LBJ's staff responded with one of the most heavy-handed, unscrupulous television ads of all time, the infamous "Daisy" ad, in which a Goldwater speech ran over images of a little girl picking daisies, ending with the flash of an atomic bomb. Yet the Gulf of Tonkin Resolution passed with no opposition at all in the House and only two senators voting against it. Senator J. William Fulbright of Arkansas—Bill Clinton's future mentor—supported the war at the time, as did virtually every liberal on Capitol Hill. Handing LBJ such authority carte blanche might have proven a master stroke in the hands of a more talented and insightful commander in chief, but consistent with his liberal leanings, Johnson had no interest in pursuing a war with the ruthlessness it demanded.

Instead, he treated it as a sideshow to his domestic agenda. "Win the war, but don't make an issue out of it," as one of his administration put it.[111] Johnson and McNamara utterly ignored the essential propagandizing necessary for a democratic society to fight a devious and relentless enemy. Neither Johnson nor the media ever demonized North Vietnam's Ho Chi Minh the way Roosevelt portrayed Hitler and the way George W. Bush later painted Saddam Hussein. This was not a trivial matter; it gave the appearance that no substantial moral or national security grounds existed for the conflict in the first place, which would play into the hands of that deceptive and destructive concept of "world opinion" and the domestic antiwar movement. Country Joe and the Fish, one of the most famous antiwar rock bands, summarized the weakness of Johnson's position with the "I-Feel-Like-I'm-Fixin'-to-Die Rag," in which they sang, "Well it's one, two, three, what are we fightin' for? Don't ask me, I don't give a damn. Next stop is Vietnam." Not only would Johnson back away from engaging in the necessary propaganda war against the North, but Western reporters aided and abetted the Communists by refusing to detail the horrors of the Viet Cong—entire villages where town leaders had their arms chopped off for supporting the government, or the ubiquitous heads on pikes. The same journalists who had railed at Diem's abuses (which seldom resulted in murder) ignored widespread atrocities by the Viet Cong and North Vietnamese because, with Jack gone, it was no longer a "good" war worth supporting.

Without the constant education of the public as to both the necessity of the conflict and, equally important, the depravity of the enemy, a flagging of public will was inevitable. Added to that, McNamara's sterile data-in, information-out approach to conducting the war might have ensured defeat on its own. As he once said in spite of mounting evidence to the contrary, "every quantitative measure we have shows we're winning this war."[112] Having been schooled in statistics during his work on World War II bombing surveys, McNamara ironically had contributed to the counterintuitive postwar consensus that strategic bombing had limited impact on the war.[113] At the same time, the former Ford president held an inflated reverence for the power of numbers and the political heft anyone wielding them could employ. Obsession with raw numbers and the unwillingness to listen to frank judgments from the Joint Chiefs of Staff muddled McNamara's ability to properly oversee the war or assess the situation on the ground. He also demanded the curtailing of operations by Army Intelligence, seeing those efforts as a duplication of the CIA's efforts.

After the war, many criticized Johnson and McNamara for failing to treat the war as a typical military conflict, or to do so aggressively enough. Admiral Thomas H. Moorer argued the United States "should have fought in the north, where everyone was the enemy, where you don't have to worry about whether or not you were shooting friendly civilians. . . . The only reason to go to war is to overthrow a government you don't like."[114] Defense Secretary James Schlesinger likewise concluded, "one of the lessons of the Vietnamese conflict is that rather than simply counter your opponent's thrusts, it is necessary to go for the heart of the opponent's power. . . ."[115]

Colonel H. R. McMaster, in a scathing and accurate history of the relationship between Presidents Kennedy and Johnson and the Joint Chiefs, concluded that the die was cast for the war's direction before the shots rang out at Dealey Plaza on November 22. Kennedy had isolated and weakened the JCS, while McNamara directly intervened to make certain reports critical of actions in the field never reached the president or General Maxwell Taylor, the chairman of the JCS (a pliable Kennedy appointee).[116] As McMaster concluded, "when the situation in Vietnam seemed to demand military action, Johnson did not turn to his military advisors . . . [but instead] to his civilian advisors to determine how to postpone a decision."[117] Shifting the responsibility for decision making away from the military to civilian analysts, attorneys, and ad hoc committees, McNamara and Johnson "place[ed] conditions and qualifications on questions they asked the Chiefs," and when the advice of the JCS did not fit McNamara's recommendations, he "lied in meetings of the National Security Council about the Chiefs' views."[118] McNamara's behavior in these critical meetings meant that the war protesters did have a point, and that the secretary of defense *should* have been prosecuted for crimes—although not those they had in mind.

Once their opinions were ignored, the Chiefs shied away from confronting the president and his civilian brain trust, which paradoxically led them to support McNamara's nonsensical "graduated pressure" strategy in an effort to escalate by degrees. On top of this formula for disaster, LBJ heaped on a half-hearted bombing of the North that turned Hanoi into the Communist equivalent of courageous Malta (the island that stood alone against assault from the air by the Nazis). McNamara's fingerprints were on the bombing campaign as well, noting that the objectives of the 1965 Rolling Thunder bombing campaign were "first, to *give us a better bargaining counter* [emphasis added] across from the North Vietnamese, and second, to interdict the flow of men and supplies from the North to the South."[119] This program of "graduated pressure," as McNamara termed it, was based on an entirely erroneous reading of the tactics used in the Cuban missile crisis. A Pentagon war game of April 1964 looked "eerily prophetic"; in response to American military involvement, the North and Viet Cong increased their aggression, and the officers who played the part of the North Vietnamese in the exercise "banked on [a lack of] American resolve" to win.[120] A second round of war games in September 1964 concluded that escalation would erode public support.

Converting bombing from an instrument of war into a tool for negotiation impelled Johnson to absorb himself in target selection and to otherwise micromanage and meddle. He lectured the Joint Chiefs, "as long as I am Commander in Chief, I am going to control from Washington."[121] The predictable deterioration of air missions meant that Johnson interfered constantly:

> [He] also stopped Rolling Thunder completely on eight occasions between March 1965 and March 1968 [then in May 1965] he halted the campaign for six days as a "propaganda effort" to demonstrate that he sought a peaceful solution to the war. . . . [I]n December 1965 and February 1967 . . . [there were] bombing pauses of thirty-seven days and six days, respectively. Johnson stopped Rolling Thunder briefly during Christmas and New

Year's in 1966 and 1967, and for twenty-four hours on Buddha's birthday in May 1967.[122]

This was warfare to impress the pacifists of the world, not to win. Administration officials engaged in heated debates over what constituted acceptable targets, disagreeing over whether a highway that had no moving vehicles was fair game. They could not even agree on the precise meaning of a *convoy*.[123] Fear of hitting Russian advisers put North Vietnamese surface-to-air missiles off limits to attacks while under construction; during each bombing pause, the Communists not only repaired their radars and guns, but reviewed and adapted their tactics so as to shoot down U.S. planes easier on the next go-round. That the United States lost only eighty aircraft during the war under such deadly disadvantages was a testament to the astounding flying skills of American pilots no less than divine providence.

Having failed to apply U.S. air power in a credible way, Johnson compounded the problems for the ground troops by refusing to interdict the resupply efforts of the Viet Cong and PAVN on the ground, especially from Red China, and almost continually through the Ho Chi Minh Trail in Laos. Even before the first American ground troops landed, China had dumped 10,000 artillery pieces and a quarter-million guns into Vietnam. Then, after America's role expanded, the Chinese grew bolder. They built railway stations, 14 tunnels, 39 bridges, laid hundreds of miles of railroad track, and shipped 327,000 Chinese troops to North Vietnam to relieve PAVN soldiers for duty in the south.[124] Far from battling a small group of guerrillas—the popular story line in newspapers—the United States found itself confronting a massive Sino-Soviet–North Vietnamese alliance, all the while hamstringing itself. The Ho Chi Minh trail ran primarily through Laos and started out as a maze of dirt roads and trails but later expanded to a four-lane paved highway and a pipeline from the North Vietnamese city of Vinh to just north of Saigon.

Laos and Cambodia became central parts of the American nonstrategy, for by preventing attacks on the Ho Chi Minh trail there, the United States gave the Communists a freeway to the south. U.S. ambassador to Laos William Sullivan, who had placed himself in command of everything to do with that country, decreed that all bombing of trails, villages, or huts in Laos required his prior approval, as did the use of defoliants (almost never approved), and all ground operations. Communist Pathet Lao forces had made consistent gains in Laos and refused to play by Sullivan's rules. This ultimately lost the country. As the American air attaché Colonel Robert

Tyrrell said, "[the Embassy staff] feels that they should always master and discipline the military."[125] Cambodia was also off-limits to bombing except by special permission. After the war, North Vietnamese colonel Bui Tin responded to a question as to how the United States could have won the war with: "block the Ho Chi Minh Trail."[126]

Civil Rights and Wrongs

JFK had been successfully detached from the war by Camelot hagiographers seeking to protect the legacy and New Left historians working to permanently discredit the war. Once it became "Johnson's War," opposition began to swell. Antiwar groups soon fused with civil rights activists in what seemed to be sister causes: fighting for the oppressed at home and abroad.

The American civil rights movement had commenced during Reconstruction (and some claimed even earlier with individuals such as Frederick Douglass), but gathered momentum in the postwar years. In 1909, a number of prominent citizens—most of them whites, including Oswald Garrison Villard and William English Walling, along with a few blacks, including W.E.B. Du Bois and Archibald Grimké—founded the National Association for the Advancement of Colored People (NAACP). The organization's chief weapon was the courts, and it used the justice system to challenge segregation laws and lobby for antilynching legislation. After World War II came a handful of important breakthroughs: President Truman integrated the U.S. armed forces in 1948, and the NAACP successfully brought *Brown v. Board of Education of Topeka, Kansas* before the U.S. Supreme Court in 1954. The *Brown* decision legally ended "separate but equal" public education.

While those were important milestones, they remained overall small steps toward racial equality in a nation where blacks, 10.5 percent of the population in 1960, not only were unequal, but did not even exist in much public life. American television featured no blacks in major roles; the famous rocker Elvis Presley was banned from southern radio stations because he "sounded black," until it was learned that he was white; and on the whole, blacks fell far below white averages in income and wealth. In the South, the numbers were noticeably worse for blacks where government power still enforced Jim Crow laws. Segregation was in effect, and blacks routinely had to drink from separate water fountains, use their own bathrooms, and attend their own schools and churches. "Mingling" at any level was frowned upon.

The wording of the *Brown* verdict generated both an excuse to resist desegregation and confusion as to what the goal was. By demanding that public schools be desegregated with "all deliberate speed," the Court handed the South a definition with which to resist, and southern governments dug in their heels, interpreting "deliberate" as meaning slow. But the Court, by stating that segregation "generates a feeling of inferiority," implied that the only way blacks could be made equal with whites was to sit next to them in schools or otherwise be in the proximity of white people. In addition, *Brown* suggested that even in voluntary arrangements, segregation would not be permissible, opening the door for private clubs to be forced to admit all colors. (These arguments would later come full circle when in the 1980s, some black activists would insist that black children were being held back by being in classrooms with whites and needed their *own* segregated schools.)

The first major incident of the civil rights movement after *Brown* occurred in 1955 in Alabama. Montgomery seamstress Rosa Parks, in defiance of a city statute, refused to give up her seat to a white passenger. While the event had more than enough drama of its own, contrary to later reports, her resistance was not spontaneous, but designed to be a test case for the law. But the means by which blacks hoped to fight the ordinance was the free market. Under the leadership of Dr. Martin Luther King, Jr., an Atlanta-born Republican pastor who had a divinity degree from Boston University, the Montgomery organizers imposed a boycott of all the Montgomery buses (which were owned and operated by a private company). The boycott lasted over a year until the Supreme Court let stand an earlier court ruling that stated "separate but equal" was not valid. Although King claimed that the losses absorbed by the company ended the boycott, the company was a monopoly in Montgomery, and insulated from the market. However, in other cases, such as the Greensboro Woolworth's sit-in, for example, where competition was abundant, the sit-ins worked. Regardless, King emerged from the episode as a national figure.

A second watershed event took place in Little Rock, Arkansas, in September 1957. Nine black students attempted to enroll in Little Rock's Central High School, only to be turned away by national guardsmen under the authority of Governor Orval Faubus, enforcing state law in defiance of a federal judge's order to desegregate. On September 20, Judge Ronald Davies issued an order for the national guardsmen to cease interfering, whereupon Faubus pulled them out and left Little Rock police in charge of what soon became a violent confrontation. President Eisenhower stepped in, sending units of the 101st Airborne to Little Rock and nationalizing the Arkansas Guard under his authority. Those troops escorted the students into the school.

King became the unifying force of the movement, and his nonviolent strategy was a brilliant and effective means of reaching the majority of compassionate Americans. He promised his enemies to "wear you down by our capacity to suffer, and in winning our freedom we will so appeal to your heart and conscience that we will win you in the process."[127] King's approach depended on the essential goodness of the majority of the American people, and borne out of his witness to the support he'd seen when hundreds of whites traveled south to join in civil rights marches, he believed that for every racist white he exposed, five nonracists would support him. King also knew that under the watchful eye of a sympathetic press and lit up by public scrutiny, even the worst of the racists would not dare kill unarmed protesters. While indeed anonymous lynchings and bombings occurred, for the most part King was right. No Amritsar massacre ever occurred.

For all the symbolism of the protests, the meat of the resistance involved changing laws. Eisenhower had proposed the Civil Rights Act of 1957, the first civil rights legislation since Reconstruction, which created a civil rights division within the Justice Department charged with prosecuting election crimes against blacks. Virtually all southern Democrats opposed the bill, and southern Democrat governors refused to enforce it. Ike admitted that the American federal system never intended Washington, D.C., to supervise county elections in Alabama—and until he (or another president) had a wider mandate, no more was possible.

Another nationally watched protest occurred at the Woolworth's lunch counter in Greensboro, North Carolina, in February 1960. Four black freshmen from North Carolina A&T sat down and demanded service; when they were refused, others joined them until the owners had to shut down the store. Other sit-ins spread across the South. Although thousands were jailed, demonstrations spread everywhere. The Congress of Racial Equality (CORE), originally founded by six people (of whom only two were black), had set up chapters in most large cities in the North. Now, CORE chapters instituted "Freedom Rides" of black and white passengers heading south to protest. More violent resistance mounted from southern whites, who beat passengers (one of them to death) and fire-bombed a bus. In 1962, James Meredith, a black student, enrolled at the University of Mississippi in defiance of state segregation laws. Attorney General Robert F. Kennedy sent in troops to provide him with an escort.

King, meanwhile, thinking that the NAACP was not the proper vehicle for his strategy, assembled more than one hundred black ministers and along with Fred Shuttlesworth, Ralph Abernathy, Bayard Rustin, and Joseph Lowery established the Southern Christian Leadership Conference (SCLC) in 1957 and became its first president. That organization would institutionalize nonviolent resistance, and, equally important, the SCLC marked the transfer of power from the descendants of northern free men of color to southern blacks who came from a legacy of slavery. King's strategy was honed even further during this time: blacks did not just have to resist and absorb the brutality of racists, but they had to do so on television so all of America witnessed it. The campaign culminated with a massive march on Washington by 200,000 blacks and white supporters on August 28, 1963. There King delivered one of the great speeches in history, "I Have a Dream," in which he said:

> I have a dream that my four little children will one day live in a nation where they will not be judged by the color of their skin but by the content of their character.[128]

Nonviolence did not appeal to all blacks, and King had his own opponents within the civil rights movement, most notably the Black Muslims and the Black Panthers. The former group had embraced Islam, but with a remarkable and often myopic twist; rather than admitting the reality of centuries of Islamic enslavement of Europeans *and* Africans, the Nation of Islam under Elijah Muhammad labeled King a tool of whites. Muhammad's teachings included the notion that the devil had created white people as lesser beings, and he recruited thousands to his religion. Whereas King sought integration, Muhammad, and his protégé Malcolm X, a burglar and street hustler, called for separation and black supremacy. "Coffee that's too black," Muhammad said, overlooking Malcolm's mixed parentage, is "too strong. . . . You integrate it with cream, you make it weak."[129] Malcolm X was assassinated in 1965, and Muhammad was generally suspected of ordering the hit. The Nation of Islam soon fell to Muhammad's successor, Louis Farrakhan, under whom the group turned vehemently anti-Semitic and antiwhite.

The Black Panthers, officially formed in 1966 in response to police brutality in Oakland's black neighborhoods, staged one of its first marches in opposition to California's new ban on certain types of weapons. Instituting community programs, food shelters, and educational initiatives, the Panthers, led by Huey Newton and Bobby Seale, were prominent in their black leather jackets and black berets and usually appeared with weapons in public. They called for federally guaranteed employment for everyone, an exemption of blacks from the draft, and reparations for slavery.[130] While all the suspicions of the FBI cannot be assumed as true, neither should its view of the Panthers as a domestic terrorist organization be dismissed. Taking advantage of the California law that allowed carrying a loaded rifle or shotgun in public, they repeatedly threatened police. Newton was pulled over for a possible traffic violation at 5:00 A.M. on October 28, 1967, and in an ensuing altercation, killed arresting officer John Frey and wounded a second policeman. The Left championed his innocence, and he was released on appeal, but he later admitted to a fellow Panther he had murdered Frey.[131] Another nine officers were killed in clashes with Panthers, and in 1969 the Panthers tortured and killed Alex Rackley, a suspected snitch, and Panthers were also heavily implicated in the murder of Black Panther bookkeeper Betty Van Patter.

Ultimately neither the Nation of Islam nor the Black Panthers changed the racial landscape a fraction compared with King and his adherents. In July 1964, Congress (largely in tribute to JFK) passed the Civil Rights Act, which abolished segregation in public places and established the Equal Employment Opportunity Commission (EEOC) to ensure fairness in hiring. A higher percentage of Republicans than Democrats supported the bill, yet Johnson and his liberal allies ensured that Democrats received all the credit. Ironically, within weeks of the Civil Rights Act's passage, large-scale riots swept Harlem, Rochester, Philadelphia, Chicago, then, in 1965, Watts, California. King, with his rhetoric of nonviolence, was in a difficult position; he was booed in Watts after the riots, and the more militant leaders insisted he was old hat. In April 1968, King gave another memorable speech, "I've Been to the Mountaintop," where he observed that "Jericho is a dangerous road." Indeed, King's road to Memphis ended with his assassination the following day, April 4.[132]

Vietnam's Deceptions

Before his death King had become a staunch opponent of the Vietnam War, both on grounds of his personal pacifism but also because he saw it as draining resources and drawing attention from domestic civil rights issues. As more troops from both sides poured in, and the press gradually repositioned itself from pro-Kennedy support to mild criticism of LBJ, the war became the focal point of virtually all youth dissent and imprecise rebellion worldwide. Thanks to television, a student in England, suffering little more than dissatisfaction with his grades, could suddenly "feel acute solidarity with guerillas in Vietnam [or] the Black Panther Party in California."[133]

Indeed, a natural alliance between civil rights groups and affluent student protesters began to unfold, allowing the radical black Left to appeal to middle-class white kids in the name of racial justice. It was an easy if erroneous argument to make—that the war absorbed resources that could have buttressed new social programs at home—and one made even easier by the myth that blacks (and draftees) were disproportionately shipped to the jungles and rice paddies. Reality was much different, but harder to translate to the public. Blacks served in Vietnam in almost the exact proportion of their percentage of the U.S. population at the time (almost 12 percent, slightly overrepresented in the Army and underrepresented in the Marines); and volunteers, not draftees, made up two thirds of those who served in Vietnam.[134]

Johnson failed to aggressively define the war (a mistake George W. Bush would repeat more than thirty years later in Iraq), leaving it to the opposition to do so. The Left eagerly produced a blizzard of propaganda that made Vietnam seem not only a draftees' war, but a *young* draftees' war, incessantly utilizing the word "kids" in protests. In fact, only 101 eighteen-year-olds died during the entire war, and 77 percent of all battle deaths were volunteers.[135] One of the demographic groups to suffer the highest death rates in Vietnam was white college graduates because of the high rate of officer and pilot casualties. Other statistics, which never reached the public, challenged the war critics' premise that Vietnam was particularly unpopular. Desertions were 55 percent lower in Vietnam than in World War II (the "Good War"). While some 10,000 American youth slogged off to Canada to avoid the draft, an astonishing 30,000 Canadians entered the U.S. military, and one third of them fought in Vietnam, alongside some 68,000 allied troops from the Philippines, Korea, Thailand, Australia, and New Zealand.[136] At one time, the Republic of Korea had 50,000 soldiers in Vietnam, or about 10 percent of the American total; Taiwan offered Johnson large numbers of forces, but he refused, afraid of provoking the Chinese.

Rice production, land under cultivation—virtually every quantitative measurement that could be employed—was positively affected by American involvement. A few graphic photos of napalmed villages or burned children severely damaged the public's determination at home, but the civilian wartime deaths from all causes, counting those resulting from actions by both sides, were about 45 percent of the total deaths, or equal to the average for twentieth-century conflicts.[137] The standard of living in American-protected areas rose rapidly; wounded had a high likelihood of surviving due to helicopter medevacs; and postwar fables about vets suffering high rates of suicide or drug addiction also turned out to be completely false. America's Vietnam-era vets, by all accounts, had similar postwar life paths as had the soldiers from earlier generations. Three of them won their party's nominations for the U.S. presidency: Al Gore (an after-action journalist who never saw combat), John Kerry (who received two Purple Hearts for self-inflicted wounds according to John O'Neill, wrote his own medal citation, and left Vietnam at his earliest opportunity), and John McCain (shot down over North Vietnam and held for five and a half years in a POW camp under unspeakable conditions). A fourth Vietnam-era military veteran who served in the Air National Guard at the time and was not sent to Vietnam, George W. Bush, won the presidency.

Hollywood chimed in to the antiwar movement, adding star power to the resistance, with no scene so memorable as Jane Fonda climbing into the gunner's seat of a North Vietnamese antiaircraft gun, when only a few miles away John McCain and other POWs languished in the "Hanoi Hilton" prison. North Vietnamese colonel Bui Tin felt the U.S. antiwar movement was essential to North Vietnamese strategy. "Support of the war from our rear was completely secure while the American rear was vulnerable. . . . America lost because of its democracy; through dissent and protest it lost the ability to mobilize a will to win."[138] Bui Tin also recalled, "Every day our leadership would listen to world news over the radio at 9 A.M. to follow the growth of the American antiwar movement. Visits to Hanoi by people like Jane Fonda and former Attorney General Ramsey Clark and ministers gave us confidence that we should hold on in the face of battlefield reverses."[139]

Certainly the news media could not be counted on to expose the enemy. *Newsweek* magazine, one of the last major weeklies to trend leftward, admitted its coverage was unpatriotic. *The New York Times* stacked its Saigon bureau with decidedly antiwar reporters, so much so that when military correspondent Hanson Baldwin arrived in Vietnam in 1965, he said, "I was appalled by the bias I found in the *Times* reporters." Liz Trotta of NBC, another new arrival, saw Charles Mohr of the *Times* threaten to beat up another reporter who voiced his support for the war.[140] One historian of *The Washington Post* noted that its journalists viewed the war as "an annoying distraction."[141] Two exceptions to the negative coverage were Don Moser's *Life* magazine piece "Eight Dedicated Men Marked for Death," which recounted the stand taken by a group of leaders in the town of Loc Dien in the summer of 1965, and Bernard Fall's article in *The New Republic*, in which he argued that the United States was winning *despite* its mistakes.[142] One study found the press had failed to sufficiently investigate the conditions that prompted the war in the first place, and certainly had not covered the North Vietnamese/Viet Cong atrocities or military disadvantages under which American forces operated.[143] Former correspondent Robert Elegant wrote, "For the first time in modern history, the outcome of a war was determined not on a battlefield, but on the printed page and, above all, on the television screen."[144]

Hamstrung without the other side of the story, namely access to the deteriorating economy in North Vietnam or the camps of the Viet Cong, where the damage by U.S. forces could be assessed, the American public got either the administration's rosy (but strategically irrelevant) updates, or the media's increasingly negative coverage. Film footage of captured weapons caches or body counts of faceless enemies did not put in perspective the significance of either—especially since the administration had no plan for victory, only fatiguing the North. Despite all that, polls found that the U.S. public overwhelmingly supported the war. In one 1966 poll, three quarters split evenly between "Keep our soldiers in Vietnam but try to end the fighting" and "Take a stronger stand even if it means invading North Vietnam," while only 9 percent wanted to "Pull out of Vietnam entirely."[145] Throughout 1967, support for escalation actually increased. And yet, an astounding story of American military might *in the absence of any real strategy* was unfolding: U.S. ground and air were routinely pulverizing the enemy.

Tet: The World's Most Unreported Victory

A single event, the January 1968 Tet Offensive by the combined Viet Cong and North Vietnamese, easily could have ended the war if followed up effectively. It was a risky gamble for the Communists: the Viet Cong deployed all their forces (estimated at more than 100,000) in a simultaneous nationwide assault on eight major population centers, supported by PAVN regulars with tanks and artillery. Many American bastions seemed doomed, particularly the Khe Sanh fire base, where Marines seemed destined to relive the French experience at Dien Bien Phu more than a decade earlier.

Defending a mile-long airstrip socked into a valley overlooked by mountains, the 10,000 Marines were surrounded by 63,000 Communists, who shelled the base relentlessly. Transport planes could no longer land, but rather pushed supply pallets off moving aircraft that skated along just a few feet off the ground. Helicopters could scarcely get the wounded out from a bunker located close to the landing strip under heavy fire from

North Vietnamese mortars, forcing the Marines underground, "living a life more similar to rats than human beings," as one officer recalled.[146] U.S. scouts could only go thirty yards outside the base, while the Viet Cong were kept at bay by B-52s flattening the jungle beyond. American air power flew 24,000 sorties, killing 10,000 enemy in one of the first major ground battles in history won almost exclusively by air power.[147] After four months, the Communists gave up on Khe Sanh. Similar failure followed throughout Vietnam for the Viet Cong and PAVNs: at the imperial city of Hue, Marines hurled back 10,000 Communists in three weeks at a cost of only 150 dead, and at Saigon, where it was wrongly asserted that the Viet Cong got inside the U.S. embassy, all the attackers were wiped out.

United States military historian Robert Leckie called Tet "the most appalling defeat in the history of the war for Hanoi—an unmitigated military disaster."[148] A top Communist general, Tran Van Tra, recognizing that the Americans had inflicted a staggering fifty-to-one casualty ratio on Communist forces, admitted, "We suffered large sacrifices and losses with regard to manpower and material, especially cadres at the various echelons, which clearly weakened us."[149] North Vietnamese general Giap stated that Communist forces in the South were almost wiped out in 1968, and that reestablishing a guerrilla force in South Vietnam took until 1971—and even that was only accomplished by inserting North Vietnamese troops as local guerrillas.[150] By their own admission, the Viet Cong were completely finished after Tet, and there could no longer be a pretense of a civil war in South Vietnam.

What should have been the final blow to the North, with massive follow-up attacks that would rip the heart out of their military and political structure once and for all, astonishingly was turned into an American defeat by the news media. For years, reporters had been staying closer to the major population centers, and none had free access to the North or Viet Cong information that would have shown the devastating losses. Moreover, having (reporters believed) passed along the Johnson administration's line that the war was almost over, they felt betrayed. (Of course, all wars have ebbs and flows. One full year after Gettysburg, Union forces lost horrific numbers of troops in bloody assaults at Cold Harbor and the Crater . . . yet stood on the precipice of victory.) Both CBS and NBC nevertheless produced half-hour news specials, "alarmist in tone" and negative in approach, which "strongly reinforced the message that Tet was a devastating defeat for the United States."[151] ABC reporter Joseph Harsch uttered a staggeringly inane conclusion: "Best estimates here are that the enemy has not yet, and *probably never will*, run out of the manpower to keep his effort going [emphasis added]."[152]

The American media turned a victory into a defeat through its slanted reporting and agenda-driven analysis. The erroneous "embassy falling" report was regurgitated endlessly, and one of the most famous photographs of the offensive was of South Vietnamese police chief Nguyen Ngoc Loan shooting a man in civilian clothes in the head at point blank range. The man was an officer in charge of a Viet Cong death squad responsible for murdering police officers and their family members. He had been captured at a mass grave containing seven police family members, and received the same summary judgment that Andrew Jackson gave to British spies in Florida over 120 years earlier. The execution photo proved the last straw for the American public, whose ire had been built up by more body bag images and the commentary of CBS News dean and closet liberal Walter Cronkite, who declared on national television that the war was now a stalemate. Cronkite's comments were echoed by Kennedy court historian Arthur Schlesinger, Jr., who warned the United States "not [to] re-enact Dien Bien Phu," or "sacrifice our brave men to the folly of generals and the obstinance of Presidents."[153]

Nary a word was reported on the near-fatal blow dealt the enemy, or how close the United States was to a truly remarkable victory in 1968. Only later that year did field producer Jack Fern recommend a three-part series describing Tet as a debacle for the Viet Cong, but, as NBC executives told Fern, "Tet was already established in the public's mind as a defeat, and, therefore, it *was* an American defeat."[154] Daniel Hallin's study of televised editorial comments revealed negative comments about the North Vietnamese plunged from 100 percent unfavorable before Tet to only 29 percent unfavorable afterward.[155] Television reporters quoted North Vietnamese officials eight times more frequently after Tet than before, while relying on American officers only slightly more than before, and the number of critical comments per hour of coverage started to eclipse the number of editorial comments about U.S. activities overall.[156]

Instead of reporting events accurately, the media now had a newfound sense of importance in their ability to *make* news and use it to change public opinion. James Reston of *The New York Times*, toward the end of the war, said, "maybe the historians will agree that the reporters and cameras were decisive in the end. They brought the issue of the war to the people . . . and forced the withdrawal of American power from Vietnam."[157] In other words, the press had moved from journalism into activism. Coverage of Tet dovetailed with growing anti-Americanism abroad and increasingly loud protests at home.

Johnson's personal approval ratings finally sagged, and in March 1968 he faced a disappointing New Hampshire primary result, a clear reflection of the Tet coverage. He was tired, in failing health, and he no longer thought he knew how to win. This, combined with the discouragement of the Tet Offensive and the loss of control over his own party, was enough. Johnson abruptly issued a surprise announcement that he would not campaign for president, nor would he accept the nomination, opening the door for doves such as Eugene McCarthy and Robert Kennedy within the Democratic Party, where they were outnumbered by the hawks. By that time, the media and intellectuals on the Left had turned on Johnson, while the hawks on the right were increasingly agitated with gradual escalation. Eugene McCarthy seemed a reasonable candidate—silver-haired, seasoned, genial—but liberals were obsessed with the Kennedy legacy, and McCarthy would have little chance against Robert Kennedy with Camelot and his family's money behind him.

The Shadow of Napoleon

Europeans viewed Vietnam as an opportunity to separate themselves from the United States, and no one was more willing to assume the mantle of European leadership than France. Still smarting from its own defeat in Indochina and seeing its last chance for greatness, France had floundered until Charles de Gaulle returned to politics in 1958 to resolve the Algerian crisis. Against the wishes of many of his supporters, he granted Algeria independence—something he had explicitly and repeatedly promised not to do. Privately, he sang a different song, and his hypocrisy was astounding. "Independence," he said, was "a folly, a monstrosity."[158] "I will never deal with those people from Cairo and Tunis," he promised. "There will be no Dien Bien Phu in Algeria."[159] In the meantime, he merely used the crisis to aggrandize himself, bring more power within the French civilian government, and push through the adoption of a constitution for the Fifth Republic, which concentrated authority in the executive as in no time since Napoleon. The Republic's new constitution included "special powers" for the president, whereupon he opened talks with those he would "never deal with," specifically the FLN (Algerian independence) leaders. In the midst of FLN terror, French generals seized power in Algeria (the so-called generals' revolt), and threatened to return to France and institute military rule once they mopped up the Muslim radicals. De Gaulle's government responded by offering independence to Algeria in 1961, starving the generals of troops as the Muslim conscripts deserted.

Terror on a level previously unseen, even from the FLN, swept Algeria as both sides sought to control the new state. De Gaulle's actions had simultaneously calcified European attitudes in Algeria as they braced for war while increasing the French civilian population's willingness to tolerate greater civil rights infringements at home to combat terror spilling over from Africa. (There were 350 convictions for insulting the head of state during de Gaulle's reign—compared with only 9 in the previous eighty-three years—including one for a man who shouted "Down with de Gaulle.")[160] France reinstituted torture as lawful. Nothing, however, could save Algeria for France once the FLN had destroyed the Muslim "moderates," whose public executions made a lasting impression on the few civic-minded holdouts. Only fifteen thousand of a quarter-million Algerian officials loyal to France managed to escape the carnage. Others were "shot without trial, used as human mine-detectors to clear the minefields along the Tunisian border, made to dig their own tombs and swallow their military decorations before being killed; some were burned alive, castrated, dragged behind trucks, fed to the dogs; there were cases where entire families including tiny children were murdered together."[161] Algeria was changed forever, turned into a terrorist hotbed, a harbinger of the anti-Christian and anti-Western radical Muslim movements that would make their presence known before the end of the century.

Abandoning Algeria did not save France or elevate de Gaulle to a position of preeminence in the free world. Rather, unloading its African colony only temporarily postponed France's slide into second-tier status. Some two million Algerians, both French and Muslim supporters of the French regime, fled Algeria for France, changing the demographic makeup of Paris forever. Some Algerian Muslims tried to assimilate. Far more became recruits for Islamic terrorists in subsequent decades, while French cities soon possessed Muslim barrios and no-go zones that were anything but French.

Determined to force respect from the United States, de Gaulle unceremoniously booted NATO out of Paris (it went to Brussels), and withdrew French military forces from NATO command in 1966—the same year France tested its own atomic bombs. With its Force de Frappe, including Mirage jets and nuclear submarines, France under de Gaulle claimed its independence from America's military protection (although French forces often continued war games with NATO).

Although France's more recent struggle was with Algeria, it was Vietnam (Indochina) that had ended any hope of the French attaining any level of prewar status. Even though de Gaulle hoped to take advantage of a temporary American vacuum derived from U.S. internal conflicts over Vietnam to increase France's stature, matters did not work out as he hoped or indeed as any Europeans thought. Certainly, the war offered a safety valve for European agitators, who could direct their ire at the United States instead of their home nations. One Swedish industrialist said, "thank God for all this . . . Vietnam protest. If there wasn't that outlet . . . all these militant youngsters would be attacking Swedish defense, or agitating for nationalization of firms like us. . . . Anti-Americanism has kept the heat off us."[162] De Gaulle campaigned worldwide against the war, contrasting the "courageous" withdrawal of French troops from Algeria with the "more and more threatening" war in Southeast Asia.[163]

France constituted the only Western nation in the 1960s capable of even partially filling the leadership void caused by America's foreign policy weaknesses, but humiliation, first in Indochina, then in Algeria, forestalled that. Even in their revived form, the bustling French and German economies could not compete with American industry. Nonetheless, Europe cheered for the Vietnamese to teach America a lesson, hopeful that their victory would allow Europe to once again dominate the world. De Gaulle had laid out the future for Europe in a speech at Strasbourg on November 23, 1959: "Yes, it is Europe, from the Atlantic to the Urals, it is the whole of Europe, that will decide the destiny of the world." Europe, from the Atlantic to the Urals— implicitly including European Russia—became the rallying cry not only for de Gaulle, but European integrationists everywhere. With the United States mired in the Far East, now was the time for Europe to reassert itself.

Yet Europe's political ideologies, its heavy state presence, and its socialist influences held back its growth. America failed to become even more dominant and powerful during this time because of its devastating domestic agenda. Lyndon Johnson accelerated America's descent with a spending program he deliberately patterned after the New Deal—but one even more ambitious in its scope.

Wars Without End, Amen

Johnson rode into office on a wave of sympathy for the martyred president John Kennedy. It is unlikely he could have won the seat in a general election on his own, for his forte was logrolling and legislating. Once in the presidency, he cared little about Europeans' opinions of the war, and only marginally more about the views of Americans. Initially, he and his advisers believed they could minimize Vietnam as an issue, and divert the public to Johnson's domestic policies, known as the Great Society. Yet there, he soon found himself enmeshed in another war he could not win—the War on Poverty.

Ginned up in large part by books such as Michael Harrington's *The Other America* (1962), the Great Society was Johnson's attempt at a second New Deal. Nicknamed the War on Poverty, Johnson's income redistribution program was hardly original in its martial characterization of economic growth. William James, addressing the Universal Peace Conference in 1904, had called on the U.S. government to conscript youths to work in poverty-stricken regions, an argument he expanded in his 1911 essay "The Moral Equivalent of War."[164] Franklin Roosevelt's National Youth Administration enlisted two million students and three million unemployed to build schools and hospitals and teach illiterate adults to read. Increasingly, poverty was viewed as an enemy which Americans had to combat.

In his first State of the Union speech, Johnson announced the most massive federal spending binge since the Great Depression. It was all based on the fraudulent notion that more Americans were falling into poverty every year. In fact, progress against poverty had been stunning since World War II, continuing steadily after the JFK tax cuts.[165] Momentum carried it a bit lower after the Great Society was announced, but beginning in 1967— once the actual poverty programs were in place—progress against poverty slowed, then eventually reversed. No sooner than Johnson declared his "war" than it was lost.

The Great Society's goals of eradicating poverty, manifested in the new food stamps and Aid to Families with Dependent Children (AFDC) programs, accomplished just the opposite, guaranteeing a new generation of "poverty moms." Incentives to get on the dole, and stay on it, proved irresistible, as social scientist Charles Murray pointed out in his 1984 book, *Losing Ground*.[166] Government AFDC programs changed the definitions of those eligible for welfare from strictly widows to any woman without a male present in the home, removing incentives to marry without doing anything about out-of-wedlock sex. Illegitimacy skyrocketed after the Great Society programs kicked in, particularly among blacks, who were easily targeted because of their concentration in large cities (whereas rural poor, mostly white, were harder to reach). Social workers combed the projects looking to enlist women. By the mid-1970s, black illegitimacy was nearing 50 percent, then it reached 57 percent by 1990, and in the inner cities, it approached 75 percent.

Johnson and the Democratic Congress scarcely even paused to catch their breath in the wave of reform, passing education bills, the Medicare Act, rent supplements, and a blizzard of other legislation, all later gushed over by historians. Old-school liberals such as Samuel Eliot Morison, Henry Steele Commager, and William E. Leuchtenburg positively beamed in their commendation of the eighty-ninth Congress, "the most productive since the New Deal," which adopted "rent subsidies, demonstration cities, a teacher corps, regional medical centers . . . and Medicaid to provide medical care for the poor. . . . Lyndon Johnson could take pride in the achievements of the 'fabulous 89th' [congress] which opened up prospects for a new era of reform."[167] John Morton Blum praised "the most impressive record of domestic legislation in a single session for 30 years," representing "the culmination of New Deal liberalism in its effort to reverse patterns of privation and inequality in American economic life."[168] From only 651,000 families on AFDC in 1950, the number exploded to 3.5 million by the time the Great Society bureaucracy hummed along in 1976. Despite spending twice as much on social welfare as on defense, the dollars had no relationship to outcome: expenditures per low-income person stood at $1,000 in 1961, then rose eightfold by 1977, with no significant change in overall poverty levels.[169] As early as 1965, with the famous Moynihan Report, undertaken by Johnson's assistant secretary of labor, Daniel Patrick Moynihan, the government was alerted to a "social pathology" of black family breakup. The report urged "the establishment of a stable family structure," which was antithetical to the incentives incorporated into AFDC.[170]

Soaring illegitimacy brought increased youth crime, specifically the proliferation of street gangs with their strong, sociopathic leaders. This was accurately prophesied and analyzed by social commentator and self-taught economist George Gilder.[171] Gilder had argued that a psychosexual ingredient of every family was the financial contribution of adult males, and in turn, males provided an absolutely essential role model for children, particularly boys. Without husbands in the home, boys gravitated to the nearest male role model, often the gang leader. Whereas Johnson insisted, "The answer for all our national problems comes in a single word: That word is education," Gilder—soon accompanied by a growing host of other sociologists and anthropologists debunking Margaret Mead's fallacious "female-headed society" reports—argued that the single word needed to save the inner city was "marriage."[172]

The Great Society was partially implemented as a means to defuse and preempt future inner-city riots after the wave that swept America in the mid-1960s. Large new multistory housing was erected and residents forced into such notorious housing facilities as Chicago's Stateway Gardens, Cabrini Green, or Robert Taylor Homes, or St. Louis's Pruitt-Igoe and Vaughn Public Housing Complex. Many of these buildings had been constructed in the decade before the Great Society, often at the behest of mayors such as Richard Daley, ostensibly to accelerate racial integration, but often actually intensifying segregation. In many cases, public housing became synonymous with drugs and gangs. Chicago's Robert Taylor Homes, planned for 11,000 residents, housed 27,000. A staggering 95 percent of them received welfare.[173] Pruitt-Igoe, one of the first urban housing projects (completed 1955, and designed by Minoru Yamasaki, who was the architect of the World Trade Center) became such a symbol of inner-city poverty and neglect that large crowds in public ceremonies cheered its demolition in 1972.[174]

Racial unrest accompanied an important and screeching subculture that linked Vietnam with other major social issues, including the sexual revolution and drugs. Like no other time in history, social change, political dissatisfaction, and the widespread access to previously unattainable narcotics coalesced to create a new subculture, the hippie generation, not just in the United States, but throughout Europe. Internationally, massive cohorts of young people, born in the aftermath of World War II, flowed into universities erected or expanded at breakneck pace to provide academics with unprecedented opportunities to shape a generation. Such leftist intellectuals as C. P. Snow, E. F. Denison, and Fritz Machlup touted the economic boost of the new "knowledge industry."[175] Berkeley's president, Clark Kerr, called education the "leading sector" in the growth of the economy. Baby boomers, those born from 1946 to 1964 during the postwar boom in birth rates, started reaching college age in 1964, filling the universities with a generation of young people who had to some extent grown up in a world without limits. Many, if not most, never lacked for any of the basics of life and in America, many had parents whose child-rearing skills were guided by Dr. Benjamin Spock's *Baby Book*, which emphasized an absence of parental discipline.

Hitler's Children

Protest and rebellion were youth sports, and America was not alone in suffering through turmoil and unrest. Vietnam proved a convenient mobilizing tool, but Europeans and Japanese found their own injustices to address. In Germany, for example, youths came of age with different baggage; "Hitler's children," as historian Tony Judt called them, rejected their parents' generation as soulless. Their "identification with America and 'the West' derived in no small measure from a wish to avoid . . . 'Germanness.' As a result, in the eyes of their sons and daughters, they stood for nothing."[176] For different reasons then, but with the same ultimate destination, Germans and some Austrian students resembled their protesting American counterparts, embracing a radical theology of free love, Spock-influenced child rearing, and nudity, and absorbing a powerful dose of anti-Semitism as derived from anticapitalist leftists (often themselves Jewish intellectuals in the United States). Thus, in one of the more stunning and remarkable developments of the modern era, the children of the authors of the Holocaust consistently failed to connect racism to the previous generation's sins, instead focusing entirely on "imperial power" and the "lackeys in Bonn." Students became the new Jews, Vietnam, the Auschwitz of America.

Even without a Vietnam to serve as the target, a rash of youth violence swept across Europe—except in France, where the eruptions proved mild under de Gaulle. But elsewhere, as in America, European student demonstrations led to student violence that resulted in murder. In June 1967, 100,000 people turned to the streets in a Berlin demonstration, leading one former critic of Bonn to warn the radicals they were "playing with fire." After a neo-Nazi shot one of the student leaders in March 1968, riots ensued, killing four and wounding 400, and forcing a government crackdown. The Turin revolution in Italy that same year saw similar bouts of activity. When plans to move part of the university into the suburbs produced a year-long reaction, the students linked up with striking workers from the Pirelli tire factories in Milan to produce the "hot autumn" of 1969.

Italian discontent took on a distinctive Maoist tone—more so than anywhere else in Europe or America—replete with rhetoric from Beijing and student mimicry of Red Chinese methods. The journal *Lotta Continua* ("Continuous Struggle") emerged as a popular mouthpiece of revolution; the most popular song, "La Violenza." During the 1968 demonstrations, Maoist-inspired slogans such as "No to social peace in the factories!" and "Only violence helps where violence reigns!" proliferated.[177] Italy got its violence when police discovered bombs at the 1969 Milan Trade Fair and the main railway station; a few months later, after the strikes were settled, the Agricultural Bank in Milan was blown up. After the riots, filmmaker Pier Paolo Pasolini observed that the "privileged children of the bourgeoisie were screaming revolutionary slogans and beating up the underpaid sons of southern sharecroppers charged with preserving civic order."[178]

The rebellion and violence were not restricted to the "white" nations: Japan endured its variant of student uprisings. Protests against the 1970 "Ampo," or Japan–United States Joint Security Treaty, constituted a renewed effort that had failed in 1960 to derail the treaty. Led by the Japan Communist Party and the New Left Party, the organizers had essentially worked for a decade to rectify their failures in earlier unsuccessful demonstrations.[179] Warming up in the mid-1960s with opposition to the Japan/Korea security treaty and the by-then-common Vietnam war protests, leftists armed students with plastic color-coded helmets and wooden poles to fight riot police. At Haneda Airport, a clash left one dead and 600 injured.[180] The 1969 University of Tokyo riots resulted in 8,500 police dispatched to seal off the Hongo campus and clear the buildings one by one, whereupon a national government crackdown followed. Where the Italian protests took on a decidedly laborite character, the Japanese demonstrators were motivated by specific campus reforms (Tokyo University's protests, for example, involved opposition to the low wages of medical students). As often as not, however, factional fighting within New Left groups proved even more deadly than clashes with the authorities; in Japan, more than a dozen members of the Red Army killed each other in internecine fighting over ideology. Bodies were found tied naked to trees where they had frozen to death.[181]

In America, however, the large-scale student protests seemed to be more appropriately defined by their opposition to specific injustices, namely racism and the war. Dating from the mid-1960s, when 25,000, many students, showed up in Washington, D.C., to protest the war in 1967, the pattern of radicalism originating on campuses was established. For some, of course, it did not move fast enough, and more radical elements always repudiated pacifism. The Weather Underground, for example, formed in 1969, was a disaffected faction of the Students for a Democratic Society whose stated goal was to overthrow the U.S. government by violent means. Early signers of their 1969 manifesto ("You Don't Need a Weatherman to Know Which Way the Wind Blows") included Mark Rudd, Bill Ayers, and Bernardine Dohrn (the last two of whom married each other). Violence, some Weather-related, some not, spread rapidly. They adopted the slogan "Bring the War Home."[182] Meeting with North Vietnamese officials, members of the Underground were implored to engage in armed action against the U.S. government.

Campuses did not need the Weathermen present to experience violence. Anarchism was a favored ideology because votes simply didn't matter anymore to many students and radicals (especially after the Chicago Democratic Convention of 1968, where the media made it appear that "the people" wanted Eugene McCarthy, but the democratic primary process clearly chose Senator Hubert Humphrey). Columbia had a raucous demonstration in 1970, one of 221 major campus disruptions that year. But the wake-up call for both naive weekend protesters and authorities alike came on August 24, 1970, when a bombing at the University of Wisconsin, connected to anti-Vietnam activists, killed a researcher, Robert Fassnacht, at the school's Sterling Hall. One of the murderers, Karleton Armstrong, interviewed in the 1990s on *America's Most Wanted* after serving seven years in prison, stated that he felt no remorse about Fassnacht's death and claimed it paled in comparison with the millions killed in Indochina. Another bomber, David Fine, was denied admission to the Oregon bar for his role in the event; a third, Leo Burt, disappeared and remained at large as of 2009; and a fourth, Dwight Armstrong, Karleton's brother, drifted into the Symbionese Liberation Army.[183]

Without question, the most memorable and tragic American student protest occurred at Kent State University in 1970. It came as a response to President Nixon's announcement of his decision on April 30 to send American troops into Cambodia to eliminate North Vietnamese sanctuaries—a long overdue protection of U.S. military lives. Students smashed some windows on May 1, but other than that, all was quiet until Saturday evening, when a rally was held on the Kent State Commons. As the crowd meandered through the campus picking up supporters, it neared the ROTC building where the protesters began to cry "Burn it" and "ROTC has got to go."[184] The building was set on fire (supposedly no one knew by whom), another group of students left to burn the college president's house down (they were thwarted by state troopers), and elements of the Ohio National Guard arrived to take control. The young guardsmen called in were pulled off of convoy duty on Interstate 80, where they had been riding shotgun on trucks driven by Teamsters, enduring sniper fire from striking Independent Steel Haulers for the last two days. Tired, jumpy, and scared, the guardsmen were in no mood to put up with more violence. There was little or no difference in age between the guardsmen and the demonstrators, but there was in education—the students were in college while the guardsmen were at best high school graduates.

A sit-in was held on Sunday evening and the administration attempted to end the protest, giving the demonstrators five minutes to disperse. When they didn't leave, approximately 110 guardsmen were ordered to move in with tear gas and bayonets. The students dispersed, although one student was slightly wounded by a bayonet. When protests resumed the following day, three thousand students assembled. They were ordered again to disperse, this time by General Robert Canterbury of the Ohio National Guard; his announcement brought a hail of rocks and obscenities from the crowd. After a skirmish line of 76 Guardsmen threw down a number of tear gas containers (which were relatively ineffective due to the wind), they retreated up a hill in ragged groups. One guardsman fired into the air as rocks pelted them, having endured ten minutes of having objects thrown at them. But then twenty-nine or thirty-one other Guardsmen, thinking there had been an order given, fired into the crowd. No order had been given. Four students were killed and nine wounded or injured; twenty-eight guardsmen were injured.

The controversy surrounding the Kent State incident continues to this day, even though a 1974 criminal trial against some of the guardsmen was dismissed, and in a federal civil trial in 1975, a jury two-to-one agreed that none of the guardsmen were legally responsible for the deaths. Some of the crowd were outsiders—career activists and agitators—and the girl in a famous photograph, kneeling over a fallen student and screaming, was not a student at all but a sixteen-year-old runaway. None of that changed the reality that young Americans had shot and killed other young Americans over ideas in what people had thought was a more civil society.[185] The assassinations of JFK, MLK, RFK, and others, combined with the urban riots and bombings, made average Americans removed from the cities and campuses feel alienated and endangered. A backlash to the student protests developed, and showing a hand with four fingers raised meant, "The score is four, and next time more." Faculty members at Kent State, one of whom had taught his class how to make a Molotov cocktail, received a torrent of letters expressing regret that they had escaped retribution. The country was truly fragmenting.

Much of this was to be anticipated. The postwar progeny had in many cases experienced the end of material hardship while at the same time absorbing the utopian vision of a peaceful world. In the United States, the mass of American college-age students arrived at the nation's universities just as the federal government dumped billions of dollars into those institutions as a result of the perceived threat of *Sputnik* and Soviet scientific capabilities. But in other ways the youth demonstrations proved universal. Across the developed countries of Europe, the numbers of university students born in the postwar birth explosion also skyrocketed. Worldwide, student numbers had increased exponentially since the 1950s. In part, the expansion occurred because some countries, including Italy and France, abolished all university entrance examinations, thus admitting virtually anyone. Europeans expanded existing universities without implementing any screening systems or requirements to winnow out the unqualified. The University of Bari in Italy saw its student body increase from 5,000 to 30,000 in the 1960s, and along with the University of Naples, at 50,000, and the University of Rome, at 60,000, had more students than in all of Italy in 1950. Germany, which had 108,000 university students in 1950, had 400,000 by 1970.[186]

American universities also grew at explosive rates. The University of Michigan, University of Wisconsin, Ohio State University, and Arizona State University all soon had student populations in excess of 40,000. (Michigan's football stadium, only slightly larger than most, held 102,000, or the entire population of Bologna, Italy.) Nothing compared with the massive University of California system, however, and its subtier of "teaching" colleges, the California State University system. UC Berkeley, which became known for its radical politics in the 1960s, actually was politically moderate compared with the more radical UC Santa Cruz. By 2005, the University of California system had 214,000 students and 170,000 faculty and staff spread across ten campuses; while its junior partner had twenty-three campuses, 450,000 students, and 46,000 faculty and staff. (This was more than all the students in 1949 in Britain, Sweden, Belgium, France, and Spain *combined*.)

Far from generating greater economic output, students consumed resources, and opting out of technical programs, entered nonproductive jobs, often in the public sector. Performance was lower yet expectations were higher. U.S. grade inflation overlapped a historical SAT test score slide of between twenty-four and fifty points (depending on the institution).[187]

Even in the Third World, similar trends could be seen and perpetuated themselves to the present. At Makerere University in Uganda, one recent study found little entrepreneurship had materialized since independence. Self-employment, the study reported, was minimal as "there are very few graduates who venture to initiate their own enterprises."[188] Indeed, by far the leading employer of graduates of Makerere was . . . schools, which consumed over 30 percent of the students. Other public sector work accounted for another 15 percent, and taken together, education and government employed more than agriculture, building/construction, mining, transportation, trade, and chemicals. Only banking and finance constituted a nongovernment employment sector that accounted for more than 10 percent. Thomas Sowell pointed out that most degrees from African universities were in political science or government, as opposed to business, agriculture, engineering, or areas in which wealth is created.[189] And if one concedes that the majority of professors in Third World colleges were hostile to the free market and enamored of government, then simply expanding the number of university students was a net loss when it came to development.

After the 1968 reforms in France undertaken as a result of the Nanterre student protest, universities admitted any high school graduate who could pass the high school exams. With a glut of college students on the market, the value of a degree plummeted, and overwhelmed by the new numbers, the French failed to invest in buildings or faculty salaries, except for the *grandes écoles*, which absorbed 30 percent of the public budget.[190] Everywhere, a familiar pattern established itself: at first, the monetary remuneration of a college degree was substantial, but as a larger share of graduates came on the market, its value fell. In 1978, most Americans already had more than a high school education, and 17 percent had a college degree. At the same time, the civil rights movement and radical feminism imposed a creeping credentialism on business. Previously, an employer could exercise his own judgment on the character of an applicant, and possibly, racism and gender perceptions caused many a good candidate to be ignored or excluded. More commonly, however, individuals who lacked a high school or college degree could be brought in on a provisionary basis, proving themselves along the way. Virtually every great female or minority entrepreneur advanced under such conditions or, denied access, created his or her own avenues around the system. Mary Kay Ash, passed over for promotions within a cosmetic company, started her own powerhouse corporation; Berry Gordy challenged the major record labels by developing a distinct Motown sound; and so on.[191] Once credentialism seeped in, the college degree became a union card of admission, greatly benefiting younger single women, often at the expense of middle-aged white and black men, who had experience but less formal education. Over time, this produced a significant obstacle to the upward mobility of married men with little education, but excellent motivation for them to return for more education that might or might not actually be useful.

Student Unrest . . . Against Communists

Behind the Iron Curtain, voices of dissent were increasingly being heard when Polish and Czech students attempted their own version of the "free speech" movement. Leszek Kołakowski, a professor of philosophy at Warsaw University, initiated the East Bloc's encounter with protesters when he gave a speech in 1956 to the History Institute denouncing Poland's missed opportunity to liberalize—for which he was promptly expelled from the party. Over the next ten years, Polish Communists became increasingly estranged from the people, and Kołakowski attained a legendary status at Warsaw University, which emerged as the new cauldron of Party criticism. The "clumsy Polish leadership, enraged by its criticism from the Left," managed to forge a powerful opposition among the university's intellectuals, which came to a head over the January 1968 cancellation of the play *Forefathers' Eve*.[192] Adam Mickiewicz's 1832 work about nineteenth-century rebels was eerily similar to the plight of modern anti-Communist freedom fighters, and its cancellation sparked a protest march in Warsaw calling for "free theater." The Poles had now co-opted the free speech movement for anti-Communist ends. Unlike Europe or America, where antidemocracy radicals were accommodated with capitulation from university or government authorities, this was the Soviet bloc. Two of the leaders were expelled from the university, and when other organizers attempted to protest their punishment in March 1968, they were met with Stalin-style sympathy in the form of genuine (not, as in the West, feigned) police repression.

If the Poles had learned anything from Saul Alinsky and the sixties radicals in America, however, it was escalate, escalate, escalate. New demonstrations followed, met with still more violent force by the authorities, under the instructions of Secretary Władisław Gomułka. Soon thereafter, more expulsions, including Kołakowski's. Trials were held, prison terms imposed, and professors and students arrested from 1968 to 1969.

Polish Communist leaders blamed *Jews* for the disturbances. Gomulka announced, "we shall not prevent Polish citizens from returning to Israel if they wish to do so. . . . We do not want a Fifth Column in our country."[193] Virtually none of Poland's tiny Jewish community (about four thousand in 1965) had ever seen Israel, and many were loyal Communists but their innocence was as irrelevant to the "forces of history" as were those purged by Stalin a half-century before. All of Poland's considerable economic problems were laid at the feet of Jews of questionable loyalty to Poland. Newspapers revived the descriptions of Jews found in the Nuremberg Laws, forcing two thirds of the nation's Jews out of the country in just over a year, while the government expelled all Jews from the Communist Party and removed them from all teaching positions in schools and universities. By doing so, Poland's Communists finished the "purification" of Poland the Nazis started, and decimated the intellectual core of the nation's universities. Some of the ease with which Gomułka carried out the persecution stemmed from the intellectuals' failure to ally with the workers, but, with the intellectuals gone, the sword now cut in the other direction. When the government hiked food prices 30 percent two years later, striking shipyard workers found themselves isolated and lacking voices in the dissident press. The old adage about "When they came for the Jews, I did nothing . . ." seemed remarkably applicable to the Poles in these years.

Czechoslovakia also learned the Polish lesson. Since the early 1960s, Czech party authorities had gradually permitted market-oriented reforms to save their stagnant economy. Incentives were offered to workers to increase output, but their greatest impact was not in Czechoslovakia's factories, but in its schools and among the cultural elites, for whom "the prospect of a loosening of the Stalinist shackles released an avalanche of criticisms, hopes and expectations."[194] Slowly, a trickle of books, plays, and pamphlets appeared that challenged or criticized the Soviet orthodoxy, especially the artificial history it had imposed on the Czechs. Still, economic reforms proceeded apace in 1967, and reform appeared to be gaining momentum with the election of First Secretary Alexander Dubček in January 1968. Here was a younger Communist, and a Slovak, who represented many of those previously disenfranchised (to the degree that communism enfranchised anyone).

The public rallied to his program—although no one really knew what he stood for—calling for freedom of the press, an end to censorship, and investigations into the 1950s purges. Slovakia was given equal status and autonomy; the Communist Party announced its Action Program, a ten-year process in which it would allow the formation of other political parties and even genuine elections. This was the so-called Prague Spring, or "Socialism with a human face." Dubcek and his more aggressive followers failed to understand there could be no third way with communism, that there was *no fundamental difference* between Stalinism and ideological communism. By its nature, a political and economic system that relied primarily on coercion, rather than an agreed-upon set of beliefs in natural law, would inevitably drift toward totalitarianism, gulags, and mass executions. To attempt to work backward from a pathological system through reform was neither logical nor without danger, as the Czechs found out. More large-scale demonstrations in favor of the reforms occurred in April 1968, followed by the official end of press censorship and the call for the formation of political parties. Czechoslovakia had crossed a line; by the summer, the Soviets could no longer ignore what was happening in Prague, and in August Leonid Brezhnev, the new Soviet dictator, assembled half a million Warsaw Pact troops to end the Czech holiday. Soviet defense minister Andrei Grechko told his fellow ministers, "The invasion will take place even if it leads to a third world war."[195]

The United States was not interested in engaging with the Soviets over Czechoslovakia at this time. Lyndon Johnson, having all but resigned with his will-not-run speech, and bogged down in Vietnam, had no inclination whatsoever to open a new front against communism. Moreover, the Soviets could look at history: a more hard-line anti-Communist such as Dwight Eisenhower had not intervened in Hungary in 1956, and the softer Johnson would not do so now.

The Prague Spring came to an abrupt end as activists submitted to "questioning," subsequently recanting their support of Dubček's reforms. Writers, playwrights, and professors received Mao-like punishments, being "forced to clean boilers and wash windows [or] stacking bricks."[196] Soviet authorities explained the resistance as a mass psychosis. A few protests against the crackdown nevertheless occurred, such as a demonstration in Red Square in August 1968 that included Pavel Litvinov, the grandson of the foreign minister under Stalin. Some of the Warsaw Pact units, particularly the Hungarians who had themselves faced Soviet correction, were withdrawn when questions about their trustworthiness were raised. Possibly the most futile protests involved the suicide-burnings of Jan Palach, a Czech student at Charles University who immolated himself at the National Museum, and Ilya Rips, a Latvian Jew, a year later. While the Western press had obsessively covered the suicides of Buddhist monks in Vietnam, to the extent that they influenced John Kennedy to acquiesce in the assassination of Diem, these anti-Communist immolations went virtually unreported in the West.

Palach and Rips were memorialized (Palach's funeral was decreed a day of Czech national mourning), but the real eulogies went unspoken, though not unnoticed. The Communist experiment was over and "never again would it be possible to maintain that Communism rested on popular consent. . . ."[197] Nonetheless, neither Poland's nor Czechoslovakia's efforts to reform communism had succeeded, although they had revealed its rotting structure and its incapacity for permanent good under any circumstances. The final, brutal illustration of what communism was all about came on August 21, 1968, when soldiers of the Red Army swarmed into a Czech party meeting and lined up behind each member, causing one official to glumly admit, "at such a moment one's concept of socialism moves to last place. But . . . you know that it has a direct connection . . . with the automatic weapon pointing at your back."[198] Soviet tanks had provided an object lesson in reality, that Stalinism was the irreversible end point of Marx's pompous theories. Contrary to the view that "the soul of Communism had died . . . in Prague," there never was a soul. It was all an illusion.

Last Days of Aquarius

In so many ways, the sixties were a "time of illusion" (as peacenik Jonathan Schell wrote) everywhere: partially due to the sheer horror possible through atomic warfare, the naïveté of the young demonstrators, and the inclination of an entire generation, for the first time, to experiment with mind-altering drugs. Like other trends in the 1960s, drug use had its origins much earlier. Long before the flower children of San Francisco began toking, before Hunter S. Thompson was "gonzo," and before Timothy Leary urged his disciples to "tune in, turn on, and drop out," English author Aldous Huxley had published *The Doors of Perception* (1954), becoming the first mainstream writer to examine psychedelic drugs (in his case, mescaline).[199] He followed that with a novel, *Island* (1962), infused with Eastern mysticism and the assumption that through mescaline, LSD, and other mind-altering drugs, he could precipitate a "revolution in Western consciousness."[200] Spiritual revelation could be attained, he claimed, and the creative process energized, by using hallucinogens; Huxley, imbibing in only low doses, had a "good trip," and pronounced such drugs harmless and useful. LSD could turn anything ordinary into something of universal import—oatmeal became the substance of the cosmos, bird droppings were Hindu death-wheels. As Huxley described acid's power, "Eternity in a flower. Infinity in four chair legs, and the Absolute in the fold of a pair of flannel trousers!"[201] Or, more realistically, madness in a chemical flake the size of a booger—but no one at the time was concerned with the evil effects of mind alteration when saving Western consciousness was at stake.

Huxley's new love of pharmaceuticals dovetailed with his readings in *The Tibetan Book of the Dead*, which he brought to the attention of a Harvard clinical psychology lecturer, Timothy Leary, in 1961. Leary claimed he had achieved astounding rehabilitation rates with criminals at Concord Prison by administering psilocybin mushrooms to prisoners. Shortly thereafter it was revealed that he experimented on Andover seminarians and undergraduates and failed to teach his classes, forcing Harvard to give him the boot in 1963. Having already gained the attention of the heirs to the Mellon fortune, Leary was given a mansion in Millbrook, New York, to continue his experiments. Leary wrote, "We saw ourselves as anthropologists from the twenty-first century inhabiting a time module set somewhere in the dark ages of the 1960s. On this space colony we were attempting to create a new paganism and a new dedication to life as art."[202] The FBI raided Leary's "space colony" repeatedly, finally shutting down Millbrook altogether. One picture of Millbrook that emerged was that of a Mansonesque orgy without the blood—nonstop tripping and crashing, interrupted by raids, many of them led by local assistant district attorney G. Gordon Liddy. (In 1982, after they both had served prison time, Leary and Liddy would share the stage in a traveling lecture show of ex-cons, debating the essence of America.) Tom Wolfe, writing about Leary in his *Electric Kool-Aid Acid Test* (1968), rode across the country with Ken Kesey and his Merry Pranksters in a Day-Glo school bus when he visited Millbrook, but claimed he didn't even see the guru, who was whacked out for three days.[203]

The Beatles also helped make drug use acceptable for the middle class, as they were the first celebrities to make reference to drug use in their lyrics and public comments. Armies of fans saw drug use as acceptable if the "clean cut" Beatles were doing it (although by the late sixties, the Beatles' look had changed substantially). Most of the band dropped acid in 1966. Four years later, John Lennon spoke of his first trip: "I did some drawings at the time. . . . I've got them somewhere—of four faces saying, 'We all agree with you.'"[204] Ray Manzarek of the Doors recalled the time he ingested LSD with singer Jim Morrison:

> There was a certain shine, a luminosity projecting out through the cornea of the devotees. The carbon-arc of the brain was flooding the entire brain pan with holy light that would . . . radiate outward through the eye sockets.[205]

Precisely because the Beatles were latecomers to the psychedelic party (although, because of their fame, they were viewed as the vanguard), they had not noticed that the hippie movement, which had swept the United States and much of Europe in the mid-1960s, was already cresting. A turning point of sorts was reached when Beatle George Harrison—one of the first pop stars to tune in through LSD—visited Haight-Ashbury in 1967, hoping to find a psychedelic paradise and expecting "to find a community of 'healthy wonderful enlightened people.'"[206] Instead, Harrison "was appalled by the squalor of the street scene, with its collection of 'drunks, down-and-outs and spotty little school kids' begging for spare change."[207] It was nothing but "'hey man' for about an hour by all these horrible people," he recalled.[208]

LSD and other psychedelic drugs had already overtaken rock music, much the way heroin and grass had compromised jazz musicians. No one could doubt that lyrics were improved, if only for the variety. Gone were the catchy ditties about "Surfin' USA" and "I'm Henry the Eighth, I am," replaced by drug-induced ramblings in which Jimi Hendrix floated on massive dragonflies and kissed the sky and Cream told of "tiny purple fishes run laughing through her fingers," how their "naked ears were tortured by the sirens sweetly singing."

Like so many other concocted fables of the 1960s, the music-as-protest myth ignored the real truth. The Jefferson Airplane, considered a protest band, in fact insisted "we didn't give a shit about politics. . . . We wanted the freedom to make our own choices."[209] The Airplane "shied away from lyrics that pointed fingers at the government, the military or other specific targets."[210] Indeed, in many ways Grace Slick, their female lead singer, was hardly the embodiment of hippiedom: a high school cheerleader and, briefly, a fashion model, Slick wore makeup, liked nice clothes, insisted on her privacy, was mortified by communal living, and hated dirt—hers or anyone else's. Beach Boy Brian Wilson summed it up: "You can always write about social issues but who gives a damn. I want to write about something these kids feel is their whole world."[211]

Antiwar protest movements did make for good theater, especially as measured in numbers; 20,000 showed up to march on the Pentagon and 250,000 came to Hyde Park, New York, to hear a free concert by the Rolling Stones. But this was the dirty little secret of many protests: if you offered plenty of free music, your crowds would come. Thus was born the mega–music festival, with hundreds of thousands of people. England's Isle of Wight held its first festival in 1968; by 1970, the festival featured one of the largest gatherings of hippiedom ever, some 600,000 fans and stars such as Jimi Hendrix, the Doors, Ten Years After, and folk legend Joan Baez. But the infamous event of the day was New York's Woodstock in 1969, made more famous thanks to the movie of the same name. Woodstock took on a legendary quality the others lacked. It was a time-delay reenactment of

Beatlemania years earlier, with "an unimaginably large crowd of young people, bound together by their shared love of rock . . . finding enough safety and power in numbers to create a fleeting state of community where the usual rules were momentarily suspended. . . ."[212] At least, that was the stated, romanticized version, perpetuated in the media and the movie.

Reality at Woodstock was much darker. Promoters originally selected the site both because of the space and privacy offered by Max Yasgur's farm, some sixty miles from the town itself, and by the prospect that Bob Dylan, who lived there, would perform (he didn't). Intended as a money maker, the event's promoters overscheduled acts, flying them in by helicopters (the roads of Sullivan County were nearly impassable after half a million hippies tramped through, backed up fifteen miles in each direction), leaving the exhausted and strung-out musicians to wait for hours while the previous acts—each encouraged to stay longer by encore demands—pushed the timetable further back.

From August 15 to 17, 1969, the world got a picture of what a hippie republic would look like. Convinced that merely a trip to Woodstock entitled the visitor to a free concert, crowds broke down the chain-link fences and scrambled inside by the thousands. A rainstorm turned the site to mud, then ninety-degree heat turned the moisture into unbearable humidity. The festival area was turned into "an undeclared disaster area, beset by the shortages of food, water, shelter, and sanitation commonly associated with floods and earthquakes."[213] A sea of people waved back and forth like a cannabis-animated cornfield; a few herky-jerked spasmodically to the music, absent any rhythm or grace. Instead of a "major planetary event," as beat poet Allen Ginsberg called it, or a "political forum for the young" as *Time* labeled it, Woodstock was a mass acid trip with its highs, lows, comedy, and terror.[214] Two years later, one radical complained that the "rapes, the bad acid burns, stealing from each other, they, too were a part of the Woodstock experience. . . ."[215] Once the haze lifted, a more reasonable interpretation suggests the concert-goers were outtasight, but not particularly insightful; tripping but not transcendent; lit, but not enlightened. Jerry Garcia, Grateful Dead guitarist, felt "the presence of the invisible time travelers from the future," but others who attended saw something much different—"kids freaking out from megadoses of acid or almost audibly buzzing from battery-acid crank like flies trapped in a soda can."[216]

Within a few years, many of those who had preached drug liberation through their songs were dead from overdoses or other consequences of their lifestyles, including the Rolling Stones' Brian Jones, Rory Storm,

Mike Bloomfield, Keith Moon, Janis Joplin, Sid Vicious, Dennis Wilson, and Jimi Hendrix, as well as the antihippie (but heavy drug user) Elvis Presley. Others, including John Bonham, Jim Morrison, Sly Stone, Gram Parsons, David Crosby, and Jack Bruce, had their careers shortened or their health destroyed by years of drug or alcohol use; two of the founding members of San Francisco's legendary Moby Grape were mental invalids, one of them committed to Bellevue. Terry Kath, Pete Ham, and Phil Ochs all committed suicide. Bassist-writer Felix Pappalardi, of Mountain, who had produced Cream's famous *Disraeli Gears* album, survived a drug overdose only to be killed by his wife a few years later. Doors keyboardist Ray Manzarek later looked back with remorse over Morrison's chronic alcoholism ("How many great lyrics got lost in that senseless flood of drunken activity?").[217] But one could have asked the same question about any of the rock geniuses. When, almost twenty years later, Don Henley asked how love could survive "in such a graceless age," it certainly seemed to apply to the Woodstock era as much as to the period he wrote about.

With almost no one hanging around to clean up, Woodstock produced one of the largest piles of garbage ever seen. It also produced considerable disillusionment among the Left: Abbie Hoffman (literally kicked off the stage by Who guitarist Pete Townshend when he attempted to commandeer a microphone for a political speech), John Sinclair, and other agitators turned on the Woodstock experience as inauthentic because it failed to advance the revolution. The event's mythology of "three days of love, peace, and happiness" was seized on by radical elements as the natural culmination of 1968 Chicago. At least, it was the society Abbie Hoffman and others hoped would emerge from a Johnson-less and Nixon-less America. "When I left Chicago," Hoffman wrote a month after the festival,

> I felt we had won a great victory [but] leaving Woodstock I was not so sure what exactly had happened. . . . Figuring out who was the enemy was not only difficult but the mere posing of the question seemed out of place. . . . Was this really the beginning of a new civilisation [sic] or the symptom of a dying one? Were we establishing a liberated zone or entering a detention camp?[218]

And as if to add insult to injury, recent research has shown that protest music never played any significant role in shaping or even reflecting anti-Vietnam attitudes until American public opinion shifted against the war in 1969, when Creedence Clearwater Revival's "Fortunate Son" and John

Lennon's "Give Peace a Chance" constituted the first true antiwar songs to make the charts. Antiwar songs made up less than 1.5 percent of the one thousand singles on the top 100s chart from 1965 through 1974. One study of teens found that only one quarter of listeners based a song's appeal on lyrics; and even the ultimate gloom-and-doom protest song, Barry Mc-Guire's "Eve of Destruction," had a message that over 40 percent of its listeners misunderstood.[219]

Flower-Power Murder

The image of flower-waving, nonviolent hippies merely searching for free love stood in sharp juxtaposition to the abstemiousness of Gandhi—whom they routinely invoked as a role model—and had a sinister side in its connection to some of the dark violence of the sixties. In the United States, while most eyes were on antiwar marches, a series of brutal and bizarre mass murders swept the nation. Between December 1968 and October 1969, a criminal known only as the Zodiac killer stalked northern California, murdering five people and sending Jack-the-Ripper-like taunting letters to the press. And just a week before Woodstock, a cult of Charles Manson's followers broke into the home of film director Roman Polanski in the Bel Air section of Los Angeles and butchered those present, smearing bloody slogans on the walls. Whereas most Americans reacted with horror and revulsion, radical Yippie leader Jerry Rubin said he fell in love with Manson's "cherub face and sparkling eyes." Bernadine Dohrn, a leader of the Weather Underground and future wife of Bill Ayers, gushed, "Dig it! First they killed those pigs, then they ate dinner in the same room with them, then they even shoved a fork into [Sharon Tate's] stomach! Wild!"[220]

That the killers frequently used drugs, and that Manson claimed to be inspired by the Beatles' song "Helter Skelter," challenged the conventional wisdom which held that drugs caused people to "mellow out." Before the killings, Beach Boy Dennis Wilson briefly put up Manson and his groupies at his house, where Manson played his songs for Wilson. Manson, perhaps for the first time, forced the hippie movement to confront its dark side:

> Most of those who sympathised [sic] with the movement, from po-
> litical activists to mellow hippies, stared into the eyes they saw on
> TV, and wondered what linked Manson's madness with their own
> imagination; what had perverted the late 1960s ideal of communal
> living, sexual freedom and musical expression to the extent that it
> could become a springboard for barbaric slaughter.[221]

It would be equally unfair, however, to assert that the drug culture was singularly responsible for the mass murder wave that struck the United States from the late 1960s to the late 1970s. Certainly more than a few killer lunatics stalked the earth before Woodstock. The notorious grave-robbing Ed Gein, for example, who decorated his Wisconsin house with human skulls, lamps made of skin, and had a belt made of noses and nipples, was captured in 1957, whereupon police raided his house and discovered his trophies. Gein became the inspiration behind such movie killers as Norman Bates in *Psycho* and Buffalo Bill in *Silence of the Lambs*. One of the most famous of the serial killers, Ted Bundy, well educated and charismatic, was an honors student with a degree in psychology, and worked for New York governor Nelson Rockefeller in his Seattle office when the New Yorker ran for president in 1968. He began murdering women at least as early as 1974, sober as a judge and crazy as a loon, kidnapping and killing coeds in Washington State at an average of one a month, before moving on to Utah and Colorado. Attending law school at the University of Utah, Bundy used disguises and feigned helplessness to get close to women, using crutches to approach victims. Bundy was every bit as ghoulish as Gein, decapitating dozens of victims with a hacksaw, applying makeup to the decomposing corpses, and having sex with the bodies. He kept their severed heads in his apartment for weeks.[222]

The Zodiac killer presaged a wave of rampages by serial killers that included Bundy and far less publicized monsters such as William Bonin (the "Freeway Killer" in LA), Dean Corll (the "Candy Man," who, with two accomplices, slaughtered more than 25 young boys in the Houston area), Juan Corona (a homosexual, machete-wielding Mexican schizophrenic), and Donald Harvey (who killed between 35 and 80 victims), followed in the early 1980s by Richard Ramirez, California's infamous "Night Stalker." Ramirez had one of the longest and most expensive trials in American history, in which 1,600 jurors were interviewed and 100 witnesses testified before a jury found him guilty on thirteen counts of murder.[223]

Mass murder by individuals, as opposed to as an outgrowth of state policy and psychotic ideologies, might be largely an American phenomenon, but other countries also had claim to a few crazed killers. One of Japan's few mass killers, Kiyoshi Okubo, "The Gentleman," operated in 1971. Norway had a single angel of death geriatric nurse, and Great Britain had the "Garden of Evil" husband and wife team of Frederick and Rosemary West, who confessed to killing thirty people, including their own daughter, whom they planted under their patio.[224] The Wests were malevolently impressive, nabbing mostly troubled girls, but also abducting a seamstress, a nanny, and a student, as well as one of Fred's former wives, for Rosemary's sadistic lesbian sex and for Fred to rape. The Brits also sparked memories of two other English mass killers, Myra Hindley and Ian Brady, who murdered children in the 1960s, and civil servant Dennis Nilsen, who dispatched fifteen young men in the early 1980s.

Italy's "Monster of Florence" stalked lovers in the Italian countryside from 1968 to 1985. Mexico featured a rare pair of sister-murderesses called *Las Poquianchis* (Sonoran for "the loose women"), who in the late 1950s and early 1960s killed more than ninety people, almost all of them prostitutes who had worked in their "bordello from hell." When the prostitutes were too badly abused or lost their looks, *Las Poquianchis* (with the help of other sisters) eliminated them, as well as a few customers who flashed large amounts of cash. In 1977, the sisters became the basis for a movie (*Las Poquianchis*) and a book (*Las Muertas*, by Jorge Ibargüengoitia).

Europe's Wild West

American violence tended toward individual acts. Senseless and mystifying as most of them were, they defied analysis by intellectuals who insisted on attempting to explain even the most irrational human behavior. Murders in the United States, especially gun violence, also enabled leftist critics to argue that it was a natural and inevitable outgrowth of the rugged individualism that, in their view, poisoned the United States. Yet similar types of violence was hardly absent in Europe. Sicily, notorious for its Mafia culture, battled mobsters for generations. Often, the entire civil structure, including mayors, police chiefs, and judges, was bought and paid for by Sicilian mob leaders. Even excluding the mob, Italy was anything but peaceful. From 1970 to 1980, assassins killed three prominent politicians, nine judges, more than sixty police, and three hundred civilians, and "not a year passed in Italy without murders, mutilations, kidnapping, assaults and sundry acts of public violence."[225] A virtual smorgasbord of terror groups sprang up— the Red Brigades were the best known, many of them funded by the KGB— with Monty Pythonesque variations on Leninist names, including the Ongoing Struggle, Workers' Power, Front Line, and Fighting Communist Unions.[226] The only ones missing from the list were the Popular People's Front or the People's Popular Front.

Italians grew increasingly numb to the daily carnage, and the nation might have descended into a Colombian-style government of thug zones had the Red Brigades not overplayed their hand in 1978 with the kidnapping of the prominent former prime minister Aldo Moro. The government refused to negotiate as the drama played out over two months, until Moro's body was discovered in a car parked in the middle of Rome. Other assassinations of notable public figures followed, despite a massive antiterror campaign by authorities. When the terrorists' acts grew so brazen that they pushed the Italian Communist Party into supporting the government, a break occurred between the radicals and the Old Left. To be sure, not all the mayhem stemmed from the Left-oriented allies of the Red Brigades. In both Germany and Italy, the fascist Right saw its opportunity to launch new attacks of its own, including the bombing of a railway station in Bologna in August 1980. One group in Italy, the P2 Lodge, counted among its members and paid associates thirty generals and forty-three deputies of parliament, plus three active ministers in the cabinet. If that were not enough, the Mafia, anxious to assert its authority, stepped up its coercion on police and judges.

Spain similarly fought a long-running war with the ETA (*Euskadi Ta Akatasuna*, or "Basquia and Freedom"), which was founded in 1958 to attain Basque independence. ETA terrorists targeted Spanish police, court authorities, and politicians, but also "moderates"—a tactic that had by then become common among all terrorists. They also sought out "symbols of 'Spanish' decadence in the region: cinemas, bars, discotheques, drug pushers, and the like."[227] In 1973, they assassinated Francisco Franco's prime minister, Luis Carrero Blanco, following that up with a Madrid bombing that killed 12 people. Attempts to offer the Basque region autonomy only exposed the terrorists for the radicals they were; after the referendum was approved, from 1979 to 1989 ETA killed 181 people in bombings and assassinations. ETA's threat grew so extreme that the government responded with its own version of extremism, stationing units of antiterrorist special forces inside the northern Basque area in France to neutralize the threat, one terrorist at a time. Perhaps the greatest irony was that a socialist government, under Prime Minister Felipe González, gave the termination orders.

Ireland was another front in terror-style violence, where the Provisional Irish Republican Army (the IRA, or, as they were called, the Provos) launched a war with British troops trying to keep order in Protestant Northern Ireland. On "Bloody Sunday," January 30, 1972, British paratroopers in Derry shot 26 civilians, killing 13, after the army, engaged in a riot-control effort (with water cannons and rubber bullets), received word of IRA snipers in the area. A year later, Ulster was the battleground: 146 police and soldiers and 321 civilians were killed.

At the same time Spain battled the ETA and the British struggled with Northern Ireland, West Germany came under assault from the Baader-Meinhof Gang (also known as the Red Army Faction). Over an eight-year period from 1970 to 1978, the Baader-Meinhof Gang was implicated in 95 killings, 162 hostage takings, and 30 bank robberies. It "pursued a strategy of deliberately random terror, assassinating soldiers, policemen and businessmen, holding up banks and kidnapping mainstream politicians."[228] Both Andreas Baader and Ulrike Meinhof were captured and both died (some say under curious circumstances) in prison, but the gang straggled along, bombing U.S. Air Force facilities at Ramstein in 1981 before fading into oblivion. Emboldened by such anarcholeftist elements, neo-Nazis disrupted the 1980 Oktoberfest with a car bomb that killed 13 and wounded 220.

Then there was the rioting, which was far more a European tradition than American, and which was normally met with brutal countermeasures. In 1961, for example, French police, struggling to contain a protest march in Paris by Algerians, killed almost 200, pushing many of them into the Seine. The police chief, Maurice Papon, was tried and condemned for crimes against humanity.[229] Indeed, all across Europe blood flowed in the streets, from all quarters, under the most absurd rationales, yet the chattering classes differentiated it from the "violent" Americans because these killings had a *purpose*. The Irish Republican Army, the ETA, the Algerian terror bombers all stood for something, whereas, the intellectuals reasoned, mayhem in the United States was personal and bereft of ideology. It was the individuality, the randomness, the lack of sense in American violence that made it so bad in the eyes of the intellectuals. One could understand—if not sympathize with—the aims of the Basques or the Algerians, but what higher value was there in the actions of Mark David Chapman (John Lennon's killer) or Zodiac? It was the Leninist-Stalinist mantra repeated and updated: killers in America were symptomatic of the larger whole because of the inherent repression of bourgeois society. Only such logical gymnastics could allow Europeans to distance themselves from their world wars and past half-century as well as exonerate themselves from the mass violence that positively engulfed them, while at the same time condemning random murders in America or the military actions in Asia as a special pathology.

Chaos in Chicago

Virtually all the mayhem and violence of 1960s America was on the Left, culminating with the 1968 Chicago Democratic National Convention which, in some ways, marked the beginning of the end of campus radical-ism and was symbolically buried by Woodstock. Protest marches and urban riots seemed to define Lyndon Johnson's presidency and, in fact, doomed it. Tet closed the casket. Yet the very structures of democracy that protesters and rioters objected to remained, and if anything continued to work against the positions of the disaffected.

When Johnson announced on March 31, 1968, that he would not ac-cept his party's nomination and, if elected, would not serve again as presi-dent, the Left within the Democratic Party assumed it had won a titanic victory. Surely, many thought, the mantle would fall to the mild-mannered Minnesota senator Eugene McCarthy. (It was a strange historical twist that both the leading candidates of the Democrats in 1968, the insider Hubert Humphrey and the "peace" candidate, McCarthy, were senators and Democrat-Farmer-Labor machine politicians from the same state.) Having chased Johnson out in the New Hampshire primary, McCarthy was undercut by Bobby Kennedy, by then a New York senator, who took dozens of key staffers with him. McCarthy fumed that Kennedy let him do the "dirty work" of forcing Johnson out, and now found himself arrayed against the Camelot myth as well as Hubert Humphrey. In a televised de-bate in California, McCarthy stumbled and began to lose his supporters to RFK. But the entire race was once again rocked on June 4, 1968, when a pro-Arab Palestinian named Sirhan Sirhan assassinated Bobby in the Am-bassador Hotel in Los Angeles. Enraged by Kennedy's support for Israel during the Six-Day War, Sirhan once claimed he killed RFK with "20 years of malice aforethought."[230]

With no supporting evidence at all, conspiracy theorists again insisted RFK was the victim of shadowy forces. With Bobby gone, the only Ken-nedy left to carry on the Camelot legacy was the youngest brother, Ted, who in short order would permanently exclude himself from a chance at the presidency through his actions at Chappaquiddick, Massachusetts. Follow-ing a private party of six men with six female RFK campaign workers in a cabin on Martha's Vineyard, he left the event with Mary Jo Kopechne and drove off a bridge into a tidal channel, where his passenger drowned. Ken-nedy left the scene, and eventually received a two-month suspended jail sentence. The investigations were slapped tight with secrecy, and although the evidence contradicted Kennedy's story, no other indictments fol-lowed.[231]

While it might have seemed logical that the antiwar McCarthy would have gained all of Bobby's supporters, some drifted even further left, to a more radical South Dakota senator, George McGovern. The moderate Democrats and the South stayed with Humphrey.

Intent on forcing the nomination of McCarthy through sheer emotion and public demonstrations, some 10,000 protesters descended on Chicago at the behest of the Yippie movement and the Students for a Democratic Society. Yippie leaders Abbie Hoffman, Jerry Rubin, and David Dellinger, among others, had planned direct and violent confrontations with police. Mayor Richard Daley intended to brook no shenanigans, and, Chicago-style, deployed almost 12,000 police, augmented by 7,500 Illinois National Guard and 1,000 FBI and Secret Service agents.

Hoffman and the others did achieve success in one aspect of their plan: they attracted the bulk of the media attention, prompting Walter Cronkite to announce he wanted to pack up the cameras and "get the devil out of here," but the radicals had no impact whatsoever inside the convention hall. If anything, the violence convinced mainstream America that the Democrats were being taken over by the lunatic fringe, even though Humphrey won the nomination easily. November's results were quite different. Humphrey lost to the resurgent Republican Richard Nixon, helped in part by a third-party candidate, George Wallace of Alabama, running to the right of Nixon, who siphoned off nearly a million Democratic ballots and forty-six electoral votes in the South. Together, Nixon and Wallace accounted for 56 percent of the total electorate, and, except for Texas, Oregon, Minnesota, Hawaii, and Michigan, gave one or the other of the two conservative candidates everything west of Pennsylvania and south of West Virginia.

Richard Nixon's multiple self-reinventions in American political history rivaled that of pop star Cher in the music industry: "in" during the House Un-American Activities Committee, then "out" prior to the "Checkers" speech that enabled Ike to take him as a vice presidential candidate, to back "in" as the Republican presidential candidate in 1960, and then "out" when he suffered another defeat in the 1962 California governor's race. Nixon crawled back in to win the GOP presidential nomination in 1968. He brushed aside Michigan governor George Romney, who claimed to have been "brainwashed" by the military into supporting the Vietnam War (the term was much more loaded then than today, implying an element of conspiracy). California governor Ronald Reagan actually had a slim 20,000-vote lead after the primaries, but lacked Nixon's delegate count, and could only stop Nixon by allying with New York's Nelson Rockefeller. The attempted union fell apart, and Nixon went on to defeat Humphrey.

The Resilient Richard Nixon

Few personalities on the Right in American history have been more paranoid—and few have had such good reasons for being so—than Richard Nixon. Following his loss in the California gubernatorial election of 1962, he uttered his famous "You don't have Nixon to kick around anymore" to the press. He blamed the media for that loss, as well as for negative coverage in the 1960 presidential election. "The press is the enemy," he told his staff. "Remember . . . they are all enemies."[232] And, of course, they were. Where they had gushed over Kennedy's intellect, or Johnson's deal-making savvy, they lampooned Nixon for his perceived lack of mental candlepower, and his staunch anticommunism. Chet Huntley, of NBC's *Nightly News*, claimed to oppose Nixon because of the president's limited intellectual capacities. "The shallowness of the man overwhelms me; the fact that he is President frightens me," Huntley told *Life* magazine in 1970.[233]

Journalists in general admitted their loathing of Nixon in unguarded moments. Tribune Publishing Company president Jack Fuller recalled that "some journalists made their reputations simply by showing hostility to the President and his men."[234] So they fed on each other: the reporters hated Nixon for his lack of trust and access, Nixon denied them access and didn't trust them because of their attacks. They were "just waiting for the chance to stick the knife in deep and twist it," he observed.[235] After attending a White House Correspondents' dinner in 1970, an event Nixon described as "three hours of pure boredom and insults," he told H. R. "Bob" Haldeman that from that point on "everybody on my staff has a responsibility to protect the office of the Presidency from such insulting incidents."[236] To many reporters, Nixon was still the man who unfairly "got" Alger Hiss (a Venona-confirmed Soviet agent), and who somehow fed Joe McCarthy's career. Film critic Pauline Kael, widely misquoted as saying "I don't know anyone who voted for Nixon," actually had a much more self-indicting comment: "I only know one person who voted for Nixon. Where [people who voted for him are] I don't know. They're outside my ken. But sometimes when I'm in a theater I can feel them."[237] But even more than a personal statement, Kael's comment showed how the press was utterly removed from American life.[238]

That Kael wouldn't know anyone who voted for Nixon wouldn't have been surprising. In the 1968 election, which he won with the smallest proportion of the popular vote since Wilson in 1912, Nixon didn't carry a single large city. Thus, to the media, his presidency always carried the scent of illegitimacy, much as George W. Bush's would in 2000. Reporter David

Broder observed, "the men and the movement that broke Lyndon Johnson's authority in 1968 are out to break Richard Nixon in 1969 . . . breaking a president is, like most feats, easier to accomplish the second time around."[239] Carefully controlling information given to the press through his press secretary, Ron Ziegler, Nixon held fewer press conferences than his predecessors (although in 1972 he had seven, more than twice the number Bill Clinton had in his last *two years* in office). Instead, he employed the radio address, somewhat similar to FDR's fireside chats, and impossible for the media to frame or reinterpret. Nor, at the time, did the opposition receive time for automatic responses. After Vice President Spiro Agnew gave a speech critical of network news fairness, ABC conducted "attitudinal surveys" of its viewers and gave TV producer Avram Westin the power to create a "news concept" that promised a "different type of fairness, a different type of balance," taking a story from the perspective of middle America rather than the Eastern liberal perspective (i.e., Kael's). Westin observed that that required "a conscious policy of reversing perspectives," essentially admitting that the networks did not see things the way middle America did.[240]

Nixon gave his "great, silent majority" speech in November 1969, and as of January 1970 had a 65 percent approval rating on his handling of the war.[241] The public, which had indeed seen itself as ignored and minimized by the press, aligned behind Nixon as one of them—a feat he had not previously been able to accomplish in his political career. In fact, Nixon exhibited few conservative traits. He employed wage and price controls (which failed) in an attempt to curb inflation. Cutting the dollar's link to gold in August 1971, Nixon astonished some of his advisers, including economist Herbert Stein, by announcing, "I am now a Keynesian in economics."[242] Instead of rolling back the Great Society programs, Nixon staffed them and provided the flesh needed to not only perpetuate but expand them. Seeking to curry favor with elites, he created the Environmental Protection Agency using an executive order, placing it under activist administrator William D. Ruckelshaus. Stein complained that the Nixon administration imposed more new regulation on the economy than at any time since the New Deal.[243] He also gave unprecedented access to unions, and although they remained a core Democratic constituency, they clearly prospered during Nixon's administration.

When Nixon ran for reelection against South Dakota senator George McGovern, it was the equivalent of the New York Yankees playing a high school softball team. Yet the unending attacks by the press and the relentless intellectual snobbery Nixon routinely confronted convinced him that he could pull no punches. This was especially true after the leak of the Pentagon Papers to *The New York Times*, in which classified Vietnam War reports were leaked to the press by Daniel Ellsberg, a former military analyst turned war opponent. Nixon insisted the *Times* halt publication, and naturally, the newspaper refused. Nixon, deeply troubled by the leaks, ordered a campaign against Ellsberg and an ongoing program to stop further leaks by a unit known as the Plumbers. Among the Plumbers were G. Gordon Liddy and E. Howard Hunt, who commenced a project to break into the office of Ellsberg's psychiatrist, Lewis Fielding, to find information to discredit him.

Nixon's Plumbers had only gotten started, although their subsequent adventures would be clouded to the present by claims and counterclaims of who ordered the infamous break-ins of the Watergate Hotel Building in June 1972. But it seemed as though nothing could derail Nixon. He had withdrawn all but a small portion of the American combat troops in Vietnam, had seemingly stifled the rage in the cities through a program of law and order, and appeared as the common-sense alternative to McGovern. But under Nixon, the United States had just momentarily gotten its head above water, and would shortly go under again—this time for almost a decade. The defining event would be called Watergate.

CHAPTER FIVE

Sex by Consent, Beauty by Consensus

TIME LINE

1968: Tet offensive; Richard Milhouse Nixon elected president

1969: Troop reductions begin in Vietnam; Americans land on the moon; Chappaquiddick incident involving Ted Kennedy; Woodstock Festival held; first ARPANET link (beginning of Internet)

1970: Lon Nol seizes power in Cambodia; first American females become generals; Polish food riots suppressed by Polish troops

1971: Weather Underground explodes bomb in U.S. Capitol building; Pentagon Papers published; Kissinger secretly visits China; United States goes off the gold standard; the U.S. dollar is devalued; Communist China replaces Taiwan in the UN

1972: Nixon opens relations with mainland China; Watergate break-in; Indo-Pakistani War ends; SALT Treaty signed; hippie culture wanes; disco music appears

1973: *Roe v. Wade* makes abortion legal; Paris Peace Accords end Vietnam War; last U.S. combat troops withdrawn from Vietnam; Allende government in Chile overthrown in coup; Vice President Spiro Agnew resigns; Yom Kippur War; OPEC oil embargo; Trans-Alaska Pipeline authorized; dollar becomes fiat currency and value allowed to float

1974:   Nixon resigns; Ford becomes president; United States allows Americans to own bullion gold

1975:   Altair 8800 microcomputer released; Microsoft founded; Khmer Rouge gain control of Cambodia; North Vietnam conquers South Vietnam; Pathet Lao (Communists) take over Laos; UN officially equates Zionism with racism

1976:   Apple Computer Company formed; Carter elected president; Cultural Revolution officially ends in China

1977:   First personal computer (Commodore) demonstrated; Department of Energy created; women integrated into the regular Navy

1978:   Camp David Accords between Israel and Egypt; Cleveland, Ohio, defaults under Mayor Dennis Kucinich; One Child Policy announced in China

1979:   Ayatollah Khomeini seizes power in Iran; China invades Vietnam; Margaret Thatcher becomes first female prime minister of England; European Parliament elected; Iran hostage crisis; Soviet Union sends troops to Afghanistan

1980:   Carter bails out the Chrysler Corporation; rescue of U.S. hostages in Iran fails; Polish food riots, worker strikes; trade union Solidarity established in Poland; Reagan defeats Carter in presidential election

Conformity, Communism, and China

As the Vietnam War wound down in July 1971, Richard Nixon's secretary of state, Henry Kissinger, undertook a secret trip to Beijing, culminating a three-year offensive on Nixon's part to open relations with the Communist giant. In 1967, Nixon had written an article in *Foreign Affairs* insisting that "we simply cannot afford to leave China forever outside the family of nations," and urged "containment without isolation."[1] Two years later he told his State Department that "we do not want 800,000,000 living in angry isolation. We want contact. . . ."[2]

In February 1972, Nixon made the first trip of a U.S. president to

China, with the intention of driving a wedge between the USSR and China. To do so, Nixon abandoned his confrontational "kitchen debate" style and concealed his hatred of communism. The president assured the Chinese, "You don't know me," and toasted Premier Zhou Enlai.[3] When he met Mao, the two clasped hands and Mao apologized ("I can't talk very well," referring to his bronchitis). "I like rightists," he said to Nixon, then joked, "Our common old friend, Generalissimo Chiang Kai-shek, doesn't approve of this."[4] But the generalissimo was hardly on Nixon's mind. Nixon's primary purpose was to get the answer he wanted from Mao when he asked, "Which is the danger that is the most frontal for China: that of aggression from the U.S., or of aggression from Russia?" Mao replied that the Soviets posed the greater threat. Nixon mistook this to mean that Mao could be something of an ally.[5] Between photo ops at the Great Wall and being serenaded by Chinese bands playing "America the Beautiful," Nixon met the Chinese at the bargaining table and produced the Shanghai Communiqué, a document that has remained the basis of Sino-American bilateral relations to this writing. The price was steep: Taiwan's seat in the United Nations was handed to Mao, Tibet was abandoned, and Nixon gained little immediate benefit in return. Although he managed his coveted extrication from Vietnam, that too came at a cost when the Chinese remained the only superpower in the region after the American withdrawal. Nixon referred to the visit as "the week that changed the world."[6] Certainly it had been an unexpected road that took Nixon—one of America's most famed Communist hunters—to the dragon's lair. Vietnam had seemingly made relations more unlikely than ever. But, with China, things were seldom as they seemed.

China's own path to the meeting had begun in World War II, in the three-way struggle between the Communists under Mao, the Nationalists (Kuomintang) under Chiang, and the Japanese. This history, detailed in the earlier volume of *A Patriot's History of the Modern World*, ended with Chiang's Nationalists being pushed off the mainland to Taiwan in 1949. Chiang, heading a quasi-socialist but utterly corrupt coalition of warlords, proved unable to unite them during both wars, against the Japanese and against the Communists. Mao, on the other hand, carefully balanced his battles against the Japanese with the conservation of his resources and preparation of his army for the real forthcoming war with Chiang. He was able, with substantial Soviet help, to take advantage of the continued Nationalist disorder, promise land reform to the peasants, and focus his army on the single purpose of defeating Chiang.

Mao Zedong, a lumbering lech of a man, was born in 1893 in Shaoshan,

Hunan province, to a farmer who eventually became a prosperous grain dealer. He briefly fought with the Revolutionary Army. Most of his life, however, was spent in or around schools, beginning with the First Provincial Normal School in Hunan, then at Peking University, where he worked as an assistant librarian. He married a professor's daughter, with whom he had knock-down, drag-out fights. (In one encounter, his wife, having caught him sleeping with a "dancing bourgeois bitch," told a friend that "he grabbed a bench and I grabbed a chair.")[7] Mao slept with an enormous number of women throughout his life, usually very young, beautiful, and from peasant backgrounds, often two to four at a time. His sexual proclivities did the women little good, however, as he had contracted genital herpes and was a carrier for *Trichomonas vaginalis*. Nor were some other habits appealing: Mao never bathed, receiving only nightly rubdowns with hot towels.[8]

Mao quickly and naturally absorbed communism, attending the National Congress of the Communist Party in 1921. His affinity for schools led him to become an organizer at the First Teachers Training School. Mao was at home in reading rooms (though he never learned to speak Mandarin), co-ops, and councils, seeking to build a movement with rickshaw pullers, peasants, students, and women. The Shanghai Congress introduced Mao to administration as well as organizing, and shortly thereafter he found himself directing a miners' strike. Unlike Marx, Mao actually visited the pits, though he was much more at home on a farm than in a mine.

It dawned on Mao that China's situation was different from textbook Marxism, although he continued to attempt to organize the lower-class proletariat. Attempts to break into industry, however, remained few and futile. One break came in 1923, when the founder of modern China, Sun Yat-sen, arranged a marriage with the Soviet Union, allowing the Chinese Communists to enter the Nationalist Party. Mao warned against any free contest of ideas: "Once freedom is given to the opposition party, it will put the cause of revolution in danger."[9] "As soon as a man talks with another man," he observed, "he is engaged in propaganda." Mao viewed the merchants as the vanguard elite of revolution as late as 1924.[10] This began to change the following year when a Japanese foreman casually killed a Chinese textile worker, causing massive strikes and protests across China. In Hong Kong, a general strike ensued for sixteen months (it constituted the longest strike in world history to that time), and for the first time, the peasants got involved. Yet it took Mao two more years before he began to write about peasant power, stating, "We have concentrated too much on the cities and ignored the peasants."[11] "If the peasants do not arise and fight in the villages . . . the power of the warlords and of imperialism can never be hurled down," he wrote.[12] Mao in particular despised landlords who hoarded grain to keep the prices up (exactly as his father had done in 1906). Although he tweaked Marxist doctrine, he firmly insisted that "the arrow of Marxism-Leninism and the Chinese Revolution is the same as between the arrow and the target. . . . [It] must be used to hit the target of the Chinese Revolution."[13]

As with almost every revolution, the Chinese variant was aided and given legs by the behavior of the opposition, in this case, Chiang Kai-shek's brutal repression of dissidents. South of the Yangtze, strikers were beheaded, their heads dangling in bamboo cages; Communist girls were shot through their vaginas, students were burned alive with kerosene; leftist agitators were tied to trees and cut thousands of times with salt rubbed into the wounds. But unlike Lenin, Mao was not unmoved by such suffering at times.

American money poured in for Chiang, to whom the official mantle of Kuomintang leadership had fallen when Sun Yat-sen died in 1925.[14] Heading the National Revolutionary Army, Chiang initially gained control by ousting several leftist opponents in a series of campaigns. Yet at the time, Chiang was known as the "Red General" in the West and in the USSR; in Russia his portrait was carried with that of Marx and Lenin. His success elicited concern in America, briefly mitigated by a 1927 purge of Communists, but he was still viewed with suspicion until the Japanese invasion of China in World War II. At that time, the United States needed any ally it could get. When Chiang withdrew westward, he left northern China to Mao and his small force of Communists supported by the USSR.

Chiang's generals were often incompetent or corrupt, or both, and increasingly the charges of corruption helped stifle American aid. Whether any amount of aid could have saved Chiang after the Japanese surrendered was debatable. There was the contribution of the Soviet Union, which handed the Communists a military organization superior to Chiang's (one dissident in the 1980s wrote that the Red Army, not Marxism, triumphed in China) and the ever-busy Soviet operatives in the Roosevelt and Truman administrations.[15] Their efforts made it somewhat fitting that in 1949, when Mao took a victory parade down the Boulevard of Eternal Peace, his car was preceded by a U.S. Sherman tank—a gift to Chiang.

Having missed or ignored the horrific crimes and failures of communism in the Soviet Union under Stalin during the 1920s and 1930s, the world would likewise ignore the similar and even more horrific crimes and failures in China under Mao Zedong. Beginning in 1949, Mao introduced social changes including allowing women to initiate divorce, and abolishing religion and the practice of female child foot binding that essentially crippled women for life. For a moment, he could have been mistaken for an agrarian reformer.

Such changes were merely window dressing for imposing total control of Chinese society, the first step of which was, of course, gaining control of the food supply. Buffaloed by Soviet-era films and phony tours of Ukraine and Kazakhstan, where Chinese visitors were shown "model" collectives with plenty of food and modern equipment, the Chinese dictator was sold on collectivization. One Chinese woman in later years recalled the propaganda effort: "We heard a lot . . . about the communes in the USSR. There were always films about the fantastic combine-harvesters with people singing in the back on their way to work."[16] Nikita Khrushchev warned Mao not to emulate Stalin, and had already begun reversing many of Stalin's agricultural policies within the USSR—but his advice had no effect on Mao. Following the Soviet model, Mao first took control of the grain supply, then collectivized farms to boost production. When people naturally fled, he introduced an internal passport system in 1956 to prevent them from leaving. Grain production plummeted 40 percent, even as Mao insisted he would double or triple previous production levels within a year.

Having not learned from the Soviet experiments, Mao collectivized China's agriculture in insidious steps, forcing all rural peasants into collectives by 1958. Initially he established "mutual aid teams" of five to ten families (think Nazi block wardens), then "elementary agricultural cooperatives" of twenty to forty families, and finally full cooperatives of one to three hundred families. He eliminated private property and the small family-owned garden plots that provided much of the food in China. Millions of recalcitrant peasants were persecuted as counterrevolutionaries, and vast numbers perished, often simply by being denied a means to survive.

The Chinese economy was entirely backward. To appreciate the ludicrousness overall, consider that in 1820, American GDP was double that of China, but within fifty years, it had swelled to *five times* that of China. By 1913, the ratio was almost ten times that of China. Matters actually got worse due to the Japanese invasion and then Mao's destructive collectivist policies, so that by 1968, an American was more than thirty times richer than an average Chinese. When actual purchasing power was factored in, the ratio was a mind-boggling seventy to one.[17]

In spite of widespread famine and starvation, Mao adopted the standard

Communist tactic of doubling down rather than admitting failure or acknowledging a faulty ideology. He instituted the Hundred Flowers policy in 1956, in theory to give greater freedom to the arts and scientific research.[18] The program catalyzed activities by China's educated citizens, and brought them to Mao's side as they believed he was liberalizing their part of society. When moderates led by Zhou Enlai criticized collectivization in the spring of 1957, Mao announced a new policy of encouraging criticisms and suggestions to meet the challenges of greater production and to encourage further liberalization. Millions of letters were received by the Communist leadership in the first six weeks after Mao's announcement, suggesting that many Chinese believed they were actually living in a free country. Whether the program was a trap from the outset, or whether Mao simply reacted to the heavy criticism of himself and his policies, the result was inevitable.[19] Those who sent criticizing letters were labeled as rightists or counterrevolutionaries, arrested, and liquidated. In one debate that reeked of Lenin's threats, Mao snapped, "heads will fall, heads will be chopped off. . . . But just think of how good communism is!"[20]

Freed from the possibility of dissent, Mao announced another new program, the Great Leap Forward, which sought to industrialize rural China and move peasants into large collectives. This Leap proved an even greater disaster than mere collectivization; China saw no growth whatsoever from 1958 to 1961 while estimates of the deaths by starvation and outright murder range from 16 million to 77 million. Historian Frank Dikötter puts the death toll at a minimum of 45 million, based on Chinese archives recently made available.[21]

Mao promoted the ideas of Soviet agriculturalist Trofim Lysenko—including faulty plant hybridization—that had proven so disastrous in Russia; they worked no better in China. The state also attempted to control the storage and distribution of all grain—a task for which it was woefully unprepared. Millions of tons of grain were contaminated by insects, eaten by rats, or lost through rot in poor storage facilities.[22] Mao's policies also abolished weddings, festivals, and funerals, and villages were razed on an incredible scale. All Chinese peasants were registered in a locality and forced to stay there; they could not leave a devastated area to seek food or employment. Even their homes were destroyed for various reasons, some 30 to 40 percent being leveled.[23] "Homes were pulled down to make fertilizer, to build canteens, to relocate villagers, to straighten roads, . . . or to simply punish their owners."[24] For a Chinese peasant, times had seldom been more horrifying. In modern times, only being a

Ukrainian peasant in the 1930s or a Cambodian during Pol Pot's murderous regime was comparable.

Under government orders, peasants had to hand over metal items to establish backyard blast furnaces that would, in theory, produce the steel necessary to make farm implements. Instead, millions of useful pots and pans were melted into worthless pig iron, unusable by the untrained Chinese steelmakers. Billions of trees were felled for the furnaces, and village lands became deserts. Deception infected every stage of the process: afraid of Mao's reaction, party officials showed him a backyard furnace that was "making" high-quality steel (but which was in fact brought in from another, real furnace).[25]

Mao was the equal of Hitler in sheer crackpottery, especially when it came to agriculture. Drafting his own list of weird and counterproductive instructions—including the use of household rubbish, such as paper and glass, for fertilizer, introducing a massive concentration of seeds that destroyed the soil, and the killing of rats and birds, which led to an explosion of insects—Mao's Great Leap Forward proved a catastrophe. No one could or would challenge or contradict him; quite the contrary, they feigned bizarre results to confirm his bizarre theories. They cross-bred sunflowers and artichokes or tomatoes and cotton; faked photographs of miracle crops with wheat so tall and dense that children sat on it (the plants were transplanted and the children sat on a concealed table); and even piled mountains of vegetables by the roadside when the leader would drive by to convince him that the peasants had abandoned the "surplus" food.[26] The entire sham reeked of Hitler's moving phantom divisions on his maps while cowed generals meekly played along, or, later, of global warming alarmists insisting the world was perishing from heat in the middle of one of the coldest decades in the century. Seeking to make fantasy reality, in 1958 the government announced to Chinese farmers that there was abundant food, and they could eat what they wanted from the communal kitchens. Months later, all food had vanished, and this time there were no baskets full of leftovers returned. Mass starvation set in the next year—some 25 million people lacking food—a horrid desperation Mao shrugged off as "tuition fees that must be paid to gain experience."[27] Vaclav Smil, reviewing the Chinese famine forty years later, concluded that "Mao's delusionary policies caused by far the largest famine in human history," and those causes "have never been discussed in the afflicted nation."[28]

As in Ukraine, the government became the enemy of the people, with the closest approximation coming in Henan province, where Communists tortured and killed thousands of "hoarders." Some were "set on fire; others had their ears cut off, were frozen to death, or were worked to death on construction projects."[29] The harvest was even smaller than the year before. No one was hiding food—there simply was no food. Socialism had again proven adept at making nothing from something. By the end of 1960, even some party officials decided they had to act, assembling evidence and statistics for Mao, though often they feared to present them. The most successful solution was to quietly install local leaders who reversed collectivization as Stalin had by private plots. They dismantled the collective kitchens, and even began to subtly question Mao. Officials lied to Mao, instituting "save yourself production" and admitting grain from Australia and Canada, so long as the packages were restamped with Chinese logos. Slowly, the Great Leap Forward reached the finish line, having killed between 30 and 40 million and making Mao Zedong the worst mass murderer in human history.

Overall, grain yields during the Leap had declined 21 percent; wheat, 41 percent. With private land—so long as farmers still met a state quota of 15 to 20 percent—agricultural production rose. Rural towns that had been nonexistent while Mao was alive accounted for 25 percent of the Chinese economy by 1990, and by 2001, China had witnessed an astonishing decline in poverty, from 33 percent in 1978 to just 3 percent.[30]

Getting to that point, however, proved rocky in the extreme. Following the catastrophe of the Great Leap Forward, Mao embarked on still another ridiculous reform effort, the Great Proletarian Cultural Revolution, in 1966. The urban worker was the favored individual in Communist China, and after having reduced rural peasants to poverty and starvation, capitalists and bourgeoisie of all stripes were now to feel the lash for the next decade. This was inciting violent class struggle to promote socialism, using naïve and fully indoctrinated students who would be unable to ameliorate their ideology with practical considerations.

Begun as a "second wave of Maoist radicalism," the Cultural Revolution represented Mao's attempt to recapture the revolutionary spirit that had swept him to power.[31] Groups of Red Guards were formed in high schools, and soon some 11 million of them were fanning out to hold their elders to account. The "Four Olds" were to be destroyed: old customs, culture, habits, and ideas. What better way than to use youth who understood none of the above to be the agents for destruction? Militants killed anyone not sufficiently radicalized, with 1,700 people beaten to death in 1966 alone. Others were forced to swallow nails. Some 85,000 were exiled to labor camps. Teachers publicly confessed their heresies and ratted on others. One anthropology professor, Pan Guangdan, explained his strategy for getting through the Cultural Revolution: "Surrender, submit and survive." Later he added "succumb."[32] For a while, the Red Guards were a law unto themselves, wielding power over local officials, the police, and the army, and even using army equipment whenever necessary. Millions of adults in various positions of authority were forced into self-criticism, and those unable to convince their youthful interrogators of their complete submission to Mao's teachings were not "reeducated" but murdered.

As one peasant put it, the revolution meant "persistent cadres holding endless meetings and telling you how to live. . . . They poked their fingers into everything." When Mao reversed his policies on population and urged birth control, one peasant complained, "Why, they even tell you when to fuck."[33] Certainly they told everyone when to worship. One explicit aim of the Culture Revolution was the obliteration of Christianity (and all other religions) from China, and this failed as miserably as the other reforms: at the end of the reign of Mao ". . . foreign missionaries and church officials were allowed back into the country. . . . The estimates then were about 60 million Christians in China."[34] Between outing associates and singing "Chairman Mao Is the Sun That Never Falls," the victims who stayed alive at least had it better than the 400,000 to 1 million who died in the Cultural Revolution. Some estimates place the victim count as high as 20 million.

Even more than Stalin, Mao built an enormous personality cult around himself, and provided his mindless followers with a "Little Red Book" of his sayings to follow. Increasingly, such demonstrations of his power came secondhand. By 1960 Mao was already becoming so impaired by drugs that he fell asleep in meetings, and according to his doctor, "his speech was slurred, his voice nearly inaudible."[35] Even at his best, Mao was anything but a deep thinker. Anyone who thought otherwise only had to listen to some of his nonsensical nostrums. "Marx was also a human being, with two eyes, two hands, and one brain. . . . Not much different from us—except that he had a lot of Marxism in his mind."[36]

As usual with such movements (as in Hitler's SA, for example), the leadership took steps to abolish the Red Guard after its usefulness had run its course. In 1969, the Red Guards were disbanded and youthful "intellectuals" (all those with a middle-school education or better) living in cities were moved to rural labor camps, to disperse their strength and render them impotent. From a historical perspective, the Cultural Revolution wreaked greater destruction than any comparable event in the entire human catalogue of injustice and carnage. Thousands, perhaps millions of buildings, historical artifacts, works of art, documents, archives, and cultural items were systematically destroyed. But it was all for naught; within a few years of Mao's death in 1976, the Chinese government had effectively reversed the policies and principles that held sway during the Cultural Revolution. Had it not, China would never have progressed to become the world's industrial giant of the twenty-first century.

Indeed, once China had begun to "capitalize," its other problem—its population—also began to stabilize. Some of the reduction in population came as a normal offshoot of wealth creation. Historically, as incomes have risen, family size has fallen. In 1970, the Indian government conducted research in Manupur in the Punjab, finding that all the men said they wanted as many sons as possible. When researchers returned to Manupur in 1982, after "green revolution" crops were introduced, only 20 percent of the men said they wanted three or more sons, and contraceptives were widely used. Wealth was the great contraceptive. But in China, the population shift came due to the one-child policy implemented in 1978, with its concomitant abortion and infanticide. Families were often allowed a second child if the first was a girl; beyond that, families had to pay stiff fines, and sexual disparities ensued. The one-child policy put procreation under government control.

Mao had practiced a kind of thought control that Stalin only dreamed about. Every aspect of private life, particularly sex, was regulated. Chinese subjects had to parrot the slogan of the day; foreign books were almost entirely absent; and "eight revolutionary operas provided the sole entertainment."[37] Loudspeakers blasted martial music from morning till night. The dour and dreary sameness of Mao's China, from its dress to its daily work, provided ironic proof that Maxim Gorky was looking the wrong direction when he called America "a machine, a cold, unseen unreasoning machine, in which man is nothing but an insignificant screw."[38] This, in fact, described Mao's China and was precisely what communism produced: identicalness, insignificance, depression, and above all, suspicion. More than a decade after the fall of the Berlin Wall, Eastern Europeans quiz anyone taking their picture, as memories of secret police remain vivid. For the most part, America dealt with China the way it dealt with the Soviet Union: hem it in, deny it additional new territory, and align with democratic neighbors. Nixon, of course, was the exception—but his overtures did not go far, and by 1976, with Mao's death, China entered an era of newer thinking. By then, however, Nixon was gone, a victim of his own paranoia and obsession with leaks.

The Press Removes a President

Richard Nixon was famous for his distrust of the press. His instincts were correct; the major newspapers and television news shows of the day were dominated not just by liberals, but liberals who had a particular burning antipathy for "Tricky Dick," as they labeled him. For Nixon, the press "are all enemies."[39]

In Vietnam, Nixon's "secret plan" had been to ramp up bombing, increase support for the South Vietnamese, and withdraw American ground troops. It worked, and by 1972 the withdrawal was almost complete and the South Vietnamese were holding their own (with American supplies). Riding on that crest, and greatly assisted by one of the weakest presidential opponents in American history—Senator George McGovern of South Dakota, who ran on a platform that included legalizing marijuana—Nixon won reelection in a landslide, carrying every state except D.C. and Massachusetts. His victory humiliated the far Left, who had their ideal candidate in McGovern. Nixon knew that McGovern represented the liberal elites in general and the media in particular, supporting "amnesty, pot, abortion, confiscation of wealth (unless it is theirs), massive increases in welfare, unilateral disarmament, reduction of our defenses and surrender in Vietnam."[40] Nixon also "loved the fact that [Abbie] Hoffman, [Jerry] Rubin, Angela Davis and others supported McGovern."[41] He told a staffer that it should be "widely publicized and used at every point . . . Nailing him to his left-wing supporters and forcing him to either repudiate them or accept their support is essential."[42]

The embarrassment delivered to the media by McGovern's overwhelming defeat only inflamed their hatred of Nixon more. One editor thundered, "There's got to be a bloodletting. We've got to make sure nobody [i.e., anyone who didn't submit themselves to the media] ever thinks of doing anything like this again."[43] Such an arrogant and pompous attitude by a member of the press had been fed by the media's role in turning a victory in Vietnam into a defeat and in the process bringing down Lyndon Johnson's presidency. Throughout the 1960s, studies of newspaper editorials show a steady leftward march, until by 1970 there were virtually no conservative voices left.[44] Filled with power and bile, the media now set its sights on Tricky Dick. Whereas with LBJ the press at least shared his social policies, it had nothing in common with Nixon, and looked for an opportunity to show him the door. Nixon obliged by forming the Plumbers, a secret group run out of an organization whose name stands as a monumental embodiment of social unawareness: CREEP (Committee to Re-Elect the President). None of the Plumbers' antileak activities were novel; Kennedy used similar measures, including bugging, and FDR invented "opposition research" in the form of an intelligence unit funded with State Department money. But neither the Kennedys nor Roosevelt were hated by a vicious press out to destroy them. Indeed, the press had completely covered up FDR's inability to walk, his mistresses, JFK's multiple trysts, the ongoing relationship with the mob under the Kennedy administration, Johnson's Bobby Baker scandal, and many others.

All that said, Nixon opened the door in his own face. Not only did he permit the Plumbers to be formed, but he allowed subordinates such as White House counsel John Dean to have authority over the unit. Dean was responsible for the infamous Watergate burglary, and, according to some sources, originated it. While history books still commonly hold that "Nixon had not only known about plans to cover up the Watergate break-in but had also ordered it," or that Nixon "certainly authorized" the break-in, the facts are less conclusive.[45] Certainly he was aware of the Plumbers unit, though likely never received detailed briefings on their shenanigans. Not until May 1972, according to G. Gordon Liddy, legal counsel for CREEP, did the Democratic National Committee headquarters become a target, and the order came from Jeb Magruder, special assistant to the president, who managed CREEP.[46] Further, in sworn testimony, Liddy said he had been "recruited by Mr. Dean to organize and deploy an . . . intelligence capability."[47] Instead of bugging the phone of DNC chairman Lawrence O'Brien, Liddy's team targeted the desk of Ida "Maxie" Wells, the secretary to Spencer Oliver, who oversaw the state party chairmen. Her desk, well away from O'Brien's office, supposedly held evidence personally injurious to Dean, and the break-in may have had nothing to do with politics.

A first break-in attempt failed on May 26. The second break-in occurred on June 17—the one most people refer to when they mention Watergate—and it was during this intrusion the burglars were caught. On June 20, H. R. "Bob" Haldeman briefed Nixon about Liddy's role in the burglary. In his memoir, RN, Nixon held fast to his assertion that June 17 was the first time he heard of the affair, and that he was shocked by the target: "I asked the same question so many times. Why bug the DNC?"[48] Even the FBI agreed that John Dean, not Nixon, was the "master manipulator of the cover up."[49] After the document shredding started, Dean called Liddy into his office: "Did anybody in the White House—are they aware of what you were doing, that you were going in there?"[50] Such a question supports Liddy's version of the events, and the fact that Dean, not Nixon, ordered the break-in. Suits by the Deans and by Maxie Wells against Liddy, for his version of the affair, resulted in one suit being thrown out of court in 1998 and a second dismissed in 2001. Liddy maintained that those dismissals proved his version of the events, though without the notebooks of E. Howard Hunt, which were destroyed, all documentary evidence linking Dean to the plot had vanished.

While certainty about who ordered the break-ins is not possible, there is no question that Nixon obstructed justice by listening to Dean and ordering the FBI to call off its investigation as a matter of national security. By then, however, both Congress and the press had gotten hold of the scandal and the Democrats on the Senate select committee began to unravel the details of the break-in and cover-up (far more so than did the celebrated journalists Bob Woodward and Carl Bernstein). Liddy refused to rat out his accomplices and was given a twenty-year prison sentence; he served five years and Dean, one. Liddy's identification of conspirators was less useful once the Senate committee learned that Nixon had installed a secret taping system in the Oval Office. A battle ensued between the president and the Senate over the tapes, wherein the courts finally sided with the Senate and ordered Nixon to turn over the tapes. One tape had a mysterious gap, caused (according to Nixon's secretary Rosemary Woods) by a secretarial accident. Many suspect it contained the infamous "smoking gun" in which Nixon implicated himself; yet no one knows for certain. It could have been several minutes of Nixonian philosophizing. Nevertheless, Nixon's downfall was assured when he had to go on television and try to convince the public that their president was "not a crook." The media had already cast him irreparably in exactly that light.

A House committee had already begun impeachment hearings, with staffer Hillary Rodham assigned to prepare a brief on exactly what legal protections the president was entitled to. (She concluded he was to have no lawyers present—a much different conclusion from that afforded her husband, Bill Clinton, in 1998 when he had no fewer than a *dozen* lawyers protecting him.) Special prosecutor Archibald Cox built a solid case of presidential mendacity during the cover-up, and the Republicans instantly knew that not only could they not stop an impeachment vote, they couldn't block a conviction in the Senate. A group of influential Republican senators, including Howard Baker and Barry Goldwater, visited Nixon and explained to him the lay of the land. He resigned in August 1974, not out of heroic sacrifice, but out of a commonsense assessment that he couldn't win.

After his resignation, and Gerald Ford's subsequent pardon, Nixon retired temporarily, only to return to public life within a decade by writing books about foreign policy. At the time of his death in 1994, he had substantially rebuilt his image, but Watergate became synonymous with presidential corruption, and the use of independent prosecutors with nearly unlimited powers became a fixture in addressing federal scandals. Nonetheless, what cases were subject to a special prosecutor continued to be politically driven. In 2012 when President Obama's administration was caught misrepresenting events in a terrorist attack on a U.S. embassy in which four Americans died, no special prosecutor was assigned due to a lack of media interest. When U.S. senators asked about the origins of the attack (known to be al-Qaeda within hours of the attack, but claimed for weeks by the Obama administration to be caused by an Internet video to help his presidential campaign), Secretary of State Hillary Clinton fumed, "What does it matter?" One wonders what chance Nixon would have had with a "what does it matter" defense in the Senate.

Europe in a Swirl

Mao died only two years after Nixon's resignation, essentially closing off both ends of the line of communications between the United States and China. China moved in a different direction which, although hardly liberal or democratic, was at least far less repressive, while President Gerald Ford and his successor Jimmy Carter showed little interest in China. Even as Nixon exited the stage, the culture bore little resemblance to the one present when he battled JFK for the White House fourteen years earlier.

Social trends from 1960 to 1980 gave the world a revolution that the hippie movement only dreamed of, transforming marriage, women's roles, increasing the distrust of government and the press, initiating the decline of established religion, and above all exhausting the willingness of Westerners to meet new challenges. Following half a decade of turmoil, street fights, riots, university takeovers, racial tension, and confrontation, the 1970s ushered in a listless period of bland politicians, declining expectations, and renewed skepticism about the marvels of open marriage and drug use. Angry anthems to revolution and militant paeans about street marches found themselves displaced on the music charts with happy, upbeat (but often sterile) disco. John Travolta in a white three-piece suit replaced John Lennon in his granny glasses as the most recognizable icon in America, while in England the Sex Pistols, with their raw, anti-everything attitude, demarcated the demise of the fun Beatles, who jokingly fell into snow banks and innocently winked at the cameras. Described as "the sour and mostly untalented end of a growing spectrum of disrespect," punk dovetailed with Britain's rising stars of comedy and film, Monty Python, whose two hits, *Monty Python and the Holy Grail* (1975) and *Monty Python's Life of Brian* (1979), while hardly Edwardian conservative, nevertheless lampooned the Left often more than the Right.[51] In *Monty Python and the Holy Grail*, Marxist rhetoric was spouted by groveling, dirty peasants to no betterment of their position, while in *Life of Brian*, the "bloody splinters" of the various "Judean People's Fronts" (a pseudonym for the PLO) are so hornswoggled by their dogma that they all commit suicide to make a statement. In France, once-idolized public figures such as Jean-Paul Sartre had been replaced by ribald television comedians. "The Seventies," wrote a socialist historian of postwar Europe, "looked backward, not forward."[52]

Europe witnessed a powerful social transformation at almost every level. Young people no longer lived with parents, or even in the same towns, while industrial expansion and employment punctured quaint villages and ethnic compounds. At the same time, immigrants swarmed in from Turkey, North Africa, and Asia, altering the character of once-isolated or homogenous neighborhoods. At first, these immigrants were mostly assimilated, but dangerous signals should have been noted when many of the Muslim arrivals created their own isolated boroughs. In France they went unnoticed among the larger shift of people as agricultural modernization depopulated the countryside while revitalizing French cities. François Mitterrand boasted, "The French are starting to understand that it is business that creates wealth, determines our standard of living, and establishes our place in global rankings."[53] Policies were put in place to provide advantages to European production, now shorn of its colonies.

European goods benefited from the artificially high value of the dollar, making Continental exports cheap and highly desirable in America. Conversely, American exports were costly to Europeans, and noncompetitive in European markets. Yet it was precisely the success and wealth of the Europeans under the protective shield of the U.S. defense budget and availability of the huge American mass market for their cheap goods that made them misinterpret their world. European states believed they could keep and even enhance their cradle-to-the-grave socialism in nonhomogenous societies, in which diverse segments vied against each other for benefits, and not pay a penalty. It was no accident that pro-socialist economists focused on tiny, homogenous Sweden to tout socialism's success. Democracy itself seemed only to work well in small European countries with homogenous populations (Norway, Sweden) or in those that granted a high degree of autonomy to homogenous regions (Belgium, Switzerland).

With traditional assimilation processes and high employment, some of the dislocations could have been ameliorated or even prevented. But at the first indication that the welfare states were unraveling, and that taxpayers were reaching the ceiling of what they could afford, much of the bloom came off the rose. Antitax parties sprang up across Europe, in some cases making notable political achievements. Norway's Progress Party established itself as a significant and growing force, while the Danish Progress Party won nearly 16 percent of the vote in 1973 within a proportional system of representation. Once stagflation set in, antitax arguments found even more support, though never on a parity with similar sentiments in the United States.

Of more import to the European political systems over the long term was the rise of Green parties with their primary focus on environmentalism and antinuclear/anti–fossil fuel energy sources. Green candidates first ran in 1973 in France and Great Britain. While attracting only 5 percent of Germany's representation, Germany's Greens were concentrated so as to capture the regional government of Hesse. Elsewhere, Greens made steady gains in some nations (from 5 to 7 percent in Belgium) but had little electoral impact in Italy and France and, predictably, consistently did their best in the pacifistic Scandinavian countries, which were largely shielded from harm by the great powers. Politically, the Greens—like the narrow antitax parties—tended to be nuisances in the short term, but over the long term, supported by think tanks of the Left and funded with mountains of cash from sympathetic donors, they began a campaign to destroy or, at the very least, severely damage the automobile culture throughout Europe and America. Indeed, an objective observer would have to admit that the intention of the environmentalists seemed to be nothing less than the deconstruction of capitalism.

As in Europe, Japan and India experienced similar postwar growth, and similarly moved toward greater centralized socialism. Japan was actually prohibited by its constitution, created during the reign of American viceroy Douglas MacArthur, from having a military in the normal sense. The constitution said that "land, sea, and air forces, as well as other war potential, will never be maintained." Since its adoption in 1947, the Japanese constitution has never been amended, and its provisions make it almost impossible to do so. Japan's military consists only of interceptor jets, ground forces lacking any invasion training or capacity, and a shallow-water navy designed to protect Japanese shores. As with European currencies, the exchange rate for the Japanese yen was extremely favorable for Japanese companies penetrating the American market, and by the 1970s Japan had returned to being an industrial powerhouse.

Japan's success came in part from its hyperattentive focus on conformity. *Wa*, meaning "harmony," is the essence of being Japanese; *fuwa* (disharmony) belongs to foreigners. By the 1980s, the population was as controlled as it was in the 1940s, following the Japanese haiku, "The nail that sticks out is the one pounded down." Yet this was not a Stalinist, government-imposed sameness, but rather a ubiquitous pressure to conform. The model for the new postmodern society in Japan was atheism, and culturally, socially, and politically uniform, progressive, and featuring a Japanese example of the New Soviet Man that Stalin attempted to build (but without Marxist class struggle) and the ideal of Nazi ideology promoted by Hitler (without race nationalism). This successful quasi-socialist state benefited enormously from its homogeneity, as it constituted the largest monocultural, monoreligious, monoracial, and monolinguistic country in the world. Japan seemed to function well for a while, and even temporarily became the envy of the industrialized West.

India was an entirely different case, adopting the tenets of socialism but being unable to make them work equitably in a polyglot nation. Even after splitting off Muslims into their own nation of Pakistan, Gandhi and Nehru's policies kept India from advancing economically. Although a relatively well-trained governmental bureaucracy was inherited from the British, it would not be until hundreds of thousands of Indians had been trained in American and European universities that India began to prosper. American companies and others seeking to expand globally turned to India and the Pacific Rim nations of Taiwan, South Korea, the Philippines, and Indonesia in the 1970s and '80s, finally bringing surprising stability and prosperity to that corner of the Third World.

As evidence of their arrival on the world stage, Asia and India created new entertainment centers to compete with Hollywood. Dating back to the turn of the century, India had developed a strong tradition of movie production. Between 1960 and 1980, India's regional governments (as well as the national government) began to subsidize Indian filmmaking, establishing the Film and Television Institute of India, but after 1980, government patronage shrank, forcing Indian producers to compete in the open market. The most popular subculture of Indian film was Bollywood, or the Hindi-language film sector, which by the year 2000 churned out a thousand movies a year, most of them musicals. So-called playback singers recorded tracks in advance, and the stars lip-synched them on screen, often in conjunction with dances, resulting in Hindu-Ziegfeld productions filmed in grandiose settings called "picturisation." Indian films featured "item numbers," allowing a beautiful starlet who was otherwise unrelated to the main plot to perform a signature song. One of the more famous item stars of the 1970s was Helen Jairag Richardson, stage name Helen, an Anglo-Burmese beauty known as "Marilyn Monroe with martyrdom." Although by the century's end Bollywood still accounted for a tiny fraction of total world film revenues ($1.3 billion to Hollywood's $51 billion), it grew at twice the rate of the American film industry and its cost per film was one twentieth that of Hollywood's.

Falling in behind Bollywood was the Hong Kong cinema, which took off in the 1970s with the Shaw Brothers studios, which specialized in kung fu movies. While comedies and musicals still remained popular, it was *The Big Boss* (1971) that introduced the world to Bruce Lee (1940–73), an American-born martial artist raised in the British colony. The son of a famous Cantonese Opera star, Lee appeared in many short films, first as a baby, then as a child actor. Although he had been in twenty films by age eighteen, he was sent back to the United States in 1959 after fighting (and whipping) a Triad gang member. Studying martial arts in America, Lee performed at a California karate tournament, where he caught the eye of a Hollywood producer, who soon hired him for a television series. But after being snubbed for the leading role in *Kung Fu*—a show based on Lee's concept—Lee returned to Hong Kong, where he played the leading role in a string of Chinese hits. No movie was more memorable than *Enter the Dragon* (1973). It was Lee's final film, for he died shortly after its completion. (Years later, his son, Brandon Lee, also a martial arts actor, was killed on the set filming *The Crow* by a blank fired at close range). Lee became a cult figure both for his unique fighting style, accompanied by high-pitched screams, and for popularizing karate in America. One of his screen opponents, Chuck Norris, would also become a film and television star of martial arts films.

Meanwhile, Hong Kong producers such as Raymond Chow and Leonard Ho, who established Golden Harvest studios in 1970, signed a new comedian and singer, Jackie Chan, who would become Asia's biggest box office draw of the century's final two decades. Hong Kong movies competed strongly in Thailand, Singapore, Malaysia, Indonesia, and South Korea, spinning off talented directors such as John Woo and actors such as

Chan, Jet Li, Jacky Cheung, and Chow Yun-fat. Yet even as Asia's movie industry began to make inroads in the West, that celluloid street ran both ways, and by the 1990s, Hollywood had aggressively entered the Asian market.

As long as the dollar remained the world's currency, such "cultural imperialism" was not only easy, it was unavoidable. American products not only offered artistic appeal, but remained relatively inexpensive to obtain. By the 1980s, this situation had begun to unwind, ending a structure built in the immediate postwar period at Bretton Woods, New Hampshire.

The End of Sound Money

International growth, as seen in the Bretton Woods Agreements, depended on the United States simultaneously keeping its currency tied to gold while lending to developing nations at an increased rate. This contradiction was impossible to maintain, and Great Society and Vietnam War spending produced deficits that slowly drove down the value of the dollar. De Gaulle denigrated this development as "America's export of her own inflation," but it had real results for the United States as well. The U.S. share of world industrial production and trade steadily backed down from postwar highs.

Then the balance of currency power began to shift. Beginning with Chinese Communist deposits in Paris at the Eurobank, the Western world began to slowly see the rise of the Eurodollar and the idea that a European currency could rival the U.S. dollar. A misnomer, in that the currency could be deposited in Tokyo or Rio, "Eurodollar" referred to any U.S. dollars deposited in non–American-controlled accounts. Taking on the auspices of "rogue" and "hip" money, Eurodollars became an instant hit, tripling from 1959 to 1960 and gaining popularity with each new government attempt to contain them. Citibank's Walter Wriston, looking back in 1979, called it a system "fathered by controls," noting that technology had made the movement of money and information nearly instantaneous and hence beyond the reach of government interference.[54] However, the dollar had its status enhanced after 1971 and 1973 agreements demarcated OPEC oil transactions in U.S. currency (now known as the petrodollar), generating a permanent demand for dollars in international markets.

Inevitably, the U.S. lost control of the old Bretton Woods system when Nixon yielded to economic reality and severed the link between the dollar and gold in 1973. By the end of 1974, U.S. citizens were allowed to own gold again, something that had been illegal since 1933. This move introduced a period of free-floating currencies—essentially an international version of what the United States had in its antebellum period during which any bank could issue money. Positioned against other currencies, the dollar dropped like a stone and triggered accelerated monetary velocity, further shocking the system. It was the realization of Triffin's Dilemma, the clash of national short-term objectives with international long-term goals in using the international reserve currency.

In 1971, the petrodollar emerged in the Tehran Agreement between twenty-two oil companies, dominated by the "seven sisters" (Standard Oil of New Jersey [later Exxon], Texaco, Standard Oil of California [later Chevron], Standard Oil of New York [later Mobil], Gulf Oil, Royal Dutch Shell, and Anglo-Persian Oil [later British Petroleum or BP]) that controlled about 85 percent of the world's oil reserves, and six Middle Eastern countries (Iran, Iraq, Saudi Arabia, Qatar, Kuwait, and the United Arab Emirates). However, this conference was hardly the start of the process of nationalizing oil production, which began with the Soviet Union in 1918, followed by Mexico in 1938, Iran in 1951, Brazil in 1953, Iraq in 1961, Indonesia in 1963, Algeria in 1971, and Libya by 1974. By 2012, few if any countries produced crude oil without either being owned by a government agency or partnership, or substantially regulated by government. Energy had become political.

Meeting in Baghdad, five oil-producing countries formed OPEC (the Organization of Petroleum Exporting Countries) in 1960: Saudi Arabia, Iran, Kuwait, Iraq, and Venezuela, which by 1971 also included Libya, Algeria, and Nigeria. At Baghdad, two important provisions were established. First, the U.S. dollar was named the currency for all oil trades, and second, the producing countries would tax oil sales so that their percentage of the take was a minimum of 55 percent. A second accord followed immediately over Mediterranean oil, supplied by Iraq, Saudi Arabia, Libya, and Algeria, and power over oil production passed forever from consuming countries to exporters.

Although a permanent demand for dollars in international markets had been created by the OPEC agreements, oil prices rose as the dollar weakened. Oil production in the United States had peaked in 1970 and imports had reached 28 percent, yet consumption continued to rise.[55] Although Sheikh Ahmed Zaki Yamani of Saudi Arabia attempted to manage the demand by Arab nationalists for additional money and power without killing the golden goose of the oil companies, he negotiated an increase in Arab ownership of the oil-producing companies, first to 25 percent, then to 51 percent in 1983.[56]

The resulting OPEC-induced "oil crisis" shook the confidence of the West and added to the impoverishment of the Third World. Arab oil money had nowhere to go in its native lands, and soon recirculated back to the United States in the form of inflation (elevated by higher oil prices). OPEC members faced as big a challenge as did the oil-dependent West, but of an entirely opposite sort: how could they employ their sudden, newfound riches? Sheikhs and royal families, of course, consumed at superhuman levels. Modern cities with astounding architecture began to go up across the Arabian peninsula. Oil billionaires spent money on yachts, ski vacations in Gstaad, and above all, gambling junkets to the Riviera. But long-term wealth-creating investment in their own nations? That proved elusive, as without the four pillars of American exceptionalism, the Middle Eastern states lacked the cultural infrastructure to employ wealth well. Indeed, most of the money ended up back in Europe or America, with an inflation premium.

Peace with Honor?

As domestic inflation began to plague the United States, exacerbated by Vietnam War spending, Nixon increasingly become handcuffed by his Watergate cover-up. Secretary of State Henry Kissinger forged ahead with talks in Paris to end American involvement in Vietnam. Whether this was a diversion from Watergate or a sincere effort, Kissinger nevertheless thought he had an understanding with North Vietnam that the North Vietnamese Army (NVA) would not attack major cities in the South, fire artillery across the Demilitarized Zone, or make threatening troop movements near the DMZ. Peace talks with the North Vietnamese constituted an attempt by Kissinger to achieve Nixon's campaign pledge of "Peace with Honor." The final agreement of the Paris Accords was signed in January 1973, and while it failed to halt the fighting, it did provide the United States with an exit plan and the return of American prisoners. For the North Vietnamese, the accords ensured that the Americans would abandon their ally, and enable them to conquer the South after a short time to maintain appearances. Kissinger and the negotiator for the North Vietnamese were awarded Nobel Peace Prizes for their work in 1973.

Senators Clifford Case and Frank Church proposed legislation a day before the Accords were signed to end direct U.S. military involvement in the war by August 15, and the Case-Church Amendment passed the U.S. Congress by more than the two-thirds majority needed to override a presidential veto. As the fighting continued, South Vietnam went on the offensive, and during 1973, made significant gains while improving the training of its army. The NVA built up its infrastructure and strength below the DMZ, and attacked major South Vietnamese positions in 1974, recovering by May what had been lost the previous year. In January 1975, the NVA captured a provincial capital, and when new president Gerald Ford requested funds from Congress to help South Vietnam, Congress refused. The lack of any American response emboldened the Communists to press forward to complete their conquest, and on April 30, the South capitulated. But the killing continued, and as the North Vietnamese began wholesale exterminations and deportation to "reeducation" camps, some million and a half people fled the country by boat, many dying or suffering harrowing experiences. Ultimately, the United States accepted more than 800,000 refugees, Canada and Australia 137,000 each, and France 96,000.[57]

Even the surrender of South Vietnam did not end the wars in Indochina, however. The Soviets continued to egg on the Vietnamese (often considered the "Prussians of the East") to further conquests in Cambodia and Laos, while China supported the Cambodian Khmer Rouge. Led by Saloth Sar, a washed-up electronics student known by his pseudonym of Pol Pot, the Communists seized the capital city of Phnom Penh in April 1975. Prince Norodom Sihanouk, former king of Cambodia from 1941 to 1955, was returned as titular head by Pol Pot. Pol Pot immediately ordered the evacuation of the entire capital city. He moved Cambodia, Gandhi-like, backward a century, proclaiming "Year Zero," abolishing markets, emptying towns, all with the goal of establishing Kampuchea, a precapitalist utopian agricultural state. Pol Pot's deindustrialization had identical results to the industrialization of the Soviet Union and China, which is to say, it produced murder on a mass scale. As Pol Pot informed the population, "To preserve you is no gain, to destroy you is no loss."[58]

Building a series of dams as his own monument, Pol Pot failed abjectly to improve daily life. Instead, everyone from doctors to teachers was examined for their "revolutionary conscience," and those found wanting were executed, often with axes or machetes, as Pol Pot's forces were short of ammunition. Men, women, and children were massacred in the fields they worked—the "killing fields"—or tortured at Toul Sleng prison. Guards and executioners often ate body parts of those they had just eliminated. Compared with Mao or Stalin, Pol Pot was a piker, killing "only" 1.5 to 2.5 million people. But Cambodia only had 7 million to begin with, thus making Pol Pot, in sheer percentages, one of the worst murderers in human history.

And just as the Ukrainians and Belarusians had disproportionately paid for their non-Russianness, so too Vietnamese and non-ethnic Cambodians were executed for their minority status. Buddhist monks, whose protests had helped overthrow Diem in Saigon, now learned what real repression was when they were targeted for having "Vietnamese minds." Border clashes with the North Vietnamese began in 1975, and a year later Vietnam sent air raids into Cambodian territory that were followed by a retaliatory mini-invasion of Vietnamese border villages by Cambodian troops. Continuing resistance by various holdouts within Cambodia was blamed on Vietnamese influence, leading Pol Pot to order a "purification" of the eastern part of the nation. This triggered a retaliatory 1978 invasion by the Vietnamese Army, and an astounding red-on-red conflict that featured Machiavellian networks in which the Chinese backed Pol Pot, the Khmer Rouge, and Sihanouk, and the Soviets and Vietnamese backed a puppet group of Cambodian Communists. Pol Pot was defeated, but cobbled together an exile government that existed until 1993, with nominal recognition from the UN as the rightful government of Cambodia. He became the beneficiary of U.S. sanctions against his enemies. In 1993, Sihanouk was restored to his throne, but all power in the nominal constitutional monarchy remained in the hands of the Vietnamese-backed Communists headed by Prime Minister Hun Sen.

In neighboring Laos, the Communist Pathet Lao, backed by the North Vietnamese and the Soviet Union, seized control of the government in 1975. The little country with four million people had set records in military history: 260 million bombs fell on it from 1964 to 1973, more than the total of all those dropped in World War II, and 80 million were still unexploded at war's end.[59] The vast majority of ordnance had fallen in the area of the Ho Chi Minh Trail where it passed through the almost uninhabited southeastern sector of the country. Casualties to Laotians had been light, but some areas were now too dangerous to enter. Laos ended relations with China during the Sino-Vietnamese war in 1979, and became more or less fully dependent on Vietnam.

Indochina had been a disaster for five American presidents over thirty-five years, costing more than fifty thousand American lives, hundreds of billions of dollars, and producing absolutely nothing to show for all that effort. And few people in America or Europe paid attention to the destruction in Southeast Asia once the Americans were gone. With American troops safe, the region fell off the front pages. Moreover, the press's inattention reflected a reality of the American antiwar movement since the early 1900s: Americans for the most part could not be moved to action by appeals concerning injustice to others—only American casualties returning home changed public perceptions. All the legitimate (or fictionalized) harangues about napalm killing innocent civilians had less of an impact on American voters than a handful of American coffins returning to Dover Air Force Base.

When it came to ignoring atrocities by Communists and other dictatorial regimes, another factor was at work within the Progressive mind-set. If the United States was the cause of all evil in the world, evil must not exist if the United States was not there. Feminists and civil rights agitators never seemed to notice that women were often the most victimized group whenever Communist dictatorships gained power, or that vast new populations literally became slaves. But with America in retreat, only Europe stood to potentially contest oppression abroad, and the new feminized Europe lacked the will to do so.

Feminizing Europe

The 1973 oil crisis ginned up by OPEC damaged America and Europe, but the root causes of weakness in both cases was inflation caused by increased spending in the public sector. Up until that point, when the oil shock descended, Europe had undergone two decades' worth of nearly unbroken prosperity, which brought with it previously unimagined pressures, including the rising feminist movement.

Women, now freed from economic ties to husbands, entered the political realm for the first time. Europe saw the election of large numbers of women to parliaments and legislatures. By 1990, almost 40 percent of the representative bodies of Finland and Sweden, and one third of the Danish deputies, were women. Their emphasis on "soft" issues of the environment, gay rights, education, welfare benefits, and above all, increased government spending, accelerated the decline of Europe's fiscal situation and productivity. By congealing the individual nations into a unified Europe, discerning the correlation between feminized politics and economic stagnation was difficult—often hidden by discrepancies between weaker states, such as the former dictatorships of Portugal and Greece, and the wealthier countries, such as Denmark and Germany. Whether Europe's increased unwillingness to use force to ensure the continuation of its own culture and national status was intertwined with the feminization of politics remains a task for political scientists (or, perhaps later, anthropologists) to sort out.

Yet in France, it was precisely those family-friendly policies that sparked the revolution and the move of women into the political arena. A 1971 petition in the weekly magazine *Le Nouvel Observateur* was signed by more than three hundred women (including actresses Jeanne Moreau and Catherine Deneuve and writer Simone de Beauvoir), stating they had had abortions in defiance of the law. (Britain had decriminalized abortion four years earlier). The government did not prosecute any of the signatories, and the following year French president Georges Pompidou stated that French law, consistent with the state Catholic Church, no longer represented public opinion on the issue. Catholic Italy attempted, in 1981, to vote in a national referendum to maintain the then-existing restrictions but make abortion legal. Spain followed, decriminalizing abortion four years later. Naturally, a "baby bust" followed, the impact of which was not evident until the 1990s when the European population shrank and native-born workers could not fill the available jobs. To a degree, abortion was directly tied to the troubling Islamification of Europe, but it was also linked to a growing desanctification of life across the continent. With this strange twist, Europe had recoiled from the massive human carnage of the two world wars only to drift at an accelerating rate into favoring only the living generation at the expense of both the past and future.

The shift of women into politics also affected domestic spending in Europe, where by 1980, the category "transfers and services" (T&S) steadily consumed larger and larger shares of European budgets. By 1982, T&S accounted for 25 percent of the GDPs of Belgium, Denmark, Italy, and Norway, and nearly 30 percent of France's and Sweden's GDP.[60] Italy's debt stood at 85 percent of its GDP, a level to be expected where more than one quarter of the population was directly employed by the state. In Britain, trade unionism had paralyzed the economy, culminating in the bitter and violent strikes of 1978–79. Whether ultimately these state-dominated welfare systems indeed nurtured more, one thing was clear: across Europe, the massive shift of resources away from the proper role of the state, namely security, into welfare and subsidies, a form of vote buying, was made possible by the umbrella of American military protection.

Hence, the big lie of the postwar European world took root, namely that the Continent had somehow found a "third way" between communism and free markets, when in fact it was nothing more than a hothouse plant shielded from aggressive expansionist elements by the martial wings of the American eagle. A phrase later used by American civil rights activists that "whites started life at third base and thought they'd hit a triple" was eerily apropos to Western Europe. Free to spend on social programs, scientific research, and education, and defended from invasion from an Evil Empire that indeed could have devoured it, Europe congratulated itself on its accomplishments while deriding its protectors. Certainly Europeans had paid a horrific price for instability, ethnic hatred, racism, and nationalism between 1914 and 1945, and without question France, Germany, Britain, and other nations had made great strides in recovering from wars. Yet the lessons they learned were not always correct, and their often-smug views of their protectors across the Atlantic led them into dangerous misperceptions, both of Soviet military intent and their own accomplishments.

Model Citizens

Women greatly influenced the hothouse fantasy, injecting a strong feminist element into politics, but also in clothing and culture, to the point of becoming the focal point of both the fashion and entertainment industries. A certain readjustment away from male influence was predictable and necessary. For too long, men had dictated female styles and set the standard for the appropriate female image, for women's clothes, and for how women should act, and a reaction was inevitable.

Such image/fashion swings had occurred before. Both male and female body types had undergone a substantial change from a century earlier, when a rotund shape for men indicated wealth and success; and centuries before that, when a plump woman was not only healthy but sexy. Then, a radical transformation in body image occurred, so that by the 1920s, the "flapper" shape of extreme thinness and absence of curves had become the rage. In America, Ida Rosenthal (born Ida Kaganovich) responded to this unnatural expectation and in the process started a clothing revolution. In 1922, Rosenthal changed women's silhouettes from the flapper look with her Maidenform brassiere, created with the help of her designer husband, William.[61] Rosenthal thought female undergarments should fit a woman's shape, not constrain it to look like a boy's. While Rosenthal originally offered her bras as a side item in her dress shop for a dollar, she soon realized that they were her biggest-selling item and ditched her other clothing lines to concentrate on brassieres, which William constantly improved with his concepts for support and lift. The company's 1942 "I Dreamed . . ." advertising campaign ("I dreamed I went shopping in my Maidenform bra") proved wildly successful, while the somewhat pointy, exaggerated shapes became an idealized and usually unattainable standard. For his part, William standardized cup sizes, while Ida patented the adjustable fastener.

Both sides of the feminist debate claimed the high ground when it came to bras. Ida's daughter, Beatrice Rosenthal Coleman, told British editor and filmmaker Harold Evans that her mother believed in liberating women, freeing them to be themselves.[62] But by the 1960s, feminists of the Betty Friedan mold claimed bras confined and suppressed the female form, artificially enhancing breasts, turning women into sex objects. Thus, designers (especially male designers) found themselves in an unwinnable situation: if they made shape-enhancing clothes for women they were sexists, and if they made unisex clothes, they disrespected femininity. It probably didn't help Ida Rosenthal's standing with the Marxist feminists of the 1960s that although she had been a socialist and a revolutionary in Russia, the Americanized Ida was a capitalist through and through, even to the point that her company thrived during the Great Depression.

Rosenthal was focused on fashion. She sought to drape the female form, not dictate its shape by what went into it. By the 1950s, however, two streams converged that sought to redesign American women, and, ultimately, the world's females. First came the fashion industry, centered in Paris and New York. Having taken a break from lecturing the public on how to look during the war years, the postwar fashion police returned with a vengeance embodied (literally) by the French sex kitten Brigitte Bardot. The Paris-born Bardot was modeling for *Elle*, the French trend-setting magazine, at age fifteen. Three years later, in 1952, Bardot appeared in the film *Crazy for Love*, becoming the toast of the European film industry and marrying French director Roger Vadim (Roger Vladimir Plemiannikov), a Belarusian émigré who had been vice consul to Egypt and who would later marry American actress and activist Jane Fonda. European film had struggled to regain its footing relative to Hollywood after World War II, and Bardot provided the needed zest, becoming one of the few money-making foreign actresses, alongside the Italian bombshells Sophia Loren, Claudia Cardinale, and Gina Lollobrigida. Whereas the Italians were clearly mature women, Bardot remained "every man's idea of the girl he'd like to meet in Paris," observed film critic Ivon Addams—with the emphasis on "girl."

Bardot's real debut as a serious actress came in 1956 with *And God Created Woman* (*Et Dieu . . . Crea la Femme*), a risqué role in which Bardot played a teenager. The Catholic League of Decency decried the film, and when it was released in the United States in 1957, Bardot's sexy barefoot table dance became an instant classic. The actress was an overnight sensation, vaulted to a level equal to the American star Marilyn Monroe, and her French accent made her even hotter to American male film-goers. One survey voted her sex goddess of the decade for the 1960s, and one cliché held that she did more for France's balance of trade than the entire French auto industry. More than simply providing on-screen eye candy, Bardot popularized the famous bikini swimwear, designed in its modern form by French engineer Louis Réard and fashion designer Jacques Heim in 1946. The Miss World Contest banned bikinis in 1951, making them a revolutionary symbol and boosting sales, which further accelerated with Bardot's film and the 1960 Brian Hyland song, "Itsy Bitsy Teenie Weenie Yellow Polka Dot Bikini."

Between bikinis and Bardot, the French fashion designers staged an American invasion. English designer Charles Frederick Worth (1826–95) had made a reputation in the United States by the turn of the century, opening the door for Christian Dior (1905–57) and Spaniard Cristóbal Balenciaga (1895–1972), who had moved his shops to Paris during the Spanish Civil War. Even during the war years, fashion-conscious socialites evaded restrictions to see his clothing lines. After the war, Dior's "New Look" hourglass shape was popular; Balenciaga countered his proportions with a tunic dress that removed the waist. Where Dior went light in his fabrics, Balenciaga went heavy and intricate. Unlike Ida Rosenthal, whose prime directive was to respect women's natural lines, Balenciaga put waists wherever he pleased, inventing the famous "baby doll" dress and the balloon skirt, and introducing a new woman's silhouette. He "regarded making dresses as a vocation, like the priesthood . . . an act of worship," observed one author. His approach was "reverential," and he wanted women to "be reluctant to part with their clothes."[63] Dior, on the other hand, epitomized the Donna Reed look of the late 1950s and early 1960s, with rounded shoulders, a tiny waist, and a full dress. Opening in 1947 with his Carolle or "figure 8" dress, Dior sought luxury. "I want to make the rich feel rich again," he said.[64] Although his lines carried on through partners and licensing agreements, Dior's death in 1957 left the fashion world to Balenciaga, Yves Saint Laurent, and Pierre Cardin.

Designers wanted to exhibit their clothes, but not particularly the women who wore them. So they turned to fashion models, who had been around for decades. Betty Grable, for example, had done her share of glamour photography in World War II. But it wasn't until after the war that designers really began to think models were mere clothing racks— something on which the artwork was hung—and that the skinnier they were, the better. English model Jean Shrimpton, in her book *The Truth About Modelling* [sic] (1964), established the maxim that the camera added ten pounds to the model, and thus photographic models had to be thinner than normal.[65]

Thus, a divergence in the image of the desirable woman occurred. American males ogled full-figured women such as Monroe, Jane Russell, Jayne Mansfield, and the Italian film sexpots, but on the runway, sizes kept dropping until Lesley Hornby, better known as Twiggy, became an international sensation in the mid-1960s. Twiggy (b. 1949) weighed ninety pounds at five-feet-six and her stick shape perfectly conjoined with the shapeless, androgynous mod fashions. She soared into stardom for her shape, but even Twiggy said of her body, "My legs—well, you know my legs. I hate them. They're so thin."[66] The miniskirt, introduced in 1964, only worked on ultrathin, girlish women, and those with shapely legs. As Marilyn Bender, the *New York Times* fashion reporter, observed in 1967, fashion used to pretend that "women were pretty, [and] had perfect bodies. . . . Pop fashion, like pop art, lays the subject on the line. Fatty knees, wrinkled elbows, ruthless natures are exposed for all to see."[67]

In fact, women at both ends of the spectrum had a great deal in common: Marilyn Monroe at 36-24-34 and Audrey Hepburn, more of a classic model body size at 31-22-31, *both* came in with a waist-to-hip ratio of .7.[68] Subsequent research covering Miss Americas from the 1920s to the 1980s and *Playboy* centerfolds from 1955 to 1965, then again from 1976 to 1990, found almost no variation in the waist-to-hip range of .72 to .68.[69] Even the so-called supermodels, with their extremely long legs, fell within this ratio. A British study of three hundred "glamour models," *Playboy* models, and fashion models all likewise varied only from .68 to .72, and even Twiggy, in her modeling heyday, scored a .73, only slightly outside the norm.[70]

The models on runways were at odds with the women on screen. Most of the popular actresses of the 1960s and 1970s, including Liz Taylor, Donna Reed, Doris Day, Ursula Andress, Raquel Welch, Janet Leigh, and Lucille Ball, were full-figured, certainly in contrast to runway models. Marilyn Monroe, at five feet five inches and between 120 and 140 pounds, with a bra size of 36D, would have worn a size-12 dress in the most recent sizing categories. Welch (born Jo Raquel Tejada), in her stunning loincloth poster shot for *One Million B.C.* (1966), likely would have been about the same dress size. Most of them wore a modern size 10 to 14, and then only after dieting and smoking regularly. Haute couture, however, rebelled against the silhouette of a real woman, celebrating instead size 4, then 2, then finally size zero models: breastless, flat-bellied, and devoid of much muscle tone. The trend was perpetuated by both sexes. Male designers, many homosexual, seemed to rebel against a fuller feminine form, further tipping fashion to make women look like twelve-year-old boys, and male fashion photographers shot the looks. But women ran the modeling agencies and schools, including Catherine Harlé in Paris and Lucie Clayton in London. Female designers, including British Mary Quant, who invented the miniskirt, and the female fashion reporters also had a hand in shaping the new look.

Barbie-arians at the Gates

Weighing in, so to speak, on the debate on femininity was the most popular toy of all time, the aforementioned Barbie doll. Sporting a sexier .54 waist-to-hip ratio, Barbie broke all the rules for dolls; she had long legs and large breasts, in contrast to the standard baby dolls of the 1950s. Barbie's marketing genius lay not in the doll itself but in the limitless clothes and fashion items that could be sold at then-exorbitant prices. Mattel Toys took a sizable risk on the product, which flunked its introduction at the New York Toy Fair in 1959. Mattel executive Ruth Handler then reached out directly to little girls through television ads, and sales exploded. Handler later realized she was selling role-playing, not a doll. "It dawned on me that this was a basic much-needed play pattern that had never before been offered by the doll industry to little girls," she observed.[71] Eventually, Barbie became the best-selling toy of any kind in history, spreading across the globe—"the most potent icon of American culture in the late 20th century," said one writer.[72] The British magazine *The Economist* put it only slightly differently: "Of all the forces against which resistance is futile, Barbie ranks right near the top."[73]

Feminists of the 1960s hated the doll. It represented an "unattainable standard," meaning Barbie was pleasant to look at but impossible to recreate in human reality. Yet where some complained that Barbie's impossible physique was oppressive to girls, and that the doll reinforced sexism, Handler countered that Barbie liberated girls by giving them a vision of future occupations. Among the many variations available, Mattel made sure Barbie had doctor's and astronaut's uniforms, pantsuits for attorneys, and police garb.[74] Others saw American imperialism at work in Barbie; feminist writer M. G. Lord complained that even the "World" collection of different-race Barbies involved "Mattel's coding of an 'American identity'" against which "aliens" were compared.[75] But feminist scholarly commentary about Barbie went unheeded by girls aged three to eleven, who, in the United States, had on average ten Barbie dolls each.[76] America's "perfect girl" went over big outside the country as well—"American imperialism," as the Marxists would insist—as Barbie was sold in forty-five countries, sometimes with slightly different stylistic twists. By 2000, the Barbie business took in $2 billion annually, "a little ahead of Armani, just behind the *Wall Street Journal*," noted British author Harold Evans.[77]

The Barbie doll continued America's march through European and, later, Asian culture. Just as soap and hygiene products in the 1920s and 1930s had "democratized bodies" through shared concepts of cleanliness under more American assumptions, so too Barbie set the standard for what perfection looked like in the female form. Yet Barbie's genius as a toy was that once again it democratized a product, bypassing the parents and going straight to the consumers—the kids. In that sense, Barbie continued the American capitalist traditions set by Cornelius Vanderbilt, Lewis Tappan, John D. Rockefeller, and Juan Trippe (and later Steve Jobs and Bill Gates) by spreading the product out through the demand of consumers and making accessible that which was previously only available to the few. The doll also captured the *other* essentially American values of independence and uniqueness through her myriad outfits. Just as Western standardized, mass-produced clothing, through endless accessorizing, made it possible for no two people to look alike, Barbie's inventory of accessories and outfits made the doll an infinitely changing toy. In that regard, Barbie presaged the on-line video game craze that began in the late 1990s where, through any combination of players, gamers had a new experience and challenge with every new play. Similarly, through the endless body piercing and tattoos that became commonplace late in the twentieth century, yet more layers of independence and differentiation emerged. The joke that Americans became distinguishable only by their personalized license plates contained a kernel of truth, and yet it was equally obvious from any parking lot that despite the dominance of mass-produced autos, virtually no two Americans drove the same exact car.

The War on Ugly

Barbie—a plastic woman—reinforced the Hollywood version of the female form just in time for medical support from the blooming field of cosmetic or plastic surgery. Reconstructive surgery had been around for at least a hundred years (some argue, much longer) and was widely used to correct deformities related to such diseases as syphilis, including deterioration or disfigurement of the nodes and tumorlike growths under facial skin.[78] Sometime in the early twentieth century, "character" found itself superseded by "personality," defined as "the quality of being Somebody" (with "personality" itself replaced by "celebrity," or the quality of being interesting, some eighty years later).[79] Personality was "implicitly social rather than autonomous; it cried out for external ornamentation and promotion in the form of appropriate speech, dress, and manners."[80] And, one could add, looks. The exceptionally ugly certainly had the deck stacked against them. One post–World War II magazine blared, "Farewell Ugliness!" and outlined mental health reasons for undergoing plastic surgery: "To the homely girl, life may seem an endless succession of Embarrassments, Frustration, and anguish until she decides . . . [to have] plastic surgery [which could] alter her personality—and her whole life."[81]

As a medical practice, elective cosmetic surgery was a relatively modern phenomenon, although by 1907 *Woman Beautiful* magazine reported the United States had four times more hairdressers than in 1890 and some 25,000 manicurists, all reflecting the democratization of beauty that put looks "squarely within America's democratic tradition of self-improvement."[82] While the American Board of Plastic Surgery (1937) was the first of the aesthetically oriented organizations, joined in 1942 by the American Association of Plastic Surgeons (now Plastic and Reconstructive Surgeons), cosmetic and reconstructive surgery accelerated after World War II as physicians set to work trying to make wounded and disfigured veterans whole again. Ironically, this masculinization of plastic surgery expanded the field and gave it new credibility and gravitas. If men were eligible for cosmetic surgery due to the ravages of combat, women saw the potential for plastic surgery to enhance their attractiveness. Dr. Charles Mayer's *Medicine in the Service of Beauty*, published in 1955 in France, gave voice to this desire for physical perfection:

> To create, or to give full value to one's beauty, it is first of all necessary to learn to triumph over one's own enemy: one's self. . . . The first rule therefore is negative: do not deliberately create ugliness. . . . [83]

By the 1950s, columnists trumpeted the amazing transformation attributable to face-lifts: "Over and over again," noted Josephine Lowman, "women have won a husband, gone ahead in a job, or just plain felt more confident and happier" after surgery.[84] One surgeon, Robert Franklyn (who wrote a biography called *Beauty Surgeon*), told a reporter that the work he did on one woman "not only saved her job but it gave her a warmer personality and a brand new attractiveness to men who previously shunned her as a 'crotchety old bag.'"[85] *Vogue* magazine described the aging process as follows: "the fading of beauty is almost imperceptible . . . a beautiful woman just seems to become plain; a desirable woman, unalluring. . . . an elusive something has vanished."[86] Naturally, though, like all things American the face-lift and other personality enhancements spread to the middle class, and it wasn't long before *Ladies' Home Journal*, a publication truly aimed at the average housewife, ran articles about women who had saved money for a face-lift: "Any really determined woman can do it," boasted one.[87] A study conducted in 1958 by Johns Hopkins University found that the typical recipient of face-lift surgery was forty-eight, white, married, Protestant, and socially active.[88]

This new appreciation for "personality enhancement" usually focused on the breasts, especially after 1953 when columnist Josephine Lowman noted the "impact of the 'sweater girl' and . . . strapless, low-cut evening gowns and swim suits."[89] Conscientious surgeons, Marguerite Clark wrote in a 1948 *McCall's*, had "neither time nor sympathy for vanity and vague longing for a beautiful body."[90] In fact, the United States was on the cusp of an aesthetic shift. One social history of the 1950s claims "big breasts, symbols of motherhood, were definitely in vogue."[91] "Mannerisms," the social historians noted, became more significant, including "walk, gestures . . . size of tits and hips."[92] Increasingly, the "too small" breasts of the 1920s flapper bodies began to be viewed as a physical problem that could be corrected by a physician. Clark's statement "dates the switch from reduction to augmentation as the central concern of aesthetic surgery of the breast. . . ."[93]

For the first time, a medical option was available to assist women in attaining the beauty they desired. Rather than lecturing women on how they should view themselves, doctors now sought to provide them with their dream body. New techniques and products were needed, and indeed they became available as beauty modification reached its critical mass. Silicon injections were first used in 1953, but for several years scientists experimented with a variety of other substances—Ivalon (polyvinylic alcohol), Polistan (polyethelyne), and Hydron (polyglycomethacrylate)—but each carried unacceptable side effects. True aesthetic augmentation became possible for the first time in March 1963 with the development of the silicon gel implant, created by Houston surgeons Thomas Cronin and Frank Gerow.[94]

Feminists were appalled at the new interest in breast augmentation, wherein "women's extreme concern with physical appearance is expressed in . . . beauty-seeking behaviors such as eating disorders and addictive plastic surgery."[95] They equated the desire to be aesthetically pleasing to a disease. Such complaints ran up against the needs of women who sought breast reconstruction and augmentation after mastectomies; was their desire to look like they previously had also a disease? It was therefore partly through the work of cancer victims that breast implants gained medical and social acceptability—but it was also the market at work. Rhinoplasties, once common among upper-class Jewish women, by the 1960s had become common among all groups.

At any rate, feminists decrying the ability of healthy women to enhance their sexuality had no more effect in reducing the popularity of breast augmentation than did the complaints about traditionalists who fretted that the popularity of "boob jobs" (as they were known in the trade) turned women into sex objects. "We live in a 'mammoriented' world," the *Journal of the American Medical Association* wryly observed in 1966.[96] *Vogue* celebrated silicon in 1971, and *Harper's Bazaar*, after a critical piece on silicon injections in 1964, positively revised its position three years later. By the time pop feminist icon Cher, who had undergone known elective plastic surgery, was celebrated in 1988 by *Ms.* magazine as "a woman who defies the conventions and expands her personal horizons," it appeared the antibeauty feminists had thrown in the loofah, as it were.[97]

There was no question the river tended to flow mostly in one direction. Mary-Lou Weisman, admitting the reality of beauty in society in an essay called "The Feminist and the Face-Lift," concluded, "I do not think . . . that too many men worry that their wives will leave them for a younger, smooth-skinned man."[98] But the quest for physical beauty and sexual advantage soon involved men nonetheless, as the silicon revolution found its way into male enhancements: the first silicon penile implant (as a treatment for impotence) was developed in 1961, and an inflatable penile implant was made available in 1972. By the 1980s, the male implant industry was growing—so to speak—at explosive rates, reaching $110 million in sales by 1989.[99]

But more popular still was liposuction, developed in France in 1977, which sucked out body fat with little scarring, could be done with minimal anesthetic, and could be repeated as desired.[100] And it was equally desired by both men and women. Before that, men had quietly sought out cosmetic surgery; perhaps not on the scale as had women, but a 1961 article in *Coronet* had reported a study of fifty-three West Coast men who had undergone face-lifts, and who had found the surgery beneficial.[101] Males, noted one plastic surgeon in 1971, were easier to work with because they had more reasonable expectations: "He's not trying to turn November back to May. He's satisfied with July or August."[102]

Overall, cosmetic surgical procedures skyrocketed, especially after improved techniques lowered postoperative pain and permitted new outpatient operations. By 1984, almost half a million aesthetic surgeries were performed in the United States, which by no means was alone in its enthusiasm for medically morphing the human body. The International Confederation for Plastic Surgery, which first met in 1955, had seventy-eight national societies representing nations from Argentina to Yugoslavia. Tokyo emerged as the Asian plastic surgery capital, sporting more than one hundred cosmetic surgery centers in 1960 alone, and specializing in the double eyelid operation. Plastic surgery in Vietnam took off during the Vietnam War as numerous Asian waitresses and dancers modified their looks to be more appealing to American soldiers. But Japanese, Koreans, then Southeast Asians, in that order, dominated the ethnic groups in Asia who sought cosmetic surgery.

Aesthetics, however, were truly in the eye of the beholder. Brazil, in hot competition with the United States as the plastic surgery capital of the world by the late twentieth century, saw a boom in parents giving their daughters breast reductions as "sweet sixteen" birthday presents. The vice president of the Brazilian Plastic Surgery Society observed, "The women who want to reduce their breasts here would probably want to increase them in the United States."[103] Brazilian plastic surgeon Ivo Pitanguy developed a popular buttocks lift in the 1970s that soon was copied worldwide, and characterized the small-breast, larger buttocks the "Brazilian look."[104] Becoming one of the hottest plastic surgery destinations for "aesthetic tourists," Brazil had 1,600 plastic surgeons and aggressively marketed its product around the world.[105] Hotels in Rio enclosed pamphlets for plastic surgery in the bedside table, right next to the Gideon Bible. (Presumably the message was that one could pray for proper financing!) While Brazilians were shrinking their cup size, Argentineans were expanding theirs, with more than a million breast enlargements performed since 1970, or one for every 30 Argentines, giving the nation the highest ratio of silicon implants per person in the world.[106]

After a decade and a half of lecturing by the likes of Naomi Wolf, efforts to minimize or diminish the importance of beauty had failed. But many of George Gilder's observations in *Sexual Suicide* (1973, reprinted in 1992 as *Men and Marriage*) had been validated.[107] American women and men continued to place a premium on beauty, large breasts, and relatively thinner bodies: the results of a 1985 survey showed that 33,000 women said they would "rather lose ten to fifteen pounds than achieve any other goal." Researchers Robin Lakoff and Raquel Scherr similarly reported that college women stated that an "overriding concern" in their lives was to lose five to twenty-five pounds.[108]

Gilder had hit upon central truths about looks and social status. Over the years, subsequent research reinforced his often intuitive conclusions. His observation that women almost never "marry down" has, even in the socially mobile late twentieth and early twenty-first century, remained almost an immutable truth. Surveys of female medical students showed that they expected to marry men with salaries equal to their own, and *not one* expressed an interest in marrying a man with a lower income for whatever reason. At the same time, some 60 percent of male medical students preferred a mate who made less money than they did, and 40 percent wanted a woman with a lower occupational status. And only by the late 1980s did the second ("trophy") wife appear, a woman who was selected as a high-income status symbol.[109]

Food, Meet Fat

Here, in the convergence of body fat, beauty, and health, the government intruded. As fashion designers, models, and actresses began to fuss about weight as an aesthetic issue, the medical profession was addressing it for an entirely different reason. It could be argued that heart disease became a national medical problem when President Dwight D. Eisenhower suffered a heart attack in September 1955. Thrust into the news, Ike's heart problems spurred millions of Americans and thousands of doctors to educate themselves in arteries, cholesterol, and diet. Although the president smoked, he had no history of heart disease and no other risk factors—he exercised regularly, was of normal weight, and had barely elevated blood pressure with below-normal cholesterol. On the advice of his doctor, Ike began a heart-healthy diet, cutting back calories, skipping meals, and eating more fruit. As his doctor, Howard Snyder, recorded, "He eats nothing for breakfast, nothing for lunch, and therefore is irritable during the noon hour. . . ."[110] The more he cut back on fats and cheese, the higher his cholesterol.

Shortly after Ike's heart problems, physiologist Ancel Keys announced a new low-fat, low-cholesterol, and high-carbohydrate diet that was quickly endorsed by the American Medical Association. By the end of the 1960s, the Keys hypothesis had become scripture, despite the fact that an increase in heart disease as separate from an increase in the *measurement* techniques and equipment (i.e., electrocardiograms) had yet to be established.[111] Indeed, the proportion of all deaths classified under "diseases of the heart" had fallen since the 1940s, some of which the medical community explained as better medical care after an event, not diet.[112] Even the World Health Organization agreed that "much of the apparent increase [of coronary heart disease] mortality may simply be due to improvements in the quality of certification and more accurate diagnosis. . . ."[113] Nevertheless, some in the medical community began to warn of a heart-disease epidemic caused by too much fat, and in particular, from eating too much meat. It seemed irrelevant to these critics that total fat consumption decreased from 1947 to 1976.[114] Cholesterol was tagged as the demon in this epidemic (even though famous heart surgeons such as Michael DeBakey found no correlation between cholesterol and heart disease in 1,700 patients), and soon fats and meats were linked to cholesterol. A massive diet change for America was in order.[115] "Diet Linked to Cut in Heart Attacks," proclaimed *The New York Times* in May 1962. Yet just nine months after that headline, the study on which the preliminary report was issued showed that twenty-six members of the dieting group had died, versus only six of the control group whose diet had not been altered.[116]

Had only issues of cholesterol, diet, and heart disease been involved, it's possible the war against meat and fat would have proven a fad no longer-lasting than the Hula Hoop, Milli Vanilli, or the pet rock. Unfortunately, the studies quickly became politicized in exactly the same way as AIDS science in the 1980s and global warming science in the 1990s. Paul Ehrlich, in his 1968 book, *The Population Bomb*, had prophesied that the world would be overpopulated and that the "battle to feed all humanity" had already been lost, despite the crop breakthroughs of researchers such as Norman Borlaug, who had virtually ended famines in southwest Asia.[117] A 1971 bestseller, *Diet for a Small Planet*, fired the opening salvos of the antimeat/anticapitalism barrage. Written by vegetarian Frances Moore Lappé, the book complained that Americans were too dependent on meat, and that livestock consumption required more soy and vegetable protein to sustain it—foods that came at the expense of the world's hungry.[118] Harvard nutritionist Jean Mayer complained that the "enormous appetite for animal products has forced the conversion (at a very poor rate) of more and more grain, soybean and even fish meal into feed for cattle, hogs and poultry, thus decreasing the amounts of food directly available for direct consumption by the poor."[119]

This was the old clean-your-plate mantra of the 1950s, well known to any American who grew up in that era, that "there are people starving in China," which linked the lack on the part of one group to the plenty on the part of another. Now, however, it wasn't just food; it was *meat*, and fat. "A shopper's decision at the meat counter in Gary, Indiana," lectured Warren Belasco, "would affect food availability in Bombay, India."[120] Rising inflation of the 1970s had also forced women into the workplace at ever-increasing rates, and this in turn had ramifications for diet at home. In 1965 one in four meals eaten by Americans was outside the home, but by 1980 half of all meals were eaten outside the home.[121] Family control over diet gave way to convenience; not necessarily a bad exchange, but one that placed control over eating habits in the hands of others, and it wasn't long until government weighed in. In 1977 George McGovern held Senate hearings to form dietary goals for the United States. McGovern's Select Committee on Nutrition and Human Needs was slated for extinction and, as the staff director noted, "[we] just thought . . . we should say something on the subject before we go out of business."[122] Seeking a return to the national diet of 1900, which the committee perceived as presumably a "healthier" era, the goals recommended an increase in carbohydrates and a reduction in fat when, in fact, as has been demonstrated, Americans ate *far* more meat and fat at that time.[123] The McGovern hearings made diet and fat a political, not personal or even scientific, issue, one with implications for obesity and body size for decades.

For example, in the 1970s, six separate studies confirmed "surprisingly" low cholesterol levels among 16,000 men who developed colon cancer.[124] This was followed by a massive study of 362,000 American men, which recorded slightly higher death rates among men who had quit smoking, consumed less cholesterol, and participated in treatments to lower blood pressure to those who hadn't. *The Wall Street Journal* accurately reported this with the headline "Heart Attacks: A Test Collapses."[125] Despite the lack of evidence that cholesterol-reducing diets had any benefit, the health lobby jumped from the premise that heavy doses of cholesterol-lowering drugs produced some benefit to the idea that cholesterol (hence fatty foods) caused heart disease. As seen on the cover of *Time* magazine in March 1984, that was illustrated as two eggs and a strip of bacon forming a frowning face. "Cholesterol . . . And Now the Bad News" warned *Time*. In fact, the results were so unconvincing as to require a "consensus conference" to determine what the consensus was.[126] That did not stop the antifat bandwagon, which was quickly supplemented by the "fiber revolution." First came the scientific study—an article in the *Journal of the American Medical Association* linking changes in fiber to a host of diseases, followed by *The Washington Post*, which championed fiber as the "tonic for our time."[127]

These debates about body image and calories were more weighty than they initially seemed because they involved a dangerous precedent of government intervention in a purely private aspect of life. The process went as follows: a group of scientists would produce a study that would be taken as conclusive rather than as a hypothesis that needed validation by multiple controlled studies. Advocates and zealots would then demand government action based on this "science," and, sensitive to the squeaky wheels, government would legislate controls or mandate behaviors.[128]

Food police such as microbiologist Michael Jacobson did not even attempt to conceal their use of the court system to impose their dietary views on the much larger majority. Like global warming twenty years later, the more accurate the study on fats, meat, and diet, the less reliable the original antifat hypothesis looked.[129] Yet despite the evidence showing the ineffectiveness of fiber in battling fat or cancer, *The Washington Post* in 1998 continued to claim "scientists have known for years that a diet rich in vegetables, fruits and fiber, and low in fat, can greatly reduce—or eliminate—the chances of developing colon cancer."[130] In 2004, when *The New York Times* caught wind of a study of thirteen subjects followed for six weeks (versus the previous studies of 47,000 and 89,000 followed for years) that showed inconclusive results, it nevertheless summarized the research as "Plenty of Reasons to Say, 'Please Pass the Fiber.' "[131]

With the cholesterol/fat/fiber research, the very nature of the science itself changed. Once government had concluded that national health (heart disease) was related to cholesterol, and that cholesterol was related to fat, and that fat was related to meat, it was inevitable that the government began trying to dictate not only diets, but science itself through funding the studies. Conditional phrases used by scientists deliberately to avoid making conclusions based on incomplete data—"could be," "may be," "are correlated with"—were snapped up by advocates to mean "are," "must be," and "are caused by."

It is worthwhile to recall the spread of Nazi eugenics under a politicized health care system:

> the greatest barriers to eugenics were those of legal rights, guaranteeing individual freedoms, Christian ethics and [in Germany] socialism. Yet all of these were flawed by organicist biology and philosophy. . . . [L]egal guarantees were no match for the extension of professional powers by state welfare experts and by professional interest groups. Law could not control science and medicine. . . .[132]

The Nazis had used the medical system not only to control health-related issues, but to employ sterilization and abortion to weed out handicaps. Ultimately, the Reich had expanded medical procedures to entire undesirable groups, including Jews and Gypsies. Nazi Germany's obsession with perfect physical traits easily became intertwined with its larger objectives of racial purity. Once the state became enmeshed in dictating diet, it was a very small step to associating other areas of life with "health," including religious practices or racial traits.

Sex, Surveys, and Science

Regardless of the supposed message about healthier diets urged as a means to improve overall health, almost without exception the marketing strategy involved selling a leaner, sexier body. Whether sex actually was becoming more important in the 1960s, or whether it was just being noticed, documented, and commented upon publicly for the first time, the widespread perception is that sexual permissiveness began then and the era of the explicit had arrived.

Geoffrey Gorer's surveys in England found that as early as 1955, 91 percent of women said sex was "very important" or "fairly important" in marriage, and those numbers remained constant over the next eighteen years.[133] One fifth of all English men Gorer interviewed had married the person with whom they first had sexual relations, and 26 percent of men and 67 percent of women were virgins when they were married. A more detailed study of 1,800 English youths found that only 12 percent of the females had engaged in intercourse, but of those who were engaged to be married, 37 percent were having sex. A separate study of British university girls found that of the 93 percent who arrived at college as virgins, only 46 percent were still virgins three years later.[134] Most of these youths didn't use any birth control at all, as reflected in the rising illegitimacy rates; from 5.8 percent in England in 1960 to 8.2 percent by the end of the decade.

Alfred Kinsey's books (*Sexual Behavior in the Human Male*, 1948, and *Sexual Behavior in the Human Female*, 1954) had less impact than William Masters and Virginia Johnson's *Human Sexual Response* (1966), which arguably documented an ongoing change rather than precipitated one. What was titillating about *Human Sexual Response* was its graphic descriptions, a sort of scientific version of the ever-popular issues of *National Geographic* featuring bare-breasted native females that young boys used for their "anthropology" homework.[135]

A curious development was also noted by anthropologists in the 1960s and 1970s, one that has generally been avoided and ignored in scholarly works to this day. White American women began to experiment with other races and foreign ethnic groups as sexual partners, often to the exclusion of their traditional white male counterparts. President Barack Obama's mother was a classic example of this trend, seeking nonwhite partners, and stating, while working in Indonesia, in reference to other Americans, "They are *not* my people [emphasis in the original]."[136] By the 1970s, racial intermarriage was no longer uncommon and certainly was no longer illegal anywhere in the United States. Although at first celebrities were slow about acknowledging interracial affairs, high-profile women including Barbara Walters eventually went public with their choices.

On college campuses, it became a rite of passage for a liberal white girl to prove her liberalism and commitment to civil rights by dating and having sexual relations with minorities. This was not missed by white males, who saw women of their own race deserting them. Yet the reverse did not occur. White males dated black females at much lower rates: a phenomenon that continued well into the twenty-first century, although there were high numbers of available black women relative to the number of black men capable of supporting them. By 2011, black men were twice as likely to marry someone of another race than black women.[137]

While women were agitating for a more nearly equal status under the law (but not with respect to divorce actions, child custody, and alimony, where they continued to be favored), many white males were becoming bewildered, resentful, and even angry. To a large number, especially middle aged and middle class, it seemed as though they were being held responsible for the ills of the world. A cultural breakdown, at the very least, in American family structure was almost unavoidable, especially given (usually) class differences between more upper-class white women and their middle- to lower-class black sex partners. This seemed to lend empirical evidence to theorists such as Masters and Johnson (not to mention Freud) who saw sex as being at the root of all human behavior. This trend was not confined to the United States; German males were confronted with large numbers of *Mischlings* or mixed-race children, French women left French men for Arabs and Africans, and Great Britain was inundated with males of other races from its former colonies seeking out English females.

Media culture celebrated the racial mixing while ignoring the class stresses, and social commentators ignored it as a cultural phenomenon. Thus, at the very time that race was emerging on college campuses as one of the explanations for *all* social unrest or disruptions, virtually no attention was paid to the most fundamental of all human activities—sex.

Sixties-era sexuality, celebrated in music, art, and movies, emerged as a fellow traveler of the hippie movement and moved effortlessly into the seventies morality. Along with drugs, free love offered a means for release from the consequences of sex. With the arrival of the Pill, sexual freedom was greatly expanded at the very time the available partner pool was shrinking due to the Vietnam War. A million U.S. males in one way or another were taken by military service, which restricted their movement and, as it were, took them out of circulation, often sending them overseas. Antiwar rallies were disproportionately dominated by women, who in a sense were protesting the nonavailability of men. Complicating the matter was the selectivity curve: women usually sought men between one and four years older than themselves, meaning that girls born in 1947 had a much smaller male pool—the 1943–44 pool—to choose from. Often, women married men their own age or slightly younger, had a child in 1967 or 1968, divorced and remarried to have another child in the mid-1970s.

The radical loosening of divorce laws virtually everywhere made such patterns more commonplace. In California, under conservative governor Ronald Reagan, "no-fault" divorce was instituted. Then there were the dislocations brought on by abortion. In 1972 the U.S. Supreme Court's *Roe v. Wade* decision legalized abortion in the United States. Due to continued immigration—especially from high-fertility groups, such as Hispanics— and strong fertility levels among certain subgroups of American women, abortion did not immediately produce in the United States the same birth dearth that it did in Europe. Abortion polarized the nation, however, particularly in the way in which it was legalized through the courts as opposed to legislation.

Perhaps surprisingly, abortion became a greater issue in Protestant America than in Catholic Europe. To a large degree, this was a matter of timing; Christianity in all mainstream denominations declined rapidly after World War II in Europe, while in the United States, evangelical Christianity absorbed much of the mainline denominations' losses until 1990. In terms of church attendees by 2000, 2,765,000 individuals were ceasing to be practicing Christians in Europe and North America every year.[138]

Phyllis Schlafly: Hear Her Roar!

Perhaps "the" women's legislation in the 1970s was not *Roe v. Wade*, decided by the courts, but the Equal Rights Amendment, which passed Congress in

1972 and went to the states for ratification. Its provisions included a controversial "equal pay for equal work" clause and the strong probability that
women would be subject to the military draft. Ironically in the end, however, the major accomplishment of the Equal Rights Amendment was the
elevation to national prominence of Phyllis Schlafly, an Illinois housewife.

Schlafly had run for Congress and lost in 1952, and had fought against
communism for years, often challenging her own party.[139] She vigorously
resisted any conciliation with the USSR, rejected Khrushchev's "peaceful
coexistence" and Brezhnev's détente. Her 1964 book supporting Barry
Goldwater for president, *A Choice Not an Echo*, sold millions of copies in a
few months, underscoring the current conservative discontent with the two
established parties ("Socialist Party A and Socialist Party B," as conservative Thomas Anderson referred to them).[140] Purged by the Republican establishment after Goldwater's crushing defeat, Schlafly continued to work
the grass roots in her position as vice president of the National Federation
of Republican Women, but was denied the presidency of that organization
in 1967 as the national party sought to distance itself from the "extremists."
But in defeat, Schlafly won a core group of committed supporters who
would serve as her foot soldiers in upcoming campaigns.

In 1967, the National Organization for Women (NOW) decided to revive the ERA, a dormant amendment for decades. After Congress passed it,
thirty states ratified it, and only eight more states were required to consent
for it to take effect. It appeared to supporters and opponents alike that the
ERA was on the fast track to ratification. Schlafly had other ideas. She created the STOP ERA movement in 1972 and laid out her case against the
ERA in her *Phyllis Schlafly Report*. She claimed the ERA would destroy the
family, erode women's rights to alimony and child support in case of divorce, and "absolutely and positively make women subject to the draft."[141]
When Oklahoma's state legislature defeated the ERA, Schlafly suddenly
had hope that the amendment could be derailed, but by 1977, only three
states needed to ratify to reach the operative number of thirty-eight.

Meanwhile, Schlafly returned to her grassroots organizations with
STOP ERA, each of which developed its own campaign strategies and
raised its own funds. STOP ERA particularly appealed to religious women
of all faiths, who were mobilized by the conservative message. Despite
claims that opponents were poorly educated or "hicks," studies showed "the
personal and political characteristics of [the anti-ERA activists] do not fit
most of the hypothesized characteristics ascribed to opponents of women's
liberation."[142] State leaders included an Austrian immigrant and refugee

from the Nazis in South Dakota, a minister's wife from Tennessee, and a Vermont McGovernite twenty-something. Elaine Donnelly, another anti-ERA activist and a housewife from Michigan, would later make herself into one of the leading experts on the American military. Schlafly deliberately used her supporters' femininity as a tool and insisted that the prettiest ones meet with the legislators, putting them in stark contrast to the mostly plain and angry ERA supporters.

When Schlafly herself could debate her opponents, she seldom lost. Meeting the leading ERA congressional advocate, Patricia Schroeder, a Progressive Democrat from the liberal enclave of Boulder, Colorado, on a televised news program, Schlafly maneuvered the congresswoman into admitting that women would be drafted for combat during wartime if the amendment passed. And when actor Alan Alda, testifying before the Illinois State Senate, said he would support his two daughters being drafted, but they would not enter the military because they were conscientious objectors, the entire equality argument became the object of ridicule.[143] As Schlafly's biographer, Donald Critchlow, noted, Schlafly won many debates due to the tendency of her feminist opponents to attack her personally rather than sticking to the issue.

The style of personal attack reflected a deeper trend in American politics in which the Left, having increasingly gained control of the major media outlets, no longer thought it was required to actually prove its positions. "Because I said so" was accepted as the only defense necessary for liberal pundits and politicians. It was the first step in a long slide of the mainstream media outlets positing leftist positions as the norm, then expressing shock when readership and viewership, not to mention public trust, all fell. When Betty Friedan in a 1973 debate with Schlafly at Illinois State University called Schlafly an "Aunt Tom" and a "traitor to your sex" whom Friedan would like to burn at the stake, Schlafly calmly pointed out the "intemperate nature of the proponents of ERA."[144] Appearing on television talk shows, and listed in *Good Housekeeping* magazine as one of the ten most admired women in America, Schlafly turned the scorn of the feminists into a reason for admiring her.

Abortion became a millstone around the neck of the ERA as well, as advocates attempted to separate reproductive rights arguments from the amendment. Schlafly's allies tied the two together whenever possible, arguing that ERA was about much more than equal rights and was in fact an attack on traditional family values, resulting in a tidal wave of STOP ERA funding, mostly from small donations. The tactics of the pro-ERA feminists, with their throwbacks to sixties-era mass demonstrations and Abbie Hoffmanesque "in your face" confrontations, alienated many women. Schlafly eagerly hyped the pro-lesbian elements within the ERA movement as characteristic of the rank-and-file.

Virtually all of Hollywood's female celebrities, including Lily Tomlin, Carol Burnett, Candice Bergen, and Marlo Thomas, actively campaigned for the amendment, as did Hugh Hefner's daughter Christie, humor columnist Erma Bombeck, and advice columnists and sisters Abigail Van Buren and Ann Landers. Even Maureen Reagan, Ronald Reagan's daughter, supported the ERA. Women's magazines stood nearly united in favor of the amendment, with thirty-two magazine editors meeting to formulate a pro-ERA strategy in their publications.[145] In addition to the intelligentsia and Hollywood, the amendment had the backing of both political parties and the new president Gerald Ford and his wife, Betty.

Schlafy, though, had her grassroots support. Almost 75 percent of the STOP ERA funding came from donations of $150 or less, and the pro-ERA side outspent STOP ERA on marketing many times over. Schlafly also had a solid strategy. Like a football team backed up to its own goal line, she had a minimum of territory to defend: only five battleground states remained in the path of ratification, including her home state of Illinois. Schlafly's forces defeated it there, but Congress extended the deadline for ratifying the amendment, changing the rules mid-game. Indiana ratified the ERA in 1977, the last state to do so—and only by a single vote under pressure from President Jimmy Carter. With the International Women's Year conference in Houston that year, in which liberals were disproportionately represented, Schlafly conceived a massive pro-family counterrally that trumped the IWY conference. Shortly thereafter, Georgia, Alabama, South Carolina, and Florida all in one way or another voted no on the ERA or refused to vote on it altogether. Clearly doomed to defeat, ERA supporters extended the ratification deadline by seven more years. Not one state ratified it during the extension, despite massive lobbying from feminist groups, while two states rescinded their ERA votes. ERA supporters, marching on Washington, threatened violence if the amendment did not pass. Yet for all the forces allied in its favor, the ERA still failed, largely due to the efforts of Phyllis Schlafly.

In the larger context, however, Schlafly failed, or more accurately, was too late; the damage done to American society by Lyndon Johnson's welfare programs had fallen disproportionately on women, pushing more of them than ever into poverty. American women increasingly became single heads of households and unable to provide for themselves and their children. Hillary Clinton might later say it took a village to raise a child, but it certainly took a father and mother, or most appropriately, a husband and wife. At the very time that women received greater latitude to terminate births or avoid pregnancy, more women than ever were becoming poor, invalidating the presumption that larger families equaled economic hardship. Lower-class women, particularly blacks, soon constituted the highest percentages of those having abortions. Black birth rates were decimated by the paired policies of the War on Poverty and abortion.

Abortion and family size became part of a greater argument about the necessity of larger numbers of children at all. That argument soon evolved into a debate over the morality of even having children. Recall that Ehrlich's *Population Bomb* (1968) had already prophesied that millions of people would starve to death in the 1970s and 1980s.[146] Keith Greiner demonstrated that conceptually, Ehrlich's projections used financial compound interest formulas, which were inapplicable to human reproduction.[147] (A few years later, Ehrlich predicted a population-induced global ice age.) Ehrlich's theories quickly collapsed, but overpopulation seemed all too real in some parts of the world, particularly China. Driven by warnings that China could not support its own population, in 1979 Deng Xiaoping instituted the one-child rule. Focused mostly on the Han Chinese in urban areas, Deng originally claimed the policy was temporary, and those in rural areas were not subject to the law. Nevertheless, it is estimated that this rule reduced China's population from what it would have been in 1999 by 300 million. (Other factors, including the failed Cultural Revolution and Red Guard activity, contributed to slowing the population growth, with 100 million suffering displacement or economic deprivation.) China's fertility rate dropped to 1.7 per couple, lower than that of the United States and barely above Germany's. Lower birth rates in democracies had another, more predictable, result: fewer young employees entered the workforce. These trends decimated the labor force in Europe, forcing an expansion of immigration from Africa, the Balkans, and the Middle East to provide necessary menial labor.

Windows of Weakness

Amid these seismic social changes in America and Europe, the cold war seemed to drift into a quiet but deadly standoff. For all intents and purposes, the war in Vietnam was over, and Southeast Asia's fate was sealed when Nixon resigned. His successor, Gerald Ford, had more in common with Jimmy Carter—his opponent in 1976—than he did with Nixon, especially when it came to national security. Under Nixon and Kissinger, the United States had negotiated a treaty known as SALT (Strategic Arms Limitation Talks, later to be SALT I), in which the total number of nuclear weapons launchers was cut (although warheads were not). The SALT accords, both a treaty and an interim agreement, signed in May 1972, froze for five years the numerical gap between the Soviet and U.S. missile forces that had developed under Kennedy and Johnson. However, due to Johnson's actions, no American programs existed that could possibly produce new missiles for at least five years. The freeze on numbers stopped no U.S. program: but it did arrest a Soviet program that was deploying more than two hundred ICBMs and SLBMs a year. For a brief time, the United States pressed forward on Trident, the B-1, Minuteman III, and MIRV. The only program to suffer was ABM, which Congress was on the verge of killing anyway.[148]

From 1973 to 1977, American foreign policy was under the firm control of Henry Kissinger, Nixon's and subsequently Ford's secretary of state. Born in Bavaria in 1923, Kissinger came to the United States in 1938 when his family was forced to flee the German persecution of Jews. In 1943, he was drafted into the army, fought in the Battle of the Bulge, and became a sergeant with the Counterintelligence Corps. He ended up at Camp King in Oberursel, Germany, at the age of twenty-three, teaching at its Intelligence School with the 970th CIC Detachment. After earning a Ph.D. at Harvard in 1954, he wrote a book, *Nuclear Weapons and Foreign Policy* (1957), in which he posited that the Soviet Union would never allow disarmament to the point that they would not enjoy hegemony vis-à-vis all neighboring nations. Yet he pursued a realpolitik strategy, believing he could negotiate with the Soviets to America's advantage. Kissinger was accused of having a greater ego than Nixon, and their relationship was sometimes rocky, like two giants continuously jockeying for leverage. He never talked with Nixon without a witness present or on the phone line, and generally seemed more comfortable with Europeans than Americans. Later, he was aghast that Reagan would scuttle détente and actively attempt to win the cold war by aggressive action.

In the four-year span beginning with the exposure of the Watergate scandal, the nation collapsed into economic, political, and moral weakness while Kissinger kept the Soviets at bay. Ford's failure and Carter's election continued a dangerous pattern in which the United States, as it had in the two decades leading up to the Civil War, would stumble through almost twenty years without a leader who combined moral and intellectual stature with the charisma and strength of will to lead. Nixon's removal and the subsequent media lampooning of Ford was evidence of the new power of a rabid press that could destroy a politician with whom it disagreed, and remove a president whom the media power brokers hated. More important, Nixon's departure meant that the only president in the twenty-year span from 1960 to 1980 who demonstrated any consistent strength of leadership internationally had left the scene, and, for a second time in an era, foreign policy was handed to amateurs and incompetents.

When Nixon resigned, Gerald Ford, a former congressman from Michigan and member of the infamous Warren Commission, assumed the presidency. Tall, bland, and the epitome of the Washington go-along-to-get-along Republican, Ford nevertheless ran a close race against Jimmy Carter in 1976. He lost on the basis of his association with Nixon, and, on the introduction of Carter's "misery index"—an invented measure that combined the inflation rate and the unemployment rate—and by Carter's central campaign question: "Are you better off today than you were four years ago?" But the main foreign policy controversy during this time was whether arms control enhanced U.S. security or damaged it. Some concerned scientists had argued that unilateral restraint would induce the Soviets to follow suit. That theory reappeared periodically and "was a contributing factor in President Carter's decision to cancel the B-1 bomber. . . . There was not the slightest proof that the Soviets operated by such a maxim, and overwhelming evidence to the contrary."[149] Carter's secretary of defense Harold Brown said in 1979, "We have found that when we build weapons, they [the Soviets] build; when we stop, they nevertheless continue to build. . . ."[150]

Another theory arose that claimed arms control created conditions where neither side could gain an advantage from a first strike because it could not avoid its own destruction during retaliation. Kissinger discounted this theory as having no supporting evidence, and stated:

> In the hands of academicians it was barely noticed that even mutual restraint had unprecedented consequences. . . . Our strategic power could no longer compensate for the Soviet superiority in conventional strength of the Soviet capacity for regional intervention . . . the democracies would have to build up their conventional strength if they wanted to avoid political blackmail. Regrettably, . . . groups favoring control of strategic weapons opposed increases in other categories of military power.[151]

Kissinger also defined the role of military personnel in arms limitation talks: "Military men cannot be expected to think creatively about restraining the arms race; nor is it desirable that they do so. Their duty is to keep the nation strong; their assignment must be to prevail should all else fail. Military men who become arms controllers are likely to neglect their primary mission."[152]

Talks continued through the 1970s but with minimal progress until Carter took over negotiations. In June of 1979, Carter and the Soviets signed SALT II, which immediately ran into problems with Senate ratification. The Senate wanted the go-ahead from the Joint Chiefs of Staff (JCS), whose approval hinged on updating all elements of America's nuclear TRIAD with new weapons. For the winged Air Force, this was a new bomber (the B-1), to replace the B-52; for the Navy, its missile submarines would continue upgrading its Polaris/Poseidon family of missiles to the Trident I missile and eventually to Trident IIs; and for the Air Force, a new missile called the MX would replace the Minuteman II and III missiles. In addition, the JCS insisted on deploying cruise missiles on numerous platforms (subs, battleships, bombers), and in creating two antiballistic missile system locations. If those upgrades were in place, they would offset the limitations on the number of launchers by making delivery of weapons more certain.[153] Kissinger again weighed in during the Senate hearings, stating, "After much reflection, I have concluded that I can support ratification, only with the following conditions. . . ." He then enumerated three conditions, the first of which was that defense spending be increased immediately, and that the treaty not be ratified until Congress approved the money for the programs desired by the JCS.[154] The Senate refused to ratify the treaty, although both sides generally respected its terms until the treaty was formally declared void by President Reagan in 1986.

"His Brain Power Is Extraordinary"

Carter's election in the United States coincided with James Callaghan's election as prime minister in England, perpetuating a phase when, for the most part, politicians of the Left governed the Anglo-American allies. James Earl "Jimmy" Carter, a former Navy submarine officer and Georgia peanut warehouseman, had been governor of Georgia from 1971 to 1975.[155] Somewhat belying his reputation for academic prowess, he first attended Georgia Southwestern College, a two-year agriculture and teachers' college, in spite of his father's wealth. He applied to the Naval Academy, but was forced to attend Georgia Tech and take additional math courses before being admitted in 1943. He graduated from Annapolis fifty-sixth in his class. After completing typical junior officer duties, he was assigned to the Navy's fledgling nuclear submarine program, and stationed at Schenectady, New York, where he took additional courses in reactor technology at Union College while writing training manuals. After seven years in the Navy, he resigned his commission, and he and his wife Rosalynn operated Carter's Warehouse, a general seed and farm supply store in Plains, Georgia.

Carter seemed anything but leftist in his biography. Married to the same woman for thirty-four years, touting his born-again Christianity, his Navy credentials, business background, and his southern heritage, Carter attracted American voters who saw him as a moral antidote to Nixon and a business-savvy opposite of Ford. Yet temperamentally he was a meddler, a micromanager who needed to be involved in details, while ideologically, his Progressivism (tempered with his own version of evangelical liberal Christianity) rivaled that of Johnson or FDR. He also exhibited substantial partisanship, referring to the Republican Party as "a party with a narrow vision, a party that is afraid of the future."[156]

Carter concealed his radical views through his purported intelligence, trumpeted by liberals in the media. Carter was "by far the most intelligent President in my lifetime," gushed *Washington Post* publisher Katherine Graham. "His brain power was extraordinary," echoed CBS's Walter Cronkite, and House Speaker Tip O'Neill called him the "smartest public official I've ever known."[157] (Others noted the sobriquets "intelligent" or "most intelligent" were often used when there was little else to recommend a politician, especially if the person in question spoke like a professor— Acheson, Stevenson, and Obama all come to mind.) A few reporters, however, admitted Carter failed to connect. "The smile is up front, but he is somewhere back in the weeds."[158] Before long, congressmen ducked his phone calls because he read to them from note cards, and he surrounded himself with his "Georgia mafia" of loyal but inexperienced subordinates. Notably, his primary adviser, his wife Rosalynn, attended cabinet meetings and seemed to be involved in every presidential decision. Not since Edith Wilson had a first lady wielded such power—and none would again until Hillary Clinton.

Despite a weak economy that grew more sluggish by the day, Carter's presidency seemed to get off to a rousing start with a major foreign policy achievement, the Camp David Accords. In many ways, the agreements at Camp David obscured the increasingly radical and violent nature of Islam, presenting a portrait of a major moderate Islamic government finally facing the reality of Israel's existence. It did mark a slight change in Egyptian willingness to accept blame for decades' worth of conflict. For years, Egypt's leaders had lied to the public about previous defeats at the hands of the Israelis. In 1948, Nasser had claimed the Saudis and the British had provided the Egyptian army with defective weapons that fired back at the soldiers firing them, and in 1967, the official line was that the American and British air forces, not the Israeli air force, had shot down Egypt's planes.

Islamic states were riddled with a culture in which acknowledging error or shortcomings was a sure way to invite severe punishment, shame, and dishonor. One Muslim commented, "In our culture, those who admit fault, even unintentional guilt, are regarded as naive or foolish. Avoiding taking any responsibility has thus become part of the national character."[159] The "moderate" Islamic world that Carter thought he dealt with was largely the creation of the Arab media and willing accomplices in the American press. One Muslim woman who fled to America later wrote that her Egyptian friend and writer Tawfik Hamid, author of *The Real Roots of Islamic Violence*, said he attempted to preach peace and nonviolence in an Egyptian mosque and was chased into the streets of Cairo with rocks and "barely escaped with his life." And this was in Egypt, not considered a hotbed of radicalism.[160]

Virtually none of the abundance that graced average Americans was understood in the Arab world. Nonie Darwish, who arrived in the United States and visited her first supermarket in 1978, recalled that "after seeing a special aisle for dog and cat food, my mother remarked, 'Even animals have more rights in America,' which she followed with a hearty 'Long live capitalism.' "[161] (These impressions greatly resembled those of Soviet MiG pilot Viktor Belenko, who escaped with his aircraft to Japan in the early 1970s, then was put under a form of witness protection by the CIA in Virginia. When he first visited a supermarket, he was convinced the CIA had staged the whole experience, as he thought it impossible for any store to have food in such abundance and in so many varieties.)[162] When Carter brokered the Camp David Accords, far from marking a sea change in Egypto-Arab attitudes, it concealed the deep hatred festering in most of the Middle Eastern states, where American abundance was seen as decadence.

Carter liked to portray himself as a nuclear engineer, although his experience was primarily from courses he took at the Naval Academy and his short service under Admiral Hyman Rickover with nuclear submarines. He resigned his naval commission after only seven years of service, and on paper, he had seemed to be a rather nontraditional politician. As a one-term governor of Georgia, he had drastically cut the number of state departments, and early in his term lowered the number of state employees. This was heavily touted as evidence of his effectiveness and fiscal responsibility, although in his last year he actually increased the Georgia employee count well above that when he took office. The consolidation of departments did not automatically increase efficiency, and many Georgians felt Carter's performance as governor was mostly smoke and mirrors.

As president, however, he slashed military programs, proving himself no friend of a strong national defense. In particular, he cut the upgraded weapons systems promised by both Nixon and Congress to the military in return for the Joint Chiefs of Staff supporting SALT II. Carter eliminated the B-1 bomber, shoved the MX missile into a delayed development (code for the weapons graveyard), reduced deployment of cruise missiles, and refused to build the antiballistic missile sites in accordance with the ABM Treaty. Carter also greatly expanded the number of federal bureaucrats with the addition of two new cabinet-level departments, Energy and Education, that became arguably, over time, the two most destructive departments in the entire federal bureaucracy.

For the conspiracy-minded, Carter provided grist for the mill. Early in his quixotic campaign for president, he came to the attention of Zbigniew Brzezinski, then working for banker David Rockefeller in setting up the Trilateral Commission (with its internationalist mission of uniting the United States, Japan, and Europe). Brzezinski vetted Carter on his globalist attitudes, introduced Carter to Rockefeller, and Carter rose from an obscure ex-governor of a southern state favored by only 4 percent of Democrats to the leading Democratic candidate for president in only two months. The media endorsed him with very favorable coverage, and the Rockefeller support was kept in the background. When Carter, a member of the Trilateral Commission, was elected president, Brzezinski was made national security advisor, and international affairs seemed to take precedence over domestic problems.

Even had any such international conspiracy existed, however, Carter's incompetence would have proven that average Americans had nothing to fear from such a cabal. Carter suddenly showed himself to be an intellectual lightweight, constantly confounded by practical politics, and was unable to address the continued stagflation and energy crisis that beset his presidency. Worst of all, he was unable to cure the "misery index" he had used in his campaign against Ford; inflation and unemployment both rose to double digits. His presidency was mired in an economic swamp and would soon become hopelessly stuck, when a host of international crises revealed that Carter was also incapable of dealing with serious foreign threats.

Light of the Aryans

Carter's biggest challenge came from a confrontation with Iran that exposed the West, for the first time, to the truly radical nature of Islamic fundamentalism. The event that triggered the altercation was the toppling of the shah of Iran.

Known as the "Light of the Aryans," "Vice Regent of God," or simply "HIM" (His Imperial Majesty), Shah Mohammad Reza Pahlavi took the throne in 1941 and proceeded to modernize Iran while at the same time governing the country with an iron fist and a great deal of corruption. His court in Tehran, according to a CIA report in the 1970s, was "a center of licentiousness and depravity, of corruption and influence peddling."[163] His butler made a fortune in real estate, his doctor became a wealthy landholder, and family members amassed extraordinary fortunes. A European visitor to the court witnessed "an atmosphere of overwhelming nouveau-riche, meretricious, chi-chi and sycophancy."[164] Darker than the graft and corruption was the brutality of the shah's regime, mainly through its SAVAK police, alleged to have tortured thousands of Iranians in the most extreme and disgusting ways. A half-million Iranians were "interviewed" between 1970 and 1975 to maintain a climate of fear and suspicion.

The shah's antithesis was a seventy-seven-year-old cleric, the Shiite Grand Ayatollah Ruhollah Khomeini (nicknamed the "Smasher of Idols" and the "one who humbles Satan"). A humorless, simple man, the ayatollah drifted into prayer sessions that lasted for days. In one such marathon, his seven-year-old daughter died and he refused to be interrupted to mourn or attend her funeral. Based in Qom, Khomeini developed a reputation as a powerful scholar, becoming an avowed enemy of the shah immediately upon Pahlavi's ascension. The two met personally only once, and intensely disliked each other immediately.

In 1963, during holy days, Khomeini told a crowd that the shah was a usurper and a tool of Satan. The following year, a new law allowed for American military personnel accused of crimes to be tried under American law, not Islamic Sharia; again, Khomeini denounced the shah, this time adding America to his list of devils. Shortly after that, Pahlavi threw the ayatollah out of the country. While in exile, Khomeini wrote *Islamic Gov-*

ernment (1971), a treatise on the superiority of a theocracy. In October 1978, Khomeini was chased out of Iraq to Paris, where he became a celebrity. Reporters flocked to his residence, where his handlers kept him carefully scripted: "We told him what to say and he memorized it and recited it ver-batim. . . ."[165] Abulhassan Banisadr, a Khomeini confidant who accompa-nied him (and would later become Iran's president), meticulously excerpted parts of the Koran that spoke to principles of equality, independence, prog-ress, and republicanism, for the ayatollah to expound upon for Westerners. Both knew full well that such views were façades for their real, more mili-tant and strict Muslim beliefs.

By that time, the shah, suffering from cancer—which he kept secret—was heavily medicated, looking shaky and staring glassy-eyed at the walls. Treasury Secretary Michael Blumenthal described him as a "zombie" after one visit. Crackdowns inside Iran intensified as opposition to the shah in-creased throughout 1978, and lines of wealthy Iranians at airports, seeking to escape, testified to the government's weakening position. American ad-visers informed the shah that he couldn't hold on to power much longer, and urged him to go into exile.

Beginning in February 1979, American officials considered a takeover by radical street elements a very real possibility and discussed it at nearly every State Department meeting. Regular protest marches numbering in the thousands routinely passed the U.S. embassy to shout "Death to Amer-ica!" In short, the eventual hostage crisis came as no surprise to those inside the Carter White House. When the shah's medical condition worsened, and he was admitted into the United States, Iran exploded. Organized by a group of Muslim students—who knew they had the full backing of the ayatollah—mobs stormed the U.S. embassy on November 4, 1979, and took sixty-three hostages, blindfolding and binding them.

Carter found himself helpless to deal with the situation, or even mar-ginally shape it. Deeply concerned about the safety of the hostages, he hes-itated to order military measures and within a short time, the hostage crisis became a national and media obsession. Brzezinski later said it was the "one thing that drove everything else in the White House."[166] Indeed, it was al-most as though Carter was hostage number sixty-four, and he proved un-able to multitask. Convinced that the key to obtaining the release of the hostages was the eviction of the shah, the administration virtually forced the sick man out, calling in favors from Panama's no-more-virtuous dicta-tor, Omar Torrijos, to take in the shah and his retinue. In December 1979, the shah's plane arrived in Panama and as the party disembarked, Torrijos whispered to a friend, "Imagine that. Twenty-five hundred years of Persian Empire reduced to ten people and two dogs."[167]

Purging himself of the shah failed to secure for Carter the release of the by then fifty-two hostages (some had been released as a supposed sign that the regime was humane). He reluctantly ordered a risky military operation, Eagle Claw, in April 1980. A phenomenally intricate and sophisticated plan, Eagle Claw involved a desert rendezvous among helicopters, C-130 transports, and a difficult extraction by Delta Force in which soldiers would blast open the compound, load the hostages on trucks, and lift them out by helicopter from a nearby soccer stadium. During the planning stages of the operation, it still wasn't clear that administration members understood that they were dealing with a potential combat situation. Colonel Charles Beckwith, of Delta Force, when briefing the president and his security team on the operation, was asked by Deputy Secretary of State Warren Christopher what would happen to the student guards. Beckwith replied that the troops would "take the guards out." Christopher asked if that meant tying them up or wounding them. Beckwith responded, "No, sir. We're going to shoot each of them twice, right between the eyes." Christopher still didn't seem to get it. "Literally?" he asked. Beckwith again explained they would "kill every guard . . . [and] put enough copper and lead in them so they wouldn't be a problem. . . ."[168]

But the operation had too many variables, not the least of which was that all of the services demanded to be included, and coordination between the Army's Delta Force, Navy helicopters and Marine pilots, the three Air Force special operations groups, and the CIA paramilitary team was poor. Command and control was never centralized, training conducted hurriedly and almost ad hoc. Personnel were unfamiliar with one another, and had never worked with the equipment provided from the other services. To make matters worse, at least eight helicopters were needed for the mission, but two scratched en route, meaning the rescue was aborted before it even began. Beckwith's team, on the ground at a remote spot in Iran, advised Carter to call off the mission. A White House response to abort quickly followed, by which time the helicopters were refueled by the transport planes. But the first chopper, which had used up some of its fuel while waiting, maneuvered to top off its tanks for the return flight to the USS *Nimitz*. One of its blades clipped the fuselage of a C-130, causing a massive explosion that engulfed the two aircraft. Eight crew members died and four others were wounded. In the moment, the standard procedure of destroying the abandoned helicopters was deemed too dangerous. As the remaining

Americans lifted off, they left behind five Sea Stallions and critical intelligence papers about the failed mission, including information that American agents were inside Tehran.

A more botched effort could hardly have been imagined, making Carter and the U.S. military the subject of ridicule by foreign military personnel. Obviously, the United States had been severely damaged by losing in Vietnam, and its military forces were no longer something to be feared. In the Pentagon, a sense of panic prevailed, with many assuming the Soviets and others would immediately test U.S. readiness and resolve. Soviet military literature blatantly discussed the advantages of a "first strike," a surprise nuclear attack, in which a weak American president would not respond against Russian cities. Admiral Stansfield Turner, Carter's director of the CIA, had just decimated the CIA's capability for human intelligence gathering, terminating more than eight hundred operational personnel in the previous fall's Halloween Massacre, and now the all-volunteer Army (set up by Nixon in January 1973) failed the first test of its readiness and had proven itself incapable of fulfilling a commando-style mission. The Soviet forces in Afghanistan were surely watching the Iranian situation very carefully, and Carter's incompetence threatened to embolden them the way Kennedy's lack of performance prior to the Cuban missile crisis had spurred on Khrushchev. It was difficult to escape the conclusion that America's security was hanging by a thread.

To add insult to injury, Texas billionaire Ross Perot, president of Electronic Data Systems, mounted an operation to rescue his employees trapped in Tehran. Two EDS executives had been arrested and incarcerated in a Tehran prison, so Perot hired retired Special Forces colonel Arthur "Bull" Simons to get them out. A rescue during a prison transfer was foiled, so an Iranian EDS employee started a riot outside the prison where the men were being held, and when the crowd stormed the prison, Simons's team swooped in, grabbed the two men, and spirited the entire crew out of the country overland to Turkey without a single casualty. The exploit was recounted in a book by Ken Follett, *On Wings of Eagles*, and made into a television miniseries. An American businessman had pulled off what the government of the United States could not.

Meanwhile, Iranian students quickly dispersed the hostages and for several months, Carter made little progress toward obtaining their release. But in September, new openings for negotiations appeared, and soon thereafter, Iraq invaded Iran, which prompted the Iranians to look for an exit strategy that would yield some of the shah's wealth. In the States, Republican campaign strategists for Ronald Reagan, then running against Carter on a platform of renewing American strength from the decline that Carter had overseen, were sure that Carter had secured a release deal and steeled themselves for an "October Surprise" in the 1980 presidential election. In fact, by late October, Tehran had yet to make any final decisions, nor did the Iranians offer any kind of solid timetable before the election. Carter's pollsters told him it would be an electoral massacre.

The networks announced Reagan had won the election barely fifteen minutes after the polls closed. That December, aware that a more conservative and stronger president would soon be in the Oval Office, the Iranians offered a deal that included allowing $2.2 billion of the assets of the Shah's estate to be transferred to the Iranian government. The Americans accepted. As a final symbol of the failure of Carter's four years, Tehran notified Washington that the hostages were leaving in the next half hour—officially freed just minutes after Ronald Reagan took the oath of office.

While all this was going on, Afghanistan, next door to Iran, saw its own stirrings of trouble. A Soviet puppet Communist government had been installed in 1978, and the United States had started supplying military aid to the mujahideen rebels. The crisis in Iran diverted U.S. attention from the deteriorating Soviet situation in Afghanistan. In December 1979, Soviet special forces assassinated the president of Afghanistan, and the Kremlin poured in ground troops, once again making Carter appear helpless. Carter's big action at the time was a boycott of the Olympics in Moscow, which arguably hurt American athletes more than it did the Soviet Union.

In addition to exposing Carter's stunning lack of leadership skills or strategic thinking, the Iranian hostage crisis laid bare Europe's increasingly marginal role in world affairs, for the Europeans were equally helpless in affecting Iranian policies. Collectively, Europe continued to seek equality among the superpowers while inching—and at times, jogging—toward state socialism. But the Europeans lacked the internal cohesion or regulatory freedom to compete with the United States.

Adding to the sluggishness, the European economic community's fiscal machinery short-circuited reforms in the 1970s, especially those recommended by the 1977 MacDougall Report. Armies of lawyers oversaw labyrinthine regulations and quotas; in 1973, the Economic Commission had a 7,000-person bureaucracy. Its legal interventions, according to a report to the Conseil d'État in 1992, included 22,445 EU regulations, 1,675 directives, 1,198 protocols and agreements, 185 recommendations of the Commission or the Council, 291 Council resolutions, and 678 special communications.[169] *The Wall Street Journal* called the new Brussels civil servant a "bureaucrat without a country . . . well paid, well fed, and universally mistrusted by the people who employed him."[170] By that time, the original six members of the Common Market (actually the European Economic Community of France, West Germany, Belgium, the Netherlands, Luxembourg, and Italy) had been joined by Great Britain, Ireland, and Denmark.

After the fall of the Soviet Union, the Treaty of the European Union at Maastricht in 1993 attempted to limit these excesses of unelected bureaucrats and streamline the process—but failed. Instead, it even further reduced the ability of the national governments to make policy, which resulted in increasingly mobile capital. This proved particularly difficult for France: any time radical students took to the streets, as in the early 1970s, it only drove capital back to the United States. Valéry Giscard d'Estaing of France and Helmut Schmidt of Germany "went to extraordinary lengths" to protect the "soft and vulnerable" French economy with the European Monetary System, even to the point of keeping details of the January/February 1978 agreement secret from the central bankers and finance ministers of the other states.[171] It did not work any better than the earlier currency agreement (called "the Snake") to keep nations within 2.25 percent above or below a dollar peg.

Europe moved steadily toward economic integration at the expense of national sovereignty, believing the only way to compete with the United States and the Soviet Union was through a larger political entity. The examples of successful smaller economies such as Korea and Hong Kong were ignored. European leaders never exhibited a scintilla of understanding about the rising threat of militant Islam, or the new economic behemoths of India and China. Integration, in fact, had created a new European provincialism, substituting regional paralysis for national inefficiency.

The Chicago Boys

While the United States and Europe struggled with sagging economies and international terrorism, the Latin American countries in the 1970s seemed to be on a different trajectory. They offered another location for investment, despite military coups in many South American countries—or, perhaps more appropriately, because of them.

In Chile, Salvador Allende had become president in 1970, leading to celebrations everywhere among the Left, for it marked one of the first times a devout Marxist had triumphed in a free election in an open society. He promptly imposed his socialist vision. In addition to nationalizing foreign assets, he appropriated all private holdings over thirty-two acres—four thousand properties by September 1973. Allende also nationalized large Chilean corporations and took all holdings of General Motors, ITT, and the Bank of America. Predictably, the Left in America applauded all Allende's actions, and he became a hero on some college campuses. But the result of his policies was even more predictable. Inflation came, which rose by 300 percent as producers fled the country and tax revenues plunged.

Allende was not without opposition, however. The *gremiolista* movement (called *Gremios* for short), which included professional organizations, truck drivers, landowners, industrialists—all of whom were being destroyed by Allende's policies—resisted. General Augusto Pinochet led a September 11, 1973, coup against Allende, and members of Allende's government were rounded up or assassinated by the Chilean secret police and military. When the coup came, the *Gremios* breathed a sigh of relief, although the subsequent political oppression under Pinochet would prove every bit as damaging as Allende's economic policies.

Pinochet, the descendant of French and Basque immigrants, had worked his way up the ranks of the Chilean military. Claiming to be one of the central plotters in the 1973 coup—an assertion other members denied—Pinochet benefited from CIA support. Many Chilean officers became CIA operatives, but no evidence exists that the United States was directly involved in Allende's removal.[172] Members of the junta fired on the presidential palace, La Moneda; Allende allegedly committed suicide, and the junta took over. As with Napoleon's Directory, the anticipated rotation of the junta members in the presidency soon gave way to Pinochet's permanent occupation of that office. Nevertheless, for all its dictatorial trappings and brutal repression (more than 1,500 killed, perhaps as many as 80,000 arrested and a third of them tortured), the junta's new constitution received a 67 percent approval in the 1980 referendum.[173] Even allowing for vote tampering and ballot shenanigans, the people had supported Pinochet.

The new president knew that above all he needed to stabilize Chile's economy, which was suffering from typical Latin American inflation. Pinochet implemented free-market policies designed by the "Chicago Boys," a group of Chilean adherents to Milton Friedman's Chicago School of market-driven economics. Led by Finance Minister Jorge Cauas and Sergio de Castro, the government attacked inflation in three rounds from 1974 to 1990. State-expropriated companies, such as ITT, Dow Chemical, and Firestone—all seized by Allende—were returned to their rightful owners, and a privatization program was launched. The Chicago Boys oversaw a 5 percent annual growth rate, and from 1982, the performance of Chile's economy surpassed that of the Latin American average (interspersed with intermittent declines under socialist governments). Inflation was brought to heel, and the Chilean poverty rate slashed in half.

At the appropriate time, Pinochet complied with the constitution, which allowed an election in 1988, and Chile returned to civilian rule when Pinochet lost 56 to 44 percent in a referendum that year. He was later arrested in England for human rights violations, and although he was released in March 2000 on medical grounds, his legacy remains mixed at best. Nevertheless, the Chilean Miracle—despite criticisms by statists such as Amartya Sen—stands as a testimony to the power of free-market principles.[174]

By the late 1970s, Brazil, Argentina, Uruguay, Bolivia, and Peru all lived under military rule. Many of these regimes reversed the destructive governmental overtures against foreign business. For example, Venezuela had stolen the foreign oil industry in its country in 1974, and in Mexico, Ford was pressured to hand over equity control of its plants in a process called "Mexicanization." The military governments, on the other hand, achieved export growth and reopened countries for foreign investment. From 1967 to 1976, for example, American investment in Brazil tripled. Under the military regimes, American banks also returned to Latin America; Bank of America, Citibank, and Chase Manhattan, plus others, loaned $6 billion by 1979. General Motors, Ford, and Chrysler all built new plants, as did Volkswagen and Toyota, with the Americans accounting for 40 percent of the auto production in Latin America by 1973. Moreover, the Americanos paid high wages.[175]

Similar results were obtained in Mexico with the *maquiladora* program beginning in 1965, which created bonded manufacturing zones where foreign companies could import duty free and assemble goods manufactured within Mexico. The exported good paid only the duty of the value added in Mexico, drastically lowering U.S. manufacturing costs. In 1967, the United States had 67 plants on the border; by 1974, it was 665 plants, exporting $450 million to the United States and causing booms in the cities of El Paso, Texas, and Ciudad Juárez, which grew to 1 million and 1.5 million respectively by 1995. Tourists also helped buoy the economies: 5 million overseas trips by 1968.

With stability of markets, even if brought by military dictatorship, came tourism, which had low start-up costs and produced a large multiplier effect on the economies. Latin American countries responded by emphasizing their local folk traditions. The United Nations even began to promote Otavalan Indian basket weaving in the Andes as a market attraction; large landowners, fearing government theft, converted their haciendas to country inns for tourists, hiring *Quimsenas* (Indian women) to dress in native garb and work at the hotel. Whether authentic or not, the result was an authentic-looking traditional expression of a Latin American way of life. By 2000, tourists had spent $16 billion in Latin America, no doubt some of it going to plastic surgery in Brazil![176]

Latin America enjoyed much of the same umbrella of freedom—even freedom to flirt with socialism—provided by American military power and prosperity. It was the same around the free world. While individuals became more liberated and prosperous on a personal level, their liberty and material condition were sheltered by a military presence whose creed and martial requirements were the antithesis of many of the personal freedoms celebrated by society at large. Protecting the West proved unpopular politically. This was sustainable in the United States, with its heritage of individual gun ownership and militia armies, but the story was different in Europe, where the moral fiber to oppose either the Soviets or the Islamic fundamentalists slowly disappeared. Full-blown libertinism and the celebrity culture were still over a decade away, but the seeds were already planted in the 1970s and early 1980s.

The West's erosion of will and discipline contrasted dramatically less with the USSR, which was already feeling the first tingles of the same liberating spirits, than with radical Islam, where that erosion was viewed with scorn, and where Western sexual liberation was viewed as contemptible. Carter's brief experience with the Iranian hostage crisis could have alerted him to the dangers of radical Islam, but he failed to grasp the larger forces at work in the Middle East.

Only a remarkable shift in the leadership of the free world could reestablish the West as a moral and military force in the world. Only a handful of powerful leaders could force the Soviets to confront the inconsistencies of their self-destructive doctrines. Had remarkable champions of freedom Margaret Thatcher, Pope John Paul II, and Ronald Reagan not appeared, the history of the cold war would certainly have been different, and quite likely, much, much longer. But while they readily saw the evil posed by the Soviet Union in its godlessness, they all missed the rising menace in the background: an aggressive, barbaric Islam.

CHAPTER SIX

Ash Heap of History

TIME LINE

1979:   Iranian hostage crisis; Margaret Thatcher becomes first female prime minister of Great Britain; Soviets invade Afghanistan

1980:   Ronald Reagan elected president; U.S. men's hockey team beats Russians in the Olympics

1981:   Iranian hostages released; unsuccessful assassination attempts on Ronald Reagan and Pope John Paul II; Reagan fires striking air traffic controllers; first *Ohio*-class submarine begins duty; Farewell intelligence operation against the Soviet Union begins

1982:   Falklands War; Equal Rights Amendment falls short of ratification

1983:   "Star Wars" initiative revealed; United States invades Grenada; Marine barracks in Beirut blown up; U.S. recession hits bottom

1984:   U.S. economy improves; Reagan reelected

1985:   Mikhail Gorbachev becomes leader of the Soviet Union.

1986:   Iran-Contra affair comes to light; Space Shuttle *Challenger* disaster; United States bombs Libya after Berlin discotheque bombing; Chernobyl nuclear power plant failure; Reykjavík, Iceland, talks between Reagan and

Gorbachev; United States passes Simpson-Mazzoli immigration amnesty bill

1987: Teenage German pilot evades Soviet defenses to land a private plane on Red Square; Reagan's Brandenburg Gate speech

1988: Soviet Union begins perestroika (economic restructuring); George H. W. Bush elected president; B-2 stealth bomber revealed; Hungary rolls up its section of the Iron Curtain fence; Bruce Springsteen plays East Berlin

1989: Solidarity union legalized in Poland; Soviets pull out of Afghanistan; Exxon *Valdez* oil spill; Tiananmen Square protests; Solidarity wins in Polish elections; Estonia, Latvia, and Lithuania demand independence from the Soviet Union; Hungarian Republic declared; Berlin Wall torn down; Bulgaria moves from Communist to socialist; non-Communist government formed in Czechoslovakia; Romanian revolution ousts Communist government

God Saves the Gipper

Waiting to the side of the Washington Hilton Hotel, the would-be assassin saw President Ronald Reagan come out of a speaking engagement. As the president, who had chosen not to wear a bulletproof vest that day, walked the thirty feet to the limousine, deranged John Hinckley, Jr., burst out from behind a rope line and fired six shots from only fifteen feet away, hitting White House press secretary James Brady, a police officer, and a Secret Service agent who shielded the president with his own body.

For a moment, Hinckley had a clear shot at the president, but he missed, due to the quick work of the Secret Service Agent in charge, who immediately shoved Reagan into the limousine. Nonetheless, one explosive bullet hit the side of the limo and ricocheted inside, striking the Gipper under the left arm, entering his lung, and coming to rest less than one inch from his heart. Reagan immediately coughed up blood. Alert when he entered the hospital emergency room, characteristically Reagan quipped to the doctors who soon were to operate on him, "I hope you're all Republicans." Dr. Joseph Giordano, a liberal Democrat, replied, "Today, Mr. President, we are all Republicans."[1]

Choosing a defining decade for the twentieth century is a daunting task, although certainly 1981 might qualify as the start of one. Overall, it is hard to imagine more significant periods in human history than those of the two world wars, let alone the most recent hundred years. But the eight years of Ronald Wilson Reagan's terms might reach that bar.

Playing "what if" is dangerous for the historian. But because individuals are so important to every clearly definable historical event, it is all the more intriguing to entertain alternative paths of the past. Where would the United States be if British captain Patrick Ferguson had not refused to shoot George Washington only a few feet away from him during the Battle of Brandywine, because it would have been ungentlemanly to shoot an unoffending individual?[2] No Union marksman felled Robert E. Lee, visibly in the midst of the Confederates fighting desperately to hold their line at Chancellorsville. If Lee had been killed, would the Civil War have ended two years earlier? If a driver had not taken a wrong turn in Sarajevo, would not the entirety of world history look *much* different, if in unpredictable ways?

Therefore, it is unrealistic neither to identify key moments in the past, nor to minimize the specific point at which individuals of titanic proportions first stride onto the world stage in their starring roles, particularly Margaret Thatcher, Ronald Reagan, and Pope John Paul II. With Britain's Thatcher, one can pinpoint that historic moment as the first meeting with her advisers on May 8, 1979, when the first order of business was to "see that both the police and the armed forces were properly paid."[3] In the near future, as matters turned out, Thatcher would need the unquestioned loyalty of both the police and the military for different purposes, and each would respond with loyalty and commitment.

Iron Lady

England changed, permanently and for the better, in 1979, substantially because of the will of Margaret Thatcher. Outside of Ronald Reagan, no figure on the Right in the twentieth century so deeply disturbed leftists—in particular, leftist academics—as the "Iron Lady."

A grocer's daughter, Thatcher was born in 1925 in Lincolnshire. She was raised Methodist and learned liberal politics from her father, who dabbled in local politics and lay preaching. After studying chemistry at Oxford, where she was president of the Oxford Conservative Association, she received an M.A. in science. Working in Colchester as a chemist for BX Plastics (and later, J. Lyons and Co.), she agreed to stand for election in 1950 as a member of Parliament. She lost her first election, although with a far smaller deficit than her predecessors. The following year, she married Denis Thatcher, a businessman, and studied law for the next two years. Thatcher thus came into politics on her own accomplishments rather than on a politician-husband's coattails or a political family name. Elected to the Finchley seat in 1958, she successfully fought for a bill to open local council meetings to the public.

Margaret Thatcher certainly represented—embodied—genuine social and political change. Unlike American feminists of the day, Thatcher reveled in her femininity. Care of her hair was a time-worthy endeavor; she liked jewelry; and always wore perfectly kept, well-tailored clothes. British historian Paul Johnson, who knew her personally, noted, "I have seldom met a woman who enjoyed being a woman more."[4] Thatcher never wore pants, and virtually never turned out except in full makeup, coiffed hair, and immaculate clothes. In part, her unabashed femininity was why she was so despised by liberal feminists. She also, however, greatly preferred the company of men to other women. When at parties, Maggie stayed with the males, and she particularly enjoyed socializing with Reagan, with whom she instinctively bonded. Yet she was completely honest and forthright. Her carefully turned-out air permeated her public persona—always in control, never frantic, never shrill. This also translated into her speech patterns as she battled in the House of Commons to make herself heard above the men.

Thatcher moved up the ranks in the Conservative Party, gaining a reputation for reasoned logic and displaying a penchant, even in the 1960s, for privatizing as much as possible. From 1970 to 1974, she was Edward Heath's secretary of state for education, eliminating the universal free-milk program and, as part of a comprehensive education reform, agreeing to school cutbacks. Under the Labour government, as a member of the minority, Thatcher honed her free-market philosophy and became the leader of the Conservative Party in February 1975. A noted anti-Communist, she gave a scathing speech against the Soviet Politburo on January 19, 1976, that caused the Communist papers to call her the "Iron Lady," a name she relished.

Some of Thatcher's political opponents recognized that the postwar system of having government provide goodies for everyone was breaking down. Prime Minister James Callaghan observed, "For too long . . . we have postponed facing up to fundamental choices and fundamental changes. . . . The cosy [sic] world we were told would go on forever, where full employment would be guaranteed at the stroke of a Chancellor's pen, cutting taxes, deficit spending—that cosy [sic] world is gone."[5] As the Labour government struggled with soaring unemployment, industrial strikes, and piles of garbage that lay in the streets (even the morticians struck, allowing dead bodies to pile up), the Conservatives saw their opportunity to take control. They ran an aggressive conservative advertising blitz, labeling the winter of 1978–79 the "Winter of Discontent" among the British citizenry. The public dissatisfaction led to a motion of no confidence in the Labour leaders and new elections were called for in 1979. Maggie Thatcher rode the subsequent Conservative majority to become the first woman prime minister, taking the reins of power just under a year ahead of Ronald Reagan in the United States.[6]

Britain had undergone a shift in attitudes toward the government—certainly not in the majority's mind yet, but in enough of a minority that it provoked the rise of new think tanks, such as the Adam Smith Institute, Centre for Policy Studies, and Institute of Economic Affairs (IEA). Even before Thatcher's ideas were fully developed, these tanks heavily influenced MP Keith Joseph, who became the free-market apostle of England. In 1974, Joseph went on a one-man speaking tour of England, appearing in front of a packed lecture hall at Oxford, promoting free enterprise, monetarism, and deregulation, in the process suffering scorn, abuse, and physical confrontations. More than one of his suits sported stains from eggs thrown at him. Joseph decisively shaped Thatcher's ideas, whose three goals were to break the power of the unions, reduce the size of the state sector, and restore confidence in the currency.[7]

In 1976, Joseph published his tract *Monetarism Is Not Enough*, calling for trade union reform. It became a guide for the 1978 "Stepping Stones," a conservative outline for the free market restoration movement in Britain. Among objectives proposed in "Stepping Stones" were balanced budgets, a shift from income taxes to sales taxes, use of the North Sea oil reserve money to keep interest rates low, and a cut in public-sector borrowing. Ideas and policy prescriptions generated by the think tanks allowed Margaret Thatcher to enter office "intellectually well prepared."[8]

She and "her Ronnie" had significant differences as leaders, especially on many social policies: Thatcher for permitting abortions, Reagan a noteworthy twentieth-century voice for the pro-life movement; Thatcher for maintaining strict divorce laws, Reagan himself divorced; Thatcher for decriminalizing homosexuality, Reagan, a traditionalist. Stylistically, she lacked Reagan's talent for employing humor as a policy weapon, and her jokes "were few and tended to be somber, with a touch of bitterness."[9]

Her public speeches usually lacked Reagan's poetry; she had to speak loudly without becoming strident or "wifely," which produced in Thatcher the unwelcome habit of odd syllable and word emphases. She adopted the tone of a lecturer—aloof, understandable, but seldom inspiring or passionate, yet had a memorable speech pattern and interesting voice. Her best lines, unlike Reagan's, which came in a natural flow that fit the energy of the moment, were droll and aristocratic. She had few memorable one-liners, and probably her best came early in her tenure. Faced with calls for her to retreat from her economic program, Thatcher, in a memorable response, told a cheering Tory convention, "You turn if you want to. The lady's not for turning." Reagan could enchant and entertain, leading the listener to conclusions he might not otherwise adopt simply out of the ease with which he journeyed there; Thatcher imposed her will through logic and repetition, perhaps pounding the audience into submission, and seldom leaving them with a sense that they enjoyed the experience.

Despite Thatcher's warm heart and kind nature—which few saw—she was "a compendium of annoying habits," which were too often on display publicly.[10] Reagan, despite his personal thoughts about his opponents, nevertheless managed to win over almost all political foes on a personal level. Reporters marveled at how they hated his policies, but still found it difficult to dislike the man. Thatcher, however, took it as a point of honor to turn opponents into fierce enemies. Unlike Reagan, who optimistically believed he could sway anyone if given enough time, Thatcher concluded her opponents would never support her policies under any circumstances, so why should she bother to befriend them personally? This policy produced remarkable hatred and vitriol among the leftists, who twenty years later still frothed against Thatcherism. It similarly opened the door for ambitious elements of her own party to throw her overboard at the first opportunity as a means of advancing their own careers. Only rarely did she misjudge people. She initially thought highly of Jimmy Carter, whom she described as a "man of marked intellectual ability with a grasp."[11]

Among other factors contributing to Thatcher's success was that she enjoyed good health throughout her career, had a safe district in North London, ensuring she didn't have to waste time running for local office, and worked her way into the cabinet without (at the time) making enemies or casting votes she would later regret. As prime minister, Thatcher carefully chose her battles, at first fighting only those she was sure she could win. Paul Johnson later characterized her as "lucky in the stupidity and loathsomeness of her public enemies," such as the Argentine dictators.[12]

Instantly upon delivering her first public speech as prime minister,

Thatcher noted "the House of Commons could expect a heavy program, designed to reverse socialism, extend choice and widen property ownership."[13] Thatcher realized the money supply growth had to be slowed and taxes lowered: the top tax rate stood at a job-killing 94 percent. The Conservatives managed to cut the top rate to 60 percent, in the process nearly doubling revenues from the Value Added Tax (a type of consumption tax that excluded the cost of raw materials from assessment). The plan worked to reverse the economic slump, and employment in England rose by 3.3 million from 1983 to 1990. Thatcher's privatization program proved wildly successful as eighty thousand houses shifted into private possession, and home ownership rose by 20 percent.[14] Thatcher's educational reform, however, met with somewhat more limited success. She introduced an educational voucher system and tried to implement testing standards; tenure was modified at universities, students were moved from a loan program to a grants system, and the government established evaluation standards.

Like Reagan, Mrs. Thatcher wanted to privatize as much as possible. Her National Enterprise Board, beginning in 1979, sold off £1 billion of government-owned assets. British Steel's Corby plant, British Leyland, Fairey Holdings, British Petroleum, British Aerospace, British Sugar Corporation, British Telecom, and British Gas: all were unloaded. Some of those firms survived in the free market but others, such as Leyland, did not. Some fifty-seven boards and commissions were eliminated in an eighteen-month period. The only major industry not privatized under Thatcher was broadcasting, where the BBC retained a stranglehold on British news.

Even critics such as liberal historian Tony Judt have grudgingly admitted "there is no doubt that Britain's economic performance *did* improve in the Thatcher years," crediting a "shakeout of inefficient firms, increased competition and the muffling of the unions."[15] It is a tribute to the success of conservatism in America and Britain that leftists adopted a bizarre argument that counted it as a "*failure* of Thatcherism to effect any far-reaching roll-back of state economic activity [emphasis in original]."[16] Such concerns on the part of the Left missed the point entirely that conservatives such as Thatcher, Reagan, Barry Goldwater, and even, to go back a few years, George Washington, understood that the issue was not how much government spent, but that its activities were restricted to those defined as proper: national security, internal stability, and protection of markets. Thatcher insisted that "there is no such thing as Society," which naturally meant "in due course people must lose respect for socially-defined goods."[17] Of course, that was partly what the debate was all about. Socially defined goods were historically seen as national defense and police, but to leftists they were everything else.

But even among their criticisms of Thatcher's impact, there is another side to the story. If public expenditure as a share of GDP only fell from 42.5 to 41.7 percent from 1977 to 1987, it was nevertheless a drop at a time when virtually every other democracy in the world saw government grow as a share of GDP. Some of Britain's increase was a direct result of downsizing the role of government, including massive commitments to unemployment insurance as the nation weathered the recession. Unemployment doubled during the first six years of Thatcher's program, as millions of miners and steel workers who had enjoyed featherbedded jobs suddenly found they had to search for real work.

The Iron Lady encountered stiff opposition when it came to unplugging unprofitable sectors of the economy from the government:

Time and again we were asked when plants and companies closed, "where will the new jobs come from?" As the months went by, we could point to the expansion of self-employment and to industrial successes in aerospace, chemicals and North Sea oil. Increasingly we could also look to foreign investment, for example in electronics and cars. But the fact is that in a market economy government does not—and cannot—know where the jobs will come from. . . .[18]

Competitiveness was where the economic battle had to be waged. Between 1978 and 1980, Britain's level of competitiveness in industry fell by half, and 60 percent of the decline was directly attributable to rising per-unit labor costs.

Mrs. Thatcher's opponents would not relent quietly, especially the unions, whose power she had methodically curtailed in several acts of Parliament. Labor, particularly, committed itself to a toxic and suicidal struggle. Given the unions' history of breaking governments—Harold Wilson's in 1969, Edward Heath's in 1974, and James Callaghan's five years later (leading to Thatcher's ascension)—the Iron Lady had cause for concern. When the engineering industry suffered a thirteen-week strike in 1979, the employers caved in, teaching Thatcher an important lesson. It "was not a political strike," she wrote in her memoirs, "nor one which threatened to bring ordinary life to a halt. But it was precisely the sort of strike which no country fighting for its industrial future could afford—an object lesson in what was wrong."[19] She vowed to learn from the experience, which, above all, taught her that the government had to carefully lay the groundwork for the kind of strike that threatened the ordinary life of Britons.

Successful in obtaining changes related to secondary picketing and protecting workers from closed shop arrangements, Thatcher went on a speaking blitz, directly targeting union families by relating the harm trade unionism was doing to them. Most of her early battles concerned immunity for strikers who were not employed by the plant they were picketing, and winning those limited the ability of unions to call strikers from sectors not immediately affected by the dispute. That was the case in the iron and steel strike of 1980. Thatcher found broad public support to implement these laws, but, after all, the beaches were often quiet before the first landing craft discharged troops on the sand. Until the government was prepared to sustain a major prolonged strike, Thatcher confided in her memoirs, she would rely on "a judicious mixture of flexibility and bluff."

War at the Bottom of the World

Thatcher might not have accomplished anything domestically, and perhaps been turned out handily, had not Argentina presented her a war "of just the right scale, in just the right place, and at just the right time."[20] For as World War I had cast a pall over all British military adventures, this was a conflict capable of changing the way Britain looked at herself in the mirror, a fight capable of reversing what Thatcher called the "Suez syndrome," in which "having previously exaggerated our power, we now exaggerated our impotence."[21] Now, the first English female to lead her country in war since Queen Victoria, Thatcher joined Golda Meir and Indira Gandhi as women who proved they could command a nation in battle.

British subjects had resided in the Falklands since 1834, when England established a permanent colony on the remote islands. The Argentines claimed sovereignty over the handful of small, lightly inhabited islands in the South Atlantic (two thirds of whose indigenous population was British) based on a failed penal colony they had attempted to establish in 1832, then abandoned. Thatcher learned—via word from amateur radio—that troops posing as unauthorized "scrap metal dealers" had landed on South Georgia Island.[22] That tiny location was home to no indigenous population and only a small British government scientific station. By March 1982, the invaders had raised the national flag of Argentina. Britain planned a show of force, but it would take weeks for British troops to arrive, leading the Argentine junta to conclude that a quick occupation of all the Falklands would present

England with a fait accompli. Fewer than one hundred Royal Marines and sailors guarded the islands when, on April 1, Argentine commandos stormed ashore and captured the government house after a brief battle. Upon news of the surrender, flag-waving crowds mobbed the Plaza de Mayo in Buenos Aires, and by the following day, all of the Falkland Islands were in Argentine hands.

Britain's task force sailed to retake the Falklands. Thatcher was rightly concerned with UN resolutions, given the "old anti-colonialist bias" of some of the Security Council's members.[23] By late April, the main UK task force arrived. British forces chased off the Argentine navy and raised the Union Jack on South Georgia Island. From there, the British launched attacks on the Falklands themselves. Limited to only three airfields on the islands, the Argentines sent air support from the mainland, at one point employing the *Escuadrón Fénix*, a fleet of civilian jets, simulating strikes on the Royal Navy to keep the combat air patrol occupied. On May 1, RAF Vulcan bombers from Ascension Island (some eight thousand nautical miles away) began bombing Argentine targets.

A single ship sinking, of the cruiser *Belgrano* on May 2 by the submarine HMS *Conqueror*, instantly turned the tide for the Brits; after that, the Argentine navy, particularly the country's only aircraft carrier, scurried back to port and was no longer a factor.[24] Two days later, however, an Argentine attack plane slammed a French Exocet missile recognized by the Royal Navy as a "friendly" into the HMS *Sheffield*, which promptly sank. Undaunted, the Royal Navy task force pressed on, landing troops at the main beachhead, San Carlos on the northwest side of the islands, in May. On May 27–28 the Brits moved inland; Stanley was assaulted on June 13, more than nine thousand Argentine troops surrendered, and the South Sandwich Islands soon followed. An embarrassed junta, led by General Leopoldo Galtieri, resigned, replaced in October 1983 by the Radical Civic Union party of Raúl Alfonsín.

The war instantly enhanced the image of Thatcher—whose government was the victim of numerous deadly leaks to the BBC by elements desperate to undermine her—and temporarily scrubbed away the Suez syndrome. Thatcher threw dirt on the coffin with her victory speech of July: "We have ceased to be a nation in retreat . . . we rejoice that Britain has rekindled that spirit which has fired her for generations past and which today has begun to burn as brightly as before."[25] In the Gulf War of 1990–91, Britain would appear once again as a player on the international scene, if in a somewhat slimmed-down version of her old imperial self. American support for Thatcher remained strong throughout the Falklands crisis—both Reagan and Defense Secretary Caspar Weinberger were knighted for their roles—but it came at a cost in Latin American relations, where the *yanqui* was again identified with colonialism. Nevertheless, it was a tradeoff the United States would make again without hesitation; for all its promise, South America had always remained only that, a promise. The Brits had proved their worth as allies time and again.

Other lessons were learned in the Falklands War. Despite the vulnerability of surface ships, which the campaign exposed with ruthless clarity, the world was reminded that aircraft carriers and the projection of air power were essential for a major power. While the British V-STOL (vertical/short takeoff and landing) Harrier jets were efficient, they were no substitute for American F-14 Tomcats and the kind of Tom Cruise *Top Gun* firepower that could be unleashed by a fleet battle carrier. These were important reminders in America for the (mostly Democratic) critics of Weinberger's buildup of the Navy, with its big carrier groups, who were calling for more spending on larger numbers of low-tech planes, ships, and ground vehicles—the same kind the Argentines had discovered were nearly worthless. But one fact went almost unnoticed in the speed of Britain's victory: the logistical difficulties of supplying thousands of men and ships over thousands of miles nearly proved insurmountable even in a short war against a mediocre foe. American planners quietly took notice, remembering this difficulty seven years later when the United States built up for Operation Desert Storm.

Most of all, victory in the Falklands bought Thatcher the time she needed for her domestic reforms to work. And work they did. As the economy recovered, Thatcher won convincing political gains. While perhaps Brits were unprepared to jump en masse to the Conservative Party, they abandoned Labour in droves. In 1983, Labour's share of the vote dropped to 27.6 percent and was reflected in a loss of 160 seats. Bolstered by the Falklands, and prepared by stockpiling coal for two years, Thatcher was ready to take on the most formidable of British unions, the National Union of Mineworkers (NUM). Led by Arthur Scargill, head of the Yorkshire chapter who was elected president of NUM in 1981, union leadership—without a democratic ballot, as required by its own rules—went to war over the National Coal Board's decision to close twenty of the worst money-losing pits. In truth, most of the coal mines were economic disasters, collectively losing 100 million pounds per year. Since 1946, coal had been publicly owned, supposedly to prevent exactly the types of strikes that the NUM now employed unceasingly.

Thatcher's government planned to examine the mines on an individual basis, closing the unprofitable ones and providing generous compensation for miners who were laid off. The government anticipated twenty thousand miners in total would lose their jobs, mostly through anticipated retirements, but the NUM would have none of their propositions. In March 1984, with the closing of the Yorkshire colliery, the NUM had its excuse to strike, and did so, using "flying pickets" (men not local to the pit to picket, made illegal in 1981). At the end of the first day, half of Britain's pits were shut down, and even those still at work faced heavy picketing. But Nottinghamshire's miners voted overwhelmingly to work, and the police, steeled for testy protests, kept their cool, giving the militant miners no propaganda images. British law held that if picketers were marched or bused to a location with the intent of causing a breach of the peace, the police were within their rights to intercept them and turn them back, which is what the local police did. Scargill, calling it the "social and industrial Battle of Britain," held on, confident that his large war chest (which contained huge sums—well over 150,000 pounds in cash—provided by Libya's Muammar Gaddafi, some of which Scargill apparently used to construct a new home) would outlast the government.[26] Violence escalated until, in May, five thousand picketers fought police at the Scunthorpe steelworks, hurling bricks and darts at the bobbies and injuring sixty-nine. In November, a taxi driver transporting nonstriking miners to work was killed.

Insistent that the judicial system be seen as quick and effective, Thatcher prodded local magistrates to try the 7,100 strikers who were charged with incitement, violence, breaking the flying picket laws, and other crimes. Almost half of them had their cases tried, with the majority convicted.[27] (All of Scargill's contempt fines were paid anonymously.)[28] "Thatcher's Laws," as they became known, were soon adopted as the standard by which to conduct industrial relations. A combination of the stockpiles, electric and nuclear energy supplies, and the working pits, combined with immediate and consistent application of Thatcher's Laws enabled the government to smash the strike. The union should have taken the deal to allow the peaceful closure of the nonperforming plants. By the time the inefficient pits were closed, 30,000 miners had been released, and the remainder of the workers had returned by February 1984.

Just a few months later, while Thatcher attended a conference at the Grand Hotel in Brighton, the Provisional Irish Republican Army detonated a bomb in the hotel. The bomb was not powerful enough to kill Thatcher, who was working on her speech in her conference suite when the bomb blew out part of her bathroom. Five people were killed, thirty others in-jured, but she escaped unharmed. There is some speculation that the bomb-ing was in retaliation for her position against the strikers as much as a statement by the IRA. Either way, the prime minister benefited from still more sympathy.

Symbolically the most important strike, in the coal pits, occupied the headlines (and Thatcher's attention), but she also managed to break a print strike and a dock strike during her early tenure. The print unions had at-tempted to storm Rupert Murdoch's massive state-of-the-art print facility, after Murdoch fired his striking print union workforce and moved all pro-duction to "Fortress Wapping," which Murdoch had designed with labor difficulties in mind. There, electrical, telecommunication, and tech unions operated the machinery.[29] Thatcher's government fully supported Mur-doch, whose plants did not lose a single day of production. It was the second major victory over unions by the Iron Lady. In each case, a deindustrializa-tion was evident. Jobs were shed, and even Thatcher was surprised at how much the British coal industry shrank when forced to compete in world markets. Not only had the unions been dealt a significant blow (Thatcher called the coal strike the most important since 1926), but the Labour Party, which never saw a strike it didn't like, suffered further embarrassment.

Freed from the manacles of unions, Britain began to witness real eco-nomic growth for the first time in decades, reaching 4 percent by 1988 after seven consecutive years of increase. British Airways achieved remarkable profitability in a tough international market. Individual shareholders now owned many companies, with the number of British stockholders growing almost fivefold in Thatcher's tenure. Direct taxation rates fell from 37 to 25 percent, and the top rates were lowered from the ridiculously self-defeating 94 percent to a still high, but reasonable, 40 percent. Home ownership soared.

However, the size of government did not shrink proportionately. Total expenditures barely fell as a share of GDP, due to the massive increase in unemployment benefits, necessitated by the long-postponed and government-cushioned restructuring of British industry. Work income as a share of household income dropped from about 80 percent in the mid-1970s to 73 percent by 1982, before Thatcher's programs really kicked in. When restructuring a state-dependent industry into a market-driven one, work initially falls as protected jobs are eliminated. As a result, it is claimed (though with little conviction) that Thatcher actually expanded the role of government. But Britain's government ownership roles shrank substantially with its disinvestment. And since welfare spending *also* fell, from 23.7 to 23.2 percent—in spite of the growth insuring process called "baseline budgeting," in which every year, departments *begin* their deliberations at last year's level then add new "budget needs"—the overall fall was quite remarkable. More of the (smaller) government budget was going to the things legitimately reserved for government to do. Thatcher profoundly changed the presumption that in England, the state was the "natural fount of legitimacy."[30] That is why, when asked what she had changed, she replied "Everything!"[31]

European Remora

More astounding than the British revival through privatization was that just across the Channel, the exact opposite was occurring. François Mitterrand was "conducting an even more ambitious . . . experiment: building Socialism in One Country."[32] His 1981 election marked the first time a socialist head of state was freely and directly elected in Europe, shattering the Communists, who withdrew from the cabinet in March 1983, and demoralizing the radical intellectual Left. Despite the phenomenal success of Thatcherism—or, given the French capacity for spite, perhaps because of it—France went the other way with a vengeance, nationalizing thirty-six private banks and eleven industrial corporations within the span of a few years. This failed to have the desired result; even after massive subsidies, investment levels had only risen 5 percent instead of the expected 50 percent. Mitterrand went far but even he knew better than to yank the nation out of international financial markets (keeping in mind that France had a total market capitalization below that of the poorest American states and only half that of IBM) because of the business panic he knew it would trigger.

More so than most developed nations, France underwent a change of character as it modernized. While Australia and Norway never ceased being Australian and Norwegian, France wrestled with a severe identity crisis during the 1970s and 1980s. As the countryside was depopulated and farm families saw their children move to the cities, terms such as *la France eternelle* began to have less meaning. In America, the absence of class identity, the presence of common law, and, above all, the chaotic and cleansing churn that was the free economy with deeds and property rights—constrained and made fair by the rule of law and Christian religious morality—meant that national identity closely correlated to the principles of the United States rather than to one's place in society. France's bureaucracy, on the other hand, achieved a level of permanence that saw a type of immortality usually associated only with vampires or deities, stretching across monarchies, republics, and empires, impervious to change or genuine control. This stood in contrast to the American views that however necessary some government may be, it was always intrusive, inefficient, and deriving its legitimacy only from voters, and above all, that standing, unelected bureaucracies were to be feared.

Modern France therefore suffered from a split personality. On the one hand, France found itself attracted (as it always had since the Revolution) to powerful, charismatic figures like de Gaulle. Whether it was Louis Philippe, Louis Napoleon, or Charles de Gaulle, individuals were elevated in the French mind to lofty positions, yet France had failed, since Napoleon Bonaparte's time, to create an administrative structure that could enable such leaders to effect change. Thus, despite what the Left heralded as a monumental breakthrough for socialism, Mitterrand was soon forced by reality and the French bureaucracy to reshape the French economy along more free-market lines to resemble that of Britain and the rest of the EC.

Across Europe in the 1970s and 1980s, social welfare networks found they could not live without market economies, and the more they sought to tax business for education, housing, health care, and the like, the more the Europeans realized that the only way to squeeze out still more was to permit companies to grow. Like any parasite, the remora fish of European socialism needed its host to stay alive, yet this development provoked not confidence or independence, but a phenomenon largely unseen in the West: self-loathing among rank-and-file liberals. The Communists and hard Left had always been hypocrites, clamoring for more equality while personally enjoying more privileges than ever. As liberalism moved into the European mainstream, however, the realization dawned on the majority that for them to dip into the pockets of their neighbors on an ever-expanding basis, some goose, somewhere, had to continue to lay golden eggs. Relying on "evil" corporations and "greedy" bankers as the ultimate source of funding for social programs produced a simmering resentment by the dependent classes. A sense of moral superiority and entitlement supplanted gratitude or an appreciation for what was supplied.

Practically, this meant that no European state could eschew economic growth for long, no matter how much socialist rhetoric filled the air. It must be kept in mind that to some degree, all the growth notched up by the Euros during the 1950s, '60s, '70s, and '80s was a tad phony. Obviously, Europe had nowhere to go but up after the devastation of the war, and indisputably, most of the Continent had put in place policies that would encourage market capitalism to thrive one way or another. It was all accomplished, however, under the protective umbrella of American troops, planes, and warships—and above all, the U.S. nuclear force. No matter what France, Germany, Britain, the Benelux countries, Italy, and the Scandinavians spent on defense (and some of their units and weapons were quite good), it was a pittance of what was required to deter Soviet expansionism. Precisely because of the presence of U.S. airbases and troops in Germany, Italy, Britain, and elsewhere, France could dedicate resources to education; Germany, to roads; Italy and Denmark, to harbors; and so on. Consequently, when historians sing the praises of the "economic miracle" of France and Germany, it was a miracle that demanded being under the safety and in the context of U.S. missiles. Likewise, when attempting to elevate the achievements of Eastern Europe relative to the West by pointing to Marshall Plan aid, historians miss the heavy direct subsidies and infrastructure support (often to enhance the Red Army's travel) provided by the USSR. In short, drawing economic equivalences during a period when security concerns completely overshadowed all else but were supplied off the books by another state becomes a futile exercise.

National, historical, and ethnic factors also shaped the disparities in privatization across Europe. In Germany, autos, chemical, electronics, and other industrial sectors were already privatized, while in England, they remained in public hands until Thatcher. Italy, which had seen wages rise by 15 percent from 1969 to 1973—twice the rate of the previous six years—and the workweek *fall* 2 percent, overcame many political obstacles to sport a rapidly growing private sector. When Alfa Romeo and other major public holding companies transformed into more traditional companies with stock ownership, Italian corporations gained efficiency and profitability. Of course, privatization in Europe was not universal. The Iberian countries seemed to regress in the 1970s; their unique answer to the deepening demands of the welfare state was to insinuate themselves into as many companies as possible. Spain's INI, or Instituto Nacional de Industria, had influential holdings in nearly 750 companies, while Portugal simply prohibited private banking, insurance, transport, electricity, and other industries. This continued until Portugal's Mário Soares (prime minister from 1976 to 1978 and 1983 to 1985) finally began to relinquish some control to the private sector in the mid-1980s. The absence of entrepreneurial spirit was so pronounced on the Iberian peninsula that as late as 1996 there was no word in either Spanish or Portuguese for "entrepreneurship."

The Union Label

Unwilling to confront the failures of government control, many Europeans took refuge in the magic bullet of integration. What had begun in the 1950s as a dual strategy of "civilizing" Germany and allowing goods and services free transit across national borders had morphed into a means to conceal (or deny) the inadequacies of national governments. The answer? Relinquish power to still larger quasi-constitutional, international bodies. By the 1970s, integration had weakened national monopolies as European Economic Community (EEC) bureaucrats in Brussels started to transcend national capitals as the source of power and largesse.[33] Not all on the Continent were enamored of the move toward integration, even those among the intellectuals known as the "institutional evolutionists." Critics included British economist Andrew Shonfield and Anglo-German sociologist Ralf Dahrendorf, along with Dutch Jacques Pelkmans, who emphasized "negative integration" to replace the old government-driven integration.[34] Pelkmans, in particular, called for less intervention.

Agriculture proved one of the most difficult sectors to manage. Four guiding principles of agricultural agreements were: 1) there were to be no barriers to inter-EEC trade; 2) there was to be a common support system of farm prices; 3) tariffs were to be raised through variable import levies; and 4) common financial responsibility was to be administered by a Community budget. Prices would be pegged to high cost producers.[35] Burdens and benefits differed wildly. European consumers paid "huge premiums" as Euro food prices (with the year 1967 equaling a baseline of 100) ranged from 131 for poultry to 483 for sugar, while farm population in participating countries fell by two thirds between 1960 and 1970. European Community agriculture budgets exploded fourfold from 1968 to 1977, then fivefold from 1977 to 1998.[36] Protection levels rose, even beyond that normally invoked by individual countries, imposing a tax of 5.6 percent on the poorest households to 2.9 percent on the rich. The productivity burden of subsidized exports amounted to about 25 percent.[37]

Despite its obvious weaknesses and threats to national sovereignty, a single European government proved difficult to resist. Its siren call reached the white cliffs of Dover, where Mrs. Thatcher's most outstanding failure was her inability to win the debate over Britain's role in the European Union (officially formed in 1993 with the Maastricht Treaty). Even though Brussels approved Britain's membership in 1972, England steadily resisted Eurofication, especially under Thatcher. She would not be alone in trying to resist full integration. Greenland, which achieved self-rule in 1979, voted in a referendum to leave the EEC, the only member to do so. Norway also stayed on the outside, in 1972 opting for limited free-trade concessions and confirming the decision in a referendum twenty years later. Most nations, however, desperately wanted in. Portugal and Spain waited nine years to join, and between 1973 and 1986, Ireland, Denmark, and Norway also entered. Greece was added; Austria and Sweden applied. Who got in, and when, largely depended on whose ox was gored by inclusion (France resisted the Iberian admission due to competition from Spanish and Portuguese growers of olives and other agricultural products). Greece benefited the most from membership precisely because Greece was poor, and by 1990 was home to half of the EU's poorest regions.[38]

The process of lifting trade barriers and redistributing money to backward or "disadvantaged" regions proved a vastly easier task than developing an integrated *polis*. By and large, a system of national vetoes in the European Council protected any member from proposals that would be disastrous to a particular nation. Instead of countries, now, there were regions within countries that received EEC subsidies and aid through the European Regional Development Fund (ERDF), wherein Italy's Mezzogiorno, Britain's Wales, Ulster, and Scotland, much of Greece, and large parts of Spain were now categorized as poor. Historian Tony Judt expressed it as a "confluence of regionalist politics *within* the separate member states and growing economic disparities *between* the states themselves."[39]

If the objective was a great leveling, it failed dismally. Using 1982 as an income level of 100, Denmark was at 126, but Greece only at 44: seven years later, Denmark was still at the top, and while Portugal had replaced Greece, the gap was still nearly the same.[40] That contrasted with the United States, where the gaps between wealthier and poorer states were much smaller, and where movement from one class to the next could be instantaneous. Not only did regional redistribution fail, it consumed more than one third of all EU expenditure by the year 2000. The result was a self-absorbed, know-it-all mentality in the governing elites, a trait Mrs. Thatcher called "the hyperactive and incestuous world of Westminster."

Armies of bureaucrats marched into Europe's poorest zones to inflict their assistance on the needy, sparking resentment and cynicism from the recipients. Adding to the confusion and graft was the constant redesignation of areas; for example, Italy's South Tyrol, classified by the EU in 1975 as "mountainous," was reclassified in 1988 as "rural," leading to multiple layers of grants, subsidies, vocational training, and environmental funds.

From 1993 to 1999, the Alto Adige/South Tyrol region of Italy therefore received the equivalent of 96 million euros (at 2005 price levels), then from 2000 to 2006 hauled in an additional 57 million euros for 83,000 residents—a population equivalent to Yuma, Arizona, or an astounding 1,844 euros per person.[41] The process of dealing money out in such amounts, and with such temptations of godlike power, not only led to exaggeration and even invention of local needs, but invited "the sorts of venal, local abuses that passed unnoticed by the Community's managers in Brussels. . . ."[42]

Some benefits of integration doubtless occurred, especially the abolition of tariff barriers between nations and the Shengen Agreement of 1985 that eliminated internal passport controls. Ultimately, however, Europe's problem lay not in the absence of better integration, but in its crushing, sclerotic bureaucracies and top-heavy welfare-oriented national governments, which the EU intended to enhance and embellish.

State employment alone constituted a debilitating weakness of the Euro economies: entrepreneurship struggled when states such as Austria employed 33 percent of the workforce in government. The Portuguese constitution prohibited private banking, transport, telecommunications or postal services, electricity production, or gasoline refining. Nonetheless, free-market fever spread into Europe in the 1980s, but with unexpected results. As a society, Italy's demand for social services combined with economic growth actually *increased* the role of the state. Thatcher's Britain saw the national government take over many of the functions of metropolitan authorities, and centralized education policy. Where control over individual corporations or sectors of the economy shrank, the scope of state authority grew, as did the share of those employed by the government: by 2 percent in Germany and Italy in the 1980s, and by more than 7 percent in Denmark.[43]

Keynesianism was proving inadequate to generate the constant growth that capitalism embodied. Across Europe after 1970, growth slowed from almost 5 percent to just over 1 percent by the mid-1980s.[44] As European industries mastered operating in the EEC and entered the world business arena, competitors took them seriously—for the first time in perhaps thirty years—and met them head on. Ministers grew obsessed with warding off unemployment and inequality, which were the handmaidens of radical economic expansion. And in each case where attempts were made to roll back the state, specific political parties had to be weakened. Labour, in Britain, was nearly broken by Thatcher's rejuvenation of capitalism, but in America the government-embedded Democratic Party was barely scratched by Reaganism. Reagan's need to prioritize and put the defeat of the Soviets at the top of the list meant that he had to quietly abandon some of his campaign promises, including the elimination of entire cabinet-level departments, such as the Department of Energy and the Department of Education. As a result, under Reagan's watch—and with his acquiescence, though not active participation—deficits soared as Democratic legislators traded the Gipper national security for unending layers of pork. In both Europe and America, the free market was winning the war of ideas, but incrementally losing ground in the trenches.

It seemed a bitter and nearly suicidal tradeoff that in order to stop Soviet domination once and for all, Western nations entered into a corrupt bargain of bread and circuses to placate the citizens long enough to accomplish the job. Whether or not the social spending of democratic states could ever be rolled back was itself problematic. Contrary to the nostrums of a golden age under Thomas Jefferson or Andrew Jackson when governments were small and largesse unseen, and excepting a handful of sharp economic downturns, *no administration* in American history had contained government or even kept per capita spending flat.[45]

Reagan, for all his rhetoric, knew from his tenure as governor of California that halting the expansion of government in peacetime constituted a single-mindedness in office that simply was not possible when confronted by the Soviet giant. Federal deficits and big government, in the long run, wouldn't matter much if the USSR succeeded in intimidating Europe or severing the nuclear link. It is not hyperbole to say that Ronald Reagan was the single most important politician of the postwar world, or that he was the last, perhaps, to understand the four pillars of exceptionalism. His 1983 speech on national defense was quite likely the most important single speech of his lifetime, surpassing even his "Time for Choosing" address in 1964. To get to that point, the lifeguard and movie actor walked an unlikely path to glory.

The Gipper's Greatness

By now, Reagan's story is oft told. Born on February 6, 1911, in Tampico, Illinois, the child slated to be called "Donald" ended up Ronald because his aunt gave birth to his cousin, Donald, first. His parents, Jack and Nelle Reagan, were poor, although their son admitted he "didn't know what that was" growing up.[46] Jack Reagan, a natural salesman, was a learned drunk, whose son grew to dread "those days when he'd take the first drink."[47] Nevertheless, he instilled in his son the values of individualism, hard work, and the value of life, which soon became apparent in the boy's success as a life-guard on the Rock River near Dixon, Illinois. A tall, lanky kid, Ronald (then known as "Dutch") was an expert swimmer and over the course of seven summers, he saved an average of eleven people from drowning each year: "One of the proudest statistics of my life is 77," he said decades later.[48]

Lifesaving instilled in Reagan a confidence that strengthened him over the years. In 1932 he graduated from Eureka College, having majored in economics. He was briefly unemployed before the University of Iowa hired him to broadcast football games and he eventually wound up in California on an assignment covering the Chicago Cubs for a Des Moines radio station. In that job, Reagan received a wire feed from Chicago that relayed only the most basic play results ("strike," "ball," "single"), leaving Reagan to recreate the play-by-play from his vivid imagination. Through a friend from Iowa, Reagan got an audition with an agent, followed by a screen test with Warner Brothers and a job offer. In the span of only a few weeks in 1937, Dutch Reagan, baseball announcer, became Ronald Reagan, actor.

Naturally good-natured and cheerful, Reagan succeeded to no small degree because he seemed to threaten no one. Extras and set people liked working with him and encouraged him. Acting came with one disconcerting element for Reagan, and that was membership in a union, the Screen Actors Guild (SAG). During World War II, Reagan served as a second lieutenant in the U.S. Army, where he was made a liaison officer in the Army Air Force's intelligence unit making training films. He prided himself on developing new methods of briefing pilots for bombing missions. Using special effects techniques he'd learned in Hollywood, his unit created a replica of Tokyo to simulate the path of bombing runs.

Reagan ended the war as a captain, then returned to moviemaking. Already a star for his roles as George Gipp in *Knute Rockne—All American* (from which he got his nickname, "The Gipper") and as an amputee in *Kings Row*, Dutch soon discovered that communism was scarcely different from the fascism he had opposed. He had "dismissed" people who had denounced the Communists as "foolish and paranoid," but now he gave new thought to the challenge communism posed to liberty.[49] Reagan discovered that the SAG was becoming thoroughly infiltrated by a front organization called the Conference of Studio Unions. In 1946, Reagan and actor William Holden crashed an organizational meeting of the communist organizers. Reagan took the floor, and held it, defending free speech but attacking communism amid boos, curses, and other interruptions. The following year, he appeared before the House Un-American Activities Committee

(HUAC) to testify about Communist infiltration, where he defended his craft and argued, "As a citizen, I would hesitate, or not like, to see any political party outlawed on the basis of its political ideology."[50] Reagan maintained the independence and integrity of free speech in the process of defeating the Communists. No less than Warner Brothers studio chief Jack Warner said Reagan "turned out to be a tower of strength, not only for the actors but for the whole industry."[51] He had broken the back of Hollywood communism, in the process riding to the rescue of a woman wrongfully investigated for Communist ties, Nancy Davis, who soon became his wife. They first met in 1949 when she found herself on the Hollywood blacklist and sought Reagan's help. Dutch found she had been confused with another actress of the same name and cleared her. They married in 1952.

Reagan's acting career, meanwhile, encountered rough water. He was offered many bad parts, but decided to hold out for higher-caliber scripts, and went for more than a year without making a movie. At one point, he resorted to performing a Las Vegas standup act. He and Nancy rejected Broadway, as they didn't want to move to New York. Finally, only television remained—in those days, a serious step down for a movie actor. But in 1954, Reagan's step down turned out to be his ticket to the stratosphere: a job with General Electric, hosting a series in which he both introduced and occasionally appeared in weekly episodes. The weekly dramatic program required as part of his contract that Reagan make public appearances at GE's 139 plants around the country. In those talks, he honed his anti-Communist message, learned to speak succinctly and from simple note cards marked with his own shorthand, and rubbed elbows with the common people, everyday Americans outside of the Hollywood bubble.

Dutch walked assembly lines, spoke with small groups, told jokes and stories, and above all, he listened. What he heard, mostly, was that government interference was choking American productivity. "No matter where I was," he recalled in his biography, "I'd find people . . . waiting to talk to me . . . and they'd all say, 'Hey, if you think things are bad in your business, let me tell you what's happening in my business. . . .'"[52] The stories were always the same: bureaucracies, taxes, and above all, what Reagan called a "permanent government never envisioned by the framers of the Constitution" that was increasingly oppressive. A New Deal, FDR Democrat, Reagan steadily moved away from his party—although his famous line was that he didn't leave the Democratic Party, it left him. In fact, the changes afoot were logical, if not inevitable, extensions of the welfare, high-tax, intrusive programs Reagan had once supported. Reagan actually started drifting from the Democratic ideology in 1950, when he campaigned for Eisenhower, although it wasn't until after the 1960 election that he formally changed his party affiliation.[53]

Critics would later complain that Reagan created a mythological America, a small-town America that never existed. No matter: he refused to demonize Franklin Roosevelt, who in his youth had appeared such a hero, despite the evidence of history. It was vintage Gipper, refusing to think ill of someone and giving everyone the benefit of the doubt. Reagan ignored Roosevelt's hostility toward business and the industrialists who created wealth; he turned a blind eye toward FDR's attempts to completely confiscate all income at higher levels; and he never confronted the reality that the New Deal maintained a heavy politically active component, created as an always campaigning election machine that made generations of voters beholden to the federal government. Dutch never would have approved of any of those things, yet just as he never said a bad word about his ex-wife Jane Wyman, neither would he criticize his former political leader. Instead, he set his face toward the sun and never looked back. Reagan never held a grudge. His diaries reveal only a single instance of reaction to back-stabbing Republicans in the early 1980s when he refused to campaign for Senators Arlen Specter of Pennsylvania and Charles "Mac" Mathias of Maryland after they helped kill the nomination of William Bradford Reynolds to the Justice Department.[54]

Barry Goldwater's political advisers asked Reagan in 1964 if he would give a speech on the senator's behalf. Reagan had routinely delivered a similar talk before smaller audiences and agreed to go on national television for Goldwater if money could be raised. In a now famous speech, "A Time for Choosing," Reagan pointed out that America stood at a crossroads, engaged in a struggle to reclaim liberty. Reagan said that "those who would trade our freedom for security have embarked on [a] downward course. . . . You and I have a rendezvous with destiny. We will preserve for our children this, the last best hope of man on earth, or we will sentence them to take the last step into a thousand years of darkness."[55] Goldwater was crushed in the election, but a political star was born. Reagan was soon persuaded to run for governor of California. He gained critical administrative experience running the largest state-level economy in the nation, and saw firsthand the crucial effect that lowering taxes had on economic growth. California politics also taught Reagan the necessity of political compromise and of prioritizing issues.

But a willingness to engage in political compromises never outweighed his top priority: defeating the Communist threat. When Reagan stepped down from the governorship in 1975 to make a presidential run, he began a series of radio addresses that touched on a wide range of subjects, all written by him personally, refuting the notion that the Gipper was a dim bulb or intellectual lightweight.[56] Explaining the dangers posed by a "World Court" in 1977, he noted that "American soldiers could be tried by this international tribunal for killing or wounding the mil[itary] forces of a warring enemy" or for other undefined human rights violations (precisely the kinds of charges Secretary of Defense Donald Rumsfeld had to entertain in European courts after Operation Iraqi Freedom).[57] In sum, Reagan's vision and understanding of world affairs was crystal clear in the early 1970s.

Reagan's self-assured and well-defined positions put him in sharp relief to Jimmy Carter, whose national security policies seemed to bounce from one blunder to the next. Carter, in Reagan's eyes, was "a disaster in the arena of national security."[58] As he told future national security advisor Richard Allen in 1977, "Dick, my idea of American policy toward the Soviet Union is simple, and some would say simplistic. It is this: We win and they lose."[59]

But Reagan also wanted, as he said in his autobiography, "to bring about a spiritual revival in America."[60] This was partly in response to Carter's "malaise" assessment of the state of the American character, but it was also because Reagan thought that defeating the Soviets demanded more than bombs and Buicks. Reagan himself was baptized in the Disciples of Christ denomination, but also attended Presbyterian churches, and most label him a nondenominational Protestant. Because he didn't carry a Bible publicly or attend church services regularly (which he attributed to the inconvenience the security precautions caused all the other worshipers), Reagan has been typically viewed as shallow in areas of faith, just as he was painted as intellectually vacant. But new work done on Reagan's spiritual side reveals a deeply religious Christian whose first thought in times of personal and national crisis was to seek God in prayer.[61]

Reagan resurrected Carter's "misery index" and even asked the same question of voters that Carter had asked four years earlier when he defeated Ford: "Are you better off now than you were four years ago?" For his part, Carter wrote in his diary, "Reagan and I have perhaps the sharpest divisions between us of any two presidential candidates in my lifetime."[62] Reagan was a bona fide leader, whose optimism caused people to follow him; Carter blamed others for their unwillingness to sign on to his pessimism.

A key moment occurred during the October 28, 1980, debate between Carter and Reagan that confirmed in the minds of Americans that Reagan was neither a radical nor senile. When Carter claimed Reagan had once opposed Medicare benefits for recipients of Social Security—a false statement—Reagan good-naturedly shook his head and blurted out, "There you go again. . . ." The debate audience laughed at Carter, who was caught on screen with a hand-in-the-cookie-jar expression, and the night belonged to Reagan. On election eve, with polls still open for two more hours in California, Carter called Reagan to concede.

Winning by more than eight million votes, the Gipper's election marked a sea change in American politics. No Democratic presidential candidate in the next twenty-four years would garner over 50 percent of the popular vote, and excluding Carter's own razor-thin 50.01 percent in 1976, no Democrat won more than half the popular vote between 1964 and 2008. Reagan won, as had Nixon, the "solid South" and the far West, forging a new Republican voting bloc that covered most of the nation except parts of the Northeast.[63, 64]

Aside from Nixon, no president since Hoover had received such consistently hostile press among the main elite media organs (though not, necessarily, in middle America's newspapers) as had Reagan. But the Gipper had too much class and too much political savvy to attack the media publicly, as Nixon had, although his presidential diaries revealed the depth of his antagonism to the press and television reporters. The contention began during the campaign, with reports about Reagan's age and energy. But in *An American Life*, Reagan noted the grueling campaign schedule "usually had members of the traveling press corps complaining of fatigue before anyone else."[65] Many nights, Reagan recalled, "I'd walk down the darkened aisle of the campaign plane after a day on the stump, and everybody would be asleep but me."[66] His attitude soured more the longer he stayed in office: "The d--n media has propagandized our people against our defense plans more than the Russians have" (1983); "Dropped in for a minute on the TV anchor men & women who were being briefed on tonite's St. of the Union [sic] address. I cannot conjure up 1 iota of respect for just about all of them" (1984).[67]

Repeatedly, the press took whatever side was aligned against Reagan. During the bombing of Libya in 1986, the press "virtually announced to [Muammar] Qaddafi that the United States was planning to attack him." The administration "tried to talk them out of revealing these state secrets," which in Reagan's view was as "crucial as it was during World War II," but "they would have none of it. Every time they got a leak, they ran with it, even though it meant risking [American] lives."[68]

Armed with his natural good humor, commonsense anecdotes, and unpretentious language, Reagan went over the heads of the media in an age when most presidential speeches were still carried in full by all networks. He connected with the mass public the way no president, not even JFK, ever had. His was an ability that angered and befuddled critics. Political strategist Stuart Spencer put it slightly differently: "Reagan's solutions to problems were always the same as the guy in the bar."[69] "Rawhide," his Secret Service code name, also reflected that common, rugged quality so many Americans latched on to: the constant public images of the Gipper clearing brush, canoeing, riding, sawing, repairing fences—these were not photo ops, but rather real-life depictions of the genuine Reagan.

Another part of Reagan's public image was his wife, Nancy. Nancy was both a constant companion yet a part of the shadows, and her presence helped Reagan significantly, although not in the same manner as Hillary Clinton's did her husband. Instead of browbeating subordinates and mapping policies, Nancy concerned herself with maximizing her Ronnie's effectiveness, aggressively protecting his time and access outside of his immediate advisers. She nevertheless allied with a group of pragmatists inside the White House, for whom Reagan was merely a marvelous front man, the face of the policies that others developed. For them—mostly Secretary of State George Shultz, Defense Secretary Caspar Weinberger, and Treasury Secretary Donald Regan—Reagan was the Great Communicator who could take the ideas of the experts and sell them to Congress and the public. It was odd, therefore, that Nancy, whose love for her Ronnie was never in question, should have had so little confidence in his real talent.[70] In the end, Reagan confounded this group and trusted his own instincts and beliefs.

"Build Up the Economy . . . Tear Down the Soviet Union"

During the campaign, Reagan addressed many issues, but privately, he had a much more tightly focused agenda. An Alabama businessman named Bob Callahan, Sr., met with Reagan aides at a fund-raiser in 1980, and asked what Reagan planned to do when he got into office. He was told by a campaign staffer, "Ronald Reagan wants to do three things: One, build up the economy. Two, build up defense. Three, he's going to bring down the Soviet Union."[71] Yet the entire moment in history might have ended on March 20, 1981, when John Hinckley put a bullet only twenty-five millimeters from the seventy-year-old president's heart. For Reagan, who lost half his blood yet recovered quickly before developing a mysterious infection that nearly killed him, the incident was nothing less than a word from the Lord Himself. Letters poured in reminding Reagan of his destiny. One read, "We need you to save the Country—remember all the lifes [sic] you saved in Lowell Park."[72] Reagan told Terence Cardinal Cooke of the Archdiocese of New York, "I have decided that whatever time I have left is for Him."[73]

Whether divine intervention or human momentum infused the new administration, it got its legs as Reagan recovered. A shift in the cold war could be seen the previous month when Reagan's staff formed an inter-agency review group on possible responses to the Soviet Union and its ob-jectives. It was significant both for the words that no longer were employed—"containment," "détente," "mutual assured destruction"—as well as the new concepts that were introduced: "rolling back Soviet power," "promoting democracy," and most of all, treating the cold war as though it were a temporary condition to be alleviated at the soonest possible moment. Reagan's near-death experience clarified for him that the real evil in the world was not the deranged Hinckleys but the institutional evil of the So-viet Union, which corrupted everything it touched.[74]

Although it had taken several months to get the new security structure organized, a study group was formed to provide the president numerous options. Where previous career bureaucrats had confidently assembled a consensus view of the world, then presented it to the president, Reagan in-sisted on genuine options, each laid out with pro and con arguments. After two months of examining the options, the group drafted the National Se-curity Decision Directive 32 (NSDD-32), a document that encapsulated a radical new strategy for winning the cold war. It proposed a full-court press on the USSR across political, diplomatic, military, economic, and informa-tion sectors. Reagan signed NSDD-32 in May and in a June 8, 1982, speech to the British Parliament in Westminster, shared his views on future en-gagement with the Soviets with the public. He became one of the first American presidents to openly note the "decay of the Soviet experiment" and pointed out that "one of the simple but overwhelming facts of our time is . . . Of all the millions of refugees . . . in the modern world, their flight is always from, not toward, the Communist world."[75]

That Reagan would be underestimated intellectually, even by many close to him, was often due to his superior public communication skills. It was a sad irony many beauty queens found themselves in: "She can't be smart. She's too pretty." But more than any American leader since Lincoln or Teddy Roosevelt, Ronald Reagan was the master of the written as well as spoken word. The evidence was abundant at the time, and yet some of his immediate staff looked right past it. Richard Pipes, a noted Harvard Sovietologist who worked closely with Reagan, marveled at the Gipper's ability to distill information to "what matters and what does not, what is right and what is wrong for his country."[76] That talent, Pipes noted, was "like perfect pitch, one is born with it."[77] One NSC staff member, John Poindexter, recalled Reagan would be presented with a stack of Soviet economic data, noting he just "loved seeing the raw intelligence," and Chief of Staff Don Regan agreed, saying, "He just loved reading that stuff. He would take that big stack and read them one by one over the weekend."[78] National Security Advisor William Clark recalled that the "decision directives" didn't come from "a workshop situation where elves sat around pounding out shoes for the king." Rather, Reagan "was very much a part of it. Not just signing, but also progression, briefing, discussion, and guidance."[79] When it came to the critical NSDD-32, which reshaped American cold war strategy, Reagan historian Paul Kengor noted, "When it was done the study and the decision were the President's."[80]

By the time NSDD-32 was ready, a national security planning group, essentially charged with ending the cold war, met regularly to dream up new methods of putting pressure on the Soviets. Whereas NSDD-32 provided the "vision statement" for achieving the task, NSDD-75 constituted the "blueprint for the endgame," according to former secretary of the Air Force Thomas Reed.[81] The key was that for the first time a president had actually made it a priority to defeat the Soviets. To alert the Soviets that he was onto their game, he announced his stance with a typically Reaganesque speech in Orlando in March 1983 before the National Association of Evangelicals, which stunned many in the audience and shocked the Kremlin. Referring to the USSR as an "evil empire," Reagan chided the more liberal clergy present for their acceptance of moral equivalence between the United States and the Soviet Union when none existed. The phrase touched off a frenzy of media criticism, outraged sputterings from Moscow, and had not won Nancy's endorsement, either. Too belligerent, she thought, a view seconded by Reagan's political adviser Stuart Spencer, who thought the language was too tough. Reagan "waved them both off. 'It *is* an evil empire. . . . It's time to close it down.'"[82]

Any military buildup necessary to force Soviet defeat, however, first demanded a fundamentally sound economic base. As early as 1968, Reagan had tied together economic soundness and national defense, saying, "The

peace and security of the world depends on the fiscal and economic stability and the defense potential of the United States."[83] Rebuilding the nation's sluggish economy required tax cuts to stimulate growth and investment and tightening the money supply to rein in inflation. The hulking, cigar-smoking Paul Volcker, brought in by Carter as the new chairman of the Federal Reserve Board, had undertaken the necessary but painful task of tightening the money supply. Interest rates had to come down for home buyers and consumers. When he assumed office, Reagan found a group of up to thirty "Blue Dog" Democrats, mostly from the South, who likewise wanted to invigorate the economy.

An early test of Reagan's will came in a June 1981 vote on his tax cuts, with the final package consisting of a three-year, 25 percent tax cut, struc-tured with a 5 percent cut in 1981, and 10 percent in each of the next two years. Squeezing out the inflation while waiting for the staggered tax cuts to kick in meant the administration would have to ride out a recession. Economist Arthur Laffer, whose supply side economics Reagan had inter-nalized (and who invented the Laffer curve, showing that tax cuts could increase government revenue), captured the dynamic of the process with the rhetorical question, "If you knew a refrigerator was going on sale tomorrow, would you buy one today?" Real investment growth would not occur until 1983.

Islamic Fanaticism, Round One

While the United States and the West were preoccupied with the Soviets, a new threat arose, that of Islamic extremism. The threat was further obscured by the fact that most Western leaders, including Reagan until the mid-1980s, saw violence by Islamic states as a subcomponent of the cold war. Even when leaders accepted that violent groups such as Hezbollah had nothing in common with the Soviets except their AK-47 rifles, the strategy for dealing with them was still tied to how support or opposition of particular Islamic states fit into the conflict with the Russians.

In June 1981, the Israelis had bombed Iraq's Osiris nuclear power plant on the grounds that it was engaged in producing materials for a nuclear weapon. Israel did not go through the United Nations, nor did the Israelis ask American permission to conduct the bombings—they staged the attack to preemptively defend themselves. Reagan understood their move. Congress threatened to investigate, concerned that Israel used American-made planes for "offensive purposes," but Reagan planned to grant a waiver if Congress acted. "I believe [the Iraqis] were preparing to build an atom bomb," he wrote. "Saddam Hussein is a 'no good nut' and I think he was trying to build nuclear weapons."[84] Congress moved on to other issues.

Of more immediate concern was Muammar Gaddafi, Libya's strongman, who had seen the Iranians run roughshod over the helpless Carter. Gaddafi had already tested Reagan's resolve in 1981 over his claims to waters in the Gulf of Sidra, a line sixty-two nautical miles out—dubbed the "Line of Death" by Gaddafi—as opposed to the generally accepted twelve nautical miles given each country. When American F-14 Tomcats flew across Gaddafi's line, Soviet-made Libyan jets attacked and the Tomcats shot them down. For the next four years, Libya was linked to the activities of numerous terror groups, culminating in the December 1985 Abu Nidal Rome and Vienna airport attacks, where Muslim gunmen killed 18 and wounded nearly 140.

A Libyan-U.S. confrontation was inevitable, and it came in 1986. An American carrier task force sailed across the "Line of Death," whereupon Gaddafi ordered a response. Before any attacks on American ships could occur, the United States destroyed Libyan radar systems and attack vessels on March 24. Gaddafi responded with a terror attack on April 5, exploding a bomb at a West Berlin disco that was frequented by American servicemen.

Two Americans were killed. American intelligence found credible evidence that Libyan agents operating out of East Germany were involved.

Gaddafi had miscalculated when it came to Reagan, and suddenly was on the receiving end of strong military action. Despite being denied over-flight rights by France and Spain (which required flying an additional 1,300 miles each way), the United States mounted a bombing raid using F-111 fighter-bombers based in England and aircraft from warships in the Gulf of Sidra. Most of the targets were military, but one landed near one of Gaddafi's residences, killing a family member and injuring two of his sons.

Gaddafi got the message, and never again challenged the United States directly, although his agents stepped up their activities, supporting Abu Nidal's hijacking of a Pan Am flight in September, followed by the horrific bombing of Pan Am 103 in 1988. (After denying its involvement for more than a decade, Libya finally accepted responsibility in 2002 and offered $2.7 billion in compensation to the families of the victims.)

Libya was only one bubble in the Middle Eastern cauldron. Two years before the final confrontation with Gaddafi, Reagan watched Lebanon deteriorate into chaos as Christians and different Muslim groups rent apart the long-standing nonaggression agreements that had made the country a model of civilization in the Middle East. After repeated attacks on Israel, in 1982 the Israelis had invaded the ravaged nation, eliminating PLO camps and Syrian bases. Following a May 1983 accord between Israel and Lebanon, an international peacekeeping force was sent in, with a large contingent of U.S. Marines, French, and Italians. In October, for the first time, Islamic Jihad used a new weapon—trucks driven by suicide bombers, laden with explosives (as opposed to bombs left in a parked truck). They attacked two barracks in Beirut, one housing the Marines and another the French. Two hundred forty-one Americans and fifty-eight French were killed, and despite pledges by both Reagan and French president François Mitterrand to stay, both nations soon pulled out after admitting the peacekeeping role was impossible.

The Beirut bombing happened just as the United States launched an invasion of the tiny Caribbean island of Grenada, where a small U.S. medical school was located, on October 25, 1983. Grenada's new government, under Bernard Coard, had taken power from Maurice Bishop and murdered him. Bishop had already aligned himself with Cuba and with funding from Cuba and the USSR had begun constructing a large airfield—which could not service commercial passenger jets, despite Bishop's claims. It looked, in other words, suspiciously like the base of a new Cuban proxy.

The coup, the member nations' requests, and the fate of American medical students at St. George's University combined with a request from the Organization of East Caribbean States to provide enough cover so the Reagan administration could act. After a three-day operation, American forces secured the island and discovered seven hundred Cubans and sixty Soviet or East Bloc advisers. U.S. troops evicted them with minimal bloodshed. Although it was a very small success, America's actions sent a signal to the Kremlin that there was a new sheriff in town.

But that success entailed a cost. Defeating the Soviet Union meant that Reagan left the rising issue of Islamic jihadism for his heirs. Until the Soviets were dealt with, Reagan could not address Muslim fundamentalism because his focus remained on the cold war. Thus to Reagan, Saddam was a "no good nut," Gaddafi a pompous, reckless dictator, and the PLO a dangerous organization which could, nevertheless, be dealt with. He professed his belief in the widespread existence of "moderate Muslims," even in such places as Saudi Arabia. In 1991, he wrote in *An American Life*,

> I don't think you can overstate the importance that the rise of Islamic fundamentalism will have to the rest of the world in the century ahead—especially if, as seems possible, its most fanatical elements get their hands on nuclear and chemical weapons and the means to deliver them against their enemies.[85]

While he was sensitive to "the rapid spread in Iran and elsewhere of the most fanatical varieties of Islamic fundamentalism," it was not clear even then that Reagan fully appreciated the inroads such radicalism had made into even the "moderate" Islamic societies. When it came to Lebanon, the solution, in his eyes, depended on negotiating with the right groups, no matter how vitriolic their rhetoric. In short, Reagan's view of Islamic fundamentalism did not differ much from Jimmy Carter's—that the jihadists were *rational*. A deeply spiritual man like Reagan should have known better; human motivations, when it comes to issues of faith, are deeply *irrational*, a trait that can make them all the more dangerous when misused.

Islamic fascism metastasized under Reagan as it had under Nixon and Carter, and would explode under George H. W. Bush and Clinton. Indeed, Reagan unwittingly fed it, because the mujahideen in Afghanistan were the only ones in the entire world actually fighting the Soviets. If Reagan, and those who came before him, can be excused for seeing the Islamic threat as less dangerous than Soviet imperialism, those who came after—particularly

Bush and Clinton and their state departments—cannot. The claxons had already sounded, and even Bush's eviction of Iraq from Kuwait in 1991 displayed an insufficient understanding of the webs of terror networks that now sought to ensnare the free world, if not the entire world. Yet leaders in Paris, Berlin, Rome, London, Washington, and even Moscow still tended to view Islamic militancy as primarily a component of the cold war, without recognizing that a quite different demon had arisen.

All of that was quite obscured in the 1980s. Certainly no one in Europe or the United States thought Iran or a bunch of renegade terrorists operating under such then-comical names as Abu Nidal or Islamic Jihad constituted a challenge to the West even remotely comparable to the USSR and its allies.

Last Days of the Evil Empire

Dealing with the Soviets proved tricky for Reagan at first, in part because Red leaders kept dying in office. This changed in 1985, when Mikhail Gorbachev assumed the position of general secretary of the Communist Party, reflecting the triumph of a group of pragmatists who knew the Soviet economy was floundering. It is not a stretch to say that Gorbachev owed his ascension to Reagan and the economic pressures he was bringing. As Georgy Shakhnazarov, one of Gorbachev's foreign policy advisers, said, the Soviet Union was "falling behind," and only "reform offered the opportunity to catch up."[86] Gorbachev had worked his way up through the Communist Party, first as a young provincial party secretary, then a deputy to the Supreme Soviet, and was elevated to the Politburo in 1979. It was a rapid rise, made faster by the successive deaths of Soviet dictators Leonid Brezhnev, Yuri Andropov, and Konstantin Chernenko in a five-year period.

Attempting, as so many of his predecessors had, to "reform" communism, in his first year Gorbachev announced a program of *glasnost* (opening up to Western ideas) and *perestroika* (restructuring). Both of his programs ensured the destruction of the Marxist system, the former because a closed society could not compete with a free one, and the latter because reform of communism was impossible without pricing—which meant private property, something no Communist would permit. As a reformer, Gorbachev was a man "sympathetic to the need for change and renewal but reluctant to assault the core tenets of [communism]."[87] Communism could not be reformed, or even improved: Gorbachev's ascension as someone who even *tried* to fix it publicly marked him as a "genetic error of the system," as an adviser described him.[88] Stalin had shot such people; Khrushchev had them committed to mental hospitals. Gorbachev's great sin was not that he admitted something was badly wrong with the worker's paradise, but that he announced it publicly.

The task was more difficult than merely reconstructing a dictatorship into a democracy. Marxism's very foundation was one of war, and the Party itself was the instrument of that war. Sovietologist William Odom noted, "Marxism is itself a theory of war."[89] Nuclear weapons had forced Soviet leaders to ignore or explain away certain aspects of Marxist-Leninist theory because nuclear war was not something the USSR could win. Increasingly, the Soviet military found itself struggling to conceive of a use for its nuclear weapons that did not entail a first strike.

Even as the general secretary sought to perform CPR on the deceased, Western fellow travelers were insisting the patient was fine. A subelement of the CIA, which had always bought into the fable of Soviet economic strength, painted in its briefings on the USSR a picture of an economically vibrant state, a diagnosis the spin doctors in the leftist media reported with considerable glee when it was leaked. Arthur Schlesinger, always good for a misguided prophecy and one who never admitted to any mistakes, intoned in 1981, "Those in the U.S. who think the Soviet Union is on the verge of economic and social collapse, ready with one small push to go over the brink, are . . . only kidding themselves."[90]

Some in the Reagan administration, however, including Thomas Reed and Bill Clark, thought otherwise, as did Herb Meyer, the vice chairman of the CIA's National Intelligence Council. An economist who had studied the Soviet economy for thirty years, Meyer drafted a memo in the fall of 1983 that completely contradicted Schlesingerian-type spouting, writing the stunning prediction that the USSR was entering a "terminal phase." Wealth had not flowed from the West as expected; the invasion of Grenada had been a "shocking setback"; and the deployment of the euromissiles would "change the balance of power in Europe back in our favor." In their death throes, Meyer warned, the Soviets might try to strike first.[91]

Reed, another skeptic of Soviet economic health, also insisted "the Soviets were going broke."[92] By the mid-1980s, the USSR had to purchase nine million tons of grain from the United States, five million from Canada, and four million from Argentina. Contrary to the conventional wisdom that the Soviets were spending only 15 percent of their gross domestic product on defense, more recent evidence concluded the true cost consumed between 35 percent and 50 percent of GDP.[93] One Soviet researcher, Boris Altshuler, argued that when all true military costs were included, So-

viet defense expenditures consumed a shocking 73 percent of national income in 1989![94] The dissenters who saw a creaky USSR were joined by
Norman Bailey, an NSC staff economist who carefully examined Soviet
hard currency shortages and discovered that Soviet oil production involved
dangerous shortcuts, sacrificing long-term gains for immediate returns,
dumping gold on the world markets, and even attempting to manipulate the
wheat exchange—all signs that the USSR was headed for a massive crash.[95]

The Soviets were not only falling behind economically but were also far
behind the West technologically. In 1994, Gorbachev's former science adviser Roald Sagdeev admitted that the USSR was a good fifteen years behind the United States in computers and microelectronics. This was in
spite of Soviet intelligence divisions mounting massive clandestine efforts
to pilfer technological and scientific knowledge, particularly related to the
new fields of computers, programming, and microelectronics, from the
United States and Europe since the 1970s.[96] Operating under the KGB's
Line X program, spies in the guise of agricultural specialists walked into
the United States through Nixon's open door of détente in 1972. Of the one
hundred members of the delegation, at least a third were known or suspected intelligence officers. Taking advantage of technicalities in the rules,
the visitors expanded their itineraries from watch factories to semiconductor firms three days before arriving, so the Defense Department did not
have time to object. A CIA assessment of Soviet tech transfer showed that
by 1980 more than five thousand Soviet research projects directly benefited
from Western technology, much of it gained through espionage.[97]

Ominously, only a very few Soviet spies were detected and neutralized
or brought to trial because to many—even in the Reagan State Department—
Communist espionage was a red herring and not to be taken seriously, and
certainly not to be prosecuted. Soviet spymaster Alexander Feklisov, the
onetime handler of Julius and Ethel Rosenberg and Klaus Fuchs, commented in his memoirs, *The Man Behind the Rosenbergs*, that most of the
spies for the Soviet Union in America were individuals who saw themselves
as citizens of the world rather than of the United States.[98] Their mission
was to enhance the flow of information to the Soviet Union to lessen the
chance of war by keeping the Soviets sufficiently powerful to act as a balance to the United States.

Nixon had been the first to place computer products on the restricted
export list, and Carter had ordered a full review of technology transfer and
canceled several equipment sales to the USSR. But it was Reagan who
turned the tables on the Soviets, using their ill-gotten gains against them.

Line X was betrayed by "Farewell," Soviet colonel Vladimir Vetrov, who photographed and supplied to the West some four thousand documents. In July 1981, François Mitterrand informed Reagan of Vetrov's activities and handed him a list of names of more than two hundred Line X officers planted in the West. In response, Reagan instantly pounced on the opportunity for a disinformation campaign and more. CIA director William Casey and NSA adviser Gus Weiss developed a plan to dispense "special" technology through front companies via Line X. That technology, including everything from oil pumping turbines to aircraft designs, would be sabotaged to perform well for a while, then fail—mostly through the insertion of computer code viruses that would trigger catastrophic failures at a future point.[99] The president instructed Casey to keep the project tightly controlled within the administration "to ensure that White House moderates did not . . . leak it to the press in order to kill the effort."[100]

Soon, a series of technologies with flawed programs were made available to the Soviets, all under the premise that they were being "stolen" by Soviet agents. These included computer chips that went into Soviet equipment, flawed turbines for gas pipelines, and extensive plans leaked that covered everything from chemical plants to tractors to a useless space shuttle design. No part of the "Farewell" program proved more successful than the effort to delay the Trans-Siberian Pipeline. Reagan had fought the pipeline tooth and nail. In a cabinet meeting as construction was starting, virtually everyone around the table, including most of the cabinet secretaries, urged Reagan to relent on credits to the Soviets for the pipeline. He listened—at times the discussion was "heated"—and finally the president said, "Well, they can have their damned pipeline. . . . But not with American equipment and not with American technology."[101] It was hardly a concession as Reagan was already taking effective action against the pipeline.

The USSR began construction early in 1982 on the massive $35 billion project to transfer its vast reserves of natural gas to Western Europe through dual 3,600-mile pipelines. Each fifty-six-inch-diameter pipe would run from producing areas in Siberia to depots in the West, moving gas to the capitalist countries and sending desperately needed hard currency to the Communists. Western European leaders, even Thatcher, had enthusiastically signed on to the promise of delivering cheap gas to the democracies well into the twenty-first century. Thus, Reagan was even isolated on the issue from many of his stalwart allies.

With help from the Canadians, who detected a KGB operative attempting to penetrate their security codes, "improved" software for operating the

Trans-Siberian Pipeline was shipped to the Soviets. That software contained a virus which reset the pump speeds and pressures above those the system could handle, resulting in the "most monumental non-nuclear explosion and fire ever seen from space."[102] Inside the White House, satellite reports suggested a three-kiloton nuclear weapon had exploded, until Weiss appeared and told the NSC staffers not to worry, although he could not tell them why. And while spooks were slipping the Kremlin high-tech lemons, Reagan's export control officials waged a merciless war on advanced technology shipments to the Iron Curtain. From a high point in 1975, when one third of all American exports were considered high-tech, Reagan's Commerce Department slashed the total to 5 percent by 1983, seizing an astounding 1,400 illegal shipments headed for Russia.

Euromissiles and Freezes

Other aspects of Reagan's cold war strategy were visible for all to see, beginning with the decision to counter the Soviets' deployment of SS-20 mobile missiles. Until then—the Soviets had begun a deployment of the missiles in 1975—the West had seen a slow deterioration of its intermediate range ballistic missile capabilities against the Warsaw Pact. While the range of the missiles suggested they could only be used against other European states, the primary target was the United States in that they were designed to "de-link" Western Europe from the U.S. atomic umbrella. The USSR was attempting nothing less than intimidating the Europeans into severing their NATO ties. Neither Gerald Ford nor Jimmy Carter took the new missiles too seriously because, for a short time, French and British bombers and American fighter-bombers stationed in Europe could offset the missiles. But as the numbers kept increasing, the West demanded an end to the deployments, to which the Soviets typically said "*Nyet.*" Reagan concluded the only option was to fight fire with fire. With Thatcher's strong support, Reagan convinced the NATO allies to accept deployment on European soil of 464 ground-launched cruise missiles and 108 Pershing II ballistic missiles, all capable of quick flights into Soviet territory with extremely limited warning time.

West Germany, Belgium, Italy, the Netherlands, and England all agreed to stationing the new missiles on their soil, provoking a storm of protests and uniting virtually every leftist group in existence. These were truly massive demonstrations, some of the largest in European history: 300,000 in Bonn alone on a single date in 1983. British demonstrators included "an enthusiastic . . . assortment of feminists, environmentalists and

[who] mounted a prolonged siege of . . . Greenham Common. . . ."[103] West German chancellor Helmut Schmidt was forced out of office for his support of the missiles—even though his successor followed through anyway. Notably, no Germans had marched for peace when the Polish Communist government declared Poland to be in a "state of war" from 1981 to 1983 (it was under martial law) or when the Soviets invaded Afghanistan. No doubt some protesters were sincere, but they were also manipulated and egged on by the KGB. One agent boasted to his embassy contact in London that "it was us, the KGB residency, who brought a quarter of a million people out onto the streets."[104] This subversion was not new, either: the Politburo, in 1976, "extolled the value of encouraging the peace movement [as a means to weaken] Western resolve," and Moscow funded protest groups that opposed the neutron bomb in 1977.[105]

Leadership of the euromissile opposition was compromised by the Soviet spy agencies. Information that surfaced after the fall of the Berlin Wall revealed that at least twenty-five members of the Bundestag (the West German Parliament) were on the Kremlin payroll. Far more were fellow travelers and willing dupes.[106] The German Peace Union received five million deutsche marks annually from the Stasi (the East German state security organization), while Sergei Grigoriev, a top official in the USSR's "International Department," funded peace groups through "public organizations and a number of communist parties. Millions of dollars were injected into the creation of all sorts of ad-hoc groups and coalitions."[107] A peace commission started by former Swedish prime minister Olof Palme named as the Soviet representative Georgy Arbatov, a KGB agent. An organization called the World Peace Council, supposedly committed to global disarmament (which, of course, never meant *Soviet* disarmament), was funded by the Politburo to the tune of $50 million a year, under strict control by the Central Committee of the Communist Party in the USSR. The KGB took pride in "stirring up the anti-military movement in countries of the west."[108]

Moscow's offensive against Reagan had started as early as the 1980 presidential campaign, when the Soviets tried to ensure his defeat. The Kremlin described him as "a dangerous confrontational foe" with a "deeply disturbing" hatred of the Communist system.[109] By 1984, it reached panic level: agents floated stories in foreign presses that Reagan's health had been "affected by his father's alcoholism," and Yuri Andropov, chairman of the KGB, ordered all his agents to put as their first priority defeating Reagan in the 1984 election.[110] Various pronouncements by the National Council of Churches against the military buildup and the deployment of the cruise missiles, in favor of the "Freeze," and against "Star Wars" (the Strategic Defense Initiative, supposedly a system operating from space as a defense against ballistic nuclear missiles) led Reagan to suspect they were infiltrated as well. He confided in his diary, "Sometimes I think (forgive me) the [National Council of Churches] believes God can be reached through Moscow."[111] Agents were immediately sent off to dig up dirt on Reagan and were instructed to popularize the slogan among the peace crowd, "*Reagan: eto voina!*" ("Reagan Means War!").[112]

Reagan, Thatcher, and NATO steadfastly moved forward with the cruise and Pershing missiles while continuing to negotiate, proving Reagan's point that the Soviets would *only* talk in good faith if forced to do so by a genuine arms race. As negotiations continued through a summit and specific arms talks—sometimes linked to Reagan's new START program (Strategic Arms Reductions Talks)—Reagan held out for a one-step-at-a-time approach in which the euromissiles would be dealt with separately from ICBMs, submarine weapons, or bombers. Naturally, Gorbachev held out for a more favorable position, repeatedly attempting to link Star Wars to the euromissiles, without success. In 1986 meetings that culminated at Reykjavík in October, the two leaders reached an understanding, finalized a year later as the Intermediate Nuclear Forces Treaty (INF). The treaty removed the euromissiles on both sides and destroyed them under the observation of representatives from both parties.

The INF Treaty constituted a stunning, overwhelming victory for Reagan and his hard-line approach, confirming that the Soviets would, in fact, back down when confronted with steel. It was no coincidence that only after Reagan held the line on the euromissiles did Gorbachev conclude "today, with the appearance of weapons of mass destruction the objective limit has arisen for class confrontation in the international arena."[113] It marked the first time in history that an entire class of nuclear weapons was destroyed, and, equally important, it came on the heels of a blistering Soviet defeat in Afghanistan.

Charlie Wilson's War

Following the installation of a pro-Soviet government in Afghanistan in 1978, an Afghan insurgency against the Russian invaders had spread from the regions north of Kabul. Harsh government crackdowns, including the execution of 27,000 political prisoners, only flamed the rebellion further, culminating in an uprising in Herat where Afghan soldiers mutinied and killed 100 Soviet advisers. Backed by Soviet air power, the People's Democratic Party of Afghanistan (PPDA) launched a massive retaliation on Herat in which 24,000 inhabitants were massacred, triggering the defection of more than half the Afghan army.[114]

Although Zbigniew Brzezinski, Jimmy Carter's national security advisor, later bragged he had helped draw the Soviet Union into "its [own] Vietnam War," Carter did little to actually support the mujahideen ("strugglers" or "people doing jihad").[115] Soviet tanks rolled into Afghanistan in December 1979, shortly after the U.S. embassy was occupied by the Iranians in Tehran. Carter was deeply disturbed by the Soviet invasion; his vice president, Walter Mondale, said it "unnerved everyone," and added, "I don't know if fear is the right word to describe our reactions." Carter declared Afghanistan the most significant foreign policy crisis since World War II, then did essentially nothing about it.[116] A trade embargo was placed on the USSR and Carter announced a boycott of the 1980 Summer Olympics, held in Moscow. (It was supremely ironic that Carter's only "victory" came when the U.S. men's hockey team—a group of collegiate players—defeated a hardened Soviet team of state-subsidized professionals in the 1980 Winter Olympics.)

When the weary and befuddled Carter stepped down, Reagan tied the fate of the Afghans to that of the Nicaraguan freedom fighters and the Poles. "Are you still trying to take over the world?" the Gipper bluntly asked Gorbachev in Geneva.[117] Of course, the United States would provide surreptitious weapons for the Afghans: CIA director Bill Casey handled that, ensuring guns and food got to the mujahideen. Aid came from unlikely places: the Chinese supplied the Afghans with AK-47s. It also came from predictable sources, which for obvious reasons wished to remain quiet: Pakistan's "safe hamlets" allowed the mujahideen to cross the border, re-arm, and reequip, receiving training from the CIA.

Democratic congressman Charlie Wilson, a hard-drinking, womanizing Texan on the House Appropriations Subcommittee on Defense, which oversaw CIA funding, made Afghanistan his personal crusade. Teaming with CIA agent Gust Avrakotos, Wilson worked with unimaginable combinations of allies, including, at one time, the Saudis (who agreed to finance double everything the United States contributed), the Egyptians (who supplied stockpiled Soviet weapons), and the Israelis (who worked on new weapons designs specifically for Wilson). Muhammad Zia-ul-Haq, Pakistan's strongman (who had come under the sway of Texas bombshell Joanne Herring), supported the Afghans despite unceasing intimidation from the Soviets.

Thanks to Wilson, the United States supplied plenty of money. Funding soared from $30 million under Carter to $2 billion under Reagan as Wilson called in favor after favor, making the guerrilla war in Afghanistan the largest CIA program in history. At the same time, Reagan had to feign separation from direct U.S. support, not only because he did not want to give the Soviets an excuse to become even more reckless, but also because it was important for the world to see the conflict as a group of rugged individualists struggling for freedom, outmanned and outgunned Muslim minutemen against the Soviet juggernaut.

Far from backing down, the Kremlin did what Marxists always do when confronted with a setback (the ideology is never wrong)—they doubled down, dispatching the Red Army's top paratroops, the special forces (*Spetsnaz*), and the KGB's best operatives to Afghanistan. Typically, the Soviets failed to understand religion, and it was no different with Islam than with Christianity. Trotsky had predicted that "the putrescent tissue of Islam will vanish at the first puff."[118] Some Afghan Communists tried to compress Islam into "the social principles of socialism," or to otherwise legitimize Islam inside Communist principles—an impossibility for a system based on a godless structure. The inability to comprehend religious motivations would plague the (later, free) Russians in Chechnya, but in 1980, it was not yet apparent to Moscow that Red Army troops had stepped into a wolves' lair. In the meantime, the Soviets' ruthlessness chased vast numbers of Afghans across the border to Pakistan; by 1985, one out of every three Afghans had left the country.

Despite raising the ante, unknown to Reagan or anyone in the West, Gorbachev was suffering from trepidation and uncertainty. He had already determined he couldn't keep Communist forces in Afghanistan very long, telling his commander he had a maximum of two years to win the war.[119] Issuing NSDD-166 in early 1985, Reagan established aid to the Afghans as American policy aimed at an outright Soviet defeat.[120] William Casey told one CIA agent, "go out and kill me 10,000 Soviets until they give up," a theme Reagan echoed, telling Casey he "wanted the numbers up, and he wanted the Soviet high command demoralized."[121] Wilson was also key in getting approval for Afghan aid from Democrats and laying the groundwork for CIA officials to authorize a transfer of between 500 and 2,000 Stinger missiles, which were added to the mix of weapons, tents, medicine, and radios Wilson had already supplied.

Afghans put the new weapons instantly to use, shooting down 275 jets and helicopters by the time the Soviets withdrew in 1989. Soviet planes vanished from Afghan skies as early as 1987 due to the threat of the Stingers, whose 80 percent shoot-to-kill effectiveness removed the Soviets' only significant advantage. Wilson almost singlehandedly rescued Afghan aid at the critical moment in July 1987, when word circulated among Hill Democrats that Pakistan had acquired key atomic bomb technology in violation of American rules on foreign aid. In a stunning, all-night session, Wilson personally buttonholed virtually every important legislator, one by one turning a vote against Pakistan—which would have doomed the Afghans—into a triumph. "Charlie did it," said Pakistan's Zia-ul-Haq to CBS. Charlie and Reagan.

Back at Langley, Champagne corks popped for a gleeful celebration of the most successful support operation in the Agency's history, to complement Farewell as the most successful intelligence operation. The raw numbers were stunning: out of 120,000 Soviet troops sent into Afghanistan, about 60 percent were casualties, including 22,939 classified as "traumatized/mutilated."[122] An unprecedented civilian protest group, the Committee of Soldiers' Mothers, succeeded in publishing information about soldiers' deaths. Lenin would have had the ringleaders arrested and shot, but Gorbachev could no longer do that. A demoralized Soviet military experienced massive draft evasion: in 1990, seven republics failed to meet their quotas.

The Reagan-Wilson offensive in Afghanistan flew so totally under the radar that the press, obsessed with creating setbacks for the Nicaraguan contras, crowed that the Democrats had achieved victory in blocking the Gipper's initiatives. It was high irony that while the Democrats spent all their energy stopping aid to twenty thousand contras, by 1986 70 percent of the CIA's operations budget was consumed with the Afghan program. Typically, the press either missed what was occurring completely or pronounced it a failure. Only a few years earlier, administration critics had claimed the Afghans "can never be strong enough to drive the Soviets out," and *The Washington Post* informed its readers the guerrillas "don't stand the slightest chance of winning."[123] Dan Rather, having donned the garb of a *mujahid*, told his *CBS Special Report* audience that the war was lost, and no other reporters would be able to go back in. Somebody needed to tell Rather he was not Cronkite, and the date was not 1968. *The New York Times*—seemingly wrong on every significant story—ran the headline "Guerrillas Are Divided and at Risk of Being Conquered."[124] Harry Reasoner, interviewing Wilson, tried to drum up sympathy . . . for the *Russian troops*. Wilson exploded on camera, "I love sticking it to the Russians. . . . They *need* to get it back, and they're getting it back. . . . And I love it!"[125]

A final incident sealed Gorbachev's determination to get out of Afghanistan quickly. In 1987, Mathias Rust, a West German youth, flew a small Cessna to Moscow and landed it behind St. Basil's Cathedral near Red Square. The stunt hit the Politburo "like a bombshell," demonstrating the shocking backwardness of Soviet air defense systems, which had not even seen Rust.[126] It also generated a "palpable change in public attitudes toward the military," as one student of the Red Army has noted.[127] All the economic sacrifices to maintain the military, it seemed, had been for naught. Rust's feat had hit the Soviets harder than Carter's failed Iranian rescue attempt had hit the United States.

A Shield, Not a Sword

If the media failed to understand what was occurring in Afghanistan or in the Kremlin, it failed on a colossal level by continually underestimating Reagan. No issue more demonstrated how out of touch the press was with both political reality and public opinion as "Star Wars," a program the media could take credit for naming.

In a 1967 meeting at Livermore National Laboratory, physicist Edward Teller provided then-governor Reagan with briefings on advances in missile defense, particularly in using explosives to shred or destroy incoming warheads. Following the meeting, Reagan had an alternative to the mutual destruction assured by the policy of massive retaliation. The two maintained a correspondence for thirteen years, with Teller sending Reagan updates on, among other technologies, lasers. (Reagan would award Teller the National Medal of Science in 1983.)

An even more recent and sobering prod to examine strategic defense came from a visit to NORAD, whereupon Reagan asked what would happen to the fortified mountain if a Soviet SS-18 landed on it. "It would blow us away," replied General James Hill. "There must be something better than this," replied the president.[128] Then came a briefing from the Pentagon that estimated 150 million Americans would be killed by a Soviet strike. Reagan had long pondered ways to eliminate nuclear weapons, but after those two experiences, he became obsessed with ridding the world of such horror.

Virtually no one in public—and few since then—has appreciated Reagan's revulsion at the very concept of nuclear weapons. Instead of the crazed warmonger his enemies portrayed him to be, Reagan found Mutual Assured Destruction (MAD) "morally abhorrent," observed his secretary of state George Shultz.[129] *Time*'s Strobe Talbott, later an undersecretary of State under Bill Clinton—no friend of Reagan and someone the Soviets considered a "special unofficial contact" (meaning he was not paid for his information)—described him as a "nuclear abolitionist."[130] Any system of defense that condemned a president to ordering a retaliatory strike that would incinerate millions of people was "simply morally untenable," according to Reagan.[131]

Information about the carnage of a nuclear exchange was not the only new intelligence presented to Reagan. He studied the Soviet missile defense effort called Red Shield, and discovered the Soviets had experimented heavily in laser and charged-particle-beam weapons in the 1970s. This was one of the reasons Gorbachev, among others, feared the Strategic Defense Initiative so much—they knew that in theory it could work, because they'd done the basic science themselves. Taken with the horrifying numbers on the impact of a nuclear war, Reagan enthusiastically embraced options to MAD. Playing his cards close to his vest, Reagan gave the ever-compromising George Shultz the text of his speech only two days before he delivered it. Shultz sat in a "rage" while he watched Reagan deliver a speech detailing a program he considered a fantasy, some sort of "cosmic joke."[132]

His program, the Strategic Defense Initiative (SDI), threatened to rock the boat from the outset. It was thoroughly mischaracterized, then and today, as a specific program of space-based lasers to shoot down enemy missiles. In fact, it was a call for an exploratory program to see which technologies would be most promising to pursue. Lasers were one component, but there were a dozen other paths available. Yet Reagan knew it was a game changer and that regardless of which technology was chosen, the United States could put it into action. Reagan considered it so controversial that he withheld releasing the news of his plans to many of his inner circle whom he knew to be part of the arms-control mind-set. The president did not want to control arms: he wanted to *eliminate* them. Contrary to some notions that Reagan went it alone and surprised everyone, the Gipper had in fact submitted the proposal to the Joint Chiefs of Staff and received their full support. Army general John Vessey, who chaired the JCS, pointed out that missile defense would "move the battle from our shores and skies."[133] Although the JCS did not design a specific form of missile defense, the members were open to any and all approaches or combinations of conventional, nuclear, and advanced technology defenses. Most of all, the Chiefs were united in their support of SDI. Reagan individually questioned each member of the JCS, assuring himself of the "complete corporate support" of that body before moving forward.[134]

Within his administration, Reagan knew there would be significant opposition. "Judge" Clark supported the idea; Robert "Bud" McFarlane, his counselor, and Shultz did not. But Reagan, like Napoleon, believed in audacity as a key element of success. On March 23, 1983, Reagan changed the cold war with a single speech. Some argue he won it with a few dozen words: "Let me share with you a vision of the future which offers hope. It is that we embark on a program to counter the awesome Soviet missile threat with measures that are defensive. . . . [What if] we could intercept and destroy strategic ballistic missiles before they reached our own soil or that of our allies?"[135] The potential for the ultimate success of such a shield came from no less a source than the Soviets: "This is not just irresponsible; it is insane," fumed Soviet dictator and former KGB director Yuri Andropov.[136]

Of course, it was neither. The Soviets' own research had proved it completely plausible (even if some of the technologies were still in the process of being refined). Moreover, the question was asked repeatedly by Star Wars supporters: if the notion was so impractical, so fantastic, then why were the Soviets so terrified of it? This question was especially valid if one considered the cost: wouldn't the Soviets (and the antiwar activists) have preferred to see the United States waste billions of dollars in nonthreatening, unusable stuff rather than directing that money into more proven weapons, such as bombers and missiles? On the contrary, Soviet leaders became frantic, placing efforts to halt SDI at the forefront of all their propaganda and intelligence activities. "Methinks," the actor Reagan could have said, "the Soviets doth protest too much" by claiming it wouldn't work. Indeed, Gorbachev made it the centerpiece of his debating points at the Reykjavík meeting, linking all other reductions in weapons to abandoning SDI. After meeting the hard-nosed Reagan in Iceland, where the president refused to put Star Wars on the negotiating table, Gorbachev never again referred to him as a "fool" or "clown," or called him incompetent. The premier had met his match.

Opposition to SDI in the United States and Europe, however, went to the barricades almost immediately. Scientists such as Carl Sagan were enlisted to hold press conferences and panels, ridiculing the program. At one such panel, Sagan showed the (admittedly simplistic) video provided by the administration as to how a future missile defense shield could work, and commented that the satellites emitted a sound "like a zzzzt, zzzzt," and the enemy missiles "just disappear—they don't even frag-*ment* [italics to show

Sagan's pronunciation]," leaving the viewer with the idea that destroying these weapons was not only easy but "fun."[137] Scholars who were nonscientists also mocked the speech. Lost in the criticisms was an amazing reality that Soviet equipment failed at very high rates, meaning that even at 80 percent effectiveness, a Star Wars system would likely be able to erase all remaining incoming threats because between 15 and 20 percent of Soviet missiles were likely never to leave the ground and those that did would see high failure rates in flight or even upon impact.

The media was unconcerned with such realities. Many of the journalists were raised in an era where applying the label "Buck Rogers" to a technology immediately made it fantasy of the lowest sort. They had failed to realize that times had changed. When Senator Ted Kennedy applied the term "Star Wars" to SDI, he meant it as a "vehicle to ridicule SDI."[138] Slavishly, the media ran with Kennedy's characterization: *The New York Times* called the speech "Reagan's answer to the film 'Star Wars.'"[139] The Kremlin also loved it, using it in all of Moscow's propaganda. Use of the term "Star Wars," instead of the accurate Strategic Defense Initiative, in the eyes of hostile reporters would expose the program to the highest skepticism and derision from the great unwashed. Reagan fretted about the phrase; it was "never mine," he complained, "and now they saddle me with it."[140]

For once, the Gipper's instincts about public perceptions were wrong. Contrary to the reactions the media hoped to produce with the term, most Americans had seen George Lucas's 1977 hit, *Star Wars*, many had witnessed the landing on the moon, and some had seen demonstrations of lasers. To them, the notion of destroying objects with deadly beams was no longer fanciful or Buck Rogers–ish but entirely within the realm of the possible. Worse for the critics, by linking SDI to *Star Wars*, the media had inadvertently moved a highly technical scientific concept into the area of practical application in the minds of the public.

This was especially true for the "greatest generation," who had in their lifetimes gone from abject poverty and the Depression to world domination and lunar landings. They often lived by the humorous maxim that the difficult was done today—the impossible takes a little longer. These were *Americans*, and as such, they confidently believed that once they set their minds to something, they could achieve anything. Polio, tuberculosis, whooping cough, and malaria had all been virtually wiped out in their lifetimes. Their parents or grandparents had ridden horses; now they climbed into jet airplanes. They recalled stories of the days when the telephone was a radical breakthrough, times before television, and life without automobiles. Time compression was a reality for them. Space was just a little ways out there, something to be conquered. "Star Wars"? Reagan could not have possibly devised a better PR slogan.

The more one examined the phrase, the more it seemed to subtly advance SDI. Despite his age, Reagan's optimism, winning smile, and energetic manner contrasted sharply with that of the Soviet leaders. Reagan was Luke Skywalker, wielding the light saber to deflect deadly attacks. When Gorbachev assumed the mantle of leadership of the USSR, he may have only loosely fit the character of Darth Vader—but the contrast nevertheless was acute, as even Gorbachev's aide noticed when the two men met at Geneva:

> I saw President Reagan coming out to greet Gorbachev in a well-tailored suit, looking young with a good haircut. . . . He projected an image of a young, dynamic leader. And Gorbachev came out of this tank-like limo . . . in a standard Politburo hat, in a scarf, in an autumn overcoat, a heavy overcoat, looking like an old guy.[141]

As for the premier's predecessors, with their grim, skeletal visages, they closely resembled the "Evil Emperor." Reagan above all understood the power of images, but he also had a deep appreciation for the common sense of the American people. No amount of vitriol from reporters, incredulity from some scientists, or wild, irrational language from Hill Democrats could change the public's perception that even if "Star Wars" was some sort of "Death Star," it was better for America to have it than the reds.

But this was not all. Other developments in Poland had in fact made the prospect of the USSR's decline a distinct possibility. Outside of Afghanistan, Poland came the closest to becoming a genuine battleground in the cold war than any other disputed ground. And events in Poland largely originated in 1980, preceding Reagan's election by only two months, with the founding of Solidarity.

Poland, the Pope, and Solidarity

In 1980, strikes began in the embers of the Ursus tractor plant and within three weeks the protests spread to all major Polish cities. In August, the shipbuilders at the Lenin Shipyards of Gdansk (previously German Danzig, the city where the first shots of World War II were fired) organized into an independent trade union called Solidarity. Drawing on *Solicitudo Rei Socialis*, a teaching of Pope John Paul II that identified with the poor and those marginalized in society, Solidarity was careful to avoid provoking a military response.

The cold war seems dominated by walls—the Berlin Wall, the Iron Curtain. So too, the Solidarity strike seemed to gain its historical place when electrician and trade-union activist Lech Wałęsa climbed over the shipyard wall to assume leadership of the strike. Solidarity practiced nonviolence, recognizing in part that violent resistance to Soviet-backed Polish forces would be folly. It became the first independent labor union in the Communist bloc, and for that, if for no other reason, it constituted a monumental threat to the Polish government and Bolshevism in general. Naturally, the government had to shut it down as quickly as possible, declaring martial law in 1981 and imposing a legal ban on the Catholic Church. Polish officials detained Wałęsa and others; phones were disconnected and mail subjected to even closer scrutiny than before. More than a dozen Poles were killed during the crackdown, which fizzled quickly. Once released, the ringleaders resumed their demands that workers have free labor unions. Polish Communists relented, but not for long. After General Wojciech Jaruzelski took power in February 1981, he moved to crush the protests before the Soviets did, declaring martial law in December and again ordering the arrests of Solidarity leaders. Solidarity's actions added one more brick to the creaking, cracked structure of Bolshevism.

Solidarity benefited immensely from the vocal support of President Reagan, who mentioned the movement incessantly in his speeches. His *Presidential Documents* contained references to Solidarity on 216 pages. Time and again he addressed the Poles directly. But the movement profited even more from its close association with Karol Wojtyła, the Cardinal of Krákow, who was elected pope as John Paul II in October 1978.

Wojtyła's rise to leadership in the Catholic Church was a particular twentieth-century story. He had lost his family, one by one, in an eleven-year period; a Pole, he had seen firsthand the oppression of the Soviets and, more generally, communism. Both young (the youngest in 140 years) and a non-Italian (the first since 1523), John Paul II was the first pope ever to come from an Iron Curtain country. That was significant, for Poland had witnessed astounding increases in the number of believers. Priests and nuns had increased by one third since 1939, monastic foundations and nunneries by 50 percent, and mass attendance in cities was up by half. Most of the population was married in, and buried by, the Church.[142]

The pope survived an assassination attempt, not by the Soviets, but by a Muslim named Mehmet Ali Ağca, who shot him four times. John Paul II's survival only enhanced his stature as "a Big Pope, taking himself and his Faith to the world."[143] Thus, within a period of three years, each of the three individuals most responsible for bringing down communism survived attempts on their lives—Margaret Thatcher, Ronald Reagan, and John Paul II.

John Paul II was also a paradox, embodying Christian existentialism and Catholic traditionalism, with its devotion to miracles, shrines, saints, and the Virgin Mary.[144] In tune with the reforms of the Second Vatican Council, which adopted liturgies in native tongues and seemed to embody a spirit of optimism and democracy, John Paul II did not address falling attendance by liberalizing further (as did the mainline Protestant denominations in the United States), but by returning to Catholicism's roots. To that end, he found it necessary to act as spokesman in chief, personally touring and making as many appearances to as many Catholics as possible. Monstrous-sized crowds came out to greet him: 3.5 million in Poland, and in Ireland, half the nation's population heard him. By 1990, he had spoken to 200 million adherents, reinvigorating Catholicism, especially in Africa and Latin America.

The fact that so many Catholics (up to 60 percent) lived in Third World countries made him particularly sensitive to issues of poverty, which made him more popular still in those parts of the world. Yet his stance on contraception was at odds with developing countries and their high birth rates. But the pope remained immensely popular, which, ironically, revealed the weak footing Catholicism stood on by the 1990s. Pope John Paul II had tapped into the culture of celebrity that consumed the United States and was starting to reach most of the world. Crowds came to see *him*, not the Vicar of Christ. In an increasingly pick-and-choose theological world, millions of Western Catholics loved the pope and ignored his teachings. Contraception was common, if not nearly universal; homosexuality in the priesthood was epidemic; and even attendance at mass, after briefly rising, started to fall in the 1980s. A Catholic variant of "love the sinner, hate the sin" took root in which people loved the man and disregarded what he stood for.

One of the pope's greatest contributions to Catholicism was his role in stopping the spread of Marxism in Latin America by endorsing the popular religion of the villagers, first by visiting the shrine of the Virgin of Guadalupe in Mexico in 1979, then by tacitly approving the spreading Catholic charismatic movement, especially in South America. In the meantime, his alignment with Solidarity gave international spiritual sanction to a specific type of liberation in action, answering Stalin's question, "How many divisions does the pope have?" with "Potentially? Hundreds." Equally important, the pope's blessing on Solidarity meant that communism had to simultaneously battle God and Ronald Reagan. That alone might have been enough to bring down Lenin's statue, when yet still other new winds began to buffet the Evil Empire.

First, there were new and largely unexpected economic pressures that accompanied the sudden plunge in gold prices, due to the Federal Reserve's anti-inflation policies. Already strapped for hard currency, the Soviets' gold reserves now declined precipitously in value. It constituted an amazing win-win for the United States, which saw domestic inflation brought down at the same time as it exerted powerful pressures on the USSR's economy. Then there was the discovery of Alaska's North Slope oil and the building of the Trans-Alaska Pipeline, which came on line in 1977, and by 1986 Russian oil revenues tumbled. Middle Eastern allies such as Saudi Arabia, concerned about Soviet ambitions in the region, collaborated in bringing down international prices, further damaging Moscow's balance sheets. And another irony: a perceived weakness of capitalism—the stock market crash of 1987, in which the Dow dropped 508 points (some 23 percent) in a day—harmed Bolshevism more, because American banks immediately became tight-fisted. No further credit flowed eastward. By that time, of course, the Iron Curtain countries had become addicted to Western loans, while at the same time they hadn't borrowed enough to exert any kind of pressure on the bankers. Eastern European shoppers saw prices rise along with their blood pressure.

Reagan kept stirring the pot, always the master of political theater. For twenty years, the Berlin Wall had stood as a doleful symbol of a divided Europe, reminding the free world that communism and slavery were just a few feet away. In June 1987, Reagan revived images of Kennedy speaking of freedom to Berliners in 1963 when he stood at the Brandenburg Gate to deliver one of his most memorable speeches. He energized the crowd and put the onus on the Soviets when he uttered the famous line, "Mr. Gorbachev, tear down this wall!" Gorbachev watched the speech on CNN, appreciating that he was losing ground by the minute.

But Reagan wasn't through: going into the lion's den, he traveled to the USSR in the spring of 1988. There he received a hero's welcome from the Soviet citizens. Strolling around the Arbat, a Moscow outdoor mall, Reagan was surrounded by crowds chanting "Reagan! Reagan!"[145] Two days later, he delivered a speech to hundreds of students at Moscow State

University—the children of the Soviet elites and nomenklatura—and Reagan spoke to the hearts of all young people everywhere by focusing on freedom, "the right to question and change the established way of doing things," as he put it. But change only came from "the eternal things, from the source of all life, which is faith." Wild applause and a standing ovation followed.[146]

These sentiments had not occurred in an intellectual vacuum, no matter how tightly the KGB attempted to clamp down on "insurrectionist" literature. They dovetailed with an ideological offensive worthy of the East Front in 1944. When Aleksandr Solzhenitsyn's book *The Gulag Archipelago* was first published in the West in 1973, it marked the last time Soviet apologists in the United States and Western Europe could deny the basic inhumanity of the Communist system. Until the publication of *The Gulag Archipelago*, some Western defenders of communism who attempted to draw a distinction between Stalinism and a "good" collectivism that was somehow possible under the auspices of a benign totalitarian state still clung to their illusions. Solzhenitsyn smashed those myths, exposing Soviet communism for the brutal dictatorship it not only had been, but still was.

Suddenly, however, a new generation of Communist youth said "No more!" Rather than storming barricades or inviting Red Army tanks to roll in, they launched their revolution with the introduction of a new language of rights and liberty—the kinds of catchphrases "firmly inscribed in every European constitution, not least those of the Peoples' Democracies."[147] A postwar rhetoric of personal liberty, spooling out from the democracies, had infiltrated communism's concrete and barbed-wire barriers. For over a century, Marxist doctrine had sidestepped a serious discussion of individual rights, as Marx did with every substantial challenge to his doctrines, by name-calling ("bourgeois") or by reformulating them solely as aspects of a proletarian workers' paradise. But someone had been listening across the ages to the words of Jefferson and Madison, and, more recently, Churchill. Freedom—individual, personal freedom—was not only real, it was *possible* and there for the taking, even if the Europeans only possessed a very limited understanding of the concept. By the 1970s, a new vocabulary of personal rights not only infused France, Germany, and England, but increasingly was detected in the works of Eastern Europeans, all without the necessary Marxist precursors of "proletarian" or "social."

Adam Michnik in Poland and Miklós Haraszti in Hungary, plus a handful of writers and playwrights in Czechoslovakia, were among the early voices to insist that these rights were a necessary part of socialism—

they were in the constitutions, after all—culminating in Michnik's 1976 essay "A New Evolutionism," which outlined a workers' resistance to communism. This attracted the attention of a young Czech, Václav Havel, the son of a Prague businessman who had lost his wealth in the Communist takeover of 1948. Always a thorn in the side of the government, Havel foreshadowed the "speak truth to power" admonitions of the 1990s, steadily becoming more political and activist. He embodied what some Western churches called "walking by faith," wherein he insisted in a 1984 essay that regardless of what the state demands, *act as though* you were free. This was more than "fake it till you make it," but rather was a means of acting on one's belief: if you truly believe you are free, your actions should reflect it. Or, as Havel told his fellow dissidents, "play at being citizens . . . make speeches as if we were grown-up and legally independent."[148] The people should tell the government how to behave, not vice versa, he insisted. He was only describing—for the first time in almost a century in Europe—America's pillar of common law.

The Poles, though, not the Czechs, were the first to act, forming a workers' committee called KOR in September 1976. This and similar organizations publicized violations of workers' rights, then, in 1979, published a "Charter of Workers' Rights." Those Communist leaders with any sense of history at all certainly must have known about the magical power seemingly inherent in any document with the words "charter," "declaration," "rights," or "liberty" used in the title. From there, the Czechs joined in, with a courageous group affixing their names to another document (labeled a "manifesto" in the West German press—another obviously loaded word), meaning that the proletariat was no longer cowed by the government. Charter 77 bore 243 signatures, but another thousand added their names over time, which still constituted an abysmally small number in Czechoslovakia. Yet just as Lenin had seized power in a nation of 160 million with a core of devout believers numbering fewer than 20,000, so too the numbers may have even seemed in favor of the dissidents.

Looking down from the high cliffs of history, the actions of a few dozen samizdat (a term referring to the copying of suppressed literature, which became a synonym for all clandestine dissident writers) take on mythic proportions. At the time, however, no one was sure what, if any, impact the underground literature was having. Certainly there was a heroic quality that the samizdat, like modern bloggers, ascribed to themselves: because it was, it was important. A Czech intellectual referred to it as the "onanistic satisfaction of publishing . . . for the same two thousand intellectuals, all of whom also write it."[149] Or, put another way, "Just because the regime didn't like you doesn't mean you were talented."[150] It did, however, increase the volume of voices crying out against communism.

Nor were the purely political scribblers the only source of journalistic opposition behind the Iron Curtain; all along, some Catholic Church newspapers had been tolerated by the Communist regimes. But aside from that, the "executioners of thought" had successfully cut off much open, public debate about anything.[151] Poet Joseph Brodsky, who would win a Nobel Prize in 1987, had been labeled a "social parasite" in 1963, and a show trial in 1965 sent Yuli Daniel and Andrei Sinyavsky to prison, providing a further object lesson for those writers with a more rebellious streak. Yet some work, most notably that of Soviet historian Roy Medvedev, slipped into publication in Western outlets from 1965 to 1970, and the samizdat grew increasingly bold, with titles such as "Arrests, Searches, and Interrogations," or "Persecution of Religion." In 1970, the KGB circulated a report warning about the "alarming political tendencies" in the dissident literature.[152]

Rock Around the Bloc

Far more subversive than literature, or even the written word, was music and culture, emanating out from the West like alien transmissions from deep space. First came the products of capitalism, unavailable behind the Iron Curtain except through the black market, most notably Levi's blue jeans. A smuggled pair, which sold for ten dollars in America, could fetch ten times that amount in dollar equivalents in the USSR. Later, after the samizdat had started probing with their verbal bayonets, came rock and roll—the ultimate art form of rebellious youth. When Andrés Segovia said that only the dog and the guitar, among all God's creations, have taken all sizes and shapes to not be separated from man, it was just as true that the music of the guitar—rock and roll—had taken all sizes and shapes not to be separated from man's spirit of freedom. In the material sense, through the form of 45 or 33 rpm vinyl records, Western rock found its way into the hands of Communist youths. Many heard Western music secondhand, with records "distributed on discarded X-ray plates—plastic photographs of bones imprinted with record grooves."[153]

Following the Nagy revolt in Hungary in 1956, the new government under János Kádár sought to neutralize the simmering revolution by permitting hundreds of Wurlitzer jukeboxes into the country. Budapest became a hotbed of bloc-rock, as did Sopot, Poland, where an aspiring journalist and club owner, Franciszek Walicki, packed his Non-Stop Club with Polish cover bands playing Jerry Lee Lewis, Carl Perkins, and Elvis. He even created the first true Polish rock act in 1958, ultimately named the Reds and the Blacks. A second band he formed, the Blues and the Blacks, featured a singer named Czesław Niemen who eventually performed in Paris and sang the first rock and roll hit songs in Poland. In Romania, officials decried the music, which aroused "animal instincts" and developed the youths' "cruelty, contempt, and destructive urges."[154] NATO strategists took notice, observing in the journal *Revue Militaire Générale* that the obsession with rock and roll was time not spent with Marx or Lenin. Elvis's arrival as a new private in Germany terrified the Communists, who saw him as a new weapon in the cold war. East Germany cracked down on rock in 1958, mandating that 60 percent of any music performed had to come from the "peoples' democracies."

Then came the Beatles, whose songs, images, and paraphernalia were everywhere from Leipzig to Leningrad. Mop-top hairstyles became common, and young people sported Beatles buttons sent to them by relatives in the West. Indeed, the Fab Four were counterculture role models—young, funny, and full of energy, in stark contrast to the aging gargoyles of the Communist elite. Riots occurred in Czechoslovakia after local Beatle look-alike bands performed. One reporter, horrified, wrote of the fan behavior, "They wriggled, they fell off the platform and crawled back onto it. . . . I expected them to bite each other at any minute."[155]

Instantly, a host of copycat Iron Curtain bands appeared, including the Illes in Hungary, Bundaratsite in Bulgaria, the Red Guitars in Poland, Czechoslovakia's Olympic, and the USSR's own Time Machine (formed when the father of the guitar player smuggled home a copy of *A Hard Day's Night*). Before the Prague Spring, Czechoslovakia even had a rock music magazine, *Melodie*. In the freest of the Soviet bloc countries, the Czechs had hundreds of bands with names such as Strangers, Buttons, and Hells' Devils—all, of course, registered with the state. But Beatlemania was everywhere: when the film *A Hard Day's Night* opened in Poland in 1965, school absenteeism was described as "rampant" and "the cinemas [were] besieged" as the *bitels* conquered Warsaw.[156] Czech schools responded to their absenteeism by offering a six-part series on modern music, including studies of Elvis and Bill Haley and the Comets. The first Iron Curtain hippies were likely Czechs known as the "little Marys" (*manicky*), but the hippie culture was not confined to any single country. One of East Germany's leading musicians, Horst Krüger, abandoned classical and jazz to only play rock and roll, and when a popular Leipzig band, the Butlers, was forcibly broken up for "damaging art," protests at the high schools had to be dispersed with troops and water cannons.

Rock was at the center of the Prague Spring, particularly a band called the Primitives, one of the earliest Soviet-bloc psychedelic bands. As Alexander Dubček liberalized Czech society, the likelihood of intervention grew, culminating in the Warsaw Pact invasion of August 20, 1968. Of course, oppression was exactly what protest singers needed. Marta Kubišová, the singer for the Golden Kids, penned the anthem of the Czech resistance with her "Prayer for Marta," which was followed by the shocking self-immolation of Jan Palach in January 1969. Another leading Czech protest song, by Moravian singer Karel Kryl, was "Close the Gate, Little Brother" (1969). It became so popular, Kryl toured Czechoslovakia performing three concerts a day, with no manager and no agent, selling 125,000 copies of his song.

In the Soviet Union, despite a relentless propaganda campaign against Western dress and music, the desire for pop music and hippie attire was insatiable. Pictures of Jagger and Hendrix were pasted over Communist slogans on walls, and a burgeoning bourgeois market appeared in Lenin's heartland. Following Beatlemania, the USSR tried a different approach— co-opting the new medium, creating state rock groups and sponsoring approved variety shows, a kind of Ed Sullivanski. Melodya, the state-run publishing house, released some of the Beatles' sheet music, and by the 1970s, hits by some Western artists, including Elvis Presley and Tom Jones, were allowed in the USSR legally. By the late 1960s, hundreds of rock bands had appeared in Moscow, although finding instruments was a challenge: when the first guitar shop opened in Moscow in 1966, the entire stock sold out in minutes.[157] A massive electric underground developed, run by the *fartsovshchiki* ("hustlers"), who hung out around Western tourist sites and cultivated contacts with smugglers. Government thugs routinely stormed concerts to seize instruments. Censors unplugged acts in mid-performance. It scarcely mattered, especially in the Baltic states (which would lead the resistance to Moscow in the early 1990s). Massive illegal concerts took place in woods and forests; musicians, required to submit lyrics to censors, shrugged them off and performed in bars, clubs, canteens, even dorm rooms without publicity so as to avoid authorities.

The Curtain came under constant pressure from inside and out. Blood, Sweat & Tears performed in Romania in 1970, greeted by chants of "U-S-A." After that, the group's concerts were watched intensely. A similar

East Berlin concert, intruded upon by police, erupted in a bloody reaction against the cops when the concertgoers "turned on the security forces, beating them, stripping them, and setting their uniforms on fire."[158]

A Czech rock and roll band, the Plastic People of the Universe, had been at the forefront of the Charter 77 movement in 1978. But getting to that point reflected the pitfalls of Iron Curtain rockdom. A state band had official sanction and received instruments from the government. It came at great cost. Charged with protecting "the red rose of Marxism," bands had to submit their lyrics to censors months before they could record them. The Plastic People of the Universe began as a sanctioned band, but their repertoire of saucy Western material cost them their protected status in the fall of 1970. They dropped out, and started their own music festivals, which attracted large crowds. During a concert in 1976, Plastic People and other musicians were arrested. The band members were given eight- to twelve-month sentences for disturbing the peace, and the band and its fans were harassed by the government for the remainder of the decade.[159]

Large-scale rock riots broke out in East Berlin in June 1987, following a concert across the Wall by Phil Collins, David Bowie, and the Eurythmics, replete with massive loudspeakers aimed eastward. When security forces tried to disperse the thousands pressed against the wall on the eastern side to listen, violence erupted. Frustrated, the East Germans scheduled several rock groups (with figure skater Katarina Witt as moderator) to counter a concert in West Berlin by Pink Floyd and Michael Jackson. That effort failed, and *Le Monde* summed it up by headlining, "East Berlin Loses the Rock War."[160]

The surrender documents were all but drawn up when the Communists invited Bruce Springsteen to perform in East Berlin before 160,000 people in 1988. While the German propagandists had actually read Springsteen's lyrics and knew that his signature song, "Born in the USA," was an antiwar song (he "uncompromisingly points out the inequity and injustices in his country," noted *Neues Deutschland* approvingly), the thousands of young people did not get the memo. Here was the flower of communism, waving American flags, raising their clenched fists, and singing along, "*Born* . . . in the USA! I was . . . *born* in the USA" as though they really *wished* they had been born in America.

Spies such as Vasili Mitrokhin, whose smuggled notes revealed the anti-Soviet influence of rock music, warned that radio broadcasts from the West were producing "unhealthy signs of interest in . . . pop stars" and "almost surreal" levels of subversion in some Russian cities.[161] Spy memos reported that 80 percent of Soviet youth listened to Western music broadcasts, which "gave young people a distorted idea of Soviet reality" (i.e., a realistic view), repeatedly noting the "treasonable nature" of such music.[162] Romanians sponsored sociologists to study the "youth problem," and officials moaned that the young had embraced materialism and cosmopolitanism.[163]

Gorbachev's glasnost policies did not create anything new, but merely reflected what was already in progress. In 1988, the government sold air time to Pepsi, which flashed commercials featuring Michael Jackson with his metal-studded jacket. Similarly, when the Soviets attempted to pick and choose Western movies to grant screenings for inside the USSR, they again badly misunderstood the messages such movies sent (as opposed to the messages they were intended by their producers to carry). Writer David Remnick, touring the Soviet Union just before it unraveled, witnessed a stunning scene in which the Communist bosses showed the then-recent Oliver Stone movie *Wall Street*. Stone's sermon to Americans was that the nation's most prominent financiers got to the top using nefarious means, with no cares for humanity. In the movie, the character played by Michael Douglas, Gordon Gekko, who was modeled after real-life bond trader and convicted felon Ivan Boesky, utters the famous line (which Boesky indeed said in a speech): "Greed is good." As Remnick recalled when he watched the screening at Lenin Hall among the audience of young Communists:

> The young acolytes, presumably the next generation of Leninist priests, reacted to this morality play of American finance in a way that would have made poor Oliver Stone weep. They did not see it as a warning about the perils of greed, not a propaganda cartoon meant to steer the best and the brightest toward a life of goodness and social work. Not at all. They audibly lusted after the goods on display [especially] the fabulous cuffs on Michael Douglas's Turnbull & Asser shirts. God, they loved those shirts. When Charlie Sheen . . . first checked out his new East Side apartment . . . you could hear the sighing of the young Leninists.[164]

When the film came to its climax, with Douglas, in his Boesky imitation, delivering the line "*Zhdanost—eto khorosho!*" ("Greed is good!"), the young Communists "went wild. There were whoops of approval."[165]

The Realities of Being Red

Defenders and apologists for the East Bloc cited any statistic that could be considered remotely positive to tout the virtues of collectivism. Historian Mark Mazower pointed out that not long after the war, the nationalization of health care in Czechoslovakia saw infant mortality fall by two thirds and that in Bulgaria the number of hospital beds doubled over the pre–World War II level.[166] Beds, of course, reflected absolutely nothing of import: in the American health care system, the number of *empty* beds and needless hospitals were scandalous, and often such hospitals could not make a profit because of the overwhelmingly high level of health care. And if child mortality fell in Communist countries, perhaps one could explain the tidal wave of Romanian street orphans? Or education: those proclaiming the wonders of communism celebrate the fact that "in Poland there were 250,000 students in higher education compared with 50,000 before the war; in Hungary some 67,000 by the early 1960s compared with a prewar 11,000."[167] However, young people—what Hungarian Paul Neuburg called "the Hero's children," who were the products of this "good Communist education"—deeply mistrusted a system that deprived them of information while preaching ideology nonstop. Moreover, the information they received was wrong. What good were schools that taught Marxist economics as the world was disproving it? It is akin to celebrating a twentieth-century nation forming a new cavalry division, fully outfitted with first-rate sabers, or adding 80,000 slingers and beaming at the fact they each have five shiny stones!

Furthermore, all of this begged the issue that no one could trust any of the numbers provided by the Communist states. Every bureaucracy and industry maintained shadow records and employed dual bookkeeping, one set for the commissars and one that reflected real activity (always much lower than the statistics fed to the government). If the "light of Stalin shines on Albanian soil," as dictator Enver Hoxha boasted in 1952, the light of truth seldom shone anywhere east of the Danube. The *real* numbers that the apologists glossed over or ignored entirely were the millions living in jails (certainly not counted in unemployment statistics) or otherwise incarcerated. Romania had 100,000 slave workers out of an industrial workforce of 361,000—just over 25 percent, or only a slightly lower percentage than the American antebellum South had black slaves. Over 100,000 forced laborers built the Baltic–White Sea Canal: investigators later discovered the teeth of the workers in camp cemeteries revealed they had eaten tree bark because of their chronically low rations. Another 40,000 workers were used up constructing the Danube–Black Sea Canal.

Added to these pressures were the internal contradictions of communism, wherein state control of the "commanding heights" proved utterly incompetent and corrupt. Economic growth ceased in almost all Iron Curtain countries: to the degree any growth could be measured, it was not Western-style increases in productivity (output per man-hour) but simply putting more hands on the tiller. Czech and East German steel could not be sold at anywhere near market prices. Absorbing resources far beyond what their products could bring, "Soviet-style economies were *subtracting* value—the raw materials they imported or dug out of the ground were worth more than the finished goods into which they were transformed."[168] East Germany, which had a population more than twice that of Austria, produced just one fiftieth the number of computers as the Austrians. The Czechs, who before the war had about as many autos per person as the Austrians, now gazed longingly across the border to their neighbors, who had three times as many cars as they did.

At root, the system was an economic black hole, absorbing capital instead of creating it, stealing from those who had already produced to redistribute to those who had not generated any real value whatsoever. It was high irony indeed that the successful entrepreneurs of the market economy through the ages were routinely derided as selfish when they alone had added to the world stock of goods, while at the same time socialist systems, by definition, could only subtract. If there had been no measuring stick, no point of comparison, perhaps in an economic sense communism could have limped along for another ten or twenty years. But the very wealth that the West generated also produced the revolution in communications that soon made instant comparisons not only possible, but inevitable. Travel, despite tight restrictions, brought with it visions of other possible worlds. Even in Yugoslavia, a faint replica of the Greek and Italian Mediterranean beaches was evolving. By the mid-1970s, more than six million people would travel to Yugoslavian beaches.[169]

Advances in communications opened the eyes of those behind the Iron Curtain, and it was clear they were losing ground to the West. An American in 1979 worked about 12.5 hours to buy a market basket of goods, while an equivalent market basket in England would have required twice as much work time. Even worse, a worker in the Soviet Union would work 42 hours for the same market basket, almost twice the time of his English counterpart.[170] But many a Soviet housewife would literally ask, "What market basket?" When she went to the grocery, it involved hours of waiting in lines. Meat and fresh vegetables were often entirely missing; entire lines of freezers, built to hold frozen meats, fish, and other products, sat empty. American women in the 1980s spoke of shopping, meaning a brief stop at a supermarket and hours of looking at clothes, jewelry, sampling perfume, or lingering over a cup of hot tea while reading *Cosmopolitan*. Shopping in the USSR meant, literally, spending most of one's day in lines to acquire the most basic staples. Remnick, who visited numerous Soviet towns and villages on loosely supervised tours, was shocked to find a level of poverty and want eclipsing that of some Latin American countries. "Byelorussian villagers scavenged scrap metal and pig fat to pay for shoes," while workers in Tyumen, "a Siberian oil region with greater resources than Kuwait, lived in shacks and shabby trailers despite winter temperatures of forty degrees below zero. . . ."[171] Poverty, as he noted, "felt normal," even among the government elites, where a "millionaire" farm chairman could not afford hot running water.

The Kremlin set the poverty line at 78 rubles a month, a level equivalent to what Americans spend on their pets. Even at that, scholars in Moscow at the time knew the real number of people living in poverty was easily double official estimates, or just under *half of the entire Soviet population*! Economist Anatoly Deryabin argued that "only 2.3 percent of all Soviet families can be called wealthy. . . . About 11.2 percent can be called middle-class or well-to-do. The rest, 86.5 percent, are simply poor."[172] Russia under Czar Nicholas II had done better. A more stunning comparison was this: the American colonies, on the eve of revolution in 1770, had a higher per capita real income than did Gorbachev's Soviet Union 220 years later![173]

Within any system where prices do not maintain a discipline of efficiency and levy a heavy penalty for waste, both are inevitable. Waste in the context of heavy industry translated directly into pollution and environmental disaster. Communist states, simply put, were the filthiest places on earth: brown coal use in Bohemia left it with smog that exceeded that of Los Angeles on its worst days, while the Czech government created a hospital service for children's respiratory problems. A third of Czech forests "were dead or dying, and one-third of all Czech watercourses were too polluted even for industrial use," both of which paled in comparison to the environmental disasters of the Soviet state, where the Aral Sea was eradicated by siphoning off water for agricultural uses.[174] Any farmer or manager who undertook pollution controls under his own initiative that might restrict output was open to punishment.[175]

No "iron law of wages" has ever existed, but a very real iron law of economics does: the money must come from somewhere. If no one would buy shabby Eastern European or Russian goods and products, and if the economies did not grow sufficiently to address even the most basic consumer needs, how could any state prevent rebellions short of Stalinist shootings and hangings? Gorbachev's answer was glasnost. Open up to a degree, and invite Western financiers in with the promise of interest payments. Credit, supplied by the International Monetary Fund, the World Bank, or even Western private bankers, flowed into the Soviet bloc countries. Poland's debt increased 3,000 percent, rising $2 billion per year. Czechoslovakia's hard currency debt rose twelvefold, and two thirds of East Germany's entire export earnings went just to service the interest on the state's borrowing. In less than a decade, the overall indebtedness of the East Bloc nations soared from just over $6 billion to $66 billion, then, astonishingly enough, it really took off, rising to $95.6 billion by 1990.

The solution, of course, was a price system, which the Communists could not permit because for prices to work, there must be a free market and private property—in essence, accepting at least two of the American pillars of exceptionalism. For any true price system to exist in the USSR would have been the equivalent of turning a horse into a marsupial: communism ceased to exist the instant real prices came into play. Lenin had said the capitalists would sell him the rope needed for the gallows, yet reality proved just the opposite. The financial nooses that Western bankers provided to East Germany, then later, the Soviet Union, strangled them by transferring "large sums of hard currency [which] unintentionally foreclosed any chance of internal change" in the East Bloc countries, most notably the German Democratic Republic.[176] The rope, in this case, caused the East Germans to dangle for years without reform, sucking away dissidents and intellectuals, making it appear all the more impossible for Communist-led transformations to occur.

Since power could not be obtained directly but only through petty (and some major) corruption that interlaced the entire population with winks, nods, and mutual cheating, it was "one of the paradoxes of the Socialist project that the absence of property tends to generate more corruption."[177] Yet faced with unsustainable debt, collapsing productivity levels, and corruption, Communist leaders could think of no alternative than to sink their ship and go down with it, carrying the anchor of communism to the seabed. Certainly Gorbachev did not think he was ending communism in the Soviet Union, contrary to the fawning assessments of modern American historians. The extent of their lack of understanding of the collapse of the Soviet Union is astounding, claiming "Gorbachev's reform policies led not only to the collapse of the Soviet empire but also to the breakup of the Soviet Union itself," or "Gorbachev also backed off Soviet imperial ambitions."[178] Praise of Gorbachev in such textbooks is so effusive as to credit him with curing everything from cancer to baldness, yet as Remnick, who viewed the USSR firsthand, rightly observed, "there is absolutely no evidence to suggest that Gorbachev was out to undermine, much less destroy, the basic tenets of ideology or statehood of the Soviet Union."[179]

Rather, Gorbachev attempted to put a modern face on Soviet communism, to make it palatable to younger generations, all the while cognizant that the Gipper had put him on a rapidly expiring hourglass as a result of the American military buildup. His restructuring (perestroika) of the Leninist model caused Western liberals to break into cheers that the Soviets were maturing: in fact, Gorbachev, in between fuming that the United States was suffering from "delusions," declared that Marxism was the wave of the future.[180] (Reagan had just put it on the "ash heap of history.") Gorbachev's book *Perestroika*, released in the West in 1987, lauded Lenin and his "ideals of socialism." Lenin, he promised, "lives on in the minds and the hearts of millions of people."[181] Now, Lenin had to be kicked to the curb, and soon, if the USSR was to survive: Russia had to become economically viable overnight, because the last vestige of power—its military might— had been yanked away. The "Upper Volta with missiles" was rapidly becoming merely the Upper Volta.

Contrary to the perception that Gorbachev acted with grit and decisiveness, he dawdled for two years until, in 1987, he finally sought a break with the past. First, at the urging of Politburo member Aleksandr Yakovlev and Foreign Minister Eduard Shevardnadze, he permitted a film, *Repentance*, to be shown. Directed by Tengiz Abuladze, an important but not iconic Russian filmmaker, *Repentance* was the story of a man unjustly condemned to prison, who finally returns home to dig up the corpse of the man who sent him away. It depicted the Stalinist camps with harsh realism, picking open the scab of the propagandized past. Gorbachev tried to buffer the impact, allowing limited screenings, leading up to his 1987 speech on the fiftieth anniversary of Red October.

He previewed the speech before the Politburo, using the opportunity to label Stalin a "criminal," and, for the first time, to lay out in detail the purges of the Stalinist terror. Party bosses panicked. Yegor Ligachev warned that exposing the specifics of Stalinism would "mean canceling our entire lives!. . . . We are opening the way for people to spit on our history."[182] The speech was given, nonetheless, on November 2, 1987, before a pavilion of Marxist celebrities, including Castro, Erich Honecker of East Germany, and Daniel Ortega of Nicaragua. "If today we look into our history with an occasionally critical gaze," he explained, "it is only because we want to get a better, fuller idea of our path into the future."[183] Whether he realized what he had done or not, Gorbachev had thrown the first shovelful of dirt on communism's grave.

Again, food proved communism's Achilles' heel. In March 1991, one of Gorbachev's aides wrote in his diary, "Yesterday the Security Council met on the food issue. . . . In Moscow and other cities there are [bread] lines like the ones two years ago for sausage. . . . I drove around Moscow . . . the bakeries are padlocked or terrifyingly empty."[184] The only exit was through a price system that would allow farmers to sell their grain for profit, and Gorbachev gave in. But it was too late.

The nationalities had rapidly broken loose, and Gorbachev had neither the will nor the troops to bring them to heel. Within months, Soviet communism was dead. Marchers in the May Day parade carried not rifles but signs reading "Socialism? No Thanks!" or "Communists: Have No Illusions. You Are Bankrupt."[185] In 2002, Gorbachev fessed up to what he knew all along:

> We, including I, were saying "Capitalism is moving toward a catastrophe, whereas we are developing well." Of course, that was pure propaganda. In fact, our country was lagging behind. . . . We did move directly [under perestroika]—but into an abyss. . . . [Soviet politicians] were discussing the problem of toothpaste . . . detergent . . . and they had to create a commission of the politburo to make sure that women have pantyhose.[186]

Gorbachev had belatedly realized that the greatest opponent of communism was neither Reagan nor Thatcher, but the inherent impossibility of any command economy or totalitarian state to possess all the answers, whereas the Gipper and the Iron Lady knew better from the outset.

Eco-Disasters of Communism

The question for history books is, "When did the cold war end?" One answer, not entirely incorrect, was given by Soviet spokesman Gennadi Gerasimov. At a joint news conference during the Malta Summit on December

3, 1989, aboard the Soviet ship *Maxim Gorky*, Gorbachev and Reagan's successor, President George H. W. Bush, declared the cold war over.[187]

However, others argued that the Soviet Union "collapsed, practically and metaphorically, at 1:23 A.M., April 26, 1986, the moment of the nuclear accident at Chernobyl."[188] During a planned test at the Ukrainian nuclear plant, an operator error shut off automatic shutdown mechanisms. When the reactor reached unstable levels, the human operators moved too slowly to react. The reactor exploded and released one hundred times the amount of radiation of Hiroshima and Nagasaki, dousing millions of Eastern and Western Europeans and killing thirty emergency personnel immediately.

Soviet bureaucrats dragged their feet in the hours after the explosion, describing it as a mishap. Before the populations were evacuated, children played in radioactive dirt, and the Young Communist League sponsored sixteen outdoor weddings the following day.[189] The annual May Day parade was held a week later in most nearby towns, even as Party officials evacuated their own families. Workers in the region received thirty-five rubles a month from the government, which they called a "coffin bonus," for laboring there. Over time, more than 30,000 have traced their diseases to the accident—more than 2,000 thyroid cancers alone—and 200,000 people eventually were evacuated, after a thirty-six-hour delay. Remnick, traveling near Narodichi in the early 1990s, interviewed farm directors who reported numerous animal deformities, including calves born without heads, ribs, and eyes, and pigs with defective skulls. Yet locals were expected to feed farm animals fodder from contaminated fields, and four years after the blast, meat from the radiated farms was shipped to stores in Siberia, turned into sausage with radiation levels ten times too high.

Since no ecological disasters were permitted in the Socialist Republic, doctors received orders that prohibited them from citing radiation poisoning as a cause of death for three years. More than two weeks after the disaster, Gorbachev finally went on television to "inform" the Soviet citizens, spending much of his time attacking Western media for covering the event. Long after the reactor had ceased to burn (having been encased in concrete), visitors with official passes had to take a "dirty" van protected against radiation before crossing into the ghost towns that had once supported workers of the power plant. Despite the danger, scavengers snuck in to strip parts from radioactive cars and sell them on the black market; cleanup personnel were limited to two-week tours of duty. One Chernobyl worker noted that only the danger the plant still posed to others kept a few "heroes" there: Chernobyl, he concluded, "could be the great monument to the Soviet empire."[190]

Certainly it wasn't the only such monument, only the one best covered by the Western press. That same year, a Soviet passenger liner, *Admiral Nakhimov*, sank in the Black Sea, claiming four hundred lives, and shortly after that, a Soviet ballistic missile submarine with its cargo of nuclear weapons vanished in the Atlantic. In 1957, a nuclear waste tank in the Urals had blown up (although this was not made public until the 1970s), dumping tons of radioactive waste into regional rivers and forcing the government to bulldoze more than twenty villages. In 1979, anthrax was accidentally discharged near the Cheliabinsk-40 chem/bio weapons facility, killing hundreds.[191]

Not only were such disasters covered up, but even when those inside the Soviet government raised red flags beforehand, no action was taken. KGB reports from 1982 and 1984 noted "shoddy" equipment used in the construction of Soviet nuclear reactors, specifically singling out two of Chernobyl's reactors (including the one that burst). Nothing was done. The report was buried. Had a massive cloud observable from space not exposed Chernobyl to the outside world, it is doubtful Gorbachev ever would have requested foreign assistance. This, in turn, revealed the superpower's utter helplessness to deal with a disaster after the fact.[192]

What Gorbachev had proclaimed as a "golden age" ahead when he took power had moved from a debacle toward a disaster. Leftist historian Tony Judt, while writing glowingly of Gorbachev, nevertheless admitted he "failed utterly" to achieve his objective of a "reformed and efficient communism."[193] Whether Gorbachev was so naive as to think his efforts at opening a totalitarian society could result in anything other than the complete destruction of such a system, or whether that was his intent in the first place, is irrelevant. If Western elites wished to credit him with vision and daring, so be it. In truth, he walked the already teetering Soviet colossus right into the bear pit laid by Reagan, with stakes reinforced by the pope, Solidarity, free expression, and rock music. Like an oyster pried apart by a squid exerting constant pressure, the weary USSR surrendered, not with a bang, but with a shrug.[194]

CHAPTER SEVEN

The Age of Boomer Ascendance

TIME LINE

1990: East and West Germany unify; Iraq invades Kuwait

1991: Gulf War liberates Kuwait; Boris Yeltsin elected president of Russia; Warsaw Pact dissolved; Soviet Union broken up

1992: Rio Earth Summit Declaration creates Agenda 21; Yugoslavia breaks up; European Union founded by Maastricht Treaty; Falun Gong organized in China; Czechoslovakia split into the Czech Republic and Slovakia; China adopts a "socialist market economy"; Bill Clinton elected president

1993: World Trade Center bombing; North American Free Trade Agreement (NAFTA) passed; Clinton administration introduces "Hillarycare"

1994: Republicans win control of both houses in Congress

1995: Clinton makes emergency loan to Mexico to avoid collapse; NATO bombing campaign against Serbia; Venona project documents made public

1996: Welfare reform passed; Clinton wins reelection; Sudan offers Osama bin Laden to Clinton administration

1997: Britain returns Hong Kong to China

1998:   Monica Lewinsky scandal; bilingual program abolished
         in California by referendum; terrorist bombings of Amer-
         ican embassies in Africa; Clinton impeached

1999:   EU establishes euro; NATO attacks Federal Republic of
         Yugoslavia (Serbia); Panama Canal turned over to Panama

2000:   India joins China in having more than a billion people;
         Clinton signs U.S. agreement to recognize World Crim-
         inal Court; USS *Cole* attacked by al-Qaeda; George W.
         Bush elected president

New Global Order

The date was 9/11, and the U.S. president, George Bush, was addressing the
nation on national security when he uttered a phrase that sent chills down
the spines of nationalists everywhere, especially old-fashioned American
patriots. Bush noted, "Out of these troubled times . . . a new world order . . .
can emerge: a new era."[1] Only the president was not George W. Bush, but
his father, George Herbert Walker Bush, and the comments had nothing to
do with terrorism or al-Qaeda, but came on September 11, 1990, when addressing a joint session of Congress about aggression by Saddam Hussein
and Iraq. Subsequently Bush would sign the North American Free Trade
Agreement, or NAFTA (which was ratified under his successor, Bill Clinton), joining Canada, Mexico, and the United States in a free trade zone
that, to conspiracy theorists, marked another step in the path to a "one
world government." Bush's phrase, then, could not have been more ominous from that perspective.

As the 1990s unfolded, change viewed as almost impossible just five
years earlier occurred rapidly. The Soviet Evil Empire fell, but an equally
malevolent ideology would take its place in the form of radical Islamic fundamentalism. Japan, once considered an unbeatable economic powerhouse,
started a slow, steady decline marked as much by its aging population as by
its lack of market and military clout. The countries of Western Europe,
desperate to place themselves on an equal footing with the (now) sole superpower, the United States, would enthusiastically embrace the destruction of
their own national sovereignties by establishing a regional authority for
governance. And America, still riding the coattails of Ronald Reagan's military buildup and economic boom, would deliberately ignore, minimize, or
excuse terrorist attacks and activity that portended a worldwide conflict just
years away.

Globalism—the catch-word of the late twentieth century—was in the air following NAFTA and the Europeans who already had done extensive groundwork for regional integration, first with the Economic Community, then with the Common Market. Their move toward integration culminated in 1992 with the Maastricht Treaty (actually only a series of amendments to previous treaties, primarily the 1957 Treaty of Rome and the 1986 Single European Act), which created the European Union, and the Treaty of Lisbon (2007), which formalized a constitution for the new superstate and permanently established regional governance by unelected elites.

Although European integration was already in progress, developments in America, especially deregulation during the Reagan administration, had a monumental impact on Europe. Velocity of growth in American entrepreneurship, new product development, and the cost of capital changed overnight, panicking Europeans who believed in the benefits of accelerating the creation of a monolithic Europe. With the Single European Act, which removed three hundred nontariff trade barriers by 1992 and included open bidding for public contracts regardless of nationality, member nations essentially adopted free trade among themselves regardless of national characteristics and diverse populations. National sovereignty took a huge hit, such as when fishing in Great Britain's territorial waters, formerly reserved strictly to British nationals, was suddenly open to all members of the European Union. Much of the impetus for integration came from the French socialist and former finance minister Jacques Delors, who became president of the European Commission in 1985. Described as a "high-strung, overbearing, rude, thin-skinned, dynamic, inexhaustible, creative, independent, deeply mystical, outwardly conventional, elusive, and maddening though irreplaceable loner," Delors favored a conservative Europe focused on trade, not growth.[2] A socialist influenced by Michel Albert's *Capitalism Against Capitalism*, an attack on American models of individuality and competition, Delors dominated the direction of European thinking on integration for the next decade.[3]

A key component of European integration was a monetary union which, although not mentioned in the European Economic Community Treaty of Rome, was implicit at the outset. The 1970 Werner Report, for example, called for a single monetary unit within ten years, and by 1988 the Hanover European Council, charged with studying and proposing specific steps to a monetary union, concluded that an economically united Europe required a single market, fiscal and budgetary discipline, and unification of money matters.[4] From such thinking emerged the euro, a common monetary unit to be enacted in 1999. Martin Feldstein, former chairman of Reagan's Council of Economic Advisers, warned that the shift toward a single currency would amount to a "dramatic and irreversible" step toward a European federal union.[5]

Resistance surfaced on several fronts, mainly because economic unity was correctly seen as ultimately forcing political unity and the loss of national sovereignty. In Denmark, popular opposition to the Maastricht Treaty "sprang up spontaneously and apparently out of nowhere."[6] France barely approved the treaty 51 to 49 percent, while Britain under Prime Minister John Major opted out of the monetary union, firing two ministers who threatened to resign if Britain did not join. In 1990, Delors received the brunt of British resistance to the Maastricht Treaty, culminating with the headline from the *Sun*, "Up Yours Delors." (Needless to say, the French translation lacked the same poetry).

Part of the opposition was concerned with a loss of national sovereignty, as the nature of the union transformed fairly rapidly from a confederation to a federation. As such arguments appeared, the Europeanists altered their vocabulary, and the Treaty of Lisbon established five categories of "areas of competence": "exclusive" to the EU; "shared," where the member states are prohibited from acting if the EU does; "shared," where EU action does not prohibit states from acting; "shared," where the EU can supplement acts by member states; and "supporting," where the Union can support, coordinate, or supplement activities of member states. The list of exclusive and shared competence areas where Union acts are determining include monetary policy and those items truly defining sovereignty. Essentially, only the areas of health, industry, culture, tourism, education, disaster prevention, research, technological development, space, development cooperation, and humanitarian aid remained under the control of the member states. Following the treaty, the EU had become a federal authority, and the member nations, although they could secede, held less sovereignty than American states.

Ironically, the greatest threat to the economic stability of the Union did not come from the nations that refused to join, but from the one looked to as the leader, Germany. Almost immediately after the Berlin Wall crumbled, East Germany held its first free elections since 1945. Helmut Kohl, a Christian Democrat who had held the chancellorship in West Germany since 1982, made a trip to Moscow in 1990 to secure Gorbachev's guarantee that the USSR would not intervene in German reunification. As the East German economy fell into paralysis, there were calls on both sides to reunify Germany. Both parliaments approved, and East Germany formally ceased to exist in October 1990. But the Federal Republic's economy was weakened by ingesting 17 million poor people with few viable industries (the former German Democratic Republic), and reunification threatened ruinous results. Easterners were promised a level of 80 percent of the wages of Westerners within five years. Money flowed out of Germany, investment money refused to stay, and unemployment in the former East rose to between 20 and 30 percent.

There were religious implications for German politics as well. From the viewpoint of the Christian Democratic Union (CDU), a primarily Catholic party, the East Germans were traditionally 95 percent Protestant, and would almost surely give the Social Democrats a permanent majority in the Bundestag. Reunification, so long a part of the CDU's party platform, was seen as the death knell of the party in practical terms by party leaders unless European integration took place and alliances could be built with other Catholic parties. From the beginning, therefore, all was not what it appeared. East Germany had been Communist, but at least as late as the middle 1960s, religion was still a powerful force that, in a sense, bound the East to the West, particularly since communism had failed to win the hearts and minds of those in the East.

Integration's promises of a "new Europe" soon dimmed with the recession of the 1990s and the seemingly inevitable oppression of paperwork and restrictions. Once the economic committee got rolling, it alone produced 1,100 regulations. Ensconced in its twenty-five-square-mile section of Brussels, the "Eurocracy" served as home to some 10,000 professional lobbyists begging for favors—one for every 1.3 officials—and more than 200 corporations established government affairs offices in Brussels. National governments found themselves serving as rubber stamps for the Brussels bureaucracy; in France, for example, almost 80 percent of its legislation by 2006 was simply enacting EU regulations and edicts. Regulations turned out by the Eurocracy's additional level of government also exacted a drag on economic growth throughout Europe. Unemployment in the EU soared up to 17 million by 1993, with some states hit harder than others. For example, between 1990 and 1993, 20 percent of Swedish industrial jobs disappeared, unemployment rose to 8 percent (not including government make-work schemes), and by 1993 Sweden's deficits (at a high of 13 percent) led Europe.

Italy, which struggled under corruption, bribery, and overstaffing in public agencies, witnessed a dampening of entrepreneurship. The government routinely overpaid for services and supplies, while bribery constituted a tax on virtually all consumption and production.[7] By the early 1990s, one fifth of the population supported the other four fifths, leading one Italian political commentator, Indro Montanelli, to glumly conclude, "Ours is a servile race, incapable of self-government, which is looking to Europe for salvation."[8] Anemic economic growth afflicted Italy throughout the decade: instead of creating more competition, Italy ended up with a quasi-monopolistic electricity industry, while taxes and labor regulations became more burdensome. Prime Minister Silvio Berlusconi came to power promising a "Copernican turn" to reinvent Italy. Instead, the "old Italy" reappeared, resplendent with a "cozy, intimate network of family dynasties who between them control the country's financial and economic life."[9]

Belgium's political class was a huge burden to the state: there were fifty-eight ministers, secretaries of state, and special commissars, each of whom was entitled to six limos, each driven by a personal chauffeur earning more than $37,000 per year. Wallonia, with only three million people, had seventeen ministers, including three for education.[10] Ever willing to invoke government as the savior, in 1993, Delors typically responded with new studies, more proposals, and expanded calls for government activism. In 1993, he presented a white paper called "Growth, Competitiveness, and Employment," promising to create 15 million new jobs, which, of course, never came close to materializing.

The inability of the EU to rescue European economies was reflected in the growing apathy of Europeans for the machinery of government. Turnout for elections to the Euro Parliament fell from 63 percent in 1979 to 49 percent in 1999 because the EU was not democratic at all—it had no real representative institutions. The EU seemed at once "pompous and threatening yet meddlesome and impotent."[11] Unable to obtain results in the real world, the EU sought to reshape perceptions, hiring Jean-Baptiste Duroselle, who wrote *Europe: A History of Its Peoples*, to write a new history presenting Europe's story as "a march of progress culminating in the benign leadership of the EU."[12] This, and other efforts at indoctrinating Europeans (and American leftists) to view the EU as the agency of salvation, had questionable results.

To see the truth of the Eurocracy, one needs to look no further than the opening line of the Lisbon Treaties that formally established the EU. Whereas the Constitution of the United States begins, "We the People of the United States . . ." the Lisbon Treaty of 2007, which amended the European Union Constitution produced in the Rome Treaty but never ratified, starts, "His Majesty the King of the Belgians, the President of the

Republic of Bulgaria . . ."[13] Even the constitution produced at Rome in 2004 started, "The states and peoples of the Union . . ." Europeans truly have a different idea of the role of the people in government than Americans. In Europe, the heads of states are sovereign (although highly limited according to the Treaty of Lisbon), whereas in the United States, sovereignty resides in the people.

To American readers the structure of the EU might look strange, as the legislative function is split between two bodies, the Parliament and Council, and the executive function between the Commission and Council. There is also a European Court that has consistently found that law made by the Union trumps national law in the member nations. The Council is made up of the member states' heads of state, and they appoint Commission members, one from each member state. They also elect the president of the Commission. The Parliament can either accept or reject the Commission as a slate, but cannot approve or disapprove individual Commission appointees. At that point, the Commission becomes the dominant power, not only because it controls the EU bureaucracy and the creation of regulations by the thousands, but also because all legislation must be initiated and written by the Commission. Parliament, directly elected by the citizens in each member's home nation, votes on the legislation, and if conflicts emerge, the bills go to the Council, acting somewhat like the American Senate, for rework and compromise. There is also a citizens' initiative allowed for petitions of a million signatures or more, but the Commission is under no obligation to take any action on such initiatives. All this tends to place primary power in the Commission, an appointed body with five-year terms (although approved by Parliament). And this structure reflects the reforms of the Treaty of Lisbon; before it, Parliament was little more than a debating society.

All the while that Europe plowed blockheadedly forward toward a federal union, examples of success through market reforms in the individual states were being ignored or discounted. The Netherlands, for example, reduced its public sector—the share of public expenditure fell from 66 percent in 1985 to 43 percent in 2000—touching off the "Dutch Miracle." Jobs increased at four times Europe's overall rate, unemployment held at 4 percent, and the Netherlands climbed from the bottom of eleven Euro northwestern countries in growth performance to number seven by 1997. Budget surpluses in 2001 led to a tax cut. Nonetheless, the march toward a union continued unabated.

Whenever the EU turned to the free market, the national economies started to revive. In response to the recession, the EU abolished 6,300 qualitative restrictions against outside imports, reduced surveillance in such areas as machine tools and electronics, and eliminated tariffs altogether for steel, paper, furniture, construction equipment, farm machinery, and pharmaceuticals. Naturally, it worked. Writing of economics around the world, economist Jeffrey Sachs noted the "puzzle is not that capitalism triumphed but that it took so long."[14] In the case of Europe, the puzzle is why statism was even considered as a solution in the first place. Its only positive effect had been to create a boom elsewhere for smaller countries outside the EU. Even those countries traditionally governed by parties of the Left (Norway, New Zealand, and Australia, for example) found themselves caught up in "sweeping changes" brought about by exposure to the international market while the EU stumbled.[15]

Nowhere were the national economic miracles more noticeable than in Finland and Ireland. Finland, by 1993, had official unemployment of 18 percent and had seen its output fall 11 percent in two years. All the major indicators were heading the wrong direction when the thirty-six-year-old Esko Aho was elected prime minister. His Reaganesque approach involved cutting taxes, reducing the budget, decentralizing the nation's educational structure, battling the unions, and lifting restrictions on foreign investment. The stock exchange soared. Foreign share ownership grew from almost zero to 20 percent. By 1994, Finland enjoyed a budget surplus, unemployment had moved down, and a shift from public to private sectors was evident. Nokia, the largest private company in Finland, had the highest capitalized value of any publicly traded Euro company. Accounting for 10 percent of Finland's GNP, with only 5 percent of its product sold in Finland, Nokia held 20 percent of the world handset market. Half of the company's employees were foreign.

The Finns, described as a nation of "technoholics," who "half-believe themselves possessed of a special e-chromosome," became the most tech-heavy nation in Europe.[16] *The Economist* in 1999 noted, "the Finns have a particular affinity with mobile phones. The air is a-twitter with personalized ring tones." People "clatter from bar to bar on skis. Even so they manage to keep their mobile phones stuck to their ears."[17] By 1999, some 92 percent of all Finnish households had cell phones, most kids received their first phone at age seven, and 1,700 electronics and electrical firms had developed to supply Nokia. One survey of the world's most competitive countries had Finland in second place, behind only the United States.

Eclipsing Finland in terms of overcoming pro-statist tendencies was

Ireland, whose economic growth was reported by virtually all as a miracle. Slashing taxes and wooing foreign investors, by the 1990s Ireland was racing past other members of the sluggish EU. For the first time, residents recalled, help wanted ads were placed overseas. Like India, Ireland largely accomplished the feat with high-tech productivity, encouraging Hewlett-Packard (which had its largest overseas plant in Ireland) and some of the largest pharmaceutical plants in the world to set up shop in the Emerald Isle.

What worked, as seen in Finland and Ireland, were free markets—when they were tried and allowed to flourish. Unable to directly challenge the economic success of places such as Margaret Thatcher's England, critics complained that, "as an *economy*, then, Thatcherized Britain was a more efficient place. But as a *society* it suffered a meltdown. . . ."[18] As usual, however, the truth was far more complex. The "fabric of social life" that observers claim was damaged by Thatcher and/or the "individualist ethic" included "socially-defined goods" such as public spaces, which "fell into neglect," or a "growing share of the population caught in permanent poverty."[19] Yet socially defined goods by their very name are determined by society: roads in the United States at one time were entirely built and maintained by the private sector, as were universities; some of the finest parks and museums in the world were (and are still being) established by individuals, not by government; and a century earlier, a walking trail or bicycle path would not have been be considered a public good by even the wildest-eyed of reformers. Moreover, recent trends toward privatizing many public functions, including garbage pickup, education, and penal systems, and even roads and highways, indicate that the public's definitions of such goods changes. And usually it changes when some can get others to pay for their social goods.

Global Gomorrah

It was not the free market but liberal policies, including allowing heavy immigration from Islamic countries, whose populations had no intention of assimilating, that produced much of the petty crime and delinquency that afflicted Britain. In the United States, where Reaganism continued to shape the economy throughout the 1990s, most of the social trends had turned around in a positive direction. This constituted a remarkable but temporary reversal of social indicators that had led former Reagan education secretary William Bennett to release his *Index of Leading Cultural Indicators* in 1993. Bennett noted that the United States had experienced "substantial social regression" over the previous three decades (1960–90), including a 500 percent increase in violent crime; 400 percent increase in illegitimate births; nearly 300 percent increase in welfare children; 100 percent increase in divorce; and a decline of seventy points on SATs. Bennett's tome was followed by Robert Bork's 1996 book, *Slouching Toward Gomorrah*, which concluded: "perhaps nothing will be done to reverse the direction of our culture . . . the degeneracy we see about us will only become worse."[20]

Bork and Bennett were not alone in predicting the collapse of Western civilization—Pat Buchanan, former Nixon adviser, perpetually led the gloomster brigade and made a cottage industry of writing about the end of America. But it really should have come as no surprise that many of the social challenges started to show improvement as the effects of a decade's worth of the Reagan economy took hold. These were then enhanced by critical policy changes forced by the 1994 Republican House of Representatives, which had come into office on the basis of the Contract with America. No change was more important than the 1995 Welfare Reform Act, which the House passed twice and which Bill Clinton vetoed twice, before polling data finally convinced him to sign it into law.

That legislation limited the time someone could be on the welfare rolls (two years at a time, five years total), ending the perpetual life on the dole. To the howls of criticism from the Left, which warned that the poor would not find jobs, but would become homeless, or that welfare mothers would have more abortions, the Republicans, led by Speaker Newt Gingrich, held firm. Within five years, the results clearly showed that most of those who left welfare went to *work*, while disincentives to having children did not result in higher abortion levels. By 2007, welfare caseloads were down 60 percent and every state had reduced welfare by one third, some by 90 percent, while abortion decreased from 1.6 million in 1990 to below 1.3 million. While the number of women on welfare absolutely declined—and contrary to what liberals claimed, the changes did not result in *more* women on welfare—the underlying dynamic of disincentives to marry remained. A 2002 study of welfare reform found that "welfare generosity appears to be positively associated with divorce," and while the research "has not reached a consensus," it was safe to say that welfare reduced incentives to marry.[21]

Other indicators were also pointing toward improvements in society. According to the National Crime Victimization Survey (NCVS), violent and property crimes fell from 1993 to 2005, reaching their lowest levels since recording began in 1973. Teen drug use moved downward, especially the use of LSD (down 50 percent) and Ecstasy (MDMA). The younger generation also seemed more conservative in some ways. Americans aged eighteen to thirty-five were the most likely of all age groups to oppose abortion, for example, while the number of high school students having sex fell by 10 percent. Teen drinking fell significantly. Education scores rose; the high school dropout rate reached a ten-year low; and SAT scores rose by eight points since 1993. But improvement had not occurred across the board, and problem areas remained. The marriage rate had fallen by half since 1970—but so had divorce rates, to their lowest level since 1970. Cohabitation was up, as was illegitimacy, constituting 37 percent of all births by 2005. Marriages became more selective, with fewer teen marriages. Pornography was as prevalent as ever, marijuana use was down, but cocaine use had dramatically increased since the 1970s. In short, there were still problems, but social indicators had made a U-turn in many areas, and some of the changes were dramatic. The data showed anything but an across-the-board social collapse. Instead, they revealed a dramatic transformation along generational lines. Like many trends in history, however, this one was destined to be short-lived. By 2012, the ever-increasing leftist assault against Christianity and the other pillars of American exceptionalism had once again put the United States on course for the "fundamental transformation" promised by President Obama.

Identifying overall trends in Europe was more difficult because individual nations still had well-defined cultures. Social indicators were bouncing all over in European states whose policies differed as starkly as the Netherlands—which allowed nearly anything—to still conservative Spain and Italy. The Dutch made abortion readily available, drugs were easily obtained, and prostitutes were unionized (as was the army). Belgium, the epicenter of the Eurocracy, had more than its share of violent crime and corruption, including the Brabant murders of twenty people around supermarkets in the Brussels area.[22]

The obsession with violence in America has largely been a function of the introspective American media, which also tended to dismiss any pathologies outside the United States as exceptions to the rule that the Europeans were better. Yet Europe had its share of horrors. The most significant Flemish case of crime and corruption was the Marc Dutroux affair. Dutroux was a convicted pedophile who abducted, drugged, imprisoned, then raped girls during the 1980s before being apprehended. Due to colossal incompetence (and some would say obvious corruption), he served only a brief stint in prison before convincing a psychiatrist that he was disabled, allowing him to receive a $2,000 per month disability pension upon his release. He also persuaded the doctor that he needed sleeping pills—which he used to keep his female prisoners sedated. With another arrest in August 1996, the investigation this time discovered the bodies of four little girls in homes he owned, as well as two other girls found alive, caged and starved. Dutroux's wife admitted she knew about the imprisoned girls because she fed the dogs in the house but was too afraid of Dutroux to either call the police or feed the girls.[23] Dutroux even told a police informer—whom he asked about acquiring young girls—that he was building a dungeon in his basement. The affair sniffed of high-level collusion and utter incompetence. Dutroux, who "had no visible means for the purchase of several homes," was "no mere solo pervert but a well-established purveyor of little girls" for patrons who had sadism and torture parties.[24] The only magistrate to advance the investigation, Jean-Marc Connerotte, was obstructed at every turn and pressured to stop. "Never before in Belgium has an investigating judge . . . been subjected to such pressure," he later said.[25]

Connerotte was eventually dismissed under conflict of interest charges after he had dinner with some of the victims' families, whereupon 300,000 outraged Belgian women dressed in white marched on the Palais de Justice in Brussels, nearly bringing down the left-center government and weakening it so that it collapsed with the next scandal (involving tainted chickens).[26] Dutroux was finally convicted in June 2004 of murder and a half-dozen other crimes, and received life imprisonment. The case was considered so infamous and evil that the name Dutroux achieved quisling-like qualities: one third of Belgians with the surname Dutroux have applied to have their name changed since 1996.[27]

Spain had its own scandals, though there was nothing in the Spanish experience as bloody as the Dutroux affair.[28] The number of articles with the word "corruption" in the title tripled from 1992 through 1996, a sure sign that Spain was not corruption free. The Boyer scandal followed two decades of economic growth in which "the working class was able for the first time to participate in consumerism . . . occasioning a kind of *embourgeoisement* of the masses [and] a partial erosion of the class barriers that strongly favored the establishment of political democracy."[29] During the growth years, however, corruption had plagued Spain's bureaucracies and politicians, with one of the most prominent scandals involving Carmen Salanueva, the publisher of the laws of parliament, who engaged in false invoicing and other swindles, including impersonating the queen of Spain.[30]

The worst, however, tainted the careers of the "two men who dictated monetarist economic policies" (labeled by *The New York Times* as "Spain's best and brightest"): Miguel Boyer, the former finance minister, and Mari-

ano Rubio, the former governor of the Bank of Spain.[31] Boyer and Rubio
were part of a new political wing (known, appropriately, as "the Beautiful")
that applied monetarist ideas to Spain's economy.[32] Overhauling Spain's an-
tiquated banking system, the new, open system allowed the stock market to
modernize and industry to thrive. And the Beautiful made for good reading: Rubio, Boyer, and their wives were often followed by the paparazzi,
whose stories of "exotic vacations and yachting excursions," with accompanying photos of their mansions at the Costa del Sol resort of Marbella,
made them the envy of average Spaniards. Boyer was "married to a knock-
out model," the former wife of singer Julio Iglesias; had a jet-set lifestyle;
and regularly graced the pages of Spanish culture glossies such as *Hola!*

After leaving office in 1985, Boyer headed some holding companies
controlled by "two fabulously wealthy sisters born with eastern European
names but in possession of proud and ancient Spanish titles, each married
to men named Alberto, who were cousins."[33] These were the famous and
beautiful Koplowitz sisters, Esther and Alicia, reported to be among the
wealthiest women in Europe. Descended from a Polish refugee who had
started the construction company Fomento de Construcciones y Contratas
(FCC), the Koplowitzes lost their father in 1962, leading the sisters to
marry early (eighteen and twenty) to "the Albertos," Alberto Cortina and
Alberto Alcocer.[34] In 1988, Alicia discovered her Alberto was having an affair with a *marquesa* while concurrently Esther learned that her Alberto was
slinking around with a former model. The sisters divorced their husbands
simultaneously on International Women's Day in March 1990 and assumed
their husbands' positions on the boards of their father's companies.

Meanwhile, Boyer's and Rubio's ties to Ibercorp, the "boutique investment bank of the Beautiful," founded in 1987, became public. The company
had benefited from government patronage, and, repaying the favor, Ibercorp provided preferential treatment for twenty-five special investors, of
course including Rubio and Boyer. The company also engaged in sham
stock purchases and sales through an intricate web of front companies.
When the structure collapsed, the losses exceeded $91 million, and Rubio
twice tried to resign as governor of the Bank of Spain, and twice Prime
Minister Felipe González refused to accept his resignation.[35] Inspection reports, however, revealed that Rubio apparently knew that Ibercorp was in
trouble even as he testified about its solvency before Parliament, and that he
was engaged in insider trading. Brought to trial, Rubio, Boyer, and their
wives appeared before a court as demonstrators gathered outside carrying a
coffin to "bury" their careers and, by extension, the "Beautiful" people who

had bewitched Spain with the *cultura del pelotazo* ("get rich quick culture").[36] Rubio was, however, acquitted of taking advantage of his office.[37] Notably, all this sordid banality in Western Europe provided a stark contrast to Eastern Europe, where communism was collapsing, people were struggling to be free, and the Evil Empire was ceasing to exist.

It had not helped that Rubio's policies, which had promised 800,000 more jobs to Spain, never materialized (the unemployment rate still hovered at 18 percent when the scandals erupted). Other socialist policies produced unexpected consequences: one law intended to encourage rentals rather than home ownership sucked in *dinero negro* ("black money") from the middle class, sending assets underground and hidden to protect ordinary Spaniards from excess taxation.[38] Mixed with the *dinero negro* came floods of Euro money seeking a foothold in Spain after it joined the EU, producing inflation in Madrid, then Barcelona and Seville, then the outlying regions, in the process further reducing home ownership.

Nevertheless, partly through a deliberate willingness to tolerate graft as an agent of economic expansion (and to avoid EU red tape), and more important, through an unwillingness to embrace French-style redistribution of wealth, Spain grew. From 1980 to 1992, real GDP rose by 40 percent. A frenetic commitment to infrastructure, associated with the Barcelona Olympic Games, the five hundredth anniversary of Columbus's voyage, and Seville's Expo '92 world's fair also contributed to a mini-revival. The Barcelona Olympics proved wildly successful, but the Quincentenary less so, as a "specially commissioned replica of the first vessel to circumnavigate the world sank as it left the slipway," and the flotilla replicating Columbus's voyage experienced a genuine mutiny.[39] The Expo '92 main pavilion burned down, and on opening night, a Franco-esque scene occurred when police fired live ammunition at demonstrators in Seville. Spain's image as a beacon of the new Europe dimmed accordingly.

Ibercorp's collapse advanced the opposition Popular Party under José María Aznar, the young and handsome tax inspector descended from a line of prominent Spanish journalists. In 1990, he emerged as the leader of the Popular Party and, after surviving a Basque bomb that detonated beneath his armored car, became president of Spain in 1996, ending more than a decade of Socialist Workers' Party rule. When the EU introduced the euro, Aznar achieved a minor victory, and after 9/11/2001, gained a reputation as a strong ally of the United States.

Certainly scandals were not unknown in more capitalist and free-market countries such as the United States or Hong Kong (the Keating Five and the Baring "rogue trader" scandals come to mind). But the capitalism understood in continental Europe and, for the most part, throughout the remainder of the world, was not free-market capitalism, but rather state crony capitalism conforming more closely to Mussolini's or Hitler's model (sans the black shirts and race hatred). In such state-dominated systems, corruption was bred as an integral part of the inner workings of government. There was no counterbalancing force such as that provided by genuine competition. The practice of *mordita* ("the little death" or bribes) in Latin America may provoke revulsion, but where the government tightly controls the economy, businesses must find a way to get government bureaucrats and politicians to represent their interests, or, at the very least, not favor their competitors.

In most of the world, corporations had to form alliances with governments to prosper, often formally organizing themselves as private-public partnerships. Unions and selected politicians were drawn into positions of comanagement and ownership, and competition was eliminated through favorable government action. Crony capitalism became enshrined in international business, perhaps best illustrated by Japan's public sector actions in the 1960s that enabled its *zaibatsu* (conglomerates of banks, autos, steel, shipbuilding, and electronics) to penetrate many segments of the American market—in some cases obtaining monopolies.

While pretending to function on behalf of the common people, socialism fostered and drove such corruption, destroying individual freedoms in the name of safety, protecting the environment, maintaining a quality of life, or other catchy, misused slogans. Political entrepreneurs, as historian Burton Folsom called them, dominated all "market entrepreneurs," engaging in "rent-seeking" activities that would win them advantages with government regulators or gain them subsidies. Even low-level enterprises (such as hairstylists or nail salons) found entry requirements raised to nearly insurmountable levels in the name of health or the environment to protect those already present in the system.

The European Union carried this concept to a new level, heretofore unseen. Member nations gradually lost almost all of their autonomy with respect to controlling their economies and business actions, ceding such power to the bureaucrats in Brussels. By 2010, corruption had become institutionalized at all levels, including the highest. The entire Commission headed by Jacques Santer was forced to resign in 1999 as a result of fraud and corruption. In 2009, the European ombudsman published statistics of citizens' complaints against EU institutions, with most of them filed against the Commission. Lack of transparency, unclear lobbyist relations, conflicts of interests, and excessive spending by the Commission were highlighted in a number of reports by auditing organizations.

At the lowest level, all occupations requiring any level of expertise or competence required a license and passing government mandated tests. Obtaining such licenses became a matter of knowing the right person or paying an appropriate sum to the right individual. At the highest level the Bilderbergs (an international, by-invitation-only group of the biggest players in finance, industry, government, and even the media) came into play, deciding on winners and losers based on their networks of friends, corporations, banks, and government officials. European elites had organized an entity to give themselves unbridled power, one in which they could not be voted out, and one easily controlled by dispensing monetary favors throughout the Union to manage the populations. An American only needs to multiply the system of earmarks, government handouts, and political corruption in the United States by an order of magnitude to understand what goes on in Europe. Life there has become an effort to gain or retain benefits and perks, literally by begging at the feet of the bureaucrats or by violent demonstrations.

Iron Curtain Sons of Liberty

Such turmoil reflects the inherent incompatibility of socialism with free markets. Sooner or later, state planners introduce instability into a functioning market, either through misguided policies or scandal, thus prompting a meltdown. These principles are not just theory; in the 1990s, Europe had already seen the Marxist future and should have realized it absolutely didn't work. The collapse of communism in Europe was nearly complete when Mikhail Gorbachev conceded a united Germany, undermining his shaky footing atop the Soviet structure.

Yet in one of the ironies of history, the United States, after more than half a century of active resistance and occasionally military opposition to the Soviet empire, found itself completely unprepared for its demise. The emasculation of the CIA under Carter had severely limited the gathering of human intelligence, and electronic surveillance alone could not determine the intent of Soviet leaders and the true condition of their country. When Boris Yeltsin became the first Politburo member in history to resign, the West was unable to grasp what was happening. Immediately prior to the breakup of the Soviet Union, Western Sovietologists were nearly unanimous in their assessment of the country as "a model of the most stable and durable regime in the world," and aside from Harvard scholar Richard Pipes, President Reagan, and a few other perceptive individuals, virtually no one expected the USSR to fall apart.[40] Quite the contrary, so strong had been the liberal themes of not destabilizing the relationship, at the very moment of victory American liberal and centrist leaders abruptly *supported* the Communist government with public statements of solidarity, while most conservatives were puzzled.

Having loaned rhetorical encouragement to the Baltic republics (Estonia, Latvia, and Lithuania) under Reagan, the new president and Reagan's former vice president, George H. W. Bush, unexpectedly balked when the independence movements became serious. The first demonstration took place in Riga in December 1986 after a rock concert, with youths chanting "Free Latvia." Six months later, another demonstration commemorated Stalin's deportations of Latvians, and in each republic a Baltic equivalent of the Sons of Liberty was founded, openly subversive and remarkably public.[41] A Lithuanian Reorganization Movement, with banners proclaiming "Red Army Go Home," took to the streets in early 1989, with all these events culminating on August 23 of that year with the "Chain of Freedom"—a chain of two million people linking hands across 370 miles through the three Baltic states.

Each new test of Soviet resolve was met, in Lenin's words, with flesh rather than the bayonet, and the Baltic states pressed forward, announcing their intention to demand independence. Gorbachev belatedly addressed the uprising without conviction in January 1990, by which time it was too late. When the Lithuanian Soviet declared independence, and tanks did not roll from Moscow, other republics smelled blood and adopted similar language asserting their sovereignty. Where the Red Army, despite its humiliation in Afghanistan, may have had a tough struggle to impose the Soviet will in Poland or East Germany, it could have easily crushed the Baltic liberation movements. But there were also riots and rebellions occurring in Armenia, Azerbaijan, Kazakhstan, Uzbekistan, and Georgia, and even demonstrations in Ukraine, Belarus, and Moldova. The Soviet Union was coming apart at the seams.

Here, Gorbachev found himself a prisoner of his own Western press clippings. Described as a reformer and a liberal, Gorbachev's very policies of openness now prevented him from acting. He observed the events with a sense of befuddlement. Warlords in the Kremlin grew uneasy; his foreign minister, Eduard Shevardnadze, resigned, cognizant of coup talk. This wasn't the way Stalin's empire reacted to piddling uprisings from pipsqueak subjects. Troops and armor put down such revolts quickly, and with blood-shed.

Precisely because of Gorbachev's weakness at home, for the first time since the Korean War, the Soviet Union failed to oppose in the United Nations Security Council a major development that clearly advanced American prestige, power, and strategic position. This historical intersection occurred just as pundits in America began speaking of a "peace dividend" caused by the thawing of U.S.-USSR relations. Bush, whose administration had failed to understand the rapid erosion of the Warsaw Pact, and which therefore had not offered encouragement to the Poles or the Germans, likewise ignored the turmoil in the Baltic states and the other republics. Bush's advisers reverted to old, outdated understandings of a bipolar world in which the United States did not "destabilize" the balance of terror—an interpretation that Reagan himself had rejected.

In hindsight, it is easy to criticize Bush and his advisers for failing to grasp the developments behind the Iron Curtain; even Reagan did not expect Soviet communism would fall so soon, though unlike Bush he was certain it was teetering. What clouded the vision of American spymasters was recent history in which uprisings in Hungary and Czechoslovakia had been crushed, and in which until only a few years earlier Russian dissidents were exiled, imprisoned in psychiatric wards, or killed. Gorbachev talked a new talk, but experience had taught U.S. administrations that Soviet leaders came in all shapes and sizes, rarely saying what they meant. What even fewer had gleaned was that internally, the Soviet Union was unraveling like a bad sweater. The "intimate bond [that existed] between force and deception [whereby] Deception becomes a method of self-defense" had started to deceive the Soviet rulers themselves.[42] That was one interpretation. Another was that the apparatchiks and nomenklatura (and even the top members of the Politburo) were no longer true believers. Communism was—as it had often been portrayed—a godless, soulless, cynical system of power invoked to justify dachas on the Black Sea and better cars, not a worldview, and certainly not a vision of the future. In essence, the sheer moral indefensibility of communism had combined with economic reality to produce, in the words of Gorbachev's chief of staff, Valery Boldin, "internal capitulation" of the leadership in the Kremlin.[43] That retreat came with stunning suddenness, for following Lithuania's independence in March 1990, thirteen other republics would declare their independence in the next twenty-one months.

Gorbachev found himself accused of "lies and deceptions" by many of his former admirers for his reluctance to smash the rebellion in the Baltic states.[44] Seeing the Baltic states loosening their tether, Ukraine soon asserted its own independence, having already founded a competitor to the Communist Party, the RUKH, in 1988. When, in April 1991, Gorbachev acknowledged reality and acquiesced to the right of secession for the republics, he became a marked man for the remaining Communist zealots, and plotting commenced.

It was not Gorbachev who led the massive transition from communism but the relatively anti-Communist Boris Yeltsin, head of the Russian Supreme Soviet and a "distinctly *Russian* politician."[45] Yeltsin had worked his way up through the party and was named to the Politburo in 1986, before rethinking the basis of communism. He voluntarily resigned from the Politburo, the first person ever to do so. In October 1987, after Gorbachev failed to take action on his resignation, he spoke at a Central Committee meeting, outlining his reasons for resigning. This was a shock and totally unheard of. For Yeltsin, the turning point came during his visit to the United States in September 1989. At a Houston supermarket, he was overwhelmed (as most first-time visitors from Communist countries were) by the endless foods and packages, everything in a dozen varieties. He was shocked by the stark contrast with relatively empty Soviet grocery store shelves.[46]

An ordinary man who had "voluntarily relinquished for himself and his family . . . the privileges of party rank," Yeltsin soon became far more popular than Gorbachev. In 1989, he won 92 percent of the vote in his election to the Congress of People's Deputies as the delegate from Moscow, and he formed the reform faction of the Congress shortly thereafter. Two years later, he challenged Gorbachev's handpicked candidate, Nikolai Ryzhkov, for the presidency of Russia, and won 60 percent of the vote, becoming the second most powerful man in the USSR behind Gorbachev. More important, Yeltsin became the first leader democratically chosen in that nation's history. A month later, President George H. W. Bush met with Yeltsin on a visit to the USSR. While hardly young and hip, Yeltsin was, at least, an outsider and not part of the problem.

Conspirators numbering less than a dozen attempted to replace Gorbachev, whom they viewed as insufficiently committed to communism, through a coup. While vacationing in the Crimea, Gorbachev was presented with an ultimatum from the plotters, including Soviet vice president Gennady Yanayev, which demanded presidential powers be turned over to an "Emergency Committee." Back in Moscow, they also imposed martial law, and optimistically prepared 300,000 arrest forms. But time had caught up to them. The aging Communists could have ridden out the storm in an earlier era, but in the television age, they neither looked appealing nor seemed responsive to the public's needs. They presented the world with a public demonstration of a crumbling, senile dictatorship.

With Gorbachev isolated in the Crimea, Yeltsin took advantage of his presence at the scene of the action to lead resistance to the coup. He organized demonstrators around the Russian parliament, entertained phone calls from world leaders, and otherwise became the man of the hour. At no time did the conspirators have the full support of the Red Army—indeed, the Soviet Union's own character, in which the military was constantly under suspicion and its top generals replaced or killed for the slightest affront to Stalin, argued against a Latin American–type coup. Although they had planned to arrest Yeltsin at his dacha near Moscow, for an unknown reason the conspirators failed to do so, and it cost them.

Party conspirators never tapped into the popular will. Quite the opposite, crowds swelled against them, and the republics, sensing their opportunity, announced independence. After one of the coup leaders committed suicide, Yeltsin perceived the time was right. He had the remaining plotters arrested and a much-relieved Gorbachev flew back to Moscow, formally resuming his powers. The man feted as one of the greatest leaders of the twentieth century had not only opened Pandora's box, but had been hypnotized by the forces it unleashed, and meekly returned through the courtesy of a loose cannon politician. Gorbachev was a step behind every major turn, still pontificating about perestroika while demonstrators called the Party a "criminal enterprise."[47]

Had the economy been sound, Gorbachev might have saved his job, but a depressing report, released in March from the Soviet planning agency, forecast a 15 percent drop in industrial production for the rest of the year and predicted Soviet GDP would shrink by over 11 percent.[48] Using phrases such as "imminent collapse" and "economic catastrophe," the Gosplan report of 1991 confirmed what Soviets had known, and what many Westerners suspected but suppressed: Soviet communism was a living demonstration of the failure of Marxist economic theory.[49] Certainly the republics did not want to be tied to the Russian anchor as it slipped beneath the waves, and in August and September 1991, the exodus of states from the Soviet Union to independence began—Ukraine, Belarus, Moldova, the "Stans," Georgia, and Armenia, each seizing power from the creaky Communist superstructure that still attempted to govern them. Scrambling to salvage any position for the Politburo and communism, Gorbachev sought new arrangements, federal systems, associations, to no avail.

Even the ludicrous (and Andrew Jacksonesque) technique of releasing government food reserves of meat and vegetables at polling places during the March 1991 referendum on unification failed to produce a friendly electorate. Absent the power of the Red Army, none of the states would again return to subservience. If they were going to be poor, they could do that without any help from Moscow. On Christmas 1991, a Russian flag replaced the hammer and sickle over the Kremlin, and on December 26, declaration 142-H of the Supreme Soviet announced the independence of all fifteen republics, as well as the creation of the Commonwealth of Independent States. The grand proletarian experiment that had cost 60 million lives flickered out of existence.

A transition to freedom, even European-style freedom, would not be easy. Free marketeers had (perhaps deliberately) avoided discussions of precisely how such a shift to market forces would occur, or how painful it would be. At a 1990 meeting of the Mont Pelerin Society, formed in 1947 by free-market economist Friedrich Hayek, economists from the former Soviet Union asked, "How do you do it? How do you get from state control to private ownership?" When it was suggested that the government simply announce that on a specified date, shares of a state-owned company would be apportioned among the employees, or put up for auction, or any of a number of alternatives, the economists countered, "But you don't understand. No one *believes* the government."[50]

Therein lay much of the problem, not for the near-term conversion of the former Iron Curtain countries to free-market republics, but for their permanent survival under the rule of law. Privatization works—but Western private property rights had evolved through thousands of small steps over a period of two hundred to five hundred years, depending on when one dates the origins of the rule of common law. Making a market required not just a buyer and seller, but competitors and a disinterested referee in the form of a government that could at least be seen as honest by most parties most of the time. Western perceptions of former East Bloc countries, misshaped to no small degree by cold warriors needing them to be "free democracies crushed under the Soviet heel," bore no connection to the pre–World War II character of Poland, Czechoslovakia, Bulgaria, and Romania. Rather, the emergent states were at best marginally democratic and at worst authoritarian aristocracies or thugocracies.

Ironically, the military stockpiles built up under Brezhnev, Andropov,

Chernenko, and Gorbachev proved to be Yeltsin's near-term salvation, and his long-term curse. The sale of those stockpiles to foreign powers cushioned the fall from a controlled economy, then, when the hardware ran out, the lack of hard assets contributed to the crash later in the decade.[51] Once the Communists lost control of the information bureaucracies and archives, the USSR's economic problems were laid bare.

Especially in the case of oil development, one could see a perfect example of Communist mismanagement. Stalin's minions had obsessively explored and mapped the rich petroleum reserves of Siberia, but once the Soviets began drilling, they crashed into the reality of stilted technology derived from a noninnovative, closed system. Drill bits, for example, proved woefully inadequate, causing the cost of drilling deep wells to soar after only a few hundred feet. Westerners, on the other hand, having used the famous Hughes drill bit as a starting point, had penetrated far deeper in harder rock.

Petroleum experts from the West, who visited some of the oil cities in Siberia, found

> cities built in the middle of nowhere [with] fountains and parks, usable only in the few short summer months, boulevards and paved roads, huge Stalinesque apartment buildings and hydroponic farms . . . with utilities added as an afterthought to the outside of buildings, fully exposed to the harsh winter weather. [The cities accommodated] not only the drilling crews, their families, and the support staffs, but the huge political overhead. . . . No Western oil-field could have supported such monstrosities.[52]

Canadian experts found wells amateurishly insulated, allowing a trillion cubic feet of gas to escape, and transmission lines leaking badly, allowing only a small percentage of the total oil and gas production to reach ports. Since the Leninist system did not permit market forces to discount cash flows, their production plans yielded overdrilling and underdrilling, slapping up structures so close to each other they sucked out the same pool of oil, or, alternatively, so far apart they left large reservoirs surrounded by water that could never be recovered. State-directed goals will always reward managers for doing one thing at the expense of most others; with Siberian drilling, the state gave managers bonuses based on the number of wells drilled, not oil produced or cost efficiency. Like the subsidized Union Pacific, which threw down railroad track with abandon to receive per-mile payments, heedless of whether the rails ran over ice, up ridiculously steep grades, or over unstable geology, the Soviet managers erected derricks and borrowed relentlessly.

Then there was the Muslim problem in Russia. Former states in the Soviet federation split off into the "Stans"—Uzbekistan, Tajikistan, Kazakhstan, and others with predominantly Muslim populations. Soviet assimilation worked no better than the French variant. Once, Russia had had a mushrooming population, growing rapidly until the arrival of the Communists. Then population growth stalled: mass murder, famine, and purges tend to have that effect on reproduction. After World War II, Russia showed some demographic growth (1.34 percent, although still below replacement level), which then slowed significantly in the 1970s, and by 1979, the USSR was no longer far ahead of the United States in relative population growth. But within Russia, the Muslim population had grown by almost one third, and Soviet Muslims had a birth rate far higher than non-Muslims. Russian population was in decline—except in the fifteen provinces dominated by Muslims.

While it was reasonable to assume that the spirit of liberty would rise in every human breast, there were wildly different non-Western notions of what true freedom—or "submission," in the Islamic world—meant. The West was about to relearn what it had forgotten while fighting the Ottoman Turks, that martial Muslim cultures did not usually embrace any of the tenets of Western culture and would resist traditional political and economic solutions.

Butcher of Baghdad

Russia's implosion triggered a short-lived global dance. Combined with Middle Eastern chaos and the flagging fortunes of Japan, it left the United States as the undisputed superpower, much to the chagrin of the emerging European Union. The first test of a world without a major Communist influence would come in a pair of tiny but important nations, Panama in 1989 and Kuwait a year later.

Reagan's vice president, George H. W. Bush, had won the presidency in a landslide over Massachusetts governor Michael Dukakis in 1988. He was tested quickly when, in 1989, a democratic election in Panama produced the defeat of strongman Manuel Noriega's handpicked successor. Noriega had planned to rig the vote, but with the help of the Catholic Church, a legitimate count of the nation's districts unfolded apart from Noriega's lackeys. Blaming foreigners for undue interference, Noriega voided the election,

Russia and Associated States, 2013

① ESTONIA	④ *East Prussia, to Russia*	⑥ UKRAINE	⑨ ARMENIA
② LATVIA		⑦ MOLDOVA	⑩ AZERBAIJAN
③ LITHUANIA	⑤ BELARUS	⑧ GEORGIA	

⑪ TAJIKISTAN
⑫ KYRGYZSTAN

and sent paramilitary troops to stop the victorious candidate from taking power. Tensions mounted between Noriega and Bush, particularly after several Americans were physically assaulted or harassed by Panamanian security forces. Matters culminated in the shooting of a U.S. Marine lieutenant in December 1989, and the United States invaded a few days later.

Despite Noriega's nullification of a UN-sanctioned election, and despite former president Jimmy Carter, sent by Bush as an observer, declaring that the election had been "stolen," the United Nations again sided with despots and the General Assembly condemned the invasion.[53] But the Panamanians—in one poll, by a 92 percent majority—supported the U.S. incursion, and three fourths said the Americans should have invaded sooner. Noriega was captured after holing up in the Vatican embassy for several days. Characteristic of the modern age, American military helicopters blasted rock music from the Australian group AC/DC at the embassy twenty-four hours a day in an effort at sleep deprivation. Noriega surrendered on January 2, 1990. Several months later when AC/DC was asked about their role, their manager said, "We were just glad to be of service."[54]

Domestically, Bush's similarity to Reagan faded fast. His campaign language of a "kinder, gentler America" implied that he thought Reagan's

America was harsh and cruel; and by supporting and signing the Americans with Disabilities Act (1990), Bush further increased the scope and intrusion of the federal government into business and the daily activities of ordinary Americans, disabled or not. The act set requirements for dozens of mandated changes in private businesses to accommodate the handicapped, to the point that one stripper in San Diego sued her place of employment because the shower was not wheelchair accessible—even though no strippers used wheelchairs! Bush's approval ratings might have fallen sooner if not for the renegade actions of Iraqi dictator Saddam Hussein.

With the Russians shattering into several federations and the West desperate to enjoy the "peace dividend" promised by the end of the cold war, Saddam sensed a power vacuum. On August 2, 1990, he launched an invasion of neighboring Kuwait, a step in his aggressive designs for which the timing seemed propitious. Saddam had benefited slightly from American favoritism of his regime over the more radical (but more predictable) Shiite Muslim theocracy in Iran. Led by ayatollahs since the 1979 revolution that resulted in the American hostage crisis, Iran seemed the more immediate threat, whereas Iraq under Saddam remained somewhat modernized and ostensibly Western (i.e., not as fundamentalist as the Iranians). But both nations exhibited the worst traits of modern Muslim states, including an abhorrence of genuine democracy, exclusion and oppression of non-Muslim religions, and a predilection for military adventurism. Thus, during the 1980s, across an eight-year war (known as the "Imposed War" by Iraqis), the two Muslim states battled to a bloody draw.

The Iran-Iraq War came as the culmination of Sunni-Shiite conflicts between the two states and as the result of bickering over borders. An agreement reached in Algiers in 1975 had affixed the borders along the Shatt al-Arab waterway, but in June 1980, Saddam delivered a war message to parliament insisting that the river have its "Iraqi-Arab identity restored." After severing diplomatic relations, Iraq invaded Iran in September, following an Iranian assassination attempt on Iraqi foreign minister Tariq Aziz. Saddam mistakenly counted on Iranian Sunnis joining the Iraqis, and accepted intelligence reports showing the Iranian military in disarray following the fall of the shah. After a quick advance by Saddam's forces, by 1982 they had been evicted from most of the territory they had gained. It was then Iran's turn, and Ayatollah Khomeini's forces crossed the border in an attempt to capture Basra, and Iraqis, fighting on the defensive, stalled the Iranian advance.

Iranian advances seemed impressive until they encountered Iraqi poison gas. After that, the struggle settled down into a seesaw affair. In 1983, Iran launched five major attacks, all of which failed; and the following year Saddam ordered air attacks on Iranian cities while increasing his use of sarin nerve gas. Scud missiles soon supplemented Iraq's traditional aircraft bombing Iranian cities—Tehran was hit in 1985—whereby Iran, having acquired Scud missiles from Libya, retaliated against Baghdad. Two years later, Saddam attacked sixty-five cities, including eight cities hit by Scud missiles. Both sides suffered serious casualties; Iran counted between 750,000 to one million killed, wounded, or missing; Iraq, 400,000.[55] In the final battle alone, Iran lost half of its remaining combat capability.

Western powers saw Saddam as the lesser of two evils, and contrary to popular perceptions, France and the Soviet Union supplied the vast majority of Saddam's weapons, with American contributions amounting to about 1 percent.[56] The West was drawn in when both sides began attacking each other's oil tankers, forcing the United States and the Soviet Union to begin chartering tankers, thus affording them military protection. It was inevitable that sooner or later the Iranians would either deliberately or inadvertently strike an American vessel and provoke a showdown. In May, an Iraqi plane attacked the USS *Stark* in the Persian Gulf, and a year later, another warship was damaged by an Iranian mine. U.S. ships, on hair-trigger alert to intruders, regularly battled Iranian gunboats pushing farther out in the Gulf.

One of the vessels engaged in opposing Iranian anti-shipping operations, the USS *Vincennes*, was involved in a hot battle with Iranian gunboats when it mistakenly shot down an Iranian civilian airliner that had not responded to four warnings and "Identification Friend or Foe" signals, killing 290 passengers. Whether or not the *Vincennes* was in Iranian waters, the willful operation of a passenger jet by the Iranians from a joint civilian/military airfield anywhere near a zone of combat operations, where it could be mistaken for an enemy, was criminal at best and deliberate at worst.[57] The airliner was almost ten miles within the normal safety zone that American warships observed, and other U.S. warships had warned that it was a possible Iranian F-14. The *Vincennes'* captain was informed the plane was descending in an attack profile and was identifying itself exclusively with codes used by military profiles.[58] " 'Don't take the first round,' was engraved in the decision-making procedure of all American ships in the Gulf," recalled the commander of the *Vincennes*.[59] Of course, the nightly news reported that human error had caused the shootdown, without specifying it was the *Iranian* human error that was responsible. NBC's Tom Brokaw thundered authoritatively, "this time we should demand a full court martial. . . . Too many people have died to brush this case of human error under the rug."[60] It was a fool's analysis, particularly when the captain of the *Vincennes* was identified on TV. Despite being completely cleared by a Navy investigation, the captain's minivan was blown up by a car bomb planted by an Iranian assassination squad on a street in San Diego (he was not injured). Brokaw and others who had "outed" the captain took no responsibility.

Meanwhile, at the end of eight years and a negotiated truce, both Iran and Iraq were exhausted. Iraq remained a harbor for international terrorists such as Abu Nidal; the Baghdad government supported Palestinian militants; and it remained, along with Iran, on the U.S. list of state sponsors of international terrorism. Having failed to obtain the Iranian lands he felt entitled to, Saddam directed his attention to his southern border, where he invoked historical (but spurious) claims on Kuwaiti territory. His real designs were on Saudi oil; Kuwait was merely the back entrance. Even as Saddam negotiated with Kuwait about the "border dispute," he stationed eight divisions of his Republican Guard south of Basra.[61] On August 2, 1990, claiming Kuwait was only technically separated from Iraq by international fiat, Saddam sent Iraqi armor across the border.

Saddam had met with the U.S. ambassador to Iraq April Glaspie in July 1990, when Glaspie reportedly indicated the United States had no position on the Iraqi-Kuwait dispute. In fact, although Glaspie was in over her head and clearly dominated by Saddam's personality, Saddam had merely read into Glaspie's words what he wanted to hear, and certainly never made any serious attempt to learn American intentions in the event of an Iraqi invasion of Kuwait. As two scholars of the Gulf War concluded,

> . . . the meeting has become a diplomatic red herring. It has been decades since policy-level communication at this level has relied on ambassadorial-level communication, without clear follow-up between senior officials at the State Department or White House Level. Both senior Iraqi and senior US officials in Washington were well aware before the meeting that Ambassador Glaspie had had little meaningful contact with Saddam Hussein during her time in Baghdad and that the US Embassy in Baghdad was not a major channel for communicating policy or receiving signals. . . .[62]

Glaspie personified the marginalization of ambassadors, who had become petty society creatures in a State Department that had become increasingly centralized, unresponsive, and less timely. Saddam didn't need an inept State Department to predict the American response. In August, he had denied exit visas to a number of Westerners, whom he was clearly treating as human shields. "Your presence, here," he noted on state television, "is meant to prevent the scourge of war."[63] Nor was there evidence of intelligence failures in appreciating the strength of the buildup: the United States knew exactly how many troops Saddam had, and where. What did catch Americans off guard was the brazenness with which the Iraqi dictator acted.

Bush met the invasion with what he thought was quick action, requesting a United Nations Security Council meeting (which produced the obligatory resolution demanding Iraqi withdrawal—followed by eleven subsequent resolutions of equal gravity), followed by an Arab League resolution also condemning the attack. Bush's willingness to enlist the UN constituted a weakness on his part, in that he was far less willing than Reagan to act unilaterally even in the case of such aggression. But it did signal that the cold war was over, as such a UN resolution never would have been possible even a decade earlier.[64] The United Nations (later called by U.S. ambassador to the UN Richard Holbrooke a "talk house . . . which simply has no importance except as a forum for speeches") wallowed in useless resolutions and futile debate, and would do nothing on its own.[65]

The United States could, and did. Within the region, Bush could wield important arguments to convince local Arab governments of their own security interests in joining a coalition. An Arab League meeting in Cairo sided overwhelmingly with Kuwait and the United States, and of the major players, only Jordan was a holdout. Anticipating that Saddam would quickly consolidate his gains, giving him 20 percent of the world's known oil reserves, then continue moving south to Saudi Arabia's Hama oil fields and claim 40 percent, Bush, much to the relief of the Saudi royal family, announced defensive operation Desert Shield to protect the kingdom. Just five days after Iraqi forces entered Kuwait, Americans landed in Saudi Arabia, marking the first time since the kingdom's independence that a large, non-Muslim body had been permitted on Saudi soil for any purpose other than construction.

The United States also engaged in a flurry of diplomacy that produced a thirty-four-nation coalition to implement UN Resolution 660 authorizing the use of force to expel Iraq if it did not comply with another resolution to withdraw. Later, after Operation Iraqi Freedom in 2003, much was made of the lack of international support for the invasion of Iraq by President

George W. Bush, yet the numbers scarcely differed—thirty-four nations for Desert Storm (many of whom were truly insignificant, including Bangladesh, Niger, Oman, Sierra Leone, and Belgium) versus forty nations for Iraqi Freedom (although only the United States, Britain, Australia, and Poland took part in the actual invasion, while the rest sent often tiny contingents to assist during the occupation). The key difference was that France and some Arab states participated in the former, but not the latter. Germany did not send forces to either fight. Japan supported the 2003 war with a token six hundred troops sent in 2004 to assist in occupation duties, but in Desert Storm, only provided $10 billion as their contribution, although afterward Japan prohibited its own contractors from bidding for work rebuilding Kuwait. Japan's actions were seen as insultingly minor by many Americans, as they had been heavily dependent on Kuwaiti oil, restored to them through American blood. Both Iran and the USSR voluntarily stood aside. Beyond that, Bush's great coup lay in convincing Israel to also sit it out, winning assurances that even if attacked by Iraqi missiles, Israel would absorb the punishment without retaliating. This allowed the Americans and the coalition to neuter Saddam once and for all without making Jewish intervention a political problem for the Arab contingent.

At the time, Desert Shield and Desert Storm (the offensive to kick the Iraqis out of Kuwait) enjoyed widespread applause as an example of collective security and United Nations effectiveness, even though the UN only passed nonbinding resolutions. Ominously, during the buildup, which received high levels of popular support in America and Britain, where it was endorsed by 75 to 80 percent of the people in polls, a dissenting faction popularized (although hardly invented) the concept of "blood for oil." Anticapitalist forces had long hated the automobile, and American Europhiles in particular waxed romantic about trains and lorries, ferries and trolley cars. Prior to becoming stockbrokers who only invested in "peace" funds or entrepreneurs who started Ben and Jerry's ice cream shops, the sixties radicals like Abbie Hoffman and Amory Lovins had championed the back-to-nature, small-is-beautiful lifestyle that promoted antipathy toward free markets.

That wing of the American political Left had been in decline during the Reagan years, many of them enjoying swelling bank accounts and rising 401(k)s. With a Middle Eastern war on the horizon, however, they reverted to form. Oil, the lifeblood of not only the American economy but the *world's* economy in the 1990s—without which many countries, particularly the poorest, would face unimaginable famines and destitution—had to flow at market prices. There was nothing mysterious, Masonic, or Opus Dei–ish about such a proposition. Despite decades' worth of research on alternative fuels, nothing was as cheap, reliable, and easy to acquire as gasoline derived from petroleum. Miracle engines that could get hundreds of miles to the gallon were pipe dreams (and practical engines that could attain such feats even twenty years later remained in the developmental stage). Eventually, "no blood for oil" officially inaugurated the final push to eliminate the automobile, later called by Vice President Al Gore the greatest threat to planet Earth.[66]

At the time, however, only a minority in Congress opposed the deployment of American force. Senator Ted Kennedy warned the fight would be a Vietnam-style disaster that would fill 45,000 body bags, Senator John Kerry typically opposed it, and Senator Daniel Patrick Moynihan claimed a Middle East fight would "wreck our military." (Saddam Hussein, it should be noted, predicted a similar number of body bags would be needed for the Americans.) Al Gore, it was later revealed by Senator Alan Simpson, "sold" his vote to whichever side gave him the most television time, finally supporting the defense of Kuwait.[67] Most Americans well appreciated the threat to the Western way of life, not to mention international stability, posed by a Middle East with Saddam Hussein's hand on the oil spigot.[68]

After a failed last-minute attempt by François Mitterrand to elevate France's position through direct negotiations with Iraq, the war was on. French and Arab armored units rounded out a contingent heavy with NATO, particularly American and British, forces. Saddam's success at holding ground with entrenched tanks and guns against Iranian human-wave infantry attacks, which lacked proper artillery and air support, had fooled him into thinking he could employ the same tactics against the Americans and their allies in the Gulf War. It was delusional thinking: Iranians used teenage boys to clear minefields by running into them, whereas the coalition would use advanced mine-clearing devices that would not cost a single life.

Excepting Grenada—hardly a war—Americans had not fought abroad in large numbers since Vietnam. Still stigmatized as a loss (debatable in all aspects except the final withdrawal), the Vietnam War had spawned a plethora of military studies and reflections, lessons learned and warnings to be heeded. Ronald Reagan had absorbed the Vietnam experience, then, after the Lebanon debacle in 1983, conceived the Reagan Doctrine of military application:

1. The United States should not commit its forces to military action overseas unless the cause is vital to our national interest.
2. If the decision is made to commit our forces to combat abroad, it must be done with the clear intent and support needed to *win*. It should not be a halfway or tentative commitment, and there must be clearly defined and realistic objectives.
3. Before we commit our troops to combat, there must be reasonable assurance that the cause we are fighting for and the actions we will take will have the support of the American people and Congress. . . .
4. Even after all these tests are met, our troops should be committed to combat abroad *only* as a last resort, when no other choice is available.[69]

Kuwait clearly met those tests. Choices in the future would not be so clear-cut. Bush spared no effort in making certain that the action would be decisive, and the victory, overwhelming. However, by aligning with the interests of the UN, and by involving the Security Council, Bush made a deal with the devil that would ensure one of Reagan's second dictums—absolute victory—was compromised by the need for "clearly defined and realistic objectives." What constitutes defeat for an enemy? When every single fighter surrenders? When the leader is killed or captured? When enemy territory is occupied? Classics historian John David Lewis has defined victory as occurring when "the fact of defeat was openly recognized and the legitimacy of the victor's terms was accepted by the vanquished."[70]

General H. Norman Schwarzkopf, the commander of CENTCOM (U.S. Central Command, located at MacDill Air Force Base in Florida) would soon discover how elusive some of those answers were. Known as "Stormin' Norman" (due to his penchant for yelling at his subordinates and staff) or simply "The Bear," Schwarzkopf's explosive reputation served as a cover for a good actor. The son of a two-star general, the four-star Schwarzkopf had nevertheless been leapfrogged in promotions by General Colin Powell, the chairman of the Joint Chiefs of Staff (JCS), and the most highly ranked African-American in U.S. military history.[71] Surprisingly, however, the two worked well together, both becoming more dovish than hawkish. Powell, a most reluctant warrior, had already privately told Prince Bandar bin Sultan of Saudi Arabia that he personally would recommend not aiding Kuwait.[72] Now, he had to coordinate a massive military buildup. Schwarzkopf, working closely with President Bush, worked out a yearlong campaign plan. He was impressed by the target-rich environment the desert provided for the use of air power, and argued that if a wild card existed, it was the havoc coalition air forces could cause across the entire Iraqi military structure.

During the long, six-month buildup in 1990–91, necessitated by the United States' traditional lack of preparedness to fight a major war overseas, Saddam had a free run at Saudi Arabia. Prince Bandar reportedly exclaimed, "Does Saddam realize he can overrun [us] this easily?"[73] Light airborne units were rushed in to hold out until reinforcements arrived. And reinforcements did arrive, as thousands of men poured ashore. Partly due to the influence of the Reagan Doctrine, Bush deliberately planned for the use of massive force, preceded by a pounding air campaign that would minimize casualties. Even then, inside the Pentagon estimates of 7,000 U.S. dead were batted about—nothing like Ted Kennedy's 45,000 body bags, but enough to rattle American public support. Privately, the conservative Schwarzkopf told Powell that offensive operations would be "dirty and bloody," and asked, "Do they know that back in Washington?"[74] He was assured they did. The general was determined not to allow Kennedy's prophecy to become a reality.[75]

On January 15, 1991, a massive, coldly technical air campaign began. New cruise missiles, Stealth F-117A fighter-bombers, and conventional fighter-bombers that had laser targeting capabilities and infrared night bombing systems sent precision weapons hurtling to their nearly helpless targets. Tanks, bridges, command and control locations, and convoys were obliterated, often without the slightest warning. Iraqi armor and trucks dared not start their engines at night, for fear of their heat signatures revealing their locations. During the day, high-altitude scout planes and satellites relayed their positions to air command with equally deadly results. Iraq had no air force—or rather, whatever air power it once possessed had been cleared from the skies in a matter of days by American fighter planes, controlled and directed by hovering EC-130 radar planes. Eventually, Saddam buried 150 fighters in the desert—they were not discovered until the 2003 invasion of Iraq—and sent still others as gifts to his former enemies, the Iranians.

Schwarzkopf was elated. Once Saddam's "eyes" were gone, the bombing campaign used high-speed antiradar missiles (HARMs) to destroy Iraq's ability to detect incoming aircraft, leaving Baghdad and other major cities vulnerable and helpless. Coalition aircraft losses of one per 1,800 sorties was a rate fourteen times lower than Vietnam's Linebacker II campaign. As an F-111B pilot put it, "If armies dig in, they die. If they come out of their holes, they die sooner."[76] In only a month, coalition air power "plinked" 1,300 of Iraq's 6,100 tanks, then accelerated the kill ratio over the next nine days to the point that when ground operations commenced, the Iraqis were losing 500 tanks per day. Powell, formerly the reluctant warrior, now blustered that the United States would "cut off the head and kill the body" of the Iraqi military. By February 23, when Schwarzkopf launched the ground offensive, coalition air forces had flown 140,000 sorties that had already made Powell's prophecy attainable.

American Marines punched a hole in the "Saddam Line" south of Kuwait City, taking Al Jabar Air Base, and were slowed only by the staggering number of prisoners they took. Egyptian and Saudi forces seized Kuwait City while the Marines stood aside to allow the Arabs the glory of liberating the city. Unable to see the vast armored columns swinging far to the west through the desert, the Iraqi army was nearly cut off from behind before mounting a desperate retreat that quickly became a rout. Conscripts at the front lines surrendered by the hundreds, then thousands, so fast American tankers threw water bottles and MREs (Meals Ready to Eat) at them and pointed them to the rear, where the detainee camps awaited.[77] One batch of starving soldiers surrendered to a CNN news crew; others deserted at rates of up to 30 percent.

By that time, there was no Iraqi army: 76 percent of the enemy tanks, 55 percent of the armored personnel carriers, and 90 percent of the dreaded Iraqi guns had been wiped out in a mere one hundred hours.[78] When pictures of the "highway of death" appeared in *Time* magazine, it gave the impression that coalition air power had simply strafed and bombed thousands of helpless Iraqis when, in fact, the Iraqis had abandoned their vehicles as soon as they realized they were sitting ducks. Allied air power annihilated the empty carcasses of Saddam's war machine.

The lethal efficiency of the campaign spooked Bush, who worried that the United States would be viewed as murderers, and he abruptly pulled the plug on the operation, a position that Powell enthusiastically supported. Schwarzkopf came out of his concrete bunker, where he had dealt with the media nonstop, and went to negotiate an end to the conflict. Of the 166 coalition dead, the largest number came from a single Scud strike on a barracks, and another unfortunate few were killed by friendly fire. Only 77 Americans died.

In his haste to conclude a stunningly successful campaign before something went wrong, Bush failed to ensure that American forces would not have to return in the future. Had he known it would be his son who would bear the brunt of political criticism for that future war, perhaps he would have instructed Schwarzkopf to march to Baghdad. Or perhaps not: pressures came from all sides to halt, including from Arab Muslim coalition members, who feared a Saddam-less Iraq would be even more unstable than a weakened Iraq with Saddam still in power (with instability being the bane of postwar security thinking).[79]

Upon conclusion of hostilities, no-fly zones were set up, the United Nations embargoed various technology sold to Iraq, and promises were made to the Kurds in the north and the Shiites in the south that international peacekeepers would protect them. Regardless, Lewis's conditions for total victory—that the loser recognize defeat and the legitimacy of the victor—were not met. When told the Americans wanted to meet to negotiate an end to the conflict, Saddam said, "Then that means we've won." In his mind, he had. He had avoided defeat, and many of his Republican Guard units were still intact, although a single day more of fighting would have eliminated them. Worse, Saddam's *potential* for deadly mischief had been abundantly demonstrated, and he was still entirely unstable and perpetually dangerous.

However brief, the Gulf War featured Iraq's use of intermediate-range Scud missiles on both Saudi Arabia and Israel. Attempts to jury-rig the Patriot antiaircraft missile to function as an antimissile missile (an early element of SDI technology) seemed quite effective at first, then less so upon further review. Perhaps no more than 10 percent of the Patriots successfully intercepted Scuds, and even allowing for higher numbers of interceptions, the shattering impact of the Patriot-Scud collision still subjected areas beneath to a shower of heavy metal debris. Nevertheless, the potential once seen by only Ronald Reagan and a handful of his advisers now had been partially tested in battle—no matter how elementary—and the principle had been proven. Now the engineering had to catch up.

A second new element was the possibility that Saddam would use chemical and biological weapons against the coalition's ground forces, leading the U.S. Army and Marines to practice relentlessly in chem-bio suits. Saddam had used such weapons against Iran and the Kurds in 1988, but did not release any chemical or biological weapons against the coalition or Israel. Nothing was known for certain, even by postwar international arms inspectors, except that the deadly potential for Saddam to place chemical or biological warheads on long-range missiles could not be ruled out.[80]

With the Gulf War, the world saw an example of international collective security that worked temporarily, one of the few times such a claim could ever be made. It worked only due to U.S. action. As Prince Khalid bin Sultan of Saudi Arabia said, "If the world is only going to have one superpower, thank God (Allah) it is the United States of America."[81] In the Gulf War, the villain could not have been more starkly drawn—Saddam had released millions of barrels of crude oil into the Persian Gulf out of spite and set the Kuwaiti oil fields on fire, constituting the worst single act of environmental terrorism in history. Throughout the 1990s, the "Butcher of Baghdad" would add to his reputation by brutally crushing the Shiites in the south (who expected the United States to come to their aid), by repeatedly violating the no-fly zones in the north and south, and by shooting at American aircraft on dozens of occasions. His brutal sons, Uday and Qusay, were placed in powerful positions in government, and gained notoriety as sociopaths. Their bloody antics included feeding dissidents to Uday's pet leopards, throwing people off buildings, and a catalogue of tortures worthy of de Sade. Yet at no time was the Gulf War held up by prominent members of the liberal elites as a model of group cooperation or international morality. In most cases (particularly in Europe), not only was the victory *not* celebrated, it was met with stunning indifference by the chattering classes.

"Get Under the Hood"

Victory in the Gulf War, which raised Bush's approval to a then-unprecedented 89 percent, also proved his undoing. With the end of the Soviet empire and Saddam's defeat, the American public impatiently expected a "peace dividend" of prosperity and domestic spending. Politicians incessantly twittered about "rebuilding America's infrastructure," despite the billions of dollars absorbed by gasoline taxes and other duties to maintain and improve roads. Bush, who lacked Reagan's conservatism, felt obliged to compromise over budget deficits. By doing so, he fractured his single most important promise to the Reagan base: "Read my lips: no new taxes." Once the Democrats in Congress had their tax hikes, they forgot about spending cuts, and Bush had the worst of both worlds—a rising deficit and higher taxes.

As a result, the president viewed as virtually unbeatable two years earlier sank like a stone in the polls, his plunge exacerbated by his seeming disconnectedness with average Americans' lives. At a grocery store he seemed baffled by an ordinary scanner, making the Democrats' elitism tag more effective. ("Poor George," Texas governor Ann Richards said at the Democratic National Convention in 1992. "He was born with a silver foot in his mouth.")[82] Bill Clinton and his running mate Albert Gore, Jr., from

Tennessee, lambasted the Republicans for the "worst economy in the last 50 years," and despite the absolute absurdity of the statement, particularly when compared with the economy under Jimmy Carter, it stuck.

Added to the political mix was a third-party candidate, Ross Perot, who rode the growing discontent with both parties' business-as-usual attitudes in D.C. A business tycoon who had created Electronic Data Systems (EDS) to provide data processing for large corporations including General Motors, Perot's initial appeal was that he was an outsider. He had financed and organized the rescue of two EDS employees held hostage in Iran while Carter's military operation failed dismally. His frequent appearances on the *Larry King Live* talk show, in which he carefully avoided specific solutions but correctly identified the problems of debt, deficits, and Washington cronyism that resonated with large numbers of people, permitted him to launch criticisms without ever having to be pinned down on answers. ("Larry," he would intone, "we need to just get under the hood and fix it.") As a political platform, Perot created the Reform Party and ran on the ticket with Vietnam veteran and POW Navy Vice Admiral James Stockdale. Perot abruptly dropped out when the media began insisting on specifics, only to reenter the race in October. While many supporters felt betrayed, Perot had cleverly avoided months of scrutiny of his positions, allowing the press to turn on Bush. Studies revealed that Perot drew evenly from both candidates, but his constant attacks on Bush meant that the incumbent president fought every battle outnumbered.

The beneficiary of Perot's mischief was William Jefferson Blythe Clinton, who won with only 43 percent of the popular vote in 1992. Over the next eight years, Clinton proved even more controversial than Ronald Reagan, less so for his actual policies than for his womanizing and incessant flirtations. One of the most gifted political opportunists of a generation, Clinton introduced America to the "politics of personal destruction," then complained he was its victim.

Born in Hope, Arkansas, three months after his biological father died in a car accident, Clinton was raised by his grandparents for a time, then by his mother and her new husband, Roger Clinton. Growing up in a dysfunctional family full of abuse and drunkenness, Clinton struck other children as a "real obnoxious little kid."[83] At school in early grades he failed "deportment" (as getting along with other kids was once termed), but according to his biographer David Maraniss soon learned to be a pleaser, a compromiser, and a peacemaker, saying whatever it took to disarm toxic confrontations—especially at home. One of his fellow Democrats, Senator Bob Kerrey of

Nebraska, in a moment of rare candor, said of Clinton, "He is an unusually good liar"—then repeated the statement for emphasis.

He played saxophone in a band, but his real forte was politics, where his hero was John F. Kennedy. Struck by racial injustice on one hand and southern Christianity on the other, Clinton developed an ability to attract both black and white supporters, choosing as his mentor Arkansas senator William Fulbright. A Rhodes scholar, where he joined "the silliest group of Americans to go abroad since the last world tour of Ringling Brothers and Barnum & Bailey Circus," Clinton landed at Oxford in 1968, while he continued to search for ways to extend his student deferment from the Vietnam War.[84] Receiving his draft notice in April 1969, Clinton hustled back to Arkansas and employed Fulbright's support to convince Colonel Eugene Holmes, the commander of the University of Arkansas's Reserve Officer Training Corps (ROTC), to defer the draft notice on Clinton's promise to serve in the ROTC the following spring. Of course, Clinton never had any intention of serving if he could help it.[85] Consequently when, in one of his first initiatives, he sought a review of the policy on homosexuals serving in the military, the red flags from his earlier draft dodging flapped noisily.

After criticizing Bush for raising taxes, Clinton increased taxes again, raising the individual income tax rate to 36 percent with a 10 percent surcharge for the top earners, increasing the corporate income tax to 35 percent, and signing the repeal of the income cap on Medicare taxes. Over the next eight years, the economy began to hum, leading the Left to argue that tax increases had caused prosperity. In fact, much larger macroeconomic factors were at work that dwarfed the negative impact of the tax hikes. First, the opening of the former Iron Curtain had provided a vast new market almost as extensive as the one created by the end of World War II. Businesses from the West flocked to Russia, Ukraine, Poland, the Czech Republic, and other "new" countries where they had previously been excluded. If banks were cautious about lending to these unstable regimes, businesses had no hesitation about setting up shop in Moscow or Prague. Second, the 1990s benefited from consistently abnormally low energy prices, especially on oil, heating oil, diesel fuel, and airplane fuel, made possible by Bush's victory over Saddam. The energy savings were passed on to consumers through lower prices, which fed ongoing spending. Every element of production was enhanced by the lower energy costs, further adding to America's growing productivity.

Perhaps the most pervasive change in the American economy came with the computer revolution, which had started to flow through the entire system, from bar code scanners at Walmart to computerized robots at Ford in auto building. In each case the introduction of computers led to lower labor costs, as the technology replaced workers. This further drove productivity improvements, from the desktop to the top of the corporation. But it did not increase unemployment, as each new use of computers not only expanded the computing industry as a whole, but began to create new and unexpected jobs that had not even existed a few years earlier. For example, by the end of the 1990s, virtually all large organizations had an IT (information technology) department that oversaw not only computer maintenance, but all the new issues of networking personal desktop computers throughout companies, schools, and hospitals.

Bill Clinton had nothing to do with leading any of those macro events. If anything, they were entirely the fruits of his two Republican predecessors, Reagan and Bush, who had opened up the former Soviet bloc and who had ensured the free flow of oil at market prices through the Gulf War. Had Clinton not raised taxes, the results would have been even more impressive, as indeed they were when the Republican Congress took over in 1994, restrained spending, and, in 1997, passed new tax cuts that generated a tsunami of venture capital. In fact, one of the most celebrated achievements of the Clinton years—the Clinton "surpluses"—never happened: while it is true that the deficit fell from $188 billion in fiscal year 1996 to $17.9 billion in FY2000, it never reached surplus status. More important, the national debt kept rising, from $4.4 trillion when Clinton came into office to $5.8 trillion when he left.[86] Social Security's "trust fund," creating the temporary surplus by being treated as revenue, had been brought under the general budget more than a decade earlier. Looming in the background was the government's massive unfunded debt, including the long-term obligations of the soon-bankrupt entities of Medicare, the Social Security Administration, and federal and military pensions and health care, which were left off such calculations, even though they were, in actuality, debt.

A Scandalous Administration

Economic dislocations that lay in the future could be ignored, and even treated with benign neglect. A much different crisis soon enveloped the Clinton White House—the Lewinsky affair—which resulted in only the second presidential impeachment in American history. It began, oddly enough, with a real estate development deal gone sour in Arkansas.

The Clintons had an interest in the Whitewater Development Corporation; it failed and generated a rather routine scandal in Arkansas, where political office was frequently associated with substantial goodies for connected individuals. A partner, David Hale, testified in a U.S. district court that Clinton had pressured him to make a fraudulent $300,000 loan to another partner, Susan McDougal. (McDougal and her husband Jim were eventually convicted of wrongdoing in the scandal, but the Clintons escaped.) When *The New York Times* ran an exposé on Whitewater in 1994, the U.S. Justice Department opened an investigation under independent counsel Robert Fiske. Fiske, however, was appointed by Clinton's attorney general, Janet Reno, and therefore was seen as having a conflict of interest. He was replaced in August 1994 by Kenneth Starr, who drafted impeachment articles for the House. The results of his inquiry contended Clinton had lied under oath about the Hale loan.

Special prosecutors in the American system have unique powers to investigate anything that seems improper related to the subject of their inquiry. Starr consolidated another suit into his purview, *Jones v. Clinton*, a 1994 case involving a sexual harassment claim by Paula Jones against Clinton from his days as Arkansas governor. She alleged that Clinton had sent an Arkansas state trooper to fetch her while she worked on his campaign at the Excelsior Hotel in Little Rock and that he pressured her to have oral sex. Clinton, now president, challenged Jones's right to bring a suit, but the U.S. Supreme Court unanimously agreed with Jones, and Clinton would eventually settle out of court for $850,000.

The Jones accusations and initial legal wrangling came before Starr while he was winding down the Whitewater investigations. The case took a serious and bizarre turn when, as part of the Jones testimony, Starr discovered in January 1998 that Clinton had denied ever having had sexual relations with women other than his wife, Hillary, while married. He also learned that Jones's attorneys had acquired evidence that Clinton in 1995 had seduced a then twenty-two-year-old White House intern named Monica Lewinsky. The smitten Lewinsky described her relationship with Clinton as a "very raw, sexual connection [which] developed into romance and tenderness," and she lit up when "POTUS" (President of the United States) appeared on her privately listed cell phone.[87]

The press, having known of Lewinsky for months, attempted to bury the story and protect Clinton the way three decades earlier they had protected JFK. But a "new media" source, the Internet *Drudge Report*, began a major exposé. Clinton suddenly faced obstruction of justice and perjury charges as well as the original Whitewater complaints. He could possibly have lied his way out of the entire episode if Lewinsky had not kept a blue dress with Clinton's semen stain on it (because she had never had it dry cleaned).[88]

That physical evidence destroyed Clinton's denial and led Starr to present a recommendation of impeachment to the U.S. House of Representatives. He was impeached on four counts of perjury and obstruction of justice, but Democratic senators, who would be needed to reach the two-thirds vote to convict, refused to even consider the evidence. Some of it was of the most heinous nature, including a claim by "Jane Doe #6" (Juanita Broaddrick) that Clinton had raped her two decades earlier, and that at least two other women, Kathleen Willey and Gennifer Flowers, had faced horrendous persecution by the Clinton team for blowing the whistle on Clinton's dalliances with them. With Democratic senators stonewalling the proceedings, Clinton was not convicted; the Senate vote was forty-five for conviction, or fifteen short of the votes necessary. But he did lose his license to practice law in another ruling by federal district judge Susan Webber Wright on a contempt of court charge.[89]

The Whitewater scandal tainted Clinton's first administration, but was seldom a distraction. But the Lewinsky affair consumed Clinton's second administration, and allegations that he engaged in foreign policy actions to divert public attention from his legal troubles were likely false, but could never be entirely dismissed. Other revelations about his sex life impinging on his official duties were more disturbing.[90] Alternatively, Clinton looked for ways to gain positive publicity at little cost. Unfortunately, the exact opposite occurred. A somewhat routine peacekeeping mission in Somalia would expose the contradictions of using the military for non-combat missions.

Death in Mogadishu

Events in Africa intervened to shape the future of the Balkans by defining President Clinton's response to crises. The stage was Mogadishu, Somalia, where a bitter internal clan war had ruined the nation's agriculture and destroyed the social structure. Starving masses flooded the cities. As video leaked out to the industrialized countries, aid followed. Tons of food shipped from the international community arrived, only to be hijacked by local warlords and used as political weapons or to trade for guns.

Just three months before Clinton would replace him, George H. W. Bush provided American military transports for a new multinational relief effort, then increased the aid again in December. Under the sanction of the United Nations, but under the control of U.S. Central Command, Marines and the Army's 10th Mountain Division arrived as part of a multinational Unified Task Force to ensure that the humanitarian aid reached the victims. Moderately successful, the task force was replaced by the United Nations Operation in Somalia II, under UN control, which changed the mission in March 1993 to one of "nation building," calling a cease-fire conference which quickly broke down, mostly due to the efforts of the leading warlord, General Mohamed Farrah Aidid. In June, a contingent of twenty-four Pakistani peacekeepers were killed in Aidid's sector of Mogadishu, leading the UN to order the arrest of those responsible. The first attempt to grab some of Aidid's leadership produced rioting that killed four journalists.

Another attempt to capture Aidid himself occurred in October, when a force consisting of American Rangers, Special Operations Forces, and Delta Force planned to drop from helicopters around Aidid's meeting place, secure him, and move into a waiting ground convoy to hustle out of the city. Matters went awry the minute the Rangers began dropping. One Ranger fell from the chopper and had to be evacuated, and at the same time, a covering Black Hawk helicopter was shot out of the sky by a rocket-propelled grenade. As more troops arrived to evacuate the wounded and injured from the downed helicopter (the pilots died, but five inside the Black Hawk survived), the situation went from bad to worse.

Forces that arrived at the downed helicopter soon found themselves surrounded and under fire. The convoy took wrong turns; a second Black Hawk was shot down; and two Delta snipers, who volunteered repeatedly until given permission, were allowed to drop into the second chopper crash site to provide cover. Both were killed and the Black Hawk pilot taken hostage. Finally, after mind-boggling delays of several hours, an armored task force with Malaysians, Pakistanis, and more Americans linked up with the beleaguered troops. As painful as the death of nineteen Americans was, more shocking were the videos of the bodies being dragged through the streets by cheering mobs.[91] It would deeply impress an emerging terrorist, Osama bin Laden, who saw the episode as evidence of America's weakness.

The Clinton administration, obsessed with public relations, knew Somalia was a disaster and tried to change the subject. "How do we get the press off of dead rangers?" Clinton adviser George Stephanopoulos asked CIA director James Woolsey.[92] Within days of the "Battle of the Black Sea," as it came to be known, Clinton directed all American forces to withdraw by March 1994. Mark Bowden's best-selling book *Black Hawk Down* (1999) would later reveal that tanks and AC-130 gunships, which the military requested for the mission, were denied from the top levels of the Clinton administration as escalation.[93] Clinton's foreign frustrations soon rendered him entirely helpless to intervene in other ongoing genocides.

For example, a shell-shocked Clinton ignored cries from Rwanda to intervene in the slaughter of Tutsis by the Hutus in 1994, deferring to the hapless United Nations. One searches in vain for a more telling account of the futility of "peacekeeping." Genocide in Rwanda was well established, and long predated the more publicized 1990s slaughter. As in most European empires, the Belgians had played one group against another, perpetuating the Germans' support of the minority Tutsis over the Hutus. The Hutus themselves were transplanted Bantu who had come from the Congo region, while the Tutsis had arrived from Ethiopia. Put another way, determining whose land it was depended entirely on one's starting point. Germany moved into the region in the late 1800s, allying with the Tutsis to place northern Rwanda under German/Tutsi control and breaking up the larger Hutu landholdings. Revolt and a fledgling independence movement began in the late 1950s, culminating in 1962 with Rwanda voting for a republic and Burundi for a constitutional monarchy. Burundi (Tutsi, despite a Hutu majority) and Rwanda (Hutu) staged ongoing raids across each other's border.

When the king of Burundi selected a Hutu prime minister, Pierre Ngendandumwe, as a gesture to the Hutus, the new prime minister was assassinated, followed by a coup engineered by the Tutsi-led army. From 1965 to 1972, the Tutsi government of Burundi exterminated more than two hundred thousand Hutus. This was followed by the massacre of another twenty thousand by the Tutsi army in 1988. Then after a Tutsi front group formed within Uganda, the RPF (Rwandan Patriotic Front) embarked on invasions.

During this bloody episode, the International Monetary Fund, citing Rwanda's "structural adjustment," continued to hand over money, and after more mayhem in 1991, poured still more loans into the country, noting "a creditable effort toward social and economic development."[94] As the Hutu bodies piled up, and millions ran for their lives to equally despotic nations on the borders, the World Bank doled out yet more credit in 1992–93, and between 1989 and 1993, foreign aid to Rwanda rose 50 percent.

Worse were the efforts—or haplessness thereof—of the UN peacekeeping forces sent into Rwanda, and the episode bears some examination for what it reveals about expectations for such an international body. Under the command of a hard-charging Canadian, Major General Roméo Dallaire, who had brought to the attention of UN officials the arming of Hutu militia, the Department of Peacekeeping Operations, then headed by Kofi Annan, insisted that any disarming of bloodthirsty militia went "beyond the mandate" entrusted to UN security forces.[95] In April 1994, the Hutu president of Rwanda, after signing the Arusha Accords to end Rwandan fighting, was killed when his plane was shot down. The Hutus sought revenge against the Tutsis, starting the genocide that confounded Clinton. A contingent of ten Belgian peacekeepers protecting the Rwandan Tutsi prime minister and her five children were surrounded and surrendered their weapons. The Hutus took the Belgians to their base and tortured them before killing them and mutilating their bodies. They executed the prime minister as well.

Belgium's UN contingent soon went from sympathetic to cowardly. Units protecting two thousand refugees at a school not only abandoned them to Hutu militia who waited outside, drinking beer and chanting "Hutu Power," but as they pulled out, they fired shots over the heads of the helpless refugees to force them back into the hands of their murderers. It wasn't only the Belgians who acted despicably. A contingent of Ghanaian UN forces, entrusted with protecting Rwandan chief justice Joseph Kavaruganda, handed him over to a death squad. They stood, laughing, while Hutus raped Kavaruganda's wife and daughters.[96] The organization's pathetic performance as peacekeepers and protectors was deplorable, but entirely understandable, given that the Human Rights Commission of the UN was chaired by Muammar Gaddafi's Libya.

International peacekeepers, led by a French commander, proved utterly useless at stopping the violence. Indeed, at times, French peacekeepers even protected war criminals. More than two million people fled Rwanda-Burundi, and even then Paul Kagame's Tutsi party sparked violence in neighboring Zaire, with Kagame supporting Laurent Kabila, a Marxist who seized power in that country in 1997. Over the next four years, another 3.8 million people were killed by one side or the other in Rwanda and another 300,000 in Burundi. As still more players got involved, Uganda joined Rwanda to invade the Democratic Republic of the Congo and oust the pro-Hutu government there, in the process seizing as much of the Congo's mineral trade as they could. Between 1998 and 2002, more than three million Congolese died in the bloodiest war since the Second World War. A tenuous Rwandan peace finally settled in under Paul Kagame, whose aides were tied to the downing of the presidential plane in 1994.

Africa's warfare was almost exclusively tribal, infected occasionally with Communist revolutionary rhetoric. It entirely frustrated traditional

Western notions of treaties between political entities. Both Somalia and Rwanda demonstrated that there was no such thing as effective international peacekeeping, and that the wheel inevitably turned back to the United States to solve bloody problems, but with new implications. First, previous American meddlers, such as Woodrow Wilson and Teddy Roosevelt, restricted their activities to America's backyard—the Caribbean and, occasionally, Latin America. Second, instantaneous international communications now could present Americans with images of mass graves, torture, or fly-infested children that struck emotional chords and proved irresistible to the public's sense of justice. That, in turn, enhanced the power of the media, which determined which crisis landed on the nightly news. And for all their moralizing, the media overwhelmingly ignored the proliferation of horrendous violence in Africa (as they would black-on-black crime in urban areas), and fixated instead on Serbian genocide.

The Balkan Quagmire

Perhaps without the "Black Hawk Down" fiasco, Clinton might have refused to get involved in the latest of many Balkan conflicts. But having appeared soft in Mogadishu, Clinton felt compelled to display American toughness, with only slightly better results.

Much of what ensued in Serbia and other states created in the wake of communism's collapse was little more than "get-even-with-'em-ism." After the death of Yugoslavia's Josip Broz (Tito) in 1980, Serbian Communist Party chairman Slobodan Milošević assumed power, and ethnic and religious tensions rapidly tore Yugoslavia apart. Tito had governed Yugoslavia since 1945, successfully maintaining his distance from Moscow. He ruled through a grid of relationships in which he distributed power among all major ethnic groups—Serbs, Slovenes, Croats, and others. He carefully avoided allowing any single group to wield too much power, and thus preserved some measure of Yugoslav unity.

Milošević ditched Tito's strategy. He targeted Slovenia, a region in northwest Yugoslavia on the Adriatic, just above Croatia. Following the Ten-Day War, won by Slovene separatists who declared Slovenian independence, the demise of Yugoslavia was acknowledged in 1991, and Milošević introduced constitutional amendments that almost eliminated representation for Albanians, of whom most were Muslim. The main antagonists were the Greek Orthodox Serbs, the Roman Catholic Croatians and Slovenians, and the Muslim Bosnians and Albanians; none of whom wished to live under what they considered foreign domination. In World War II the Croatians and Bosnians had generally supported Hitler, while the Serbs were allied with the Soviet Union. Prior to that, the Bosnian Muslims had enjoyed a privileged status under the Muslim Ottoman Empire, and had been overlords to both the Croatians and Serbs. In short, the country could only be held together by a strong central government, and that had been what Tito furnished. With Tito gone, the country shattered, and anyone caught in the wrong place at the wrong time often was summarily killed.

Milošević tested the Slovenes by using a redistribution scheme that used federal money (of which Slovenia contributed a quarter) to provide back pay for state workers (of which Slovenes were a small minority). When the Slovenes resisted, the Yugoslavian People's Army (JNA) commenced its offensive. In the process, both Slovenian and Croat soldiers left the Yugoslav army, ending any pretense of a national campaign to put down domestic rebellions and providing an object lesson once again in the folly of collective security on the part of groups that have little in common.

A 1992 cease-fire negotiated by the United Nations proved tenuous, with action on all sides continuing until the Dayton Agreement of 1995. While that brew was bubbling, in 1993 fighting broke out between the Croats and Muslims *within* Bosnia. Convinced the world was sufficiently distracted or uninterested in his region, Milošević attacked the province of Kosovo within Serbian Bosnia, with its large and rapidly growing Muslim population.

What followed was "ethnic cleansing," in which each state attempted to reconfigure itself based on ethnicity by expelling (or, if necessary, killing) other groups unwilling to leave. In its worst form, ethnic cleansing involved helicopter attacks on helpless villages and lines of civilians shot and buried Katyn-style. Exiles during the first year of the Croatian and Bosnian wars numbered more than three million, and estimates of the total dead exceeded three hundred thousand, all taking place under the noses of the "new Europe" and perpetually ineffective United Nations. The chest-thumping anti-Americanism, accompanied by language suggesting that Europe was fully capable of governing itself, disappeared into the mass graves of Kosovo. In fact, while several European countries recognized Croatia's and Slovenia's independence, only Germany actively sought to halt Serb advances.

By and large, "Old Europe" feared the Serbs and painted them as Nazis—even as the Communists and devout Left rose to their defense. Serbia, in their eyes, remained a holdout against the "New World Order," a place where a form of socialism still had a chance. Thus the struggle was largely interpreted within the context of the global economy and the European Union, not religion or even nationality. The Communist parties of Greece, Bulgaria, and even Albania supported Serbia in its claims to Kosovo based on the region's history, reflecting an odd, 180-degree turn in which many Communists and socialists in Europe had adopted some positions Americans would call conservative. Despite the contradictions, many socialists were church members, fought homosexual rights, and opposed abortion, whereas the term "liberal" had come to refer to the globalization crowd that met at Davos, Switzerland.

These conflicts, picking up from pre–World War I conflicts, illustrated two disquieting facts of Europe in the late twentieth century. First, the American experiment in multiethnic melting had succeeded only because immigrants dribbled in, then blended with the larger stew. Conclaves of Irish, German, Jamaican, and Hispanic immigrants became Americanized in language, manners, and above all, expectations. Singers such as Gloria Estefan, Jennifer Lopez, and Marc Anthony displayed their Latino heritage while folding it into the broader values of the American Dream in the same way that Dean Martin and Tony Bennett had done with their Italian heritage two generations earlier. No such concept had ever taken root in Yugoslavia or even in parts of Spain, where the Basques held out for independence. National identities in England, Germany, and France were strong, but who was an Albanian? A Yugoslav? Attempting to ameliorate powerful ethnic differences by virtue of international mandate and goodwill (Versailles), raw power (Tito), and now "special interest" democracy had all failed.

A second, more disturbing trend was buried with the dead in the Balkans, and that was the religious character of the Kosovo and Bosnian conflicts. Historians have downplayed the Muslim influence in those events, but documents captured after the wars revealed terrorists had poured money into the region. The enthusiasm with which Croats (Roman Catholic), Bosnians (Muslim), Serbs (Greek Orthodox), and Slovenians (Roman Catholic) killed one another remained the defining characteristic of the wars. But the willingness of the West and the Clinton administration in particular to disregard the fundamentalist overtones of the Kosovars' language allowed pundits to set the Balkans aside as a separate security issue from the real threat facing the United States. Specifically, the Clinton administration treated the rhetoric used by the Serbs of a Muslim jihad as silly talk, a mask to cover their own vile bloodlust.

Far from international mediation or even force, what reined in Serbia initially was old-fashioned effective military resistance from Croatia and

Bosnia. Typically, however, the United Nations and NATO found themselves unwilling to identify the aggressor, in the process turning UN peacekeepers into hostages in Krajina, where the Serbs held 350 UN soldiers. The UN's humiliation was complete in July 1995 when a 400-strong Dutch contingent, supposedly protecting the Bosnian town of Srebrenica, meekly handed over its weapons to the Serbs.

UN peacekeepers transformed themselves from hapless bystanders to active accomplices in systematic carnage. Denied air support, UN forces under Lieutenant Colonel Thomas Karremans offered no resistance to the advancing Serbs in Srebrenica, where scenes of "unimaginable savagery" followed: "thousands of men [were] executed and buried in mass graves, hundreds of men buried alive, men and women mutilated and slaughtered . . . a grandfather forced to eat the liver of his own grandson."[97] Dutch soldiers high-tailed it out along with a two-mile column of refugees, having "crassly celebrated their evacuation . . . to Zagreb . . . even while the massacre persisted."[98] Met by Crown Prince Willem-Alexander of the Netherlands, the soldiers partied with Dutch officials, dancing in a chorus line to a forty-two-piece band playing Glenn Miller songs while the people they were charged with protecting fell in pools of blood. Nearly 7,400 Bosnian males were herded into the fields outside of Srebrenica and killed. It was a scene eerily reminiscent of the École Technique Officielle school slaughter in Rwanda.

The bombing finally forced Milošević to accept the Dayton Peace Agreement, the culmination of negotiations between Croat, Bosnian, and Serb leaders. Under the agreement, Bosnia and Herzegovina shared a federation with a Serbian entity (Republika Srpska), each overseeing half of the country and having equal constitutional status.

While the Dayton outcome did preserve Bosnia as a state, thanks to a permanent NATO force of sixty thousand, most of the preinvasion Muslims did not return. If it was Bosnia, it was a Serbianized Bosnia that was much different from the state that started the war. Moreover, its continued existence depended almost entirely on World Bank funding and the services provided by outside agencies. Jacques Poos, the Luxembourg representative at the peace process, boasted, "This is the Hour of Europe, not of America."[99] It was hardly anyone's hour. Contrary to popular impressions, the Dayton Peace Agreement did not end the bloodshed in the region, and indeed did not bring peace at all. If anything, Euro meddling convinced the Serbs that outside forces were against them, causing them to interpret nonthreatening developments in the worst possible light.

The quick recognition of Croatia and Slovenia by the Europeans had played on the Serbs' worst fears, strengthening the position of Milošević. Limited to two terms as president of Serbia, he took the position of president of the Federal Republic in 1997, but remained the prime mover in the Serbian government. When a revolt broke out in Kosovo against Serbia in 1997, and a Kosovo Liberation Army (KLA) staged attacks on Yugoslav army units (i.e., Serbian units), Serb forces moved in. More than 150,000 Kosovars were evicted. A new round of NATO bombing ensued in 1999, carefully avoiding placing any U.S. ground troops in the region. NATO spokesmen trumpeted the operation's goals as "Serbs out, peacekeepers in, refugees back." Serbia stepped up its efforts to remove the Kosovars before the bombing campaign ended—the bombs falling about them did nothing to reassure the Kosovars that it made good sense to stay—and the KLA encouraged the exodus. But the Serbs were, first and foremost, responsible for the relocations (and occasional exterminations, as at Peć). When they had substantially dispersed the population of Kosovo—up to a million Albanians—Milošević agreed to conditions.

None of the accords, agreements, plans, programs, or understandings stilled the violence, which erupted anew in March 2004 with the shooting of a Serb teenager, which in turn led to protest marches, followed by the retaliatory drowning of three Albanian children. Albanian mobs gathered at the Kosovska Mitrovica, separating the Serb and Albanian sections, with NATO peacekeepers armed with rubber bullets caught in between. Both the Albanians and Serbs had real bullets. Once gunfire started, the peacekeepers were merely targets. Six people were killed, three hundred wounded (including eleven peacekeepers), and the violence soon spread to include attacks on dozens of churches and mosques. Eventually the passions subsided, but it was a stark reminder that little had been solved by the interventions in the Balkans, and that, ultimately, the aggressive use of force determined history's winners and losers, not international peacekeeping forces and agreements. Milošević was eventually ousted by the Serbs themselves, then arrested and turned over to the UN International Criminal Court at the Hague to be tried for war crimes.

Lions of Allah

Bosnia and Kosovo constituted unique problems for the Europeans because in both states Islam made the conflict a religious war as well as a political struggle. The Europeans had gone out of their way for three hundred years to minimize religious differences—indeed, to pretend they did not even exist. Thus, the threat of radical Islam was not taken seriously anywhere because Islam itself was not taken seriously throughout the West. It did not occur to increasingly secularized Westerners (even Russians) that Muslims actually believed in their religion, and, more important, that many believed it was a call to violent action. Yet all that was needed were a few Muslim lightning rods to attract popular support for jihad throughout Islamic nations.

The first of those was Sayyid Qutb, a leading member of the Muslim Brotherhood (a forerunner of al-Qaeda). Qutb was deeply traumatized by his time in the United States at Colorado State College of Education (now Northern Colorado University). Arriving in the United States in 1948 as a less than devout Muslim, the Egyptian student and former bureaucrat found that he had many Western tastes, including a love of Hollywood movies and French novels. However, the ubiquitous sex available and flaunted in America deeply troubled him. He saw sex as "the main enemy of salvation," and thought "sexual mixing led inevitably to perversion."[100] If a "girl looks at you," he wrote, "appearing as if she were an enchanting nymph . . . you sense only the screaming instinct inside her, and you can smell her burning body, not the scent of her perfume but flesh, only flesh. . . ."[101] Although he spent only six months in Greeley before visiting other cities, Qutb nevertheless returned from America in 1950 fully radicalized, absorbed with "the white man in Europe or America" as "our number-one enemy."[102] Whether it was gyrating girls at parties or sporting events, Qutb found American culture profoundly demonic:

> This primitiveness can be seen in the spectacle of the fans as they follow a game of football . . . or watch boxing matches or bloody, monstrous wrestling matches. . . . This spectacle leaves no room for doubt as to the primitiveness of the feelings of those who are enamored with muscular strength and desire it.[103]

Back in Egypt, Qutb found himself in jail for his connections with the Muslim Brotherhood, where he wrote a manifesto ("Milestones"), the Muslim equivalent of Lenin's 1902 "What Is to Be Done?" There was no "Muslim community," he complained, only an Islamic revival that he would lead. From 1948 until the 1970s, the Muslim Brotherhood engaged in a number of bombings and assassination attempts, particularly the failed attack on Egyptian president Nasser in 1954. Nasser rounded up Qutb and others for their crimes. Released a decade later, Qutb was arrested again in August of

1965 for plotting the overthrow of the government. In June 1966, Qutb was given the death sentence, which he welcomed as "martyrdom." The government realized its mistake after demonstrators filled Cairo's streets, and sought to release him if he would appeal the sentence. But Qutb was determined to die for the cause, and the Egyptian government finally obliged by hanging him.

Another Egyptian, an innocent-looking bespectacled surgeon named Ayman al-Zawahiri, followed in Qutb's footsteps. Born in a Cairo suburb to a prominent doctor, Zawahiri formed his own radical Islamic cell at age fifteen, identifying Jews and Americans as the twin devils to be expunged. He soon was printing leaflets to support the Iranian revolution, and when Anwar Sadat, the president of Egypt, moved to dissolve student radical organizations and end the jihad camps, Zawahiri was inflamed. On October 6, 1981, plotters associated with Zawahiri assassinated Sadat while he reviewed marching army units, although Zawahiri later said he had not learned of the plot until a few hours before. Like his spiritual mentor Qutb, Zawahiri was hauled off to jail. His trial, and that of his conspirators, lasted three years, matching his sentence. Released in 1984, Zawahiri had transformed from a peaceful doctor into a "hardened radical whose beliefs had been hammered into brilliant resolve."[104]

He soon found himself in Saudi Arabia, where he became acquainted with Mohammed bin Laden, a wealthy developer, and his son, Osama. A tall, gangly youth, Osama bin Laden had been briefly arrested by the Saudi government for affiliation with those who staged the attack at the Grand Mosque in 1980. That siege, finally crushed by the Saudi government, resulted in sixty-three beheadings performed in eight different Saudi cities—the largest execution ever carried out in the country. Already, bin Laden longed to join the Afghan resistance against the Soviet Union, but couldn't get permission from the Saudi authorities to leave the country. Falling under the influence of the "warrior priest" Sheikh Abdullah Azzam—whose slogan was "Jihad and the rifle alone; no negotiations, no conferences, no dialogues"—bin Laden hatched a plan in September 1984 to provide fodder for the war against the Soviets. He offered an airline ticket, lodging, and living expenses for every Arab (and his family) who joined the mujahideen.[105] Azzam supported the offer when he published a fatwa, "Defense of the Muslim Lands," in which he portrayed fighting in Afghanistan as the equivalent of the holy pilgrimage to Mecca, even taking precedence over the Palestinian struggle.[106]

Bin Laden joined the jihad himself in 1986, moving to a Pakistani camp to cross into Afghanistan, where he was soon reunited with Zawahiri. Two years later, they formed al-Qaeda, or "the Base," an organization devoted to expunging any Russian presence in Afghanistan. But by that time the Soviets were already withdrawing and another enemy had to be found. Obsessed with cleansing the Muslim world of unbelievers—both heretical Muslims and non-Muslims—bin Laden was energized by Saddam Hussein's invasion of Kuwait. Seeing himself as Islam's savior, bin Laden lobbied Saudi officials to let the mujahideen expel the Iraqis. Instead, the House of Saud turned to the Americans and the West. From that point on, the United States became bin Laden's mortal enemy.

By all accounts, the tripwire for attacks on U.S. soil—and the earliest indicator that al-Qaeda was operating in America—occurred in November 1990, with the assassination of Jewish Defense League founder Rabbi Meir Kahane in Manhattan by an Egyptian, El Sayyid Nosair. Police investigating the murder found multiple New Jersey driver's licenses in Nosair's apartment and turned up lists of other prominent Jews in the United States who were apparently targets. A battle over jurisdiction between the New York police and the FBI obscured the fact that FBI agents had spotted Nosair at a shooting range two years earlier and photographed him. As one New York–based FBI agent said, "you couldn't get anybody to take terrorism seriously. . . . Even after Kahane, nobody felt it could happen here. . . ."[107]

In 1992, bin Laden relocated to the Sudan, taking up residence in Khartoum, where a previous Mahdi had engaged in terrorism against helpless civilians a century earlier. Whether bin Laden actually dispatched Ramzi Yousef to blow up the World Trade Center in 1993 or not, it is clear that Yousef was trained at an Afghanistan al-Qaeda camp. Yousef intended to blow out the support columns of one World Trade Center tower and collapse it onto the other. His crew rented a Ryder truck, filled it with explosives, and on February 26, 1993, parked it next to the predetermined spot, then left. The explosion shook the building and killed eight, but failed to bring down the tower where it was set, let alone both. Investigators were able to find the vehicle identification number of the truck, trace it back to the terrorists (one of whom had actually tried to get his money back because the truck was destroyed "in an accident"), and easily learn the names of the conspirators.

Yet it scarcely made a dent in the attitude toward terrorist attacks on Americans. At the hearings for the new attorney general nominee a few weeks later, neither the senators nor nominee Janet Reno even mentioned the event, and the newly appointed director of the FBI, Louis Freeh, found "there was no White House interest in conducting a wide-ranging probe to determine whether the Trade Center bombing was state sponsored."[108] CIA director James Woolsey concurred: "No one wanted to hear the bad news that the first World Trade Center attack might just be the beginning."[109]

Yousef, whom former Clinton adviser on Iraq Laurie Mylroie claimed was linked to Saddam Hussein, was a Palestinian/Pakistani from an affluent family and had studied in Wales. Following the bombing, he fled to Pakistan (where he failed to assassinate Benazir Bhutto, Pakistan's prime minister), then staged a bombing of a Shiite Muslim shrine in Iran. In doing so, he demonstrated that the schisms within Islam were as vicious as those separating radical Muslims from the West. He then traveled to the Philippines to plan the Bojinka attack with his uncle, Khalid Sheikh Mohammed, a squat, disgusting man whose only trait in common with Yousef was his hatred of America.

The Bojinka plot demonstrated the cell-like nature of al-Qaeda. While bin Laden ostensibly orchestrated operations, individual cells carried out attacks, frequently at the same time, and occasionally without coordination. Bojinka involved simultaneous bombings of a dozen U.S. jumbo jets over the Pacific, which would bring air travel to a halt. Around the same time, bin Laden also contacted Yousef to inquire about a plan to assassinate Bill Clinton when he visited Manila in November 1994. Perhaps these plots would have succeeded had not Yousef's momentary incompetence—he allowed the chemicals in his apartment to catch fire—halted the planning. Manila police found his apartment because of the fire and seized his computer with the Bojinka and Clinton plans on it.

After Clinton refused to authorize an operation to capture bin Laden in Sudan and also rejected an offer by Sudan's defense minister to hand bin Laden over to U.S. control, the terror chief decided in 1996 to exit Khartoum for Afghanistan.[110] There, bin Laden became the guest of the Taliban government—an ultraradical Islamic sect that meticulously followed Sharia law. They imposed ruthless, often murderous, sentences on those guilty of the slightest infractions. Music, movies, dancing, photographs, dolls, smoking, even flying kites were serious offenses, and all men were subject to "beard patrols." People caught in the act of unmarried sex were stoned to death in public stadiums. Thieves received the traditional amputation of a hand. Women were singled out for special horrors, including public beatings. They were banned from schools and had to wear the head-to-toe covering called the burqa. The national museum of Afghanistan was sacked and destroyed. But none other than future Bush administration critic and counterterrorism czar in both the Bush and Clinton administrations Richard Clarke noted that a source had revealed that Iraq had also offered bin Laden asylum.[111]

Bin Laden and Zawahiri had absorbed the key ingredient necessary to being a star twentieth-century terrorist: good theater. Killing not only had to be big and bloody, but symbolic. Shock and humiliation were also desired elements. The Bojinka plan intrigued bin Laden and Khalid Sheikh Mohammed and remained in their imagination from that point on. They soon modified their plan to fly airliners into the Twin Towers and, at the same time, al-Qaeda sought to procure uranium.[112]

In June of 1996, al-Qaeda terrorists detonated a fuel truck at the Khobar Towers in Saudi Arabia, the barracks of the 4404th Airlift Wing, killing nineteen Americans and injuring hundreds. The 9/11 Commission suspected both Iran and bin Laden were involved, with the explosives and timing devices coming from the former and the perpetrators supplied by the latter.[113]

Slowly, Western media's awareness of bin Laden went from "Who?" to "Wow." He was depicted as a multimillionaire "James Bond villain," living in "a vast, underground lair that would put Dr. No's to shame."[114] He was said to be on a kidney dialysis machine. But popular reports of a $300 million fortune proved a myth. Saudi Arabia froze bin Laden's assets in 1994, and the 9/11 Commission reported that never were "bin Laden's assets in Sudan a source of money for al Qaeda [sic]."[115] Sudan expropriated all his businesses and froze all his accounts when he left in 1996.

In many ways, bin Laden was extremely typical of the new breed of Islamist murderers in that he was unwilling to risk his own life in the kinds of suicidal martyrdom to which he consigned his minions. Where he was thoroughly typical was in his Qutb-like devout hatred of the West. He, Zawahiri, Khalid Sheikh Mohammed—all of them saw America as the locus of evil because it was the main and, in many ways, sole, Christian nation on earth. As an evangelizing nation for Christianity, one which sent missionaries abroad and even into Muslim lands, it was the main threat to Islam. Christianity "was not just a rival, it was the archenemy," and America was its engine.[116] As bin Laden put it to the Americans, "You are terrorists" who had to withdraw from intervention against Muslims anywhere and everywhere "in the whole world."[117] His comments were echoed by numerous other groups, including the famous fatwa by the International Islamic Front for Jihad in February 1998, which declared that killing all

Americans and their allies was a holy act and "individual duty for every Muslim who can do it."

By then, prototype al-Qaeda bombings, assassinations, and murder missions began to occur with deadly frequency:

- November 1997, Luxor Temple, Egypt. Target: tourists visiting the ruins. Sixty-two people were slaughtered, then the killers committed suicide.

- August 1998, Nairobi, Kenya, and Dar es Salaam, Tanzania. Target: U.S. embassies, in al-Qaeda's first multiple bombing strike. (In fact, five embassies had been targeted, and intelligence had saved three.) Hundreds were killed, a thousand wounded.

- January 2000, Aden, Yemen. Target: USS *The Sullivans*, which was saved by an accident when fishermen discovered the al-Qaeda vessel that would be used to attack the American ship and pillaged what they thought was hashish. It was explosives, and the plot was foiled.

- October 2000, Aden, Yemen. Target: USS *Cole*. A bomb killed seventeen U.S. servicemen and badly damaged the *Cole*.

- September 2001, New York City. Targets: the World Trade Center, Pentagon, and White House or Congress. More than three thousand civilians died, both towers were destroyed, and the Pentagon was badly damaged in the worst attack on U.S. soil since 1941.

Unconnected Dots

Throughout this period, American intelligence agencies—particularly the FBI and the CIA—studiously avoided sharing information. Some of this was institutional and embedded in the nature of intelligence organizations. Some was structural, based on the different missions and powers each possessed. But much of it was bureaucratic and political. The July 1995 "Wall" memo, issued by Clinton's attorney general Janet Reno and designed by Deputy Attorney General Jamie Gorelick, essentially prohibited exchanges of critical information between the FBI and the CIA. It was by some accounts intended to sidetrack investigations into political contributions to the Clinton-Gore campaign from shady donors such as John Huang and

Charlie Trie, which could have exposed Clinton to yet another special prosecutor—but the effects were lethal to U.S. counterterrorism efforts. Although the 9/11 Commission, on which Gorelick served as a commissioner, would seek to spin her obstructionism as developing "procedures aimed at managing information," in fact the procedures *limited and controlled* the information flow.[118] The Clinton administration had approached terrorism with a law enforcement model, and even the 9/11 Commission acknowledged that court rules had hamstrung the sharing of information; the FAA's intelligence unit produced threat assessments that its administrator, Jane Garvey, never even saw. Not even until 1995 did the Defense Department heavily invest in planning for domestic terror incidents dealing with nuclear, chemical, or biological weapons.[119]

After the Beirut truck bombing in 1983, Ronald Reagan had shifted the government from passive to active counterterrorism measures and was the first to declare terrorism an "act of war."[120] But under Clinton, antiterrorism was downgraded to what one staffer called "drugs and thugs." Clinton's 1996 "defer, defeat, and respond vigorously" Decision Directive 39 further wedded the United States to crime-prevention models, while, according to the 9/11 Report, Congress "had a distinct tendency to push questions of emerging national security threats off its own plate." Bin Laden didn't get his own special unit inside the CIA until after 1996, and a capture plan wasn't approved until 1998. Indeed, Clinton shut down a 1995 investigation of Islamic charities out of concern that it would expose Saudi Arabia's ties to terrorist money-laundering operations that funded suicide bombers.[121]

Meanwhile, domestic terrorists Timothy McVeigh and Terry Nichols exploded a truck bomb outside the Murrah Federal Building in Oklahoma City in April 1995. This instantly rerouted the entire law enforcement and investigation apparatus of the federal government away from al-Qaeda and to home-grown extremists. Their grievance was that the federal government was trampling on the rights of citizens, both at Waco, Texas (when the Branch Davidian religious compound was attacked) and at Ruby Ridge, Idaho, where a separatist's wife was killed by a government sniper while she stood holding her baby behind a door. Even a liberal Democratic congressman such as John Conyers of Michigan referred to the Bureau of Alcohol, Tobacco, and Firearms as "jack-booted thugs."

McVeigh and Nichols not only bear full guilt for the 168 souls they killed in Oklahoma, but also share a small part of the blame for the nation's unpreparedness for 9/11. It is also true that Attorney General Janet Reno and subsequent attorneys general (aside, briefly, from John Ashcroft) have shown significantly more interest in pursuing right-wing militias in the United States than in uncovering terror cells of Muslim radicals. Later the emphasis would be shifted further to fundamentalist Christians and returning military veterans under Obama. President Bill Clinton on April 19 even blamed a variant of talk radio for encouraging antigovernment extremism, lumping Islamic terrorism in with right-wingers. He claimed "loud and angry voices" inflamed the public debate, and called those who were on the "nation's airwaves" "reckless" and "purveyors of hatred and division."[122]

Although Clinton was very vocal against the perpetrators of the Oklahoma City bombing, he had no comment when five days afterward, a timber lobbyist became the third victim of a mail bomb campaign. The explosive was sent by a man known as the Unabomber for his personal bomb deliveries (bombs designed to send an "environmentally friendly" message). When the bomber, Ted Kaczynski, was captured a year later, he had a copy of Vice President Al Gore's book on the environment, *Earth in the Balance*, in his apartment. Nonetheless, environmental terrorists of the Left were not targeted by Clinton's Justice Department. McVeigh, meanwhile, was tried in Denver, the city in the United States with the second highest number of federal employees (Washington, D.C., of course, was first), guaranteeing not only a conviction but the death penalty.

Even when Clinton did focus on Islamic terror, his target was not bin Laden but Saddam Hussein. Amazingly, he was prodded to invade Iraq and topple Hussein by future Bush critics Edward Kennedy and John Kerry. This was where the murkiness came in: while almost all those in the intelligence communities could see something was going on, no one was certain yet if there was an organized effort that connected bin Laden, Iran, and Iraq (as well as the warlords in Mogadishu and Kosovo), or if the jihadists were isolated radicals who just got lucky once in a while. Larry Johnson, a former CIA officer and Clinton's deputy director of the State Department's Counterterrorism Office, made public appearances in early 2001 scoffing at the terrorist threat. "Americans are bedeviled by fantasies about terrorism," he wrote in a *New York Times* op-ed titled "The Declining Terrorist Threat."[123] Others, however, including Clinton's CIA director, George Tenet, who was retained by the Bush administration, were deeply concerned, with Tenet warning about a "major attack" by al-Qaeda in the near future.[124]

Thus, by the late 1990s, while intellectuals such as Edward Said waxed eloquently about global "interconnectedness" and Thomas Friedman, whose predictions were as stunningly wrong as they were prolific, advanced his "Golden Arches" theory—his claim that no two countries with a Mc-Donald's ever went to war against each other, rendered null and void almost immediately by a Serb-Croat war—a shockingly obvious disparity between Islamic states and Western nations had appeared. There was, in fact, little in common between the two: virtually all scientific, technological, and cultural advances of any sort were coming from the westernized countries, while Muslim states were being "re-primitivized" at a rapid rate. A 2002 United Nations report noted that more books were translated into Spanish in a single year than have been translated into Arabic in the last millennium, and that among those books that did cross the Arabic-language line were *Mein Kampf* and the *Protocols of the Elders of Zion*.[125]After the 1979 Grand Mosque attack in Saudi Arabia, an already rigid society became positively oppressive: most music disappeared, television was "dominated by bearded men debating fine points of religious law," movie theaters were closed, and the Riyadh concert hall, completed in 1989, never witnessed a performance.[126] Of even more importance were the growing reports of the stoning of women, the murder of missionaries, and the overall retrenching of much of the Middle East into a medieval society along the lines of Sharia law. Far from liberating people through religion, the fundamentalist imams were returning the region to the times of Muhammad, quite literally.

Sunset in the Pacific

If any society in recent memory had approximated the fanaticism of the radical jihadists, it was Imperial Japan. Suicide bombings, after all, had been part and parcel of Japan's final moments in World War II. Yet Japan seemed unconcerned with the rise of radical Muslim nations on its back doorstep. Instead, the land of the Rising Sun turned inward, increasingly concerned with its flagging economy.

After 1990s, the once-feared Asian economic colossus revealed its clay feet. Just as America's economic boom after the Second World War originated with the automobile, so too the automobile had given Japan its greatest entrée into world markets. The first reliable Japanese cars hit the American auto market at the very time the Volkswagen craze hit its apex.[127] When Detroit's compact models fizzled in the mid-1960s, auto executives wrongly concluded that there would never be a market for such cars. U.S. automakers added weight and length to even the "pony cars," stretching the once-nimble Mustangs and Camaros into full-blown sedan sizes while the world was on the cusp of a massive shift: from 1968 to 1974, the small car market rose from 10 percent of the total to 50 percent.[128]

Like the Europeans, Japan had chosen a state-planning model, run through the Ministry of International Trade and Industry (MITI, created in 1949) to protect domestic industries and, most important, to develop an export policy. High tariffs or debilitating restrictions were put on American imports, especially for steel and cars, while MITI organized bank loans and trade deals for the Japanese producers. Hailed as a great success, MITI shepherded the export of, first, Datsun (later Nissan) and then Toyota models.

Predictably, though, it was not a government planner or even an auto executive who enabled Japanese autos to break into the American market. Nobe Wakatsuki, a trading specialist and grandson of a former Japanese prime minister, had represented the Marubeni Trading Company in Japan since 1954. A keen observer of American life, he found that Americans identified with their cars and that an auto was the equivalent to the Japanese *geta* or sandal (everyone needed sandals). When he visited the California Chamber of Commerce and asked about importing Japanese cars, the American official was stunned and said, "I thought they got their cars from Jimmy [General Motors]."[129]

Nobe watched the first Datsuns make their appearance at a Los Angeles auto show. People asked, "What is a Datsun?" to which Nobe responded, "It's a Japanese car," and the customer would always reply, "I didn't know the Japanese made cars."[130] Datsun began by establishing a small pickup market, marketing at first to Japanese landscapers. Then, Japanese designers sought to compete in the consumer sedan market, and did so with some success because of low prices. Still, Datsun's first teams in America became acutely aware of the differences in taste that separated their cultures—differences that Japan had to incorporate into its cars. Americans wanted more room; and above all, more horsepower.

MITI played a key role in marketing Japanese cars to the world, but the real competitive edge had already been imposed on Japanese industry through ruthless domestic competition. All Japanese manufacturers benefited in a perverse irony from wartime bombing: with factories destroyed, companies had to invest in new equipment. Nissan, for example, was still making autos by hand in 1960 before erecting new factories with automated welding machines. Production soared from 33,000 cars in 1959 to 213,000 in 1964.

American observers and consultants to Japan, such as writer James Abegglen, warned U.S. manufacturers that the rapidly rising prosperity of postwar Japan would so greatly expand its domestic car production that its companies would modernize and retool rapidly, and with American access, the Japanese companies would achieve an instant export base of millions of quality-conscious consumers.[131] In an odd precursor to the Detroit observers of Japanese production lines twenty years later, swarms of Japanese engineers and executives toured American plants, searching for any quality edge they could find. As David Halberstam noted, "they measured, they photographed, they sketched, and they tape-recorded everything they could. Their questions were precise."[132] Americans, they thought, were condescending—sharing openly because their visitors were Asians, and not to be taken seriously. The visitors leveraged those prejudices, playing the "poor little Asian" role to perfection.

Japan's strategy in shipbuilding and steel had been the same. First, engineers and executives studied foreign technology; then, they purchased the best equipment they could, even if it meant buying single machines. In some cases, the Japanese bought whole American factories with state-of-the-art technology, such as the world's most modern copper tube mill located in Euclid, Ohio, and owned by Chase Brass and Copper, which had never reached its potential due to engineering problems, union wage structures, and opposition to automation. It was purchased by a *zaibatsu* and put into production in Japan. Companies sacrificed profits for market share, first, inside Japan (a market then twice the size of West Germany), then internationally. In the 1960s, the Japanese applied this strategy to automobiles. They not only adopted foreign technology, they adopted foreign ideas. When an American statistician came to them with suggestions for improving their management structures, they listened intently.

If any one American changed Japan more than General Douglas MacArthur, it was W. Edwards Deming, a statistician sent to Japan in the late 1940s to work on the Japanese census. His expertise, however, was in quality control techniques, and he soon began lecturing. To his surprise, not only did managers attend, but they were attentive. He promised them results, and as one executive wrote, "in order not to lose face, we did what we were told and it worked."[133] Quickly attaining the role of guru, Deming found the Japanese obsessed with following his recommendations. In 1951 the Japanese government went so far as to establish a quality-control prize in his name.

Yet for all the consultants and MITI planners, one competitor stood out as having received no government support. Soichiro Honda, a mechanic who pioneered new piston rings, went into the manufacture of powered bicycles after World War II. Operating from a wooden shack, Honda Motor Company opened for business in 1948, producing motorcycles and scooters. In motorcycle production and sales, Honda displayed a savage ruthlessness that would later typify all the Japanese companies. When he entered the competition for motorcycles, Tohatsu controlled 22 percent of the market and Honda, 20 percent. Building a better motorcycle, and using aggressive marketing, Honda soon controlled 44 percent of the market, and Tohatsu was bankrupt. Honda founded the American Honda Company ten years later, with its highly popular motorcycles, when Honda contemplated moving into the auto market. Honda had to rely solely on quality to sell his product. He accomplished the impossible: Honda not only broke into the Japanese auto market, but the American market as well.

In 1952, the typical Japanese car cost nearly double that of an American model. By 1959, the difference had fallen to only $200 in the Americans' favor, but by 1970, an American car cost $1,000 more than a Japanese car.[134] American union demands (and corporate acquiescence—hypnotized, as the executives were, by the seemingly unending sticker price increases they were able to inflict on consumers) afflicted the auto industry with a slow-growing cancer that would prove fatal to American auto, and industrial, dominance. Medical insurance and retirement programs, even in the 1970s, were simply unsustainable.

During the 1980s, although American autos staged a recovery (Chrysler with a federal bailout), Japanese firms retained a quality edge. Toyota vied with General Motors for the position of largest automaker in the world. In shipbuilding, steel, robots, and electronics, Japanese firms either took the lead or equaled American competitors, although significantly, in every area where the Japanese staged rapid advances, they had produced *more* competitors inside Japan, not fewer. This constituted a direct refutation of the notion that the planned MITI economy would thrive with government picking winners and losers. While autos continued to do well, the other stars in MITI's crown began to falter. Unable to export its way to sustained growth, the Japanese economy entered a long, slow downward spiral. Data from the Japanese economy, the world's second largest, turned "relentlessly bleak" by the early twenty-first century, down to 1.5 percent per year from earlier estimates of 2.6 percent. By 2009, the unemployment rate reached unheard of levels at 4.4 percent, as 1980s powerhouses such as Honda, Panasonic, Sony, and NEC laid off thousands. Toyota, having just become the number one car manufacturer in the world, posted a loss for the first time since the Great Depression, and forecasts were for things to get worse. The suicide rate—a "barometer of financial distress in shame-conscious

Japan"—was rising fast, as more than 33,000 Japanese killed themselves, most of them unemployed.[135] Japan's legendary lifetime employment had been replaced with short-term contracts, which by 2009 made up a third of all Japanese employment.

Japan provided yet another example of the fallacy of Keynesian spending to prop up a crumbling economy: gross government debt as a percentage of GDP rose from 45 percent in 1989 to 170 percent in 2009, with no real effect. By 2010, even *The New York Times*—which had led the chorus of dire warnings about the Japanese threat in the 1980s—reported "Japan Goes from Dynamic to Disheartened."[136] The Japanese middle class had shrunk under a collapse that neither massive Keynesian spending nor the vaunted export-led industry could stifle, making the nation "little more than an afterthought in the global economy."[137] By 2009, the Nikkei stock market index had dropped to 1983 levels.

More troubling still, Japan was an aging nation, one filled with "disenchanted youth." This included hundreds of thousands of youths, mostly males, who withdrew from society out of fully informed views of Japan's "economic and spiritual crisis."[138] Like all government agencies, MITI—once the darling of American intellectuals who longed for a similar American "office of industrial policy"—had no answers for one of the most basic questions of national existence: what happens when you stop producing more people?

Japan's demographic decline began to affect all elements of the culture. The United States, in contrast, had partly through legal and partly through illegal immigration continued to see its population grow. Japan had showed that its planned structure could prosper for a short time, until all of the associated ills of a deeply regimented society crashed in on it. Not only did the population decline affect obvious trends in aging and elderly care, but it leeched the creativity, energy, and vision from the society.

America, Adrift

Despite having superficially imposed a peace in the Balkans, America's superpower image had become badly tarnished by Mogadishu, Rwanda, and the Serb campaign. Muslim radicals were emboldened, African dictators unafraid, and Europeans, unimpressed. Moreover, the new sole superpower status of the United States produced a bafflingly inconsistent set of criticisms of American culture.

Europeans and Third Worlders seemed unable to decide if Americans were vulgar, decadent, contemptible, weak, feminized—or shrewd, oppressive, powerful, brutal, and ruthless. The United States was simultaneously portrayed as a land of hideous inequality where the "plutocrats trample the silently suffering and impoverished into dust," yet at the same time subject to complaints that a sea of rabble determined the tastes of everything.[139] Were American women Amazonian man-killers without femininity, or seducers who slept with any man they could find? Were American males sissified, feminized metrosexuals, or domineering, gun-toting, mach cowboys? Were Americans Puritans who censored the pleasurable, or hedonistic, drug-absorbed, sex-crazed suburbanites who spent all day chasing each other's wives? Was America "fundamentalist Christian," or was it "ruled by the Jew"?[140]

If America's persona seemed Janus-faced, much of the Western world likewise had descended into schizophrenic and mutually incompatible tendencies. Throughout the West, feminism and economic growth had combined to reduce fertility rates and family sizes. Not only were there fewer children, but there were fewer children with fathers present in the home— even among prosperous groups. Birth control, the holy grail of the sexual revolution, had been augmented by its opposite, fertility treatments among upper-class women anxious to experience motherhood without a husband.

Writer Joyce Winer observed, "If the sixties was all about sex without babies, the nineties is all about babies without sex."[141] Especially in Hollywood, a spate of single mothers raising children graced the popular magazine covers. In the television show *Murphy Brown*, which featured Candice Bergen as a single newswoman, the plot line had Brown become pregnant, then go it alone with a child when her boyfriend didn't want to give up his freedom for fatherhood. Then–vice president Dan Quayle commented on the inappropriate messages such a plot delivered, for which he was ridiculed. (A few years later, sociologist Barbara Dafoe Whitehead produced an article summarizing all the recent sociological studies under the title "Dan Quayle Was Right.")

In fact, while the trends had been in place, the 1990s kicked off the "unmarriage revolution."[142] The collapse of marriage translated into the collapse of the family, or more appropriately, the separation of the United States into two nations: one of old-fashioned married couples with children and one of single-parent families (largely female headed). This split divided sharply along education lines: a woman with a college education or a high school diploma and some college fell heavily into the first group, while a woman without a high school diploma more often ended up as a single mother. And while the United States continued "to be the teen-mommy capital of the Western world," the rate of teen motherhood actually fell in the 1990s. Increasingly, low-income thirty-somethings were having babies.[143] By 2000, the gap had become stunning: only 10 percent of women who had graduated from college were living without husbands, but three and a half times that many women with less education were alone. That statistic, in turn, correlated almost *exactly* with the 36 percent of female-headed families below the poverty line. As traditional as it sounded, a woman without a husband had a very good chance of being poor—all the more so if she was uneducated.[144]

Marriage—not welfare—determined whether a woman was poor. England, with its much more generous welfare programs, had similar rates of poverty among single mothers. At the time (the 1990s), there was an increase in cohabitation, especially among low-income couples, leading to fewer marriage-willing males. Most of all, however, better-educated women realized that they needed a husband to ensure that their children succeeded academically. Research by Kay Hymowitz found that "children of single mothers have lower grades and educational attainment than kids who grow up with married parents, even after controlling for race, family background, and IQ."[145] Contrary to the assertions of *Murphy Brown*, educated women view the question of what man will become their husband *and* the father of their children as possibly the most important decision of their lives.

What welfare incentives didn't affect, the courts did, exacerbating the single-mother disaster with the 1972 *Stanley v. Illinois* case, which ruled that fathers who had never married the mother had the same custody rights as a former husband. This further frayed the threads of marriage and child rearing. Marriage taught children the values of a nuclear family, with both a father and a mother, one or both being breadwinners, and both involved in child rearing; children who went to school and learned values and skills from both parents then gained desirable employment. In contrast, children of the ghetto—more than those in rural areas, which often did not have the same concentration of female-headed homes—absorbed none of those lessons. Rather, they learned that marriage wasn't important, fathers were invisible, jobs were undesirable, and education was irrelevant. Daniel Patrick Moynihan had observed this already occurring in 1965, when he issued his Moynihan Report, which stated that by and large single mothers in the ghetto were unlikely to "shape their children's character and ability in ways that lead to upward mobility."[146]

But in the two decades since Moynihan's report appeared, scholars had turned cartwheels to legitimize single-parent families as normal, citing child abuse statistics, battered wife complaints, and other data demonizing dads. Novelist Toni Morrison went so far as to claim that the "strong black woman" (i.e., single mother) was "superior in terms of [her] ability to function healthily in the world."[147] Such stunningly imbecilic comments might have been humorous had they not contributed to an epidemic of single-motherhood and illegitimate children.

A subtheme of the defense of single-motherhood was the emerging "children's rights" field in law, which viewed children as virtually independent from and unassociated with family units. This was a feature of Communist ideology which stated that children do not belong to their parents or families, but to the state. Not surprising, this position was unabashedly advocated in the United States by a number of leftists, including in 2013 black professor Melissa Harris-Perry, the host of a weekend show on MSNBC on which she said, "We have to break through our kind of private idea that kids belong to their parents and recognize that kids belong to whole communities. . . . We haven't had a very collective notion that these are our children." Children of single mothers were also thought more likely to look to the state for parenting than those in a traditional family, and thereby to favor Progressivism. Liberal children's advocates, therefore, were not about to train their guns on welfare-queen mothers. Bill Clinton, however reluctantly, signed legislation that sought to increase the number of children living with their two married parents. That, however, had not solved the problem of Progressive scholars, who continued to churn out antimarriage books that viewed marriage as a source of female oppression and bad for their cause.

The data, however, demolished the notion that marriage and class didn't matter for child development and future successes. One study found that the average number of words per hour heard by professors' kids was 2,150, for the children in a welfare family 620.[148] Moreover, middle-class parents interacted in decisively different ways with their children as they read, prompting the kids to develop other thoughts around words. Another researcher found that poor mothers, when urged to talk to their babies, often replied, "Why would I talk to him? He can't answer me."[149]

Collapsing marriage rates played an important role in slowly eroding the American economy (not to mention undermining the entire society). Other powerful cultural changes were also at work, gaining reckless momentum in the 1990s. A clear segregation of those who attended Ivy League schools and "everyone else" had made itself felt more than at any other time in America's past. This merged with a coagulation of wealthier groups into small, nearly self-contained and hermetically sealed enclaves (called by sociologist Charles Murray "superzips," meaning zip codes with a combination of high income and a high preponderance of Ivy League degrees).[150] Whereas a mere three decades earlier some of the wealthiest people in towns lived in the same neighborhood as the average citizen, by 1995 much of that had changed. The highly educated and wealthy not only gravitated toward each other, but they systematically began to exclude others to the point that in some Washington, D.C., neighborhoods virtually every person had graduated from an Ivy League school. These elite bubbles were often not only isolated within themselves, but were further surrounded by other "superzips" that ensured that, with few exceptions, a person could go days on end without ever encountering someone of a different socioeconomic stratum except in a service capacity.[151]

A divergence of socioeconomic cultures also produced drastic differences in attitudes toward work, where, beginning in 1990, the number of working-age adult men who dropped out of the labor force began to shoot upward.[152] In previous eras, such activity (or, more appropriately, inactivity) would have been met with horrific public scorn and ostracism. An able-bodied man would find a job out of embarrassment if for no other reason. But as the skill levels demanded by tech jobs increased, larger and larger numbers of low-educated men of lesser cognitive ability began to find it difficult to fill genuine full-time jobs. Their material well-being and self-respect could not be substantially improved by government assistance. Where such men, if married, would have been pressured to take any job (and in so doing, fulfill at least one important role as family provider), the destruction of marriage closed off that pressure and fulfillment. Increasingly these men would cite "disability" as the reason they were not in the workforce, but the fact was that most were disabled only by their inability to find wives.

The inverse of the men's dilemma was, on the surface, positive: more women went to college, more entered the workforce, more obtained high-salary jobs. Yet neither was this what it seemed. By the twenty-first century, women under thirty were outearning men. In New York, they averaged 117 percent of a man's salary, in Dallas, 120 percent. Childless women outearned men in all but three of America's largest cities by 2008.[153] Women became majorities at most major universities; began owning real estate more than men; and almost 60 percent of women were in the workforce by 1995.[154]

While the American economy of the 1990s bore no resemblance at all to that of the 1970s, in attitude and ambition, the USA had reverted to its disco-era form. Content to let the United Nations solve international disputes whose overtones threatened regional war and state-sponsored carnage, complacent about the inevitability of economic growth in the wake of Japan's decline, and culturally bereft of moorings—so that a U.S. president could engage in oral sex with a young intern in the White House Oval Office and somehow stay in office—the United States looked every bit as wobbly as the Soviet empire that had just collapsed. Worse, the rest of the West still followed America, even on a trip with Thanatos.

CHAPTER EIGHT

Jihad

TIME LINE

2000: George W. Bush elected president; Y2K scare

2001: Demonstrations against globalization at G8 summit in Italy; 9/11 terrorist attack on World Trade Center and Pentagon; anthrax mail attacks in Washington, D.C.; China admitted to World Trade Organization; dot-com bust

2002: Euro coins and notes issued in European Union; U.S. intervention in Afghanistan; UN World Summit on Sustainable Development; Department of Homeland Security established

2003: United States invades Iraq; Saddam Hussein captured and his sons killed; Muslim suicide bombings proliferate worldwide

2004: Kosovo violence, eight thousand Serb homes and three hundred churches burned; Estonia, Latvia, Lithuania, Slovakia, Slovenia, Romania, and Bulgaria join NATO; EU adds Poland, Estonia, Latvia, Lithuania, the Czech Republic, Slovakia, Hungary, Slovenia, Cyprus, and Malta; EU Constitution written but not ratified; Bush reelected; Republicans gain both houses of Congress

2005: Kyoto Protocol to the United Nations Framework Convention on Climate Change goes into effect without the United States

2006:   Iran starts uranium enrichment with Russia; North Korea conducts nuclear test; sectarian violence in Iraq accelerates; U.S. "surge" adds more troops; Anbar Awakening in Iraq; Democrats gain both houses of U.S. Congress

2007:   Bulgaria and Romania join the EU; Treaty of Lisbon establishes EU Constitution

2008:   Crude oil price exceeds $100 per barrel; gasoline prices reach $4 per gallon in United States; real estate bubble bursts; global financial crisis; Dow Jones Industrial Average falls from 13,000 to below 7,500; TARP bailout of banks and businesses; Barack Obama elected president

2009:   Stimulus bill passes; rise of Tea Party protest movement; Congress fails to pass a budget for the first time; Dow Jones Average hits low of 6,443

2010:   "Obamacare" national health care law passed in United States; Republicans regain House; U.S. national debt exceeds $13.5 trillion; economic slowdown in China; record number of Americans on food stamps; tallest man-made building (2,722 feet) opens in Dubai; first EU bailouts of member countries (Greece, Ireland)

2011:   Arab Spring in Egypt ousts Hosni Mubarak; Muammar Gaddafi overthrown in Libya and killed; Tunisian government falls; Osama bin Laden killed

2012:   U.S. national debt exceeds $16.4 trillion; unfunded national debt from entitlement programs exceeds $87 trillion; Americans on food stamps exceed 47.7 million; American ambassador killed by Islamic terrorists in Libya; Barack Obama reelected; Chinese spacecraft docks with space station

2013:   U.S. National debt exceeds $17 trillion; IRS admits targeting Tea Party groups; Justice Department resurrects Espionage Act of 1917 and targets reporter records and communications

Prosperity Revolution

Europe and Japan's decline in the late twentieth century owed much to its aging—and shrinking—population. Demographic changes posed as big a challenge to the modern world as did thermonuclear war, but not in the way commonly proposed by such alarmist overpopulation writers as Paul Ehrlich.

In the thirty years since Ehrlich's book *The Population Bomb*, which warned of overpopulation that would cause oceans to run out of fish and massive starvation, a remarkable development occurred: the main threat to future prosperity was underpopulation in advanced countries, not overpopulation in the developing ones. With the exception of Muslim countries, birthrates worldwide stabilized, and then began to fall, leading *The Wall Street Journal* in 2003 to note "a global population decline may be in sight."[1] The population was on track to level off at 9 billion by 2050 (up from 6 billion in 2003), and well below the 12 billion projected in 1993. Nations with large populations, including India and China, saw their birthrates fall dramatically, but not nearly as dramatically as Europe or Japan. Even in high-birthrate countries such as Mexico, where seven births per family in the 1970s plunged to just two by 2010, the trend was the same. How these upheavals affected the world promised to dictate much of the course of the twenty-first century and determine the success of a radical renewed movement in Islam, the call to jihad.

The head of the UN's population division, Joseph Chamie, attributed the fall in birthrates to a "revolution in fertility"—or more properly a revolution in prosperity—whereby richer nations became more self-focused and selfish, looking toward present pleasures as opposed to investments in future human family capital. In 2000, Chamie's division forecast a fall in the fertility rate in the key group of major developing countries to 2.1 by the mid-twenty-first century, but in 2002, they were forced to revise their forecast downwards to 1.85.[2] At those rates, world population would peak sometime in the middle of the twenty-first century and begin a decline.

As writer Mark Steyn noted, "The single most important fact about the early twenty-first century is the rapid aging of almost every developed nation other than the United States (which still had reasonable marriage rates and a large Catholic population): Canada, Europe, and Japan are getting old fast, older than any functioning society has ever been and faster than it has ever aged."[3] Japan, with the world's longest life expectancy, would be affected later than some other nations, but by the 1990s its economy was already feeling what Masahiro Yamada of Tokyo's Gakugei University called the first "low birth-rate recession."[4] China, viewed by pundits as the next colossus, was rapidly aging and would get old before it got rich.[5] Older societies took fewer risks, invented less, innovated less, and had less social energy—along with less crime and pathological behavior. Overall, however, an overly aged society was a dying society. And no place was dying faster than Europe.

In the last part of the twentieth century and the first years of the twenty-first, a few Europeans woke up to the fact of their own demographic cataclysm. A number of authors lamented the decline in fertility and its implications for a diminishing European influence in the world. Jean-Claude Chesnais, a French demographer, published *Revenge of the Third World* (1987) and *The Twilight of the Occident* (1995), while his mentor, Alfred Sauvy, the best-known of France's demographers, produced *The Aging of Nations* (2000). German anthropologist Herwig Birg wrote *Die demographische Zeitenwende* (*The Demographic Turning Point in History*, 2001); journalist Frank Schirrmacher wrote *Das Methusalem-Komplott* (*The Methuselah Conspiracy*, 2004); and the German-born professor Walter Laqueur capped it off with *The Last Days of Europe* in 2007.

Whether through the comfort provided by prosperity or the inconvenience of raising children, the collapse of Europe's native-born population was stunning. The United Nations projected in 2001 that by century's end, France's population would fall by one third (and the number of native Frenchmen much faster), while Germany's population was expected to decline from 82 million in 2001 to 61 million by 2050. Italy would be shrunk by almost three fourths in a century, and Spain by even more.[6] Russia stood to lose one third of its numbers within fifty years, and Russians actually had to consider the possibility that the Turks would soon outnumber them. Thousands of Russian villages had literally disappeared by 2012, and nearly a third of the population east of Moscow had left Siberia an even more empty and frozen desert than it had been previously.

Writer Claire Berlinski observed that birthrates dropped faster in the former Axis powers than anywhere else in the world. "It is tempting to wonder," she wrote, "whether, in some way, the experiences of the Second World War convinced people in these countries, at a deep, inarticulate level, that they do not deserve to exist."[7] On the other hand, the Axis countries stressed population growth during their years of power, and this principle may have become rejected with the remainder of their totalitarian doctrines. An even simpler explanation is that having seen so much sacrifice in the first half of the twentieth century, Germans were going to enjoy the second half. As the frequently spoken German attitude indicated, "We fought the last two wars, you (Americans) can fight the next one."

A voluntary decimation of population on this scale had never occurred before in human history. Then again, neither had self-absorption ever been so widespread, or family life and structures received such little attention from government. Paul Demeny, a demographer warning about the precipitous collapse of Western birthrates, noted that in contrast, certain Muslim states were growing at unprecedented rates. In 1950, Yemen had only 4 million people but by 2007 had 20 million and is projected to have 100 million by 2050; Algeria, in 1962, had 10 million people, but by 2006 it had 33 million.[8] Not only were Muslim nations poorer than European countries, but the heavy emphasis on having a son (or sons) contributed to growing populations.

Muslims in Europe were outpacing their mostly white counterparts, but their populations swelled further due to immigration from Islamic countries. By 2007, warnings about Europeans being inundated in a sea of immigrants started to gain ground, making Jean Raspail's 1973 novel, *The Camp of the Saints*, seem eerily prophetic. Raspail portrayed waves of impoverished immigrants (although mostly from India and Africa, not Muslim countries) landing on European beaches. Europeans, out of guilt and basic humanity, could not muster the fortitude to prevent them from overwhelming their countries by the sheer presence of their bodies—and society collapsed for all.[9] In reality, by 2010 the population growth was coming from Muslim countries (or India), and forecasts of Europe becoming Muslim and adopting Sharia law in the twenty-first century were no longer hollow warnings. Many European countries did not permit asking an immigrant his religion, so in some places, numbers are unreliable. Nonetheless, Muslim numbers were clearly growing, such as in Albania, where it was already estimated that Muslims constituted 70 percent of the population.[10]

Population decline in the West—or, more accurately, the decline of birthrates among nonimmigrant groups—exacerbated the growing "Muslim problem" of Europe in which Islamic immigrants and their children resisted assimilation into their new homes. Their religion and culture were largely incompatible with Christianity, which they often viewed as satanic, and they insisted on living according to Sharia law rather than adapting to secular civil law. The presence of so many young people, especially young Muslim men, also made these populations volatile, and difficult for civil authorities to control.

Whereas in most Western European nations the average share of the population over sixty-five was over 12 percent (in Italy, nearly 25 percent), in Third World countries only 5 to 6 percent of the populations were over sixty-five. In 2006, Spain and Germany's under-fifteen population was 14 percent; Britain's 18 percent; and the United States, 21 percent. By 2050, the median age in Europe will be fifty-two. In shocking contrast, some 40 percent of Pakistanis and Saudis were under fifteen in 2006, Pakistan's median age was under twenty, and Yemen's under-fifteen numbers were above 47 percent! It was no coincidence that when the United States saw its economy growing at remarkable levels and Britain was leading the world in medical and scientific breakthroughs, their populations were young. Yet at the same time, both were thoroughly grounded in Western concepts of law, private property rights, personal freedom, and above all a Christian God. And in the first decade of the twenty-first century, only the United States was reproducing herself. This was not the result of Hispanic immigration, as some suggest, but of white women in America (the majority group) having 1.85 children. That rate far exceeded that of white European or Canadian women, although the higher fertility of immigrants pushed the overall fertility rate above that needed for population replacement.

Each Muslim woman in the EU was producing more than twice as many children as the typical European woman, giving substance to Muammar Gaddafi's claim that "fifty million Muslims of Europe will turn it into a Muslim continent in a few decades."[11] Across the Arab world, fertility rates held at similar levels: Somalia, 6.76; Yemen, 6.58; Sudan, 4.72; Libya, 3.28; and Pakistan and Saudi Arabia, 4.[12] It was worth noting that the highest fertility rates resided in the most economically backward of Muslim states; Algeria, Tunisia, Egypt, and Turkey all had significantly lower birthrates. Even in Palestinian territory, the rates differed between the Gaza Strip and the West Bank.[13] Nevertheless, these were all significantly higher than any European nation, and, if nothing else, radical Islam had "demography on its side."[14] The greatest strength of Islam is the focus by its women to produce babies, rather than equal rights. Western women may have attained the greatest level of equality between the sexes in the history of mankind, but without progeny, their achievement will soon be a footnote for future historians relating the disappearance of the West.

Was Europe doomed to G. K. Chesterton's cycle of defeating its enemies, only to become enslaved by them? He described the cycle as "Victory over barbarians. Employment of barbarians. Alliance with barbarians. Conquest by barbarians." This certainly was the history of the Boers in

South Africa. Now the operative principles were spreading. Europe and Canada has "outsourced its entire future to the Third World," to the point that Canadians celebrated their own low birthrates by "continuing to encourage the immigration of talented people . . . from overcrowded parts of the world."[15] Put in terms of political economy, people were too costly to reproduce at home, and Islam was the largest supplier of new Europeans and the second largest supplier of new Canadians.

This marked a fundamental and dangerous reversal of all previous European and American immigration principles in the past two centuries, when it was assumed that immigrants would assimilate. Rotterdam's Muslim population topped 40 percent by 2012, and the most popular boy's name in Amsterdam and Malmo, Sweden—and indeed all of Belgium—was Mohammed. In Brussels, ten of the seventeen members of the ruling Socialist Party sported Muslim names.

But these were not "new Europeans" or "new Canadians." Far from assimilating, the new Islamic immigrants were "looking for ways to build institutions that will allow Muslims to practice their religion in a way that is compatible with social integration."[16] How would that be possible when, according to polls done in the early twenty-first century, one fifth to one quarter of British Muslims did not identify with England in any way?[17] If integration was to occur, the non-Muslims would have to socially integrate with the Muslims, not the other way around. Merely in world outlook, these new immigrants were light-years away from the views of the host nation: in Canada, after the 9/11 attacks, polls of Canadian imams found only two who thought Muslims had *any role* in the attacks; and in 2006, a British poll revealed that 83 percent of Muslims living in Britain shared the view that Muslims played no part in the attacks.[18]

Forging French nationalism among Muslim immigrants has proved equally elusive to date. In France, only a handful of "Francofied" leaders exist in the Muslim community, and only 4 percent of imams are French citizens. Most of them cannot even speak French. Eager to appease the waves of Muslim immigrants, French governments have established organizations to construct and maintain mosques. Across the border to the east, Turks who came to Germany were allowed to retain Turkish citizenship even if they became German, while to the west, Spain entered into an arrangement with the Comisión Islamica de España—"a Concordat, much like those agreed between nation-states and the Catholic Church."[19] Such actions often not only failed to win allies or produce loyal citizens, but convinced Muslims of the Europeans' lack of conviction.

Euro-Slam

France was one of the fulcrums of clashes between European and Islamic cultures. Despite the reputation of having the most unfriendly locals in Europe (though rated the most romantic and having the best cuisine, shopping, and parks), Paris still attracted tourists.[20] They flocked to La Grande Arche and the Louvre, and drove through La Défense, or Centre Pompidou, but had to carefully avoid any of the 751 areas (officially called "Sensitive Urban Zones") where even the French police dared not enter without heavy backup. This was not only true of Paris, but also Carcassonne, Marseilles, Nice, Tours, Caen, and virtually every other major French city.

These immigrant-dominated danger zones were labeled differently in each European nation, but all featured identical problems. France called them no-go zones, and estimated over five million Muslims lived in these zones; Germans labeled them "fear zones," and they included Brandenburg and the formerly Communist Berlin district of Wedding. London's West End and Oldham reported growing numbers of British citizens being attacked for "walking while white." Holland published a list of its top forty no-go zones, all ruled by Muslim radicals, including five in Rotterdam.[21] Twenty percent of the Belgian capital of Brussels was Muslim, as was 25 percent of the Swedish city of Malmo.

Yet even to acknowledge the existence of such Islamic zones was dangerous. The Anglican bishop of Rochester, Michael Nazir-Ali, a Christian born in Pakistan who held dual citizenship from Pakistan and Great Britain, was threatened after he claimed Islamic extremism made some areas no-go areas for non-Muslims. Nazir-Ali accused Church of England authorities of not confronting the "spiritual and moral vacuum" issue Islam had created in Britain.[22] British, French, and Italian non-Muslim women routinely covered their heads out of fear while in areas with heavy Muslim populations. Amsterdam's Slotervaart district experienced rioting nightly when a female police officer shot and killed the mentally deranged Moroccan friend of Mohammed Bouyeri, jihadist murderer of Dutch filmmaker Theo van Gogh. In November 2006, Lyon became so dangerous that police demonstrated "against the forces of disorder." Writer Amir Taheri observed "a de facto millet system" in place in parts of France, where "all women are obliged to wear the standardized Islamist hajib."[23] French shopkeepers, dance halls and pornographic movie houses, discos, and establishments selling pork were all driven out by radicals. Taheri noted the observations of a reporter who had visited Clichy, Bondy, Aulany-sous-Bois, and Bobigny, who heard a "single overarching message: The French authorities should keep out."[24]

Scandinavia witnessed extensive disruptions. An Oslo policeman was termed an "intruder" and had to run from angry crowds in the Furuset shopping center. A sociological survey of the crime rate in Malmo, Sweden (nine times higher than in similar cities), was entitled "We're Waging a War Against the Swedes." Interviewing immigrants in Malmo who were involved in crime, the survey revealed that they saw the recent crime wave as part of a culture war against Sweden itself—one could say, a jihad.[25] One Muslim thief laughed at the cowardly response of his victims, saying, "The Swedes don't do anything, they just give us the stuff." Another said, "We rob, every single day, as often as we want to, whenever we want to." Yet another said, "Power for me means that the Swedes shall look at me, lie down on the ground and kiss my feet."[26]

Entire cities have been virtually overtaken by (mostly Muslim) immigrants, including Rosengard and Tensta in Sweden and much of the Catalonia province in Spain. Continually rising numbers led demographers to predict that Cologne, Düsseldorf, and Duisburg would be nearly half Muslim by 2015.[27] Cologne, with 120,000 mostly Turkish Muslims in 2009, is the largest Muslim city in Germany and is on a pace to be two-thirds foreign by 2020.[28] Brussels's "Little Morocco" or Sint-Jans-Molenbeek section by 2006 was already not a "part of Belgium but . . . an area under Islamic jurisdiction in which Belgians [were] not welcome."[29] France's interior minister in 2005 (later president), Nicolas Sarkozy, noted that "The police presence in the suburbs is vital. . . . If they don't do [the job], who will replace them? Mafias or *integristes* [fundamentalists]." Another official added, the "hoodlums of North African descent smoke marijuana, wear Nikes and drive BMWs, [but] many of them also admire Bin Laden. . . . They share turf and services with extremists. . . ."[30]

Paradoxically, not only did Muslims reject the European radical Left, they displaced it, both ideologically and geographically.[31] Conversions to Islam often constituted a protest against "what is." As Philip Jenkins noted, "many [Spanish converts were] veterans of the radical left of the 1960s and 1970s who were attracted by Islam's mystical tradition."[32] The young, especially, found Islam appealing as an alternative to capitalism or communism, and many clearly considered it a "political ideological belief," not a religion.[33]

Briefly, leftists thought that they could forge an alliance with Islam. But the marriage was generally forced. Marxist godlessness did not grow well in

Islamic soil, regardless of their common nourishment—a suspicion or hatred of Western liberty. And mutual hatred of America and the West was
hardly a strong enough bond to maintain a relationship.

While so-called Muslim moderates often denounced extremism to
British, French, or German audiences, they said something quite different
in front of Muslim groups. Inayat Bunglawala, for example, a member of
the post-7/7 bombing's "road show" sent out by the British government to
put a Muslim face on the government's denouncing of terrorism, had over
the years "left a lengthy paper trail of distinctly non-moderate comments,"
to the point of celebrating Osama bin Laden as a "freedom fighter."[34] Top
Muslim officials—even those embraced by the British government—joined
in calling for the death of Salman Rushdie in 1988 and demanded censorship of the film *Submission* (2004). None of the leading Muslim voices in
Europe ever condemned the terrorism of the Chechnyan rebels, the inti-
fada or suicide bombings in Palestine, or the Muslim violence in Kashmir.
No British or European Islamic version of the antiwar group Not In Our
Name or Code Pink ever appeared, anywhere, in any Muslim European
subsociety. Despite this, top British officials (such as Labour's "Red Ken"
Livingstone) continued to praise "moderates" such as Sheikh Yusuf al-
Qaradawi, who routinely attacked Jews and celebrated suicide bombings in
Israel: "The Israelis might have nuclear bombs but we have the children
bomb," he observed.[35] And while France's "moderate" Muslim clergy at-
tempted to quell the 2005 riots, they had little impact.

Some observers offered evidence for thinking that a radicalized Islam
was less than omnipotent. Mosque attendance varied, as high as 60 percent
in some areas, or as low as 10 percent in others, but at any rate most immigrants didn't understand the sermons, because they were in Arabic or Urdu
(not French). Less than one third of French Muslims said they prayed daily
(far lower than the numbers reported by American Christians), although
twice that number observed the Ramadan fast. Although the trends were
ominous, some delusional Europeans claimed that Islam's presence in Europe was not as sinister and threatening as it seemed. Mosques looked full
because there were relatively few of them compared with churches, and a
nonobservant Muslim culture had emerged in which a mere 5 percent of
French Muslims attended mosques with regularity.[36] A handful of modernizing reformist groups had appeared within European Islam, and a few
states, such as Morocco, had enacted westernized laws that expanded wom-
en's rights and which sought to pry Islam away from the militants. The
requirement of the pilgrimage to Mecca saw low levels of participation—

twenty thousand from Britain and seventeen thousand from Germany—despite the fact that Muslim organizations subsidized the travel fares. One poll of Turks in England found only 7 percent considered themselves "very orthodox."

Yet how did Europeans expect Muslims to celebrate "Frenchness" or "Dutchness" when for sixty years the Europeans had deliberately downplayed nationalism, seen as the root cause of two world wars? A French writer expressed the difficulty of applying the American dream to Europe, where "There is no French, Dutch or other European dream. You emigrate here to escape poverty and nothing more."[37] Unwilling to champion their own self-worth, Europeans were shocked that Muslims would see little value in European law or traditions. Polls showed Muslims in the United Kingdom felt no loyalty to Britain (only 26 percent in one poll did), and 40 percent favored introducing Sharia law in England, 47 percent supported terror bombing in Israel, and 40 percent said Jews in Britain were legitimate targets for terror.[38]

And while mosque attendance remained unimpressive, many mosques served as terrorist recruitment centers (such as Finsbury Park and Brixton in London). They were neither the largest, nor the most religiously orthodox worship centers. Nevertheless, they had disproportional influence, especially the famed Hamburg mosque where Mohamed Atta and the 9/11 plotters worshiped.[39] The Finsbury Park mosque, known as the "suicide factory," became the home for the radical Muhajiroun sect, where numerous plots were hatched, including one by Djamel Beghal to fly a helicopter full of explosives into the American embassy in Paris.

The most notorious radical from the Finsbury Park mosque was Abu Hamza, "Old Hooky," as the British media called him. He loved the spotlight and, waving his hook of a hand, took center stage at any anti-Western protest. Abu Hamza was aided and abetted by Abu Qatada, a Palestinian called "al-Qaeda's spiritual ambassador in Europe."[40] Another radical, Omar Bakri Muhammad, a Syrian, arrived in England in the 1980s and soon became a fixture known as the "Tottenham Ayatollah." Bakri called the September 11 attacks "magnificent" and described London's subway bombers as the "fantastic four."[41] Together, the three formed what security experts termed "Londonistan's unholy trinity."[42]

Fortunately, many radical Muslims plots were foiled, including attacks on Madrid's National Court, Barcelona's World Trade Center, an attack on an Italian coastal city with a ship "as big as the *Titanic*," and a number of schemes to blow up airliners. British intelligence investigated thirty conspiracies in 2006 alone.[43] One of the most dangerous plots, discovered by a 2003 London raid, involved massive quantities of castor oil beans, which were the raw materials for making ricin, along with all the equipment needed to refine and produce ricin, cyanide, and a host of other poisons.[44] But the most chilling scenario remained the "dirty bomb" or nuclear threat, which virtually every intelligence service in the world took seriously.[45]

Intellectuals frequently cited poverty and ignorance as among the causes of terrorism. "I have six root causes [for terrorism, and] poverty is *the* main factor," claimed former CIA senior analyst and pro-Palestinian Bill Christison while Australian leftist Bob Carr flatly stated, "Poverty is a cause of terrorism."[46] Former Clinton economic adviser Laura Tyson described "a world so interconnected that poverty and despair in a remote region can harbor a network of terrorism," and President George W. Bush intoned, "We fight against poverty because hope is an answer to terror."[47] A Dutch security expert claimed "the breeding grounds [for terrorism were] websites, prisons, and mosques," and as in America, the Muslim movement remained powerful in the prison setting.[48] Consequently, European leaders expended no small amount of energy examining poverty as a causal factor in Islamic terrorism.

For a while, it appeared there might be a connection between poverty and violence, at least in the form of urban unrest. Between 1989 and 1990, for example, when urban unrest became more common in Europe, Turkish unemployment in Berlin was more than double that of Germans and Arab unemployment in France doubled that of French. In Sweden, unemployment rates among immigrant groups commonly topped 50 percent, and Muslim immigrants in England were far more likely to be in poverty than anyone else, including immigrants from other nations, regardless of color.[49] Many of Europe's cities found themselves with American-style suburbs and ghettos, including Malmo, Sweden, where the Rosengard projects resembled Cabrini Green.

Even then, the Muslims generally lived at a much higher standard of living than in their home countries, and certainly, government assistance was vastly greater. While poverty did not breed terrorists in the sense that social scientists claimed (most of the twentieth- and twenty-first-century hijackers were well educated and at least middle class), it contributed to worsening urban decay. *The Economist* noted that many of Europe's immigrant residential areas contained "rain-streaked concrete high-rise estates; multiple faiths, tongues and colors; and the usual cocktail of joblessness, broken families, truancy and drug-dealing."[50]

After 9/11, however, studies began to refute the poverty explanation.[51] Lawrence Wright's intricate history of al-Qaeda establishes that the terror organization's founding had virtually nothing to do with wealth, income, or even Israel, but with a festering moral outrage ultimately grounded in a hatred of Western sexual mores.[52] Several of the 9/11 perpetrators visited strip clubs before the attack to confirm their hatred and repugnance for the decadent and immoral United States and harden their hearts. Meghnad Desai, in *Rethinking Islam*, correctly describes Islamism as "a political ideology" which appeals "to a deep hurt in the Muslim psyche. . . ."[53] Europe became a haven for Muslim terrorist masterminds, just as Western Europe had once been home to Third World revolutionaries such as Ho Chi Minh. Mullah Krekar, the leader of Ansar al Islam, lived in Norway; Abu Talal al-Qasimi, an Egyptian jihadist, moved to Denmark in 1993; Abdelghani Mzoudi and Mounir el-Motassadeq were part of the 9/11 Hamburg cell; and Abu Hamza al-Mizri propagandized out of the Finsbury mosque. Liberal asylum laws in the West permitted militants being hunted by their own governments to set up shop in London, Paris, Berlin, Rotterdam, and Hamburg and plot terror strikes against their hosts.

Committed jihadists were joined by those flirting with Islamic militancy, for whom the movement took on an aura of romantic heroism, and, certainly, anti-Americanism. Berliners watched immigrant neighborhoods set off firecrackers to celebrate the 9/11 attacks. More than a third of Dutch Muslims approved of the terror strikes on the United States, and when an Algerian soccer team started to lose to the French team, the immigrants in the stands began chanting "Bin Laden! Bin Laden!"[54] A Hamburg imam, Moroccan Mohamed Fizazi, urged killing all Christians and Jews, "no matter if it's a man, a woman or a child."[55] Although Pew polls taken in 2006 showed high levels of support for the notion that there was no conflict between being a Muslim and living in a modern secular society, the young routinely held more radical views.[56] One third of Turkish youth in Germany said Islam should govern every nation, and majorities approved of the murder of filmmaker Theo van Gogh on the grounds that "If you insult Islam, you have to pay."[57]

Moderate Muslims looked at the polls and found that 75 percent of Muslims opposed suicide bombings under any circumstances, but increasingly Muslims in England turned to satellite television and Muslim news channels because of a distrust of the BBC, a disturbing trend given the network's eagerness to appear sympathetic to Islamic causes. Fed hatred and distortions from radical Arab media outlets, no wonder only 17 percent of British Muslims thought Arabs carried out the 9/11 terror attacks, and after the 7/7 bombings in London, more than one third denied that the attacks were carried out by Muslims.[58] Increasingly, Americans and Israelis were the targets of almost all international terrorist attacks: between 1991 and 2001, 10 percent of all attacks have been directed at U.S. citizens.[59]

Of course, Jews were always convenient villains for Muslim radicals. French Muslim youth killed Israelis and French Jews at least as early as 2005 when Ilan Halimi, a young Israeli, was kidnapped, tortured, and finally killed by a Muslim group called the "Barbarians." In a telephone call to the family, the Barbarians' leader, Youssouf Fofana, an African Muslim, read verses from the Koran as his captive was screaming in the background. Apologists claimed the Barbarians were not just Muslims, and downplayed the Islam connection, as they would with a 2006 attack by a gang of forty mostly Arab males on a train near Nice-Lyon.[60] Topping it off, a new Muslim "gangsta rap" had become popular throughout Europe, whose lyrics made American black hip-hop artists' own obscene rhymes pale by comparison. In French *banlieues*, an average of ninety cars per night were set on fire in the first months of 2005. In Britain, gangs of Muslim background have largely replaced the Afro-Caribbeans as drug pushers, and the percentage of young Muslims in European prisons far exceeds their portion of the population.[61] Some 70 percent of French prisoners are Muslims; and Berlin's police chief stated that one third of the young immigrants (mostly Muslims) in his city had a criminal record.

The culmination of this clash of cultures came not in the Madrid or London bombings, but in the November 2005 French riots, when two youths fleeing police were killed in Clichy-sous-Bois in the 93rd district. Thousands of cars were burned (1,400 on the night of November 7 alone) in what was considered the worst public-order crisis in France since the 1968 riots. The Associated Press and other liberal news organizations deemphasized the use of the term "Muslim" in their reports. While the majority of the rioters were Muslims, a low level of Islamic presence was obvious. There were few religious slogans shouted; none of the prominent Muslim leaders supported the crimes; and many claimed the riots constituted class warfare, not a clash of religions. Nevertheless, a sober look at the trends in Europe suggested that there was clearly an Islamic nature to the violence, and, indeed, to the overall reshaping of the Continent and England. Overwhelmingly, world violence took on a Muslim versus non-Muslim shape in the twenty-first century, even when groups such as al-Qaeda were not obviously present, as in the 2008 Mumbai hostage taking and bombing of the Taj Hotel.

None of this should have been a surprise. A foretaste of what the radicals had in store was evident when Salman Rushdie published his novel about Islam, *The Satanic Verses*, in 1988. The Bombay-born, Cambridge-educated Rushdie was already an established novelist who dealt with political issues in Pakistan when he published his supposedly irreverent depiction of Muhammad. A few months after publication of *The Satanic Verses*, Ayatollah Ruhollah Khomeini, the spiritual dictator of Iran, called the book "blasphemous" and issued a fatwa calling for Rushdie's death and offering a bounty for his head. Britain and Iran severed diplomatic relations over Rushdie, as copies of his books were burned and riots broke out in both countries. Following Khomeini's death, subsequent religious leaders reaffirmed the death sentence, and as late as February 2006 Rushdie received what he called a "Valentine's card" from the militants reminding him of the fatwa. According to terrorism officials, at least one London bomb explosion, in 1989, was directed at Rushdie. A 1990 Pakistani film, *International Guerrillas*, featured a Rushdie-like hero who schemed to destroy Pakistan. Attacked by a quartet of holy books at the end of the film, the hero's head explodes into flame. None of this fazed Britain, which knighted Rushdie in 2007, yet at the same time clung to the view that peaceful Muslims were in the majority.

Rushdie's name was invoked during another jihad, the violent row over cartoons in a Danish newspaper, *Jyllands-Posten*, in September 2006. Twelve cartoons depicting Muhammad—including one showing the Prophet wearing a bomb as his turban—set off extensive protests, which led to more than one hundred deaths. Norwegian and Danish embassies in the Middle East were burned, more death threats issued, and Hezbollah leader Hassan Nasrallah stated that if Rushdie had been killed as called for in the fatwa, "this rabble who insult our Prophet Mohammed in Denmark, Norway and France would not have dared to do so."[62] Bounties were placed on the heads of the cartoonists, and many nations including Saudi Arabia and other Middle Eastern states launched boycotts (a "cartoon intifada") against Denmark. Protesters in England marched with placards reading, "Europe you will pay—9/11 is on its way," and "Remember, remember the Eleventh of September."

Many Europeans suddenly realized that their neighbors were anything but Europeanized. In an effort to assuage the militants, the Danish government brought charges against *Jyllands-Posten* for disturbing public order and for degrading people based on religious or ethnic grounds. Denmark's courts ultimately rejected the notion that publication of the cartoons constituted a crime, and reiterated the principle that freedom of speech had to be observed (but within limits of providing information as an aspect of the "public interest"). Protests did not stop, forcing the newspaper to issue an apology and the artist to produce an "explanation." Thus, a relatively insignificant illustrated joke, published in a paper with minimal circulation, did more to expose Europeans to the threat of fundamentalist Islam than had several terror bombings and assassinations.

Euro-fears and political correctness, however, still prohibited a rational and open discussion of Islam in the twenty-first century. Evangelists such as Åke Green and Franklin Graham, who called Islam a "very evil and wicked religion," flirted with the justice system merely by expressing their concerns about Islamic practices. British member of Parliament Nick Griffin was acquitted (after a trial) for depicting Islam as a "wicked, vicious faith . . . [that had] expanded from a handful of cranky lunatics about 1,300 years ago."[63] Oriana Fallaci, the Italian journalist, excoriated Pope John Paul II for not taking a tougher stand on Muslims, and in *The Force of Reason*, which sold 800,000 copies in Italy alone, she warned that Europe was becoming "more and more a province of Islam, a colony of Islam. . . . In each one of our cities there is a second city. . . . A Muslim city, a city ruled by the Koran."[64] Another anti-Islamic book by Fallaci, *The Rage and the Pride*, sold more than 1.5 million copies worldwide. She also famously stated, "Asking a Moslem about his women is like asking him about a secret vice," and in 2005 called Europe "Eurabia." Christian religious leaders found themselves drawing lines in the sand. Pope Benedict XVI flatly stated "there must not be any conflict in the content of . . . teaching with respect to our Constitution, for example regarding civil rights, starting with religious liberty, or equality between men and women, or marriage."[65] At a speech in Bavaria, Benedict went further, questioning what Muhammad brought that "was new," adding, "there you will find things only evil and inhuman, such as his command to spread by the sword the faith he preached."

The Iron Veil

Europeans seemed most ruffled by Islam's treatment of women, instead of its terror attacks. Publication of the book *Women in Islam*, by the imam of Fuengirola, which advocated beating wives so as not to leave a mark, resulted in the author's prosecution, but other Muslim commentators routinely pointed to Koranic verse supporting such actions by husbands. This was preceded by Samira Bellil's *In the Hell of the Tournantes*, which recounted gang rape by Muslims of girls who were too westernized.[66] Germany's Necla Kelek's book *The Foreign Bride* (2005) was an exposé of honor killings and arranged Muslim marriages, while the French book *Ni Putes Ni Soumises* (*Neither Whores Nor Doormats*, 2003) became the French equivalent of *The Female Eunuch*. Divorce in Holland by Moroccan and Turkish women rose rapidly in the late twentieth century, indicating some change. Overall, however, the Churchillian Iron Curtain of the Cold War era had been replaced by the Iron Veil of Islam.

Women under Islam in the West saw the promise of liberty doused by the cold reality of life as a Muslim. Islamic scholars across Europe routinely defended rape when it involved "provocative" behavior by women. Honor killings rose in Germany in the 1990s; a police investigation in the case of a Turkish woman who was killed after discarding her headscarf found that neighbors shrugged the murder off by saying, "The Whore lived like a German."[67] The most notorious example of Islamic intolerance toward women was exemplified by the murder of Dutch filmmaker Theo van Gogh, who was in the process of completing *Submission*, a film about women under Muslim law. In 2004, Mohammed Bouyeri assassinated van Gogh, pinning a note to his body admitting the deed and promising to kill the woman who was featured in the film, Ayaan Hirsi Ali, as well.

"Honor killings," largely by Muslims, had increased worldwide from 1989 to 2009 by five thousand a year, according to the United Nations.[68] Almost 60 percent of those murdered were killed for being "too Western," and most were killed by several perpetrators, or gangs of men. Attempts were made by European and American intellectuals to pass this off as no different from Western domestic violence. But researchers found that in fact most were murdered because they refused to wear the *hijab*.

Western European homosexuality also drew the ire of Muslim commentators, such as Khalil el-Moumni, a Moroccan exiled to Holland who said in 1998, "The Europeans stand lower than dogs and pigs" because of homosexuality.[69] Western liberalism, particularly in its defense of feminism and homosexual rights, increasingly came into conflict with tolerance for Muslim religious values, with most observers unwilling to admit there was a fundamental impasse. It was the issue of values, especially when it came to homosexuality, however, where European civil law found itself supporting the morality of both Muslims and Christians (which, of course, was irreconcilable). In a 2001 Dutch case, a Muslim preacher was acquitted when the court agreed he could ground his denunciations of homosexuality in the Koran, while the Swedish Supreme Court reached a similar decision in the case of Åke Green in 2004 for his sermons against homosexuality. Both, however, were close-run things, as such was the power of the homosexual movement in Europe.[70]

In other areas of public life, particularly when it came to Muslim complaints about blasphemy in the case of television shows or cartoons that in any way criticized Muhammad, European police and courts have unofficially sided with Muslims. Producers, directors, and writers have generally withdrawn "offensive" material after it was made clear the police would not (or could not) protect them. This had disastrous repercussions: Germany and France found that their unwillingness to apply laws fairly and equally to all religions and ethnic groups gave rise to new neo-Nazi groups.

Soothsayers of both the Left and Right noted the trends with horror. The homosexual writer and literary critic Bruce Bawer foresaw the time that Dutch social mores, including same-sex marriage and liberal drug policies, would become crimes under Sharia law, under which homosexuals and adulteresses would be stoned to death.[71] Dutch sociologist Pim Fortuyn's *Against the Islamicization of Our Culture* similarly inveighed against the imposition of fundamentalist Muslim values. George Weigel predicted "a Europe in which the *muezzin* summons the faithful to prayer from the central loggia of St. Peter's in Rome, while Notre Dame has been transformed into Hagia Sophia on the Seine. . . ."[72] Islamic scholar Bassam Tibi predicted "either Islam gets Europeanized, or Europe gets Islamized. . . . [the only question is] which Islam—Sharia Islam or Euro-Islam—is to dominate Europe," a sentiment shared by Bernard Lewis, the noted Arabist, who in 2004 told *Die Welt* that at then-current trends, Europe "will be part of the Arab west—the Maghreb."[73] EU Commissioner Frits Bolkestein observed in 2004 that Europe's time was past: the "USA will remain the only superpower . . . Europe is being Islamicized."[74]

The Empty Church

These, and other dire pronouncements, certainly captured the sentiment of many Europeans in the twenty-first century. To a small degree, however, by 2006 a secularized Islam, ignored by some in the West and vehemently denounced by fanatical Muslims, had taken root much the same way a secularized Christianity had once appeared, but in terms of impact, it remained a shadow compared with the violent extremists' substance. A dose of political reality had contributed to some reassessment among Muslims, symbolized by Turkey's appeal for admission into the European Union, which sparked fierce resistance.

Nevertheless, the ominous decline of devout Christianity on the Continent constituted a vacuum-producing dynamic enabling the rise of Islam, wherein street preachers and Pentecostals were viewed as more dangerous than mullahs and jihadists. George Weigel's *The Cube and the Cathedral* referred to a "Christophobia" rampant in Europe, and pointed to a demise of respect for the spiritual world that had reached such proportions that during the heat wave of 2003, French left for their summer vacation spots while their unburied dead parents lay in refrigerated lockers.[75] In Germany, deaths were no longer recorded in the newspapers, and many Germans opted out of funeral services. A Swedish firm went even further, providing a human compost service that used liquid nitrogen to freeze the cadaver before ultrasound waves were used to blast the body into tiny bits that were freeze-dried and used for fertilizer.[76] Paul Johnson, who in the first edition of his magisterial book, *Modern Times*, had described a resurgence of religion as one of the great unreported stories of the age, was much more restrained and cautious in his second edition, glumly noting a "widespread retreat from the churches and established religious bodies. . . ."[77]

Surveys of the period are quite revealing. When asked if religion played an important role in their lives, only 21 percent of Europeans answered "yes," while in the United States the average was 60 percent. This gulf accounted in part for the condescending attitude by many Europeans toward Americans and their "childlike" belief in Christianity—something the Europeans saw themselves as having outgrown. For example, approximately 34 percent of French in 1994 and 35 percent of Britons in 2004 claimed no religion or no belief in God or thought that Jesus even lived at all.[78] Another authority, London resident and pastor Jono Millar, stated on August 31, 2011, that whereas in 1900 95 percent of Britons attended church regularly, in 2000, 95 percent did not attend church regularly. The Church of Sweden estimated in 2008 that fewer than 2 percent of its membership attended church regularly in Sweden.[79] European church attendance was only half that of American attendance, but some countries had incredibly high rates of nonattendance. Some 60 percent of French never went to church. In England, the number of young people attending church had fallen by half since 1979. Between 1900 and 1984, the number of Anglican clerics was cut in half and just over 5 percent of the British population were members of an Anglican church, leading the former Archbishop of Canterbury to say that if the Anglican Church were a person, "the last rites would be administered at any moment."[80]

Throughout Europe—especially in what might be considered the most devout nations of Italy and Spain—a precipitous decline in the public expression of Christian faith has taken place during the past forty years. Even Ireland, which turned out a million people to greet Pope John Paul II when he visited in 1979, saw participation in mass fall by almost half since his visit. Combined with the demographic trends, where the elderly remained faithful but the younger generations left the faith, the reality was, as Cardinal Joachim Meisner of Cologne said, "for every one baptism, there are three funerals."[81] As the faithful aged, so did the clergy, leaving not only a shrinking base of priests and pastors but a much older one. France's fifty thousand priests in 1970 were reduced by half over the next thirty years. Maynooth seminary in Ireland once had had five hundred pupils, but by 2006 held only sixty. Dublin's archdiocese, responsible for a million adherents, ordained only one new priest per year. American Catholic numbers were not much better. From a high point in the late 1960s, when men studying to be priests in all religious orders in the United States neared twenty-five thousand, by 2000 fewer than one fifth that number were in seminaries.[82]

Poison Within

Infecting this malaise within the faith was ongoing pedophilia, actually often simple homosexuality, within the priesthood, some of which the Catholic Church covered up—and virtually all of which it denied—over the past half century.

This phenomenon was epitomized by the bishop of Bayeux-Lisieux, who in 2001 was given a suspended sentence for protecting a priest who raped one boy and had sexual relations with ten others while under his authority. Austrian cardinal Hans Hermann Groer resigned after it was revealed he had sexually molested students at the seminary; six years later, pictures of priests engaging in sex with seminarians surfaced on a seminary computer. English Catholics were horrified by the scandal at the Ampleforth boarding school, which revealed a thirty-year period of sexual abuse. A Polish archbishop had to quit because he engaged in sex with younger priests. By 2006, 250 Irish priests were under investigation for pedophilia.[83] Dublin's diocese alone handled a hundred cases of sexual abuse.[84] The worst, however, was probably the Ferns diocese, whose crimes came to light after the suicide of Father Sean Fortune in 1999. Ferns officials covered up sexual predations that had been going on over a forty-year period, with allegations leveled at twenty-one priests, leading the normally sympathetic Irish media to label it the "devil's diocese" and the "horror of Ferns."

Pedophilia's poison was not limited to Ireland. In the American Catholic Church, the crime grew so widespread and destructive that lawsuits forced the body of Catholic bishops, in 2002, to approve a "Charter for the Protection of Children and Young People," commissioning a national review board to conduct a study of sexual misconduct under the auspices of the John Jay College of Criminal Justice.[85] More than 10,600 victims made allegations against the Catholic Church, leading to legal fees and compensation of over $570 million. In 1994 alone, the Chicago Archdiocese spent more than $4 million on legal fees related to sex scandals.[86] One Catholic journalist who followed the first wave of American pedophile and homosexual abuse cases that originated in Louisiana found an "ecclesiastical culture that has become a magnet to men with pathological problems."[87]

Other studies painted a picture of severe personality disorder among seminarians. Personality tests of seminarians found them shockingly similar in their answers to the responses given by psychopaths. A study by Vincent Herr reported great variance for seminarians in personality tests from the responses of most males in that the seminarians were substantially more feminine in character. A 1968 study described 70 percent of male candidates for the clergy as "psychosexually immature, exhibiting traits of heterosexual retardation, confusion concerning sexual role, fear of sexuality, effeminacy and potentially homosexual dispositions" with a full 8 percent "sexually deviant."[88] Conrad Baars in 1972 claimed 20 to 25 percent of his sample of priests had "serious psychiatric difficulties" and that "heterosexual retardation was a common threat."[89] The Church first acknowledged a problem existed in a ninety-two-page report in 1985, "The Problem of Sexual Molestations by Roman Catholic Clergy: Meeting the Problem in a Comprehensive and Responsible Manner."[90]

Moreover, the unacknowledged character of the abuse was that it was homosexual in nature. This was not a psychiatric disorder as often alleged by using the term "pedophilia"—it was simply homosexuality involving children. John Jay's report found 81 percent of the victims were boys, and the very title of the study—"The Nature and Scope of Sexual Abuse of Minors by Catholic Priests and Deacons . . . ," with *nuns* left out—indicated the unwelcome and unstated reality that primarily this remained a male homosexual issue, not an issue of just child abuse.[91] Where single incidents were involved, a higher percentage of females were in the victim category, but repeat offenders chose boys to abuse.[92] Some priests practiced their perverse behavior for as long as forty-one years. Other indicators were equally disturbing: of the 114 dioceses and religious institutes responsible for six or more priests, no action at all was taken against 8 percent of the accused clerics, 55 percent were referred "for evaluation," and 7 percent were "reprimanded and returned."[93] Bishops, including Daniel Ryan of Springfield, Illinois, and Anthony O'Connell (who had replaced sex abuser Joseph Keith Symons) of Palm Beach, Florida, resigned over sex charges (Ryan with a teenage male prostitute, O'Connell with a former seminarian). AIDS was rampant among priests—four per ten thousand, or a rate four times that of the general population.[94]

Peter McDonough and Eugene C. Bianchi reported a homosexual subculture flourished within the Jesuits, a claim first made public in a serious way in the 1992 bestseller *Lead Us Not into Temptation* by Jason Berry, who followed the case of St. Francis Seminary in California.[95] Based on his interviews, Berry claimed one third of the seminarians were homosexual, a similar fraction as the estimates of other church observers.[96] Father Donald B. Cozzens warned that the American priesthood was becoming a "gay profession."[97] Rose's interviews with students revealed that the homosexual subculture was so prominent that seminaries were routinely referred to by nicknames such as Notre Flame (Notre Dame), the Pink Palace (St. Mary's in Baltimore), or the Theological Closet (Theological College at Catholic University of America in Washington, D.C.), as opposed to those deigned merely hopelessly liberal, such as Mary Inaccurate (Mary Immaculate in Pennsylvania).[98] St. Mary of the Lake in Mundelein, Illinois, became so debauched that in 1996 a priest from the Archdiocese of Chicago, Father Wayne Wurst, took to the radio to denounce it, noting that "there were madams, pimps, and prostitutes all in a major seminary system."[99] Joseph Kellenyi estimated half of his fellow students at Mundelein were homosexuals; Father Norman Weslin, in his autobiography, put the number of "practicing homosexuals" at Sacred Heart Seminary in Wisconsin at 40 percent.[100] Priests were forced into counseling as "homosexuals in denial" for *not* embracing (figuratively and literally) the homosexual lifestyle.[101]

Individual orders also suffered from a gay mafia. A highly publicized northern California case involved a discrimination in the workplace suit by a Jesuit scholastic who alleged that his superiors subjected him to such sexual harassment (including superiors sending him greeting cards with sexually aroused naked men), he could not remain in the order.[102] John Bollard told *60 Minutes* that a dozen Jesuit priests made sexual advances to him and invited him to cruise gay bars.[103] Mark Jordan, a "self-proclaimed Thomist and homosexual," authored *The Silence of Sodom*, in which he claimed the Catholic priesthood had long been essentially homosexual.[104]

Were child abuse, pedophilia, and rampant homosexuality within the ranks of the clergy causes of the decline of Christianity in Europe and, to a far smaller degree, in the United States? Or were they merely fellow travelers of a religious culture gone badly astray, culminating in "Christophobia"? Or was it just part of the secularization of Europe? Some have argued the radicalization of parts of the church was a psychological backlash to the liberation movements of 1989, in which a nonviolent revolution, strongly influenced by Christianity and decisively directed by Pope John Paul II and Christian leaders throughout the West and the Iron Curtain countries, succeeded in toppling the paragon of hypersecularism, communism.[105] The fall of godless communism precipitated a severe denial and angry reactions from the faithful who had worshiped the golden calf of Marxism. Instead of celebrating the human liberty brought about by the fall of the Berlin Wall, many left-wing intellectuals gnashed their teeth and redoubled their efforts to exterminate the source of that freedom. That source was Christianity.

Missionaries to the Europeans

Whereas at one time, Europe and America evangelized the world, by 1990 the fastest-growing churches—especially Protestant churches—were African or Latin American. Indeed, it seemed the only salvation for Europe's Christianity was the lands Europeans had once Christianized. In 2005, the new Archbishop of York was John Sentamu, a Ugandan (inaugurated in a ceremony featuring African dancers and drums); one of the most rapidly growing Ukrainian ministries was that of Sunday Adelaja, a Nigerian; and a Zairian priest led the mass for French president Jacques Chirac in 1996. Matthew Ashimolowo, who founded the Kingsway International Christian Centre in London in 1992, boasted 12,000 in attendance by 2006. His was the largest church created in Britain since 1861, whose auditorium was double the capacity of St. Paul's Cathedral or Westminster Abbey.[106] Kensington Temple claimed more than 5,500 members, as did Hillsong, an Australian-based ministry led by a black pastor in London.[107] Many of the new African churches in England had dual ministries that reached out to local Britons but which also, via television, reached a wide audience in Nigeria, Ghana, South Africa, Malawi, Uganda, Sierra Leone, and the Caribbean.

Both the Aladura movement and the Alpha Enterprise represented the new face of immigrant Christianity. Aladura (a Yoruba word for "owners of prayer"), a Pentecostal variant, emphasized prayer, fasting, spiritual warfare, charismatic gifts, and healing. The English-based Alpha movement, created at Holy Trinity Church in Brompton in the 1980s by Nicky Gumbel, resembled the American nondenominational "seeker churches" that used a series of lectures and discussions to introduce people to Jesus in a nonthreatening setting.[108] The Archbishop of Paris called the Alpha movement, along with the charismatic movement, the two greatest gifts Protestants have given to Catholics.[109] A critical evaluation of the Alpha movement nevertheless admitted that "many church leaders in the UK [regarded it] as the most important initiative of its time."[110] Beginning with four courses in 1991 (which were basic Bible studies without the Bible, asking, "Who is Jesus?," "What is sin?," and so on), the program exploded to reach 7,300 by 2001 and had extended to the United States. Advertised in Britain through billboards, leaflets, street posters—all supported by personal contact—the initiative was possibly the most significant development during the so-called Decade of Evangelism. The message on the billboards greatly resembled the "God messages" seen in America in the early 2000s, with simple statements or questions that had no overt link to Christianity ("You're born. You live. You die. End of story?")

In addition, hundreds of new African-initiated churches populated Europe.[111] London, Kiev, and Paris saw black-originated churches springing up under the auspices of a number of organizations, including the Redeemed Christian Church of God and the Congolese Kimbanguist church, as well as a few Latin American churches, such as the Universal Church of the Kingdom of God, based in Brazil. Ethnic Protestants, particularly Pentecostals, had begun reevangelizing Europe. By 2007, Paris contained some 250 mostly black Protestant churches. Within the postal zone known as 93rd (Seine-Saint-Denis), at least 60 evangelical churches operated, of which one fifth were members of the Communauté des Églises d'Expressions Africaines de France (CEAF), a Congolese Christian organization. St. Denis alone had four congregations associated with the CEAF. Rome saw its all-Italian churches being infiltrated by as many as 100,000 Filipinos; St. Andrews Presbyterian Church in Scotland played home to Korean evangelists; and Germany featured 1,100 foreign language Protestant churches, including many Nigerian churches.

Immigrants were not the only source of revitalization in the Christian Church, as numerous internal sects and movements injected life into the somnambulant body. Many of these were Catholic and Protestant charismatics, including the Rinnovamento nello Spirito (RnS) in Italy, which claimed a quarter-million adherents in some 1,300 congregations.[112] A related movement in France emphasized the Virgin Mary and the veneration of the pilgrimage site Paray-le-Monial, the location of the Sacred Heart vision. Czech priest Vladimir Miklucia and Slovakian Silvo Krcmery led Catholic charismatic revivals with operations that reached millions. Opus Dei, demonized in the best-selling book *The Da Vinci Code*, has produced talented businesspeople who advised governments. Other new ecclesiastical movements were brought together by the Catholic Church in May 1998 at St. Peter's Square in the first-ever such mass gathering of these groups.[113]

Indicators of Europe's cultural leftism often failed to capture the underlying conservatism that reflected the influence of the Church. While most European countries had liberal abortion laws, for example, the time limit for pregnancy termination in Britain has shrunk from twenty-eight weeks in 1967 to twenty-four and was heading toward further limitation. France, the UK, Germany, and the Netherlands all had lower—in some nations, far lower—abortion rates than the United States.[114] Nor were all indicators of the health of Christianity declining. From 1999 to 2005, the number of men studying for the priesthood in Poland rose from 4,500 to 7,000, and the ratio of seminarians to ordained priests was 22.5, or enough to maintain the priest population (contrary to the United States and Italy, where the ratios were 10 and 11.6, or France [5.6] or Ireland [3.6]).[115]

Still, most of the trends were not encouraging: between 1970 and 2005 the Catholic Church closed 1,700 churches (10 percent of its total), and between 2001 and 2007, some 500 London churches of all denominations were closed. Europe once accounted for almost 40 percent of all candidates for the priesthood worldwide, a number that has fallen to only 22 percent. Whereas France alone ordained 566 priests in 1966, only 40 priests were ordained four decades later; and the numbers entering French seminaries dropped by one fourth. Perhaps the greatest indicator of the decline of Europe's Christianity, however, lies in a simple anecdote about Czechs visiting an art gallery with paintings of Christ. Having to be informed as to who the man on the cross was, one girl asked, "Who did that to him?" A friend responded, "The Communists."[116]

Revival in Christendom

Christianity was thriving in Latin America and Africa where, of twenty-two countries whose Catholic population exceeded 10 million in 2010, fifteen were in the Third World, led by Brazil, which by the 1990s had a Catholic population of 125 million and 330 bishops. Whereas 48.75 percent of all Catholics lived in the Americas, until March 2013, no pope had ever come from anywhere but Europe (which contains only 26.37 percent of all Catholics). Pope Francis's ascension in 2013 (from Argentina) marked a sharp departure by the College of Cardinals from its practice of selecting popes from Europe and a recognition of the New World's dominance of Catholicism.

Africa added 100 million Christians between 1950 and the 1975, and the number of Catholics alone reached 125 million by the 1990s. The Basilica of Our Lady of Peace of Yamoussoukro in the Ivory Coast was (depending on the definition) the largest Christian structure in the world, able to accommodate 18,000 worshipers. As the largest domed church in the world, the 30,000-square-meter facility was one third larger than St. Peter's Basilica.

Christianity in Africa had grown despite persecutions. Nigeria was home to some of the largest revivals in human history in Africa, including a six-day Nigerian crusade by German evangelist Reinhard Bonnke that counted 6.6 million in attendance, with a single-crusade high of 1.5 million. Between 1995 to 2000, Boennke's crusades, many of them in Africa where he expressed a special calling, numbered over 28 million.[117] With the rise in the number of Christians in nations such as Nigeria, however, came a revival of violence reminiscent of the Nigerian-Biafran war of 1967, this time with religious overtones as Muslims trying to enforce Sharia law killed hundreds of Christian Igbos.[118]

As in Africa and Latin America, Pentecostalism soared in some parts of Asia, most notably South Korea. In sheer membership, nothing came close to Yoido Full Gospel Church in Seoul, South Korea, which counted 830,000 members as of 2007. Asia represented fertile ground indeed for Christ's gospel. Known as the "sacred doctrine," the Bible—not Mao's little red book—became a bestseller in China in the twenty-first century. With only a single authorized publisher in the nation, Amity Printing, some 50 million Bibles were printed in China, and even printing one book per second, the publisher was unable to keep up with demand.[119] As of 2007, there were 40 million Christians in China, whose vast population made it the richest evangelical field in human history. China was on track to become the most Christian nation on earth in total numbers by 2020, eclipsing the United States.

Meanwhile, a stream of Protestant, particularly Pentecostal, missionaries into Latin America in mid-century turned into a flood by the end of the millennium and made deep inroads into Latin America, accounting for one fourth of all South American Christians by 1940.[120] Just over a decade later, there were already four thousand Protestant missionaries on the continent, including many Seventh Day Adventists. Aimee Semple McPherson's Four-square Gospel church sent a wave of missionaries to Brazil in 1953. These and other Pentecostal missionaries helped the Latins "cope emotionally with the wrenching changes that . . . modernization would bring to their lives."[121] Financed in part by American televangelists and aided by the lifting of prohibitions against non-Catholic faiths in many countries, the Protestant expansion continued with a new generation of home-grown Latin American evangelists. By 1997, some 60 million Latins identified themselves as evangelicals (two thirds of whom were Pentecostals), and even critics admitted that these Protestant faiths addressed the people's needs of healing, battling evil spirits, and attacking poverty.[122]

The Catholic variant of this grassroots evangelicalism was the *religiosidad popular*, a type of Catholic fundamentalism emphasizing saints, shrines, and relics and borrowing heavily from local Indian and African traditions. Receiving the papal endorsement in 1979 when John Paul II visited the shrine of the Virgin of Guadalupe in Mexico, these movements swelled Christianity's numbers in Spanish-speaking countries. Overall, however, the Catholic Church appeared somewhat behind the curve when it came to finding solutions for Latin America's problems. It was El Salvadoran and Nicaraguan Pentecostals who supported the removal of Communists and dictators (American televangelist Jimmy Swaggart called the removal of the Marxist Allende "one of the great acts of this century") at the time when American Catholics were supporting the communist regimes.[123] Time and again, when Catholic priests stood "in solidarity with the poor," they were in reality ensuring the continued poverty of the people they claimed to support—just like various American politicians who fight for welfare programs to keep their constituencies beholden to them. Before long, many Latin Americans had picked up on this fact.

Many of those priests devoted to the "church of social action," whether Catholic or some of the more liberal Protestant varieties, had forsaken the primary purpose of the church in the first place—saving the lost. Nonetheless, the job still got done by lay members and the unofficial church, through grassroots missionary efforts and by tapping into technology. One of the most successful, the Jesus Film Project, produced 1,011 different translations of the *Jesus* film with 1,026 audio and video translations, having distributed 43 million videocassettes and 14 million audio cassettes worldwide. Into the first decade of the twenty-first century, then, the Christian God was alive and well on Planet Earth, although His primary residence had moved, from Europe to the Americas, and expanding rapidly into Africa and China.

Believers, whether African, North American, Chinese, or Latin American, sought genuine spiritual connections, not liberalized mush. Christianity's decline in Europe was accelerated because of its departure from authentic (one might say, fundamentalist) principles.[124]

This resulted in an exodus from traditional churches. "Presbyterians, Methodists, and Episcopalians [lost] nearly half their young people for good," with almost half of all Presbyterian youth leaving church altogether.[125] Despite efforts to be "inclusive" (i.e., to condone sexual immorality and homosexuality, and ordain women; or to water down doctrine to the point where it was unrecognizable as Christian), mainline churches in America saw their memberships plummet. One third of American Methodist churches performed no baptisms at all in 1985. Major denominations to experience substantial enrollment decline from 1990 to 2000 included the United Church of Christ (14 percent), Presbyterians (11.6 percent), and Methodists (6.7 percent). Meanwhile, fundamentalist denominations, such as Baptists and Pentecostals, grew: Assemblies of God (18.5 percent), Christian Missionary Alliance (21.8 percent), Church of God (40 percent), and Evangelical Free Church (57 percent).[126]

Criticisms of these church members—that they were uneducated or resorted to fundamentalist doctrines because they were poor—didn't wash. Almost 30 percent of self-defined evangelical adults in the United States had a college degree, a number higher than the national average, and one quarter of the adult born-again Christians came from households making $60,000 or more a year.[127] And if Christianity wasn't always reflected in church attendance, it still was seen in poll responses. In 1991, Gallup reported that 86 percent said they believed Jesus was God or the Son of God and 81 percent agreed that the Bible was either the literal or inspired word of God.[128] Surveys taken in 1994 similarly showed two thirds of Americans went to church at least once a month.[129]

Hollywood and the American media certainly have not helped Christianity in the United States and particularly not Protestantism. Many moviegoers have seen multiple bar mitzvahs and Jewish weddings on the screen (*A Serious Man, Keeping Up with the Steins, Sixty Six*, and more), but one would search in vain for a Protestant confirmation or noninfant baptism. Nor have Protestant ministers usually been portrayed in a positive light—more commonly they have been shown to be hypocrites, especially concerning racial issues, and often philanderers, sex addicts, or crooks (*Footloose, Monsignor, True Confessions, There Will Be Blood, Night of the Hunter, Hawaii*, etc., and such as con man/preacher Jonas Nightengale, played by Steve

Martin in the 1992 movie *Leap of Faith*). Once again, the sophisticates on the Left have deprecated Christianity and its adherents to promote socialism and statism.

A path-breaking exception to that trend was *The Passion of the Christ* (2004), directed by Mel Gibson, a practicing Catholic. Made for what was, by Hollywood standards, a small budget ($30 million), *Passion* grossed over $600 million worldwide—netting $83 million on the first weekend alone—all accomplished without traditional Hollywood marketing budgets by going straight to audiences through church screenings. Gibson not only demonstrated that a vast religious market existed for feature films, even one quite gory and lacking any sex or romance at all, but that the tested, high-dollar advertising campaigns were not necessarily needed. By implication, *Passion* suggested that well-made conservative and free-market films would find sizable audiences previously ignored by the industry.

Nevertheless, obtaining a "faith picture" of Americans at the end of the millennium remained a difficult task, as polls yielded conflicting evidence. Christian pollster George Barna, while noting in 1992 that almost 80 percent of Americans said religion was "very important" to them, and at least 65 percent of any particular age group agreed that the Bible was "totally accurate," also discovered that less than 10 percent of all born-again adults had a "biblical worldview" based on core teachings of Christianity.[130] On one hand, Bible sales topped $400 million per year, and Christian book sales were already growing dramatically *before* the publication of the phenomenally popular *Left Behind* series, beginning in 1995.[131] Christian concerts and record sales set records, seeing rising attendance when secular concerts were flagging.[132] On the other hand, Christians in America tended to divorce at the same rate as non-Christians and had almost as much trouble with alcoholism and other addictions and attended church on a steadily decreasing trajectory.[133]

How does one reconcile such history? Had Christianity become mere entertainment? The truth seems to lie in George Barna's research, which defined a core group of "Revolutionaries" in late twentieth-century American religious life. He estimated that these Revolutionaries comprised between 10 and 30 percent of self-identified Christians. Those Revolutionaries were far more committed but far less traditional in their style of worship, displaying a passion for intimate worship, faith-based conversations, and intentional (often self-directed) spiritual growth.[134] By 2025, he predicted, "alternative faith-based communities would account for as much of the spiritual experience and expression" as the local church.[135] Indeed, even at the megachurches, such as Chicago's Willow Creek, which had made its reputation on "seeker-friendly" services, surveys found that fully 25 percent of the members thought the church was standing in the *way* of their further spiritual growth.[136] The upshot was that no one could yet proclaim the death of Christianity, but certainly the traditional church of a half-century earlier was becoming radically transformed. This was, of course, one more transformation of American Christianity, no different from the change from Anglican services of the 1790s to the campfire revivals of the 1840s.

Uncle Sam Bashing

If "Revolutionaries" existed at all in Europe, they made little impact on the declining church-going European Christian community. America's continued Christian character reflected the reality that the "faith gap" between the United States and Europe had widened. But the chasm was not only in the area of religion, and it coincided with a rising tone of anti-Americanism across the Continent.

European disapproval of American foreign policy reached 58 percent in Germany, 63 percent in Spain, 66 percent in France, and 41 percent in Britain. Greece and Turkey recorded disapproval rates of 70 to 80 percent, and even so-called right-wing leaders, such as Jörg Haider in Austria or Jean-Marie Le Pen in France, made political hay out of bashing Uncle Sam, framing their nationalism in a hate-everybody rhetoric. It was telling, however, that *no one* ever polled Americans on their approval of Spanish, French, British, or even Russian foreign policy. Critics cited the war on terror as the reason for the worldwide uptick in anti-Americanism, especially within Muslim states, despite American intervention in the Balkans that helped save the Bosnian Muslims.

Leftist British playwright Harold Pinter, who had just survived an operation for cancer in 2002, recalled:

> I found that to emerge from a personal nightmare was to enter an infinitely more pervasive public nightmare—the nightmare of American hysteria, ignorance, stupidity, and belligerence. The most powerful nation the world has ever known effectively waging war against the rest of the world. . . . The US administration is now a bloodthirsty wild animal.[137]

Novelist Margaret Drabble similarly expressed views that bordered on deranged, saying, "My anti-Americanism has become almost uncontrolla-

ble. It has possessed me, like a disease." She continued, "I detest Disneyfi-
cation. I detest Coca-Cola. I detest burgers. I detest sentimental and violent
Hollywood movies that tell lies about history. I detest American imperialism, American infantilism, and American triumphalism about victories it
didn't even win."[138] After George Bush was reelected, Brian Reade of the
Mirror fumed that Americans were "self-righteous, gun-totin', military lo-
vin', sister marryin', abortion hatin', gay-loathin', foreigner despisin', non-
passport-ownin' rednecks. . . ."[139]

Anti-Americanism, however, did not translate into Euro patriotism, if
such a thing is possible for a nonstate. Instead, 2004 polls showed that two
thirds of British and Eastern Europeans said they would not miss the European Union were it to disappear, and less than half of the Continental Europeans thought membership in the EU was beneficial—a percentage that
kept falling. By 2006, only one third of Austrians favored membership in
the EU, and with good reason, as private sector initiatives had halted. Just
as André Siegfried, a European intellectual, warned in 1935 that "Europe
without her individuality would be only one continent among many; she
would cease to be the yeast which leavens the rest of the world" (assuming
Europe was the yeast, and not the United States), it was equally true that a
unified Europe would cease to be Europe at all in the traditional sense—
namely a disparate collection of identities—and would become something
fundamentally different.[140] But unity may not be possible, if Esperanto's
history means anything. The artificially constructed language thought to
be the answer for linguistically polyglot Europe has been a failure, achieving essentially a negligible number of fluent speakers over its 130 years of
existence. And there is America. Europeans for decades had struggled
against what they called "Babbittry," or the cultural imperialism of American markets, and in the 1990s, renewed complaints about the encroachment
of Americanism arose. With those complaints came a rising anxiety that
Europe would never catch America.

Books like *Why Europe Will Run the 21st Century, The End of the American Era*, or *Europe's Mighty Economy* were replaced by titles such as *Can Germany Still Be Saved?, The Collapse of France*, Robert Samuelson's *End of
Europe*, and Fareed Zakaria's *Decline and Fall of Europe*.[141] *The Economist*, il-
lustrating Ronald Reagan's quip that he'd like to meet a one-armed economist (so that he wouldn't hear, "On the other hand . . ."), published two
contrasting editorials in a six-month period—one touting a brilliant future
for Germany, followed by a gloomy editorial proclaiming Germany was
finished!

For almost a century, European theorists have explained American exceptionalism in terms of the absence of socialism. Werner Sombart's famous line that American socialism smashed onto the "shoals of roast beef and apple pie" suggested that workers accustomed themselves to the comfortable life of capitalism and its associated absence of class stigma. Yet by the late twentieth century, one could argue the opposite; that as the sumptuary lines between classes disintegrated, class envy rose to new levels in certain areas. With every television show such as *Celebrity Cribs* or the older *Lifestyles of the Rich and Famous* came renewed angst about the inadequacies of middle-class life if a strong religious underpinning was absent.

Class envy was inevitable, and most pronounced in secular and self-absorbed California, where the disparities between classes were most fully on display.[142] Whereas some saw capitalism as resulting in a more ethical society through consumption—where people no longer had to fight over scraps—tension between income groups rose with each new acquisition if no other mediating force existed to intervene.[143] California attempted to buy its way into prosperity, utterly failing, and becoming the butt of jokes like "We should sell California to the Chinese to get out of debt—but they have to agree to take the people."

Surplus Males

In the Far East, other trends were taking place that were perhaps even more significant than Europe's Islamification or America's secularization. In both China and India, families were practicing infanticide: in India's case voluntarily, deliberately limiting family size, and in China's because only a single child was allowed per family by the government, beginning in 1979. In both, female babies were aborted and male children were much favored. By 2010, this practice had resulted in China's having a surplus of three hundred million males, mostly young, and for whom there would be no females available. Western observers have noted these males would be available for military service.

China's sleeping giant appeared to have awoken with the new millennium, and initially a formidable giant it appeared to be. With 160 cities having a population of a million or more, China had the capacity to tap into an unprecedented labor supply. What was missing was the incentive of the market—until Deng Xiaoping embarked on a stunning break with Marxist doctrines. In the early 1990s, after negotiations were concluded that would give China control of capitalist Hong Kong in 1997, Deng began to seriously modify Chinese communism into state capitalism under the control and regulation of the Communist party. His pragmatism was of long standing; even before the Cultural Revolution he had argued against collectivism and promoted land leasing and entrepreneurship. With respect to introducing capitalist markets, he quoted an old Chinese saying, "It doesn't matter whether a cat is white or black as long as it catches mice."[144] When China joined the World Trade Organization, the WTO rule book sold *two million copies* in a matter of weeks.

Applying the world's largest labor force to the tiller, for years China's productivity nevertheless remained low. When Deng released the "cats" through growing internal economic freedom, that began to change radically. The private sector of Chinese industry increased productivity at a mind-boggling 17 percent *annually* between 1995 and 2002. Thirty years ago, Datang, a Chinese city, was primarily responsible for rice production, although its inhabitants sewed socks in their spare time. After Deng Xiaoping's opening of the Chinese markets, Datang was responsible for producing nine billion pairs of socks annually, or one third of the world total. A small area north of Hong Kong, the Zhu Jiang Delta, was home to 50,000 electronics firms. China added 350,000 engineers *per year* to its employment rolls.

All growth is accompanied by a cost, and so it was with China, which experienced an explosion in car sales. Beijing alone had over 1,400 cars a day added to the city's streets. The price was pollution, with sixteen of the world's twenty worst polluted cities residing in China. As typically happened in developing economies, heavy industries shed jobs, and China was no different, losing 15 million manufacturing jobs as its manufacturing productivity soared. At the same time, China found itself outsourcing to areas deeper in the countryside. One factory owner, showing the president of the U.S. Chamber of Commerce a pair of socks that sold for eleven cents, acknowledged that he was "uncompetitive" and had to relocate his factory inland to get the price down by almost half. Worldwide, products were assessed a "China price"—what it would cost the manufacturer to make it in China. On China's end, however, the result was a rising tide, not a lowering level. In 1990, the World Bank reported 375 million people in China living in poverty—a number that had fallen in 2000 to 212 million, with projections that it would fall further to only 16 million by 2015.[145] However, all definitions of poverty rely heavily on accurate reporting by the government under scrutiny, and are subject to political influence.

American producers were not deprived of the benefits of trade whether domestic or global in orientation. However, large corporations increasingly located facilities abroad and adopted international management structures. Service-related call centers for banks, reservations, and other help lines were particularly attractive targets for relocation. By January 2004, U.S. companies that operated abroad generated 56 percent of American exports and accounted for 60 percent of all manufacturing employment.[146] Hewlett-Packard, for example, had 150,000 employees in 170 countries and was the largest information technology company in Europe, Russia, the Middle East, and South Africa. Ireland, whose Green Miracle saw the country's workforce nearly double in fifteen years with no noticeable unemployment, received more direct investment by American businesses than did China. America's Dell Computer was Ireland's largest exporter.[147] It didn't hurt Ireland's growth that the government slashed taxes to 12.5 percent, or far below the levels of Europe or America.

In addition to China and Ireland, free trade unleashed an industrial revolution in India, whose trade with the United States soared by 400 percent from 1990 to 2006, although still only a tenth of the Sino-American trade. The Indian economy grew at a rate of 5.5 percent between 1975 and 2007 (compared with its twenty-year rate under collectivist economics of 3.4 percent and its anemic rate of 2.6 percent in the early 1970s). In the last decade alone, India grew at the unprecedented rate of 8 percent.

Globalization had come to India, changing not only the living standards but the character of India as well. By 2010 India had more English-speaking individuals than any other country while one of its ancient native tongues, Sanskrit, had virtually vanished, except in America, whose universities turned out more Sanskrit scholars than did India's![148] The tech revolution had also brought about the rise of a new class of Indian techies called "Zippies," young city or suburban residents who belonged to Generation Z. The Zippies saw nothing wrong with making or spending money, desiring not only good jobs but the good life. Indian entrepreneurs such as Nandan Nilekani, the former CEO of Indian information powerhouse Infosys, observed a new attitude had overtaken the subcontinent: "we are going to break out of this trap. There's a sense that our future can be better for our children than for us."[149]

As late as 1968, one middle-class Indian recalled, every morning "the milkman came around with his cow," and the only way to keep cool was to sit under a "crazily beating fan." Forty years later, his relatives lived in a booming New Delhi suburb with two refrigerators, air conditioners, and a flat-screen television. Construction sites, however, still featured women toting heavy baskets of cement on their heads to men on rickety scaffolding who, in turn, trotted upward to apply it. A single view from a hotel could include the sparkling glass Cisco building and a sprawling shantytown of tin-roofed shacks. Although many Indians still wanted to emigrate to the United States, increasing numbers thought they could succeed in their home country.

Low-wage, high-skilled Indians proved irresistible to American information technology companies needing to slash costs in the 1990s, leading them to export jobs to English-speaking Indian Zippies, many trained to perfect a flat midwestern dialect. (When one Indian writer spoke her native language to a group of college kids from the subcontinent, she was stunned to hear them say, "Actually, ma'am, we're not allowed. We have to speak English only.")[150] Doordarshan, the Indian television network that reaches 90 percent of the subcontinent's population (the world's largest television market, with 119 million viewers), features extensive English-only programming.

"India Shining," the slogan of the tech-oriented globalist Bharatiya Janata Party that reflected the high-tech India movement, marked India's arrival as a world economic force. Bharat Forge, Suzlon, Wipro, and Tata—all Indian companies—owned firms in Sweden, Germany, Britain, China, France, and the United States. When Tata, the Indian steel company, bought Europe's steel giant Mittal in 2006, former chief executive of Arcelor, Guy Dollé, described the takeover as "a company full of Indians [using] monkey money."[151] Not long thereafter, Tata spent another $8.1 billion of that "monkey money" to buy the Anglo-Dutch steel company Corus, and Tata's tea subdivision bought American food producers Good Earth and Eight O'Clock Coffee between 2005 and 2006. Infosys, a Bangalore-based company notorious for outsourced jobs, grew at a Silicon Valley rate of 50 percent a year in the twenty-first century, with astonishing wage differences: $5,000 for an Indian engineer, $60,000 for an American. In Bangalore, India's new technical center, the more highly paid workers lived in gated communities ("Dollar Colony," for example), and office parks and shopping centers (literally translated, "shopping complicated") popped up as soon as old buildings could be ripped down.[152]

For all of India's growth, the United States *every year* still grew at nearly the equivalent of India's total GNP. The Americanization of the world remained evident even in Bollywood, where new uploading technologies made possible "the globalization of the local."[153] Pundit Thomas Friedman argued arrogantly and unconvincingly in *The World Is Flat* that the flat-world platforms would enhance local culture and prevent the Americanization of the globe, but more than ever, Bollywood wanted to be Hollywood. There were Indian versions of *American Idol* and game shows, culminating in the 2008 sleeper hit *Slumdog Millionaire*, which featured an Indian version of "Who Wants to Be a Millionaire?" But even proponents of the "new India" message admitted that "Bollywood . . . put no value on script writing." Despite claims that Bollywood's creativity was "pent up," and would "explode," as of 2008 a creativity gap with California's movie industry still remained.[154] The American market was what counted, and remained what moviemakers in Bali, Calcutta, Hong Kong, and Prague all wanted to crack. American shows, such as Disney's *That's So Raven* and *Lizzie McGuire*, dominated Indian children's and teen programming. Indeed, as one American noted while searching for the qualities of happiness around the world, "if anything . . . India is aping America. Shopping malls, gated communities, fast food. They're all here now."[155]

Nor had the "India Shining" movement reached much of the rural countryside. Alcoholism and corruption were rampant, female infanticide was rising, and the only mouse many of the children encountered was the furry rodent, not the computer device.[156] Daily, millions of children picked through trash piles for food or to find items to sell in the market. Pockets of utter destitution dotted India, where 800 million still survived on less than $2 a day, and, to paraphrase Mark Twain, every life was sacred except human life. More than half of Indian women and a third of Indian males still were illiterate by 2008, including a quarter of all fifteen- to twenty-four-year-olds. But with a remarkably common American symbol—the gate in front of a restricted-access community—India also displayed its numerous wealthy communities, with their private militias and personal security companies.

Other indicators of technological progress revealed both the promise and continuing plight of India. With more than 78 million mobile phone users, and a subscription base growing at nearly 300 percent a year, India appeared to have joined the "flat world." Yet the reality of rapid growth often only underscored the nature of the challenge: counting 50 million Internet users in 2006—a tenfold increase in just a half decade—India's nonwired population still constituted 95 percent of the population. Those Internet cafés that did exist often were mere fronts for porn viewing and antigovernment blogs. In 2006, the government shut down a private website as contributing to "inflammatory postings." A couple was threatened with jail for kissing each other publicly during their wedding ceremony (forbidden in Rajasthan), and a film starlet had to apologize publicly for commenting in Tamil that premarital sex existed. India's cultural differences could not be easily bridged despite Infosys and Cisco.

Change and "Un-Change"

Elsewhere, however, the world in the first decade of the twenty-first century continued to look much as it had in the 1980s. Virtually no change could be detected on Egypt's skyline, which resembled its silhouette from 1970; Mexico City, likewise, had been largely unchanged. Stagnant, state-controlled economies resulted in a landscape that seldom changed. The high irony was that the charge of "traditionalism," always leveled against conservatives "because they fear change," proved entirely to be the domain of the Left. It was the absence of capitalist-driven economic growth that caused stagnation, and the only states clinging to the past were those still employing socialist policies.

Aside from endemic internecine warfare, regulatory obstruction continued to retard Third World growth. Starting a business in Haiti took an average of 203 days, and in the Congo, 215 days, compared with just 2 days in Australia, according to the International Finance Corporation.[157] Nigeria had 21 procedures to register property, Norway and Sweden, one. In the United States it only cost half a percent of property value to legally register property, but in Syria, it cost nearly one third and in Senegal, 34 percent.[158] Whereas it only took a day to register private property in Norway or two days in New Zealand, it took at least a year to do so in Angola, the former Ivory Coast, Rwanda, and Ghana, and nearly three years in Croatia.[159] Virtually all property was registered in Denmark and Costa Rica, but nearly none in Togo or Pakistan. Enforcement of a contract in Tunisia took only a week, but required 1,500 days in Guatemala; and the cost of enforcement was less than 1 percent of the disputed amount in countries such as Austria, Canada, and Britain, but more than 100 percent in the Dominican Republic, Indonesia, and the Philippines.[160] The most expensive states to create collateral for a loan were, as might be expected, those in the Middle East and sub-Saharan Africa, which comprised all ten of the most expensive and difficult places to create and register a security instrument.[161]

Another type of traditionalism, however, hung like a millstone around the necks of the Middle East—Islam. Islamic states continued to languish in the lower depths of developing countries, and the Muslim world was noteworthy for its lack of contributions to science, literature, or business. Between 1980 and 1999, only 171 international patents emerged from Arab countries, in contrast to the 16,328 coming from South Korea alone.[162] America's Hewlett-Packard Corporation registered 11 patents per day, equaling the output of all the Arab world in less than a month.

Similar stunning numbers reflect the Islamic world's impenetrability when it comes to technology. On average, there were less than 400 scientists and engineers working in research per million people in Arabic countries, whereas even including Latin America and Africa, the rest of the world averaged 979 per million. When Arab youths did acquire advanced university training in computers or technology, they left for the West. With only 18 computers per 1,000 people (versus 78 per 1,000 worldwide), Arab countries looked to drift further behind. Despite having 5 percent of the world population, Arabs accounted for only 1 percent of the books published and had more than one fourth of all unemployed males between fifteen and twenty-four.[163]

One could still see an antiscientific, antiprogress character on display in much of the modern Islamic world. As former USAID diplomat Lawrence Harrison noted, "when it comes to the relationship between religion and human progress, I find compelling evidence that some religions do better than others in promoting the goals of democratic politics, social justice and prosperity."[164] Voices calling for a Muslim equivalent of the Protestant Reformation have not yet been heard. The further behind Muslim nations got, however, the economically weaker they became and the more their humiliation; at the same time, the higher their population growth rates, the more their demographic power.

A common solution—education, or lack of it—proved inadequate to advance many Middle Eastern societies. As noted earlier, a number of Islamic terrorists had solid educations and college degrees. Increasingly, Islamic societies directed both young men and women into the sciences and even entrepreneurship. This constituted a dramatic contrast to Africa, where a high percentage of college graduates were still receiving degrees in political science or economics. Economist Thomas Sowell has demonstrated how even in America wage statistics purportedly showing racial discrepancies actually reflect educational differences.[165] Education was the key, but neither Africa nor the more backward countries in the Middle East were directing large numbers of their best and brightest into creative pursuits, engineering, science, and business, where their efforts would have the greatest positive effects for their people.

Yet even the education of governing elites that was occurring did not diminish the level of want and sheer backwardness found in many Middle

Eastern societies. Cairo, for example, with its 18 million people, was so noisy people routinely screamed to be heard. Studies of noise levels there found it not uncommon for sound levels to reach ninety-five decibels—the equivalent of standing next to a jackhammer or Eric Clapton's amplifier. Streets, alive twenty-four hours a day, were a cacophony of braying mules, honking cars, muezzins' prayer calls blaring from loudspeakers, air horns, and construction work.[166] Cairo, Calcutta, Mexico City, and other Third World cities also were notorious for their pungent odors of food, feces, and burning fuel. Neither noise nor smells seemed to affect the hundreds of thousands of homeless who slept in cemeteries each night. Merely having educated leaders—without the robust support of the pillars of American exceptionalism—proved futile in overall economic improvement for average people.

In other areas, some improvement was evident. Poverty in South Asia (India, Pakistan, and Bangladesh) fell from 462 million living on less than $1 a day (adjusted for inflation) in the mid-twentieth century to 431 million by 2001, with estimates placing the number at 216 million by 2015. Africa saw the number of cell phones increase tenfold every three years, and the ownership of radios went from under 200 per 10,000 persons in 1964 to more than 1,600 by 1998.[167] Televisions per capita rose faster than radios, reaching nearly 1,800 per 10,000 persons by 1998.[168] While lagging Europe and Asia badly, Africa's Internet usage soared from one per 27,000 people in 1996 to one per 138 in less than ten years. Whether China, India, Africa, Latin America, or South Asia, the questions were greater in 2008 than the answers: could these places prosper and thrive in spite of their spiritual, cultural, and economic contradictions? More specifically, could they compete with—even think of surpassing—the United States without adopting the four pillars of American exceptionalism?

One difficulty in catching the United States was that the USA did not stand still. By the twenty-first century, despite the dot-com bust, 9/11 terrorism, costs of foreign wars, and the home-mortgage market meltdown, America remained remarkably prosperous. Wall Street still accounted for more market capitalization than the *next five exchanges combined*.[169] Average home sizes had nearly doubled from fifteen years earlier, up to more than 2,400 square feet, which stood in stark contrast to the just over 1,000-square-foot average Japanese, Swedish, Portuguese, Italian, or British home.[170] And Americans did not own just one home: by 2005, more than one quarter of American homeowners bought or sold a home in which they had no plans to reside (including rentals), and owned 6.8 million vacation homes.[171]

Due to their freedom, prosperity, and unsurpassed standard of living, despite highly touted global polls showing other nations with higher living standards (as measured by numerous dubious benchmarks, such as number of family leave days, or questionable environmental quality measures), Americans remained far more optimistic and had a higher life satisfaction than Europeans. While "happiness surveys" put the United States a little down the list (ranking in the mid-teens to mid-twenties out of some one hundred countries where studies were done), Americans were uniquely optimistic. A 2003 Eurobarometer survey of fifteen EU countries showed that Americans were more likely to believe their lives had improved, and that almost 60 percent were "very satisfied" with their lives. Whereas only 40 percent of Europeans thought their lives would improve in the next five years, a stunning 63 percent of Americans said life would be better. Only Denmark (64 percent) had a higher satisfaction level than Americans.[172] And of all major nations subjected to psychological experiments involving fewer or more choices, only Americans consistently said they preferred more choices.[173]

Americans looked forward to expanding their horizons, while all other nationalities were happy to retrench on what they had and knew. Americans, confident in their individualism, were not daunted by greater options. These attitudes were directly related to American exceptionalism and the view that here, "things can—and will—be different."

Millennium of Fear

The world of computers has come a long way from the development of the world's first electronic general purpose computer, ENIAC (Electronic Numerical Integrator and Computer), at the University of Pennsylvania, put into operation in 1947. Perhaps befitting an invention that so greatly changed the course of the world, the assignment of credit to the developer(s) or inventor(s) of the world's first computer is still marred by controversy.

Using binary arithmetic, Harvard's Howard Aiken designed and IBM engineers built the Mark I computing machine in 1944. The Mark I gave the world Commander Grace Hopper, generally reputed to be the grandmother of computer programming, and the primary developer of COBOL (COmmon Business Oriented Language). Added to these efforts, the University of Pennsylvania's ENIAC project, headed by John Mauchly and J. Presper Eckert, produced an electronic computer using vacuum tubes that eliminated relays and switches. However, renowned mathematician John von Neumann had become interested in ENIAC and inserted himself as a consultant, publishing a draft report under his own name. As a result, computers using stored programs became known as von Neumann machines.[174]

A dozen business machine and computing companies were soon in business. By the 1960s, however, the world of computers was dominated by International Business Machines (IBM)—which at one point held 80 percent of the world computer market—although pushed by others such as Univac, Burroughs, Honeywell, and NCR.[175] IBM's 360 computer became the standard against which all others were measured, and its sales force was second to none. Although in coming decades the personal computer seized the industry, IBM remained the largest of the large-enterprise computer companies.

Even before the advent of the personal computer, though, a revolution was literally in the air. A theory of the growth in computing power with time was expressed by Gordon Moore (Moore's law), roughly stated as "computing power doubled every two years." Moore's law accelerated with the introduction of the first highly successful, mass-produced personal computer (PC), the Apple II, invented and built by Steve Wozniak in 1977 and marketed by Steve Jobs, after the introduction of Wozniak's early prototype, the Apple I, unveiled in 1976. Six years later, a variant of a PC beat a giant Cray supercomputer in chess, demonstrating that computing power had now been condensed so much that networks would dominate individual machines. By the 1990s, computing power rapidly overtook cost, then a yawning chasm opened up as silicon chips (the guts of computing) became dirt cheap.

Yet no sooner had the computer revolution begun to infiltrate every aspect of life in modern societies than it heralded a new and potentially terrifying problem. Sometime in the late 1990s, computer programmers began to express concerns that the programs for most of the world's computer systems—which had been designed over the previous four decades—had neglected a critical flaw in the storage of dates that would make itself known on midnight of January 1, 2000. The calendars inside computers were programmed to roll over to the next year, but dates were stored as six digits (YYMMDD, or for example 950331 for March 31, 1995) with no provision for centuries. With no space having been reserved for a two-digit century, the calendars would flip back to 1900, causing calculations using dates to malfunction and possibly shut down systems entirely. Many of the IBM mainframes were still running programs that emulated code written for earlier machines that had not been touched for decades, and no one knew anymore where they were or what they did. Scenarios appeared in newspapers and the new blogs (Web logs) prophesied utter chaos, with jails opening as computer locks failed, Social Security checks not going out, gas dispensers, lacking proper codes, ceasing to work, and so on.

Corporate America (and indeed, business around the globe) took the Y2K bug extremely seriously, and hiring of computer professionals sky-rocketed. It was a good time to be a programmer, and retirees were avidly sought by companies to rewrite programs and rebuild databases with eight-digit dates on a massive scale. Ultimately, they succeeded, and the new year arrived with few noticing any problem except in accessing older, legacy systems that had not been updated.

This panic programming effort coincided with another crash unrelated to Y2K, the dot-com bust. As use of the Internet skyrocketed in the late 1990s, companies scrambled to stake out a claim to Internet services and technology. As services became available across a large number of Web sites, the need for portals, or Internet service providers (ISPs), arose, causing the creation of companies like Mindspring and America OnLine (AOL). Many of these companies announced their technological expertise and industry by using their Internet domain names, like Amazon.com, where ".com" is their domain (site) suffix (*com* stood for commercial, as distinguished from *edu*, education, or *gov*, government), as their corporate name. Once again, personal computers fell in price while increasing in capabilities and speed, users grew from the hundreds of thousands to the hundreds of millions, and services were increasingly offered on the World Wide Web.[176] Entrepreneurs saw opportunities here, not least the ability to search the Web by subject to find information on suppliers or markets.

Every young computer programmer seemed to have an idea that would make millions of dollars as people would subscribe to his site or use his service. Increasingly, good sites were seen as advertising bonanzas, and every person accessing a site would have to see a spread of advertisements. The only question was which sites or services would prove popular and thereby profitable. There was no way to test-market an idea; one simply had to have faith. Since this was all new and open to everyone, it was thought that a company had to grow faster than its competitors to achieve a higher market share regardless of the cost. Once a user base was locked in, then subscription prices could be raised or advertising increased. Amazon.com, for example, lost money for years as it built up a dominant place in the market, not only for books but for music, electronics, and products of all sorts.

There seemed to be no limit to the amount of investor capital available for a good idea. Initial public offerings of stock were made with great fan-fare, often by a company that had yet to show a profit, or was not even then in operation.[177] But having little or no business experience, entrepreneurs often spent lavishly on themselves and their employees, throwing away vast sums on vacations, automobiles, and palatial facilities. Stock prices ad-vanced broadly, and sometimes spectacularly. Mindspring stock went from $9.00 per share to over $125.00 within two years. Cisco stock likewise rose rapidly. The name of the game was growth, not profits. Companies proudly reported their increases in employees and customers and found excuses for their losses. The entire United States seemed enamored with the young dot-com millionaires, and a number of films or TV movies celebrated com-puter geeks, including *Triumph of the Nerds* (1996) and *The Pirates of Silicon Valley* (1999). Far more, of course, portrayed a dark future dominated or controlled by computers.[178]

As of the late 1990s, however, the commercial potential of the Internet was all rank speculation and had only been proven as a business model in a few cases. A concerned Federal Reserve raised interest rates six times during 1999 and 2000 to rein in the speculators. Retribution was not long in com-ing. Collapse began in March 2000, and within a year many of the dot-coms had burned through their capital investment and were forced to declare bankruptcy. It was a scenario much like the auto industry had endured a century earlier, but the weeding out of losers was substantially faster.

Although a large number of dot-com companies survived—often under much reduced circumstances—public confidence in the Internet as a way to make money went into hiding for a decade. It was a demonstration of both rampant greed and the perils of attempting to profit from a radical new technology. The simple lesson to all was to be on the leading edge of tech-nology, not the bleeding edge.

Despite struggling through Y2K, the downsizing of the defense indus-try after the cold war, and the continued bloated demands of retirement and health care, American prosperity seemed poised to rebound. The statistics of progress were abundant. In 1985, there had been 2.1 million personal computers in the United States, but by 2007 the number had soared to 243 million. Cell phone usage had risen to the same level. Some three quarters of Americans owned a car, and one third owned two; and 46 percent owned their own homes. Average living space for a poor person was 721 square feet, compared with only 430 in Sweden and 92 in Mexico. Infant mortality was down from twenty deaths per thousand in 1970 to seven by 2002, and life expectancy reached seventy-eight years. Despite international surveys that claimed the American health care system was behind others, in fact it was so far ahead that its doctors routinely attempted to save infants and elderly who in other societies would be denied treatment through rationing. For example, one study suggested that infant mortality in the United States was overstated by as much as 40 percent.[179]

Improving health and longevity were to be expected by applying computing power to health care; just as everything seemed to improve, and costs seem to be lowered. In fact, for a number of reasons, most notably the separation of the user of health care (the patient), the provider (a doctor or hospital), and the payee (usually an insurance company), for the only time in recent memory the application of new technology to an industry failed to drive prices down. In fact, health care costs continued to rise, everywhere, although this had everything to do with the artificial availability of scarce medical resources concealed by third-party payers, and nothing to do with the advances of the technology itself. Certainly, computers greatly increased detection of disease, location of tumors, analysis of blood and urine, and the transfer and sharing of medical records.

Indeed, the Internet made possible the sharing of absolutely every type of information—even that which individuals wished to keep private. This trend had been foreseen early in the 1990s, when George Gilder prophesied that what flowed by wires would soon travel through the air, and what went through air (especially television) would soon move by wire, thus opening up the spectrum to incredible carrying capacity. That inversion began to appear by the early twenty-first century as computing capabilities continued to soar.

Moore's law of doubling computing power was proven time and again, and electronic storage per unit cost increased logarithmically. The "exaflood," or the torrent of Internet and Internet Protocol (IP) traffic, had arrived.[180] An exabyte (a one-quintillion unit of information storage 50,000 times larger than the entire digitized Library of Congress, or 10 to the 18th power) potential had emerged, permitting wireless networks to transmit high-definition television shows, YouTube videos, and any number of other individual computing operations. By 2006, the United States traffic alone equaled 10 exabytes, but the Discovery Institute estimated the U.S. Internet would grow *fifty times* larger within a decade, somewhere around 1,000 exabytes (a sextillion bytes), requiring upwards of $100 billion in investment capital.

Whether the promises of technology materialized or not, of course, depended greatly on the continued freedom secured by the United States and her allies throughout the world. All the developed nations operated on the assumption that the developing nations wanted freedom and prosperity as well—in short, that they sought progress. But in the new millennium, those assumptions were challenged by blood and fire.

Bush Wins a Contested Election . . . by 537 Votes

Few saw George W. Bush as a leader who would take the United States and the West as a whole in a dramatically new direction, much less a crusade. He was a president who had not won a majority of the popular vote (under mitigating circumstances) and who had avoided foreign policy as an issue during his campaign.

Bush, son of the forty-first president, George Herbert Walker Bush, like Bill Clinton was a baby boomer. Born in 1946 to a patrician family, Bush attended Yale University and received an MBA from the Harvard Business School (and, contrary to claims by the Left, had good grades, even better than Barack Obama). After working in the oil business and co-owning the Texas Rangers baseball team, he won the Texas governorship in 1994. Running for president in 2000, Bush emphasized educational reform and "compassionate" conservatism.[181]

The 2000 election was, depending on how one viewed it, the closest election in American history, rivaled only by the fraudulent 1876 election of Rutherford B. Hayes and the likely fraudulent Kennedy-Nixon decision in 1960.[182] Bush was aided by a left-wing third-party candidate, activist Ralph Nader, who siphoned off 2.74 percent of the vote that surely would have gone to Democratic candidate Vice President Al Gore. Although Bush held a lead in the polls, on the final weekend of the campaign an old arrest record surfaced at a time most convenient to the Gore campaign, showing a conviction for drunk driving during Bush's college days. The news threw the race into an absolute tie.

On election night, the networks, relying on exit polls (questions asked of people who had just voted), showed Bush ahead, but neither man could win the electoral college without Florida. Fox News and other outlets called Florida for Gore before the votes had been tallied—but it became clear in the late hours that night that Bush had narrowly won Florida. The final margin of victory was 537 votes, although the early call of the state to Gore had occurred *before* polls had closed in the Florida Panhandle, a Republican sector of the state, as well as every time zone other than Eastern Standard Time. Postelection analysis suggested that the early call cost Bush 15,000 Florida votes. Bob Beckel, a Democratic strategist, later said the premature award of Florida (and the presidency) to Gore may have cost Bush one million votes nationally, particularly on the West Coast where the polls would be open for over two more hours, Alaska three, and Hawaii five—and a victory in the popular vote as well as the electoral college.

Gore conceded to Bush at one point, then retracted his concession and asked for a recount, which, by law, he was allowed to do. Except Gore did not want a statewide recount—that would have given Bush a substantial win—but only a recount of three selected Democrat-heavy counties. David Boies, Gore's legal adviser, said the strategy was simple: "Do everything you can to put numbers on the board. Whether they're erased or chiseled in granite, get them on the board."[183] Unfortunately for Gore, the laws of the state of Florida and the U.S. Constitution set deadlines for certifying the results of the election. On November 26, Republican Katherine Harris, the Florida secretary of state, certified the election with Bush as the winner (by which time the ballots had been counted three times, every time with Bush the winner by different margins). A desperate Gore now called for a statewide recount, for which there was simply not enough time. Assisted by a Democrat-dominated Florida state supreme court ruling, which called for only recounting the 43,000 ballots where no vote was detectable, the state had plunged itself into the impossible task of determining voters' intent. Gore thought he could still win, but the time-consuming process of an election board evaluating *every single ballot* where there was no vote proved hopeless and boards simply gave up.

Gore continued to press for an extension and counting all disputed ballots, but Bush sued on the grounds of constitutionality: it violated "one man, one vote," in that *only* ballots in Gore-friendly counties were to be recounted. The U.S. Supreme Court, in a fast-tracked decision, agreed with Bush 7–2. This was the key decision, even though the second decision handed down, a 5–4 vote that ruled there was insufficient time to count all votes, was viewed as controversial and partisan. Polls showed the public thought the Court had acted on the basis of the law, not favoritism toward Bush.[184] Subsequent analysis involving numerous media-sponsored recounts found that Bush would have won by almost any standard, and usually by a larger margin.

Almost unnoticed was that had Bush lost Florida, he could not have contested the election as Gore did. In 1981, during the gubernatorial election in New Jersey, a lawsuit was brought against the Republican National Committee et al., accusing them of violating the Voting Rights Act of 1965, and the Fourteenth and Fifteenth amendments to the Constitution of the

United States. To settle the lawsuit, in 1982 the RNC entered into a consent decree, which was national in scope, forbidding the RNC and all subsidiary and affiliated organizations from engaging in activities to ensure ballot integrity, ballot security, or other efforts to prevent or remedy vote fraud unless the RNC obtained court approval in advance. This little-known agreement opened the door for Democrat Party fraud that could not be contested by the Republicans. An appeal affirmed the lower court's decision, and since 1982, the consent decree has been renewed every year by the original district judge, a Democrat appointee.[185]

What did not go unnoticed by Democrat operatives (and the finance man George Soros) was the power of the Florida secretary of state, indeed all state secretaries of state, in determining the results of close or disputed elections. A stealth campaign to gain control of the secretary of state offices was undertaken from the national level, and in tandem with the Republican consent decree, close elections began increasingly to fall to the Democrat candidate. In 2008, this campaign bore spectacular fruit: the Democrat-Farmer-Labor Party secretary of state in Minnesota, Mark Ritchie, played a pivotal part in the Senate recount. Improbably large changes in DFL-controlled St. Paul, nearly all in favor of the DFL Senate candidate, comedian Al Franken, ultimately allowed Ritchie to certify Franken the winner by 312 votes. In the presidential election of 2012, once again Republicans noted substantial anomalies in heavily Democratic areas, but were unable to challenge the results due to the consent decree and hostile secretaries of state.

The U.S. 2000 election produced two long-lasting trends in American politics. First, the Democrats invoked the mantra that Bush was "selected," not elected, and therefore viewed his presidency as illegitimate (much as the Tildenites referred to Hayes as "His Fraudulency" in 1877). This supposedly legitimized the showing of more disrespect to Bush at home and abroad than any previous presidents had ever experienced. It also provided the rationale for the Democrat Party to pursue an attack strategy of criticizing every aspect, statement, or action of the Bush administration. In the long run, the attacks proved debilitating to the administration, especially after Democrats gained the Senate in 2006.[186] A second major development of the 2000 election was a map that broke the nation down by counties, which revealed an overwhelming county support for Bush (the Republican counties shown in red for enemy) and a handful of high-population enclaves, mostly on the East and West coasts (shown in blue for friendly), for Democrats. The result was the division of the United States by political pundits into "red state/blue state" personas. While this seemed to be an accurate characterization for a time, ignoring the implied meaning of the colors, before long writers were pointing to "purple" states that were neither heavily Republican nor heavily Democrat.

Bush made a number of selections or appointments that would later prove critical (in both a positive and negative sense) after 9/11: Donald Rumsfeld at Defense, Dick Cheney as vice president, Colin Powell as secretary of state, and Condoleezza Rice as national security advisor. Both Cheney and Rumsfeld had excellent management experience—Cheney as George H. W. Bush's secretary of defense—but Powell would prove a thorn in Bush's side. Even though he dutifully presented the case against Iraq and its weapons of mass destruction in 2002, Powell was suspected of being a leaker of information damaging to the president, and it was Powell's undersecretary, Richard Armitage, who leaked the name of covert operative Valerie Plame in 2003.[187] The Bush administration had barely settled down to run the government, however, when the Islamic terror attacks of 9/11 shook the entire world.

Clear the Skies!

It is not "Americentric" to say that the world changed on September 11, 2001. Many specific years mark calendars—some mostly in the West, such as 1453, 1571, or 1789—but few *days* are recorded. December 7, 1941, for Americans, June 6, 1944, perhaps, remains a date of shared memory for both Europeans and Americans, while August 6, 1945, is etched in the minds of Japanese. With the advent of worldwide instant communications and television, however, parts of the globe that would not have learned of the events in New York City, Washington, and Pennsylvania for days, if ever, saw the images within hours. Virtually no people were unaffected by the terrorist attacks on the United States, given the reach of Islamic expansion into even parts of Africa and Asia. September 11 became the first event of significance experienced worldwide nearly simultaneously.

On the morning of September 11, 2001, Americans in New York, Washington, D.C., and in airports in Boston and New Jersey were going about their daily routines, unaware of the horror about to be visited on them. Particularly in New York, that Tuesday was a beautiful day. A film crew by chance took actual video footage of the first plane crashing into World Trade Center 1 (WTC, or North Tower). The crew had accompanied a truck from the New York Fire Department, sent to investigate a gas leak, and had its cameras rolling—pointed down—when at 8:42 A.M. a jet's roar caused the photographers to aim upward, just in time to see a plane fly straight into the building. Anyone who had watched the flight path knew it was deliberate, but at the time, most thought that a small plane—a Cessna or Piper Cub—had gotten badly off course and hit the building in an accident. Americans automatically assumed the most optimistic and benign cause for the calamity—it was not a deliberate evil, but an accident beyond the capacity of man to avoid.

The aircraft hit the tower around the eighty-ninth floor and smoke instantly poured out of the building. Within minutes, people were hanging out of windows, desperately waving shirts for help. Few knew that most of the stairwells had been immolated and some of the escalators rendered nonfunctional. Emergency vehicles flocked to the site, but no one at the moment suspected terrorism, and some employees in the South Tower (WTC 2) were admonished to stay at work, even as others began to evacuate. It became apparent that the entire top of Tower 1 was beyond assistance. Fire crews couldn't get to the higher floors from the ground, and smoke and wires on the roof prevented any helicopter rescues. Hundreds were condemned to a fiery death; some leaped rather than face the inevitable smoke and flames.

Only minutes earlier, a radio signal from American Airlines Flight 11 had been heard in the Boston regional air traffic control center—an ominous voice saying, "We have some planes." FAA officials had treated the incident as it had previous hijackings, expecting to see the plane headed for Cuba. But this was no ordinary hijacking. Flight 11, with eighty-one passengers and eleven crew members, had been flown directly into the North Tower on a suicide mission, engulfing the 110-story building in a ball of flame and smoke above the hundredth floor, and sending temperatures soaring above 1,800 degrees. Those emerging at ground level looked up and, as one recalled, "I knew it was a terrorist attack the moment I looked up and saw the smoke. . . . I saw the face of evil."[188] As firefighters raced into the North Tower to perform their duty, cameras caught the second jumbo jet (United Flight 175 from Boston to Los Angeles with fifty-six passengers and nine crew members) hurtling into WTC 2, consuming it in a massive fireball as well.

By then it was clear that America was under attack. Already emergency responders at both towers found carnage and mayhem: "There's a lot of bodies," said one fireman, as he reached the forty-fifth floor of WTC 2.[189] Only sixteen people survived from the South Tower above the ninetieth floor, just above where the plane hit; none survived above the seventy-eighth-floor crash line in the North Tower. The buildings had been designed to sustain accidental aircraft impacts, but never to hold up under deliberate terror bombing using airplanes as weapons. Even so, the towers had been built extremely well, and stood longer than engineers expected. Thousands of people escaped before the towers collapsed. Both buildings "pancaked," coming almost straight down in a swirl of debris, a ghastly cloud of dust, and parts of human bodies. When they collapsed, the World Trade Center buildings buried hundreds of firemen and rescue teams who had set up headquarters close by.

More than 4,200 planes were airborne in the United States that morning and all had to be landed and accounted for. Officials decided at 9:38 A.M. to "clear the skies" even before United Flight 175 flew into the South Tower. As they started landing planes, they learned another plane was in the hands of hijackers—American Flight 77, bound for Los Angeles from Washington with 58 passengers and 8 crew members—and it soon crashed into the Pentagon, killing all aboard and 125 people inside the building.

But the dying was not over. United Airlines Flight 93, bound for San Francisco with 45 people aboard, failed to respond to air traffic controllers, and soon plunged into the ground near Shanksville, Pennsylvania, after several courageous passengers sought to take the plane back from the terrorists.[190] Later it was learned the primary target for this plane was the Capitol, its secondary the White House. Individual, ordinary Americans had ignored Progressive teaching that citizens were to let the authorities always handle everything, and had risen up to fight with their bare hands, saving their representatives in Congress at the cost of their own lives. Before the day was over, more than 3,000 Americans would be dead, although some bodies were vaporized and it would forever be impossible to know exactly how many died on that day.

President Bush was visiting a Florida elementary school that morning, and reading with children when his chief of staff, Andy Card, quietly walked in and whispered in the president's ear. He had waited until after the second attack, whereupon it was clearly a terrorist strike, and Bush remained in place for a few minutes so as not to alarm the children. Shortly thereafter, a shaken Bush, after making a brief television appearance, was hustled onto *Air Force One*, which itself was thought to be under attack.[191] The Secret Service had received a report that *Air Force One* was a target because "chatter" was picked up by intelligence agencies indicating the terrorists knew the airplane's code sign for the day. From his command post in the sky, Bush spoke to Vice President Dick Cheney: "We're going to find out who did this and we're going to kick their asses."[192] Bush later remembered thinking, "They had declared war on us, and I made up my mind at that moment we were going to war."[193]

Interceptors raced into the skies within minutes of the FAA's decision to ground all airplanes and receiving its calls to Air Force bases for backup. Only *four* interceptors were available on the entire East Coast, and some of them did not even have weapons. They were given instructions to bring down any aircraft that did not respond to air traffic controllers' orders, even if it meant ramming the passenger jet with their own plane. Despite going to afterburners, none of the interceptors had reached United 93 when the passengers' revolt brought it down.

It took little time for the CIA and the FBI to confirm that the hijackings were the work of Osama bin Laden and al-Qaeda. CIA head George Tenet thought it was bin Laden almost immediately.[194] It took even less time for some liberals, notably Hollywood leftists, to concoct an elaborate justification for the attacks, claiming that bin Laden was only responding to the U.S. presence in the Gulf, or American forces on "holy Islamic soil," or offer other implausible explanations for the attacks.[195]

Bin Laden was already committed to guerrilla war and terrorism on America (the "far enemy," as he called the United States) as early as 1989.[196] There was no question how he viewed the murder of three thousand people: "Its greatest buildings were destroyed," bin Laden exclaimed. "America! Full of fear. . . . Thank God for that."[197] Bin Laden had used a cell led by an Egyptian (and one of the few non-Saudis), Mohamed Atta, to execute the scheme, but it was designed by the devout terrorist Khalid Sheikh Mohammed ("KSM" as he was known) as an upgraded version of his failed Bojinka plot. He and bin Laden had plotted for years, reviewing the failure of the 1993 WTC bombing. Initially, KSM and bin Laden planned for a much more ambitious attack to hit ten U.S. targets, but scaled back when Zacarias Moussaoui, another al-Qaeda member and (some thought) a replacement for one of the original twenty who was denied an entry visa, was arrested in August.

Throughout 2001, nineteen Muslim men, most of them from Saudi Arabia, many of them middle class and well educated, infiltrated the country. They obtained normal jobs and acquired dozens of driver's licenses. Told to blend in, the terrorists worked out of four separate cells, each of which included a pilot who had not been trained to land an airplane, only steer it. Each plane was to have five terrorists, of whom one had a phony bomb strapped to him to keep passengers at bay while the others seized control of the cockpit. (Flight 93 had only four.)

Six months after the attacks, FBI agents, diplomats, and reporters unveiled evidence that many warning signs had been missed, and the buzz phrase in Washington was "we failed to connect the dots." In fact, the intelligence agencies—for all their lack of coordination and cooperation—had to sift through three million pieces of intelligence information accumulated *per day* by the CIA and National Security Agency alone. Clinton's "Wall" memo, prohibiting the FBI and CIA from sharing information, made such interagency assistance almost impossible, and was not substantially improved by Bush's creation of yet another department, the Department of Homeland Security. Aspects of the Patriot Act, passed in 2001 by wide majorities in both houses of Congress, enhanced law enforcement agencies' ability to search e-mails, phone records, financial data, or other records, while at the same time broadening the police powers to investigate, detain, and deport suspected terrorists. Some of those functions were doubtless necessary, although simply using the terrorist profiling system employed by the Israelis would have prevented 9/11. Hamstrung by fears of appearing politically incorrect and incurring the wrath of the Left, American politicians chose to burden everyone and curtail individual liberties.

In the months that followed, seeking answers for why the United States was taken by surprise became a national pastime. In November 2002, Bush appointed a blue-ribbon, bipartisan commission to study the intelligence failures leading up to 9/11. It concluded there had been "pervasive problems of managing and sharing information across a large and unwieldy government . . . built in a different era. . . ."[198] Ahmed Ressam, an Algerian who attempted to enter the United States from Canada, provided details about al-Qaeda that President Bush received in August 2001 under the ominous title of a leaked memo, "Bin Laden Determined to Strike US."[199] In fact, the somewhat less than sensational actual memo said "Bin Laden Determined to Strike *in* US," and everyone knew he already had, in 1993. The memo provided no important details about any airplane hijackings or any other specifics—but that remained well in the future.

But there were other signs—again ignored by Clinton as well as Bush— that al-Qaeda had just been getting started. Following the failed attempt to destroy *The Sullivans*, in October 2000 al-Qaeda launched a suicide boat bombing of the USS *Cole*, a guided missile destroyer that had stopped in the Yemeni port of Aden for refueling. After the vessel off-loaded garbage onto two of the three garbage barges it had ordered, a rubber dinghy pulled alongside, with two persons aboard waving at the crew. As the dinghy brushed the *Cole*'s side where the previous garbage barge had been, a terrific explosion vaporized the dinghy and its occupants, blew a thirty-five-by-thirty-six-foot hole in the *Cole*'s side, and killed seventeen U.S. sailors and injured thirty-nine. The attack somewhat resembled the subsequent bombing of the French tanker *Limburg*. Bin Laden not only claimed credit for the attacks, but, still thinking he could draw the United States into a fatal conflict in Afghanistan, expressed disappointment that the U.S. government did not attempt to retaliate.[200] Now, he had his moment. Not only had he destroyed two symbols of American prosperity, damaged the symbol of American military might, and shocked the nation, but the economic impact of the attacks equaled that of the OPEC oil embargo in the 1970s, compressed into a shorter period.[201]

"The Rest of the World Hears You!"

In the immediate aftermath of 9/11, Bush had to rally the country while comforting the victims' families. He had two iconic moments in the days that followed the attack. First, he visited Ground Zero on September 14, viewing the wreckage with retired firefighter Bob Beckwith at his side. He climbed atop a heap of rubble to make a few comments through a bullhorn. As he began, a rescue worker shouted, "I can't hear you!" Bush turned and forcefully said, "I can hear you! I can hear you! The rest of the world hears you! And the people . . . who knocked these buildings down will hear all of us soon!" The crowd of rescue workers erupted into chants of "USA, USA." Bush's second shining moment came at his National Cathedral address on September 14, where he stated, "This conflict was begun on the timing and terms of others; it will end in a way and at an hour of our choosing." He cited America's freedoms as the object of the al-Qaeda attacks: "They have attacked America because we are freedom's home and defender, and the commitment of our fathers is now the calling of our time."[202]

To his advisers, Bush emphasized he wanted aggressive action, and soon. He had already told them he was "tired of swatting flies," and instead ordered a new, bold strategy to eliminate al-Qaeda. Meeting with his war cabinet the following day, Bush outlined the Bush Doctrine, in which if the Taliban government in Afghanistan—who harbored al-Qaeda—did not immediately hand over bin Laden and his thugs, the United States would eliminate the Taliban as well. Bush told the press he wanted bin Laden "dead or alive," and in an address to the nation stated in no uncertain terms that the nations of the world were either "with us, or with the terrorists." There was no middle ground. Congress had already authorized action with a joint resolution on September 14, and air strikes for Operation Enduring Freedom began on October 7. Secretary of Defense Donald Rumsfeld had successfully lobbied hard for a nontraditional approach of CIA and special forces, aided by British allies, working with the anti-Taliban coalition in Afghanistan, and Americans were soon on the ground working with the Northern Alliance of friendly Afghan forces.

Typically, the press began conjuring up images of Vietnam, producing a litany of reasons why the United States would fail in Afghanistan (other nations failed to secure it, it was too hot, it was too mountainous, and so on). But military analyst Victor Davis Hanson summed up the reality of the situation facing al-Qaeda and the Taliban: "Glad we are not fighting us." Within months, the Taliban were crushed and al-Qaeda, including bin Laden, fled into the Tora Bora Mountains. Whether anyone could have stopped him from escaping is in dispute. Rumsfeld argued that even a massive force, had it been available—which it was not—could not have covered every valley or escape route.[203]

In the year following September 2001, the United States slammed shut al-Qaeda's operations in Afghanistan and better secured the airlines and other domestic targets, while terrorists made renewed attempts to follow up. Richard Reid (Muslim name: Riady), an al-Qaeda-connected shoe bomber, attempted to blow up a passenger jet with explosives smuggled aboard in his shoes. In October 2002, a resort on the island vacation area of Bali was rocked by an al-Qaeda bomb that killed 181. Adding to the terror—although not directly linked to the terrorist network—a series of shootings in the Virginia and Maryland area soon proved to be the work of a Muslim sniper and his young apprentice (known as the "D.C. Sniper" because of the assumption it was one person, not a team). After a year and a half, no other direct attacks on U.S. soil had occurred (unless one counted the D.C. Sniper). Both Riady and José Padilla (the "dirty bomber") had been arrested and their attempts foiled, and al-Qaeda cells in several cities were crushed. Khalid Sheikh Mohammed himself was captured in March 2003 by Pakistani secret police with CIA intelligence—and subjected to "waterboarding" treatment, where he quickly broke and yielded a treasure trove of intelligence. Surprised interrogators found he "even use[d] a chalkboard at times."[204]

Bush and his British ally, Prime Minister Tony Blair, were soon joined by NATO members, including Italian president Silvio Berlusconi and Spanish president José María Aznar. The NATO Treaty had been declared in force almost immediately after 9/11, meaning that all NATO members were obliged to assist the United States, which had been attacked. Blair, Berlusconi, and Aznar all agreed that the larger issue was not just terrorists unattached to a particular state, but the possibility of anti-Western nations providing the terrorists with weapons of mass destruction (WMDs) and other support.

Most notably, the West was concerned about the weapons-making capability of Iraq, Iran, and Libya. In his January 2002 State of the Union speech, Bush specifically identified Iraq, Iran, and (likely in an effort to appear to include non-Muslims) North Korea as an "axis of evil."[205] Most of those rogue states had been given limp warnings by the United Nations, but virtually none had paid a price. Bush now put them on alert that they were all in the crosshairs. Some foreign policy experts, particularly Michael Ledeen, a consultant to national security in several administrations, had argued that Iran was the central threat. If those within the Bush administration agreed, certainly they knew that both Iraq and Afghanistan would be needed as staging bases if any action against Iran was ever undertaken.

Virtually every important leader in the Democrat Party over the previous five years had insisted that Saddam Hussein had WMDs. Clinton and Gore both strongly warned about Iraq's WMD capacity, and in 1998, a group of Democrat senators, including John Kerry and Ted Kennedy, wrote Clinton a letter urging him to invade Iraq if necessary due to the threat. A 1999 joint intelligence report from the Clinton administration stated, "We believe that Iraq possesses chemical agent stockpiles that can be, or already are, weaponized." Two months before Bush took office, the intelligence community said, "Our main judgments about what remains of Iraq's original WMD programs, agent stockpiles, and delivery systems have changed little [since the end of the Gulf War]. Iraq retains stockpiles of chemical and biological agents and munitions."[206] Democrat senator Jay Rockefeller, who later would criticize Bush for attacking Iraq, said in a floor speech on October 10, 2002,

> There has been some debate over how "imminent" a threat Iraq poses. I do believe that Iraq poses an imminent threat, but I also believe that after September 11, that question is increasingly outdated. It is in the nature of these weapons, and the way they are targeted against civilian populations, that documented capability and demonstrated intent may be the only warning we get. . . . Can we afford to take that chance? We cannot.[207]

By 2002, every major national intelligence service from France, Britain, Russia, China, Israel, Egypt, and Jordan had agreed that Saddam had WMDs, and even the UN's inspectors admitted that there was no proof that Saddam had ever destroyed his anthrax stocks and that "at least some of this was retained [after the Gulf War]." Bush prepared the ground for war with Iraq by addressing the United Nations in September 2002. In a blunt, nonapologetic speech, he methodically outlined violation after violation by Iraq of UN mandates, embarrassing the international body and displaying its lack of resolve. Subsequently, the UN passed Resolution 1441, which required new inspections and "full disclosure" by Iraq—something Saddam had never permitted before, nor would now. Bush rightfully chafed at notions that he "rushed to war," and in his 2010 memoir recounted the multiple efforts he made to find a peaceful solution enforced by the UN.[208]

On March 17, 2003, Bush gave Saddam and his two evil sons forty-eight hours to leave Iraq. They refused, and three days later, based on intelligence showing Saddam's location, a targeted missile strike hit a compound where Saddam was supposedly located. The information proved wrong, but the dictator knew his days were numbered. Coalition forces plunged into Iraq, finding little resistance, and armored units seized Baghdad after only two weeks of ground fighting. Iraqis threw flowers and cheered American troops with "Bush, Bush, Bush"; U.S. soldiers, aided by cranes and Iraqi civilians, pulled down the massive statue of Saddam in the center of Baghdad. Iraqis dragged the head around town as people beat it with their shoes. So far, the ground war had been a perfect demonstration of the Western way of war, or a "Mesopotamian show and tell" as one Middle Eastern commentator called it.

Bush's approval rating neared 90 percent after the 9/11 attacks, and again reached high levels after the Iraq invasion. But the early successes came in part because the Iraqi military had dissolved rather than fight, and Saddam had left behind his fedayeen guerrilla squads to wreak havoc on civilian areas in hopes of fomenting a civil war. Moreover, every jihadist in the Middle East saw an opportunity to attack the "Great Satan" and flooded into Iraq. In retrospect, no better strategy to fight terrorism could ever have been devised: rather than invading state after state—an impossibility— Bush had inadvertently sucked nearly every Islamic terrorist in the world into Iraq. In the meantime, however, order collapsed, neighborhoods fell into the hands of hooligans, and Sunnis and Shiites began to plot ways to attack each other. The United States was caught in the middle of what promised to be a nasty conflict. Compounding Bush's problems, no massive piles of WMDs were discovered—no countless vats of sarin or boxes full of anthrax. Rather than focus on what was discovered in Iraq, namely terrorists of every stripe, the Bush administration remained mute. Bush adviser Karl Rove would later admit that "our weak response in defense of the president and in setting the record straight [was] one of the biggest mistakes of the Bush years. . . . We should have seen this for what it was: a poison-tipped dagger aimed at the heart of the Bush presidency."[209]

Rove stated in his memoir that he doubted the Iraq War would have been launched without the claim of WMDs, and Rumsfeld, in his memoir, would admit to being mistaken on the presence of WMDs. Yet already the United States had extracted *550 tons* of uranium (which could easily have been converted into weapons-grade material) from Iraq, and as of 2011, no one had yet determined what was in the semi-tractor trailers that left various weapons sites in Iraq for the Syrian border immediately prior to the invasion. Indeed in 2012, when all agreed the Syrians had chemical and biological weapons, no one could explain how they got them. Actually, in the wake of 9/11, no president could realistically have allowed Saddam to stay in power with the possibility of having WMDs that he could use to support terrorists. In addition, the Iraq invasion immediately produced an unintended side effect, namely that Muammar Gaddafi announced he would voluntarily give up his own WMD stockpiles.

Lawfare

The war on terror, given public lip service by most European governments, was taken quite seriously by the French. Contrary to the stereotype of French weakness and incompetence gained during the Bosnian conflict—where French troops made such an extremely poor showing—by 2007, France national police and military had become "the most accomplished counterterrorism practitioner in Europe."[210]

While security services in Germany and Great Britain were slow to appreciate the threat of homegrown Islamic terrorists, France's intellectuals had long analyzed the problem of European Muslim jihadists. Indeed, France had a level of communication between journalists and security forces exceeding that of the United States when it came to terrorists. In 2005, the French parliament issued the Marsaud Report, examining the threat and the nation's counterterrorism capabilities, outlining the number of attacks against France since 9/11, including the May 2002 strike in Karachi against Direction des Constructions Navales, a major shipbuilder, and

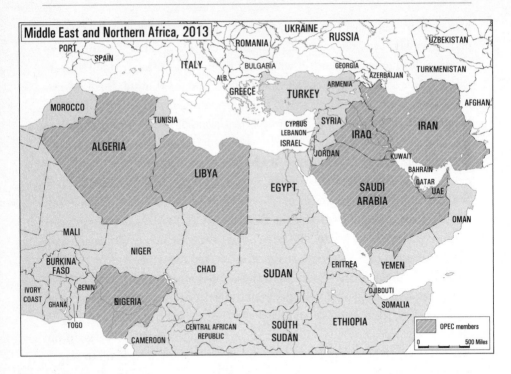

the attack on the *Limburg*, a French oil tanker off Yemen in October of that year.

France's Direction de la Surveillance du Territoire (DST), and its counterterrorist investigative magistrates (*juges d'instruction*), had no American parallel, providing extensive latitude for French magistrates to handle classified materials and take actions prohibited by law in the United States. This allowed French counterterrorist officials to "concentrate the combined resources of the state quickly," whether in the form of wiretaps or electronic interception.[211] The French interpretation of "probable cause" differed vastly from that of American requirements, whereby French officials could jail citizens without sufficient grounds for charging them in court, holding them secretly, and allowing wide latitude in interrogation methods. None of this would have worked in the U.S. system of separation of powers, and it shows how different the European concepts of freedom and individual rights are from those of the United States.

But French actions and capabilities aside, the Euros in general drifted toward a dangerous policy of "lawfare," a term created by Donald Rumsfeld to apply international law to American efforts at self-defense. "As never before in history," he wrote, "today lawyers and legal considerations pervade every aspect of U.S. military operations."[212] Detaining terrorists at

Guantánamo Bay, Cuba ("Gitmo"), opened the door to both international civil-rights crusaders and American antiwar activists to end the process of military tribunals that the Bush administration had established in line with long-held traditions of war. In *Hamdi v. Rumsfeld*, a habeas corpus case brought on behalf of a U.S. citizen being defined as an "illegal enemy combatant," the U.S. Supreme Court curbed the power of the government to detain American citizens who were enemy combatants, and theoretically extended those rights to all detainees. The ruling (and two subsequent rulings in the same vein) constituted a severe threat to American security and the nation's ability to segregate violent terrorists from mainstream society in accordance with the Geneva Convention. But it was entirely predictable from a Court that barely held a conservative majority in most matters and almost always trended liberal on issues of civil rights.

Europeans, with their schizophrenic approach to dealing with Islamic terrorism—brushing aside civil liberties and offering quick trials, but, due to public political correctness, permitting hostile Islamic enclaves—had experienced mixed results. Both the Palestinians and Algerians had sought to effect change in their own regions through terrorist acts on the Continent, with the Palestinian strikes between 1970 and 1976 peaking at the 1972 Munich Olympics. Having freed herself from Algeria in 1962, France suddenly found the Algerian war of the 1990s brought new terror attacks, particularly on French transport systems in mid-decade. In 1994, hijackers also planned to crash an airliner into the Eiffel Tower, anticipating the World Trade Center attacks of 9/11. Some of the plotters, including Khaled Kelkal of Lyon (who was killed in a 1995 street battle), soon allied with al-Qaeda.[213]

But no nation had more experience in dealing with Arab terrorism than Israel, where the number and scope of attacks over the years dwarfed anything other than the 9/11 attack. Israel continued to struggle for its existence in the late twentieth and early twenty-first centuries. Gone were the wars of mass armies sponsored by Syria, Egypt, Jordan, or other states. In their place came the intifada and hit-and-run strikes by terror organizations such as Hamas and Hezbollah. Although al-Qaeda terrorism could hardly be considered as pursuing a civil war, it also did not fit the classical situation where one sovereign nation warred against another.

Hamas, a Palestinian government organization, was long suspected by the Israelis and the CIA as being merely a front for terrorism. Hezbollah, a Shiite political/terrorist group from Lebanon, was more open about its terrorist methods. Both groups copied the model of the Assassins, an order of the Nizari Ismailis based at Alamut in Iran from the late eleventh century until eradicated by the Mongol Ilkhan Hulagu. In exterminating the Is-maili threat to stability in the Muslim world, the Mongols and Mamluks campaigned against them ruthlessly until their power through assassina-tion and intimation was broken. As the Assassins made extensive use of suicide attackers and respected no conventions of warfare, they and their women and children were killed wherever found without mercy. The his-torical precedent was there for all to see, but the West remained obstinate in refusing to acknowledge the different culture behind Islamic terrorism and its basic contrast with Western principles of right to life.

Some of the unrest in the Muslim world indeed properly belonged to the civil war category, most notably the never-ending conflict between dif-ferent Islamic groups in Lebanon (including Sunni Syrians, Palestinians, the unorthodox Druze, and some Shiites). Defining "civil war," thus calcu-lating the number of such conflicts, has proven elusive, but using the lan-guage of conflict resolution specialists, there had been a minimum of fifty-five civil wars between 1945 and 1973.[214] The American Civil War is an outstanding example of the kind of peaceful society that can be created when revenge and punishment are eschewed by the victor. But achieving such a dénouement is difficult. One authority on peacekeeping, scholar Roy Licklider, noted, "We may [assume] that only a 'just' settlement will really assure a lasting peace, but the empirical evidence for this proposition is unclear."[215]

Quite the contrary, civil wars rarely end in negotiated settlements. The problem of how people live and work with others who have recently killed their families and burned their towns has been, to say the least, thorny. Perhaps unsurprising, numerous scholars have concluded that civil wars are less likely to end in negotiated settlements than other wars.[216] In a home-grown example, the American Civil War continued in northern Arkansas and southern Missouri for over a decade following Appomattox, with mur-ders, bushwhackings, and terrorist acts being committed on both sides until finally petering out from combatant exhaustion and the death of most of the hard-core participants. On the other hand, a foreign power imposing a peace—the modern model to end such conflicts—has produced few suc-cesses and several instances of genocide and shame.

Cool It

Civil wars, oppression, genocide—all were linked in the minds of the mod-ern Left as the toxic fruit of capitalism. As the narrative went, if only man-kind returned to a simpler life, the world would be a more peaceful place.

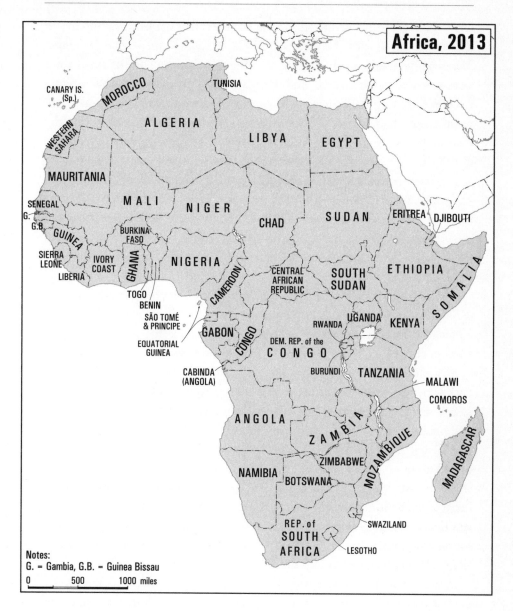

Africa, 2013

CANARY IS.
(Sp.)
MOROCCO
TUNISIA
WESTERN SAHARA
ALGERIA
LIBYA
EGYPT
MAURITANIA
MALI
NIGER
SENEGAL
G.
G.B.
GUINEA
BURKINA FASO
CHAD
SUDAN
ERITREA
DJIBOUTI
SIERRA LEONE
IVORY COAST
GHANA
NIGERIA
CENTRAL AFRICAN REPUBLIC
SOUTH SUDAN
ETHIOPIA
SOMALIA
LIBERIA
TOGO
BENIN
CAMEROON
SÃO TOMÉ & PRINCIPE
GABON
CONGO
RWANDA
UGANDA
KENYA
EQUATORIAL GUINEA
DEM. REP. of the CONGO
CABINDA (ANGOLA)
BURUNDI
TANZANIA
MALAWI
COMOROS
ANGOLA
ZAMBIA
MOZAMBIQUE
MADAGASCAR
ZIMBABWE
NAMIBIA
BOTSWANA
REP. of SOUTH AFRICA
SWAZILAND
LESOTHO

Notes:
G. = Gambia, G.B. = Guinea Bissau
0   500   1000 miles

    The outcry against global warming was a continuation of the anticapi-
talist campaign launched in the 1970s against hybrid food production and
was given a great boost at the Rio de Janeiro earth summit in 1992 that
produced Agenda 21. Indeed, in the minds of activists, environmentalism,
population growth, global warming, and food were all tied together. Once
purely scientific, but now highly politicized, journals such as *Science* warned
that obesity had become an epidemic resulting from "improved prosper-

ity."[217] Nutritionists David and Marcia Pimentel lent academic credibility to the war on meat with their 2003 study in the *American Journal of Clinical Nutrition*, in which they claimed that meat eating and use of fossil fuels were inexorably intertwined, and the salvation of the planet lay in a vegetarian diet.[218] Basing their analysis on American *overpopulation* (at a time when most nations had a more serious *underpopulation* problem to deal with), the Pimentels gave academic cover to the radical vegan movement, which was already partly supported by the antifat, heart-disease lobby. Then came *Scientific American*, which had already signed on to the global warming theories with its alarmist article "How Meat Contributes to Global Warming."[219] Cow flatulence, farms that "give rise to greenhouse gases," and the idea that raising just one pound of beef for the dinner table requires ten pounds of plant protein became great problems that required government intervention.

At root of all this meat hate was human hate, for the authors were always quick to point out that even an ounce of asparagus absorbed a "CO_2 equivalent of 3.2 ounces."[220] Clearly, even mandating a meatless diet wouldn't be sufficient for the zealots, who would then attack vegan diets as "un-earth-friendly" (some activists even insisted plants "screamed" when cut). If people were the ultimate target, "Big Food"—capitalism embodied in caloric intake—was the immediate villain. Movies such as *Super Size Me* and books such as *Fast Food Nation* began the assault on Big Food through implausible diet regimens and selective hysteria-ridden "facts." Larger food giants, though, would soon be in the crosshairs. Supposedly food corporations marketed foods low in nutritional value, duping children into buying cereals for the toys contained in the boxes. Unstated in these charges was a fundamental contradiction, given that most of the experts believed in evolution: if evolution meant for people to be less active and use their brains more, weren't heavier people "natural"?

Such thoughts apparently never crossed the mind of Yale's Kelly Brownell, who headed the school's center for weight disorders, and who complained that American culture "encourages overeating and physical inactivity."[221] Unfortunately for the "blame corporate America first" mentality, from 1971 to 2000, average caloric intake only rose by 150 in the United States, while men's intake of fat decreased and women's intake only increased slightly.[222] At the same time, the Centers for Disease Control offered evidence that Americans were "no less active at the end of the 1990s than they were at the beginning of that decade. . . ."[223] More than 40 million Americans belonged to health clubs (which had revenues of some $16 billion by 2005), and as early as 1977 *The New York Times* noted an "exercise explosion" and three years later *The Washington Post* proclaimed a "fitness revolution."[224] Sporting goods sales in America topped $52 billion. Yet even so, Americans remained decidedly heavier than Europeans and both bigger and heavier than Asians, and had been since 1776 according to Revolutionary War records, mainly due to a healthier (and meatier) diet.

If obesity was a Western and specifically American problem, other maladies afflicted the underdeveloped world. Despite unimaginable transfers of wealth to the Third World to improve health, by 2008 many health care problems in undeveloped countries seemed as impervious to Western medicine and aid as the nations' political systems were to reform. The disease of the day was AIDS, largely because so many Western homosexuals had contracted it, and they sought to use it as a tool both to force governments to pour money into finding a cure on the one hand, and to employ it as leverage for the social acceptance of homosexuality on the other.

There was no question Africa was already experiencing an AIDS epidemic (whose origins to date are lacking a satisfactory explanation) and that by the late 1970s the disease was rapidly spreading. But American cries for assistance to Africa were noticeably absent until the American homosexual community began contracting AIDS. Only then did celebrities such as the singer Bono and actress Ashley Judd call for action against AIDS in Africa, where in 2002 more than two million died of the disease. Estimates put the total number of HIV-infected Africans at 3.5 million: in many eastern and southern countries on the continent up to 25 percent of the population was HIV-positive. In Botswana, Lesotho, Swaziland, and Zimbabwe nearly a third of the adult population was infected.[225]

Western campaigns to address AIDS, including George W. Bush's astounding call for $15 billion in foreign aid for fighting AIDS in his 2003 State of the Union message, constituted ongoing reactions to a combination of homosexual lobbying, genuine compassion, and the continuing assumption that money would solve all deeper problems. Two massive obstacles confronted Western attempts to stop AIDS in Africa. First, the cost of the medicines was astronomical while the likelihood of recovery was next to zero. (Only a few individuals, such as the highly visible basketball star Earvin "Magic" Johnson, had gone into near-full remission after being diagnosed as HIV positive.) This meant that the money absorbed by AIDS was likely to have little real impact. Second, funding AIDS meant reduced amounts of money were available to combat diseases that were less politically correct or chic. It has been argued, for example, that had no money been directed at AIDS, malaria and sleeping sickness could have been nearly eliminated with a net increase in lives saved, all through the introduction of netting and clean water. Indeed, that has been an initiative of the Bill and Melinda Gates Foundation, namely simple widespread improvements that increase life expectancy on an extensive basis. Many of those diseases were easily and inexpensively controlled by Western medicine. Measles, for example, had been almost eliminated in Africa through routine (and inexpensive) immunization of children. Polio and smallpox, of course, had been wiped out altogether. Individual success stories were even more impressive. Trachoma, a leading preventable cause of blindness, was reduced 90 percent in a single program in Morocco; Sri Lanka slashed deaths during childbirth by a similar percentage; China cut tuberculosis cases by 40 percent in the decade of the 1990s; spraying programs curtailed the spread of Chagas disease in many parts of South America.[226] Still, many diseases remained to be treated, and in short, AIDS sucked up resources in astronomical proportions to other diseases, and with far less hope of success, whereas visible progress was being made on numerous other medical and health fronts.

Nor was it a case (as the Left argued) that the West ignored AIDS until it was too late. The fact is, earlier intervention, particularly in Africa, would have been *more* costly and even *less* effective than efforts in the late twentieth century because far less was known about the disease. Worse still, claims by such bodies as the World Bank that AIDS is completely preventable assume that individuals and societies wanted to make social and cultural choices that would, in fact, prevent AIDS.

Bush's 2003 proposal, labeled PEPFAR (the President's Emergency Plan for AIDS Relief), in addition to funding, stressed the ABC solution of abstinence, being faithful, and condom use—a solution laden with moral values about monogamy and virginity before marriage. Dealing with AIDS in Africa involved daunting cultural and social roadblocks for such a strategy. The practices of polygamy, rape, and sex with very young girls were common across the continent. Tribal customs, including witchcraft, were "taboo in aid agencies, as nobody want[ed] to reinforce ill-informed stereotypes."[227] In Soweto, South Africa, witchcraft was commonly thought to cause AIDS, and government assistance and UN programs deliberately obstructed Christian evangelism and its abstinence programs, which were the *only* guarantee of stopping the disease. The ABC solution was denigrated because it failed to address "sexual coercion and violence, taboos surrounding discussing sex, [and] economic pressures . . . to have sex."[228] Yet even African Center for Disease Control doctors admitted it was an "important strategy." The ongoing issue was the fact that as of 2006, African women still had "limited access to female controlled methods that [would] enable them to control their own sexual health," and with their sexual health went that of the continent.[229] And there was substantial opposition: surveys in Kenya, for example, reported

> There were some responses about the negative perceived physical effects of abstinence and being faithful—that regular sexual activity with a number of partners was a natural healthy thing to do and that restraining it was unhealthy. There were also negative views about condoms and a sense of fatalism about becoming HIV infected despite adopting safer sexual behavior.[230]

Health care professionals found that even in *churches*, polygamy was endorsed, and that reducing the number of multiple wives was a significant challenge. One study learned that virgins were particularly susceptible to rape precisely because boys knew they would not be HIV carriers.[231] Reformers found themselves in the conundrum of whether they needed to empower women or change men. In short, the missionaries' original goals—often demonized as ill informed or unrealistic—increasingly looked like the *only* solution for Africa, where only a massive cultural and moral transformation could eradicate a disease far too costly for human medicine.

Overcoming the activism of the do-gooders and planners constituted a formidable hurdle for actually addressing medical needs in the Third World. Grassroots health workers had found that tuberculosis medicines cost only about $10 per person infected, and yet three million a year died from the disease. Almost one quarter of the world suffered from intestinal worms, which by simply eating diatomaceous earth could be eradicated at a cost of a dollar a year per person and a similar amount could cure even the worst strains of malaria. At the other end of the spectrum were AIDS drugs, which at best only prolong the life of the victim a few years at the cost of $1,500 per person. Some experts finally began to admit as much: in 2002, Harvard professor Michael Kremer found that for a single person treated for one year with AIDS antiviral therapy, up to 110 life years could be gained with either prevention efforts or vaccination of others with more easily curable diseases.[232]

Big-planner solutions, such as those trumpeted by Harvard's Jeffrey Sachs (*The End of Poverty*), typified the presumptuousness of Western elites.[233] Bono was one of the few who came to "humbling" realizations about the necessity for capitalism, profits, and economic growth to save the underdeveloped world. In 2012 he told a conference that "job creators and innovators are just the key." "As one who got into all this as a righteous anger activist with all the clichés," Bono admitted it was "a humbling thing" to realize the importance of capitalism and entrepreneurship.[234] And the patronizing attitude of the Western elites was seldom lost on the Third World. One Cameroonian noted of the Live 8 concerts—a series of world-wide simultaneous concerts to raise money to fight Third World poverty—that the organizers "still believe us to be like the children they must save."[235]

In the case of Africans, however, the evidence was that they wanted to be saved from AIDS, which was not necessarily the case with some American homosexuals. San Francisco's HIV incubation capital spawned the astounding phenomenon of homosexual males having unprotected sex *in order to become infected* with HIV. Known as "bug chasers, they dismissed HIV as a minor annoyance . . . like diabetes," treating HIV-tainted semen as "liquid gold."[236] Contracting AIDS put those males "into the brotherhood," and becoming HIV-positive was referred to as getting "knocked up." A single Web chat room that provided a site for men wanting to "join the club" sported more than 1,400 members before it was closed down by Yahoo! in 2002. Reporters surveying the Stop AIDS Project or the San Francisco AIDS Foundation learned that such groups were reluctant to even admit bug chasing occurred, let alone that it was a problem.[237]

At the same time, the hysterically hyped "heterosexual AIDS crisis" of the 1980s never developed, as indeed predicted by Michael Fumento.[238] It wasn't until 2008, however, that World Health Organization (WHO) officials finally admitted that the "threat of a global heterosexual pandemic has disappeared."[239] By that time, health officials of world organizations were concerned that money had been "misplaced" outside of Africa, a point Fumento and others made twenty years earlier.

A good example of misplaced efforts, bureaucratic malfeasance, bad science, and the effect of agency-controlled propaganda was malaria. The deadly disease had reemerged with a vengeance in Africa while the focus was on AIDS, killing more than a million people per year on that continent alone.[240] This occurred due to the UN's ban on the pesticide DDT, which had drastically reduced the incidence of malaria by decimating the mosquito population. The environmentalists used fear and phony science to make their case against DDT, as no evidence ever surfaced to show that it was harmful to humans. In fact, it was just the opposite; one proponent routinely ate DDT during his lectures, and suffered no ill effects. Rachel

Carson had started the war on DDT with her book *Silent Spring* (1962), which was shown to contain many falsehoods and exaggerations. Entomologist J. Gordon Edwards of San Jose State University in 1992 exposed much of Carson's fraud, yet her polemic unabatedly shaped environmental policy in the United States and throughout the world. By the second decade of the twenty-first century, UN bureaucrats continued to destroy millions of lives every year through their ban on DDT.[241]

Of course, the Left and the environmental movement continued to blame health problems of all sorts, especially cancer, on capitalism, industrialism, and the West. The WHO and its International Agency for Research on Cancer (IARC), beginning in the 1950s, had studied cancer rates in Africa and compared them with those in the United States and some European nations, concluding that most human cancers were caused by environmental factors and were preventable.[242] But when Oxford epidemiologists Richard Doll and Richard Peto examined this claim, their conclusions in 1981 were that man-made chemicals (in pollution, food additives, or occupational exposure) played a minimal role in human cancers. Diet was the determining factor, causing 35 percent of all cancers.[243]

Despite the WHO's frequent reference to environmental factors, even John Higginson, who had originated the African cancer studies, repeatedly pointed out that "man-made chemicals" played a minor role, and that "only a very small part of the total cancer burden can be directly related to industrialization."[244] This correlated well with other research showing that a nonindustrial city such as Geneva, Switzerland, had more cancer than a "polluted" city such as Birmingham, England, or why prostate cancer rates were ten times higher in the relatively lightly industrialized nation of Sweden than in highly industrialized Japan.[245] By 1979, Higginson blew the whistle on the cancer/environment lobby: "If they could possibly make people believe that cancer was going to result from pollution, this would enable them to facilitate the clean-up of the air; or whatever it is," he explained to an interviewer from *Science* magazine. To make "cancer the whipping boy for every environmental evil may prevent effective action when it does matter."[246]

Precisely because the American food industry expanded worldwide, it became a target for consumer advocates and health zealots, resulting in the demonization of such fast-food companies as McDonald's. Leading the charge were polemics such as *Fast Food Nation*, aided and abetted by such supposed public interest firms as Michael Jacobson's Center for Science in the Public Interest. By the 1990s, tort lawyers had piled on, bringing suits against food corporations for causing obesity. The U.S. Congress passed legislation protecting companies from such frivolous suits before any tobacco-type pattern could set in. Nonetheless, even business practices were attacked by the food police: "Our culture's apparent obsession with 'getting the best value' may underlie the increased offering and selection of larger portions. . . ."[247]

Surprisingly, some firms escaped attacks if the advertising was benign and they didn't affect the environment. Left out of the media and activists' gunsights was the international coffee giant, Starbucks, which had some five thousand stores in forty-one countries outside the United States. Indeed, throughout the Middle East, including Qatar, Saudi Arabia, Bahrain, the United Arab Emirates, and Turkey, which at one time was noted for its coffee, Starbucks and McDonald's had replaced Coca-Cola as perhaps the most familiar American products in the world. To anti-American voices, however, these constituted sources of American cultural imperialism. Of course, American "imperialism" of this sort had occurred for more than a century, but it had moved well beyond the postwar European notions that Coca-Cola was part of the American intelligence apparatus. American marketers hit upon a perfect formula, noting that their products were impossible to resist when the products were easily obtained and tweaked for local taste buds (Coke), and when they were portable enough that American soldiers could introduce the product anywhere (cigarettes). American marketing continued to impact everyone the world over, and the dominance of Hollywood movie stars in the international arena further heightened the fears on the part of some Europeans and Asians that they were becoming absorbed into a giant American cash register.

Premature Obituary

Ironically, European concerns about American dominance occurred at a time when many were writing the obituary of the American economy. High international debt levels, the sinking dollar, the low numbers of American math and science graduates—all relentlessly pounded by pundits such as Thomas Friedman—constituted genuine problems, but they also masked a silent transformation in other parts of the economy.

Steel, for example, had entered a new era of prosperity after the downturn of the 1980s. Having slashed four hundred thousand employees (and their health costs) from their expenses, the industry met new soaring global demand and invited foreign companies to "build American." Led by Nucor and its electric arc process and AK Steel, American companies outperformed the stock market by wide margins and drove down production costs. By the late 1990s, several American companies were topping archrival Japan in cost per ton. Steel prices, meanwhile, continued to rise (70 percent in 2007 alone), partly due to the demand of exploding economies in India and China. The high profits led foreign companies to invest in American facilities; German steelmaker ThyssenKrupp, for one, built a $4 billion plant in Alabama, while Honda and Toyota built state-of-the-art auto facilities in Ohio and Kentucky. Nucor did not stand still either, laying plans to build a $2 billion plant in Louisiana.[248] Likewise, publishing, once dominated by a handful of major companies, saw the top few merge while dozens of niche competitors run by entrepreneurs sprang up, specializing in everything from travel to food to computer games.

Both industries reflected a small part of the transformation of the U.S. economy from a big-company economy to a small-business entrepreneurship economy, and a rebound in small-business starts. This was seen in the rise of entrepreneurship courses in business schools around the nation. By 2008, some 70 percent of high schoolers said they intended to start their own business, and half of all college graduates said self-employment was more secure than a full-time job. Those age eighteen to twenty-four were starting companies at a faster rate than those a decade older; Gen Y business owners, by a large majority, saw themselves as "serial entrepreneurs," and 80 percent of American universities offered courses in entrepreneurship.[249]

At the same time, the once-popular legal profession lost its luster. Attorneys were incredibly cynical and depressed: the California state bar in the 1990s found a large majority of attorneys thought their profession lacked honor and were "profoundly pessimistic" about the law. Two thirds said that modern attorneys "compromise their professionalism" over money, and four fifths said the state bar failed to punish bad-apple attorneys. Half said they would not become lawyers again if they could start over.[250] A similar study in Maryland unearthed an overwhelming malaise within the profession, typified by attorneys who were "irritable, short-tempered, argumentative, and verbally abusive," as well as "detached, withdrawn, preoccupied, or distracted."[251] A review by the Florida bar found "a substantial minority" of its members were "money-grabbing, too clever, tricky, sneaky, and not trustworthy; who had little regard for the truth or fairness, willing to distort, manipulate, and conceal to win; arrogant, condescending, and abusive."[252]

More than just the legal profession displayed these attitudes; by the

1990s they were already being seen in overall attitudes among the young. One organization surveyed 387 urban middle and high school students from New York, Washington, Camden, Philadelphia, and East Oakland and conducted focus groups with 295 others in 1991.[253] The results showed an overwhelming sense of hopelessness and cynicism in the future among these inner-city youth. Risk taking and dangerous/destructive behavior were common, celebrating promiscuity, drug abuse, gangs, and violence. Urban youth laughed at attempts to reach them through traditional mediums of communication. Researchers were stunned to find the "Hip-Hop generation" did not revere Martin Luther King, nor any other civil rights icons. They did, however, crave authenticity: traditional public service approaches were useless.[254] A more optimistic picture was painted by the Sloan Study of Youth and Social Development, done a few years later, which found that 80 percent of high school seniors expected to work in a professional job, 71 percent expected to be millionaires, and 40 percent thought they would become millionaires before age forty. If those were "expectations of an insanely high level" (and certainly far higher than those of students forty years earlier), they nevertheless reflected an astonishing level of optimism, if somewhat devoid of realism.[255]

Was the United States falling into a situation like that in the Soviet Union, where no one believed the federal government, politicians, or the media? Was there a correlation between the decline in professional honesty and trustworthiness at all levels—the "Enron problem"—and falling rates of religiosity in American society? Scientific surveys actually concluded there was, with one study discovering that merely the moral reminder of writing down as many of the Ten Commandments as one could remember before undertaking a trustworthiness exercise significantly increased the subject's honesty.[256] Trust and happiness also were discovered to be fellow travelers. Happier nations tended to be those with high trust levels, although they also tended to have wider income distributions (possibly because the opportunity to get rich was more important than having similar incomes), and, surprisingly to some, the most homogenous—not the most diverse—societies tended to be the happiest.[257] And the old saw that money doesn't buy happiness? It was correct, but only to a point. Research found average happiness indexes had increased slightly in richer countries and decreased markedly in poorer nations, reinforcing the "hierarchy of needs" first elaborated by Abraham Maslow in 1943.[258] Until basic needs of food, shelter, and security were met, it was unlikely too many people in a society would be happy.

Yet for almost three decades, a Liberal Western Consensus (LWC) had insisted that poorer nations would see the necessity of, in the view of LWC advocates, restraining their own economic, social, and cultural growth for the broader benefit of mankind, defined as "protecting the environment." China, in particular, which was one of the largest (if not *the* largest) polluter in the world, was seen by the LWC as a state that could be reasoned with and persuaded *not* to grow fast.

But even issues such as the environment lose their luster over time, and such causes as global warming lessened in vogue. Even among those in the West, other issues slowly surged ahead of global warming and its corollary restrictions on world economies. For example, the Copenhagen Consensus Center, a think tank including five Nobel Prize–winning economists that weighs proposals to improve the world by spending $75 billion over four years, found that global warming was already moving down its priority list. In 2008, it ranked only thirtieth. The highest single proposal related to climate change was research into low-carbon energy, which ranked fourteenth. But more traditional wealth-creation concepts, such as the benefits of freer trade, were seen as more likely to improve world prosperity. The adoption of free-trade policies by additional nations was estimated to boost wealth in developing countries by $113 trillion in the twenty-first century, with an estimated 80 percent of all new wealth generated in the next one hundred years from expanded trade going to undeveloped countries.[259] But would free trade, an expansion of capitalism, and a reassertion of American exceptionalism, which had produced many of the advances already blessing the rest of the world, be the mainstay of policies after 2008?

Even under Bush, the elements of American exceptionalism had eroded. Liberty was infringed by body searches and X-ray scans at airports. Deficits swelled. Abroad, Europeans (except for Britons) seemed cowed by terrorist attacks. Spain left the Iraq coalition, and the UN had pulled out of Baghdad after its personnel were hit by a deadly suicide bombing. Bush's approval ratings fell. American prestige, especially after claims of WMDs in Iraq were not verified, dropped precipitously. The core pillar of exceptionalism, the Christian religion, appeared in decline not only in Europe but in America as well.

America had aged. The air that once had been fragrant with liberty seemed stale, and the skies once inscribed with honor grew gray. Citizens who had fought in World War II, the Korean War, and the cold war now demanded their rewards and sought to cash in on promises made by government. But the society that made the promises was no longer the society charged with paying for them. Demanding what the nation simply did not have, the greatest generation sounded more like greedy geezers. Yet these Depression-era products had achieved amazing things, performed heroic feats, quite unlike the baby boomers who followed. Boomers demonstrated their clout again and again when it came to commercial products, entertainment, and lifestyle choices, and their generation dominated the world with its tastes and political selections. What it did not do was demonstrate that it could sacrifice or deny itself benefits that would otherwise come at heavy costs for future generations. And most of all, it had not shown that it had a vision of the future or could lead the world into the next millennium. History has a way of forcing those choices on the reluctant and the procrastinators. It would soon do so again.

CHAPTER NINE

Fastest to the Bottom

TIME LINE

2004: Chechen attack on theater in Beslan, Russia; *SpaceShip-One* makes first privately funded space flight; Bush administration abandons amnesty plan for illegal aliens

2006: Bush plan for small restructuring of Social Security fails; Democrats win U.S. Senate

2007: Jokela, Finland, school shooting; Virginia Tech school shooting

2008: Barack Obama elected president; TARP bailout for banks "too big to fail"; Kauhajoki, Finland, school shooting; U.S. annual deficit exceeds $1 trillion; Democrats win both houses of Congress

2009: Banking crisis continues; stimulus bailout passed in United States; federal government purchases General Motors; Tea Party demonstrations; financial crises in Greece, Spain, Portugal, Ireland; AIDS cases in Africa top 22 million, deaths from AIDS in Africa exceed 1.3 million

2010: National Health Care ("Obamacare") passes; Republicans regain House; EU bails out Greece, Ireland, and Spain; Obama announces end of U.S. manned space program; U.S. economic growth stalls at under 2 percent average

2011:   Revolts in Yemen, Egypt, Tunisia overthrow dictator-
          ships (Arab Spring); gold, silver, gas prices reach new
          highs in United States; U.S. debt tops $15 trillion; U.S.
          Navy SEALs kill Osama bin Laden; U.S. troops with-
          draw from Iraq; Oslo, Norway, summer camp massacre

2012:   Aurora, Colorado, theater shooting; U.S. Supreme Court
          rules Obamacare legal as a tax; Newtown, Connecticut,
          school shooting; Muslim Brotherhood candidate seizes
          power in Egypt; *Dragon* private spacecraft connects to In-
          ternational Space Station; number of Americans on food
          stamps hits record (47.7 million); U.S. real unemployment
          rate tops 15 percent; U.S. federal debt tops $16 trillion;
          fourth consecutive year of $1 trillion annual deficits; U.S.
          embassy in Benghazi, Libya, assaulted, ambassador killed;
          International Atomic Energy Commission reports Iran
          close to functional nuclear weapons

Descent of the West?

By 2008, if not earlier, it had become fashionable across the political spectrum to proclaim the "descent of the West." Conservatives such as Niall
Ferguson, Pat Buchanan, and Mark Steyn, and liberal advocates of globalism such as Thomas Friedman all saw abundant economic, moral, and social indicators that wherever one looked in the West, the direction was
negative. Many conservatives cited either the demographic changes of the
Islamic/Asian/Indian world relative to that of the Europeans, or the "superior" productivity gains of the emerging nations, or the decline of Western
morality.

Such pronouncements were nothing new—Oswald Spengler's *Decline of
the West* in 1918, which offered a cyclical view of history, or Michael Harrington's *Twilight of Capitalism* (1976), which declared the arrival of socialism's triumph, both typified the views that the West was finished.
Furthermore, as Ferguson pointed out, it was precisely concerns about ethnic or racial imbalances that had aided and abetted the rise of the totalitarians in the past. Hitler and Mussolini had garnered support by citing the
need to establish strong governments for security against threats inside and
out. Meanwhile, leftists proclaimed the inevitable final collapse of capitalism due to its internal contradictions.

Oddly, for half a century, liberals had argued that multiculturalism and ethnoracial mixing would prevent conflict. Had not Francis Fukuyama argued just a decade earlier that we had arrived at "the end of history"? In 1992, he asserted the world had not seen just the "passing of a particular period of post-war history, but the end of history as such: that is, the end point of mankind's ideological evolution and the universalization of Western liberal democracy as the final form of human government."[1] Admitting his premise originated with Marx, for whom the end of history meant the termination of class struggle with the triumph of the proletariat, Fukuyama rejected a materialistic explanation in favor of an ideological one, namely that the world had accepted the triumph of Western values. Here, he claimed even China had succumbed to liberalism's penetration, and in his words, "can no longer act as a beacon for illiberal forces."[2] Fukuyama, of course, had ignored the Islamic threat, which would quickly replace communism as the next true ideological force. This new worldview was captured in Benjamin Barber's book, with its catchy title, *Jihad vs. McWorld*.[3] Certainly, however, the Europeans, Chinese, and Japanese did not think that they were being conquered by either Islam or crass capitalism.

For most "declinist" critics on the Left, however, in the same breath that they decried American society as racist and imperialist, they celebrated the racial and ethnic assimilation—the "melting pot" of the American experience—that would erase all differences. How a melting pot could be both racist and yet desirable was not explained. In fact, the lesson of the twenty-first century was that assimilation without other modifying factors was a dismal failure. German/Jewish weddings in 1920 were common, as were Tutsi/Hutu marriages in Rwanda seventy years later; but Pole/Jew, Serb/Slovene, Czech/German, Tutsi/Hutu all went out the window when the killing started. As Ferguson noted, the lesson of the Balkans and Rwanda was that history was set back to the beginning of the twentieth century. Only those who viewed history as constantly progressive—toward final utopian perfection—would believe that merely placing different groups, with historically and sometimes radically different religions, languages, cultures, and objectives, side by side would somehow produce lasting harmony. But Friedman and Ferguson pointed to other disturbing trends that indicated Asian dominance, especially the fact that the ratio of European to East Asian per capita GDP had rapidly shrunk since 1970. Only a half century ago, the gap was decried as evidence of capitalism's failure and immorality; once that gap narrowed it was evidence of European/American decline.

The notion that Europe's and America's rise had only been possible through the decadence of non-Western empires and their exploitation by inhuman Western imperialistic nations was preposterous. Were all the Incas, the Aztecs, the North American Indians, the dozens of major African tribes, the Chinese, the Japanese, and eventually the Arabs and Persians decadent? Or were they surpassed by an ideology of liberty that unleashed both superior technology and governmental organization? To come to such a conclusion would invalidate the entire multiculturalist perspective.

Evidence from the former Third World mounted, showing in fact that Western institutions and values were critical to sustained economic prosperity. Nobel Prize winner Amartya Sen, an Indian economist, wrote an essay in 1999 in which he argued that "in the terrible history of famines in the world, no substantial famine has ever occurred in any independent and democratic country with a relatively free press."[4] Calling democracy a "universal value" and "the preeminent development" of the twentieth century, Sen continued: "We cannot find exceptions to this rule, no matter where we look: the recent famines of Ethiopia, Somalia, or other dictatorial regimes; famines in the Soviet Union of the 1930s; China's 1958–61 famine . . . or, earlier still, the famines in Ireland or India under alien rule."[5] The last famine he saw, as a child, ended abruptly in 1943 with the establishment of a multiparty democracy and a free press. Ethiopia's 1982–85 famine arose as a "combination of military and agricultural policies by the Ethiopian government," noted the *Journal of Peace Research*.[6]

It was perhaps, then, significant that, over time, freedom spread as the West surged in its dominance of food production and overall wealth. Israel, which did not even exist in 1946, and which by 2008 had only seven million people, counted 7,200 millionaires and national assets of $35 billion, with a GDP nearly double that of any other Middle Eastern country, *even including* oil wealth.[7]

Asia, especially China, had similarly begun producing its share of wealthy individuals. As a region, Asia had come full circle. Once the world's wealthiest region, Asia accounted for 75 percent of estimated world economic output in A.D. 1, then declined sharply by 1870 and fell behind the United States and Europe altogether in 1950.[8] This reversal of places was due to a massive productivity increase in Western agriculture, especially on American farms. In 1945, the United States easily supported 140 million Americans and most of war-torn Europe and many in the Far East on 365 million acres of cultivated land, while China, with four times as many people, struggled to stave off mass starvation. The average American farm even then was nearly 160 acres, contrasted with the typical Chinese farm of only

4 acres.[9] Abundant and low-cost food was taken for granted in the United States, and the trend continued, to the point that by the late twentieth century, the average American spent less than 20 percent of his income on food, lower than in any other country.[10]

Cauldron on the Dark Continent

Food, of course, remained one of the most potent weapons any society possessed and was brutally used by dictators, particularly in Africa. Zimbabwe's Robert Mugabe, who presided over a disastrous decline in his country's agriculture, imitated old Communist tactics, turning a once productive regional breadbasket into a basket case. From 2000 to 2008, agricultural output dropped 80 percent, unemployment rose to 90 percent, and inflation topped 100,000 percent.[11] The average Zimbabwean, for example, could expect to live to be only forty years old, and one fifth of the population fled. Mugabe responded by trading food ration documents for votes in the election.

Hell-pits such as Zimbabwe were all too common in Africa, with only a few bright spots—one of them Rwanda, which had staged something of an economic miracle. In the twenty-first century, according to the World Bank Doing Business Index, Rwanda ranked as the number-one reformer (in 2009) and had averaged 8 percent growth since 2004. Most important, it had slashed its reliance on foreign aid from 100 percent to just 40 percent, and was tied with the United States as the easiest country in which to start a business on the World Bank's scale. A business registration process could be completed in twenty-four hours, and the nation's government considered instituting a flat tax. The state had sold off sixty-two of its seventy-two state-owned businesses; cut paperwork and red tape; and joined Kenya, Burundi, Tanzania, and Uganda in a free-trade zone. Although Rwanda had some ways to go even to reach parity with neighboring Kenya (per-capita GDP of $535 compared with Kenya's $911), the Rwandan achievements—for a nation that had been mired in genocide just a decade earlier—constituted an astounding accomplishment and provided a light for the rest of Africa.[12] Unfortunagely, states such as Rwanda were too few to lift Africa in the same way China, South Korea, and Japan were lifting Asia, largely because the other African states still often ignored property rights.

The entire continent had been a battleground during the cold war, with both the Americans and the Soviets attempting to woo, cajole, or bribe virtually every African state into the superpowers' orbit. Ironically, inside America, interest in Africa came from across the political spectrum, but for different reasons. U.S. black activists of the sixties were surprised to learn that Africans were seeking to abandon tribal dress and culture at the very time blacks in the United States were celebrating their Africanness. One Nigerian tribal leader, Fela Kuti, found the newfound affinity for Africa among Americans "crazy," and recalled, "we were even ashamed to go around in national dress until we saw pictures of [American] blacks wearing dashikis on 125th Street."[13] In fact, Africans often wanted little to do with American customs, black or white: Tanzania had banned American soul music in 1969 as subversive.

Throughout Africa, the U.S. government employed other techniques to push newly emerging states into cooperation, including food aid, which often was rendered under entirely humanitarian intentions but produced a cold war result. Almost all of the U.S. assistance to Somalia in the 1960s and 1970s, for example, had been nonmilitary, and by 1988, a World Bank study discovered that food aid was growing fourteen times faster than food consumption in Somalia, fostering corruption at outrageous levels.[14] By 1988, both the West and the Soviets were finished with Somalia for a time, although they would return in the Mogadishu fiasco of 1993.[15]

Meanwhile, the struggle for Africa had shifted to Angola, which the Portuguese essentially abandoned in 1975, convinced that the coming civil war would not treat Europeans with kindness no matter who won. With the Soviet threat gone, American aid to the pro-Western Jonas Savimbi ended in 1991, whereupon a peace treaty between the warring parties was signed. It barely lasted a decade before new fighting erupted in 2002, Savimbi was killed and the Angolan economy—along with its only chance for a Western-style market-oriented government—disintegrated. By the first part of the twenty-first century, Angola was as backward as ever: 25 percent of children died before their fifth birthday, and provincial capitals had not seen electricity in a decade. However unpleasant the Portuguese imperialists were, they had raised per capita incomes by about $300 between 1960 and 2000. Since the Americans abandoned Savimbi, incomes plummeted by two thirds.[16]

Angola's decline also vaporized one of the buffers for white-dominated South Africa. Mozambique had fallen in the 1980s, and in the process some 200,000 whites abandoned their homes, farms, and factories at the prospect of the takeover by the Marxist-Leninist Samora Machel. Yet Machel confounded his Soviet sponsors in 1984 by signing a nonaggression pact with South African president P. W. Botha.

On South Africa's third border, however, Rhodesia posed a much different problem of instability. There, Robert Mugabe led a revolution in which he emerged from the independence movement in 1980 as the last leader standing, becoming head of state in 1987. That left South Africa alone as a white-controlled island in a black sea.

South Africa had held out as long as it did, and against heavier odds, than any of the other white-dominated outposts in Africa, partly because it was insulated against world opinion by geography and its own self-sufficiency (it possessed some of the largest reserves of diamonds, gold, phosphates, iron ore, manganese, tin, uranium, zinc, and vanadium in the world). Ironically, Western liberals—who detested the South African regime—had propped it up for almost twenty years through their inflationary welfare spending, which caused the price of South African gold to skyrocket. Between 1972 and 1980, a gold ingot's value rose tenfold. Moreover, South Africa's economy *was* growing, and even benefiting the black underclass living in apartheid. Indeed, one of the little-discussed curiosities of the era was that South Africa saw a net in-migration from its black neighbors, many of whom ignored the boycott called by the Organization for African Unity (in place since 1964, with little impact). Some deliberately courted South African favor, including Malawi, whose capital city and Cabora Bassa Dam were built by the hated apartheid regime.

Botha's successor, F. W. de Klerk, nevertheless knew that white dominance could not be sustained. He removed the ban on the African National Congress (ANC) and released ANC leader Nelson Mandela from jail in early 1990. Two years later the white electorate voted overwhelmingly to dismantle apartheid. A new draft constitution was negotiated with black leaders, and in 1994, South Africa held its first multiracial election, in which Mandela became president and de Klerk vice president. That year, hoping to "undo the wrongs of apartheid" by taking land from whites and giving it to native blacks, the South African government began a program in 1994 which would turn 30 percent of the commercial farmland over to blacks by 2014. Yet by 2012, the government had only handed over 8 percent of the land—and most of that land was considered "unproductive."[17]

Unlike Zimbabwe, the South African government resisted seizing lands by force, regardless of its political rhetoric, realizing that it would lose the whites' capital and expertise. Instead it attempted to rent land to natives, but, as one of the key object lessons of American exceptionalism showed, property is almost without value unless ownership is provable by titles and deeds. Without an incentive to improve the land, and without paper instruments to prove their interests, farmers found bank loans were unobtainable due to a lack of collateral. Moreover, experience in what crops to grow, and when to market them, came over time and demanded substantial numbers of failures to build experience—another reality the statist South African government sought to avoid.

Taken as a whole, then, by 2012, Africa remained as economically stunted and politically adrift as ever. In the few nations where any significant growth had occurred, as in the Ivory Coast from the 1960s to the mid-1980s, it ended or even reversed with civil wars and coups. Ghana, the Ivory Coast's neighbor, which once lagged far behind, recovered and passed the Ivory Coast by the twenty-first century. Yet how stable was Ghana? Or Rwanda? Or any of the nations that at present had shown some progress? Based on the last seventy years, the answer would have to be "not very."

Two Steps Back

Africa learned some of the lessons of Western success, but seemed unable to employ them consistently or across multiple nations. Latin America in the twenty-first century, while better on scales of entrepreneurship, property ownership, and barriers to starting a business, remained an "unfulfilled promise," according to a leading scholar of South America.[18]

Since 1928, only Brazil, Mexico, Peru, Puerto Rico, and Venezuela have recorded even adequate economic performances. A few countries, including Uruguay and Argentina, achieved somewhat higher GDP growth while El Salvador, Nicaragua, and Ecuador were among the lowest. Only Argentina witnessed widespread vertical integration of its businesses—a practice that had been adopted in the United States 150 years earlier. When Richard Nixon said, "Latin America's had 150 years of trying . . . and they don't have much going on down there," he captured a political reality that Americans officially skirted.[19] More significantly, foreign investors remained noticeably absent. "The swashbuckling entrepreneur who cut a swath through the tropical jungle in pursuit of profit may have captured the imagination of the outside world, but no foreign capitalists and very few domestic ones have ever invested a cent before the ground rules have been agreed on with the government," noted one survey of South America's economy.[20]

Only a few South American leaders responded to decades of low growth with market reforms: Óscar Arias in Costa Rica, Carlos Menem in Argentina, Sixto Durán Ballén in Ecuador, Víctor Paz Estenssoro in Bolivia, César Gaviria in Colombia, and Carlos Andrés Pérez in Venezuela in his second term. More often than not, the pattern of Latin America in the late twentieth century was protectionism, statism, collectivism, and high taxation. Reagan helped the region as best he could. A massive restructuring of Latin American loans was begun in the 1980s with his Caribbean Initiative, which gave duty-free access on a range of goods to the United States. Attempting to stimulate American investment, he unveiled the "Brady Bond," a zero coupon Treasury bill that could be exchanged for lower face value national bonds and gave American banks an escape hatch from their exposure in South America. Nonetheless, Latin America as a whole remained at a big disadvantage in the "knowledge economy," possessing only 34 computers per 1,000 people versus 311 per 1,000 in the United States at the turn of the new millennium.

Mexico in particular disappointed Western liberals, remaining impervious to reform even though it saw somewhat higher growth than other Latin American states and its economic progress tended to lift the entire region of Central America. Part of this growth reflected the billions of dollars transmitted back to Mexico by Mexican workers in the United States, legally or illegally. Through the North American Free Trade Agreement (NAFTA), Mexico was closely tied to America's fortunes, and generally did better than other Latin American countries (as did Panama). In the 1990s, Mexican exports to America accounted for one quarter of all of its exports.

Mexico also suffered from a renewed wave of violence in the late twentieth century. The socialist and state-endorsed PRI party (Partido Revolucionario Institucional) had held power for seventy-one years, but increasing frustration with its grasp on political life led to a series of assassinations. PRI candidate Luis Donaldo Colosio was gunned down in 1994, followed by José Francisco Ruiz Massieu, an ally of Colosio's successor, Ernesto Zedillo Ponce de León. Historian Peter Smith claimed the endemic violence "inflicted a devastating blow to Mexico's international image."[21] Mexico could no longer be seen as an up-and-coming country on the brink of joining the advanced nations. Instead, it looked like a Third World country that was coming apart at the seams.

Mexico was not alone in drifting into chaos and tyranny. In Venezuela, Hugo Chávez, a former paratrooper who gained the presidency, seized the Venezuelan assets of American-owned oil companies in 1998. Seizing Venezuela's oil company Petroleos de Venezuela as well, Chávez used his country's oil wealth to launch a guerrilla war on neighboring Colombia by supporting the Colombian Communist insurgency (FARC). Over the years, Chávez delivered 90,000 barrels of oil into Cuba, giving it a staggering subsidy worth $3 billion. In return Fidel Castro pumped security forces, doctors, and other specialists into Venezuela. Governing with a never-ending stream of invective against the United States, Chávez crushed internal opposition and controlled the media. Seeking broad new constitutional powers, he was defeated in a referendum in 2007, although he still held on to his office. Indeed, he was feted at the United Nations, where, referring to President George W. Bush as "the devil," Chávez told the delegates that the podium from which Bush spoke "still smells from sulfur."[22] Then in 2009 at the Copenhagen climate change conference, he launched into a diatribe against America and capitalism that received the most enthusiastic reaction of all the speeches, even more than that of President Barack Obama. "I'm still a subversive," he crowed.[23] With the largest army in Latin America, oil reserves second only to those of Saudi Arabia, and control over more hard assets than most foreign powers, Chávez declared himself the "enemy of the American empire."[24] "We have to . . . see the gringos as enemies. . . ."[25] Clinton and Bush ignored him; Obama embraced him (and even sent an official delegation to his 2013 funeral).

Latin American critics (and enemies) of the United States such as Chávez continued to receive theoretical support from academics such as Brazilian sociologist (and two-term president) Fernando Henrique Cardoso, who claimed the plight of undeveloped countries stemmed from their position as peripheral regions. A battle had raged for thirty years in Latin America between the structuralists (who called for new taxes and the reform of the land-tenures system) and the monetarists from the University of Chicago (known as the Chicago School), who were obsessed with deficits and money supply. Neither addressed the real problems of Latin America or any of the other undeveloped regions, namely the absence of entrepreneurship and property titles, due to the oppressive and repeated state intervention in the private sector. It was all too easy for demagogues such as Chávez to catch the dancing eye of the masses with the quick fix of socialism.

The so-called Five Republics (Costa Rica, Ecuador, El Salvador, Nicaragua, and Venezuela) all had managed to increase their share of world trade after World War II through export-led growth.[26] Then, in the 1970s, the Latin countries diversified. Peru moved into zinc, copper, lead, and iron; its fish, fishmeal, and hog industries were dynamic, and by the end of the decade, one third of all Peruvian export earnings came from fish (as opposed to only 1 percent in 1945). Similarly, Ecuador captured one fourth of the world's market in bananas. Guatemalan farmers experimented with the herb cardamom (in the ginger family), controlling 80 percent of the world's exports. Nonetheless, only Colombia established a traditional labor-intensive export growth that affected income distribution. For all its oil, mineral, and agricultural advantages, South America remained well behind the European countries and America—an astounding indictment of statist policies, given that Latin America (with the exception of Colombia) was untouched by warfare for sixty years, had benefited from wartime demand for its goods, lacked any interstate conflict to speak of since 1900, and held a near-monopoly on so many raw materials.

There were good reasons for South America's perpetually slow growth. Tariffs were not only high, they varied wildly from country to country, transport remained poor, and national restrictions on truckers and railroad shippers meant excruciatingly long delays at frontiers for loading and un-loading. Red tape discouraged entrepreneurial activity. The panacea of a re-gional trade agreement vanished as consumers found themselves substituting low-cost goods from abroad for high-cost goods made in Latin America. Attempts to lower trade barriers failed, and while interregional trade grew somewhat, it did so at a price. The private sector, unwilling to invest given the business restrictions, proved equally unable to free up markets. Even where governments reduced tariffs, they failed on the other side of the equa-tion to control the money supply, as in the case of the "southern cone coun-tries," which had slashed tariffs by one third, but saw inflation and high interest rates destroy investment. Banks raised interest rates up to 20 percent, and the debt-service ratio in some countries rose as high as 59 percent.[27]

Most nations with a socialist bent should have looked to their Carib-bean neighbor, Cuba, and seen that Cuba had not generated a whit of eco-nomic growth after forty years of socialism refined to full-blown communism. Westerners such as Michael Moore and singer Stephen Stills championed Fidel Castro and his Cuban "miracle," yet according to one detailed study, after Castro's vast redistribution of assets, the country had shown virtually no improvement in basic needs (food, clothing, housing, and education).[28] As Castro clung to life in helpless infirmity, his brother Raúl assumed the presidency, formally receiving power from Fidel in 2006. Raúl then shocked socialists everywhere by announcing a series of pro-capitalist reforms, permitting a number of prohibited items (DVD players, computers, cooking equipment) to be sold openly and, Thatcher-style, sell-ing off state-owned industries.[29] Even more stunning, Raúl told actor Sean Penn, who interviewed him for *The Nation*, "The American people are among our closest neighbors. We should respect each other. We have never held anything against the American people. Good relations would be mu-tually advantageous. Perhaps we cannot solve all of our problems, but we can solve a good many of them."[30]

Despite Cuba's early and obvious signs of floundering, state-owned enterprises became the rage in Latin America by the end of the 1970s. Brazil established more than 650 by 1980, and virtually all foreign auto manufacturers had to buy from state-owned industries, which soon extended to tourism and nightclubs. State-owned corporations became the most favored clients of the banks—PEMEX in Mexico received massive loans—and the entrepreneurship problem remained unmet.[31] A few bright spots existed: Panama saw growth in sugar, shrimp, oil, and services (offshore banking had 120 banks with $43 billion in deposits by 1982). The number of Panamanian-registered ships also rose. With the Carter-Torrijos treaties in 1977, income from the Canal Zone (owned by the United States) shifted to the nation of Panama itself, providing another healthy boost.[32]

The wake-up call came in 1982 when Mexico failed to meet its foreign debt obligations, throwing Western banks into a panic. Bank of America, heavily leveraged south of the border, nearly collapsed.[33] At the same time, Colombia entered the third prolonged period of internal warfare it had experienced in the twentieth century. From 1899 to 1901, the nation had a civil war (the "War of a Thousand Days"), then from 1946 to 1965 suffered a second internal war, fought mostly in rural areas, called *La Violencia*. But the drug wars that began in the 1980s constituted an order of magnitude departure from previous localized conflicts, drawing in Communist guerrilla cells that acted as mercenaries and hangers-on for the drug cartels. In 1989, the Medellín cartel assassinated Colombian senator Luis Carlos Galán, then a presidential candidate who promised to crush the drug lords. Outrage in Colombia was immediate and resulted in the 1993 killing of cartel head Pablo Escobar by Colombian police. Two years later, the Orejuela brothers, who headed the Cali cartel, were arrested. But quelling the violence and reclaiming control over drug territories proved nearly impossible; in 2001 alone, the 481-mile-long Caño Limón–Coveñas Pipeline owned by Occidental Petroleum was bombed 170 times by guerrillas.[34]

Throughout Latin America, inflation and debt remained crushing problems, addressed by the so-called Washington consensus of the early 1990s in which American and Western banks agreed to write down Latin debts if those countries would open their economies, shrink their governments, and allow easier access for foreign corporations. Particularly after NAFTA was passed in the early 1990s, the consensus seemed to be working. Whereas inflation rates had ranged from 20 to 50 percent in the 1980s in Latin America, after adoption of the Washington consensus, most inflation rates fell to under 20 percent. United States investment tripled under

NAFTA. And despite the 1982 default, banks continued to pour money into Mexico.

Still, massive obstacles to Latin American/Central American/Mexican growth remained. For example, Mexican banks could roll over loans that borrowers failed to repay without even declaring them in default.[35] The nation's arcane bankruptcy laws meant that it could take banks up to seven years to recover collateral from borrowers—another defect in the system that worked against entrepreneurship and growth. Moreover, with so many Latin American economies dependent on one or two goods, a sudden shift in world markets could spell disaster, as occurred in the 1990s when coffee prices plunged.

Argentina in particular became a model for what happens under fiscal mismanagement. It sold off nearly all its nationally held telecommunications companies, but still suffered from high inflation due to government policies. In 2001, its economy collapsed: the country went on a barter economy, its currency was devalued, large areas became police no-go zones, and many European descendants migrated back to the Continent. A better modern object lesson for what happens to a society when government gets out of hand could not be imagined.

Overall, South America had shown much improvement since World War II. Its population was rising, health indicators were improving, urban centers were growing, and unemployment overall declined, despite the fact that large numbers of women finally began to enter the workforce. Wage and income disparities remained sharp—much higher than in the United States or Europe—but the poor were better off, even as the rich got richer faster. Tourism began to take hold across the southern hemisphere, dampened only by the drug cartels and kooky dictators. Unfortunately, something else grew in Latin America: state bureaucracies and quasi-dictatorial government, which, by 2010, showed no sign of yielding to true democracy or free markets.

The absence of common law, the political and economic instability, and the stubborn poverty that afflicted Mexico, Central America, and much of South America gave rise to other pathologies. Mexico battled infestations of drug lords who had taken to leaving heads on city streets as warnings. Juárez—directly across the Rio Grande from El Paso, Texas—became little safer than Baghdad with more than 2,600 murders in 2009. Mexican police and *federales* were routinely assassinated throughout the country; in response, President Felipe Calderón launched a crackdown on the drug cartels in 2006, deploying 50,000 troops to the worst drug regions. By 2010, some 28,000 people had died in drug-related violence in Mexico. The *Los Angeles Times* published travel updates for Americans, warning that certain beach resorts, including Ixtapa and Zihuatenejo, should be avoided. An April 2010 shootout in Acapulco killed three bystanders, and the U.S. consulate in Nuevo Laredo prohibited its own employees from entering the section of that city called "Boy's Town."[36]

Drug violence seemed unaffected by the expansion of American cultural influence and morals. American movies made up 80 percent of the movies in Latin American video stores; a large American-style shopping center opened in Tucumán, Argentina, in 1994, and the Hipermercado Libertad (Liberty Hypermarket) featured the Statue of Liberty as its logo. Coca-Cola, with its brilliant product placement in a popular Brazilian television show called *Duas Vidas* ("Two Lives"), was thought of as "Latin." Haitians thought Coke revived the dead, and in Chiapas, Mexico, it was used to get rid of evil spirits. Culture, however, could only truly flourish in a relatively free society where people could import American products, surf the Web for American entertainment, and have access to Western ideas of freedom and dissent. By 2012, in states such as Venezuela, these liberties were at risk, while in Cuba, for the first time, they were being enjoyed. Which vision of the future would endure remained an open question.

Amnesty, Amigo

If the Latin Americans embraced many American products and trends, they nevertheless continued to pour into the United States in staggering numbers. Ronald Reagan had attempted to end illegal immigration in 1986 with the Immigration Reform and Control Act (known as "Simpson-Mazzoli"), allowing an estimated three million illegal aliens to acquire amnesty on the grounds that the one-time legislation would tighten the borders. It failed miserably. According to immigrationcounters.com, by 2010, there were 23 million illegal aliens in the United States (and only 591,000 were not Mexican).[37]

What had begun after World War II as a stream became a flood, creating a massive subgroup of immigrants; 43 percent of those who immigrated since 1990 were Hispanic. This constituted a stunning lack of diversity (the liberal buzzword of the late twentieth century) in immigration policy. These immigrants, however, were different from the previous waves of immigrants in that the Hispanics failed to develop an American mind-set and character of their ethnicity that could allow them to assimilate into the dominant culture, possibly in large part because many or most were here illegally. The immigration problem quickly became a budget problem as the cost of social services and other government expenses connected with illegals rose dramatically, reaching $113 billion in 2010 as reported by the Federation for American Immigration Reform, including $84 billion absorbed by state and local government, with much of that due to the more than five million illegal immigrant children in public schools.

The Simpson-Mazzoli bill was labeled as immigration reform, but it did no such thing: more illegals poured across the border waiting for the next "reform." Instead of assimilating, they segregated themselves into pockets of festering anti-Americanism. This became evident when "Mexican-Americans" (thousands of whom were in fact not Americans at all but Mexican illegals) across the country marched in the hundreds of thousands in 2006 after Arizona senator John McCain proposed yet another new "comprehensive immigration reform" bill. Supported by President George Bush, McCain's plan essentially called for a new amnesty to "bring people out of the shadows." Yet there was no way to enforce documenting those illegally in the country. If they couldn't be deported before, how could they be deported later? While the media slavishly reported on the marches, the cameramen apparently failed to notice that the overwhelming number of flags being waved by the marchers were Mexican—an odd choice given that, supposedly, they wanted out of Mexico and into the United States. One Mexican television reporter crowed, "this shows that Los Angeles has never stopped being ours." In 2010, when the number of Mexican children constituted a majority in the Los Angeles school district, that boast seemed accurate.[38]

Politically, a swift and stunning backlash to what was perceived as an amnesty movement occurred. Talk shows exploded with angry callers, and Congress's switchboards lit up like seldom before. The issue helped permanently wreck the Bush presidency and temporarily swamped the Capitol Hill switchboard until Congress backed down. During the illegal immigration debate, it became disturbingly obvious to many who had never taken note before that there were very large pockets of illegal Mexican immigrants in the United States, particularly in Arizona, California, and Texas. Many Mexicans in the United States perpetuated their Mexican culture, Spanish language, and loyalty to the place of their birth, effectively rejecting all things American. Univision, founded in 1986 to become the largest Spanish-language network in the United States, and Telemundo, a Puerto Rican television station, carved out substantial American markets. Almost

80 percent of Hispanics watched one channel or the other, with half of them citing these outlets as their primary television viewing.[39]

Efforts proliferated to provide bilingual schooling, in which students would be taught in Spanish first and slowly acclimated to English. In actuality, Spanish simply remained the language of choice for the students, and increasingly, these programs doomed students to menial jobs and second-class status. Mexicans in the United States simply refused to "melt." Furthermore, Mexican immigrants, unlike most other ethnic groups, did not celebrate their culture by creating institutions that benefited all. Los Angeles, with its massive Mexican population, did not have a single Mexican hospital, college, cemetery, or charity. Contrast that with the Irish Catholic presence, or any of the earlier waves of ethnic and religious institutions, and the problem was obvious.[40]

Hispanics had the lowest rates of any immigrant group when it came to acquiring citizenship, were the least educated of all immigrant groups, and possessed the lowest level of entrepreneurship of any immigrant subpopulation. Yet surprisingly, the fertility rates of Mexican women who moved to America were *higher* than those of Mexican women in Mexico, despite the myth that by acquiring more opportunities and education they would have fewer children.[41]

More than a few Mexican writers boasted about Mexico "recovering the territories ceded to the United States with migratory tactics," or called the migration "The Great Invasion: Mexico Recovers Its Own."[42] In this respect a new myth was born, that the southwestern United States was the homeland of the Aztecs. Agitation began for the creation of a new country called Aztlán, comprising California, Nevada, Arizona, New Mexico, parts of Texas, and the six northernmost Mexican states. Activists understood that ethnic populations had demanded plebiscites in Europe to determine a region's national affiliation, and that the United States had supported such votes in the past. Once Mexicans became the majority in the southwestern United States, they could demand the formation of this new, entirely fictional, country. (Whom, after all, did the Spaniards get the land from? And before them, the Aztecs? And before them . . . the logic was never ending.) American politicians, unwilling to offend a large voter block, simply ignored this minefield, even as states such as Arizona desperately sought to control the border and the crime that followed the illegals. In 2011, Hispanics and liberals in southern Arizona sought to secede from the state and form "Baja Arizona," the fifty-first state, making the Aztlán movement less ridiculous than it may have seemed.[43]

Furiously promoting diversity, government, Hollywood, and academics produced anything but a truly mixed culture. As one wag put it, diversity was only good when looking for a place to eat. Indeed, studies in the early twenty-first century produced shocking results: diversity was badly fragmenting American society. As Robert Putnam, author of *Bowling Alone*, noted, "inhabitants of diverse communities tend to withdraw from collective life, to distrust their neighbors, regardless of the color of their skin . . . to volunteer less, give less to charity and work on community projects less often, to register to vote less, [but] agitate for social reform *more*. . . ."[44] Other findings by a team at MIT and the Fletcher School of Law and Diplomacy concluded, "all these studies have the same punch line: heterogeneity reduces civic engagement. In more diverse communities, people participate less. . . ." A study in Germany put it even more bluntly, noting a significant "anti-social effect" on society brought about by low-skill immigration.[45] One poll found that 90 percent of Mexican immigrants would vote in the next *Mexican* election, suggesting more than a little that their loyalties hardly resided with the USA.[46]

This was the kind of "transnationalism" (or, better yet, nonnationalism) that Samuel Huntington warned about in his *Clash of Civilizations*. His 1993 thesis, first published in *Foreign Affairs* and later in book form, made him among the first to identify the cultural elites—philanthropists, educators, politicians, journalists, and industrialists—as abandoning a "commitment to their nation and their fellow citizens and argu[ing] the moral superiority of identifying with humanity at large."[47] Seeing themselves as "citizens of the world," they no longer identified with the United States. Notably, that was exactly the same characteristic the Soviet KGB had looked for when scouting potential agents. Of all people, consumer gadfly Ralph Nader exposed the elites' lack of patriotism in a letter to the top companies in the Fortune 500 list, in which he asked the CEOs to open their next shareholders' meeting with the Pledge of Allegiance. Not one CEO accepted the idea, and even Ford, which at one time had preached Americanism as a central element in its company, wrote back, "We do not believe that the concept of 'corporate allegiance' is possible."[48]

America, contrary to popular views, had not always thrown its doors open to immigrants. Immigration laws in 1921 and 1924 reduced immigration by three fourths of its 1914 levels, and it remained low for sixty-five years. Even Franklin Roosevelt stated, "We have within our shores today the materials out of which we shall continue to build an even better home for liberty," while twenty years later, Lyndon Johnson insisted, "The days of unlimited immigration are past."[49] In fact, it had just started. As of 1970, the number of foreign-born Americans was under 10 million (5 percent of the total population), but by 2007, that had skyrocketed to 38 million (or over 12 percent).

Previous generations of immigrants were expected to adopt "patriotic assimilation," identifying with the United States over their country of origin and "cultivating an emotional attachment" to America.[50] This became increasingly difficult when, over the last half of the twentieth century, intellectuals and elites in the United States began to devalue American history and culture, embracing multinationalism. Politicians did the same, but for different purposes—identifying immigrants as minorities that needed government assistance allowed them to build constituencies out of these groups, and by fighting for these groups (but not always producing results), politicians balkanized American politics to a previously unimaginable degree.

Illegal aliens posed a growing financial and economic threat to the nation as well. They constituted massive drains on social services, particularly in an age when everything from Viagra to sexual identity counseling was paid for by the state. They contributed in particular to the massive deficits that California began to run in the first decade of the twenty-first century, and their presence meant that until they could be effectively dealt with, there could be no fiscal responsibility in the state.

Broker Than Bankrupt

Virtually no one at any level seemed to have fiscal responsibility by the end of the twentieth century. In 2002, the European finance ministers abandoned balanced budgets entirely. The United States had become a perennial debtor nation much earlier, in the 1980s, and never looked back. Particularly oppressive were the Social Security and Medicare programs, scheduled to abandon the baby boomers when they slipped into the red early in the twenty-first century.

Projections showed that by 2030 there would be 84 million Americans on Social Security, up 68 percent from 2008, and Medicare was slated to nearly double by 2030—a total $50 *trillion* obligation that was simply unfundable. Social Security was projected to go into a theoretical deficit by 2017 and would be bankrupt by 2041, ignoring the fact that all money in the spurious "trust fund" had already been spent, many times over. The economic recession of 2007–8, made much worse by the Obama stimulus program, health care reform, and other policies, accelerated those projections, adding $600 billion to the final price tag for every year that the nation waited to deal with the impending crisis.[51]

Even worse, with lengthening life spans and increasing medical costs, every year over $7 trillion was added to the unfunded debt of the United States in future Social Security and Medicare obligations that the government refused to report to the people. That didn't even count other obligations including defaulting student loans, government pension plans, the unrecoverable Fannie Mae and Freddie Mac debt, and the Federal Reserve assets in worthless paper, all figured on a net present value basis. By the end of 2012, the recorded debt was over $16 trillion, although a conservative estimate of the unfunded debt placed it at $87 trillion, and combinations of all debt reached as high as $200 trillion.[52]

No logic was more twisted than the twenty-first-century Progressive mantra that government costs had exploded due to skyrocketing costs of health care in the *private* sector. President Barack Obama ran on such tortured reasoning in 2008, and in July 2009 insisted that to "rescue this economy from a full-blown crisis, we must rebuild it stronger than before. And health insurance reform is central to that effort. . . ."[53] It was, of course, never actually explained how spending hundreds of billions of dollars more would *reduce* current spending, although a month earlier he had tied the need to control health care costs to soaring future Medicare and Medicaid costs.[54] Reality came from the IRS when it estimated that the health insurance costs for an average family through insurance exchanges under Obamacare would be $20,000 per year, and from California, which calculated individual premiums would rise from 64 to 146 percent. Polls quickly showed the plan was grossly unpopular, and the more that people learned of the details, the more unpopular it became. Even liberal pollsters such as the Kaiser Family Foundation showed a 46–40 disapproval/approval for the health care law in 2010, but by 2012—just before the Supreme Court decision—almost two thirds wanted to see all or part of the plan struck down, according to a *New York Times*/CBS News poll.[55] Regardless, Obama stuck with his logic and doubled down, ignoring the outrage and the polls. Backed by the Democrat Speaker of the House Nancy Pelosi of California and Senate majority leader Democrat Harry Reid of Nevada, Obama staked much of his presidency on the domestic equivalent of an eighteen-month Tet Offensive, sacrificing more than sixty Democrats in the House and six in the Senate to a rising voter insurrection over a national government health care plan passed in March 2010.

In June 2012, with polling showing Obamacare unpopular by (in some surveys) two to one, the United States Supreme Court ruled it constitutional, with Chief Justice John Roberts arguing that it was not up to the Court to save voters from themselves.[56] Nevertheless, the Supreme Court struck down three key elements of Obamacare: one that said it was permitted by the commerce clause, which constituted, long term, a serious blow to expansion of government; another allowed states to opt out of the insurance exchanges created in the law, in a strong boost to states' rights; and finally the Court redefined the legislation as a tax, which had originated in the Senate, itself unconstitutional and under challenge. Some thirty states took advantage of the opt-out clause, gutting the funding mechanism of the legislation and making it difficult, if not impossible, to fund. In the short term, however, Obamacare threatened to drive out armies of doctors and to bankrupt insurance companies due to the preexisting condition coverage that was required. If the Britain-style single-payer, government-funded health care system was his goal, Barack Obama had taken critical steps toward achieving that.

Republican vice presidential candidate Sarah Palin had warned in 2008 that Obamacare would involve "death panels" and was ridiculed for her comments, yet already various procedures were being rationed in England for obese individuals or smokers. In September 2012, with Obama's reelection seeming more certain, Steven Rattner, a top Democratic strategist, was blunt in stating that mandatory rationing for the elderly under Obamacare was inevitable. "We need death panels," he wrote in *The New York Times*, and "unless we start allocating health care resources more prudently— rationing, by its proper name."[57] When that rationing is determined by the secretary of health and human services, as *all* elements of the Obamacare law were, the actual makeup of the death panel would be irrelevant. Yet actually that was already resolved in April 2011, when it was announced that Medicare costs would be kept under control by the Independent Payment Advisory Board (IPAB), which would ration funding. In an ominous statement of intent, Obama said he would "give the *independent commission* the authority to make additional savings by further improving Medicare."[58] Another Democratic journalist, trying to pave the way for the acceptance of government-administered death panels, argued, "Death panels exist, they will exist in any conceivable system of health-care delivery," although the patient, the family, and the family doctor did not seem remotely like a death panel to most sensible Americans.[59]

Britain had already moved indirectly to death panels by funding hospitals that hit targets for placing people in a service called Liverpool Care

Pathway (LCP), an "end of life" service that had "been involved in the deaths of 130,000 patients who were elderly, terminally ill, or seriously ill but not dying."[60] LCP used heavy doses of morphine to control pain, except it was revealed that only 5 percent of its patients required such high levels to control pain. Instead of compassion and comfort, the British practice had simply led to more death. The same was true in the Netherlands, which had enacted a euthanasia law in 2002 and has seen an increase in nonvoluntary deaths in the several years since.[61] Moreover, researchers reported that in one fifth of the cases doctors failed to report euthanasia. Death panels were seen in Belgium, whose courts approved the odious notion of "wrongful life" in 2010. The Belgian euthanasia law permitted doctors to kill disabled people, although a court ruled that compensation was due for "the fact of being born with . . . disabilities."[62] Belgium's penal code authorizing thera-peutic abortions, the court held, was intended to "help avoid giving birth to children with abnormalities," and parents were entitled to damages from doctors if a misdiagnosis had failed to find disabilities before birth. Thus, even as the West confronted a birth dearth and stared at collapsing econo-mies, policies were being expanded that enabled individuals to sue for *any* abnormality in a child deemed "unwanted" that had been allowed to escape abortion. As we saw in volume 1, this was the Nazi concept of "life unwor-thy of life"—which is always ultimately applied to entire groups.

Ultimately, the intrusion of government into medical decisions im-posed its own tortured logic, namely that because the state ultimately was responsible for a person's health, so too it must be the guardian and master of a person's body in all aspects of life. The easiest of these elements to control was food, where the federal government's subsidies had for genera-tions wormed their way into the agricultural process. Made worse by the early-twentieth-century campaigns against meat, Coca-Cola, and finally alcohol, the government's influence had expanded in the wake of Eisenhow-er's heart attack through various dietary guidelines. It seemed the limits of absurdity had been reached by New York mayor Michael Bloomberg in 2012 when he announced a ban on soda drinks of over sixteen ounces, all in the name of better health. Early in 2013 a state supreme court judge, Milton Tingling, threw out the regulation as "arbitrary and capricious" because it was enacted through Bloomberg's executive order, not through legislation. The judge did not, however, note that the ruling was a massive invasion of free will and human choice, not to mention market liberties.

And food regulation inevitably ran up against individuals' desires to look a certain way. The effort seemed doomed to pathetic failure worldwide. Across Asia, especially in Hong Kong, extreme dieting became the latest fashion fad. Dieters flooded slimming centers that used infrared radiation, ultrasound, and other treatments to take off fat. At one clinic, the number of patients admitted for eating disorders doubled in the ten-year period from 1998 to 2007. Dieting in Asia, *USA Today* reported, was "more extreme than in the West because of cultural perceptions of beauty."[63] In Hong Kong, the paper reported, "scores of skinny women seem always to be looking for ways to get even skinnier," trying to get under the magic number of one hundred pounds.

Allowing government to dictate food choices—or any other choices, for that matter—based on health care costs was demonstrated to be all the more unreliable and problematic given that much of this legislation was based on faulty research. In 2011, a former researcher at Amgen pharmaceuticals revealed that over 64 percent of the cancer studies could not be replicated and another 12 percent could only be partially replicated.[64] In April 2011, Bayer published a paper in which it announced it had ceased two thirds of its early drug projects because it could not reproduce claims found in the literature.[65] These were significant findings, meaning that if researchers could not be confident in studies that were extremely tightly controlled and that studied microlevel data, how could they have any confidence whatsoever in studies of heart disease or fat in massive sample sizes or, even more absurdly, in predicting weather patterns based on human influences?

Terror Stalks Liberty

Whether it was dictating food choices, defining optimal body shapes and sizes, gobbling up land through restrictions and zoning, or telling businesses how to operate, governments at all levels and in all nations were careening out of control in the twenty-first century. Yet neither major American political party sensed a danger in the creeping intrusion by the state into private lives. As is often the case, the first expansions came when national security was invoked—and with good reason. Shortly after the 9/11 attacks, Bush asked Congress for the Patriot Act, designed to stop future terrorism on American soil, and Congress complied. Over the next several years, Patriot Act authority led to numerous foiled terrorist plots that were made public (and likely dozens of others kept secret).

But infringement on personal rights slowly increased. Airport security—which, had existing rules been correctly implemented, could have stopped the 9/11 attacks, especially if the information sharing between the FBI and CIA had occurred—witnessed a steady expansion of privacy incursions. First came the scanning of bags, then, following the unsuccessful shoe bombing terror attempt by Richard Reid, with scanning of clothing items such as shoes and coats, then ultimately the introduction of scanners that revealed a naked body's outline. Each new (failed) terrorist incident brought new inconveniences and more intrusions on privacy. Random searches were instituted; bags were opened and checked for explosives; and finally a near revolt by passengers arose over personal searches by Transportation Safety Administration agents who were alleged to have "groped." As *The Washington Post* put it, "the examinations routinely involve[d] the touching of breasts and genitals, invasive searches designed to find weapons and suspicious items."[66] Consumer advocate Ralph Nader called the frisks "extremely voyeuristic and intrusive."[67]

The irony of the ever-tightening security was that many of the attacks that had been foiled since 9/11 were stopped by accident or in spite of government protections. Several involved heroic passengers and flight attendants. Reid was grabbed by passengers who tied him up while a doctor gave him a tranquilizer. On a 2009 Northwest Airlines flight, a Nigerian would-be terrorist named Umar Farouk Abdulmutallab (who somehow managed to board the flight despite being on the no-fly list) was subdued by a heroic passenger.[68] The Times Square bomber's device, left in an SUV, failed to go off successfully and a street vendor spotted the smoke from the fuse, then alerted police. Other plots were broken up by routine city police activities: the Brooklyn Bridge terrorist was identified and captured by New York City police, as were the New York Republican National Convention bombers and the "Synagogue Terror bombers." The FBI also had success in infiltrating a number of mosques and Muslim terror groups beforehand (as with Michael Fenton, the attempted bomber in Chicago) or, as with the CIA's eavesdropping, picking up clues that led to the "Lackawanna Six" arrests. Arrests almost never occurred in the airport, at the lines set up to catch terrorists.

The Quagmire That Wasn't

Victories in the war on terror, accidental or otherwise, came against the backdrop of tremendous improvements in Iraq due to the surge strategy. Far from becoming "another Vietnam," by 2007 the Iraqi success spread far beyond the Iraq theater of the war on terror (always, and deliberately, misnamed by the press as the Iraq War), shifting attitudes not only of Iraqis, but also of large segments of the Muslim world. It was a transformation so remarkable as to invite studies of its methods for years to come.

Following the 2003 invasion that deposed Saddam and scattered his army, the United States had accomplished a near-impossible feat of traveling several hundred miles through enemy territory in less than a week to defeat a larger military while suffering under two hundred total battle deaths (including accidents). At that point, the conflict morphed into a quasi-guerrilla war, part insurrection, part civil war. Such constant battlefield change occurred because, as General Tommy Franks said, "the enemy always gets a vote." Again, as it had in Afghanistan, the press rushed to invoke Vietnam analogies. The word "quagmire" was bandied about, possibly more than any other word in the English language, in the pages of *The New York Times* and *The Washington Post* from 2003 to 2006, completely absent of any historical context.

The United States had conducted much longer successful military actions, having "stayed continuously in Haiti for 19 years, in Nicaragua for 23 years, in the Philippines for 44 years, in China for almost 100 years," noted military historian Max Boot.[69] World War II was an anomaly: historically many wars had lasted decades, bearing names such as the Thirty Years' War and the Hundred Years' War. But the jihadists understood the post-Vietnam mind-set, especially of the American media: string it out, inflict some casualties, and you have a chance. Saddam's remnant army, combined with some twenty thousand al-Qaeda volunteers from virtually every country in the Middle East, took to the ground and instituted a broad guerrilla war. Only the scale of violence against noncombatants differed from the atrocities of the Viet Cong: families were assassinated for cooperating with the Americans; civilian contractors were killed, burned, and mutilated; captive journalists and other Westerners were beheaded on videotape.

Secretary of Defense Donald Rumsfeld had steadfastly maintained that a "small footprint" was needed to allow the Iraqis to gain confidence and responsibility for their own defense.[70] But that proved impossible when the population cowered in fear of a new bombing or assassination. After the midterm elections in 2006, Rumsfeld resigned and Bush accepted the recommendations of the Iraq Study Group (and the similar, but independent, proposal of military expert Fred Kagan), which recommended not only increasing U.S. troop strength in Iraq, but specifically adding more combat forces (as opposed to logistics and training).[71]

As more Iraqis felt secure, two things occurred. First, life returned to the streets, and Iraqi society, even in Baghdad, again seemed normal. In 2008, for example, there was a street fair in Baghdad featuring carnivals, shops, and massive crowds—all without violence. Sectarian battles between

Shiite and Sunni diminished as the terrorist-instigated incidents fell, removing a further source of tension and in turn strengthening the Iraqi government. Second, al-Qaeda grew more desperate in those zones it thought it controlled, especially Anbar province.

Once considered lost by the U.S. military, Anbar made a U-turn as al-Qaeda grew more bold and murderous. In fact, most al-Qaeda "insurgents" were not Iraqis at all and their disregard of the local sheikhs' power, local customs, and morals in the province proved a massive error. The terrorists attempted to institute Sharia law, against which even devout Muslims recoiled. With each new al-Qaeda attempt at intimidation (such as the bombing of a mosque in Habbaniyah in February 2006, where a cleric preached against al-Qaeda) the sheikhs grew more convinced that their future lay with the U.S. military. *Sahawah Al Anbar*—the Anbar Awakening, as it was labeled, was in fact the direct result of the surge, driving al-Qaeda to Anbar, and of al-Qaeda's desperation. Beginning in the summer of 2006, the Jazeera Council in Ramadi threw in its lot with the Americans, raising the Stars and Stripes along with the Iraqi flag in its headquarters.

The Anbar Awakening produced local security forces (Provincial Security Forces, or PSFs) that provided information to Americans and, when no Americans were nearby, handled matters themselves. Al-Qaeda guerrillas were killed, hunted down, and chased out. Haditha and Ramadi became quiet, streets were cleaned for the first time, market forces returned. Most of Fallujah, the early turning point of the Iraq conflict in 2004, was calm. One journalist/blogger who had remained in Iraq wrote that the progress was "unthinkable just one year ago," and the "turning of the tribes against al Qaeda is a crucial piece of the puzzle, but so was the perseverance of U.S. forces in the region."[72] Fallujah had fully functioning local police by that time, using their own vehicles on patrol.

These direct results of the surge led to another worldwide attitude shift—one the American media virtually ignored—in which terrorism in general, and Osama bin Laden in particular, suddenly became the object of clerics' hostility. This was accompanied by Muslim intellectuals abandoning the jihad as a legitimate form of expression in what one former presidential adviser called "the single most important ideological development in recent years."[73] Sayyed Imam Al-Sharif, in his *Rationalizations on Jihad in Egypt and the World*, called the 9/11 attacks a "catastrophe for all Muslims." He argued that the use of violence against Islamic governments by Muslims was unlawful, and proposed a special Islamic court to try bin Laden and his confederate, al-Zawahiri. Saudi Arabia's leading cleric, Sheikh Abd Al-'Aziz bin Abdallah, issued a fatwa, with the "obvious target" being bin Laden, that prohibited Saudis from engaging in jihad abroad, and of being "drawn to arbitrary opinions and [religious] zeal that is not based on religious knowledge."[74] Another Saudi sheikh wrote a highly critical open letter to bin Laden, claiming he had caused the "ruin of an entire people."

By January 2008, less than one fourth of Pakistanis approved of bin Laden (down from almost half the previous August), and support of al-Qaeda dropped by a similar amount, from 33 percent to just 18 percent. Meanwhile, the Pew Global Attitudes Project in July 2007 found "large and growing numbers of Muslims in the Middle East . . . [are] rejecting Islamic extremism." The percentage of Muslims who agreed that suicide bombing was justifiable in the defense of Islam declined in all but one Islamic country, and in some places the decline was startling, down from 74 percent in Lebanon in 2002 to 34 percent in 2007.[75] In May 2011, one of the early—and most pressing—objectives in the war on terror was achieved when the CIA tracked down Osama bin Laden and the al-Qaeda leader was shot and killed in a daring strike conducted by Navy SEALs. Following years of surveillance of his compound in Abbottabad, Pakistan, the SEALs used two Stealth Hawk (nearly soundless) helicopters to fly directly over his house. They were to drop by rope onto the roof of "Geronimo's" (the code-name for bin Laden) compound from one, while the other landed and assaulted the building from the ground. The first helicopter was affected by the heat and high walls, forcing its pilot to crash-land the aircraft while the second helicopter landed outside the compound. Nonetheless, the assault took place without American casualties, and bin Laden and four others were killed. SEALs took photos and DNA samples and immediately transmitted them back to headquarters. After twenty-four hours of jubilation, the event was quickly pushed into the background in the West (although some media recklessly reported the names of the SEALs, putting their lives and the lives of their families in danger).

President Barack Obama repeatedly took credit for the operation, which was made possible entirely by the intelligence methods he decried during his 2008 campaign. Even so, he received a smaller poll bump from bin Laden's death than former president Bush received after 9/11. But the most significant development was that bin Laden's death didn't particularly affect the larger war on terror at all. The al-Qaeda leader had already been neutered for years, bottled up in a hideout.

When the United States withdrew from Iraq in December 2011, it was one of the most unreported events of the war on terror—the quagmire that never developed. Bush had signed the agreement to withdraw American forces with the Iraqi government in 2008. Unwisely, Bush did not insist on a permanent military base in Iraq, something that likely would be needed to disarm the growing threat of Iran. Meanwhile, in Afghanistan, Obama tried to shift the burden of fighting al-Qaeda onto the NATO allies, who had much different approaches to fighting terrorism; stories abounded of NATO troops in Afghanistan shunning combat. In addition, Obama's Afghanistan strategy involved reopening relations with the Taliban. It constituted a sharp break from Bush's "You're either with us or you're with the terrorists" approach. Whether this accounted for the high suicide rate among American troops—which exceeded combat deaths in 2012—was not clear, but morale among U.S. forces clearly dropped.[76]

Ascending Decline?

Even as the West increasingly doubted its own self-worth and moral standing, its accomplishments in music, art, business, and architecture continued to lead the world. It was as if a dynamic within Western societies refused to be suppressed, even by the guilty and self-loathing elites who preached against American exceptionalism and Western civilization.

Western self-expression, obvious in architecture, achieved jarring levels in 2007. The winner of a competition for Prague's new library design, by Jan Kaplický, consisted of a giant, lime-green-with-purple-dots half-ameba, half-octopus shape. Set amid 1600s-style traditional European buildings, the ameba-library was, to say the least, a shocking divorce from the past. Architecture of the West often shrieked irresistibly the attitudes of the day or the rebellion against them. Thus, when it came time to rebuild the World Trade Center, some jokesters suggested a four-building structure with the third building extended doubly over the rest—the "bird," in popular vernacular—indicating to the rest of the world (politely) "up yours." That design did not win, but the Freedom Tower that was selected would exceed in height the original WTC (although it would be only one building, not two), its airiness and light symbolizing the undying spirit of liberty in America. That is, if it ever got built: seven years after the attack, not a hole had been dug or concrete poured as various interests continued to bicker (and the government was involved; it was not simply left up to private industry to rebuild).

Meanwhile, in five years, Dubai had constructed the largest purely hotel-use building in the world, the astounding Burj Al Arab. Designed by architect Tom Wright and built by British engineers, the Burj Al Arab was intended to resemble the sail of a dhow. Merely establishing the foundation—an artificial island more than two hundred yards offshore—demanded contractors build a new surface. Its Teflon-coated fiberglass sail permitted a constant, soft light to enter, while the inside of the hotel featured the world's tallest atrium. Many critics hated it ("fabulous, hideous," wrote one, and, like the city, a monument to "the triumph of money over practicality," snorted another).[77]

In fact, it represented both a bold, new style and, sitting on its man-made island, a continuation of other architectural styles seen on an increasing basis where man refused to let nature or geography define his limits. Dubai also featured the famous Palm Islands resort and residences, begun in 2001 and built into the ocean along a ten-mile breakwater. Its Palm Jueirah Island in the center radiates out "palm fronds" of land. Other similar palms (Palm Jebel Ali) were also under construction, while an even more ambitious "world islands" project involved the construction (again, entirely on reclaimed ocean) of an archipelago of two hundred islands built in the shape of the world map. Hotels were just the newest structures carved out of the ocean: typical of this genre were the offshore airports in Japan, such as Kansai (designed by an Italian architect) or Chubu Central Japan International Airport at Nagoya (designed by the Western firm HOK). These architectural marvels (and three other offshore airports) were literally reclamation projects, each occupying chunks of land approximately four miles by one mile, reclaimed entirely out of the ocean and anchored by monstrous concrete revetments on the seabed. Repeatedly, the West had provided the design skills and often the construction expertise to make these architectural designs into structural reality.

Construction worldwide began to slow, however, and the sound of building and growth grew faint. Cranes in the United Arab Emirates soon were idled. Japan had already seen its economy slow in the 1990s. Between the dot-com bust and 9/11, the United States had only slowly recovered.

Beginning in 2008 and growing worse in 2009, however, a worldwide slowdown left some wondering if the "World" would ever be completed, and its stagnation seemed symbolic. As Greece, Ireland, and other European countries faced draconian cuts in long-expected social services (their military budgets having been eviscerated decades ago), the halt to construction in Dubai illustrated that even the richest nations were not immune to economic realities.

Some Americans thought the United States might somehow escape the worldwide slowdown and return to the vibrant activity of the 1980s and

1990s. Under Bush, the U.S. economy added a respectable six million jobs. Following the housing collapse and the failures of investment institutions Lehman Brothers and AIG, business activity dropped to recessionary levels in 2008, then plummeted under Obama. Unemployment reached 13 million in a few months after he took office (24 million if one correctly includes all those who were no longer looking for work). Congress, with Obama's blessing, continued to extend unemployment benefits, ensuring that those receiving government help would not be looking for jobs.

Nevertheless, foreign confidence in the United States remained high, perhaps because there was simply nowhere else to go. In 2007 alone, foreign investors poured $276 billion into the U.S. economy, a fivefold increase since 2002. A host of gloomsters continued to insist that America had drifted into "flatness," and had lost its technological lead. Harvard economist Richard Freeman warned that American technological competitiveness would soon be threatened by developing nations, such as China and India; politician after politician promised more spending on science and technology. Yet one study of supposedly globalized companies found 60 percent derived almost all of their revenues from the United States, and a third received all revenues from U.S. clients.[78]

Other trends were also visible, some ominous for America's future. At a time when success came from extraordinary execution of ideas or processes already established, fewer than 5 percent of the founders of *Inc.* companies reported filing a patent.[79] For years, economists had warned of a drain of the most talented people into law and financial services, and out of science, technology, and engineering, claiming it was "one of the sources of [America's] low productivity growth."[80] Perennial alarmist Clyde Prestowitz, in his *America's Technology Future at Risk* (2006), insisted the United States was "well on its way to surrendering leadership in advanced telecom products and services."[81] Bachelor of science degrees had fallen to pre-1983 levels in the United States, well below the levels in Japan, China, India, and Korea, and professional engineer degrees had disappeared. By 2001, European Union institutions granted 54 percent more Ph.D.s than the United States; the share of American-originated papers in scientific journals had fallen, along with a drop in the number of citations of U.S. articles. American-originated papers counted in the Chemical Abstract Service dropped by nearly half from 1983 to 2003.[82] (On the other hand, Norway, which had relatively fewer publications than any of its Scandinavian neighbors, nevertheless had the highest labor productivity in the world.)[83]

At almost the same time as the dire warnings about America falling behind arose, across the Atlantic the Europeans were making the very same arguments. Indeed, the Lisbon Agenda, set out as a developmental plan by the EU in 2000, sought to invest more in science and research to catch the United States, claiming that the EU invested less than the USA.[84] More puzzling, no decline in U.S. per capita incomes in either absolute or relative terms had taken place during this period of supposed weakness. European countries still remained at 75 percent of U.S. income, Japan at about 80 percent. Even manufacturing in the United States seemed to be holding its own. Americans still made more " 'stuff' than any other nation on earth, and by a wide margin."[85] American manufacturing output was $2.15 trillion in 2009, more than China's $1.48 trillion, and the American percentage of world manufacturing had scarcely changed since 1990.

How did one explain the seeming contradictions of falling science and math levels in America with the persistent technological breakthroughs? Economist Amar Bhidé argued that midlevel innovators, who were less geographically mobile than high-end producers, contributed to a widespread optimization of benefits to American consumers. More important, consumers, by interacting with the product (in terms of demands for functions), became a part of the innovation process.[86] MIT's Eric von Hippel found that lead users often were the first to develop many and perhaps most new industrial consumer products. These consumers, he claimed, accounted for 80 percent of the most important innovations in scientific equipment and semiconductor processing.[87] In consumer sports products such as windsurf-boards, mountain bikes, and snow boards, the users accounted for almost all of the advances. This was not, however, widespread: usually the value added came in another form. Apple's iPod music player, for example, was produced in the Far East, but virtually all tertiary activities, which took place in the United States, added the value. Dockworkers unloaded the containers, truck drivers transported the units, domestic retailers sold them, staff provided after-sale service, and most important, the infrastructure of iTunes was developed by lawyers, accountants, music professionals, and so on. Most important, however, American music tastes, movies, and celebrities drove the content of iTunes and, soon, the iPad. In a sense, due to the almost instantaneous transmission of information, American consumers—for all their crassness and lack of sophistication— had become codesigners of the technologies.

Thus the rate of labor productivity growth between 1995 and 2001 in services (2.6 percent) exceeded that in goods production (2.3 percent), and was widespread across U.S. industries. In one study, productivity grew in twenty-four of the twenty-nine sectors examined.[88] American exports were also strong: in 1900, the United States only exported about 15 percent of the merchandise it produced, but by 1997, it exported 40 percent.[89] And the trend has been across almost all the Organization of Economic Co-operation and Development (OECD) countries, that services have become the most important sector: the share of the service sector has increased to almost 70 percent of the total value added by most OECD countries by 2000.[90] Another study by McKinsey Global Institute found that six of the economies' fifty-nine sectors accounted for all of the net productivity growth in the United States from 1995 to 1999, all in the service sector.

If the United States was losing its place as world leader, other parts of the world often did not think so. In a conference on entrepreneurship in England, one economist observed "speaker after speaker emphasized the importance of securing U.S. sales—but there was virtually no mention of the equally populous and more proximate market in continental Europe."[91] As for the threat of immigration and its low-cost labor in America, immigrants with college degrees tended to have a wage premium slightly above that of native-born Americans, undercutting the notion that they provided a low-cost substitute for highly paid U.S. workers.[92] The threat was never from highly skilled Indians or Chinese, but from unskilled Mexican illegals. Indeed, America's high-tech industry seemed to accelerate. More than one third of the world's largest telecom companies were American, and half the nations on earth relied on Hollywood for their movies.[93]

Shopaholics

Though the American economy had not shrunk, it had certainly undergone a radical transformation, and this was nowhere more apparent than in retail shopping. Although numerous marketplaces, arcades, and indoor malls had been built in America, historians generally consider Country Club Plaza in Kansas City (opened 1924) to be the first shopping mall designed to accommodate shoppers who arrived by car. Southdale, near Minneapolis, opened in 1956 and became the first enclosed, fully climate-controlled shopping mall.

The concept of the mall, which contained several anchor stores (large department stores), combined with dozens—or even hundreds—of smaller, more specialized shops and restaurants, became hugely popular in the 1960s and 1970s. American malls entirely tailored themselves to auto shopping: gas stations and restaurants surrounded them on a periphery, while the spacious parking lots and wide doors ensured easy entry. Becoming places of entertainment and community, malls were locations for Saturday evening strolls, elderly fitness walkers, teens seeking independence within safe confines, and, of course, endless retail sales. In decades when most families remained intact and suburban crime stayed low, malls offered nearly complete social and entertainment services. Anchor stores often had their own spas, nail salons, and beauty salons; and for men, Sears (one of the stalwarts of the American mall system) had an auto repair shop where the husband could have a new battery or set of tires installed while he shopped with his wife.

Three factors brought malls under assault. As previously noted, the war on the automobile had never truly ended. By the late 1980s, environmentalists renewed the attack by targeting SUVs (sport utility vehicles) and minivans. The attractive features of the SUV included space for several children and sports equipment, fold-down backseats for storage, and upward-tilting rear hatches for easy access. SUVs had become sexy in the 1980s, and constituted a total surprise to the auto industry, which originally failed to appreciate their appeal. But Detroit caught on quickly, adding a decade-long bounce to American auto sales and inspiring the Japanese, who disdained larger cars, to scramble for their share of the market.

Second, the old-but-new concept of the walking mall, mostly situated outside, was revived. Fitting well with yuppie enviro-friendly notions (though hardly any different in terms of actual environmental impact), walking malls such as Easton Station in Columbus, Ohio, or Town Square in Las Vegas, Nevada, were built. Despite their initial popularity, these shopping centers faced serious problems, reminding people why climate-controlled malls were built in the first place: Columbus is freezing for months out of the year, while Las Vegas can be blistering hot. Nevertheless, beginning in the 1990s, outdoor malls made a resurgence.

Third, the explosion of retail giants such as Walmart, Target, and Costco meant that many staple clothing items, as well as appliances and auto parts, could be found in a single location. This dampened the allure of the anchor stores—Sears, JCPenney—and thereby diminished the profitability of all the interior mall stores that relied on the anchors to bring in traffic. These factors, combined with the general economic malaise that gripped the nation late in Bush's second term and throughout the Obama presidency, toppled large stores like ten-pins at a bowling tourney. In 2008 alone, six thousand recognizable chain stores went out of business, constituting the largest percentage drop in fifteen years.[94] Starbucks closed nearly one thousand stores, while Foot Locker, Home Depot, Ann Taylor, and

Zales shuttered hundreds. Circuit City went into bankruptcy; Home Depot and Kohl's announced cutbacks.

Certainly the rise of online shopping, with Amazon.com, LandsEnd .com, Teleflora.com, and individual companies such as Office Depot played an important part in the decline of bricks-and-mortar stores. Amazon dramatically cut into the profits of book sellers such as Barnes and Noble and Borders (which went out of business in 2011). According to one industry analyst, online shopping accounted for over $42 billion in Christmas sales in 2012—an increase of 14 percent over the previous period in 2011.[95] Overall, e-commerce in America topped $259 billion in 2012, up from $256 billion a year earlier. UK shoppers spent over $70 billion online.

"I Have Thrown Away My 'Red Cap'"

Recessions in America were often blamed on foreign competition, and the Americanization of the world often drifted out of view during such downturns. Japan's threat during the late 1980s largely proved hollow, except in autos and electronics, where even Japan felt powerful competition from Korea.

China found itself with enclaves of capitalism that resembled Levittown and a middle class that dreamed of moving to the suburbs and decorating their homes like "homes in the United States."[96] Retailers such as Ikea and Home Depot made impressive inroads into the Chinese market as disposable income in urban areas doubled. By the late 1990s, *BusinessWeek* touted China's "New Capitalism," which thrived "as the state sector crumbles."[97] State-owned companies made up less than half of China's economy at the end of the millennium, while more than 111,000 private enterprises, including banking, telecom, and wholesaling, took the stage. "Now I have thrown away my 'red cap,'" said one sign company president, typical of the thousands of Chinese entrepreneurs who ceased hiding their entrepreneurial status. One obstacle to further growth was that the government had started to consider ways to help, always a harbinger of increased regulation and interference. But barring such aid, villages such as Huaxi rapidly became richer: its average family assets of $150,000 (in a nation where by 2009 per capita income stood at $2,000) were a testimony to the power of capitalism. Every family had at least one car as part of the city's interest in the Huaxi Group, a "commune corporation" listed on the Chinese stock market with enterprises in steel, iron, and textiles that brought in $7.3 billion a year.[98]

At one point, China's economy was growing at a rate of 9.5 percent per

year, and it had doubled three times over in the thirty years since reform.[99]
By 2003, China was already selling the United States over $150 billion more
in goods than it bought, shipping out of Shanghai, the world's second-
busiest port. Shanghai became a largely Western city, attractive to tourists
and foreign businessmen, and the Chinese played on the appeal by building
the Grand Theater and the Shanghai Museum. Surprisingly, many of the
new investors and immigrants came from Taiwan—the so-called overseas
Chinese.

Much of China's economic miracle had its origins with the legendary
"Eighteen Farmers" in the 1970s. Fed up with collectivism, eighteen farmers desperate for a better life divided up their collective into private plots
that would have made John Smith at Jamestown beam with pride. By 1978,
they were engaging in full-scale capitalism (although the amount of land
involved was small.) The Chinese government noted that the yields from
the land soared, and Deng Xiaoping ordered comparable agreements
across the nation. Like a Chinese Declaration of Independence, the agreement of the Eighteen Farmers is now "enshrined in the Museum of the
Chinese Revolution in Beijing."[100]

Still, not all were convinced about the miracle of Chinese growth. A
report by China's own Ministry of Finance found that almost 90 percent of
the state enterprises cooked their profit and loss statements and that in fact
many were "uneconomic."[101] Subsidized overproduction of manufactured
goods accounted for, by some estimates, 2 to 3 percent of GNP, and in
2012, *Forbes* described China as "the World's Next Rust Belt," noting "the
country faces the prospect of decades of de-industrialization."[102] In the
spirit of the Chinese proverb that says "No feast lasts forever," China's
growth began to slow down. The workforce actually peaked in 2012, with
the result being the onset of higher wages. Low-wage labor had always been
China's advantage, and almost immediately, some labor-intensive garment
work began being transferred back to the United States, although most
ended up in Jordan, Honduras, El Salvador, Kenya, Egypt, and Cambodia.
But the potential for China to utterly dominate a low-wage market was un-
arguable: some eight thousand of the world's nine thousand cement producers were located in China, most under some form of government protection
against competition.[103]

China had determined over the course of two decades that its population could be a resource instead of a burden, and that in a capitalist society,
not only were more people good, but more educated people were even better. This led to the creation of hundreds of universities and research insti-

tutes, serving millions of students. However, as many as 75 percent of students left for developed countries upon graduation.[104] Most Chinese workers earned as little as $100 a month and lived in dorms, bearing no resemblance to the American middle class.[105]

AIDS presented another significant threat to Chinese growth. When AIDS was detected in the United States in the 1980s, the Chinese Ministry of Health cited it as a symptom of capitalist excesses and stated that China was immune to the disease. Early AIDS cases in China were ascribed to drug addiction, while in fact hundreds of thousands of Chinese were afflicted by selling their blood.[106] As late as 1994, AIDS remained unacknowledged in China. Henan province especially had a lucrative trade from the "blood heads" (those who sold blood routinely), with people using the proceeds to pay fines for having more than two children. Only after *The New York Times* and the French paper *Liberation* sent reporters to cover the story did Beijing ban the sale and purchase of blood.[107] As for those infected, the government finally admitted the disease existed in 2000, when it quarantined the affected areas, redrew maps without showing contaminated districts, and waited for the victims to die. China's propaganda ministry set up a story for foreign journalists that touted a tritherapy cure, and the press reported a new model cure. Chinese hospitals registered a million new AIDS patients per year, even as the government insisted there were only one million afflicted with AIDS across the entire nation. Former president Bill Clinton was allowed to visit Henan in 2005, but as part of an agreement with the Chinese government, he stayed away from photo sessions in the worst regions in return for permission to set up an anti-AIDS foundation.[108]

Façades were maintained in a number of areas in Chinese society, including in sexual relations. China in the twenty-first century seemed to remain immune to the sexual liberation movement. As late as 1990, an extramarital sexual relationship could result in prison; yet despite a public ban on prostitution, the profession was exploding. One Chinese researcher—the first sexologist in China, Pan Suiming—identified a well-defined structure in which courtesans were selected and assigned to their benefactors. Taiwanese entrepreneurs received second wives; European and American visitors were permitted higher-class call girls; and migrant workers who labored on construction sites and in factories were given unemployed peasant girls.[109] One Beijing student who worked as a prostitute joked that she was "contributing to national development," but the reality was more sobering. Nearly all of the Taiwanese males who invested in China were revealed to have had a second wife there who received a monthly allowance, and in fact she was viewed as a perk for doing business on the mainland.[110] The status of sex in the "new" China seemed a throwback to Mao's personal practices, yet without official sanction.

As for the economy, China's supposed jewel, the nation still was composed mainly of peasants who were likely to remain uneducated for some time. (By 2010, only 20 percent of Chinese university students came from rural backgrounds.) Significant productivity increases had indeed occurred in the agricultural sector by applying Western technology, but even then Chinese farm productivity remained well below that of the West. A large exodus to the cities had ensued, further distorting the numbers ("a man with a machine is more productive than a man working with a sickle," one authority noted).[111]

All that progress nevertheless left China with a per-capita income only one-twentieth of Europe's, a GDP about the size of Italy's, and an economy that had "not created any brand, innovation, or manufacturing process of world standard."[112] Capitalist progress must permit failure, and rising incomes must permit poverty: China saw 53 million people lose their jobs between 1996 and 2001, and, to adjust to the free market, the government had to fire 21 million workers in just four years.[113] The turmoil made China's population difficult to count, with more than 100 million (and perhaps 300 million) transient workers who constantly moved for work.

China had become the world's fifth nuclear power (after the United States, Soviet Union, Great Britain, and France) in 1964 when it exploded its first atomic bomb, largely due to its intelligence services' penetration of all three Western nuclear nations. After Mao's debacles in the 1960s, technology transfer from the United States became an obsession, and Chinese agents took everything not nailed down. After the fall of the Soviet Union, China took its place in espionage activities. Using the Internet, it created havoc not only hacking into U.S. government computers, but also private industry as well. In the twenty-first century, China added a new twist to ensure its technological competitiveness: American companies seeking to sell to China had to agree to three stipulations. First, sales to China had to be made through a subsidiary in China, owned at least 51 percent by Chinese. (In practice, this meant the Chinese Communist government.) Second, all technology owned by the American parent had to be transferred to the Chinese subsidiary, which would have full and unlimited rights and use of that technology. And third, the American parent had to agree to transfer all its technology in the future to the Chinese subsidiary, without limit. In effect, to do business in China meant giving away all a corporation's secrets and technology, current and future, to the Communist Chinese government. Surprisingly, many American companies agreed, notably the avionics division of General Electric and Westinghouse's nuclear power division.

Most of the goods China exported were indeed assembled there, but not designed in China. Factories in Guangdong bought cloth from the Philippines and accessories from Korea to sew American and European designs. Whereas Japan and Korea had gone through a similar phase, each had some institutions that encouraged the entrepreneurial and innovative spirit. One of the factors most retarding true productivity growth in China was that the massive population continued to flood into the factories in the reverse of the American model in the early 1800s, where the availability of land pushed up wages and forced businesses to mechanize. All the global economy did was to forge a modus operandi in which Westerners postponed demands for serious, long-term political change in return for access to markets on the backs of the Chinese peasants. Here communism and capitalism forged an alliance to oppress in the manner Marx saw as specific to the free market.

How could this occur in mainland China, when nearby Taiwan and South Korea had both made a largely successful transition to some degree of political freedom and middle-class prosperity? Both nations had a cold war imperative to liberalize, and to remain on the side of human rights and liberty to one degree or another. Taiwan never lost its civil society the way Red China had, and religion was not stifled. Some churches, particularly the Presbyterian church, toiled actively for religious and political freedoms in Taiwan (even as the Vatican deliberated over breaking diplomatic ties with Taipei to court Beijing).

The answer to the question about the different paths of Taiwan, South Korea, and China lies in the presence of property rights with titles and deeds supported by a free market in the former, and the absence of those structures in the latter. Where did one find guarantees for market safety? Certainly not in the Chinese legal system, which was unreliable; nor in intellectual property rights, which were routinely violated; nor in the tax structure, which existed at the whim of the Communist Party.

Little of this absence of market structures could be detected simply by looking at Shanghai, China's display window to the world. The city sported flashy skyscrapers, elevated roadways, lots of glass and shiny steel, all of which was intended to lure in foreign capital. Yet half of the city's 17 million inhabitants lacked proper sanitation. Intended to rival Hong Kong, Shanghai underscored China's dependence on the West. Its French-designed opera house staged imported Broadway musicals. Hong Kong's financial district vastly outstripped Shanghai's, and the Hong Kong stock market routinely won the competition with Shanghai to have stocks listed on its board. In a microcosm of Western developments, Hong Kong's assembly lines and physical production largely relocated inland, but its consulting and financial services, with their more highly educated and higher-paid workers, have continued to grow in the city.

By 2010, little hope existed of seeing a thriving middle class in China any time in the near future. Like most struggling economies, China did not have reliable property rights but rather "occupation rights" in which people could live in an apartment or operate an enterprise. Even when apartment dwellers owned space in a collective housing block, the building itself sat on land granted a limited lease by the state. For those with connections (called *guanxi*), one way to move up was by getting a loan and not paying it back, although merely obtaining such a loan involved a web of bribes and kickbacks. But the "nonrepayable" loan itself existed at the pleasure of the Communist Party, and could be withdrawn at any time.

Few experts could also deny China's environmental destruction, which by some accounts equaled 10 percent of total production value (and which, in the world of accounting, would normally be deducted from China's growth statistics). The explosion in Chinese energy production, particularly coal, contributed greatly to worldwide pollution. By 2008, China added a new coal plant every ten days—each with enough power for an American city the size of Dallas—and burned more coal every year than Japan, Europe, and the United States combined.[114] Few of these had modern scrubbers or clean-air devices. By 2010, China was on pace to account for half of global coal production and consumption, and the government even considered capping domestic output between 2011 and 2015 because of a fear the nation was running out of reserves.[115] Western intellectuals and environmental activists, however, continued to pretend that China was not the world's largest environmental problem, choosing instead to see capitalism in general and the United States in particular as the world's worst offender.

Aside from cheap goods and environmental degradation, China also was home to another growth industry, Christianity. By 2010, estimates put the number of Chinese Christians at 80 million, all meeting below the radar in "house churches" and other unsanctioned gatherings. Some predicted that within a few years, China would have more Christians than any nation on earth. In what was described as "China's 'Come to Jesus' moment," Wang Zuoan, the director of the State Administration for Religious Affairs, told a Kenyan cleric that "religion is good for development."[116] The Puritans in New England could not have said it any better.

Yet it was not only development that sparked a stirring of Christianity in China, but concerns about the nation's soul. In October 2011, in the city of Foshan, a van ran over a nine-year-old girl, then drove over her again (the driver saying he was liable for less penalty with a dead girl than an injured one). The incident ignited a firestorm of concern over China's moral compass. Business owners began to notice that Christian workers were motivated not only by positive reinforcement, but by guilt over doing a job badly: "they feel guilty," said one factory owner. "That's the difference."[117] When combined with what the Chinese viewed as the Christian underpinnings of business success, Christianity gained a foothold it had not had since the early part of the twentieth century.[118]

World of the Spirit

It appeared that China's Christianity, while more vibrant than in parts of the West, represented a small but important revival around the world. Many, if not most, formal American church organizations had hit a plateau where shrinking slowed. As in China, some of this renewed interest coincided with the rise of the "house church" as an alternative to the traditional church. George Barna's research organization found that one in five adult Americans (or, about 70 million) attended a house church at least once a month, and on a given weekend, roughly 20 million met in a house church.[119] This contention remains controversial, but certainly small, informal churches are making a comeback. Meanwhile, church attendance in England also may have bottomed out, as weekly mass attendance in the Roman Catholic Church stabilized after 2005 and even increased slightly, and likewise the Church of England saw very modest gains. Baptists in England witnessed growth, especially among young people, and one survey in 2010 showed that 63 percent of all British citizens saw themselves as Christians.[120]

The numbers also reflected the fact that Gen-Xers were more likely to adhere to religion than baby boomers.[121] Others indicated there was new interest (especially among American youth) in the Bible: one study found that young adults (eighteen to twenty-four) showed the greatest surge in Bible reading, which reached its highest level since 1995 (up to 40 percent from 31 percent). Barna found even stronger numbers, reporting that 47 percent of American adults read their Bibles at least once a week outside

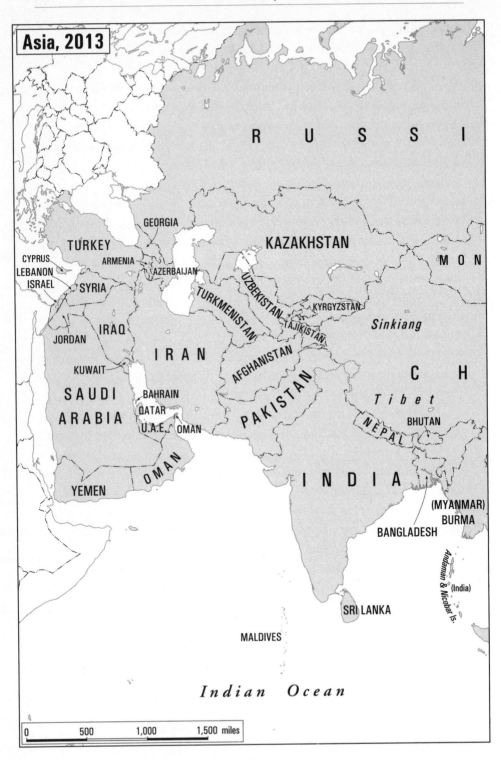

Asia, 2013

RUSSI

GEORGIA

KAZAKHSTAN

MON

TURKEY

CYPRUS
LEBANON
ISRAEL

ARMENIA

AZERBAIJAN

UZBEKISTAN

KYRGYZSTAN

SYRIA

TURKMENISTAN

TAJIKISTAN

Sinkiang

IRAQ

JORDAN

IRAN

AFGHANISTAN

C H

KUWAIT

Tibet

SAUDI
ARABIA

BAHRAIN
QATAR
U.A.E. OMAN

PAKISTAN

NEPAL

BHUTAN

YEMEN

OMAN

INDIA

(MYANMAR)
BURMA

BANGLADESH

Andaman & Nicobar Is.

(India)

SRI LANKA

MALDIVES

Indian Ocean

0   500   1,000   1,500 miles

church, and Gallup in 2000 had found that while the number of those reading the Bible had fallen since 1980, it still remained close to 60 percent.[122]

There were other, less favorable, changes occurring with American youth, however. In 2011, scientists reported that girls were maturing faster than ever, with 15 percent of U.S. females hitting puberty by age seven. Over the last thirty years, the childhood of young girls was shortened by about a year and a half.[123] These statistics hinted at profound implications in the social structure, whereby illegitimacy—especially among blacks—remained at epidemic levels. At the very time that smaller families were an economic necessity, and when single motherhood was one of the most likely predictors of poverty, girls could get pregnant easier and were sexually active sooner than ever before. Indeed, as economic conditions worsened and as the job market looked bleaker, the likelihood that even college graduates would move back in with their parents became more pronounced. By 2011, some 85 percent of college grads had returned home. For a pregnant girl, all that meant was that her mother would end up watching the child as the daughter went back into the low-wage workforce, introducing a new cycle of poverty to onetime middle-class children.[124] If the grandmother had to work as well, children were left to watch other children.

Even as prosperity drove advanced nations to smaller families, that, too, had an unwelcome side effect, for aging societies became less dynamic and innovative. No better case existed than Japan. Once feared as an invincible economic giant, by 2010 Japan prompted a *New York Times* headline that blared, "Japan Goes from Dynamic to Disheartened."[125] Japan failed to grow at all in the twenty-first century as the statist policies of the Ministry of International Trade and Industry (MITI) lost their luster. "Somewhere along the way," Mitsuo Ohashi, a Japanese businessman, commented, "Japan lost its animal spirits." But it also lost its youth, leaving an aging society to be cared for in an inverted pyramid by a shrinking number of young workers at the bottom—a fate that awaited virtually all of Europe, tempered only by immigration from Muslim states. "Japan used to be so flashy and upbeat," Ohashi observed, "but now everyone must live in a dark and subdued way."[126] In 2012, sales of adult diapers exceeded those of baby diapers.[127] In an even more bizarre turn, an increasing number of Japanese youths practiced *hikikomori*, or "pulling inward or being confined," literally retreating to their rooms for up to a decade![128] One shut-in spent his entire day in a tiny room, watching television and listening to "anything that was dark and sounded desperate."[129] Estimates were that up to 1 percent of Japan's young men were *hikikomori*. Needless to say, these men were hardly likely to find mates or reproduce. The combination of already-low birth-rates, an increasing number of Japanese single men choosing celibacy, and new surveys that showed Japanese single women preferred to stay single in overwhelming numbers, meant that Japan faced a daunting challenge in repopulating and reinvigorating itself.

Taken together, the trends in China and Japan, combined with the rising economic might of India, constituted a complex tapestry, more complicated than the mere switching of economic positions between Japan and China. In the political sphere, Japan, an ally since World War II, could usually be counted on to act in the interest of liberty and democratic government. Such was not the case with China. Its surging exports to the United States made China the single largest foreign holder of American debt—perhaps as high as $2 trillion by 2010. Not only did this make the United States vulnerable to manipulation by the Chinese, but it meant that America had little influence over the very policies she hoped to change by developing a deeper relationship. Moreover, if anything occurred that caused China to rethink its position as lender, it could instantly cause the value of American government securities to plummet by dumping them on the open market.

Anything that placed still more debt in China's hands constituted a grave threat to American national security. Yet from 2000 to 2012—and especially in the administration of Barack Obama—U.S. debt levels shot up, surging past $1 trillion a year. After one year in office, Obama's annual deficits exceeded the entire federal debt only a decade earlier, and with no end in sight. Far from seeking to redress the situation, Obama deepened the hole with unprecedented levels of spending. The struggling U.S. economy had not seen its troubles start under Obama, but he made matters dramatically worse.

No Money Down

In 2008, George W. Bush played out his string as the lamest of ducks. His popularity hovered at barely 30 percent, and his party was given the boot from its majorities in both houses of Congress in 2006. The Republicans had squandered their mandate by spending like Democrats. First came a new Medicare prescription drug benefit that polls showed few people wanted, which added a half-trillion dollars to the deficit. Next, Bush sought a marginal improvement in the Social Security system by privatizing an infinitesimal portion of the individual's contribution, but the Democrats promised to block that, and it went nowhere. Then Bush, McCain, and other Republicans had supported the new amnesty bill for illegals.

The final nail in the Republicans' coffin involved the collapse of the housing bubble in 2007–8, which had its roots in several flawed behaviors by government, banks, and homeowners. First and foremost, for almost twenty years the federal government had made it a goal to encourage everyone to own a home, whether they were creditworthy or not. Federal Reserve policy underwrote this by keeping interest rates artificially low for several years of the first decade of the century, encouraging a "house flipping" mentality in which people purchased homes not primarily to live in but to speculate on. Not all markets acted the same, but in particularly hot markets, such as California, Arizona, Virginia, and Las Vegas, home prices soared. In San Mateo, California, housing prices rose at a rate of $2,000 a *day*; the 2006 median home price in California for a 1,600-square-foot home was $561,000.[130] Average home prices rose nationwide at a strong 13 percent a year clip, but in certain spots, such as Arizona, it was not uncommon to see one's home triple in value over a year.

Rising home values led to a second behavior, in which homeowners, thinking their home values would go nowhere but up, borrowed against their equity for vacations, cars, or appliances, ratcheting up their overall housing debt. Houses became big-ticket ATMs. Government also insisted on peddling houses to low-income borrowers who had no capability to repay their loans. As early as 1995, regulators strong-armed banks into making a requisite number of affordable housing loans to minorities. To make the application forms fit even new, flexible bank requirements, bankers contorted the loans further through interest-only loans and no-down-payment loans. Representative Barney Frank and Senator Christopher Dodd, both long-serving Democrats from New England, were especially culpable in loosening standards through two government-created, privately owned institutions, Fannie Mae (the Federal National Mortgage Association) and Freddie Mac (the Federal Home Loan Mortgage Corporation). These lenders bought mortgages from the commercial and mortgage banks at an increasingly voracious level: in 2004, Fannie and Freddie had gobbled up *one trillion dollars' worth of subprime mortgages*, holding at some point up to two thirds of all mortgages and becoming the largest holders of junk debt in the United States.

Inevitably, the housing market turned down. This began in 2007 as foreclosure rates leaped 87 percent over the previous year. California saw fantastic drops: the average home price fell $100,000 in a single year. Freddie and Fannie, who held many of these bad loans, found themselves in need of a bailout but so did many large investment banks, including JPMorgan Chase, Wells Fargo, AIG, Bank of America, Lehman Brothers, and others. Bush's economic advisers, including Treasury Secretary Henry Paulson and Fed chairman Ben Bernanke, informed him that if more of the investment banks failed like Bear Stearns and Lehman Brothers did, another Great Depression would ensue. Calling it a "breathtaking intervention in the free market," Bush nevertheless approved of the Troubled Asset Relief Program (TARP) to pour $700 billion into the banking sector.[131] Echoing FDR, he would later write, "It flew against all my instincts . . . [but] it was necessary to pull the country out of the panic. I decided the only way to preserve the free market in the long run was to intervene in the short run."[132] Some argued it worked: there were no massive bank runs. Others argued the bank runs never would have occurred anyway, and that taxpayers were stuck now with monstrously large bills. Far from giving Bush credit for preserving the free market, as Bush thought he had done, Democratic candidate Barack Obama campaigned against the incumbent for his actions and continued to do so four years after Bush left office.

"It's Not About Me"

Republicans suffered a shellacking at the hands of Barack Obama and the Democrats, which allowed the new administration to exploit the chaos to advance still more big government schemes. And few other candidates in American history were as radical—and hid their radical character so well—as Barack Hussein Obama.

Obama, whose place of birth continued to be questioned in lawsuits two years after his election, was born to a Kenyan father and an American mother. His father and his mother's parents were all Communists, as was his primary mentor, Frank Marshall Davis. As a child (then going by Barry Soetoro), he lived in Indonesia, where he attended public and Catholic schools in Jakarta, and Hawaii, where he attended private schools, became heavily involved with drugs, and graduated from high school with a very undistinguished record. Obama moved to Los Angeles and attended Occidental College for two years, earning mediocre grades and continuing his radical and Communist associations before transferring to Columbia University, where he was a virtual ghost. Almost none of his classmates recalled seeing him or meeting him. In 1985, after college, he moved to Chicago to take a job as a community organizer before his admittance to Harvard Law School, where he was the first black president of the *Harvard Law Review* although he never actually wrote anything for the publication. Obama left few footprints and made even fewer friends. (Those he did make, such as terror-bomber Bill Ayers and the radical preacher Jeremiah Wright, Obama later attempted to discard.) The *Law Review* position did land him a lucrative book contract for a memoir/biography, *Dreams from My Father* (1995), a work laced with racial grievances. He worked as a lawyer in Chicago representing slum landlords before running for the Illinois state senate in 1996.

In the state senate, his most common vote was "present" (to avoid taking a stand on controversial issues), and on this record, he ran for the U.S. Senate seat in 2006. Except for his congressional primary race against Democratic incumbent Bobby Rush, Obama either was able to get his opponents removed from the ballot through some legal pretense, or his opponent's campaign was efficiently derailed. During the 2004 Illinois senate election, the sealed divorce records of his opponent, Jack Ryan (married to the actress Jeri Ryan, known best for her *Star Trek* role as Seven of Nine), which involved a sex scandal, were "unsealed" by the Obama-friendly media. (Obama was careful never to actually have to campaign against a serious candidate except Rush, when he lost badly.) A humiliated Ryan left the race shortly thereafter, leaving the Republicans to hastily find a replacement, and Obama won easily. Protected, coddled, and groomed, Obama gave the keynote speech in the 2004 Democratic National Convention, at which time it was apparent he would be running for president in the near future. Few, however, expected him to successfully challenge Hillary Clinton for the nomination in 2008. Clinton, although considered the overwhelming favorite not only for the nomination but for the presidency, carried the anchor of her pro-war vote on Iraq in 2003. That vote sent the far left wing of the Democratic Party into hysterical fits of opposition.

Neither Hillary nor, after her defeat in the primaries, the woefully inept Republican nominee John McCain enjoyed the fawning, even "slobbering" media love heaped on Obama.[133] McCain's campaign manager specifically instructed his staff not to attack Obama out of fear of racism charges. Briefly, McCain's firebrand vice presidential nominee, Sarah Palin, the governor of Alaska, launched some verbal missiles, to no avail. The press covered up for Obama—his origins, his education, and most of all, his worldview—more than it ever had forty years earlier with JFK's sexual dalliances, which were of far lesser import.

Because of his race and youth, the world greeted him as a messiah as well. His July 2008 speech at Berlin's Victory Column brought out thousands (with the promise of a rock concert to occur afterward). Officially titled "A World That Stands as One," the speech laid out a dark vision of America as usurper and polluter. Obama subscribed without hesitation to the flawed (and many would say, fraudulent) notion of global warming, stating that "cars in Boston and factories in Beijing are melting the ice caps in the Arctic, shrinking coastlines in the Atlantic, and bringing drought to farms from Kansas to Kenya."[134] In what became the first of many "apology" speeches, Obama noted Americans had "made our share of mistakes, and there are times when our actions around the world have not lived up to our best intentions." The Europeans ate it up, praising Obama as visionary and bold. Only two years later, *Der Spiegel* would reassess him, calling him "cold, arrogant and elitist."[135]

Virtually no reporters seriously questioned his affiliations with the terrorist Ayers, his twenty-year tutelage under the radical Wright (who preached that America deserved the 9/11 attacks and was the "U.S. of KKK A"), his pampered college career, or his Communist background and associations. Journalists disregarded his utter absence of foreign policy experience, let alone ideas, and his track record as a freshman senator (who spent less than two years in the Upper Chamber before devoting himself to campaigning for president) was nearly nonexistent and entirely undecipherable. He strongly criticized detaining prisoners at Guantánamo Bay (but later would perpetuate that policy), insisted the United States should immediately pull out of Iraq (and later rescinded that idea), and intoned that terrorists should be dealt with in the U.S. legal system (and changed that tune in a hurry as well). Rather, he framed his entire campaign around broad and meaningless slogans: "hope," "change you can believe in," and above all, youthful grandiose phrases such as "yes we can."

Obama dwelled endlessly on himself. In his first eight months in office, he gave 41 major speeches (far more than most presidents) in which he referred to himself almost 1,200 times.[136] During a visit to Ohio in January 2010, where he supposedly was touting his new jobs program, he "referred to himself no fewer than 132 times and, in the same speech, had the unwittingly humorous audacity to proclaim, 'It's not about me.'"[137] The media played along, giving him more favorable coverage than Bush and Clinton put together in his first months: *Time* magazine placed him on half its covers after November 2008, while *Newsweek* put him on 12 of 52 covers. Even a liberal radio host was taken aback by the West Wing "shrine" to Obama, his pictures covering the walls, one after another.[138] Aides referred to the new president as "Black Jesus." One voter gushed about how he would pay her mortgage out of his "stash." Elementary school children were directed to sing songs about him, clapping and snapping their fingers in rhythm: "Bar-ack Hus-sein O-bam-a . . . um, um, um."[139]

In many ways, however, Obama continued the all-too-common career path of those in government who never held a responsible job in a profit-making company (other than being a slumlord lawyer). At least George Bush had been president of a baseball team, but neither Hillary Clinton (except for the Rose law firm in Little Rock), nor Bill (outside of teaching at the University of Arkansas very briefly), nor Al Gore nor John Kerry—other recent contenders for the presidency—had ever worked in the private sector. To them, the process of meeting payrolls, the burden of taxes, and the necessity to make a profit in order to stay in business were entirely foreign. Obama reinforced this trend with his cabinet appointments, of whom only 11 percent had ever worked in a real business—the lowest percentage of any president in history. When he drew up a "Jobs Panel" to advise him on how to create jobs, not one of the members had ever worked in the private sector or created a job. All were political hacks, bureaucrats, or academics.

Only the so-called new media outlets, including Rush Limbaugh's hugely popular talk radio show and its imitators, the Fox News television channel, and the Internet provided a counterweight to the liberal dominance of information. And it was indeed a formidable liberal alliance that included all the major broadcast networks and CNN, the printed press (especially *The New York Times* and *The Washington Post*), and the fast-disappearing news magazines, such as *Time* and *Newsweek*.

There was, however, another set of new media in play that distinctly favored Obama, namely the social networking media of YouTube, Facebook, and Twitter. These demanded active participation by the candidate, and unlike ABC or CBS News, were costless in monetary terms but not in time and effort. The Obama campaign engaged these outlets heavily. According to Jason Mattera, by election day Obama had 2.3 million Facebook friends, McCain, 622,000. The Obama campaign Web site had four times as many visitors as McCain's and had posted six times as many campaign-made videos to YouTube; and in the number of views of videos mentioned online about either candidate, Obama had a lead of *300 million*.[140] Obama had 125,000 Twitter followers to McCain's 5,300, while in the number of online references to the campaign's voter contact operation Obama had a staggering 479,000 to 325 lead. Daytime television's dominant diva, Oprah Winfrey, worked hard for Obama; economists, analyzing sales of the Oprah

Book Club selections of his book and subscriptions to her magazine *O*, "estimated she captured about 1 million additional votes for Obama in the primary election."[141]

With only the new media to expose Obama's radicalism, and with the latent white guilt of so many Americans who wanted the race issue resolved once and for all in the manner of Martin Luther King's "content of their character" goal, Obama cruised to an easy victory with a nine million popular vote advantage, and the Democrats attained a filibuster-proof Senate to go along with their large majority in the House. Blacks voted in high numbers, and for the first time ever, the youth vote came out in force for the Democrats.[142]

As FDR had half a century earlier, Obama had a blank check to do what he wanted. Americans expected change, which meant to them an economic turnaround and a resolution to the war on terror, but also some relief to falling home prices. Moreover, a deeper concern that jobs were going overseas and that the United States did not manufacture things anymore underlay the anxiety that elected Obama. Rarely mentioned in the campaign, however, had been the free spending that had doomed the Republicans in 2006 and which the Democrats now planned to accelerate. TARP could be charged to Bush—even though Obama and McCain both endorsed it—but immediately upon taking office Obama and the Democrats rammed through a Keynesian-style stimulus bill so laden with pet projects that it became known as the "porkulus." Obama promised "shovel ready" jobs, of which few materialized. Most of the money went to favored companies such as Solyndra and other "green" firms, or to preserving government jobs at the expense of the private sector or union jobs at higher costs than more lower-paying nonunion jobs. Every government job created or saved was another drain on the private sector, and actually decreased jobs overall. But they did generate more debt. Deficits swelled with each new expenditure, and by the end of Obama's first year, the annual budget deficit exceeded $1 trillion. Meanwhile, TARP regulations essentially forgave many people their mortgages in addition to sending huge amounts of money to foreign banks.

Tea, Anyone?

Then, one of those seemingly insignificant incidents took place that shook the nation. During the broadcast of a cable news business show from the floor of the Chicago Mercantile Exchange in February 2009, a reporter named Rick Santelli burst into a tirade about how Americans were tired of paying other people's defaulted mortgages, and that perhaps it was time for a new "tea party." Cheering broke out on the floor of the exchange.

His rant went viral in the new media, with Fox News and the radio talk shows (particularly Rush Limbaugh, with his audience of 20 million) all replaying his phrases constantly—not to mention the huge Internet attention his speech received. Overnight, massive protests erupted, coinciding with Tax Day (April 15—when taxes were paid, not "Tax Freedom Day," a month later, when Americans had finished working for the government for the year and began working for themselves). At parks and courthouses and gymnasiums across the country, hundreds of thousands of people of all political stripes turned out to launch the new Tea Party, with "TEA" standing for Taxed Enough Already. Instead of operating like one of the two established parties, the Tea Party movement, while nominally independent, nevertheless focused its main energy on recapturing the Republican Party for conservatism and educating citizens. For the first time in generations, Americans became avid readers of the Constitution. *Atlas Shrugged* and *The Road to Serfdom* shot to the top of the bestseller lists.

Initially and predictably dismissed by the chattering classes, the Tea Party movement grew throughout 2009, especially as the Democrats continued spending, worsening economic conditions. Free-market economists had predicted a souring economy. The stimulus passed in early 2009 stimulated only more unemployment, leaving the private sector with 2.6 million *fewer* jobs, contrasted with the Bush administration's record of 6 million net new jobs, or Reagan's great legacy of 14 million. Federal employment, however, rose, as did federal spending per U.S. household, to over $12,000 more than pre-Obama levels.[143] Worse still, government intervention doused investor and entrepreneurial ardor, provoking a capital strike. Although the Fed tamped interest rates down to almost zero, no one wanted to borrow money. New factory building halted. In scenes reminiscent of the Great Depression, the wealthy had money but weren't spending it. Even the upper middle class that had spent lavishly on clothes, entertainment, and vacations now curtailed their expenses except for investments in gold and other precious metals. No one created jobs with supply-side investment, and unemployment hovered at 10 percent (the official rate) or the estimated unemployment/underemployment (and discouraged worker) rate of over 24 percent.

In fact, the government rapidly deleted workers from the workforce to keep the unemployment percentage halfway reasonable, and by 2012, 5.6 million workers had been erased from the official compilation. Although the Congressional Budget Office estimated in 2011 that the stimulus had saved or created 500,000 to 3.3 million jobs, such a wide gap between the two numbers meant that the government essentially had no idea how many, if any, jobs had been created or saved. One fourth to one third of American workers were either unemployed, discouraged, underemployed, or had dropped out of the workforce.

Obama's signature issue was a nationalized health care program based on failed European models, and it was extremely unpopular. Hillary Clinton had been crushed by her attempt to nationalize health care, but Obama now had a much more radical Congress at his beck and call. Many congressmen acknowledged they would lose their seats if they voted for Obamacare, but ideologically the program constituted a once-in-a-lifetime opportunity to expand government, and they committed political hara-kiri. Yet as it marched through the congressional committees, the bill steadily gained opposition, and was more unpopular by 2012 than when it was passed.[144]

Despite Obama's claims that the monstrosity was anything other than a single-payer nationalized system, he was already on record as favoring "single-payer universal health care."[145] Employing transparent bribes reminiscent of FDR's use of New Deal money to secure reelection, Obama got the necessary votes. But knowing how unpopular the legislation was, during the deliberation period, legislators hid from constituents, barred entry to opponents in town meetings, and ducked public appearances. Over the next two years, hundreds of companies (most of them Democrat favorites), several states, and, of course, the unions would all receive waivers from having to participate in Obamacare.

No aspect of American life seemed outside the grasp of the U.S. government. General Motors, the flagging auto giant, neared bankruptcy during the Bush administration. Bush told president-elect Obama he "wouldn't let the automaker fail," and backed a massive $50 billion loan/bailout plan.[146] Chrysler, also struggling, wanted money too. Under the guise of saving jobs, the bailout passed Congress in the spring of 2009, whereupon the two auto companies closed 2,500 dealerships (some based on politics) and eliminated 100,000 jobs. Obama claimed he had "no interest [in] running GM," but at the time he said that, he had already called the mayor of Detroit to assure him that GM would be headquartered there, pressured GM to eliminate its GMC truck brand (one of its most profitable lines), forced out the GM CEO Rick Wagoner, and bossed Chrysler around in the same vein.[147] Back in the heyday of sixties student activism, actor Peter Coyote complained that the protest movement was ineffectual because "the country has become the equivalent of fascist. It's General Motors Fascism," he said. It was ironic that a radical liberal, Barack Obama, actually produced "General Motors Fascism" by nationalizing the car giant in 2009 and giving ownership preference to its union.[148]

The GM bailout joined the stimulus bill and TARP as the focus of Tea Party ire. By the time the Tea Party had mobilized in April 2009, it had gained the momentum of a tidal wave. On tax day, April 15, rallies across the country—virtually all of them spontaneous and springing up without any support from the established Republican Party (sometimes actually in spite of the traditional party)—stunned the news media with their turnout and enthusiasm. Cities across the country saw rallies drawing giant crowds. Many of the attendees had never engaged in political action before.

"Liberty Groups" quickly formed to follow up with change at the polls in 2010, mobilizing quickly enough to affect the Republican primaries and give conservative candidates victories. Tea Parties then followed up the primary victories with successful general election efforts, reclaiming the House and replacing moderate Republicans with much more conservative individuals. They came up short, however, in capturing the Senate, and thus for two years the Senate successfully blocked all House legislation and refused to even pass a (constitutionally required) budget.

Apologizing for Liberty

When not attempting to remake the U.S. economy along socialist models, Obama used foreign trips as a platform to criticize the United States, its past, and, in his view, its legacy of racism. These apology tours continued his comments from the 2008 Berlin speech.

Obama also minimized or ridiculed American exceptionalism. A June 2009 Cairo address designed to soften America's image in the Islamic world included Obama's homage to "civilization's debt to Islam." The Islamic religion, he told the audience, "is not part of the problem in combating violent extremism," despite the fact that the overwhelming majority of terrorist incidents in the previous thirty years had been committed by Muslims with little response from so-called mainstream Islamic clerics.[149] His outreach to the Islamic world had little effect, and indeed one could hardly tell the difference in Muslim reaction between Obama and the much-hated George W. Bush. Pew polling in February 2009 showed that only 15 percent of Palestinians had a favorable view of the United States; even after the Cairo speech, only 27 percent were favorable. In Pakistan, negative perceptions of the United States *rose* during Obama's first year in office.[150]

Recounting America's sins did not end with the Islamic world. As apologist-in-chief, Obama told the G20 meeting in London, "You're starting to see some restoration of America's standing in the world."[151] The United States, he told the French, had been "arrogant," "dismissive," and "derisive." He repeated the charges later in Trinidad, claiming the United States had been "dictatorial" and "disengaged," and apologized to Mexican president Felipe Calderón for Arizona's attempt to control rampant crime and illegal immigration.[152] As with the Muslim populations, the apologies netted scorn rather than goodwill, and indicated a lack of conviction about America's significance in the world on the president's part. British newspapers condemned his "rudeness" and "appalling" behavior during the visit of Prime Minister Gordon Brown in March 2009. French resident Nicolas Sarkozy, humiliated when the Obamas declined his dinner invitation, soon described him as naive and inexperienced—but then Obama also snubbed German chancellor Angela Merkel, so Sarkozy was not alone.[153] Sarkozy later mocked Obama's address to the United Nations as foolish and unrealistic. When it came to Obama's view of Iran, the French president described it as "utterly immature" and called Obama "arrogant."[154] As if to underscore the phrase, the New Delhi *Sunday Pioneer* labeled Obama "arrogant" and "abrasive," reserving his "acid tongue for those . . . considered close allies of the U.S."[155] And where Obama had most focused his rhetoric—the Middle East—his approval numbers fell lower than George Bush's, to an astonishingly low 16 percent, according to Pew.[156] Even some of Obama's allies began to desert him. Mort Zuckerman, one of his staunchest press pals, observed that in the previous months, Obama had come across "as a young man in a grown-up's game—impressive but not presidential . . . managing American policy at home and American power abroad with disturbing amateurishness."[157]

Through all his apologies, Obama reflected an anti-Americanism that rested on the "singular idea that something associated with the United States, something at the core of American life, [was] deeply wrong and threatening to the rest of the world."[158] This anti-Americanism had a long, lamentable history. The very term highlighted a stunning reality, that *no one* spoke of "Venezuelanization," "Sovietization," or "New Zealandization," or even "Arabization." Indeed, no country, reaching as far back as Rome, has been so conflated with a group of values (or perceived flaws) as the United States. It all came back to the four pillars of American exceptionalism, which neither Obama nor most Democrats (and many Republicans) wanted to genuinely address.

Others joined Obama in criticizing America, claiming the United States was obsessed with materialism and practicality and thus deserved some of the tragedies that had struck. Much earlier the disciples of Friedrich Nietzsche, including Arthur Moeller Van den Bruck, for example, complained that everything in America was practical and standardized—"the national Taylor system."[159] Certainly one could accuse Americans throughout their history of being practical—everything from their language to their cooking to their shopping testified to that trait. Yet it was not pragmatism that drew legions of immigrants to American shores; people around the world were attracted to the concepts of freedom and liberty. That didn't stop intellectuals such as Martin Heidegger from insisting as early as 1935 that, from "a metaphysical point of view, Russia and America are the same, with the same dreary technological frenzy and the same unrestricted organization of the average man."[160] The moral equivalence of a murderous dictatorial regime and a representative democracy was therefore established even before World War II. Holding such views was not unique to the Europeans, nor to intellectuals. President Jimmy Carter, in his famous "malaise" speech of July 15, 1979, had scolded his fellow citizens, "all the legislation in the world can't fix *what's wrong* with America" (emphasis ours).[161]

The Tea Party wasn't upset with America, only its leaders in government. This was a strong reaction to America's drift into debt and nonsuperpower status that had propelled the new political movement—a self-correction the American system always seemed to produce when absolutely necessary. Nor had Americans entirely lost confidence in the United States as an ideal. On the World Values Survey, for example, Americans ranked well near the top of eighty countries in the category of "happiness." The overall happiness of the American public continued to surprise pundits.[162] (As one might possibly expect, significant majorities of people in North Africa and the Islamic world were dissatisfied with their lives.)[163] The old maxim that money can't buy happiness was certainly true as far as it went, but the evidence was also overwhelming that more prosperous nations with higher standards of living scored higher on almost every measure of "happiness." One obvious reason was that nations achieved prosperity *because of* systems of trust and a responsible legal structure.

Federal deficits and debt seemed to be the elephant in the room, particularly entitlements, which rotted every aspect of American society. A 2008 study of trends in leisure found, not surprisingly, that there had been an increase in Americans' leisure time since 1965 and that the largest increase came among the poor and less educated, contributing to the growing inequality gap.[164] In Obama's first term, food stamp use rose to record levels while the number of people receiving some form of government income reached nearly 50 percent. Entitlements drove debt far more than the military expenditures so frequently cited by the Left.

One of the most critical ongoing debilitating traits of the chronic unemployment under Obama was the "mancession"—the dramatic plunge in employment among men sixteen and over. Since 1995, following a steady climb upward from the Reagan years, men had been employed at levels of almost 70 percent. But beginning in 2007, male employment fell to barely over 60 percent. Much of this was due to the perpetual extension of unemployment benefits, which Democrats insisted created jobs. With so many men paid not to work, it was not surprising that they accepted that option in record numbers. Added to that was an epidemic of "disability" among working-age men, who, as Charles Murray pointed out, could be found doing any number of strenuous and high-risk activities outside the workforce. To many observers, it seemed that Max Weber's Protestant work ethic had become a thing of the past.

Yet there was a staggering caveat to all this, in that for more than thirty years, despite fostering social pathologies, including sloth, dependence, family breakup, and illegitimacy, the warnings about America's debt crisis had not produced any noticeable *financial* effects. This was especially true when it came to the monetarist warnings of inflation: from 2001 to 2012, inflation remained extremely low and interest rates hovered at near-record low levels. Home mortgages could be acquired at 4 percent or even less; auto loans at 5 percent.

Explanations included the "deflation" theory—that the United States after the housing bust had seen such dramatic declines in asset values that the nation was still teetering on deflation. Another theory held that China was absorbing all the American debt, and once the Chinese decided further acquisitions were too risky, they would cease and interest rates would skyrocket. Or, alternatively, if China's economy slowed down, there would be no place to put U.S. debt. All of these explanations had some validity, but the most obvious answer was that however poor the state of the American economy, almost everyone else's was worse by 2012.

Additionally, Americans no longer responded to the Puritan ethic of thrift and not borrowing money. And—despite claims of moral collapse—these attitudes were not new. Consumer credit, available since the early 1800s, had transformed the mercantile business of Lewis Tappan into the credit reporting firm of Dun & Bradstreet; Cyrus McCormick sold reapers for a down payment of $35 and $90 due after harvest; Singer offered terms in 1856; and the per capita debt level of Americans rose every year after 1896. Total debt in the 1920s doubled, and accelerated rapidly in the 1980s and 1990s.[165] Earlier Americans had moved heaven and earth to pay what they owed and maintain good credit; now they looked increasingly to the government to provide for them.

Whether it was fast food or faith, the rest of the world looked more like America than America looked like it, even after millions of immigrants came ashore. Where American youth still wore Che Guevara T-shirts—designed in America, almost certainly produced in Mexico, China, or Vietnam—few knew who he was, or what he stood for. As music critic Peter Doggett complained, Che "was nothing more potent or threatening than an outlaw symbol, removed from the class-warfare milieu that he had inhabited."[166] English had become the global language, in large part because of the Americanization of products (Xerox, Coke, Starbucks, which became synonymous with copying a document, soft drinks, and coffee). A utilitarian core of about 1,500 English words were used by Asians, Latinos, Africans, and Anglo-Europeans, and while some referred to the international dialect as "globish," in reality it was "Americanish."[167]

All this returns us to the "Clash of Civilizations."[168] Samuel Huntington decried the declining influence of the West, brought about in large part by the West's new universalist principles that themselves posed a threat to the Islamic world and China. The survival of the West, he wrote in his book, *The Clash of Civilizations and the Remaking of the World* (1996), depended on "Americans reaffirming their Western identity and Westerners accepting their civilization as unique and universal. . . ."[169] Arguing that for the first time in history, political confrontations had become both multipolar and multicivilizational, Huntington warned that the major threats to world peace would come from intercivilizational clashes between (mostly) either the West and the Sino-Asian civilization; the West and Islam; or Islam and the Asian groups. Or, as he bluntly put it, "the fault lines between civilizations will be the battle lines of the future."[170]

Arab Spring, Bitter Winter

Cross-cultural conflict with Islam was inevitable. Liberals, however, pointed to so-called moderate Arabs who were largely westernized—just like us, but in kaffiyehs and veils. All it took, according to that interpretation of Islam, was for the moderates to rise up and overthrow the fundamentalists and dictators.

On December 17, 2010, the hopes of such an uprising seemed to be taking shape as waves of demonstrations began to sweep Tunisia, Egypt, Libya, Yemen, and other parts of the Islamic world. While protests had been building, especially in Algeria and the western Sahara, the spark that ignited the flames came when a Tunisian named Mohamed Bouazizi, an out-of-work fruit seller, had his products seized by the government. Bouaziz set himself aflame in protest. The following day, Tunisia was rocked with unrest, whereupon its president, Zine El Abidine Ben Ali, abdicated and fled to Saudi Arabia.

In February, similar large protests hit Egypt, focused in Tahrir Square in Cairo. The protesters forced the resignation of Egyptian president Hosni Mubarak. Egyptian protests were fomented largely by "a surprisingly small clique of young bloggers and activists . . . under the age of thirty. . . ."[171] Youth agitation in Islamic countries was not unusual, given that younger people were a decisive majority in all twenty-two Arab countries—in Egypt the median age was twenty-four, and in Gaza and Yemen it was eighteen. Like Egypt, Yemen also witnessed a quasi-voluntary resignation in which the president, Ali Abdullah Saleh, turned power over to Abd al-Rab Mansur al-Hadi in exchange for a deal to avoid jail. In one of the most stunning developments in the region, Libyan strongman Muammar Gaddafi was forced out in August 2011 and was killed in October by rebels. In almost every major Islamic nation, demonstrations forced reorganizations of governments, dismissals of ministers, "voluntary" retirement of leaders in office, or other major political changes.

Yet the Arab Spring—supposedly a time when more liberal, freedom-loving governments would replace the old dictatorships—fizzled rapidly. Egypt was the worst case, where strongman Mubarak was replaced by a government headed by Mohamed Morsi, with ties to the Muslim Brotherhood (an al-Qaeda-like group). The Muslim Brotherhood's motto was "Allah is our objective; the Quran is our law, the Prophet is our leader; Jihad is our way; and death for the sake of Allah is the highest of aspirations." It sought to install Sharia law in all Islamic countries, and hoped to inspire a "millions of martyrs march toward Jerusalem."[172] It did not take long for many Egyptians to realize that they had merely traded a secular dictator for a theocracy.[173] Christianity, of course, was the hardest hit by the revolts. A study by the think tank Civitas in 2012 warned that Christianity was "close to extinction" in the Middle East and that persecution around the world—but especially in the Middle East and Africa—had increased.[174]

Many searching for moderate Islamic reformation pointed to Islamic youth, who they hoped would resemble Western younger generations and demand liberalization. In fact, Islamic youth were in the forefront of terror, jihad, and persecution. While this was often explained in terms of unemployment or poor education, aforementioned studies of terrorists found no shortage of well-off or highly educated young people active in terrorist cells.

Speaking Truth to Youth

If Islamic youth were susceptible to the call of the madrassas, Western—and especially American—generations born after 1960 had gone through much different changes. Generation X, the generation born after the baby boom, had witnessed the longest period of sustained economic expansion in the history of the United States—largely attributable to almost ten years of low taxes under Reagan and Bush. It was a generation tempered by rapid change, and the varying importance of large social issues. Yet it was also a generation filled with hypocrisy, especially among the wealthy and the celebrities, who lectured the public about global warming while flying across the country in private jets to luncheons. A more heterogeneous generation, Gen X did not appreciate the necessity of Americanizing immigrants or of a common cultural heritage. They were also the first generation since 1900 to earn less than their fathers—significantly less. Various think tanks produced policy papers assuring Gen-Xers that it was acceptable.[175]

Those in the successor generation, Generation Y (or Millennials), born starting in the 1980s, have experienced higher birthrates than originally estimated.[176] Neither generation had the likelihood of doing as well as their parents, but Y was decidedly more interested in becoming wealthy, and far less concerned with the environment or "developing a meaningful philosophy of life."[177] They also were much better educated, but had far fewer jobs.

The continued Obama recession took a deep toll on the voters who supported Obama the most. Gen-Y professionals saw a yawning earnings and employment gap between themselves and their parents, and dimmed hopes for a brighter future.[178] Although they did not blame Obama, their attitudes correlated with overall historic levels of negativity toward the U.S. government. In September 2011, Gallup found that 81 percent of Americans were dissatisfied with government, while trust and confidence in those in political office fell dramatically.[179] In 2010, Social Security ran a deficit for the first time since 1982, but even before, polls of younger people found that more were likely to believe in UFOs than to think they would ever receive a Social Security check.[180]

Yet Gen-X and Gen-Y Americans continued to support Obama and the Democrat Party, especially on social issues. But even on economic issues, everything was not as it seemed, for the crushing levels of debt the nation faced were not viewed as a problem for a generation who "actually [felt] empowered by their credit card and education debts." One researcher concluded, "Young people seem to view debt mostly in just positive terms than as a potential burden."[181] Oddly, young adults received a boost of self-esteem from debt. Moreover, when Obama repeatedly promised to address the "student aid problem," it meant to younger generations that they would not have to pay off their student loans after all.

Perhaps not surprising, the Age of Entitlement had produced a generation of kids who thought themselves "more special than *ever*" (emphasis in original), according to the UK *Mail*. An analysis of American college freshmen who came into college in 2012 revealed that no matter their ability (or lack thereof), the students were more likely to think of themselves as "special" or "gifted" than any generation yet recorded.[182] The study found a 20 percent rise in narcissism—the highest since 1979—and, drawing on a 2006 study, warned that "ambition inflation" (in which students have unrealistic expectations) had led to an increase in anxiety and depression.

Still, the future looked anything but bright based on the last twenty years for those teenagers and young adults. A certain hopelessness and cynicism descended over an entire generation, which could be seen in part in the obsession with the celebrity culture—not just in America, but around the world. Average (and under-average) youth, possessing a desperate desire to become celebrities, elevated shows such as *American Idol* and *Keeping Up with the Kardashians* to top ratings. Man-on-the-street interviews showed more people could name stars of a reality show than a member of the U.S. Supreme Court, and entertainment channels such as E! perpetuated the notion that being a celebrity was a talent unto itself. Amid this culture—where Prince William was featured on the cover of every magazine, or where YouTube videos made instant stars out of people such as Justin Bieber—a disturbing dark side arose.

Murderers Stalk America

Beginning in 1999 with the Columbine High School massacre, this maelstrom of omnipresent uncertainty, family breakdown, the expulsion of religion, and the possibility of eternal life through celebrity status manifested itself. Two teen malcontents, seeking (as they wrote in their journal entries) to "outdo" the Oklahoma City bombing and the Waco siege, killed thirteen (mostly teenagers) and injured twenty-four others.[183] While some pointed to bullying of the pair by others as the cause of the spree, the killers did not specifically target those who had bullied them, but rather murdered people randomly. A similar scene was repeated at Virginia Tech University in 2007 when Seung-Hui Cho killed thirty-two people and wounded seventeen. The mentally ill Cho had already been ordered to treatment, which, of course, he avoided. In his suicide note, he expressed his hatred of the rich and, according to the Virginia Tech Review Panel, he immersed himself in a fantasy in which "he would be remembered as the savior of the oppressed, the downtrodden, the poor, and the rejected."[184]

In Cho's case—as in the case of the killer who marched into a Connecticut elementary school and gunned down twenty-six people, mostly children, in December 2012—there was another factor at work: mental illness. The U.S. Supreme Court (*O'Connor v. Donaldson*, 1975) had deinstitutionalized mentally ill people who were deemed nondangerous and capable of surviving by themselves. This made it almost impossible to keep truly dangerous lunatics off the streets until they committed a heinous act, because, after all, merely saying "dangerous" things could be dismissed as imagination or pretending. A renewed, but somewhat muffled, discussion of how to deal with the mentally ill was revived, but largely buried under calls for more gun control laws. Of the many spree shootings that had occurred since 1990, however, most had been stopped by an armed civilian or when the perpetrator killed himself upon the arrival of armed police. The difference in fatalities between civilian and police action, however, was stunning. In almost a dozen cases where an armed civilian stopped the assailant, an average of just over two people died; when victims had to wait for the police, the number of fatalities skyrocketed to over twelve.

These kinds of statistics did not concern the media or the Democrat Party, both of which went on a frenetic crusade in 2012 to eliminate firearms. Yet the actual number of mass killings had declined since widespread use of "concealed carry" laws in the various states, and homicide rates, which rose after gun control laws were enacted in the mid-1960s, fell sharply after concealed carry permits were enacted by states beginning in 1993. In the 1990s, there were forty-three cases of non–drug-related mass killings, but from 2000 to 2012, the number fell by almost half.[185] Such realities hardly stifled the frenzy over guns. National Rifle Association executive director Wayne LaPierre was ridiculed in December 2012 when he called for stationing an armed policeman in every American school. Yet President Obama's own daughters already attended a school with eleven armed guards, virtually all celebrities calling for more gun control were protected constantly by armed security, and public schools in Texas, Delaware, New Mexico, and Florida already had armed police. Instead of confronting the real problems—mental illness and the inability to violate the civil rights of the insane—liberals continued to focus on the sideshow of guns. And the likelihood of reducing anxiety levels through higher employment and lower debt seemed light-years away as Barack Obama was reelected in 2012.

"You Didn't Build That!"

Perhaps one of the most unexpected political events of the last seventy-five years occurred in 2012 when Barack Obama won reelection. He did so despite virtually every leading indicator signaling he would lose: pollsters found that well over 60 percent of people said the country was on the wrong track, unemployment was the highest ever for a non-Depression president, personal wealth and income had stagnated, and both the middle class and the poor had lost significant ground over the previous four years. Most of all, despite a weak Republican candidate in former Massachusetts governor Mitt Romney (who repelled the conservative base), Obama continued to commit public gaffes that would have sunk most politicians. In July 2012, Obama told a Virginia audience,

> If you were successful, somebody along the line gave you some help. There was a great teacher somewhere in your life. Somebody helped to create this unbelievable American system that we have that allowed you to thrive. Somebody invested in roads and bridges. If you've got a business—*you didn't build that. Somebody else made that happen.*[186]

To any entrepreneur, such words were objectionable and insulting at a minimum. People who had worked sixty hours a week, taking no vacations and earning no profit for years, saw Obama's comment as one more indicator that he despised free-market businesses. Worse, Obama's phrase by then encapsulated the Keynesian and even quasi-socialist views of the mainstream Democrat Party that economic growth emanated from government, not the private sector.

Astoundingly, the comment did not sink Obama's campaign, in part because one of Mitt Romney's own comments—for entirely different reasons—proved more divisive: Romney, in a private meeting with fundraisers, said 47 percent of Americans were "dependent on government" and that they believed they were "victims." While he referred to the 47 percent of the citizenry that paid no income taxes, the words seemed to imply that Social Security recipients or the military were part of the group. In fact, however, Romney's comments were off in the other direction: the top 50 percent of American taxpayers paid almost *all* federal income taxes, and the bottom 50 percent paid almost none.

Obama seized upon the opportunity to pit one group of Americans against another based on wealth. Repeatedly slamming Republicans as supporting only "tax cuts for the rich," Obama dodged any discussion of accomplishments in his first administration, ran away from his stimulus (except in front of union audiences), and ignored the debt. For four years, Democrats had consistently blamed the economy on Bush, even after White House data showed that the Bush tax cuts actually *narrowed* the deficit gap.[187] In November, Obama won reelection by a narrower margin than in 2008, beating Romney by almost five million votes (as opposed to the nine million he tallied against McCain in 2008), and losing only Indiana and North Carolina from his 2008 electoral college total. For the first time in recent memory, the losing candidate carried the independent voters and by a solid margin. Although the votes in Ohio, Florida, Colorado, and Virginia—which could have given Romney a narrow win—were extremely close, he failed to reach McCain's level of turnout in many key areas. Post-election analysis showed that while Obama lost almost eight million from his totals in 2008, he had produced another four million new voters in the interim—mostly Hispanics and youth.[188] In doing so, he became the only post–World War II president to be reelected with an unemployment rate over 5 percent and the only Democrat since Roosevelt in 1944 to win re-election with 50 percent of the vote. Even the popular Bill Clinton fell short in 1996. Nevertheless, Obama had out-organized Romney at the grassroots level and successfully demonized his ideas, if not the man himself.

A new phenomenon, the "low information voter," had appeared in the 2012 election. Media pundits used the phrase to refer to those who did not closely follow politics, and who only picked up snippets of political news. In fact, the demise of the major news organizations had contributed to the decline in political information. In the 1960s, if only by osmosis, even passive voters assimilated news information from the only entertainment on at the dinner hour: network news. As cable television, talk radio, and Internet news sites appeared, the power of those networks to control information disappeared, but so did much of the even passing political knowledge of large numbers of citizens. Therefore, it was a mixed blessing: the "big three" networks could no longer propagandize, but fewer people were getting any information at all—a danger of a different sort.

Although the 2012 elections left the Republicans with the House, the Democrats held the Senate, rendering any attempt to repeal Obamacare or address entitlements utterly impossible. Obama's only negotiating points over the 2013 budget were finding ways to tax wealthier Americans more. Nevertheless, armed with the Supreme Court approval, Obama entered his second term with no reason to compromise and every reason to accelerate his transformation of the United States into a European-style socialist country.

Circling the Drain

This approach, of course, was already a path blazed in Europe, particularly France, where the Socialist candidate François Hollande had won the presidency in May 2012. France sharply raised taxes on capital gains, dividends, and income (which reached 75 percent). French millionaires began to flee, and in 2012, famed French actor Gérard Depardieu moved to lower-tax Belgium after issuing a volatile statement against government tax burdens. But in December 2012, the French high court rejected the tax plan in a "stinging rebuke" of Hollande's policies, calling it "unfair and unconstitutional."[189] Unfazed, Hollande moved ahead with government-sponsored stimulus-type construction plans.

History (and common sense) showed that these efforts would impede economic growth. Already other European countries were verging on collapse after following such policies. Greece was the worst of the sovereign-debt crisis nations. When rating services downgraded Greek bonds to junk levels in 2009, other European nations, especially Germany, stepped in to force austerity measures in return for a loan from the International Monetary Fund (essentially U.S. dollars). Greek citizens—having been accustomed to entitlements—resisted, and in May 2012 Greece threatened to withdraw from the EU.[190] This potential "Grexit" affected international market behavior and forced countless negotiations and restructurings of the debt. Polls showed that Greeks simultaneously wanted to remain in the EU, but also wanted to default while Germany simply insisted Greece remain in the eurozone.[191] Spain, Portugal, Cyprus, and Italy were in scarcely better shape, with legions receiving entitlements from others, and Spain referring to a "lost generation" of nonworking adults. Predictably, the Spanish European commissioner insisted that the wealthier European states keep the needy countries in the EU and that richer countries needed to "reduce imbalances" to maintain the EU.[192] Cyprus and other nations teetered near the precipice as well.

Across Europe, almost two thirds of those surveyed said their national economy was "bad" or "very bad"; in Spain the number of those who believed their national economy was in dire shape reached 95 percent. By November 2012, just as Obama won an election on the notion that government could be a job creator, the eurozone reached new highs in unemployment at 10.6 percent (with Spain at 26 percent). The eurozone was home to almost 19 million unemployed people. Youth unemployment exceeded 25 percent.[193] For perspective, consider that Ronald Reagan's policies led to the creation of 14 million *net* new jobs in just eight years. By the end of George H. W. Bush's term, the United States had generated enough jobs to employ *all* the unemployed Europeans today! But that was the United States of yesteryear. Whether America could still reverse course and regain her moral, political, and spiritual compass—which would in turn produce a revival in her economy—remained an open question.

One shining bright light came, oddly enough, in the field of energy, where despite Obama's obsessive support for "green energy" companies such as the bankrupt Solyndra, a genuine revolution was occurring. A Bank of America/Merrill Lynch "Energy Outlook" for 2013 captured the prospects adeptly:

> Surging US shale oil output creates the risk of $50 [a barrel oil]. America's energy supplies are surging while the rest of the world continues to fight for scarce molecules of oil and gas. . . . [O]nshore US crude oil output now vastly exceeds previous growth rates in liquids and nat[ural] gas. . . . [194]

North Dakota became a mecca for energy production, at least temporarily escaping Obama's regulatory nets. Its Bakken shale oil formation covered 200,000 square miles, and early estimates from the U.S. government were that North Dakota alone would produce 350,000 barrels of oil a day by 2035. Yet even those estimates were constantly revised upward. Production reached 458,000 barrels per day in 2010, so that in 2013 the U.S. Geological Survey said that the field was the largest ever discovered in North America and could produce over seven *billion* barrels of oil. Still others thought the number too low by a factor of four or five.[195] In addition, the existing oil fields in the United States, if permitted unrestricted production and exploration, could generate almost 50 million barrels a day, reaching a minimum of 17 million barrels per day by 2020 after factoring in depletion rates. This, according to a Harvard Business School analysis, "would represent the most significant increase in any decade since the 1980s."[196] The once-fashionable "peak oil" theory—which held that we had already tapped all available oil— had been quietly discarded by 2012 in all but the most extremist environmental circles. Harvard's study flatly stated, "Oil is not in short supply. . . . Technology may turn today's expensive oil into tomorrow's cheap oil."[197]

"Fracking," or hydraulic fracturing of rock layers, had opened up vast expanses of obtainable oil. Predictably, environmental groups opposed fracking as well as normal drilling, ostensibly because it damaged the rock layers, but in reality because the main goal of most modern environmentalists was to eliminate any facet of the capitalist economy that ran on oil and would continue to do so for the foreseeable future. Yet even better, new fracking technologies using freezing processes that dramatically reduced the amount of water and sand used to create pressures had already been tested. Hence, an even more environmentally friendly process had already been developed. Technically, the energy future looks bright if the government will allow private enterprise to extract and produce what is now known to be within U.S. borders.

Of course, independence through American oil could not come without intense opposition from the liberals and Obama, who admitted in 2008 that he favored higher oil prices.[198] His energy secretary, Steven Chu, added, "Somehow we have to . . . boost the price of gasoline to levels in Europe"— to $8 a gallon when Americans paid less than $4.[199] Transportation Secretary Ray LaHood wanted to "coerce people out of their cars," and he appeared to have the perfect crisis for his platform when a BP oil platform in the Gulf of Mexico exploded and had a massive spill.[200] Obama imposed a six-month moratorium on drilling permits for deep-water rigs, and even though a federal judge ordered the moratorium lifted, Obama ignored the ruling. The moratorium cost Louisiana an estimated $2 billion in wages and forfeited tax revenues. Overall, more than thirteen thousand jobs were lost due to the moratorium—yet at exactly the same time, Obama's administration handed Mexico's state oil company $1 billion in federal loans, and he told Brazilian officials "we want to help with technology to develop [your] oil reserves."[201] Obama's new regulations added $1.4 million to each new deep-water well project, and then tacked on another seven-year moratorium on exploration in the eastern Gulf. As to be expected, when fracking promised to make America energy independent, Obama unleashed new regulations against shale, even while he insisted that government invented the fracking process (which in fact was developed long before government ever got involved). Possibly the most outrageous and transparent effort on Obama's part to ensure that the United States did not achieve energy independence came when, citing environmental concerns, he blocked construction of the Keystone XL pipeline from Canada to Texas. Once again, environmental activists won out over American energy independence.

All the while, Obama's stimulus bill had pumped hundreds of millions of dollars into Department of Energy "green" companies such as Abengoa Solar, Abound Solar, and of course, Solyndra (the investment worked out to $1.3 million *per job created*).[202] Solyndra proved the most embarrassing of the Obama-backed green energy fiascos, and was likely in violation of numerous laws, as the Obama administration had already received warnings from its own officials that Solyndra was "infused with politics at every level" and was hardly a "smart bet."[203] Hardly a smart bet indeed: in 2011, Solyndra let all its employees go and filed for bankruptcy—but it was just one of many Obama-backed green companies that came nowhere close to making a profit, even with government money. With indications the company was sinking, the administration sought still *more* loan guarantees from Congress, and deliberately strong-armed the company to withhold its bankruptcy announcement until after the November midterm elections.[204]

Such shortsightedness and/or deliberate destruction of the American energy industry underscored the potential of American energy deposits to, astoundingly enough, make the United States not only energy independent in the near future, but the world's largest energy supplier. The implications were staggering. The Middle East would lose its grip on politics immediately; Europe, Japan, and China would have to rely on the United States for oil; and the American economy would witness a boom like it had not seen in three decades.

That energy potential only constituted a small part of what could be with policies in place designed to restore American strength and exceptionalism. Surprisingly enough, one only had to look across the border to Canada—long considered America's quasi-socialist neighbor—to see conservative governments succeed. For over a decade, they had reduced Canada's overall spending by 8.8 percent and reduced the size of the federal government from 16.2 percent of GDP to 13.1 percent.[205] More important, Canada had addressed the elephant in the room—entitlements—even reforming its social security system in such a way as to make it viable again. Of all the nations close to possessing the four pillars, by 2012 Canada remains one of the best examples of what those foundations implied when correctly employed.

Future Shock

History does not happen when random and isolated events suddenly alter the course of mankind, but rather within large sweeps that ebb and flow. These movements fostering events, discovery, and innovation are sometimes inspired, sometimes due to ignorance and folly. By 2012, some trends

Europe, 2013

Country Abbreviations:
Alb. = Albania
Belg. = Belgium
K. = Kosovo
Li. = Liechtenstein
Lux. = Luxembourg
M. = Montenegro
Mac. = Macedonia
Mon. = Monaco
Neth. = Netherlands
Slov. = Slovenia
S.M. = San Marino
Switz. = Switzerland

0   500 Miles

European Union members

were easily discernible in the world, although they were not uniform across all nations: the rise of Islam and atheism and the decline of Christianity; the rebirth of fascism/statism and the decline of communism and anarchism; the universality of products and technology and the decline of multicultural political entities; the rise of alternative multinational criminal organizations and the decline of local governments; the rise of countries with youthful demographics and the decline of those tied to aging populations; and finally, an increasing awareness that the resources of the Earth are finite, and conflict between disparate groups for "wasting assets" ensures that wars will continue to be endemic for some time to come.

Although the nineteenth century belonged to Europe, with its innovative technologies and burgeoning population that enabled it to generate vast colonial empires, the twentieth century belonged to the United States. America, with its political heritage of individual liberty, private property laws, spirit of innovation, and above all, religious vitality, proved flexible and dynamic enough to overcome a German-Japanese alliance whose ideas greatly resembled those of the Soviet Union—the other foe the United States vanquished in a forty-five-year period. Whether the United States can retain its superpower status in the twenty-first century remains to be seen. Threats from populous nations with relatively homogenous citizenries (China and India) and statism in various flavors will become the general basis for governing the vast majority of nations, and the United States will again find itself apart and exceptional.

Precisely because of American prosperity, success, and openness, the United States absorbed a large immigrant wave in the nineteenth century from societies unfamiliar with true individual liberty for the masses. America had developed democratic institutions almost unique in the annals of history, where private property was widely held throughout the country by its population, and property rights were secured by law from arbitrary seizure by governments or the masses. Until the New Deal, government regulations were held to a minimum, and common people participated in upholding the law, actually determined by them under the United States' system of common law, derived from the customs and desires of the people, codified and administered by elected representatives (legislatures, sheriffs, coroners, judges, etc.), and assisted through various levels of vigilantism. Such power residing in the citizenry was unknown in Europe and poorly understood on the Continent, which continued to function under civil law, whereby all laws went down rather than up.

This situation enabled the United States to rapidly and easily surpass anything Europe (or anyone else) could do. The result of the cataclysms of the twentieth century was the destruction of nine empires (Ottoman, British, French, Russian, Belgian, Dutch, Italian, Austria-Hungarian, and in the East, Japanese). What was left were two superpowers representing radically conflicting economic systems, socialism and capitalism; two diametrically opposed political ideologies, statism and representative democracy; and two vastly opposite theological principles, one that God governed man's life and one that insisted there was no God at all. By the end of the century, the USSR had collapsed, dying of a terminally unworkable economic system and a flawed theological construct. But in its death throes, it somehow left its political ideology dormant for assumption in other societies.

From the late 1800s on, however, the United States steadily flirted with statism as elites, ever more convinced of their superior intellect and morality, saw the growth of a powerful middle class as threatening their positions of authority. Many simply wished to have the power they saw wielded in Europe by aristocrats and elites as their just due in some form of state capitalism as had been developed under Italian fascism. Civil rights legislation in the 1960s, loudly proclaimed as beneficial to minorities and the poor, actually increased the elites' control of those same minorities and poor and institutionalized their status. Poverty activists perverted Martin Luther King, Jr.'s teachings after his death into a mechanism for establishing and controlling a permanent underclass, while increasing government regulations, taxation, and restrictions decimated the middle class. For the first time, a broad gulf between poor and rich was created, with politicians of the Left seeking to exacerbate it at every turn.

The stage was set by 2008 for class warfare, with the remnants of the middle class desiring to return to the days before government played such a huge role in people's lives. Elites had come quite close to pushing the U.S. population into a condition of state dependency through combinations of income tax withholding, mortgage interest deductions, school loans, and hundreds of other insidious tentacles that wound their way through the liberty of the individual and family. This was Mitt Romney's 47 percent, not all of whom were on welfare, but all of whom were in one way or another beholden to government. Local and state governments found themselves almost powerless to function without help from the federal government, unable to even enforce their own border security. At the same time, the presidency itself had become more and more imperial, usurping the prerogatives of Congress by legislating through executive orders and regulations in bureaucratic departments.

At that point, the United States again confronted foreign enemies and radical ideologies. Islamic fundamentalism—an ideology without a particular state—joined China and India while Europe increasingly was sidetracked into "saving" the planet through "sustainable development," which would be of little value if jihad succeeded or if China (the most polluting nation in history) dominated the world economy. Indeed, it was the slowing of the European economic engine that had rejuvenated Islam as a worldwide force when Muslim immigrants began to swamp Europeans in their home countries, hastening the demise of Christian, and especially Catholic, Europe. In the western hemisphere, Islam's progress was confined to the United States and Canada, with the number of Muslims approximating the number of Jews in the United States by 2012. The war on terror was minimized by the Obama administration; the term "terrorist" (and certainly "Islamic terrorist") was forbidden in government statements; and Obama's Cairo speech signaled that the United States was ready to adopt the Muslims' interpretation of an imperialist and oppressive history on the part of the United States toward the Middle East.

Domestically, American debt, under Obama reaching many trillions of dollars, empowered China with the wherewithal and position to dictate American monetary policy. With the demonstrable failure of the European Union in a few years, there will be no impetus for Latin America to federalize, if indeed the wide differences in culture and ethnicity would allow it. Mexico alone periodically exhibits difficulties keeping itself together, and not even Simón Bolívar was able to bring about any unity in South America. If Latin America is doomed to be mired in statism and repression throughout the twenty-first century, there remains the distinct possibility that there will be new pressures by Hispanic activists to partition off the American Southwest to form Aztlán with some of the northern Mexican states. Yet American politicians, and the judiciary in particular, seem unwilling to confront the reality of a Hispanicized American Southwest.

In short, the very pillars of American exceptionalism that made the United States into the world's first sole superpower in the twentieth century must be restored, and quickly. Perhaps even before they can be restored, they need to once again be *recognized*, understood, and appreciated. They were not anachronistic baubles that could be discarded for newer fashion, but rather the essence of what made America, and what made America great. Such an awareness demands a restoration of the very concept of greatness, which far too many political leaders on all sides today think long past.

Perhaps the most difficult and most important pillar to recognize and restore is the self-reliant culture based on Protestant Christianity. Roman Catholicism is, in 2013, the largest Christian denomination, and the one the media and Hollywood favors. It could on the one hand be easily attacked for the pedophilia scandals—making it easier to delegitimize—and of all the Christian denominations it is the least democratic. Its hierarchical structure in the form of the pope and a clergy could be paralleled, or, better yet, replaced by an atheistic, secular government. This weakness is precisely what the Puritans had rebelled against. To empower the people in a Christian society, the religious leaders must be elected by the people, not imposed on them by a high religious authority. In that sense, Christianity and common law overlapped in the form of the congregational church structure.

The second pillar, that of common law, remained in place, but was often undermined by state and national politicians in order to increase their power. They did not acknowledge that the law comes from God to the people, and they were servants of the sovereign people, able to codify and administer that law on the people's behalf. As mere instruments of the people, they should be severely limited in regard to the time they may serve, a principle recognized as far back in time as the fifth century B.C. in Athens. Mercy Otis Warren, a political activist and propagandist during the American Revolution, pointed out this flaw in the Constitution in 1788. She argued at the time that even a Bill of Rights would not be sufficient to prevent the expansion of government, ultimately to the point of tyranny. Even the most noble of men, she warned, would be unable to resist the lure of perpetual office where they could wield power. Two centuries later, economist Milton Friedman would put it only slightly differently, referring to the "tyranny of the status quo" when it came to the difficulty of *ever* rolling back government even in the smallest degree.[206]

It took the disastrous Progressive presidency of Franklin Roosevelt to convince the majority of Americans she was right, and even then, the reform was limited to presidential term limits. Many states have term limits, but the U.S. Supreme Court struck down the limitations on federal service as unconstitutional, insisting that the ballot box was the proper remedy for abuse.

The third pillar of the sanctity of private property has also been substantially undercut by elitist lawmakers seeking to establish control of the people through eminent domain or new means of extracting revenue to increase the size and role of government. James Otis said in 1761 that a citizen's rights to his life, liberty, and property were inherent and inalienable, yet by the twenty-first century, a citizen's home, totally paid for and owned by the citizen, was not only subject to the whim of a vast army of government bureaucrats, but accounted to little more than a lease, subject to the annual payment of property taxes. In DuPage County, Illinois, a single tax notice is mailed out by regular mail in the spring of each year, and if the tax is not fully paid by the deadline date in September of that same year, a penalty is added. Certified funds only are accepted after a date in October, and after the second week in November, no payment will be accepted, regardless of postmark. The very next day, the tax sale begins.[207] Procedures such as these are designed to confiscate a homeowner's property at the earliest possible moment, and violate the spirit in which the United States was founded. Moreover, much of the property tax in any state goes to pay pensions of local government employees, and people who possess insufficient funds to invest in a pension for themselves are required to pay for the retirements of government employees who, in theory, serve them. This is the very essence of serfdom.

Last, the fourth pillar of exceptionalism, free-market capitalism, has been under assault from the beginning of the Progressive era in 1900. Brought into the White House by Theodore Roosevelt, this attack went on steroids under Woodrow Wilson, Franklin Roosevelt, Lyndon Johnson, and Barack Obama. By 2012, entrepreneurship was fading fast; the Kaufman research group found a drop of over 5 percent in new ventures just between 2010 to 2011, and the "establishment birth rate" for creating new ventures had dropped by one third since 1996.[208] This was to be expected when the rising business model was crony or state capitalism. Government regulations stifled business and economic growth at every level, and Obama's re-election showed the voters possessed little stomach for returning to the Protestant work ethic and free competition, preferring to work and live under ever-stricter government controls. The federal government had become a monster permeating every activity of American life at an enormous cost—and no different from the EU government, which increasingly ground its subjects into serfdom.

Simply propping up the structure on one leg (fiscal solvency) would be a colossal failure, for fiscal solvency itself depends, as the Founders knew, on an honest citizenry driven most of the time by virtue. Why should anyone adhere to contracts if the U.S. government can cheat General Motors' bondholders? Why should everyday homeowners repay debts to banks if American politicians simply write off billions of dollars in mortgage debt because it inconvenienced the wrong voting blocs? Why should businesses reinvest in America when the United States devalues its dollar in such a way as to destroy those businesses? What entrepreneur would consider starting a new factory in America—with its thousands of pages of environmental laws—when the Chinese or Indians would welcome such a facility with no debilitating restrictions? Why should American collegians view entrepreneurship as a career path when the first lady of the United States scorned it and urged students to go into government service instead? Why should *any* American think himself, or his country, as special—and most notably defend it in the U.S. military—when three decades' worth of Hollywood movies and television shows have reinforced the charge that America is the central problem in the world, not the solution? Or when Hollywood stars without exception avoided military service in the war on terror?[209]

These are blunt, even confrontational questions, but they demand answers. They demand honesty from both voters and public officials. If Americans are willing to trade a few more years' worth of comfort as their standard of living declines and their culture is fatally eroded, then the finale is already written and the play ends as a one-act tragedy. If, on the other hand, that same unrelenting minority that fomented a revolution against a king, that abolished slavery, that saved Europe, twice, and that saw a way to defeat communism when all others said "coexist" can survive, revive, then flourish, the nation's epic and exceptional story has only begun.

CONCLUSION

A beautiful, but hardened and resourceful heroine. A tyrannical government claiming only to have the "welfare of the people" in mind. A futuristic world, plagued by government-imposed food shortages, dreary sameness, mindless rules, and ruthless punishment, that saps the energy from all but those most fiercely determined to survive and succeed. A pair of lovers refusing to allow the state to dictate their passions or pursuits.

This is the plot line for not one, but two influential books, both written by women—almost fifty years apart. One was meant as a clarion call to resistance, the other as teenage entertainment. Both sold fabulously well. One author was a Russian immigrant, the other an American-born writer for children's television. For one writer, love was an unnecessary moral code, obsolete in the new world; for the other, love was the cornerstone upon which all rested, including the lives of literally thousands of people.

Atlas Shrugged and *The Hunger Games* both appealed—in vastly different ways—to youth and its rebellion, frustration, and above all, impatience with the evils perpetrated by government. Ayn Rand, the author of *Atlas Shrugged*, had come to America in 1926 from the USSR, already in the throes of horrific oppression and mass murder by the Communists. Able to obtain a visa to visit relatives, she arrived in the United States and headed for Hollywood where she became a screenwriter, then the head of costumes at RKO studios. She published a number of books, including *The Fountainhead* (1943), which dealt with the struggle between the individual and the state. But it was *Atlas Shrugged* (1957) that laid out in sharp contours the consequences of a society that demonizes excellence and penalizes achievement.[1]

Her heroine, Dagny Taggart, along with other industrialists such as Hank Rearden, finally refuses to support society any longer with her talent and genius. Led by John Galt (who ultimately becomes Taggart's love interest), those individuals who were the engines of industry drop out to live in "Galt's Gulch." It is at that point that Atlas indeed shrugs, refusing any longer to carry the world on his shoulders. The book, even with its dauntingly stilted multipage monologues, especially resonated with young adults in the late 1950s, and entrenched itself as a cult classic until it enjoyed a revival in the early twenty-first century.

Suzanne Collins, a Roman Catholic Air Force brat educated in the heartland of America, wrote for children's television shows before conceiving of her best-selling trilogy. *The Hunger Games* became an overnight success, especially among late teens, and dominated the new e-book market, making Collins the best-selling Kindle author of all time as of this writing. As with *Atlas Shrugged*, *The Hunger Games* pits a pretty, tough heroine, Katniss Everdeen, not against her "tribute" opponents in the Games themselves (organized by the government to teach an annual lesson to once-rebellious districts by requiring each to send two child-gladiators to fight to the death in specially designed futuristic arenas), but against the oppressive government of Panem and its rules. Ultimately, Katniss rebels against the games and the state of Panem itself. In the finale, when only Katniss and her fellow tribute, Peeta, remain, the games called for one to kill the other. Instead, Katniss and Peeta threaten to simultaneously eat poisonous berries rather than satisfy the game's government-sanctioned council. Panem is forced to allow the two to live, though in subsequent volumes of the trilogy the government attempts to take its revenge.[2]

Both stories highlighted a voice of dissent against the slow but steady expansion of the Leviathan state in the late twentieth and early twenty-first centuries. Taken together, they represented a remarkable full circle of literary prophecy-turned-reality in the modern era. While no one—yet—has forced teenagers to fight to the death for entertainment as a means of ensuring their region's survival, radical Islamic societies have increasingly enlisted brainwashed children as suicide bombers, and the notorious Joseph Kony in Sudan kidnapped hundreds of children to serve in his murderous bands. Nor was either book particularly new in depicting a harsh future of government oppression: George Orwell had done that in 1949 with *Nineteen Eighty-Four*. But both authors—one looking at her contemporary times, one looking forward—addressed the overarching issue of human freedom in an increasingly less-free world.

Were these works off target, merely dark fantasies by writers seeking plots? By 2012, most free world governments were not yet tyrannical. But the world had transformed rather radically from the supposedly free societies that emerged from the end of the Second World War into a large-scale conglomeration in the case of the European Union; an often-lawless Russia; a socialist China with numerous pockets of protected state capitalism; a series of thugocracies in the Middle East and Africa; a crime-ridden Mexico and Latin America; and a United States substantially different in character from the exceptional nation that won World War II with its steel and blood. Could any Frenchman have dreamed in 1945 that Brussels—or Berlin— would dictate tariff rates, child behavior, education standards, and currency values for France? Would any American who risked his life on the sands of a Pacific island have done so for a nation that permitted rogue mayors to ban the sale of soft drinks, or Congress to tax people who did *not* buy a product? Would the residents of India, upon gaining independence, dream that in sixty years their nation would still in many ways be a third-rate economic power? Would *any* of the wise men who oversaw the postwar peace have predicted that most of Africa would still be run by gangster dictators, and that the few strongmen who held power in the Middle East would be overthrown by radical Islamic militants?

Shocking changes in the past century to the world landscape were even more difficult to digest when they came largely through nonviolent revolutions and normal legislative processes. Both Nazi Germany and Fascist Italy had arisen also through legal legislative processes. Japan's imperial tyranny by the 1930s maintained the façade of a legislative body (the Diet), but could in no way be considered a free and democratic society. Yet by 1930, most still remained convinced that Europe had learned its lesson and that Japan would come around. Obviously, that was not the case.

Seeing what's ahead is difficult, even for so-called experts. "Always in motion is the future," observes Yoda in the *Star Wars* movie series. Things can, and do, change in an instant. But the current trends are disturbing, to say the least. The submission of vast swaths of humanity under some form of authoritarianism was unprecedented in human history. From the soft tyranny of land and business regulations in the United States to the meek submission to the rules of a bureaucratic EU to the relatively effortless takeovers of Libya, Egypt, and Iran by radical Islamic parties in the first decade of the twenty-first century, freedom was steadily receding.

By 1990, the successful Western victory in the cold war, achieved largely by the United States under Ronald Reagan and undergirded by

Western culture as a force for freedom, seemed again to promise a new horizon of liberty. The Soviet empire had crumbled, and Germany was united, while simultaneously, in one of the first truly united efforts by the United Nations to enforce collective security, Saddam Hussein's army was unceremoniously kicked out of Kuwait. Indeed, at the time, the European Union had not even yet been formally ratified by the Treaty of Maastricht, and South Africa had held multiracial elections, culminating with the first nonwhite ever to hold that nation's highest office. Only pockets of ideological repression—mostly Communist, Cuba and North Korea being the most notable—still remained. Everywhere else, or so the theory went, Western-style democracy (ignoring the substantial differences between the United States and almost all other Western nations) was going to be accepted sooner or later. Francis Fukuyama, in his 1992 book *The End of History*, insisted that the advent of liberal democracies across the globe signaled the final stage of humanity's sociocultural revolution.[3]

But, of course, there was no such thing as the "end of history." The claxons were already sounding in states such as Zimbabwe, which attained its independence in 1980, and which promptly began to drive out whites. The country descended into murder and economic stagnation. Even as Fukuyama wrote, the Balkans were erupting yet again. Islamic radicals continued to account for the overwhelming majority of terrorist acts in the world, with no other group even coming close. Soviet-style communism may have disappeared in most modern nations, but it began to mutate in China into a stringent, yet carefully concealed, authoritarianism that permitted some capitalism on the one hand while imposing mandatory abortions and draconian limits on family size on the other. Russia descended into a mafia state in possession of nuclear weapons, while the Europeans religiously refused to stand against oppression almost anywhere.

From Japan and China to Western Europe to the United States, nations seemed to be reaching the end of growth when using state planning or heavy regulatory models. Instead of the end of history, the world was rapidly coming to the end of freedom, at least temporarily. A dark age appeared imminent, and how long it might last was, again, "in motion." But there was no question it fell to the United States to lead the way out.

In 2012, however, Americans had, for the time being, accepted the soft slavery of entitlements and the silver shackles of government support. The United States remained a republic, and it still had a free market. But both its status as a republic and its free market were under assault. States consistently lost powers to the federal government, and the federal government had begun to cede authority to international bodies through Agenda 21 and other agreements. Whether one defined the "welfare" class as all those who received government checks or merely those designated as public assistance, the sphere of control by Washington had swollen so substantially that even leaders from just fifty years ago would have been hard-pressed to recognize the nation—let alone Franklin, Jefferson, or Washington.

The pillars of property rights and the Christian religion were also under unrelenting attack, the former mostly from environmentalists and the latter from culture warriors bent on forcing homosexual marriage, abortion, and other elements of social collapse onto the body politic. (As an example, in January 2013, a New York public school teacher was ordered to remove a sticky note on her desk featuring a quotation from Ronald Reagan, "If we ever forget that we are One Nation Under God, then we will be a Nation gone under," and received a "counseling letter."[4]) As these pillars eroded, so too did common law, which was ignored, trampled, and redefined at every opportunity to fit the new progressive ideology of the state.

Still, the twentieth century was the American century. It began with— for its time—a period of government intrusion as foreign to the Americans of 1899 as the current one is to Americans of 1959. The Progressives' efforts to ban alcohol, impose an income tax, establish a central bank with virtually no government oversight, were all radical for their day, and the United States, while damaged, managed to recover and indeed prosper. Whether the twenty-first century will still see an exceptional America that can lead the world, or whether the United States "Europeanizes" is "in motion." The cover of the January 5, 2013, issue of *The Economist* said it all; featuring a French-looking President Obama and a German-dressed Speaker Boehner, the headline blared, "America turns European: A broken system, a lousy deal and no end in sight."[5] The accompanying article accurately described the similarities of Washington's mismanagement and that of eurozone nations.

We end with a pair of references, at least in part, from the Bible. Solomon, claimed by the Judeo-Christian heritage to be the wisest man who ever lived, said in Proverbs 18:21 that "death and life are in the power of the tongue." Margaret Thatcher put this somewhat differently: "Watch your thoughts, for they become words. Watch your words, for they become actions. Watch your actions, for they become habits. Watch your habits, for they become your character. And watch your character, for it becomes your destiny!" Historical revisionism by leftists is dangerous for this very reason: by rewriting America's past, they have redefined her character, and therefore are reshaping her destiny. They have, literally, spoken death to American history by portraying her Founders as materialist, racist, and entirely selfish; by describing her champions of freedom as imperialist; and by calling her titans of industry greedy and uncaring. By reshaping America's past, they have minimized, ridiculed, and otherwise damaged American exceptionalism—which is essential to America's destiny in the twenty-first century. And as we've seen, with America goes the world.

A second story from the Bible, whether taken as metaphor or literally, bears a close approximation to the current circumstances in America in 2013. The children of Israel, having been brought out of slavery by the Lord, were given a government by judges. Israel was alone among nations—one could say "exceptional"—in having judges govern the nation instead of a king. Yet in 1 Samuel 8, a tale unfolds in which the Israelites demanded a king. Samuel warned the people that such a king would claim their properties, seize their boys for war and their daughters as slaves, and take a tenth of everything they owned (in addition to what they had to tithe to the Lord). But they were undeterred. "We want a king over us. Then we will be like all the other nations, with a king to lead us and go out before us and fight our battles." This sounds much like America in 2013, which wants a government to "fight our battles" and take care of everyone, needy or not. Israel lost much of its exceptional status when it was granted a king, as God no longer heard His people. Let us hope the United States does not get its wish, for once the shining city on a hill sees its light dimmed, all mankind will pay the price.

ACKNOWLEDGMENTS

A year after volume one of *A Patriot's History of the Modern World* appeared, the state of the planet appears in more peril than ever. Dave Dougherty and I were torn between optimism and pessimism at the end of writing volume one, but now events seem to have shifted us toward the latter, at least temporarily. This volume, however, is actually lighter and in many ways was more enjoyable to write simply because it did not contain two wars. That did not free us from needing intensive editing, for which we thank Natalie Horbachevsky. Her rearranging left us with, we hope, a much tighter final product.

As with volume one, both Michael Allen and David Limbaugh read parts of the manuscript, and we thank both of them. And as in volume one, Philip Schwartzberg continued to provide excellent maps and illustrations. Our agent, Roger Williams of New England Publishing Associates, has remained the watchdog of our rights and interests.

The Patriot's History series, which is now trademarked and includes a Reader and a television series in preproduction, has been given timely boosts by everyone from Kathryn Lopez at National Review Online to Matt Spaulding at the Heritage Foundation to Glenn Beck and Rush Limbaugh. Specifically, research for this volume was aided by work from Adam Schweikart, Brian Bennett, Christ Castelitz, and Stephen Majkowski. The University of Dayton has continued its generous support for my work, especially the dean of Arts and Sciences, Paul Benson, and history department chairmen Julius Amin and Juan Santamarina.

Dee Schweikart takes immense pleasure in my writing for it allows her time to shop while I pore through books in shopping malls. And while they were not involved in anything actually connected with this book, I need to thank my lifelong friends Bud (Ian) Kirk, Randy Gage, and John Tatum— musicians all—for their faith in my work. Finally, thanks to my coauthor Dave Dougherty for a nearly effortless writing relationship. Both Mike Allen and Dave have been exceptional coauthors, and no one could wish for better writing partners.

—Larry Schweikart

Although I am the senior partner in terms of age, my friend Larry Schweikart is certainly my senior as an author and writer. This last year, one of the few bright spots has been our collaboration, as Larry teaches and informs in everything he does. I am privileged to be his coauthor.

One must continually seek out such individuals as Larry, in order to confront the assault on American exceptionalism we experience every day, particularly when that attack directly assails and marginalizes Christianity, a factor without parallel in my life. Past caring for myself in this great battle, I am called to protect those I love: my son, David Henry Ralph Dougherty, my brother, Ralph Harding Dougherty, and my partner in all other things, Shirley Wunderlich. They inspire me daily to the greatest efforts my humble talents and knowledge allow, and it is to them that I dedicate this work.

Uncommonly for an American in this day and age, all of my direct ancestors were present in the United States at the time the shot was fired that was heard around the world. My family took part in nearly all the wars America has fought, and my great-great-great-grandfather James Dougherty spent eight years in the Continental Army fighting for his liberties and for all who came after him. Others helped turned back England in the War of 1812, two were killed by Indians, two served on opposite sides in the Civil War, and so forth down to my own service in the U.S. Army. To quit now would be to betray all those who have gone before me, and render my own life a nullity. Someday I hope my spirit will meet up with James's, and I cannot tell him that I stood by, did nothing, and simply watched the United States sink into the cesspool of nations that allowed their societies to rot into oblivion. That was my motivation behind this endeavor, and if my writing is poor, possibly some of my passion for my country will redeem the deficiencies in my work.

—Dave Dougherty

NOTES

Introduction

1. Interview with Gabe Bohm; *Rockin' the Wall*, documentary film produced by Larry Schweikart and Marc Leif, 2009.

2. Comments from musicians who toured the Iron Curtain countries in the 1970s, in ibid.

3. Rudiger Overmans, *Deutsche militärische Verluste im Zweiten Weltkrieg* (Munich: Oldenbourg, 2000).

4. Barack Obama, "A New Beginning," Cairo, Egypt, June 4, 2009.

5. Ibid. If that wasn't enough, Obama insisted Islam "has demonstrated . . . the possibilities of religious tolerance and racial equality," an astounding statement given the *dhimmitude* of all non-Islamic people living in Muslim societies and the fact that Islam led the world in the slave trade up to the 1600s, and is leading it again.

6. *The Economist*, July 14, 2012.

7. R. J. Rummel, *Death by Government* (New Brunswick, NJ: Transaction Publishers, 1994) and R. J. Rummel, *Statistics of Democide* (New Brunswick, NJ: Transaction Publishers, 1997).

8. David B. Barrett, George T. Kurian, and Todd M. Johnson, *World Christian Encyclopedia*, 2nd Edition, Volume 1 (New York: Oxford University Press, 2001), 772.

9. Pew Research Center, poll conducted June 28–July 9, 2012, www.pewforum.org/Politics -and-Elections/2012-Opinions-on-for-gay-marriage-unchanged-after-obamas -announcement.aspx.

10. "Most Catholic Women Use Birth Control Banned by Church," Reuters, April 13, 2011.

11. Peter Ferrara, "Reaganomics vs. Obamanomics: Facts and Figures," *Forbes*, May 5, 2011. C. Cooper, J. Steinberg, and M. Shires, "The Evolution of the European Economy: Implications for Transatlantic Relations," RAND Corporation, 1992, suggests that it was in fact worse for Europe: as a share of working age population, employment actually declined (13).

12. David B. Barrett, George T. Kurian, and Todd M. Johnson, *World Christian Encyclopedia*, 2nd ed., 2 vols. (New York: Oxford University Press, 2001), 1:191.

13. "Changing Adolescence Programme Briefing Paper: Social Trends and Mental Health: Introducing the Main Findings," Nuffield Foundation, 2005, http://www.nuffieldfoundation .org/sites/default/files/files/Changing%20Adolescence_Social%20trends%20and%20 mental%20health_introducing%20the%20main%20findings.pdf.

14. "European Youth Trend Report '09," Youth Partnership EU, http://youth-partnership-eu .coe.int/youth-partnership/documents/EKCYP/Youth_Policy/docs/Better_understanding /Research/European-Youth-Trend-Report-x09-.pdf. Interestingly, with the exception of

only one age category in Britain, *every* youth subgroup drank Coke as its number one beverage.

15. Thomas Jefferson, *The Writings of Thomas Jefferson*, Vol. XVI, edited by Albert Ellery Bergh (Washington, DC: Thomas Jefferson Memorial Association of the United States, 1907), 320–21, contains the full and correct letter. Survey performed by Dave Dougherty, 2010.

16. Larry Schweikart, *Seven Events That Made America America* (New York: Sentinel, 2010).

17. Gordon Wood, "Introduction," *The Idea of America*, online Kindle ed., http://www.amazon .com/Idea-America-Reflections-United-States/dp/1594202907#reader_B004IYIUFG.

18. Alexis de Tocqueville, *Democracy in America*, 2 vols., ed. J. P. Mayer, trans. George Lawrence (New York: HarperPerennial, 1988), 2:455–56.

Chapter 1: Hot Spots, Cold War

1. "Akihiro Takahashi: Bore Witness to Hiroshima Attack," December 13, 2011, http://articles .boston.com/2011-12-13/bostonglobe/30512635_1_hiroshima-peace-memorial-museum -hiroshima-attack-hiroshima-survivor. In an attempt to undercut American exceptionalism, the Progressives have cited Hiroshima as an example of why the United States is no different from any other nation. In fact, the reality is that the United States offered ample opportunities for the Japanese to surrender, especially after the first bomb was dropped, and that the Japanese did not is indicative of the wisdom of Truman's decision. Moreover, the phenomenal restraint the United States has used in all subsequent wars—some not involving the USSR (such as Afghanistan or Iraq)—is further evidence of the exceptional restraint imposed by America's Christian morality.

2. Michael Beschloss, *The Conquerors: Roosevelt, Truman and the Destruction of Hitler's Germany, 1941–1945* (New York: Simon and Schuster, 2003); Wilson D. Miscamble, *From Roosevelt to Truman: Potsdam, Hiroshima, and the Cold War* (Cambridge: Cambridge University Press, 2007).

3. "The Change in the Soviet Union," (Kennan) to the Secretary of State, February 22, 1946, http://www.gwu.edu/~nsarchiv/coldwar/documents/episode-1/kennan.htm.

4. George F. Kennan, *Memoirs, 1925–1950* (Boston: Little Brown, 1967), 354–56.

5. Tony Judt, *Postwar: The History of Europe Since 1945* (New York: Penguin, 2005), 16–17.

6. Jeffery K. Olick, *In the House of the Hangman* (Chicago: University of Chicago Press, 2005), 100.

7. James Bacque, *Other Losses*, 2nd Revised Edition (Boston: Little, Brown & Co., 2004), 33.

8. Ibid., xxxiv.

9. Judt, *Postwar*, 21.

10. Ibid., 22.

11. Ibid., 20.

12. Beschloss, *The Conquerors*, 277.

13. Richard W. Walton, *Henry Wallace, Harry Truman, and the Cold War* (New York: Viking, 1976), 63–64; Robert James Maddox, *From War to Cold War* (Boulder, CO: Westview Press, 1989).

14. Roosevelt's comments appear in Robert E. Sherwood, *Roosevelt and Hopkins: An Intimate History*, 2 vols., (New York: G. P. Putnam's Sons, 1950); Paul Johnson, *A History of the American People* (New York: HarperCollins, 1997), 790; "Bush and Putin: Best of Friends," BBC News, http://usproxy.bbc.com/2/hi/europe/1392791.stm. John F. Kennedy thought much the same thing when he bargained with Khrushchev in Vienna.

15. Roman Blackman, *The Secret File of Joseph Stalin: A Hidden Life* (London: Frank Cass, 2001), 360.

16. Ibid.

17. Blackman, *Secret File of Joseph Stalin*, 360; Lord Moran, *Churchill: The Struggle for Survival, 1940–44* (London: Sphere, 1968), 154; Johnson, *History of the American People*, 791.

18. Johnson, *History of the American People*, 791.

19. Robert Leckie, *The Wars of America* (New York: HarperCollins, 1992), 837; Samuel Eliot Morison, *The Two-Ocean War* (Boston: Little, Brown, 1963), 1046.

20. "Interview Transcripts: Truman's Soviet Policy," http://www.pbs.org/wgbh/amex/truman/filmmore/it_1.html; Harry S. Truman, *Memoirs*, 2 vols. (New York: Doubleday, 1956); Johnson, *History of the American People*, 805.

21. Johnson nevertheless admitted Truman was "surprisingly slow" to react to Stalin's provocations (Johnson, *History of the American People*, 806).

22. Greg Behrman, *The Most Noble Adventure: The Marshall Plan and the Time when America Helped Save Europe* (New York: The Free Press, 2007), 20.

23. Ibid., 21.

24. Johnson, *History of the American People*, 807.

25. Ted Morgan, *FDR: A Biography* (New York: Simon & Schuster, 1985), 473, 613–15, 621.

26. Behrman, *The Most Noble Adventure*, 69.

27. William I. Hitchcock, *The Bitter Road to Freedom: A New History of the Liberation of Europe* (New York: The Free Press, 2008), 216.

28. Victoria de Grazia, *Irresistible Empire: America's Advance Through Twentieth-Century Europe* (Cambridge, MA: Belknap, 2005), 336.

29. Ibid., 340.

30. Behrman, *The Most Noble Adventure*, 164.

31. Ibid., 184.

32. Ibid.,157.

33. Ibid., 226.

34. John Earl Haynes and Harvey Klehr, *Venona: Decoding Soviet Espionage in America* (New Haven, CT: Yale University Press, 2000), 369.

35. Diane Canwell, *The Berlin Airlift* (Gretna, LA: Pelican Publishing, 2008); Roger Gene Miller, *To Save a City: The Berlin Airlift, 1948–1949* (College Station, TX: Texas A&M University Press, 2000).

36. D. M. Giangreco and Robert E. Griffin, *Airbridge to Berlin: The Berlin Crisis of 1948, Its Origins and Aftermath* (New York: Presidio Press, 1988).

37. Peter H. Smith, *Talons of the Eagle: Dynamics of U.S.–Latin American Relations* (New York: Oxford, 1996), 130.

38. Smith, *Talons of the Eagle*, 140.

39. Ibid.

40. Albert C. Wedemeyer, *Wedemeyer Reports!* (New York: Henry Holt & Co., 1958).

41. Robert Higgs, "From Central Planning to the Market: The American Transition, 1945–1947," *Journal of Economic History* 59 (September 1999): 600–623.

42. Clay Blair, *The Forgotten War* (Annapolis, MD: Naval Institute Press, 1987), 4–8.

43. David R. Henderson, "The U.S. Postwar Miracle," Mercatus Center, working paper #10-67, November 2010, 8.

44. Michael Dobbs, *Six Months in 1945* (New York: Alfred A. Knopf, 2012), 354; also Joseph C. Goulden, *Korea: The Untold Story of the War* (New York: Times Books, 1982), 19; and Kim Young-Sik, "A Brief History of the US-Korea Relations Prior to 1945," May 15, 2003, paper presented at the University of Oregon.

45. Goulden, *Korea*, 24.

46. Ibid., 53.

47. J. Lawton Collins, *War in Peacetime* (Boston: Houghton Mifflin, 1969), 30–31.

48. Korean Institute of Military History, *The Korean War*, Volume I (New York: Bison Books, 2000), 109–10.

49. Blair, *Forgotten War*, 55.

50. Collins, *War in Peacetime*, 14.

51. Matthew M. Aid, *The Secret Sentry: The Untold History of the National Security Agency* (New York: Bloomsbury Press, 2009), 27.

52. Ibid.

53. Ibid.

54. Ibid., 377.

55. Martin Russ, *Breakout: The Chosin Reservoir Campaign, Korea 1950* (New York: Penguin Books, 2000), 293–94.

56. Niall Ferguson, *Colossus: The Rise and Fall of the American Empire* (London: Allan Lane, 2004), 89.

57. Ibid., 91.

58. Rosemary Foot, *The Wrong War: American Policy and the Dimensions of the Korean Conflict, 1950–1953* (Ithaca, NY: Cornell University Press, 1985), 25.

59. John E. Mueller, *War, Presidents and Public Opinion* (New York: John Wiley, 1973), 105.

60. Earl J. McGill, *Black Tuesday over Namsi* (Solihull, England: Helion & Company, 2012), 63.

61. Ibid., 187.

62. John Patrick Finnegan, *Military Intelligence* (Washington, DC: U.S. Army Center of Military History, 1998), 101, 107.

63. Reinhard Gehlen, *The Service* (New York: World Publishing, 1972), 119–35.

64. Patrick Seale and Maureen McConnville, *Philby: The Long Road to Moscow* (New York: Simon & Schuster, 1973), 209.

65. Ibid.

66. John Fisher, *Burgess and Maclean: A New Look at the Foreign Office Spies* (London: Hale, 1977), 193.

67. Andrew Boyle, *The Fourth Man: The Definitive Account of Kim Philby, Guy Burgess, and Donald Maclean and Who Recruited Them to Spy for Russia* (New York: Dial Press, 1979), 432.

68. Haynes and Klehr, *Venona*, 126.

69. Ibid., 141.

70. Ibid., 142.

71. Edward Mark, "Who was VENONA's ALES? Cryptanalysis and the Hiss Case," *IONS* 18 (Autumn 2003); John R. Schindler, "Hiss in VENONA: The Continuing Controversy," paper presented at Symposium of Center for Cryptologic History, October 27, 2005, Laurel, MD.

72. John Earl Haynes and Harvey Klehr, "Hiss Was Guilty," historynewsnetwork, April 16, 2007, http://hnn.us/articles/37456.htm. Also see Nathaniel Weyl, *Treason: The Story of Disloyalty and Betrayal in American History* (Washington, DC: Public Affairs Press, 1950), and Christopher Andrew and Oleg Gordievsky, *KGB: The Inside Story of Its Foreign Operations from Lenin to Gorbachev* (New York: HarperCollins, 1990), 287.

73. G. Edward White, *Alger Hiss's Looking-Glass War* (New York: Oxford University Press, 2005), 82–83; White's relatively short rendition of Hiss and his life is perhaps the best single book on Hiss, but see also John Earl Haynes, Harvey Klehr, and Alexander Vassiliev, *Spies: The Rise and Fall of the KGB in America* (New Haven, CT: Yale University Press, 2009); Allen Weinstein, *Perjury*, 2nd ed. (New York: Random House, 1997); Allen Weinstein and Alexander Vassiliev, *The Haunted Wood* (New York: The Modern Library, 1999); and Jerrold and Leona Schecter, *Shared Secrets* (Washington, DC: Brassey's Inc., 2003); all agree there is no question Hiss was a Communist and Soviet agent.

74. Larry Schweikart, *48 Liberal Lies about American History (That You Probably Learned in School)* (New York: Sentinel, 2008), 245–46.

75. "Russian General Retreats on Hiss," *New York Times*, December 17, 1992.

76. Schecter and Schecter, *Shared Secrets*, 29; David Rees, *Harry Dexter White: A Study in Paradox* (New York: Coward, McCann, and Geoghegan, 1973), 114.

77. Haynes and Klehr, *Venona*, 149–50.

78. Schweikart, *48 Liberal Lies*, 104.

79. Aleksandr Felkisov and Sergei Kostin, *The Man Behind the Rosenbergs* (New York: Enigma Books, 2001), 40–47.

80. "Judge Kaufman's Statement Upon Sentencing the Rosenbergs," April 1951, University of Missouri–Kansas City, http://law2.umkc.edu/faculty/projects/ftrials/rosenb/ROS_SENT.HTM.

81. "Case Closed: The Rosenbergs Were Soviet Spies," *Los Angeles Times*, September 17, 2008.

82. "Khrushchev on Rosenbergs: Stoking Old Embers," *New York Times*, September 25, 1990. Khrushchev went on to say, "Let this be a worthy tribute to the memory of those people. Let my words serve as an expression of gratitude to those who sacrificed their lives to a great cause of the Soviet state . . .'"

83. Senator Joseph McCarthy, Speech at Wheeling, West Virginia, 1950, http://faculty.tnstate.edu/tcorse/h2020/senator_joseph_mccarthy.htm.

84. Arthur Herman, *Joseph McCarthy: Reexamining the Life and Legacy of America's Most Hated Senator* (New York: Free Press, 1999).

85. Ibid., 115.

86. Ibid.

87. "Joseph McCarthy," http://www.conservapedia.com/Joseph_McCarthy#Communist_Issue.

88. See, for example, the claims by a standard college textbook that "McCarthy never uncovered a single Communist agent in government" (George Brown Tindall and David E. Shi, *America: A Narrative History* [New York: Norton, 2004], 1041). Contrasted with M. Stanton Evans, *Blacklisted by History: The Untold Story of Senator Joe McCarthy and His Fight Against America's Enemies* (New York: Crown, 2007), who proves without a doubt that the "Annie Lee Moss" claimed by the Left to have been falsely identified as a Communist was by the CPUSA's own records . . . a Communist! (529–35).

89. Herman, *Joseph McCarthy*, 146, 160.

90. Haynes and Klehr, *Venona*, 339.

91. Memorandum, Belmont to Boardman, Nov. 27, 1957, 2–4, FBI Venona Files, FBI FOIA Reading Room, Washington, DC; Matthew M. Aid, *The Secret Sentry* (New York: Bloomsbury Press: 2009), 324.

92. Larry Schweikart and Michael Allen, *A Patriot's History of the United States: From Columbus's Great Discovery to the War on Terror*, 2nd ed. (New York: Sentinel, 2007), 646.

93. Anthony Summers, *Official and Confidential: The Secret Life of J. Edgar Hoover* (New York: G. P. Putnam's Sons, 1993), 191.

94. Guenter Lewy, *The Cause That Failed: Communism in American Political Life* (New York: Oxford University Press, 1990), 101.

95. Harvey Klehr and Earl Haynes, *The American Communist Movement: Storming Heaven Itself* (New York: Twayne, 1992), 181.

96. Herbert Romerstein and Eric Breindel, *The Venona Secrets* (Washington, DC: Regnery Publishing: 2000), 449.

97. Ibid., 434–39.

98. Ibid.

99. Schweikart, *48 Liberal Lies*, 93–96, 104–8, 145–48.

100. Haynes and Klehr, *Venona*, 35.

101. Aid, *Silent Sentry*, 13, 17.

102. Amy Knight, *How the Cold War Began* (New York: Carroll & Graf, 2006), 35.

103. Ibid., 243.

104. Ron Radosh, "What Ronald Reagan Accomplished in His Hollywood Years: A New *LA Times* Article Tells Us the Real Story," PJMedia.com, Feb. 4, 2012, http://pjmedia.com/ronradosh/2012/02/04/what-ronald-reagan-accomplished-in-his-hollywood-years-a-new-la-times-articles-tells-us-the-real-story/.

105. Ronald Reagan, *An American Life* (New York: Pocket Books, 1990), 112.

Chapter 2: Dark Continents

1. Stephen F. Ambrose, *The Supreme Commander: The War Years of General Dwight D. Eisenhower* (Garden City, NY: Doubleday & Company, 1970), 583.

2. Stanley Weintraub, *15 Stars: Eisenhower, MacArthur, Marshall, Three Generals Who Saved the American Century* (New York: The Free Press, 2007), 313.

3. Stanley Wolpert, *Gandhi's Passion: The Life and Legacy of Mahatma Gandhi* (Oxford: Oxford University Press, 2001), 17.

4. Ibid., 26.

5. Carroll Quigley, *Tragedy & Hope: A History of the World in Our Time* (New York: Macmillan, 1966), 169.

6. Wolpert, *Gandhi's Passion*, 23.

7. Quigley, *Tragedy & Hope*, 169.

8. Wolpert, *Gandhi's Passion*, 73.

9. Ibid., 227; Diary, January 2, 1947, in Mohandas K. Gandhi, *The Collected Works of Mahatma Gandhi* (Ahmedabad: Navajivan Trust, 1967–1984), 86:302.

10. Quigley, *Tragedy & Hope*, 170.

11. Ibid., 172.

12. Ibid., 100.

13. Ibid., 107–9.

14. Paul Johnson, *Modern Times: A History of the World from the Twenties to the Nineties* (New York: HarperCollins, 1991), 471; Mohandas K. Gandhi, *The Story of My Experiments with Truth*, http://www.nalanda.nitc.ac.in/resources/english/etext-project/biography/gandhi/part4.chapter7.html; Adolf Just, *Return to Nature: Paradise Regained* (New York: E. P. Dutton, 1912), original translator B. Lust.

15. Ibid., 123.

16. Ibid., 149.

17. Ibid., 123.

18. Ibid., 128.

19. Johnson, *Modern Times*, 471.

20. Ibid., 39.

21. "In God's Name," http://www.time.com/time/magazine/article/0,9171,777380,00.html?iid=chix-sphere.

22. Wolpert, *Gandhi's Passion*, 197.

23. Daniel Yergin and Joseph Stanislaw, *The Commanding Heights: The Battle for the World Economy* (New York: Touchstone, 2002), 51.

24. M. J. Akbar, *Nehru: The Making of India* (New York: Viking Penguin, 1988), 129, quoted in Yergin and Stanislaw, *Commanding Heights*, 52.

25. Jawaharlal Nehru, *An Autobiography* (London: John Lane, 1936), 82; Stanley Wolpert, *Nehru: A Tryst with Destiny* (New York: Oxford, 1996), 46.

26. Akbar, *Nehru*, 122, quoted in Yergin and Stanislaw, *Commanding Heights*, 52.

27. Wolpert, *Nehru*, 283.

28. Ibid., 283.

29. Ibid.

30. Ibid., 129.

31. Ibid., 256.

32. "Working Committee Resolution on the War," September 14, 1939, in S. Gopal, ed., *Selected Works of Jawaharlal Nehru*, 15 vols. (New Dehli: Orient Longman, 1972–1982), 10:122–35; Stanley Wolpert, *Shameful Flight: The Last Years of the British Empire in India* (Oxford: Oxford University Press, 2006).

33. Wolpert, *Nehru*, 258.

34. Quoted in ibid., 301.

35. Ibid., 310.

36. Wolpert, *Gandhi's Passion*, 202.

37. Wolpert, *Nehru*, 311.

38. Ibid., 314.

39. Wolpert, *Shameful Flight*, 17. This is contrary to Paul Johnson's claim that Nehru "almost until the last minute . . . refused to believe . . . that if the British Raj handed over power to [the Indian Congress] the Muslims would demand a separate state" (Johnson, *Modern Times*, 473).

40. William Easterly, *White Man's Burden: Why the West's Efforts to Aid the Rest Have Done So Much Ill and So Little Good* (New York: Penguin, 2006), 299.

41. Archibald Percival Wavell to Leo Amery, June 25, 1945, #537, in Nicholas Mansergh and E.W.R. Lumby, eds., *The Transfer of Power, 1942–1947*, 12 vols. (London: HMSO, 1983), 5:1154–57.

42. Wavell to Lord Penthick-Lawrence, October 9, 1945, *Transfer of Power*, 6:319–20.

43. Ibid.

44. Wolpert, *Nehru*, 386.

45. See, for example, Jane Caplan and John Torpey, eds., *Documenting Individual Identity: The Development of State Practices in the Modern World* (Princeton, NJ: Princeton University Press, 2001).

46. Wolpert, *Nehru*, 401.

47. "Speech at Prayers," September 17, 1947, in Mohandas K. Gandhi, *Collected Works of Mahatma Gandhi*, vols. 23–90 (Ahmedabad: Navajivan Trust, 1967–1984), 89:183–86.

48. Alastair Lamb, *Kashmir: A Disputed Legacy, 1846–1990* (Hertingfordbury, England: Roxford Books, 1991).

49. Johnson, *Modern Times*, 474.

50. Jawaharlal Nehru, *Visit to America* (New York: John Day, 1950).

51. Wolpert, *Shameful Flight*, 2, quoting *The* [London] *Spectator*, September 4, 2004, John Osman's e-mail about Mountbatten.

52. Jawaharal Nehru, *The Discovery of India* (New Dehli: Oxford, 1989), 29.

53. Ibid., 372.

54. Quoted in Yergin and Stanislaw, *Commanding Heights*, 53.

55. Nehru, *Discovery of India*, 398.

56. Nehru, *Visit to America*, 5.

57. Ibid., 6.

58. Johnson, *Modern Times*, 475.

59. Nehru, *Visit to America*, 31–33.

60. Ibid., 50.

61. "Chinese Deception, Nehru's Naivete Led to '62 War: CIA Papers," *Times of India*, June 27, 2007.

62. Ibid.

63. Jung Chang and Jon Halliday, *Mao: The Unknown Story* (New York: Anchor, 2006), 568, 579.

64. John W. Garver, "China's Decision for War with India in 1962," http://www.people.fas.harvard.edu/~johnston/garver.pdf.

65. R. Sukumaran, "The 1962 India-China War and Kargil 1999: Restrictions on the Use of Air Power," *Strategic Analysis* 27 (July–September, 2003), http://www.ciaonet.org/olj/sa/sa_jul03/sa_jul03sur01.html#txt1.

66. P. B. Sinha, A. A. Athale, with S. N. Prasad, eds., *History of the Conflict with China, 1962* (New Delhi: History Division, Ministry of Defence, Government of India, 1992), 430.

67. John Rowland, *A History of Sino-Indian Relations* (Princeton, NJ: Van Nostrand, 1967), xv.

68. Johnson, *Modern Times*, 167–73; David Gadd, *The Loving Friends: A Portrait of Bloomsbury* (New York: Harcourt Brace, 1974).

69. Johnson, *Modern Times*, 168.

70. Virginia Woolf, "A Sketch of the Past," 1939, unfinished memoir available at www.woolfonline.com.

71. William Graham Sumner, *What the Social Classes Owe Each Other* (Caldwell, ID: Caxton Printers, 1974), 15.

72. Andrew Carnegie, *The Gospel of Wealth* (London: F. C. Hagen & Co., 1889).

73. Sumner, *What Social Classes Owe to Each Other*, 13–24, 113–21, 157–68.

74. Ludwig von Mises, *Socialism: An Economic and Sociological Analysis*, trans. J. Kahane (New Haven, CT: Yale University Press).

75. W. Ross Ashby, *An Introduction to Cybernetics* (New York: Chapman, 1956), 29–30.

76. Von Mises, *Socialism*, http://www.econlib.org/library/Mises/msSApp.html.

77. Peter Klein, ed., *The Fortunes of Liberalism: The Collected Works of F. A. Hayek* (London: Routledge, 1993), 170.

78. W. W. Bartley and Stephen Kresge, *F. A. Hayek: The Trend of Economic Thinking* (London: Routledge, 1991), 40.

79. Ludwig von Mises, *Omnipotent Government: The Rise of the Total State and Total War* (New Haven, CT: Yale University Press), 1944.

80. Yergin and Stanislaw, *Commanding Heights*, 124–45.

81. Richard Crokett, *Thinking the Unthinkable: Think-tanks and the Economic Counter Revolution* (London: Fontana Press, 1995), 89–90.

82. Frederich A. Von Hayek, *The Constitution of Liberty* (Chicago: University of Chicago Press, 1960).

83. Yergin and Stanislaw, *Commanding Heights*, 128; Melvin Reder, "Chicago Economics: Permanence and Change," *Journal of Economic Literature*, March 1982, 1–38.

84. Gerald M. Meier, "The Formative Period," in Gerald M. Meier and Dudley Seers, eds., *Pioneers in Development* (New York: Oxford University Press, 1984), 240–45, 277; Sukhamoy Chakravarty, *Development Planning: The Indian Experience* (Oxford University Press, 1966).

85. Alexander Gerschenkron, *Economic Backwardness in Historical Perspective* (Cambridge, MA: Belknap, 1962 [1951]).

86. W. W. Rostow, *Stages of Economic Growth: a Non-Communist Manifesto* (Cambridge: Cambridge University Press, 1960), and Peter Thomas Bauer and Basil S. Yamey, *The Economics of Under-developed Countries* (Cambridge: Cambridge University Press, 1957).

87. Yergin and Stanislaw, *Commanding Heights*, 64.

88. Ron Chernow, *Titan: The Life of John D. Rockefeller* (New York: Vintage, 1998).

89. See the discussion in Larry Schweikart and Michael Allen, *A Patriot's History of the United States from Columbus's Great Discovery to the War on Terror* (New York: Sentinel, 2006), 155–58, 182–84, 186–89; Larry Schweikart, *The Entrepreneurial Adventure: A History of Business in the United States* (Fort Worth, TX: Harcourt, 2000), ch. 3.

90. Alfred D. Chandler, Jr., *Visible Hand: The Managerial Revolution in American Business* (Cambridge, MA: Belknap, 1977); Burton W. Folsom, Jr., *The Myth of the Robber Barons* (Herndon, VA: Young America's Foundation, 1991).

91. Easterly, *White Man's Burden*, 165.

92. Ibid., 190.

93. David Dougherty and C. Specter in 1981 studied business investment policy in developing nations. Categorizing various models of government and expected sales growth by international businesses, they found that the emergence of a strong leader or seizure of power by a military junta indicated a favorable environment for investment, whereas internal strife and movement toward increased socialism called for a phasing out of in-country investments. (D. M. Dougherty and C. Specter, "Intervention Analysis: A Tool for Improved Risk Analysis in International Business," *Management International Review* 22 (1982): 9–21.)

94. Tony Killick, *Development Economics in Action: A Study of Economic Policies in Ghana* (London: Thomas Nelson and Sons, 1961), 34.

95. Martin Meredith, *The Fate of Africa: A History of Fifty Years of Independence* (New York: Public Affairs, 2005), 163.

96. John F. Kennedy, "Remarks of Welcome to President Nkrumah of Ghana at the Washington National Airport," March 8, 1961.

97. Yergin and Stanislaw, *Commanding Heights*, 69.

98. Tony Judt, *Postwar: A History of Europe Since 1945* (New York: Penguin, 2005), 280.

99. Ibid., 278–79.

100. Ibid., 282.

101. Meredith, *Fate of Africa*, 5.

102. Ibid., 5–6.

103. Ibid., 4.

104. Ibid., 8.

105. Ibid.

106. Johnson, *Modern Times*, 508.

107. Steward Easton, *The Twilight of European Colonialism* (London: Methuen, 1961), 31.

108. Johnson, *Modern Times*, 508.

109. Aaron Klein interview, February 27, 2011, http://www.wnd.com/index.php?pageId=268989.

110. Thomas Sowell, *Ethnic America* (New York: Basic Books, 1981), 31.

111. Jonathan Derrick, *Africa's Agitators: Militant Anti-Colonialism in Africa and the West, 1918–1939* (New York: Columbia University Press, 2008), 83 ("Declaration of the Rights of the Negro Peoples of the World").

112. Johnson, *Modern Times*, 481.

113. Quoted in *Obsession: Radical Islam's War Against the West*, Wayne Kopping, director, 2007.

114. Netanel Lorch, *The Edge of the Sword: Israel's War of Independence, 1947-1949* (Norwalk, CT: Easton Press, 1961), 25.

115. Howard Morely Sachar, *A History of Israel: From the Rise of Zionism to Our Time* (New York: Knopf, 2007), 265–66.

116. David Jeremiah, *What in the World Is Going On?* (Nashville: Thomas Nelson, 2008), 22.

117. David McCullough, *Truman* (New York: Simon and Schuster, 1992), 620.

118. Harry S. Truman, *Memoirs: 1945: Year of Decisions* (New York: Konecky and Konecky, 1955), 69.

119. Truman, *Memoirs: 1945*, 69.

120. Gary Frazier, *Signs of the Coming of Christ* (Arlington, TX: Discovery Ministries, 1998), 67.

121. Larry Schweikart and Dave Dougherty, *A Patriot's History of the Modern World, From America's Exceptional Ascent to the Atomic Bomb, 1898-1945* (New York: Sentinel, 2012), 198–99.

122. Christopher Andrew and Vasili Mitrokhin, *The World Was Going Our Way: The KGB and the Battle for the Third World* (New York: Basic Books, 2005), 427.

123. Kwame Nkrumah, *I Speak of Freedom: A Statement of African Ideology* (London: Heinemann, 1961), 262–63.

124. Said K. Aburish, *Nasser, the Last Arab* (New York: St. Martin's Press, 2004), 18.

125. Andrew and Mitrokhin, *The World Was Going Our Way*, 146.

126. Ibid., 149.

127. Ibid., 150.

128. Ibid., 150.

129. Ibid., 153.

130. Johnson, *Modern Times*, 492.

131. Ibid.

132. Andrew and Mitrokhkin, *The World Was Going Our Way*, 152.

133. Nelson Mandela, *Long Walk to Freedom* (London: Little, Brown 1994), 123–24, 137–38, 436, 562.

134. Andrew and Mitrokhin, *The World Was Going Our Way*, 428.

135. Ibid., 445.

136. William Finnegan, *A Complicated War: The Harrowing of Mozambique* (Berkeley: University of California Press, 1992), 108–13.

137. Barack H. Obama [Senior], "Another Critique of Sessional Paper No. 10, Problems Facing Our Socialism," *East Africa Journal*, July 1965, 1–10 (quotation on 8).

138. Ibid., 9.

139. Andrew and Mitrokhin, *The World Was Going Our Way*, 434.

140. Ibid., 436.

141. Ibid., 437.

142. Bruce D. Larkin, *China and Africa 1949–1970: The Foreign Policy of the People's Republic of China* (Berkeley: University of California Press, 1971), 2; Philip Snow, *The Star Raft: China's Encounter with Africa* (London: Weidenfeld & Nicolson, 1988), 100–101.

143. Andrew and Mitrokhin, *The World Was Going Our Way*, 444.

144. Easterly, *White Man's Burden*, 4.

145. Thomas W. Dichter, *Despite Good Intentions* (Amherst: University of Massachusetts Press, 2003), ix.

146. Craig Burnside and David Dollar, "Aid, Policies, and Growth," *American Economic Review* 90 (September 2000): 847–68.

147. Easterly, *White Man's Burden*, 48, and his "Can Aid Buy Growth?," *Journal of Economic Perspectives* 17 (Summer 2003): 23–48; William Easterly, Ross Levine, and David Roodman, "New Data, New Doubts: Comment on 'Aid, Policies, and Growth,' (2000) by Burnside and Dollar," *American Economic Review* 94 (June 2004): 774–80.

148. Peter Boone's 1996 study, cited in Easterly, *White Man's Burden*, 45.

149. Raghuram G. Rajan and Arvind Subramanian, "Aid and Growth: What Does the Cross-Country Evidence Really Show?," IMF mimeograph, April 2005, cited in Easterly, *White Man's Burden*, 49.

150. Easterly, *White Man's Burden*, 45.

151. Stephen C. Smith, *Ending Global Poverty: A Guide to What Works* (New York: Palgrave Macmillan, 2005), 59.

152. Hernando De Soto, *The Mystery of Capital: Why Capitalism Triumphs in the West and Fails Everywhere Else* (New York: Basic Books, 2003).

153. World Bank, *Doing Business in 2005: Removing Obstacles to Growth* (Washington, DC: World Bank, International Finance Corporation and Oxford University Press, 2005), 3.

154. Easterly, *White Man's Burden*, 95.

155. Paul J. Zak and Stephen Knack, "Trust and Growth," World Bank, Development Research Group, September 18, 1998; Stephen Knack and Paul J. Zak, "Building Trust: Public Policy, Interpersonal Trust, and Economic Development," March 2002, http://ssrn.com/abstract=304640; Steve Knack, "Groups, Growth, and Trust," *Public Choice* 117 (2003): 341–55.

156. Easterly, *White Man's Burden*, 82.

157. Larry Schweikart, *Banking in the American South from the Age of Jackson to Reconstruction* (Baton Rouge: Louisiana State University Press, 1987).

158. Naomi Lamoreaux, *Insider Lending: Banks, Personal Connections, and Economic Development in Industrial New England* (Cambridge: Cambridge University Press, 1996).

159. Harold Evans with Gail Buckland and David Lefer, *They Made America* (New York: Little Brown, 2004), 118–24.

160. Rowena Olegario, *A Culture of Credit: Embedding Trust and Transparency in American Business* (Cambridge, MA: Harvard University Press, 2006), 45.

161. Ibid., 80.

162. Schweikart and Allen, *A Patriot's History of the United States from Columbus's Great Discovery to the War on Terror*, introduction.

163. Philippe Aghion, Alberto Alesina, and Francesco Trebbi, "Endogenous Political Institutions," 2004, cited in Easterly, *White Man's Burden*, 120.

164. William Easterly, R. Gatti, and S. Kurlar, "Democracy, Development, and Mass Killings," New York University Development Research Institute Working Paper, 2004. In a revival of Beardianism, Daron Acemoglu and James Robinson argue that democracies result from an agreement between a rich minority and a poor majority, whereby the majority agrees to share power with the minority to avoid revolution, conditional upon checks and balances of the redistributive power of the majority. See Daren Acemoglu and James A. Robinson, *Economic Origins of Dictatorship and Democracy* (Cambridge: Cambridge University Press, 2006).

165. Daron Acemoglu, "The Form of Property Rights: Oligarchic vs. Democratic Societies," cited in Easterly, *White Man's Burden*, 121.

166. William Easterly, "The Middle-Class Consensus and Economic Development," *Journal of Economic Growth* 6 (December 2001): 317–36.

167. Harry S. Truman, *Years of Trial and Hope*, vol. 2, *Memoirs* (Garden City, NY: Doubleday, 1956), 232; Dichter, *Despite Good Intentions*, 55.

168. Dichter, *Despite Good Intentions*, 68–69.

169. Ibid., 109.

170. Willard L. Thorp, *The Reality of Foreign Aid* (New York: Praeger, 1971), 11.

171. James Piereson, *Camelot and the Cultural Revolution: How the Assassination of John F. Kennedy Shattered American Liberalism* (New York: Encounter Books, 2007), 209.

172. Eugene W. Castle, *The Great Giveaway* (Chicago: Henry Regnery Company, 1957), 37.

173. Easterly, *White Man's Burden*, 133.

174. Alberto Alesina and Beatrice Weder, "Do Corrupt Governments Receive Less Foreign Aid?," *American Economic Review* 92 (September 2002): 1126–37.

175. Quotations, mostly from World Bank officials, cited in Easterly, *White Man's Burden*, 138–39.

176. William Easterly, *White Man's Burden*, 218.

177. Michael Hunt, *Ideology and U.S. Foreign Policy* (New Haven, CT: Yale University Press, 1987), 164.

178. Richard D. Mahoney, *JFK: Ordeal in Africa* (New York: Oxford, 1983), 35.

179. Amin, *Peace Corps in Cameroon*, 43.

180. John F. Kennedy, Inaugural Address, January 20, 1961, http://www.bartleby.com/124/pres56.html.

181. Julius Amin, *The Peace Corps in Cameroon* (Kent, OH: Kent State University Press, 1992), 15.

182. Ibid., 19.

183. "Speech of Senator John F. Kennedy," Cow Palace, San Francisco, CA, November 2, 1960, U.S. Subcommittee on *Freedom of Communications*, part 1, The Speeches, Remarks, Press Conferences and Statements of Senator John F. Kennedy, August 1–November 7, 1960, 87th Cong., 1st sess. (Washington, DC: Government Printing Office, 1961), 865.

184. Dichter, *Despite Good Intentions*, 60, referring to William Lederer's and Eugene Burdick's 1958 book, *The Ugly American* (New York: Norton, 1958). On the Peace Corps, see Gerard T. Rice, *The Bold Experiment: JFK'S Peace Corps* (Notre Dame, IN: University of Notre Dame Press, 1985); Coates Redmond, *Come as You Are: The Peace Corps Story* (San Diego: Harcourt Brace Jovanovich, 1986); and Milton Viorst, ed., *Making a Difference: The Peace Corps at Twenty-five* (New York: Weidenfeld & Nicholson, 1986).

185. Quoted in Amin, *Peace Corps in Cameroon*, 4.

186. Rice, *Bold Experiment*, 2.

187. Amin, *Peace Corps in Cameroon*, 18.

188. Dichter, *Despite Good Intentions*, 61.

189. Henry Fairlie, *The Kennedy Promise: The Politics of Expectation* (New York: Doubleday, 1973), 180–81.

190. Amin, *Peace Corps in Cameroon*, 121.

191. Viorst, *Making a Difference*, 34; *New York Herald Tribune*, March 27, 1961; Rice, *Bold Experiment*, 70.

192. Jody Olson, "The Volunteer," in Viorst, *Making a Difference*, 48.

193. Amin, *Peace Corps in Cameroon*, 25; Fairlie, *The Kennedy Promise*, 180–81.

194. Amin, *Peace Corps in Cameroon*, 26.

195. Viorst, *Making a Difference*, 59.

196. "An Exchange Between President Kennedy and Tom Scanlon," 1962, in Viorst, *Making a Difference*, 42–43.

197. Viorst, *Making a Difference*, 119.

198. Arthur M. Schlesinger, Jr., *The Crisis of Confidence* (New York: Houghton Mifflin, 1969), 153.

199. Fairlie, *The Kennedy Promise*, 22; Walter Lippmann, *The National Purpose* (New York: Holt, Rinehart & Winston, 1960).

200. Arthur M. Schlesinger, Jr., "The Shape of National Politics to Come," cited in Rice, *Bold Experiment*, 27.

Chapter 3: Freedom's Chariots

1. Daniel Yergin and Joseph Stanislaw, *The Commanding Heights: The Battle for the World Economy* (New York: Touchstone, 2002), 15.

2. John Gillingham, *European Integration, 1950–2003* (Cambridge: Cambridge University Press, 2003), 12.

3. Yergin and Stanislaw, *Commanding Heights*, 18.

4. Jeffrey K. Olick, *In the House of the Hangman: The Agonies of German Defeat, 1947–1949* (Chicago: University of Chicago Press, 2005), 43.

5. Giles MacDonogh, *After the Reich* (New York: Basic Books, 2007), 394.

6. Ibid., 395.

7. Gillingham, *European Integration*, passim.

8. Gillingham, *European Integration*, 15, 20–21.

9. Herbert Giersch et al., *The Fading Miracle: Four Decades of Market Economy in Germany* (Cambridge: Cambridge University Press, 1992), 88.

10. Gillingham, *European Integration*, 55.

11. Ibid., 56.

12. Victor Sebestven, *Twelve Days: The Story of the 1956 Hungarian Revolution* (New York: Pantheon Books, 2006), 264.

13. Paul Johnson, *Modern Times: A History of the World from the Twenties to the Nineties*, 2nd ed. (New York: HarperColllins, 1991), 578.

14. Konrad Adenauer, *Memoirs, 1945–1953* (Washington, DC: Regnery, 1965); Charles Williams, *Adenauer: The Father of the New Germany* (New York: John Wiley, 2001); Hans-Peter Schwarz, *Konrad Adenauer: A German Politician and Statesman in a Period of War, Revolution and Reconstruction: from the German Empire to the Federal Republic, 1876–1952*, vol. 1 (Oxford: Berghahn Books, 1995).

15. Olick, *In the House of the Hangman*, 251. On Adenauer, see Williams, *Adenauer: The Father of the New Germany*; Schwartz, *Konrad Adenauer: A German Politician*; and Paul Weymar, *Adenauer: His Authorized Biography* (New York: Dutton, 1957).

16. Olick, *In the House of the Hangman*, 251.

17. Ibid., 253.

18. Ibid., 251.

19. Ibid., 255.

20. Johnson, *Modern Times*, 582.

21. Ibid., 585.

22. C. L. Sulzberger, *The Last of the Giants* (New York: Macmillan, 1970), 13.

23. Jean Lacouture, *De Gaulle the Rebel 1890–1944* (New York: W. W. Norton, 1990), 137.

24. Johnson, *Modern Times*, 588. Numbers range from 75,000 to a few hundred.

25. Sulzberger, *The Last of the Giants*, 29. He also noted that "the big trouble with France is that in one hundred and fifty years it has had thirteen constitutions and has been invaded six times" (25). De Gaulle started with 1814.

26. Sulzberger, *Last of the Giants*, 19.

27. Ibid., 107.

28. Johnson, *Modern Times*, 594.

29. Sulzberger, *Last of the Giants*, 23.

30. Paul Johnson, *Heroes* (New York: HarperCollins, 2007), 232.

31. Christopher G. L. Hall, *Steel Phoenix: The Fall and Rise of the U.S. Steel Industry* (New York: St. Martin's, 1997), 37.

32. Henry R. Nau, *The Myth of America's Decline: Leading the World Economy into the 1990s* (New York: Oxford University Press, 1992), 63.

33. Ibid., 53.

34. Ibid., 54.

35. Cotten Seiler, *Republic of Drivers: A Cultural History of Automobility in America* (Chicago: University of Chicago Press, 2008), 2.

36. Martin E. Marty, "The Altar of Automobility," *The Christian Century* 75 (January 22, 1958): 95.

37. Ruth Brandon, *How the Car Changed Life* (London: Macmillan, 2002), 2; Loren E. Lomasky, "Autonomy and Automobility," *Independent Review* 2 (1997): 8–9.

38. Jeff Jacoby, "Our Passion for Automobility," *Boston Globe*, August 10, 1995.

39. Seiler, *Republic of Drivers*, 45.

40. Ibid., 100.

41. Marty, "Altar of Automobility," 95.

42. John Heitmann, "The Automobile and American Life," 2007, manuscript in author's possession, chapter 7:3; David Gartman, *Auto Opium: A Social History of the American Automobile Design* (London: Routledge, 1994), and his "Three Ages of the Automobile: the Cultural Logistics of the Car," *Theory, Culture & Society* 21 (2004): 169ff.; John Keats, *The Insolent Chariots* (Greenwich, CT: Fawcett, 1959), 26; David L. Lewis and Laurence Goldstein, eds., *The Automobile and American Culture* (Ann Arbor: University of Michigan Press, 1983).

43. Vance Packard: *The Hidden Persuaders* (New York: D. McKay, 1957); Keats, *The Insolent Chariots*, passim; B. Bruce-Briggs, *The War Against the Automobile* (New York: Dutton, 1977).

44. Lewis H. Siegebaum, *Cars for Comrades: The Life of the Soviet Automobile* (Ithaca, NY: Cornell University Press, 2008), 2, 14.

45. Ibid., 40.

46. Ibid., 20.

47. Ibid., 52.

48. Ibid., 225.

49. Ibid., 127.

50. Ibid., 257.

51. Ibid., 253–54.

52. Time lists, "1975 Trabant," http://www.time.com/time/specials/2007/article/0,28804,1658545_1658533_1658030,00.html.

53. Bernhard Rieger, "From People's Car to New Beetle: The Transatlantic Journeys of the Volkswagen Beetle," *Journal of American History*, June 2010, 91–115.

54. Ibid., 94.

55. Ibid., 98.

56. Ibid., passim.

57. "Tripping Down the Hippie Highway," *Newsweek*, July 27, 1970, 22–24.

58. Tony Judt, *Postwar: A History of Europe Since 1945* (New York: Penguin Press, 2005), 339.

59. Ibid., 341.

60. Seiler, *Republic of Drivers*, 71.

61. Ken Purdy, "The Unbelieving Auto Inventor," *Catholic Digest* 16 (September 1952): 72–74.

62. National Safety Research Council, "Motor-Vehicle Deaths and Rates," *Accident Facts*, 1998, 104. The incredible tale of Dean's Porsche 550 Spyder after his death remains grist for the writing mills of those inclined toward the supernatural: when a car customizer bought it, the Porsche rolled off a truck and broke a mechanic's legs; broken up for parts, the engine wound up in a doctor's Porsche, who was killed in a crash on his first outing; and a doctor who bought the Dean transmission also ended up in a nonfatal crash, while a New Yorker who purchased the Dean Porsche's tires had them both blow out simultaneously and also was in a nonfatal crash. Finally, the shell of the Porsche, while en route to sale, was stolen after the transporter was in a crash and the driver killed.

63. Special thanks to John Heitmann for this material in his manuscript, "The Automobile in American Life." See also Stephen Bayley, *Sex, Drink and Fast Cars* (New York: Pantheon, 1986), 52–57.

64. In 2004, the song was ranked #18 on *Rolling Stone* magazine's five hundred greatest songs of all time.

65. Heitmann, "Automobile in American Life," 160.

66. Alfred Kinsey, et al., *Sexual Behavior in the Human Female* (Philadelphia: W. B. Saunders Company, 1953), 310. A 2006 survey of Brits found 68 percent had engaged in sex in a car, 10 percent actually had sex while driving, and 6 percent had damaged their car DWC (driving while copulating). Asked to name their favorite "passion wagon," Brits voted the Volvo Estate number one ("Volvo Estate Named 'Best Passion Wagon,'" *Daily Mail*, May 10, 2006, http://www.dailymail.co.uk/pages/text/print.html?in_article_id=408674&in_page_id+1770). Likewise, car critics could not resist the sexual imagery. Peter March and Peter Collett, *Driving Passion: The Psychology of the Car* (Boston and London: Faber and Faber, 1987), 201. The car works as a metaphor of the most basic aspect of human behavior for both males and females past the point of puberty. The symbolism evoked by its shape is fused with inevitable connotations of its mechanical functions. In the internal combustion engine pistons pump reciprocatingly in lubricated cylinders. So close are the parallels that they arouse embarrassment.

67. Ibid., 325.

68. Ibid., 325, 331.

69. Ibid.

70. Judt, *Postwar*, 338.

71. Ibid., 338–39.

72. Mark Mazower, *Dark Continent: Europe's Twentieth Century* (New York: Knopf, 1998), 279.

73. Ibid., 281.

74. James J. Flink, "Three Stages of American Automobile Consciousness," *American Quarterly* 24 (October 1972): 451–73 (quotations on 452, 454).

75. Everett S. Lee, "The Turner Thesis Reexamined," *American Quarterly* 14 (Summer 1962): 275–89.

76. Thomas C. Cochran, *The American Business System* (Cambridge, MA: Harvard University Press, 1957), 44.

77. Alan Petigny, *The Permissive Society: America, 1941–1965* (Cambridge: Cambridge University Press, 2009), 8.

78. Charles L. Sanford, "The Intellectual Origins and New-Worldliness of American Industry," *Journal of Economic History* 18 (March 1958): 1–16 (quotation on 2).

79. Victoria de Grazia, *Irresistible Empire: America's Advance Through Twentieth-Century Europe* (Cambridge, MA: Belknap Press, 2005), 398.

80. Ibid., 347, 361.

81. Ibid., 347, 364.

82. Ibid., 395.

83. Ibid., 403–4.

84. Ibid., 449.

85. Harold Evans with Gail Buckland and David Lefer, *They Made America: From the Steam Engine to the Search Engine: Two Centuries of Innovators* (New York: Little, Brown, 2004), 388–92.

86. Mira Kamdar, *Planet India: How the Fastest Growing Democracy Is Transforming America and the World* (New York: Scribner, 2007), 59; Evans et al., *They Made America*, 392.

87. Christiane Diehl Taylor, "The Worth of Wives: 1950s Corporate America 'Discovers' Spousal Social Capital," in Lynne Pierson Doti, ed., *Essays in Economic and Business History*, 26, 2008, 33–46 (quotation on 41).

88. U.S. Department of Commerce, Bureau of the Census, "Series D 182-232, Major Occupation Group of Experienced Civilian Labor Force, by Sex, 1900–1970, *Historical Statistics of the United States: Colonial Times to 1970* (Washington, DC: Department of Commerce, Bureau of the Census, 1975); Claudia Golden, *Understanding the Gender Gap: Economic History of American Women* (New York: Oxford University Press, 1990), 175–76.

89. Ferdinand Lundberg and Marynia F. Farnham, *Modern Woman: The Lost Sex* (New York: Harper and Brothers, 1947), v–15.

90. Petigny, *The Permissive Society*, 106–7.

91. Taylor, "Worth of Wives," 35.

92. E. M. Ryan, "Executive Wives in a Growing Business," *American Business*, July 1957, 14.

93. William H. Whyte, Jr., "The Wives of Management," *Fortune*, October 1951, 86–88, 204–13, and "The Corporation and the Wife," *Fortune*, November 1951, 109–11; Laurence A. Appley, "Wife, Home Greatly Affect Personal Progress," *Personnel Journal* 32 (May 1953): 10–14; and C. F. Johnson, "When the Boss's Wife Should Have Stayed Home," *American Business*, August 1958, 15.

94. Eli Zaretsky, "Charisma or Rationalization? Domesticity and Psychoanalysis in the United States in the 1950s," *Critical Inquiry* 26 (Winter 2000): 328–54.

95. T. B. Johannis, Jr., and J. M. Rollins, "Teenager Perception of Family Decision-making," *The Coordinator*, June 1959, 70–74; M. I. Kohn, "Social Class and Exercise of Parental Authority," *American Sociological Review*, June 1959, 352–66; and Robert O. Blood., Jr., and Donald M. Wolfe, *Husbands and Wives: The Dynamics of Married Living* (Glencoe, IL: Free Press, 1960).

96. Blood and Wolfe, *Husbands and Wives*, 28–29.

97. William G. Dyer and Dick Urban, "The Institutionalization of Equalitarian Family Norms," *Marriage and Family Living*, February 1958, 53–58.

98. Ruth Rosen, *The World Split Open: How the Modern Women's Movement Changed America* (New York: Viking, 2000), 36.

99. Steven Mintz and Susan Kellogg, *Domestic Revolutions: A Social History of American Family Life* (New York: Free Press, 1988), 186–87.

100. Lizabeth Cohen, *A Consumers' Republic: The Politics of Mass Consumption in Postwar America* (New York: Vintage, 2003), 148.

101. Elizabeth H. Wolgast, "Do Husbands or Wives Make the Purchasing Decisions?" *Journal of Marketing*, October 1958, 151–58.

102. Carl Abbott, *The New Urban America: Growth and Politics in Sunbelt Cities* (Chapel Hill: University of North Carolina Press, 1987); Joel Kotkin and Fred Siegel, *Digital Geography : The Remaking of City and Countryside in the New Economy* (Washington: Hudson Institute, 2000).

103. David M. Dougherty, "El Paso: A Travel Time Quality View to Growth," *Southwest Business and Economic Review*, University of Texas at El Paso Bureau of Business and Economic Research 20 (August 1982): 1–14.

104. David H. McDonald, "Saving America's Cities," 2009, unpublished manuscript in Larry Schweikart's possession, courtesy of David H. McDonald, 16–17.

105. Andrew A. Beveridge and Fredrica Rudell, "A Review: An Evaluation of 'Public Attitudes Toward Science and Technology' in Science Indicators: The 1985 Report," in *Public Opinion Quarterly*, Autumn 1988, 374–85 (quotation on 382).

106. Petigny, *The Permissive Society*, 10.

107. Ibid., 111; Donald T. Critchlow, *Intended Consequences: Birth Control, Abortion, and the Federal Government in Modern America* (New York: Oxford University Press, 1999).

108. Elaine Tyler May, *Homeward Bound: American Families in the Cold War Era* (New York: Basic Books, 1988); John D'Emilio and Estelle Freedman, *Intimate Matters: A History of Sexuality in America* (Chicago: University of Chicago Press, 1988).

109. Petigny, *The Permissive Society*, 117.

110. Ibid., 201.

111. Typical of the traditional views are Steven Seidman, *Embattled Eros: Sexual Politics and Ethics in Contemporary America* (New York: Routledge, 1992); John Heindry, *What Wild Ecstasy: The Rise and Fall of the Sexual Revolution* (New York: Simon & Schuster, 1997); and Arlene Skonick, *Embattled Paradise: The American Family in an Age of Uncertainty* (New York: Basic Books, 1991).

112. Charles J. Caput, "Contraception: A Symposium," *First Things*, December 1988, 19–20; Harvey Mansfield, "The Legacy of the Late 1960s," in Steven Macedo, ed., *Reassessing the Sixties: Debating the Political and Cultural Legacy* (New York: W. W. Norton, 1997), 21–31; Mona Charen, "Paying Dues for the Sexual Revolution," *Newsday*, January 22, 1990, 46; William Bennett, *Index of Leading Cultural Indicators: Facts and Figures on the State of American Society* (New York: Touchstone, 1994); Robert Bork, *Slouching Toward Gomorrah: Modern Liberalism and American Decline* (New York: Regan Books, 1996); and Gertrude Himmelfarb, "A De-Moralized Society: The British/American Experience," in Mark Gerson, ed., *The Essential Neo-Conservative Reader* (New York: Addison-Wesley, 1996), 412–13. Bennett doesn't mention any statistics for single motherhood prior to 1960, for example.

113. Bernard Asbell, *The Pill: A Biography of the Drug That Changed the World* (New York: Random House, 1995).

114. Mary Ryan, *Mysteries of Sex: Tracing Women and Men Through American History* (Chapel Hill: University of North Carolina Press, 2006), 263.

115. Beth Bailey, "Prescribing the Pill: Politics, Culture, and the Sexual Revolution in America's Heartland," *Journal of Social History* 30 (Summer 1997): 827–56, and her *From Front Porch to Back Seat: Courtship in Twentieth-Century America* (Baltimore: Johns Hopkins University Press, 1988); Elizabeth Siegel Watkins, *On the Pill: A Social History of Oral Contraceptives, 1950–1970* (Baltimore: Johns Hopkins University Press, 1998); "The Pill on Campus," *Newsweek*, October 11, 1965, 93.

116. John F. Katner and Melvin Zelnik, "Contraception and Pregnancy: Experience of Young Married Women in the United States," *Family Planning Perspectives* 5 (Winter 1973): 21–35.

117. Philip Rieff, *The Triumph of the Therapeutic: Uses of Faith After Freud* (Chicago: University of Chicago Press, 1966).

118. Ian Stevenson, "Tranquilizers and the Mind," *Harpers*, July 1957, 26; Urie Bronfenbrenner, "Socialization and Social Class Through Time and Space," in Eleanor Maccoby, et al., eds., *Readings in Social Psychology* (New York: Holt, Rinehart & Winston, 1958), 400–425.

119. Petigny, *The Permissive Society*, 81.

120. "Concordia University Student William Groombridge Sues Over B+ Grade," *Huffington Post*, November 13, 2012, http://www.huffingtonpost.com/2012/11/13/concordia-university-william-groombridge_n_2121723.html; "'C+' in Chemistry Leads to Lawsuit Against School District," *Albany Patch*, July 24, 2012; http://albany.patch.com/articles/c-in-chemistry-leads-to-lawsuit-against-school-district.

121. Hunter James Davison, *Evangelicalism: The Coming Generation* (Chicago: University of Chicago Press, 1987), 59.

122. Petigny, *Permissive Society*, 199.

123. John Modell, *Into One's Own: From Youth to Adulthood in the United States, 1920–1975* (Berkeley: University of California Press, 1988), 228. See, for the common mistreatment of teen attitudes, John Patrick Diggins, *The Proud Decade: America in War and Peace, 1941–1960* (New York: W. W. Norton, 1989).

124. Institute for Social Research, *A Study of Adolescent Boys* (New Brunswick, NJ: Boy Scouts of America, 1955).

125. R. H. Remmers and D. H. Radler, *The American Teenager* (Indianapolis: Bobbs-Merrill Co., 1957), 171–74.

126. Joseph F. Kett, *Rites of Passage: Adolescence in America, 1970 to the Present* (New York: Basic Books, 1977).

127. Anna Wolf, "Can a Child Be Too Good?" *National Parent-Teacher*, September 1958, 7–8; "Adolescence: Time of the Rebel," *New York Times*, October 9, 1960.

128. Maria Reidelbach, *Completely MAD: A History of the Comic Book and Magazine* (New York: MJF Books, 1998).

129. Ibid., 143.

130. Kristin L. Matthews, "A MAD Proposition in Postwar America," *Journal of American Culture* 30 (June 2007): 212–21.

131. Sanford, "The Intellectual Origins and New-Worldliness of American Industry," 16; quoting *New York Herald Tribune*, July 20, 1953.

132. Mark Erickson, *Into the Unknown Together: The DOD, NASA, and Early Spaceflight* (Maxwell Air Force Base, AL: Air University Press, 2005).

133. Walter A. McDougall, *The Heavens and the Earth: A Political History of the Space Age* (New York: Basic Books, 1985), xvi–xvii.

134. Ibid., 131.

135. Ibid., 6.

136. Ibid., 130–31.

137. Ibid., 145.

138. Johnson, *Modern Times*, 629.

139. John F. Kennedy, "Special Message to the Congress on Urgent National Needs, May 25, 1961," http://www.jfklibrary.org/Research/Ready-Reference/JFK-Speeches/Special-Message-to-the-Congress-on-Urgent-National-Needs-May-25-1961.aspx.

140. Ibid.

141. John F. Kennedy, Speech at Rice Stadium, September 12, 1962, http://er.jsc.nasa.gov/seh/ricetalk.htm.

142. Ibid.

Chapter 4: Castles Made of Sand

1. Nigel Hamilton, *JFK: Reckless Youth* (New York: Random House, 1992), 373.

2. Jack Olsen, *Aphrodite: Desperate Mission* (New York: G. P. Putnam's Sons, 1970), passim.

3. Ibid., 253.

4. John H. Davis, *The Kennedys: Dynasty and Disaster* (New York: McGraw-Hill, 1984).

5. Thomas C. Reeves, *A Question of Character: A Life of John F. Kennedy* (New York: Forum, 1997), 63.

6. Joan and Clay Blair, Jr., *The Search for JFK* (New York: Berkeley, 1976), 238–44.

7. Robert J. Donovan, *PT 109: John F. Kennedy in WW II* (New York: McGraw-Hill, 2001), 104–5.

8. Reeves, *A Question of Character*, 64–66.

9. James Bradley, *Flags of Our Fathers* (New York: Bantam, 2006).

10. Reeves, *A Question of Character*, 49.

11. Ibid., 81.

12. Robert Dallek, *An Unfinished Life: John F. Kennedy, 1917–1963* (New York: Back Bay Books, 2003), 130.

13. Few have explored the possibility that Kennedy's Addison's disease may have affected his military service, and particularly his command immediately preceding the shredding of PT-109. If so, clearly Kennedy rose above the challenge for the rescue of his crewman.

14. Dallek, *An Unfinished Life*, 74–75. In one case, he had five in a single day!

15. Reeves, *A Question of Character*, 38.

16. Michael Beschloss, *The Crisis Years: Kennedy and Khrushchev, 1960–1963* (New York: Edward Burlingame Books, 1991), 189.

17. Ibid., 187.

18. *New York Times,* July 5, 1960.

19. Beschloss, *The Crisis Years*, 187.

20. Jeanette Walls, *Dish: The Inside Story on the World of Gossip* (New York: Avon Books, 2000), 34.

21. Reeves, *Question of Character*, 202.

22. Dallek, *An Unfinished Life*, 286.

23. Ibid., 277.

24. Ibid.

25. Ibid., 449.

26. Steve Sailer, "The Inside Story of How JFK Won Illinois in 1960," http://www.isteve.com/2000_Inside_Story_of_How_JFK_Won_Illinois.htm.

27. Stephen E. Ambrose, *Nixon: Volume 1–The Education of a Politician, 1913–1962* (New York: Simon and Schuster, 1988), 606.

28. Ibid., I:606.

29. Ibid., I:606–7.

30. Edmund F. Kallina, Jr., *Kennedy v. Nixon: The Presidential Election of 1960* (Gainesville: University Press of Florida, 2011).

31. Dallek, *An Unfinished Life*, 295–96.

32. David Greenberg, "Was Nixon Robbed: The Legend of the Stolen 1960 Presidential Election," *Slate*, October 18, 2000. Not surprisingly, either, the left-wing coauthor of *Freakonomics* tasked a research assistant to spend a "month going through old voting records," without finding anything. Steven D. Levitt, "Did Richard Daley Steal the 1960 Election for Kennedy?," *New York Times*, November 3, 2005.

33. Peter Carlson, "Another Race to the Finish: 1960's Election Was Close But Nixon Didn't Haggle," *Washington Post*, November 17, 2000. Richard Daley would later justify his actions by saying Democratic fraud in Chicago was no different from Republican fraud downstate. Circuit court judge Thomas Kluczynski, who handled the Republican National Committee's lawsuit, dismissed it, and was promptly awarded an appointment to the federal bench by President Kennedy. Only later did an election judge confess to vote tampering in Chicago's twenty-eighth ward, by which time it was too late. Earl Mazo, a correspondent for the New York *Herald Tribune* (a mostly Republican paper), found a cemetery full of the names of people who had voted, a gutted house where 56 Kennedy voters had listed their address, and massive other fraud. But a twelve-part series the paper had planned was called off by Nixon, who implored the editors to "stop running the damn thing." Mazo was stunned, meeting Nixon in person and thinking, "He's a goddamn fool." In fact, Mazo's research had turned up shocking numbers. Fannin County, Texas, had just under 4,900 voters registered, yet somehow 6,138 managed to vote, of which 75 percent voted for JFK; Angelina County, Texas, had a precinct with only 86 people, yet 147 voted for Kennedy, 24 for Nixon. Astoundingly, the Texas Election Board, Democrats all, found no irregularities. A federal investigation into fraud agreed—no hanky-panky. That investigation was headed by the new attorney general, Robert F. Kennedy, who for all intents and purposes was JFK's deputy president.

34. Beschloss, *The Crisis Years*, 406.

35. Ibid., 63.

36. Ibid., 109.

37. Ibid., 375. Beschloss claimed, without a named source, that the CIA under Kennedy initiated more covert actions than under any other president (376).

38. Ibid., 135–42.

39. Reeves, *A Question of Character*, 277.

40. Ibid., 277–78.

41. Dallek, *An Unfinished Life*, 519.

42. Lamar Waldron with Thom Harmann, *Legacy of Secrecy: The Long Shadow of the JFK Assassination* (Berkeley: Counterpoint, 2009).

43. Peter Wyden, *Bay of Pigs: The Untold Story* (New York: Simon & Schuster, 1979), 96.

44. Ibid., 167.

45. Beschloss, *The Crisis Years*, 114.

46. Ibid., 130.

47. Ibid., 132–33.

48. Waldron and Harmann, *Legacy of Secrecy*, 15.

49. Kenneth Conboy with James Morrison, *Shadow War: The CIA's Secret War in Laos* (Boulder, CO: Paladin Press, 1995), 52.

50. Ibid., 59–97.

51. Dallek, *An Unfinished Life*, 305.

52. Beschloss, *The Crisis Years*, 234–35. Lyndon Johnson told his friends, "Khrushchev scared the poor little fellow dead."

53. Ibid., 228.

54. Ibid., 233, 241.

55. Ibid., 274.

56. Dallek, *An Unfinished Life*, 533.

57. Curtis Cate, *The Ides of August: The Berlin Wall Crisis—1961* (New York: M. Evans & Company, 1978), 469–72.

58. Michael Dobbs, *One Minute to Midnight: Kennedy, Khrushchev, and Castro on the Brink of Nuclear War* (New York: Alfred A. Knopf, 2008), 7.

59. Dallek, *An Unfinished Life*, 505.

60. Ibid., 505.

61. Beschloss, *The Crisis Years*, 411.

62. Nina Khrushcheva, "The Case of Khrushchev's Shoe," *New Statesman*, October 2, 2000, http://www.newstatesman.com/200010020025. Nina Khrushcheva was Nikita's granddaughter.

63. Beschloss, *The Crisis Years*, 390.

64. Sheldon M. Stern, *The Week the World Stood Still: Inside the Secret Cuban Missile Crisis* (Stanford, CA: Stanford University Pres, 2005), 39.

65. Ibid., 47.

66. Ibid., 64.

67. Dobbs, *One Minute to Midnight*, 352.

68. Ibid., 27.

69. Stern, *The Week the World Stood Still*, 74.

70. Beschloss, *The Crisis Years*, 435. Subsequent research by Beschloss has shown that the only thing that prevented Kennedy from approving an immediate surprise air strike on Cuba was the likelihood that it could not guarantee the destruction of all the missiles, and still would have to be followed by an invasion. Ironically, Senator William Fulbright, later famous as a Vietnam dove, argued strongly for an invasion as *less* risky. Throughout, Kennedy remained convinced the Russians would counterstrike in Berlin.

71. Alexander Feklisov, *The Man Behind the Rosenbergs* (New York: Enigma Books, 2001), 380.

72. Dobbs, *One Minute to Midnight*, 165.

73. Stern, *The Week the World Stood Still*, 146.

74. Beschloss, *The Crisis Years*, 523.

75. Dobbs, *One Minute to Midnight*, 322

76. Beschloss, *The Crisis Years*, 541.

77. Ibid., 398–99.

78. Paul Johnson, *Modern Times: A History of the World From the Twenties to the Nineties*, rev. ed. (New York: HarperCollins, 1991), 627.

79. Strobe R. Talbott, ed., *Khrushchev Remembers* (Boston: Little, Brown, 1970), 511.

80. Johnson, *Modern Times*, 627–28.

81. Beschloss, *The Crisis Years*, 392–93.

82. John Gillingham, *European Integration, 1950–2003* (Cambridge: Cambridge University Press, 2003), 66–67.

83. Dallek, *An Unfinished Life*, 525.

84. Ibid., 531.

85. Michael MacLear, *The Ten Thousand Day War: Vietnam: 1945–1975* (New York: St. Martin's Press, 1981), 13.

86. Johnson, *Modern Times*, 633.

87. Lawrence S. Wittner, *Cold War America from Hiroshima to Watergate* (New York: Praeger, 1974), 229.

88. "President Kennedy's Remarks at the Yellowstone County Fairgrounds," Billings, Montana, Sept. 25, 1963, http://www.mtholyoke.edu/acad/intrel/pentagon2/ps40.htm; Richard J. Walton, *Cold War and Counterrevolution: The Foreign Policy of John F. Kennedy* (New York: Viking, 1972), 201.

89. John Newman, *JFK and Vietnam* (New York: Warner Books, 1992); David Kaiser, *American Tragedy: Kennedy, Johnson and the Origins of the Vietnam War* (Cambridge, MA: Belknap Press, 2006).

90. Dallek, *An Unfinished Life*, 529.

91. Ibid.

92. *Editor and Publisher*, November 12, 1960, 7; Tom Wicker, *On Press* (New York: Viking, 1978), 125–26.

93. Thomas Brown, *JFK: History of an Image* (Bloomington, IN: Indiana University Press, 1988), 17.

94. Paul B. Fay, Jr., *The Pleasure of His Company* (New York: Harper and Row, 1966), 35–37, 95, 196, 202–3, 208.

95. Boylan, "Declarations of Independence," *Columbia Journalism Review*, November/December 1986, 29–45; Robert Shogan, *Bad News: Where the Press Goes Wrong in the Making of the President* (Chicago: Ivan R. Dee, 2001), 23; Alsop quoted in James T. Graham, "Kennedy, Cuba, and the Press," *Journalism History* 24 (Summer 1998): 60–71, quotation on 61.

96. Charles Roberts, "JFK and the Press," in K.W. Thompson, ed., *Ten Presidents and the Press* (Lanham, MD: University Press of America, 1983), cited in David Broder, *Behind the Front Page* (New York: Touchstone, 1987), 158. Kennedy had only one minor opposition press to deal with, the New York *Herald Tribune*, which closed its doors in 1966. See Christopher D. McKenna, "Two Strikes and You're Out: The Demise of the New York *Herald Tribune*," *Historian* 63 (Winter 2001): 287–308.

97. Philip B. Kunhardt, Jr., ed., *Life in Camelot* (New York: Time-Life Books, 1988), 6.

98. William Hammond, *Reporting Vietnam* (Lawrence: University of Kansas Press, 1998), 5.

99. John P. Roche, "Indochina Revisited: The Demise of Liberal Internationalism," *National Review* 37 (May 3, 1985): 26–44, http://findarticles.com/p/articles/mi_m1282/is_v37/ai_3760849/pg_5/?tag=content;col1.

100. Stanley Karnow, "The Fall of the House of Ngo Dinh," in *Reporting Vietnam: Part One: American Journalism, 1959–1969* (New York: Library of America, 1998), 94.

101. William Colby with James McCargor, *Lost Victory: A Firsthand Account of America's Sixteen-Year Involvement in Vietnam* (Chicago: Contemporary Books, 1989), 158.

102. Roche, "Indochina Revisited."

103. Johnson, *Modern Times*, 636.

104. James Piereson, *Camelot and the Cultural Revolution* (New York: Encounter, 2007), 2.

105. "Ruby Asks World to Take His Word," *New York Times*, Dec. 20, 1966.

106. Refer to n. 45, page 887, in the paperback edition of Larry Schweikart and Michael Allen, *A Patriot's History of the United States, from Columbus's Great Discovery to the War on Terror*, 2nd ed. (New York: Sentinel, 2007).

107. Piereson, *Camelot and the Cultural Revolution*, xi.

108. Ibid., x.

109. Robert F. Turner, "Reassessing the Causes," *Washington Times*, August 2, 2009.

110. Ibid.

111. Roche, "Indochina Revisited."

112. Arthur Schlesinger and David Sobel, *A Thousand Days: John F. Kennedy in the White House* (New York: Mariner Books, 2002), 203.

113. Henry Trewhitt, *McNamara* (New York: Harper & Row, 1971); William W. Kaufman, *The McNamara Strategy* (New York: Harper & Row, 1964); and Larry Schweikart, "Robert McNamara," in Larry Schweikart, ed., *The Encyclopedia of American Business History and Biography: Banking and Finance Since 1913* (New York: Facts on File, 1990), 251–67.

114. Stanley Karnow, *Vietnam: A History* (London: Viking, 1994), 19.

115. George C. Herring, *America's Longest War: The United States and Vietnam, 1950–1975* (New York: Knopf, 1979), 268.

116. H. R. McMaster, *Dereliction of Duty: Johnson, McNamara and the Joint Chiefs of Staff, and the Lies That Led to Vietnam* (New York: HarperPerennial, 1998).

117. Ibid., 225.

118. Ibid., 329.

119. Mark Clodfelter, *The Limits of Air Power: The American Bombing of North Vietnam* (New York: Free Press, 1989), 70.

120. McMaster, *Dereliction of Duty*, 90.

121. Ibid., 266.

122. Clodfelter, *Limits of Air Power*, 119.

123. Ibid., 121.

124. Michael Lind, *Vietnam: The Necessary War* (New York: Touchstone, 1999), 19.

125. Conboy and Morrison, *Shadow War*, 210.

126. Bui Tin, *Following Ho Chi Minh: Memoirs of a North Vietnamese Colonel* (Annapolis, MD: Naval Institute Press, 2002), 64, retrieved from http://en.citizendium.org/wiki/Bui_Tin.

127. Larry Schweikart and Michael Allen, *A Patriot's History of the United States: From Columbus's Great Discovery to the War on Terror* (New York: Sentinel, 2007), 664; Juan Williams, *Eyes on the Prize: America's Civil Rights Years, 1954–1965* (New York: Penguin, 1988); Taylor Branch, *Parting the Waters: America in the King Years, 1954–63* (New York: Simon & Schuster, 1963).

128. Martin Luther King, Jr., "I Have a Dream," August 28, 1963, http://historywired.si.edu/detail.cfm?ID=501.

129. Winthrop Jordan and Leon Litwak, *The United States*, 7th ed., combined ed. (Englewood Cliffs, NJ: Prentice-Hall, 1991), 724.

130. "The Ten Point Program," http://en.wikipedia.org/wiki/Ten-Point_Program#The_Ten_Point_Program.

131. Hugh Pearson, *The Shadow of the Panther: Huey Newton and the Price of Black Power in America* (Cambridge, MA: Da Capo Press, 1994), 3–4, 283–91.

132. Despite the name of the speech, King did not actually utter the phrase, "I have been to the mountaintop." He said that God "allowed me to go up the mountain" (http://en.wikipedia.org/wiki/I%27ve_Been_to_the_Mountaintop).

133. Peter Doggett, *There's a Riot Going On: Revolutionaries, Rock Stars, and the Rise and Fall of the '60s* (New York: Canongate, 2007), 3.

134. James F. Dunnigan and Albert A. Nofi, *Dirty Little Secrets of the Vietnam War: Military Information You're Not Supposed to Know* (New York: St. Martin's Griffin, 1999), 7–8; Harry G. Summers, *Vietnam War Almanac* (New York: Facts on File, 1985), 108.

135. Summers, *Vietnam War Almanac*, 108.

136. Ibid.; Dunnigan and Nofi, *Dirty Little Secrets of the Vietnam War*, 65.

137. Johnson, *Modern Times*, 636.

138. Bui Tin, "How North Vietnam Won the War," *Wall Street Journal*, August 3, 1995.

139. Lewis Sorley, *A Better War: The Unexamined Victories and Final Tragedy of America's Last Years in Vietnam* (San Diego: Harvest Books, 1999), 93.

140. Kennedy, *Military and the Media*, 102.

141. Chalmers Roberts, *The* Washington Post: *The First 100 Years* (Boston: Houghton Mifflin, 1977),

142. Don Moser, "Eight Dedicated Men Marked for Death," *Life* Magazine, September 3, 1965, 28–33, 68–70, 72, 75–76; Bernard B. Fall, "Vietnam Blitz: A Report on the Impersonal War," *New Republic*, October 9, 1965, 17–21.

143. Patterson, "Television's Living Room War," 39.

144. Robert Elegant, "How to Lose a War: Reflections of a War Correspondent," *Encounter*, August 1981, 73–90, quotation on 73.

145. John E. Mueller, *War, Presidents and Public Opinion* (New York: John Wiley, 1973), 87.

146. Larry Schweikart, *America's Victories: Why the U.S. Wins Wars and Will Win the War on Terror* (New York: Sentinel, 2006), 35.

147. Benjamin S. Lambeth, *The Transformation of American Air Power* (Ithaca, NY: Cornell University Press, 2000), 23.

148. Robert Leckie, *The Wars of America*, rev. ed. (New York: Harper & Row, 1981), 1006–7.

149. Victor Davis Hanson, *Carnage and Culture: Landmark Battles in the Rise of Western Power* (New York: Doubleday, 2001), 404.

150. Bui Tin, *Following Ho Chi Minh* (Honolulu: University of Hawaii Press, 1995), 62; "How North Vietnam Won the War"; and Bui Tin, *From Enemy to Friend* (Annapolis, MD: Naval Institute Press, 2002), 64.

151. Rodger Streitmatter, *Mightier Than the Sword: How the News Media Have Shaped American History* (Boulder, CO: Westview Press, 2011), 194.

152. Ibid., 194–95.

153. Hanson, *Carnage and Culture*, 401.

154. Edward Jay Epstein, *Between Fact and Fiction* (New York: Vintage, 1975), 225.

155. Daniel Hallin, "The Media, the War in Vietnam, and Political Support; A Critique of the Thesis of an Oppositional Media," *Journal of Politics* 46 (February 1984): 2–24, table on 8.

156. Hallin, "Media, the War in Vietnam, and Political Support," passim.

157. "Vietnam and Electronic Journalism," *Broadcasting*, May 19, 1975, 26.

158. Johnson, *Modern Times*, 502.

159. Ibid., 502.

160. Johnson, *Heroes*, 232.

161. Ibid., 504.

162. Roland Huntford, *The New Totalitarians* (New York: Stein and Day, 1980), 152.

163. Thomas Alan Schwartz, *Lyndon Johnson and Europe: In the Shadow of Vietnam* (Cambridge, MA: Harvard University Press, 2003), 141.

164. William James, *Memories and Studies* (New York: Longmans, Green & Co., 1911), 267–96.

165. Robert Rector and William Lauber, *America's Failed $5.4 Trillion War on Poverty* (Washington, DC: Heritage Foundation, 1995), Table 1, 92–93.

166. Charles Murray, *Losing Ground: American Social Policy, 1950–1980* (New York: Basic Books, 1984).

167. Samuel Eliot Morison, Henry Steele Commager, and William E. Leuchtenburg, *A Concise History of the American Republic*, 2nd ed. (New York: Oxford University Press, 1983), 734.

168. John Morton Blum, et al., *The National Experience: A History of the United States*, 7th ed. (New York: Harcourt Brace Jovanovich, 1989), 755–57. Modern textbooks, such as David Harrell's *Unto a Good Land*, are no better, claiming, "Many of the programs put in place during the sixties remain pillars in the American welfare state. If Johnson's programs fell short of eliminating poverty in the nation, they nevertheless changed many lives for the better" (David Edwin Harrell, et al., *Unto a Good Land: A History of the American People* [Grand Rapids, MI: William B. Eerdmans, 2005], 1098).

169. Rector and Lauber, *America's Failed $5.4 Trillion War on Poverty*, 92–95; Warren Brookes, *The Economy in Mind* (New York: Universe Publishers, November 1982), tables 7-3 and 7-5; Michael Tanner, *The End of Welfare* (Washington, DC: Cato Institute, 1996), 70.

170. Reprinted as Daniel Patrick Moynihan, *The Negro Family* (Washington, DC: United States Department of Labor, 1965). See also his *Maximum Feasible Misunderstanding: Community Action in the War on Poverty* (New York: Free Press, 1969).

171. George Gilder, *Men and Marriage* (Gretna, LA: Pelican, 1992).

172. Johnson, *Modern Times*, 640; Margaret Mead, *Coming of Age in Samoa* (New York: Harper-Collins, 1973) was dismantled by Derek Freeman, *Margaret Mead and Samoa: The Making and Unmaking of an Anthropological Myth* (Cambridge, MA: Harvard University Press, 1983) and *The Fateful Hoaxing of Margaret Mead* (Boulder, CO: Westview Press, 1999).

173. "Midst the Handguns' Red Glare—Chicago's Robert Taylor Homes, a public housing development," *Whole Earth*, Summer 1999, http://findarticles.com/p/articles/mi_m0GER/is_1999_Summer/ai_55127438/.

174. Julia Vitullo-Martin, "Lessons in Public Housing," *Forbes*, May 5, 2009.

175. Johnson, *Modern Times*. 641.

176. Tony Judt, *Postwar: A History of Europe Since 1945* (New York: Penguin Press, 2005), 417.

177. Ibid., 415.

178. Ibid., 416.

179. Stuart Dowsey, *Zengakuren: Japan's Revolutionary Students* (Berkeley, CA: The Ishi Press, 1970).

180. Patricia G. Steinhoff, "Student Protest in the 1960s," *Social Science Japan*, March 15, 1999, 3–6; Thomas R. H. Havens, *Fire Across the Sea: The Vietnam War and Japan, 1965–1975* (Princeton, NJ: Princeton University Press, 1987).

181. Louis D. Hayes, *Introduction to Japanese Politics* (Missoula: University of Montana, 1992), 120.

182. Kirkpatrick Sale, *SDS* (New York: Vintage Books, 1974).

183. Tom Bates, *RADS: The 1970 Bombing of the Army Math Research Center at the University of Wisconsin–Madison and Its Aftermath* (New York: Perennial, 1993).

184. Peter Davies, *The Truth About Kent State* (New York: Farrar, Straus and Giroux, 1973), 17.

185. James A. Michener, *Kent State: What Happened and Why* (New York: Random House, 1971), 515.

186. Judt, *Postwar*, 393.

187. Rex Jackson, Appendix to *On Further Examination*, "Comparison of SAT Score Trends in Selected Schools Judged to Have Traditional or Experimental Orientations" (Princeton, NJ: College Entrance Examination Board, 1977).

188. Muhammad K. Mayanja, "Graduate Employment: Investing in the Service Mandate of the African University," April 2002, http://www.codesria.org/Links/conferences/universities/Muhammad_Mayanja.pdf.

189. Thomas Sowell, *The Economics and Politics of Race* (New York: Quill/Basic Books, 1983), 236.

190. "Higher Learning in France Clings to Its Old Ways," *New York Times*, May 12, 2006.

191. Larry Schweikart, *The Entrepreneurial Adventure: A History of Business in the United States* (New York: Harcourt, 2000), 397–98.

192. Judt, *Postwar*, 433.

193. Ibid., 435.

194. Ibid., 437.

195. Ibid., 444.

196. Ibid., 446.

197. Ibid.

198. Ibid., 447.

199. Aldous Huxley, *The Doors of Perception and Heaven and Hell* (London: Chatto & Windus, 1960).

200. Jonathan Gould, *Can't Buy Me Love: The Beatles, Britain, and America* (New York: Harmony Books, 2007), 318.

201. Huxley, *Doors of Perception*, 36–37.

202. Jay Stevens, *Storming Heaven: LSD and the American Dream* (New York: Grove Press, 1998), 208.

203. Tom Wolfe, *The Electric Kool-Aid Acid Test* (New York: Bantam, 1999).

204. Jann Wenner, *John Lennon Remembers* (New York: Popular Library, 1971), 140; Hunter Davies, *The Beatles: The Authorized Biography* (New York: McGraw-Hill, 1968), 289.

205. Ray Manzarek, *Light My Fire: My Life with the Doors* (New York: Berkley Press, 1999), 123.

206. Gould, *Can't Buy Me Love*, 432.

207. Ibid.

208. Ibid.

209. Ibid., 97.

210. Jeff Tamarkin, *Got a Revolution!: The Turbulent Flight of Jefferson Airplane* (New York: Atria Books, 2003), 73.

211. Glenn C. Altschuler, *All Shook Up: How Rock 'n' Roll Changed America* (Oxford: Oxford University Press, 2003), 175.

212. Gould, *Can't Buy Me Love*, 567.

213. Ibid., 566.

214. Altschuler, *All Shook Up*, 188.

215. Doggett, *There's a Riot Going On*, 277.

216. David Dalton, "Finally, the Shocking Truth About Woodstock Can Be Told, or Kill It Before It Clones Itself," *The Gadfly*, August 1999, http://gadfly.org/1999-08/toc.asp.

217. Manzarek, *Light My Fire*, 11.

218. Abbie Hoffman, *Woodstock Nation* (New York: Vintage, 1969), 91; Doggett, *There's a Riot Going On*, 275.

219. Kenneth J. Bindas and Craig Houston, " 'Takin' Care of Business': Rock Music, Vietnam and the Protest Myth," *Historian* 52 (November 1989): 1–23; Emily Edwards and Michael Singletary, "Mass Media Images in Popular Music: An Examination of Media Images in Student Music Collections and Student Attitudes Toward Media Performance," *Popular Music and Society* 9 (1984): 17-26; R. Serge Denisoff and Mark H. Levine, "Youth and Popular Music: A Test of the Taste Culture Hypothesis," *Youth Society* 4 (1972): 237–55. Buffalo Springfield's "For What It's Worth," though later rationalized by Stephen Stills as an antiwar song, was about a riot on Sunset Boulevard.

220. Martin Lee and Bruce Shlain, *Acid Dreams* (New York: Grove Press, 1992), 257.

221. Doggett, *There's a Riot Going On*, 309.

222. Robert Keppel, *The Riverman: Ted Bundy and I Hunt for the Green River Killer* (New York: Pocket Books, 1995); Ann Rule, *The Stranger Beside Me* (New York: Signet, 2000).

223. Philip Carlo, *The Night Stalker: The Life and Crimes of Richard Ramirez* (New York: Kensington, 1996).

224. Howard Sounes, *Fred and Rose: The Full Story of Fred and Rose West and the Gloucester House of Horrors* (London: Warner Books, 1995).

225. Judt, *Postwar*, 474.

226. Ibid., 477.

227. Ibid., 465.

228. Ibid., 470.

229. Ibid., 463.

230. "Sirhan Sirhan Denied Parole for 12th Time," http://www.signonsandiego.com/news/state/20030306-2018-ca-sirhanparole.html.

231. Joe McGinnis, *The Last Brother* (New York: Simon & Schuster, 1993); Burton Hersh, *Ted Kennedy: An Intimate Biography* (Berkeley, CA: Counterpoint, 2010).

232. Johnson, *Modern Times*, 647.

233. Joseph Charles Keeley, *The Left-Leaning Antenna: Political Bias in Television* (New York: Arlington House, 1971), 148.

234. Jack Fuller, *News Values: Ideas for an Information Age* (Chicago: University of Chicago Press, 1996), 192.

235. Jeffery A. Smith, *War and Press Freedom: The Problem of Prerogative Power* (New York: Oxford University Press, 1999), 185.

236. Ibid.

237. Israel Shenker, "2 Critics Here Focus on Films as Language Conference Opens," *New York Times*, December 28, 1972.

238. If possible, scholars hated Nixon more than the media. *A Concise History of the American Republic* describes Nixon as a man "known neither for his imagination nor his scruples," and says he was "long thought of as a 'born loser.' "(Samuel Eliot Morison, Henry Steele Commager, and William E. Leuchtenberg, *A Concise History of the American Republic*, 2nd ed. [New York: Oxford University Press, 1983], 745.) In fact, Nixon's 1960 loss had been razor thin, and, as we have seen, largely the result of fraud and ballot tampering, and his 1968 race was close only because a third-party candidate siphoned votes from Nixon's right. In 1972, he won one of the largest blowouts in presidential election history. The only ones who thought Nixon was a "born loser" were academics and members of the press.

239. Paul Johnson, *A History of the American People* (New York: HarperCollins, 1997), 888.

240. Smith, *War and Press Freedom*, 185. Cram, "Toward More Conservative News Coverage," www.MediaWars.com, June 18, 2000; Robert Shogan, *Bad News: Where the Press Goes Wrong in the Making of the President* (Chicago: Ivan R. Dee, 2001).

241. William Safire, *Before the Fall: An Inside View of the Pre-Watergate White House* (New York: Doubleday, 1975), 117–18.

242. The original phrase is attributed to Milton Friedman in December 1965, in which he said, "In one sense, we are all Keynesians now; in another, nobody is any longer a Keynesian." *Time*, December 31, 1965, and follow-up letter February 4, 1966.

243. Daniel Yergin and Joseph Stanislaw, *The Commanding Heights: The Battle for the World Economy* (New York: Touchstone, 2002), 46.

Chapter 5: Sex by Consent, Beauty by Consensus

1. Richard M. Nixon, "Asia After Viet Nam," *Foreign Affairs* 46 (October 1967): 111–25 (quotation on 125).

2. Memorandum from President Nixon to his Assistant for National Security Affairs (Kissinger), February 1, 1969, *Foreign Relations of the United States, 1969–1976: Volume XVII, China, 1969–72*, Document 3, http://history.state.gov/historicaldocuments/frus1969-76v17/d3.

3. Niall Ferguson, *The War of the World* (New York: Penguin, 2006), 621.

4. Ross Terrill, *Mao: A Biography* (Stanford, CA: Stanford University Press, 1999), 393.

5. Ibid., 396.

6. "1972 Year in Review," http://www.upi.com/Audio/Year_in_Review/Events-of-1972/Events-of-1972/12305688736666-1/.

7. Terrill, *Mao*, 184.

8. Li Zhisui, *The Private Life of Chairman Mao* (New York: Random House, 1994), 364.

9. Terrill, *Mao*, 96.

10. Ibid., 98.

11. Ibid., 105.

12. Ibid.

13. Ibid., 199.

14. Jay Taylor, *The Generalissimo: Chaing Kai-Shek and the Struggle for Modern China* (Cambridge, MA: Belknap Press, 2009).

15. Guy Sorman, *The Empire of Lies: The Truth About China in the Twenty-First Century* (New York: Encounter Books, 2008), 16.

16. Tom Standage, *An Edible History of Humanity* (New York: Walker & Company, 2009), 182.

17. Niall Ferguson, *Civilization: The West and the Rest* (New York: Penguin, 2011), 304.

18. Jung Chang, *Wild Swans* (New York: Touchstone, 2003), 211.

19. Li Zhisui, *Private Life of Chairman Mao*, 197–202.

20. Terrill, *Mao*, 76.

21. Frank Dikoetter, *Mao's Great Famine: The History of China's Most Devastating Catastrophe* (New York: Walker & Company, 2010), 333.

22. Ibid., 137.

23. Ibid., 167.

24. Ibid., xi–xii.

25. Terrill noted that this deception was willingly embraced by the West: "A tendency to believe the best about Mao was one reason why Western Sinology was for some years disinclined to see the pathological in [him]" (Terrill, *Mao*, 15).

26. Ibid., 184.

27. Ibid., 185; Vaclav Smil, "China's Great Famine 40 Years Later," *British Medical Journal* 319 (1999): 1619–21.

28. Smil, "China's Great Famine 40 Years Later," 1620.

29. Standage, *An Edible History of Humanity*, 186.

30. Ibid.

31. Ferguson, *War of the World*, 620.

32. Ibid.

33. Terrill, *Mao*, 262.

34. Alan Hirsch, *The Forgotten Ways: Reactivating the Missional Church* (Grand Rapids, MI: Brazos Press, 2006), 19; Philip Yancey, "Discreet and Dynamic: Why, with No Apparent Resources, Chinese Churches Thrive," *Christianity Today*, July 2004, 72, at http://www.christianitytoday.com/ct/2004/July/16.72.html.

35. Terrill, *Mao*, 17.

36. Ibid., 296.

37. Sorman, *Empire of Lies*, 17.

38. William Russell Mead, *God and Gold: Britain, America, and the Making of the Modern World* (New York: Knopf, 2007), 59.

39. Paul Johnson, *Modern Times: A History of the World from the Twenties to the Nineties*, rev. ed. (New York: HarperCollins, 1991), 647.

40. Ibid., 649.

41. Peter Doggett, *There's a Riot Going On: Revolutionaries, Rock Stars, and the Rise and Fall of the '60s* (New York: Canongate, 2007), 488.

42. Arthur Marwick, *Beauty in History: Society, Politics, and Personal Appearance c. 1500 to the Present* (Gloucester, England: Thames and Hudson, 1988).

43. William Safire, *Before the Fall: An Inside View of the Pre-Watergate White House* (New York: Doubleday, 1975), 264.

44. Unpublished research by Larry Schweikart and Jim Kuypers, newspaper editorials, 1958–1970, in Schweikart's possession.

45. David E. Harrell, et al., *Unto a Good Land: A History of the American People* (Grand Rapids, MI: William B. Eerdmans, 2005), 11; John Mack Faragher, et al., *One of Many*, combined vol., 4th ed., TLC ed. (Upper Saddle River, NJ: Pearson, 2006), 82.

46. *Maureen K. Dean and John Dean v. St. Martin's Press, Inc., Len Colodny, Robert Gettlin, G. Gordon Liddy, and Phillip Makin Bailley* (1996), http://www.Nixonera.com/media/transcripts/likely.pdf.

47. Ibid.

48. Richard Nixon, *RN: The Memoirs of Richard Nixon* (New York: Grosset & Dunlap, 1978), 632; Larry Schweikart, *48 Liberal Lies About American History (That You Probably Learned in School)* (New York: Sentinel, 2009), 140–44; "Liddy Case Dismissed," CBS News, February 2, 2001.

49. Federal Bureau of Investigation, Office of Planning and Valuation. FBI Watergate Investigation: OPE Analysis, July 5, 1974. File Number 139-4089, 11.

50. *Dean v. St. Martin's*, 119.

51. Tony Judt, *Postwar: A History of Europe Since 1945* (New York: Penguin, 2005), 482.

52. Ibid., 483.

53. Ibid., 535.

54. Walter Wriston Speech Before the International Monetary Conference, June 11, 1979, quoted in Anthony Sampson, *The Money Lenders: Bankers in a Dangerous World* (London: Hodder and Stoughton, 1981), 106ff.

55. Anthony Sampson, *The Seven Sisters* (New York: PFD, 2009), retrieved from www. http://journeytoforever.org/biofuel_library/sevensisters/7sisters11.html.

56. Daniel Yergin, *The Prize: The Epic Quest of Oil, Money, and Power* (New York: The Free Press, 2008), 566.

57. Lewis Sorley, *A Better War: The Unexamined Victories and Final Tragedy of America's Last Years in Vietnam* (San Diego: Harvest Books, 2007).

58. Ferguson, *War of the World*, 621.

59. http://www.guardian.co.uk/world/2008/dec/03/laos-cluster-bombs-uxo-deaths, Dec. 2, 2008.

60. Henry R. Nau, *The Myth of America's Decline* (New York: Oxford, 1990), table 6-2.

61. Harold Evans, *They Made America: Two Centuries of Innovators from the Steam Engine to the Search Engine* (New York: Little Brown, 2004), 308–17.

62. Harold Evans, "They Made America," http://www.pbs.org/wgbh/theymadeamerica/whomade/rosenthal_hi.html.

63. Paul Johnson, *Creators: From Chaucer and Dürer to Picasso and Disney* (New York: HarperCollins, 2006), 239, 241. Lest anyone get too romantic about the designers, it should be noted that Hugo Boss designed the Nazis' infamous uniforms.

64. Ibid., 236.

65. Jean Shrimpton, *The Truth About Modelling* (New York: Bantam Books, 1965 [1964]).

66. Twiggy, *Twiggy: An Autobiography* (London: Hart-Davis, MacGibbon, 1975), 29.

67. Marilyn Bender, *The Beautiful People* (New York: Coward, 1967), 23.

68. Nancy Etcoff, *Survival of the Prettiest: The Science of Beauty* (New York: Doubleday, 1999), 192–93; Dev Singh, "Adaptive Significance of Female Physical Attractiveness: Role of Waist-to-Hip Ratio," *Journal of Personality and Social Psychology* 65 (1993): 293–307, and Dev Singh with S. Luis, "Ethnic and Gender Consensus for the Effect of Waist-to-Hip Ratio on Judgment of Women's Attractiveness," *Human Nature* 6 (1995): 51–65, and Dev Singh with R. K. Young, "Body Weight, Waist-to-Hip Ratio, Breasts, and Hips: Role in Judgments of Female Attractiveness and Desirability for Relationships," *Ethology and Sociobiology* 16 (1995): 483–507.

69. Singh's studies, cited in the previous note, apply here.

70. Etcoff, *Survival of the Prettiest*, 193; M. J. Tovee, et al., "Supermodels: Stick Insects or Hour-Glasses?" *Lancet* 350 (1997): 1474–75.

71. Evans, *They Made America*, 391.

72. Ibid., 392.

73. Ibid.

74. Ibid., 388–92.

75. M. G. Lord, *Forever Barbie: The Unauthorized Biography of a Real Doll* (New York: William Morrow, 1994), 177.

76. Evans, *They Made America*, 388.

77. Ibid.

78. Sander L. Gilman, *Making the Body Beautiful: A Cultural History of Aesthetic Surgery* (Princeton, NJ: Princeton University Press, 1999).

79. Warren Susman, " 'Personality' and the Making of Twentieth Century Culture," in his *Culture as History: The Transformation of American Society in the Twentieth Century* (New York: Pantheon, 1984), 277–80.

80. Elizabeth Haiken, *Venus Envy: A History of Cosmetic Surgery* (Baltimore: Johns Hopkins University Press, 1997), 100.

81. Robert Potter, "Farewell to Ugliness," *American Weekly*, April 7 and 14, 1946.

82. Haiken, *Venus Envy*, 23.

83. Mayer, quoted in Marwick, *Beauty in History*, 332.

84. Josephine Lowman, "Why Grow Old?" *Oakland Tribune*, April 27, 1953.

85. Haiken, *Venus Envy*, 149.

86. "The Imagined Image," *Vogue*, September 15, 1961.

87. Haiken, *Venus Envy*, 153.

88. Ibid., 154.

89. Lowman, "Why Grow Old?"

90. Marguerite Clark, "Breast Surgery," *McCall's* 75 (1948): 2.

91. Douglas T. Miller and Marion Nowak, *The Fifties: The Way We Really Were* (Garden City, NY: Doubleday, 1977), 8.

92. Ibid., 329.

93. Gilman, *Making the Body Beautiful*, 238.

94. E. S. Truppman and B. M. Schwarz, "Aesthetic Breast Surgery," *Journal of the Florida Medical Association* 76 (1989): 609–12.

95. Kimberly Ellena Bergman, "Women's Ideas About Beauty (Physical Attractiveness)," Ph.D. dissertation, California School of Professional Psychology, Los Angeles, 1990.

96. "Abreast of the Times," *Journal of the American Medical Association* 195 (March 7, 1966): 863.

97. "Cheers for Cher," *Ms.*, July 1988, 53.

98. Mary Lou Weisman, "The Feminist and the Face-Lift," *San Francisco Chronicle*, January 5, 1984.

99. "Explosive Market Growth Forecast in Soft Tissue Implant Industry," *Hospitals* 59 (1985): 74.

100. C. M. Lewis, "Early History of Lipoplasty in the United States," *Aesthetic Plastic Surgery* 14 (1990): 123–26; Ricardo Baroudi and Mario Moraes, "Philosophy, Technical Principles, Selection, and Indication in Body Contouring Surgery," *Aesthetic Plastic Surgery* 15 (1991): 1–18; Gregory P. Hetter, *Lipoplasty: The Theory and Practice of Blunt Suction Lipectomy* (Boston: Little, Brown, 1990), 21.

101. "Plastic Surgery for Men," *Coronet*, May 1961, 100–104.

102. Everett R. Hollis, "Face-Lifting Erases Age in Men, Too," *New York Times*, June 28, 1971.

103. Gilman, *Making the Body Beautiful*, 255.

104. Ibid., 215; Martha Gil-Montero, "Ivo Pitanguy: Master of Artful Surgery," *America's* 43 (1991): 24; Ricardo Baroudi, "Why Aesthetic Plastic Surgery Became Popular in Brazil?" *Annals of Plastic Surgery* 27 (1991): 396–97.

105. Gilman, *Making the Body Beautiful*, 216.

106. "In Argentina, Cosmetic Surgery Tops Popular Conversation Topics," *Dallas Morning News*, May 26, 1996.

107. George Gilder, *Men and Marriage* (Gretna, LA: Pelican Publishing, 1992).

108. Naomi Wolf, *The Beauty Myth* (New York: William Morrow, 1991), 10; Robin Lakoff and Raquel Scherr, *Face Value: The Politics of Beauty* (Boston: Routledge, 1984); Joan Jacobs Brumberg, *Fasting Girls: The History of Anorexia Nervosa* (New York: New American Library, 1988).

109. J. M. Townsend, "Mate Selection Criteria: A Pilot Study," *Ethology and Sociobiology* 10 (1989): 241–53, and with G. D. Levy, "Effect of Potential Partners' Physical Attractiveness and Socioeconomic Status on Sexuality and Partner Selection," *Journal of Sexual Behavior* 19 (1990): 149–64; M. W. Weiderman and E. R. Allgeier, "Gender Differences in Mate Selection Criteria: Sociobiological or Socioeconomic Explanation?" *Ethology and Sociobiology* 13 (1992): 115–24.

110. Gary Taubes, *Good Calories, Bad Calories: Challenging the Conventional Wisdom on Diet, Weight Control, and Disease* (New York: Knopf, 2007), 4.

111. Ibid., 8.

112. A. E. Harper, "Dietary Guidelines in Perspective," *Journal of Nutrition* 126 (April 1996 supplement): 1042–48.

113. R. Lozano, et al., "Miscoding and Misclassification of Ischaemic Heart Disease Mortality," World Health Organization, 2001, http://www.who.int/entity/healthinfo/paper12.pdf, 14.

114. B. L. Friend, et al., "Food Consumption Patterns, U.S.A.: 1909–13 to 1976," in R. I. Levy, et al., *Nutrition, Lipids, and Coronary Heart Disease: A Global View* (New York: Raven Press, 1979), 489–522.

115. H. E. Garrett, E. C. Horning, B. G. Creech, and Michael De Bakey, "Serum Cholesterol Values in Patients Treated Surgically for Atherosclerosis," *Journal of the American Medical Association* 189 (August 31, 1964): 655–59.

116. Note the differences between the reporting of the first, preliminary study, in G. Christakis, et al., "The Anti-Coronary Club: A Dietary Approach to the Prevention of Coronary Heart Disease—a Seven Year Report," *American Journal of Public Health and the Nation's Health* 56 (February 1966): 299–314, and their November final report, "Effect of the Anti-Coronary Club Program on Coronary Heart Disease: Risk-Factor Status," *Journal of the American Medical Association* 198 (November 7, 1966): 597–604.

117. Paul Ehrlich, *The Population Bomb* (New York: Ballantine, 1968), 11; Greg Easterbrook, "Forgotten Benefactor of Humanity," *Atlantic Monthly*, January 1996, 75–82; R. E. Evenson and D. Gollin, "Assessing the Impact of the Green Revolution, 1960–2000," *Science*, New Series, 300 (May 2, 2003): 758–62.

118. Francis Moore Lappé, *Diet for a Small Planet* (New York: Ballantine, 1971), 7–9.

119. Jean Mayer, "By Bread Alone," *New York Times Book Review*, December 15, 1974.

120. Warren Belasco, *Appetite for Change: How the Counterculture Took on the Food Industry, 1966–1988* (New York: Pantheon, 1989), 57. This rationale became even more pronounced over time: by 2009, one researcher claimed that 800 million people could be fed on the grain used to feed animals alone, and this, of course, was directly tied to "fossil fuels, which consumed oil." See David Pimentel and Marcia Pimentel, *American Journal of Clinical Nutrition* 78 (September 2003 supplemental): 660–63. In fact, the Pimentels claim that the population of the United States is "projected to double" and that population increase is the biggest threat to survival—when in fact the United States is one of the few—if not the only—industrialized nations worldwide to even hold its population level. All others are decreasing.

121. Waverly Root and Richard de Rochemont, *Eating in America: A History* (New York: Ecco Press, 1995), 447.

122. Taubes, *Good Calories, Bad Calories*, 45.

123. U.S. Senate Select Committee on Nutrition and Human Needs of the United States, *Dietary Goals for the United States* (Washington, DC: U.S. Government Printing Office, 1977), 37–42; Root and de Rochemont, *Eating in America*, passim; Taubes, *Good Calories, Bad Calories*, passim.

124. Taubes, *Good Calories, Bad Calories*, 54.

125. "Heart Attacks: A Test Collapses," *Wall Street Journal*, October 6, 1982. Among the various studies, for example, a Framingham, Massachusetts, study over twenty-four years showed no relationship between cholesterol and sudden cardiac death; and a Harvard study by William Taylor found that men with a "high" risk of heart disease might gain one extra year of life by avoiding all saturated fat—provided there were no other risk factors that the study hadn't accounted for. Healthy men might—might!—gain as much as three days of life. See W. C. Taylor, et al., "Cholesterol Reduction and Life Expectancy: A Model Incorporating Multiple Risk Factors," *Annals of Internal Medicine* 106 (April 1987): 605–14.

126. See "Lowering Blood Cholesterol to Prevent Heart Disease," NIH Consensus Development Conference, December 10–12, 1984, program and abstracts, National Heart, Lung, and Blood Institute and the NIH Office of Medical Applications Research.

127. "Roughing It—Tonic for Our Time," *Washington Post*, August 19, 1974; D. P. Burkitt and N. S. Painter, "Dietary Fiber and Disease," *Journal of the American Medical Association* 229 (August 19, 1974): 1068–74.

128. In the late twentieth century, Michael Jacobson at the Center for Science in the Public Interest jumped on this transformation of science, for now science could be manipulated by first determining what was in the "public interest" and then corralling the necessary researchers to support it. Jacobson, a Naderite, was a vegetarian who refused to even eat a cookie for its fat content. An animal-rights extremist, he was a board member of the "Great American Meatout," and CSPI's in-house eating policy reached the absurd point that he even once announced he would remove the office coffee machine until most of the staffers threatened to resign. Founding CSPI in 1971 with the goal of applying regulation through litigation, Jacobson attacked what Paul Johnson termed the "soft underbelly of the establishment" by claiming concern for public health. The pseudo-scientific nature of his jihads seldom involved real data or studies: in 2003, he claimed (without any evidence) that a chemical found in potato chips caused "tens of thousands" of cancers among Canadians. Jacobson subsequently attacked green tea as causing hypertension—when studies found just the opposite; claimed salt was only "good for funeral directors and coffin makers," even though the data linking sodium to various health outcomes are inconsistent. See "Michael Jacobson, Biography," http://www.activistcash.com/biography.cfm/bid/1284.

129. Two observational studies conducted from 1994 to 2000 of some 129,000 subjects in different groups found no relationship between levels of fiber in the diet and colon cancer, nor did "more fiber" lead to weight loss. See E. Giovannucci et al., "Intake of Fat, Meat, and Fiber in Relation to Risk of Colon Cancer in Men," *Cancer Research* 54 (May 1, 1994): 290–97.

130. "The First Line of Defense: Those Old Standbys, Diet and Exercise, Are Key Weapons in the Fight Against Cancer," *Washington Post*, February 10, 1998.

131. "Plenty of Reasons to Say 'Please Pass the Fiber,' " *New York Times*, April 26, 2004.

132. Paul Weindling, *Health, Race and German Politics Between National Unification and Nazism, 1870–1945* (New York: Cambridge University Press, 1989), 481.

133. Geoffrey Gorer, *Exploring English Character* (New York: Criterion, 1955), 122, and his *Sex and Marriage in England Today: A Study of the Views and Experience of the Under-45s* (London: Nelson, 1971).

134. Michael Schofield, *Sexual Behaviour of Young People* (Boston: Little, Brown, 1965).

135. William H. Masters and Virginia Johnson, *Human Sexual Response* (St. Louis: Little, Brown, 1966).

136. Barack Obama, *Dreams from My Father*, rev. ed. (New York: Three Rivers Press, 2004), 47.

137. "A Shortage of Eligible Black Men," *New York Times*, January 20, 2012. See also "Reasons Why Black Women Don't Date White Men," *Madam Noire*, January 4, 2012.

138. David B. Barrett, George T. Kurian, and Todd M. Johnson, *World Christian Encyclopedia*, 2nd ed., vol. 1 (New York: Oxford University Press, 2001), 5.

139. Donald T. Critchlow, *Phyllis Schlafly and Grassroots Conservatism: A Woman's Crusade* (Princeton, NJ: Princeton University Press, 2005).

140. Ibid., 110.

141. Ibid., 218.

142. Theodore S. Arrington and Patricia A. Kyle, "Equal Rights Amendment Activists in North Carolina," *Signs* 3 (Spring 1978): 666–80 (quotation on 678).

143. Critchlow, *Phyllis Schlafly and Grassroots Conservatism*, 213.

144. Ibid., 227.

145. Ibid., 232.

146. Paul R. Ehrlich and David Brower, *The Population Bomb* (New York: Ballantine, 1968).

147. Keith Greiner, "The Baby Boom Generation and How They Grew," *Chance: A Magazine of the American Statistical Association*, Winter 1994, 17-19.

148. Henry A. Kissinger, *White House Years* (Boston: Little, Brown, 1979), 821.

149. Henry A. Kissinger, *Years of Upheaval* (Boston: Little, Brown, 1982), 1008.

150. Statement of Secretary of Defense Harold Brown before the Senate Foreign Relations Committee, July 9, 1979, in U.S. Congress, Senate, Hearings on the Salt II Treaty before the Committee on Foreign Relations, 96th Cong., 1st session., Part 1, p. 111.

151. Kissinger, *Years of Upheaval*, 1009.

152. Ibid., 1175.

153. United States Congress, Senate, Committee on Foreign Affairs, The SALT II Treaty: Hearings before the Committee on Foreign Relations, United States Senate, Ninety-Sixth Congress, first session, on Ex. Y, 96 1 (Volume 3) (Ann Arbor: University of Michigan Library, 1979); Kissinger, *White House Years*; Henry A. Kissinger, *Nuclear Weapons and Foreign Policy* (Boston: W. W. Norton, 1969).

154. Thomas Pettit, (Reporter), and John Chancellor, (Anchor), July 31, 1979, "Kissinger Recommends Ratification of SALT II Treaty" [Television series episode]. *NBC Nightly News*. Retrieved from https://archives.nbclearn.com/portal/site/k-12/browse/?cuecard=2746.

155. Carter tells his own boyhood story in *In an Hour Before Daylight* (New York: Simon & Schuster, 2001) and of his time in the White House in *White House Diary* (New York: Farrar, Straus and Giroux, 2010), and in his memoirs, *Keeping Faith: Memoirs of a President* (Little Rock: University of Arkansas Press, 1995). His biographies include Frye Galliard and David C. Carter, *Prophet from Plains: Jimmy Carter and His Legacy* (Athens: University of Georgia Press, 2009) and Julian E. Zelizer, Arthur M. Schlesinger, and Sean Wilentz, *Jimmy Carter* (American Presidents) (New York: Times Books, 2010).

156. Edward Walsh, "Carter Attacks Reagan Tax Cut, Seeks Debates," *Washington Post*, July 18, 1980, referring to comments made at a Democrat Party fund-raiser in Hollywood, Florida.

157. David Harris, *The Crisis: The President, the Prophet, and the Shah—1979 and the Coming of Militant Islam* (New York: Little, Brown, 2004), 51.

158. Ibid.

159. Nonie Darwish, *Now They Call Me Infidel* (New York: Sentinel, 2006).

160. Ibid., 151.

161. Ibid.

162. John Barron, *MiG Pilot: The Final Escape of Lieutenant Belenko* (New York: Avon, 1983).

163. Harris, *The Crisis*, 13.

164. Ibid., 23.

165. Ibid., 108.

166. Ibid., 214.

167. Ibid.

168. Ibid., 346.

169. John Gillingham, *European Integration, 1950–2003* (Cambridge: Cambridge University Press, 2003), 132; Fritz W. Scharpf, *Governing in Europe: Effective and Democratic* (Oxford: Oxford University Press, 1999).

170. Ibid, 258.

171. Ibid., 134.

172. Frank Church, et al., *Covert Action in Chile, 1963–1973* (Washington, DC: Government Printing Office, 1975).

173. For Pinochet's repression, see the "Rettig Report" (United States Institute of Peace, "Report of the Chilean National Commission on Truth and Reconciliation," 1993), http://www.usip.org/files/resources/collections/truth_commissions/Chile90-Report/Chile90 -Report.pdf.

174. Gary S. Becker, "What Latin America Owes the Chicago Boys," in Peter Robinson, ed., *Hoover Digest* 4 (1997); Jean Dreze and Amartya Sen, *Hunger and Public Action* (New York: Oxford University Press, 1991).

175. Thomas F. O'Brien, *Making the Americas: The United States and Latin America in the Age of Revolutions to the Era of Globalization* (Albuquerque: University of New Mexico Press, 2007).

176. Ibid., 262.

Chapter 6: Ash Heap of History

1. Office of Inspection, "Reagan Assassination Attempt Interview Reports," May 4, 1981, http://www.secretservice.gov/Reagan%20Assassination%20Attempt%20Interview%20Reports.pdf; Sean Wilentz, *The Age of Reagan: A History, 1974–2008* (New York: HarperCollins, 2008).

2. Bruce E. Mowday, *September 11, 1777: Washington's Defeat at Brandywine Dooms Philadelphia* (Shippenburg, PA: White Mane Books, 2002), 97.

3. Margaret Thatcher, *Downing Street Years* (London: HarperCollins, 1993), 32.

4. Paul Johnson, *Heroes: From Alexander the Great and Julius Caesar to Churchill and De Gaulle* (New York: HarperCollins, 2007), 262.

5. Richard Crockett, *Thinking the Unthinkable: Think-tanks and the Economic Counter-revolution, 1932–1983* (London: HarperCollins, 1995), 187.

6. Typically, historians of the Left used the same tactics with Thatcher as they would with Reagan to attempt to minimize her impact. First, they tried to make it appear that the Conservative Party "did not so much win elections as watch Labour lose them. . . ." (Tony Judt, *Postwar: A History of Europe Since 1945* [New York: Penguin, 2005], 541.) Next they tried to argue that the state actually grew under Thatcher, and that government spending was high. (See Mark Mazower, *Dark Continent: Europe's Twentieth Century* [New York: Vintage, 1998].)

7. John Gillingham, *European Integration, 1950–2003* (Cambridge: Cambridge University Press, 2003), 138.

8. Ibid., 168. Hostility toward Ronald Reagan among intellectuals—even among ostensibly free-market scholars—was so great that John Gillingham, who praised Thatcher's training, did not give Ronald Reagan the same credit, despite the fact that not only had Reagan read the same types of debates and solutions, but he had in fact *proposed* many of them long before Thatcher ever came into office! See, for example, Reagan's extensive commentaries for his radio show: George P. Schultz, Kiron K. Skinner, Annelise Anderson, and Martin Anderson, *Reagan, In His Own Hand: The Writings of Ronald Reagan That Reveal His Revolutionary Vision for America* (New York: Free Press, 2001).

9. Johnson, *Heroes*, 263.

10. Ibid., 266.

11. Thatcher, *Downing Street Years*, 68.

12. Johnson, *Heroes*, 269.

13. Thatcher, *Downing Street Years*, 39.

14. Gillingham, *European Integration*, 170.

15. Judt, *Postwar*, 542.

16. Mazower, *Dark Continent*, 333.

17. Judt, *Postwar*, 543.

18. Thatcher, *Downing Street Years*, 93.

19. Ibid., 98.

20. Ibid., 71–90; Gillingham, *European Integration*, 136–37.

21. Thatcher, *Downing Street Years*, 8.

22. Max Hastings and Simon Jenkins, *The Battle for the Falklands* (New York: W. W. Norton, 1983), 7.

23. Thatcher, *Downing Street Years*, 182.

24. Lawrence Freedman, *The Official History of the Falklands Campaign*, 2 vols. (London: Routledge, 2005).

25. Thatcher, *Downing Street Years*, 235.

26. Ibid., 369. The London *Sunday Times* on October 28, 1984, reported that the union had appealed to Libya for support and that Scargill had met a Libyan labor official in Paris. Whether Scargill used the money to pay off his own mortgages is debated, but evidence seems clear that Libyan funds reached the coal miners.

27. Johnson, *Modern Times*, 742.

28. Thatcher, *Downing Street Years*, 368.

29. Paul Johnson, *Modern Times: A History of the World from the Twenties to the Nineties*, rev. ed. (New York: HarperCollins, 1991), 744.

30. Judt, *Postwar*, 547.

31. Mazower, *Dark Continent*, 333.

32. Gillingham, *European Integration*, 137–40.

33. Ibid., 82.

34. Andrew Shonfield, *Europe: Journey to an Unknown Destination* (London: Allen Lane, 1973); Ralf Dahrendorf, *Plädoyer für die Europäische Union* ("Pleas for the European Union," Munich, 1973).

35. Richard Howarth, "The Common Agricultural Policy," in P. Minford, ed., *The Cost of Europe* (Manchester: Manchester University Press, 1992), 51–83.

36. Gillingham, *European Integration*, 122–24.

37. Ibid.

38. Judt, *Postwar*, 526–28.

39. Ibid., 530.

40. Ibid., 531.

41. Ibid., 532–33.

42. Ibid., 533.

43. Ibid., 545–58.

44. Mazower, *Dark Continent*, 363.

45. Jefferson had instructed his secretary of the treasury, Albert Gallatin, to concoct a massive program of federally funded transportation projects that amounted to double the size of the *entire federal budget*, and even Martin Van Buren, hailed by some as the epitome of small-government ideas, not only saw spending and employment increase in his term, but enacted policies that in the long run guaranteed massive job giveaways by candidates to get elected. Larry Schweikart and Lynne Pierson Doti, *American Entrepreneur* (New York: Amacom, 2009), 82, and on Van Buren, Schweikart and Michael Allen, *A Patriot's History of the United States from Columbus's Great Discovery to the War on Terror* (New York: Sentinel, 2006), 179–248.

46. Ronald Reagan, *An American Life* (New York: Pocket Books, 1990), 28.

47. Ibid., 34.

48. Paul Kengor, *The Crusader: Ronald Reagan and the Fall of Communism* (New York: Regan Books, 2006), 7.

49. Reagan, *An American Life*, 106.

50. Kengor, *The Crusader*, 16.

51. Ibid., 19.

52. Reagan, *An American Life*, 129.

53. Ibid., 134.

54. Douglas Brinkley, ed., *The Reagan Diaries* (New York: HarperCollins, 2007), 339.

55. Reagan, *An American Life*, 142.

56. Skinner, et al., eds., *Reagan: In His Own Hand*.

57. Ibid., 166.

58. Reagan, *An American Life*, 205.

59. Kengor, *The Crusader*, 54.

60. Reagan, *An American Life*, 219.

61. Paul Kengor, *God and Ronald Reagan: A Spiritual Life* (New York: Regan Books, 2004).

62. Quoted in David Harris, *The Crisis: The President, the Prophet, and the Shah—1979 and the Coming of Militant Islam* (New York: Little, Brown, 2004), 380.

63. Critics have grasped at anything to minimize the impact of Reagan's election. Textbooks emphasized the "low turnout." "Where had all the voters gone?" asked historians George Tindall and David Shi. "The 1980 election reflected . . . 'the largest mass movement of our time'—nonvoting" (George Brown Tindall and David E. Shi, *America: A Narrative History*, brief 6th ed. [New York: Norton, 2004], 1176). New Deal liberals such as Samuel Eliot Morison, Henry Steele Commager, and William Leuchtenburg asserted that "the favorite candidate of millions of Americans, unhappy with Carter but distrustful of the right-wing ideologue Reagan, was 'None of the above.'" (Samuel Eliot Morison, Henry Steele Commager, and William E. Leuchtenburg, *Concise History of the American Republic*, 2nd ed. [New York: Oxford, 1983], 761). "The election results," observed liberal historians Winthrop Jordan and Leon Litwack, "revealed a new low in voter turnout [and] the new president entered the White House having received a 'landslide' of only 26 percent of the electorate" (Winthrop D. Jordan and Leon F. Litwack, *The United States: Combined Edition*, 7th ed. [Englewood Cliffs, NJ: Prentice Hall, 1991], 866). None of these texts bothered to mention that not only did Reagan get a higher percentage of the vote than did Bill Clinton twelve years later, but Clinton only had one million more votes than Reagan even though the nation had added almost 22 million more people!

64. Reagan, *An American Life*, 227.

65. Ibid., 209.

66. Ibid., 210.

67. Ibid., 135, 215.

68. Ronald Reagan, *An American Life* (New York: Pocket Books, 1990), 519.

69. Quoted in Cannon, "Reagan's Big Idea."

70. Thomas C. Reed, *At the Abyss: An Insider's History of the Cold War* (New York: Ballantine, 2004), 263–64.

71. Kengor, *The Crusader*, 69.

72. Edmund Morris, *Dutch: A Memoir of Ronald Reagan* (New York: HarperCollins, 1999), 435.

73. Kengor, *God and Ronald Reagan*, 200.

74. Morris, *Dutch*, 434–35.

75. Ronald Reagan, "Address to Members of the British Parliament," June 8, 1982, http://www .heritage.org/research/reports/2002/06/reagans-westminster-speech.

76. Kengor, *The Crusader*, 117.

77. Ibid.

78. Ibid., 118.

79. Ibid., 126.

80. Ibid., 130.

81. Reed, *At the Abyss*, 240.

82. Ibid., 240.

83. Ronald Reagan, "Speech to Members of the Platform Committee," Republican National Convention, July 31, 1968, Reagan Library, "RWR—Speeches and Articles (1968)," vertical files.

84. Brinkley, *Reagan Diaries*, 25.

85. Reagan, *An American Life*, 409.

86. Peter Schweizer, *Reagan's War: The Epic Story of His Forty-Year Struggle and Final Triumph over Communism* (New York: Anchor, 2002), 245.

87. Judt, *Postwar*, 602.

88. Ibid., 603.

89. William E. Odom, *The Collapse of the Soviet Military* (New Haven, CT: Yale University Press, 1998), 2.

90. Kengor, *The Crusader*, 149.

91. Schweizer, *Reagan's War*, 232.

92. Reed, *At the Abyss*, 213.

93. Thomas Sowell, *Basic Economics*, 4th ed. (New York: Basic Books, 2011), 17–25, and Vladimir Popov and Nicolai Shemelev, *The Turning Point in the Soviet Economy* (New York: Doubleday, 1989).

94. Reed, *At the Abyss*, 219.

95. Ibid., 214.

96. Gus W. Weiss, "CSI: The Farewell Dossier—Duping the Soviets," [Central Intelligence Agency] *Studies in Intelligence*, 1996, https://www.cia.gov/library/center-for-the-study-of-intelligence/csi-publications/csi-studies/studies/96unclass/farewell.htm.

97. Odom, *Collapse of the Soviet Military*, 64.

98. Alexander Feklisov, *The Man Behind the Rosenbergs* (New York: Enigma Books, 2001), 66.

99. Kengor, *The Crusader*, 124–25.

100. David E. Hoffman, "Reagan Approved Plan to Sabotage Soviets," *Washington Post*, February 27, 2004; Kengor, *The Crusader*, 124–25. Kengor relies heavily on direct communications with Weiss and documents provided by Weiss, including an article printed in the CIA journal, *Studies in Intelligence*, 1996, called "Duping the Soviets: The Farewell Dossier."

101. Kengor, *The Crusader*, 150.

102. Reed, *At the Abyss*, 268–69.

103. Judt, *Postwar*, 591.

104. Christopher Andrew and Oleg Gordievsky, *KGB: The Inside Story* (New York: HarperPerennial, 1990), 585. In this case, the boast was wrong. Evidence shows that the KGB participated in the London demonstration, but did not organize it. Indeed, one operation set up by the KGB in London to direct such operations found that the Western peace movements enthusiastically and reliably mounted anti-U.S. campaigns completely on their own.

105. Schweizer, *Reagan's War*, 181.

106. Judt, *Postwar*, 591; Jeffrey Herf, *War by Other Means: Soviet Power, West German Resistance, and the Battle of the Euromissiles* (New York: Free Press, 1991).

107. Schweizer, *Reagan's War*, 181–82.

108. Ibid., 226.

109. Morris, *Dutch*, 454.

110. Christopher Andrew and Vasili Mitrokhin, *The Sword and the Shield: The Mitrokhin Archive and the Secret History of the KGB* (New York: Basic Books, 1999), 242–43.

111. Brinkley, *Reagan Diaries*, 13.

112. Andrew and Gordievsky, *KGB*, 590.

113. Odom, *Collapse of the Soviet Military*, 112.

114. Larry P. Goodson, *Afghanistan's Endless War: State Failure, Regional Politics, and the Rise of the Taliban* (Seattle: University of Washington Press, 2001), 57.

115. "The CIA's Intervention in Afghanistan," *Le Nouvel Observateur*, January 15, 1988, http://www.globalresearch.ca/articles/BRZ110A.html.

116. George Crile, *Charlie Wilson's War* (New York: Grove Press, 2003), 14.

117. Morris does not include the phrase, but Kenneth Adelman, who was Reagan's arms control director, called the exchange the most "harsh indictment of Soviet behavior ever delivered" to any Russian dictator. Kenneth Adelman, *The Great Universal Embrace* (New York: Simon and Schuster, 1989), 136–41.

118. Johnson, *Modern Times*, 720.

119. Odom, *Collapse of the Soviet Military*, 103.

120. Peter Schweizer, ed., *The Fall of the Berlin Wall* (Stanford, CA: Hoover Institution Press, 2000), 19.

121. Kengor, *The Crusader*, 234–35.

122. Oddly, Tony Judt, who pointed out that "one in five veterans of the Afghan wars were confirmed alcoholics," seemed to miss the fact that one in *three* Soviet men died drunk, whether they were veterans or not! Thus, serving in Afghanistan may have *lowered* a Russian male's chances of becoming a lush (Judt, *Postwar*, 593).

123. "Inside Afghanistan," *Newsweek*, June 11, 1984; "Why Aid Afghanistan?" *Washington Post*, January 2, 1985.

124. Crile, *Charlie Wilson's War*, 424.

125. Ibid., 499.

126. Odom, *Collapse of the Soviet Military*, 107.

127. Ibid., 108.

128. Kengor, *The Crusader*, 178.

129. Ibid.

130. William Pemberton, *Exit with Honor: The Life and Presidency of Ronald Reagan* (Armonk, NY: Sharpe, 1997), 131.

131. Ronald Reagan, "Remarks to the Institute for Foreign Policy Analysis at a Conference on the Strategic Defense Initiative," March 14, 1988; Caspar W. Weinberger, *Fighting for Peace: Seven Critical Years in the Pentagon* (New York: Warner Books, 1991), 304.

132. Morris, *Dutch*, 476. Indeed, Shultz dined with Reagan on February 12, and while the topic was mutual assured destruction, and while Shultz understood how deeply Reagan opposed it, he still claimed to have no intimation of the impending Strategic Defense Initiative at that time. See Paul Lettow, *Ronald Reagan and His Quest to Abolish Nuclear Weapons* (New York: Random House, 2005), 100–101. Shultz fumed that only a "lunatic" such as Keyworth could have foisted SDI off on the president, without realizing that the whole concept was largely Reagan's—and his instincts were right, and Shultz's wrong.

133. Lettow, *Ronald Reagan and His Quest to Abolish Nuclear Weapons*, 98.

134. Ibid., 99.

135. "Address to the Nation on Defense and National Security," March 23, 1983, http://www .cnn.com/SPECIALS/cold.war/episodes/22/documents/starwars.speech/.

136. Morris, *Dutch*, 478.

137. Sagan is seen in *Reagan: The Cold War and a Speech*, a film by Bob Parks, with screenplay by Larry Schweikart, in author's possession, 2007.

138. "President Seeks Futuristic Defense Against Missiles," *Washington Post*, March 24, 1983; Kengor, *The Crusader*, 181.

139. "Now, Talk of New Strains Among Top Aides," *New York Times*, March 31, 1983.

140. Kengor, *The Crusader*, 182.

141. Schweizer, *Reagan's War*, 249.

142. Johnson, *Modern Times*, 702.

143. Judt, *Postwar*, 586.

144. Johnson, *Modern Times*, 702.

145. Schweizer, *Reagan's War*, 273.

146. Ibid., 212.

147. Judt, *Postwar*, 564.

148. Ibid., 568.

149. Ibid., 572.

150. Ibid.

151. Ibid., 571.

152. "Excerpt from Protokol N. 119, Paragraph IIc of the Secretariat of the TsK [Central Committee, CPSU]," analysis of the so-called *samizdat* literature in distribution among intelligentsia and youth, http://psi.ece.jhu.edu/~kaplan/IRUSS/BUK/GBARC/pdfs/dis70/ct119-71.pdf.

153. Artemy Troitsky, "Rock in the USSR: The True Story of Rock in Russia," http://www.planetaquarium.com/eng/pub/doc_at1.html.

154. Timothy W. Ryback, *Rock Around the Bloc: A History of Rock Music in Eastern Europe and the Soviet Union* (New York: Oxford, 1990), 26.

155. Ibid., 58. Also see Larry Schweikart, *Seven Events That Made America America* (New York: Sentinel, 2010), 117–50.

156. Ryback, *Rock Around the Bloc*, 50–58 and passim.

157. Ibid., 109.

158. Ibid., 5.

159. Ibid., 141–48.

160. "East Berlin Loses the Rock War," *Le Monde*, June 21, 1988.

161. Andrew and Mitrokhin, *The Sword and the Shield*, 548.

162. Ibid.

163. Mazower, *Dark Continent*, 181.

164. David Remnick, *Lenin's Tomb: The Last Days of the Soviet Empire* (New York: Random House, 1993), 307.

165. Ibid.

166. Mazower, *Dark Continent*, 278.

167. Ibid., 279.

168. Judt, *Postwar*, 578.

169. Mazower, *Dark Continent*, 282.

170. Judt, *Postwar*, 581.

171. Remnick, *Lenin's Tomb*, 203.

172. Ibid.

173. Schweikart and Doti, *American Entrepreneur*, 40.

174. Judt, *Postwar*, 570–71.

175. Ibid., 571.

176. Ibid., 573.

177. Ibid., 579.

178. James West Davidson, et al., *Nation of Nations: A Concise Narrative of the American Republic*, vol. II: *Since 1865* (New York: McGraw-Hill, 2002), 952; George Brown Tindall and David E. Shi, *America: A Narrative History*, brief 6th ed. (New York: W. W. Norton, 2004), 1196.

179. Remnick, *Lenin's Tomb*, 47.

180. Mikhail Gorbachev, *Perestroika* (New York: Harper & Row, 1987), 24, 58, 62–64, 161, 252–54.

181. Kengor, *The Crusader*, 124.

182. Remnick, *Lenin's Tomb*, 48.

183. Ibid., 50.

184. Tom Standage, *An Edible History of Humanity* (New York: Walker & Company, 2009), 191.

185. Remnick, *Lenin's Tomb*, 326.

186. "Mikhail Gorbachev: Communism was 'Pure Propaganda,'" Associated Press, March 11, 2002, in speech to Columbia University.

187. "1989: Malta Summit Ends Cold War," http://news.bbc.co.uk/onthisday/hi/dates/stories/december/3/newsid_4119000/4119950.stm.

188. Remnick, *Lenin's Tomb*, 244.

189. Ibid., 245; Judt, *Postwar*, 597.

190. Remnick, *Lenin's Tomb*, 247.

191. Zhores A. Medvedev, *Nuclear Disaster in the Urals*, trans. George Saunders (New York: W. W. Norton, 1979); Judt, *Postwar*, 598.

192. Judt, *Postwar*, 598.

193. Ibid., 603.

194. The contortions leftist historians have gone through to salvage anything from the collapse of communism are enduringly humorous. Mark Mazower, for example, argued that while the USSR fell, it was "hardly of the kind or in the manner anticipated." The "almost universal failure to predict the collapse of communism drove a large nail into the coffin of Western political science," he claimed (*Dark Continent*, 361–62). A former political science major, Larry Schweikart could not identify any models that would have predicted communism's implosion—but there is certainly a very good economic model and it's called capitalism, which anticipated the Soviet Union's demise perfectly. Sooner or later, people will demand human liberty, and this will most likely appear in the form of a steady, subtle pressure for the basics of life, including decent food, housing, and transportation. Every housewife and farmer will not readily ascend the barricades to demand freedom of speech or even religious liberty, but each will quietly erode totalitarian economic controls until there are no excuses left to be made. Adam Smith, Friedrich Hayek, and Milton Friedman all could have predicted the certainty of the Marxist demise, if not its precise timing.

Chapter 7: The Age of Boomer Ascendance

1. George H. W. Bush Address Before a Joint Session of Congress on the Persian Gulf Crisis, September 11, 1990, http://bushlibrary.tamu.edu/research/public_papers.php?id=2217&-year=1990&month=9.

2. John Gillingham, *European Integration, 1950–2003* (Cambridge: Cambridge University Press, 2003), 157.

3. Michel Albert, *Capitalism Versus Capitalism: How America's Obsession with Individual Achievement and Short-term Profit Has Led It to the Brink of Collapse* (New York: Four Walls Eight Windows, 1993).

4. Ibid., 272.

5. Ibid., 276.

6. Ibid., 286.

7. Patrick McCarthy, *The Crisis of the Italian State: From the Origins of the Cold War to the Fall of Berlusconi* (New York: St. Martin's, 1995), 2–4, 61–80, 82, 91–94, 174–75.

8. Ibid., 367.

9. "Dynasties Run Italy from Politics to Finance," London *Times*, August 4, 2001.

10. Gillingham, *European Integration*, 325.

11. Ibid., 305.

12. Ibid., 349.

13. "Treaty of Lisbon," http://eur-lex.europa.eu/JOHtml.do?uri=OJ:C:2007:306:SOM:EN:HTML.

14. Jeffrey Sachs, "Consolidating Capitalism," *Foreign Policy* 98 (Spring 1995): 50–59.

15. Herman Schwartz, "Small States in Big Trouble: State Reorganization in Australia, Denmark, New Zealand, and Sweden in the 1980s," *World Politics* 46 (July 1994): 527–55 (quotation on 547).

16. Gillingham, *European Integration*, 363.

17. "Telecommunications to the Finland Station," *The Economist*, October 9, 1999.

18. Tony Judt, *Postwar: A History of Europe Since 1945* (New York: Penguin Press, 2005), 543.

19. Ibid., 543–44.

20. Peter Wehner and Yuval Levin, "Crime, Drugs, Welfare—and Other Good News," *Commentary*, December 2007, 19–24.

21. Marianne P. Bitler, Jonah B. Gelback, Hilary W. Hoynes, and Madeline Zavodny, "The Impact of Welfare Reform on Marriage and Divorce," Federal Reserve Bank of Atlanta Working Paper 2002-9, June 2002, 1.

22. Gillingham, *European Integration*, 326.

23. Ibid., 326–27.

24. Ibid.

25. "Judge Tells of Murder Plots to Block Dutroux Investigation," UK *Telegraph*, May 3, 2004.

26. "Something Rotten," *The Economist*, September 14, 1996; "Child Murders Could Provoke New Revolution," *Daily Telegraph*, January 23, 2002; "Dutroux Trial Over Six Years in the Making," *Sunday Tribune*, June 2, 2002.

27. Gillingham, *European Integration*, 327.

28. Paul M. Heywood, "Corruption in Contemporary Spain," *PS: Political Science & Politics* 40 (2007): 695–99.

29. Gillingham, *European Integration*, 212; Omar Encarnación, "Social Concentration in Democratic and Market Transitions: Comparative Lessons from Spain," *Comparative Political Studies* 30 (August 1997): 387–420.

30. Ibid., 220.

31. "Spain's Insiders in Insider Scandal," *New York Times*, May 23, 1992.

32. Ibid.

33. Gillingham, *European Integration*, 220.

34. "Superwomen Sisters Split at Last in Battle of Spanish Succession," London *Independent*, February 15, 1998.

35. Heywood, "Corruption in Contemporary Spain," passim.

36. Antonio Argandona, "Ethics in Finance and Public Policy, the Ibercorp Affair," Research Paper No. 369, October 1998, University of Navarra, Barcelona, 12.

37. Antonio Argandona, "Ethics in Finance and Public Policy: The Ibercorp Case," *Journal of Business Ethics* 22 (1999) 219–31.

38. John Hooper, *The New Spaniards*, 2nd ed. (New York: Penguin, 2006), 55.

39. Ibid., 62.

40. Paul Hollander, *Political Will and Personal Belief: The Decline and Fall of Soviet Communism* (New Haven, CT: Yale University Press, 1999), 7; coauthor Dave Dougherty in an unpublished novel, "Gnosis," also predicted in 1985 the fall of the Berlin Wall, the dissolution of the Warsaw Pact, and a restructuring of the Soviet Union to take place in 1991, almost exactly on schedule.

41. Judt, *Postwar*, 644–45.

42. Hollander, *Political Will*, 22.

43. Ibid., 4.

44. Judt, *Postwar*, 647.

45. Ibid., 653.

46. Thomas Sowell, *Basic Economics: A Common Sense Guide to the Economy* (New York: Basic Books, 2011), 18–19.

47. Ibid., 656.

48. Paul Johnson, *Modern Times: A History of the World from the Twenties to the Nineties* (New York: HarperCollins, 1991), 768.

49. Ibid.

50. Comments to the author from various Soviet economists, Mont Pelerin Society Meeting, 1990, Munich.

51. Thomas C. Reed, *At the Abyss: An Insider's History of the Cold War* (New York: Ballantime, 2004), 214.

52. Ibid., 217.

53. R. M. Koster and Guillermo Sánchez, *In the Time of the Tyrants: Panama, 1968–1990* (New York City: Norton, 1990).

54. Murray Engleheart with Arnaud Durieux, *AC/DC: Maximum Rock and Roll* (New York: Harper Entertainment, 2008), 398.

55. Anthony Cordesman and Abraham R. Wagner, *The Lessons of Modern War: Volume Two—The Iran-Iraq Conflict* (Boulder, CO: Westview, 1990).

56. Stockholm International Peace Research Institute, http://projects.sign.se/armstrade/atrig_data.html.

57. Sharon Rogers, Will Rogers, and Gene Gregston, *Storm Center: The USS Vincennes and Iran Air Flight 655: A Personal Account of Tragedy and Terrorism* (Annapolis, MD: U.S. Naval Institute Press, 1992).

58. United States Navy, "Formal Investigation into the Circumstances Surrounding the Downing of Iran Air Flight 655 on 3 July 1988," 19 August 1988, 4–5, http://www.dod.mil/pubs/foi/reading_room/172.pdf.

59. Rogers, Rogers, and Gregston, *Storm Center*, 11.

60. Ibid., 159.

61. Cordesman and Wagner, *Lessons of Modern War*, 39.

62. Ibid., 45.

63. "1990: Outrage at Iraqi TV Hostage Show," August 23, 1990, http://news.bbc.co.uk/onthisday/hi/dates/stories/august/23/newsid_2512000/2512289.stm.

64. Johnson, *Modern Times*, 770.

65. Dore Gold, *Tower of Babble: How the United Nations Has Fueled Global Chaos* (New York: Crown, 2004), 40.

66. Al Gore, *Earth in the Balance: Ecology and the Human Spirit* (New York: Houghton Mifflin, 2000).

67. "Gore's Persian Gulf War Vote," WorldNetDaily, October 6, 2000. This claim has been researched by Snopes.com and is labeled "undetermined," but Simpson stands by his claim.

68. Jennifer Verner, "Ted Kennedy's Jihad," frontpagemagazine.com, May 31, 2004, http://frontpagemag.com/Articles/Read.aspx?GUID={2F90CDBB-7C84-4AA4-87F3-42929BE56C8C}.

69. Ronald Reagan, *An American Life* (New York: Pocket Books, 1990), 466.

70. John David Lewis, *Nothing Less Than Victory: Decisive Wars and the Lessons of History* (Princeton, NJ: Princeton University Press, 2010), 287.

71. Bob Woodward, *The Commanders* (New York: Simon and Schuster, 1991), 208–9.

72. Ibid., 214.

73. Ibid., 278.

74. Ibid., 310.

75. Ibid., 349. Schwarzkopf dismissed the 7,000-casualty estimate as unrealistic, even at worst.

76. Benjamin S. Lambeth, *The Transformation of American Air Power* (Ithaca, NY: Cornell University Press, 2000), 112–23; Michael J. Brodner and William W. Bruner III, "Tank Plinking," *Air Force Magazine*, October 1993, 31; Richard Reynolds, *Heart of the Storm: The Genesis of the Air Power in the Persian Gulf* (Maxwell Air Force Base, AL: Air University Press, 1995).

77. Interviews with various soldiers from *Inside the Kill Box*, Discovery Channel, 2005.

78. Tom Keaney and Eliot Cohen, *Evolution in Warfare?* (Annapolis, MD: Naval Institute Press, 1995), 91–92.

79. Norman Schwarzkopf with Peter Petre, *It Doesn't Take a Hero* (New York: Bantam Books, 1992), 470.

80. Robert Rabil, "Genocide in Iraq," http://www.hrw.org/reports/1993/iraqanfal/#Table%20of.

81. Schwarzkopf, *It Doesn't Take a Hero*, 503.

82. Democratic National Convention address by Ann Richards, http://gos.sbc.edu/r/richards.html.

83. Nigel Hamilton, *Bill Clinton: An American Journey, Great Expectations* (New York: Ballantine, 2003), 52. Biographer David Maraniss doesn't mention an incident where Clinton broke his leg jumping rope (David Maraniss, *First in His Class: The Biography of Bill Clinton* [New York: Touchstone, 1995]), and Clinton himself (Bill Clinton, *My Life, Vol. I, The Early Years* [New York: Vintage, 2005], 23) claims it was an accident because he didn't take off his boots, but Hamilton suggests the other children deliberately tripped him.

84. Hamilton, *Bill Clinton*, 176.

85. Ibid., 198.

86. Craig Steiner, "The Myth of the Clinton Surplus," October 31, 2007, http://www.craig steiner.us/ and also at http://www.treasuredirect.gov/NP/BPDLogin?application=np.

87. Andrew Morton, *Monica's Story* (New York: St. Martin's, 1999), 73, 69. In his grand jury testimony, Clinton deliberately wore one of the ties Lewinsky gave him, a sign she took of his deep affection for her.

88. Ibid., 143–44.

89. *Washington Post* and Kenneth W. Starr, *The Starr Report: The Official Report of the Independent Counsel's Investigation of the President* (Rocklin, CA: Forum, 1998); Ann Coulter, *High Crimes and Misdemeanors: The Case Against Bill Clinton* (Washington, DC: Regnery, 1998); David Schippers, *Sellout: The Inside Story of President Clinton's Impeachment* (Washington, DC: Regnery, 2001); Morton, *Monica's Story*; Marvin L. Kalb, *One Scandalous Story: Clinton, Lewinsky, and Thirteen Days That Tarnished American Journalism* (New York: Free Press, 2007).

90. According to the *St. Petersburg Times* (September 12, 1998), Clinton was on the phone with Representative Sonny Callahan discussing troop deployment in Bosnia while Lewinsky performed oral sex on him.

91. Mark Bowden, *Black Hawk Down: A Story of Modern War* (New York: Atlantic Monthly Press, 1999); Jonathan Stevenson, *Losing Mogadishu: Testing U.S. Policy in Somalia* (Annapolis, MD: Naval Institute Press, 1995).

92. Gerald Posner, *Why America Slept: The Failure to Prevent 9/11* (New York: Random House, 2003), 66.

93. Clinton did not heed polls that said that the public would have supported a more aggressive response than Clinton offered: in a subsequent study, two political scientists concluded, "Had the administration chosen to galvanize public opposition to Somali warlord Farah Aideed . . . Americans would have tolerated an expanded effort to catch and punish him" (Peter D. Feaver and Richard K. Kohn, "Digest of Findings and Studies," Project on the Gap Between the Military and Civilian Society, Triangle Institute for Security Studies, June 2000, and their "A Look at Casualty Aversion: How Many Deaths Are Acceptable? A Surprising Answer," *Washington Post*, November 7, 1999.)

94. William Easterly, *The White Man's Burden: Why the West's Efforts to Aid the Rest Have Done So Much Ill and So Little Good* (New York: Penguin, 2006), 150.

95. Gold, *Tower of Babble*, 139.

96. Ibid., 145.

97. Ibid., 158.

98. Ibid., 159.

99. Gillingham, *European Integration*, 282.

100. Lawrence Wright, *The Looming Tower: Al-Qaeda and the Road to 9/11* (New York: Knopf, 2006), 11–12.

101. Ibid., 12.

102. Ibid., 23.

103. Walter Russell Mead, *God and Gold: Britain, America, and the Making of the Modern World* (New York: Alfred A. Knopf, 2007), 67.

104. Wright, *The Looming Tower*, 58.

105. Ibid.; Peter L. Bergen, *Holy War, Inc.: Inside the Secret World of Osama bin Laden* (New York: Free Press, 2001), 88.

106. Wright, *The Looming Tower*, 102.

107. Interview with Charles Calomiris, September 18, 2001.

108. "America's Chaotic Road to War," www.washingtonpost.com, January 27, 2002.

109. Ibid.

110. Monsoor Ijaz, a Pakistani and a Clinton donor, identified himself as the go-between in these meetings (Posner, *Why America Slept*, 102).

111. Ibid., 134.

112. "The 9/11 Commission Report," June 22, 2004, http://www.9-11commission.gov/report/911Report.pdf. 60; Wright, *The Looming Tower*, 236.

113. William Perry, U.S. secretary of defense at the time, said in 2007 he thought al-Qaeda, not Iran, was behind the attack ("Perry: U.S. Eyed Iran Attack After Bombing," United Press International, June 6, 2007, http://www.upi.com/Security_Terrorism/Briefing/2007/06/06/perry_us_eyed_iran_attack_after_bombing/7045/.

114. Richard Minitier, *Disinformation: 22 Media Myths That Undermine the War on Terror* (Washington, DC: Regnery, 2005), 23.

115. Ibid., 27; "The 9/11 Commission Report," 62.

116. Wright, *The Looming Tower*, 171.

117. Ibid., 247.

118. "The 9/11 Commission Report," 79.

119. Ibid., 97.

120. Larry Schweikart, *Seven Events That Made America America* (New York: Sentinel, 2010).

121. "Clinton White House Axed Terror Fund Probe," *Washington Times*, April 2, 2002.

122. "Bill Clinton and Echoes of 1995," http://www.washingtonpost.com/wp-dyn/content/article/2010/04/20/AR2010042001456.html.

123. Larry C. Johnson, "The Declining Terrorist Threat," *New York Times*, July 10, 2001.

124. Peter Lance, *1000 Years for Revenge: International Terrorism and the FBI—the Untold Story* (New York: William Morrow, 2003), 408.

125. "America's Chaotic Road to War"; Mark Steyn, *America Alone: The End of the World as We Know It* (Washington, DC: Regnery, 2006), 16.

126. Wright, *The Looming Tower*, 170.

127. James Flink, *The American Automobile Industry Since 1945* (Cambridge, MA: Harvard University Press, 1971), and his "Three Stages of American Automobile Consciousness," *American Quarterly* 24 (October 1972): 451–73.

128. John Heitmann, *The Automobile and American Life* (Jefferson, NC: McFarland, 2009), chapter 7.

129. David Halberstam, *The Reckoning* (New York: Avon, 1986), 295.

130. Ibid., 296.

131. Ibid., 305–9.

132. Ibid., 311.

133. Ibid., 318.

134. Ibid., 309.

135. "Japan Falls into Spiral of Despair," *London Sunday Times*, February 22, 2009, http://business.timesonline.co.uk/tol/business/economics/article5780318.ece.

136. "Japan Goes from Dynamic to Disheartened," *New York Times*, October 17, 2010.

137. Ibid.

138. Review of *A Nation in Retreat* by Michael Zielenziger (New York: Doubleday, 2006), http://www.washingtonpost.com/wp-dyn/content/article/2006/09/18/AR2006091801192.html.

139. Walter Russell Mead, *God and Gold: Britain, America and the Making of the Modern World* (New York: Knopf, 2007), 72.

140. Ibid., 73.

141. Joyce Winer, "The Floating Lightbulb," in Patricia Foster, ed., *Minding the Body: Women Writers on Body and Soul* (New York: Anchor, 1994), 47.

142. Kay S. Hymowitz, *Marriage and Caste in America: Separate and Unequal Families in a Post-Marital Age* (Chicago: Ivan R. Dee, 2006), 6.

143. Ibid., 20

144. Ibid., 21–22.

145. Ibid., 25.

146. Ibid., 55; Office of Policy Planning and Research, United States Department of Labor, "The Negro Family: The Case for National Action," March 1965.

147. Hymowitz, *Marriage and Caste in America*, 61.

148. Todd R. Risley, Betty Hart, and Louis Bloom, *Meaningful Differences in the Everyday Experience of Young Children* (Baltimore: Paul H. Brookes, 1995).

149. Hymowitz, *Marriage and Caste in America*, 84.

150. Charles Murray, *Coming Apart: The State of White America, 1960–2010* (New York: Crown, 2012).

151. Ibid., 88–94.

152. Ibid., 174.

153. Kay S. Hymowitz, *Manning Up: How the Rise of Women Has Turned Men into Boys* (New York: Basic Books, 2011), 55.

154. Ibid., 65–66.

Chapter 8: Jihad

1. "Fertility Revolution Lowers Birth Rates," *Wall Street Journal*, January 24, 2003.

2. Joseph Chamie, quoted in the *Wall Street Journal*, January 24, 2003, retrieved from http://online.wsj.com/article/0,SB104334616761507264,00.html.

3. Mark Steyn, *America Alone* (Washington, DC: Regnery, 2006), 4.

4. Ibid., 2.

5. Ibid.

6. United Nations, ed., *World Population Prospects: The 1998 Revisions. The 2001 Revisions* (New York: United Nations, n.d. [2001]), and its *World Population in 2300*, both cited in Walter Laqueur, *The Last Days of Europe* (New York: Thomas Dunne, 2007), 24–25.

7. Claire Berlinski, *Menace in Europe* (New York: Three Rivers Press, 2007), 141.

8. Paul Demeny, "Population Policy Dilemmas in Europe at the Dawn of the Twenty-first Century," in *Population and Development Review* 29 (March 2003): 1–28.

9. Jean Raspail, *The Camp of the Saints* (Petosky, MI: Social Contract Press, 1994 [1973]).

10. "Albania," Religious Intelligence. United States Department of State, http://www.state.gov/j/drl/rls/irf/2006/71364.htm.

11. Philip Jenkins, *God's Continent: Christianity, Islam, and Europe's Religious Crisis* (Oxford: Oxford University Press, 2007), 8.

12. Ibid.

13. Ibid, 21.

14. Niall Ferguson, *The War of the World* (London: Allen Lane, 2006), quoted in Jenkins, *God's Continent*, 9.

15. Steyn, *America Alone*, 12.

16. Jytte Klausen, *The Islamic Challenge* (New York: Oxford University Press, 2005), 3, 7.

17. "It's Paranoia, not Islamophobia," UK *Guardian*, July 15, 2005.

18. Steyn, *America Alone*, 17.

19. Jenkins, *God's Continent*, 250; www.mju.es/asuntos_religiosos/ar_n08_e.htm; Jonathan Laurence and Justin Vaisse, *Integrating Islam* (Washington, DC: Brookings Institution Press, 2006).

20. "London Most Expensive, Dirty City in Europe," Survey, March 12, 2008, http://afp.google.com/article/ALeqM5hWqM8M4Kubw9PsasW0u2VFw5wyzQ.

21. Soeren Kern, *European 'No-Go' Zones for Non-Muslims Proliferating*, Gatestone Institute, http://www.gatestoneinstitute.org/2367/european-muslim-no-go-zones.

22. "'No-Go' Bishop Defends Comments," BBC News, February 24, 2008.

23. Amir Taheri, "France's Ticking Time Bomb," *Arab News*, November 5, 2005, www.benador associates/com/article/18823; "As Muslims Call Europe Home, Dangerous Isolation Takes Root," *Wall Street Journal*, July 11, 2005; "Sharia Law? Don't Even Think About It," UK *Guardian*, February 20, 2006.

24. Taheri, "France's Ticking Time Bomb."

25. "Swedish Welfare State Collapses as Immigrants Wage War," *Brussels Journal*, March 28, 2006.

26. Ibid.

27. Laqueur, *Last Days of Europe*, 41.

28. Isabelle de Pommereau, "Germans Wary as Mosque Rises in Cologne," *Christian Science Monitor*, http://www.csmonitor.com/World/Europe/2009/0810/p06s16-woeu.html.

29. Peter Schneider, "The New Berlin Wall," *New York Times Magazine*, December 4, 2005; Hind Fraihi, *Undercover in Klein-Marokko* (Leuven: Van Halewyck, 2006); Lowell Ponte, "Goodbye Europe," Frontpagemagazine.com, March 28, 2006.

30. Jenkins, *God's Continent*, 225; Hisham Aidi, "Let Us Be Moors," www.columbia.edu/cu/ccbh/pdfs/Souls.Let_Us_Be_Moors.pdf.

31. "Europe's Muslims May Be Headed Where the Marxists Went Before," *New York Times*, December 26, 2004; Gilles Kepel, *Jihad: The Trail of Political Islam* (Cambridge, MA: Belknap Press, 2002).

32. Jenkins, *God's Continent*, 227.

33. Ibid.

34. Inayat Bunglawala, "It's Getting Harder to Be a British Muslim," London *Observer*, May 19, 2002; "Top Job Fighting Extremism for Muslim Who Praised Bomber," London *Daily Telegraph*, September 25, 2006.

35. "Sheik Yusuf al-Qaradawi: Theologian of Terror," August 1, 2005, www.adl.org/main_Arab_World/al_Qaradawi_report_20041110.htm?Multi_page_sections=sHeading_2.

36. Jenkins, *God's Continent*, 122.

37. Ibid., 247; Remy Leveau, Khadija Mohsen-Finan, and Cathering Wihtol de Wenden, eds., *New European Identity and Citizenship* (Aldershot, England: Ashgate, 2002).

38. Laqueur, *Last Days of Europe*, 72. However, as Laqueur points out, polls often yield contradictory results—another poll in 2006 reported that 91 percent of Muslims in Britain expressed loyalty to the UK, but even of those, up to 20 percent felt "sympathy" for the 2005 bombers.

39. "Hamburg's Cauldron of Terror," *Washington Post*, September 11, 2002.

40. Sean O'Neill and Daniel McGrory, *The Suicide Factory* (London: HarperPerennial, 2006), 107; "Wooing the Next Wave of Holy Warriors," *Los Angeles Times*, March 2, 2003.

41. Jenkins, *God's Continent*, 218.

42. O'Neill and McGrory, *Suicide Factory*, 106.

43. "Italy: Algerian Suspects Allegedly Planned to Kill 10,000," *La Stampa*, November 19, 2005; Philip Jenkins, *Images of Terror* (Hawthorne, NY: Aldine De Gruyter, 2003).

44. Jenkins, *God's Continent*, 213.

45. "Al-Qaeda Plotting Nuclear Attack on UK Officials Warn," UK *Guardian*, November 14, 2006. Many observers questioned why such a "dirty bomb" attack had not already occurred, especially in the United States, with its porous southern border (in the 2006 elections, a congressional candidate in Texas drove three full-sized elephants across the border without detection!). If fiction anticipates reality, some insight into the "why not" question may reside in novels, such as Nelson DeMille's *Wildfire* (Harrisonville, VA: Vision Publishers, 2007), which postulated that the U.S. government had informed Arab capitals that a nuclear attack of any sort on American soil would result in an automatic destruction of Mecca. While there was some logic to this kind of tit-for-tat, it presumes that Arab/Middle Eastern governments

actually had some degree of control over al-Qaeda and other terrorists. The assassination of Benazir Bhutto in Pakistan in late 2007, just as an example, called that premise into question.

46. Christison quoted in *Washington Post*, April 10, 2002, http://foi.missouri.edu/terrorbkgd/rootcauses.html; Carr in *New South Wales Iraq Appeal*, June 8, 2003, http://www.catholic weekly.com.au/03/jun/8/04.html.

47. George W. Bush, March 22, 2002, http://whitehouse.gov/news/releases/2002/03/200203221 .html; Tyson quoted from "It's Time to Step Up the Global War on Poverty," *BusinessWeek*, 2001, in Richard Miniter, *Disinformation: Media Myths That Undermine the War on Terror* (Washington, DC: Regnery, 2005), 125.

48. Brian Moynahan, "Putting the Fear of God into Holland," quoted in Jenkins, *God's Continent*, 160.

49. "Young Muslims and Terrorism," British Home Office and British Foreign Office, www .globalsecurity.org/security/library/report/2004/muslimext-uk.htm; "Europe Meets the New Face of Terrorism," *New York Times*, August 1, 2005.

50. "An Underclass Rebellion," *Economist*, November 14, 2005; Christopher Caldwell, "Islam on the Outskirts of the Welfare State," *New York Times Magazine*, February 5, 2006.

51. Alberto Abadie, working with the National Bureau of Economic Research, found the risk of terrorism was not significantly higher for poorer countries, and that a nation's level of political freedom is a more important factor (Alberto Abadie, "Poverty, Political Education, and the Roots of Terrorism," National Bureau of Economic Research Working Paper No. 10859), while Alan Krueger and Jitka Maleckova concluded "there was little reason for optimism that a reduction in poverty or an increase in educational attainment would meaningfully reduce international terrorism" (Alan B. Krueger and Jitka Maleckova, "Education, Poverty and Terrorism: Is There a Causal Connection?," *The Journal of Economic Perspectives* 17 (Autumn 2003): 119–44 [quotation on 119]).

52. Lawrence Wright, *The Looming Tower: Al-Qaeda and the Road to 9/11* (New York: Knopf, 2006), 7.

53. Meghnad Desai, *Rethinking Islamism* (New York: I. B. Tauris, 2006), 133.

54. "Putting the Fear of God into Holland," in Jenkins, *God's Continent*, 162; "New Berlin Wall," passim.

55. "Moroccan Preacher Said to Have Met with 9/11 Plotters," *Los Angeles Times*, July 6, 2005.

56. "The Great Divide," Pew Global Attitudes Project (Washington, DC: Pew Research Center, 2006).

57. "Stoned to Death," London *Times*, December 4, 2004.

58. Dilwar Hussein, "The Impact of 9/11 on British Muslim Identity," in Ron Geaves, et al., eds., *Islam and the West Post–September 11th* (Burlington, VT: Ashgate, 2005), 115–29.

59. Niall Ferguson, *Colossus: The Rise and Fall of the American Empire* (London: Allan Lane, 2004), 126.

60. Jenkins, *God's Continent*, 170.

61. Laqueur, *Last Days of Europe*, 46.

62. "Hezbollah: Rushdie Death Would Stop Prophet Insults," Agence France-Press, February 2, 2006.

63. "BNP Leader Warned of Multiracial Hell Hole," UK *Guardian*, January 19, 2006.

64. Jenkins, *God's Continent*, 244; Oriana Fallaci, *The Force of Reason* (New York: Rizzoli, 2006), 34–35.

65. "Pope Calls West Divorced from Faith, Adding a Blunt Footnote on Jihad," *New York Times*, September 13, 2006; John L. Allen, Jr., "The Word from Rome," *National Catholic Reporter*, March 24, 2006.

66. Samira Bellil, *Dans l'enfer des tournantes* (Paris: Gallimard, 2003); Sharon Lapkin, "Western Muslims' Racist Rape Spree," FrontPageMagazine.com, December 27, 2005.

67. "The Whore Lived Like a German," *Der Spiegel*, March 2, 2005.

68. "Ending Violence Against Women and Girls," State of the World Population 2000 (New York: United Nations Population Fund, 2000); Phyllis Chesler, "Worldwide Trends in Honor Killings," *Middle East Quarterly*, Spring 2010, 3–11.

69. "Khalil el-Moumni," http://en.wikipedia.org/wiki/Khalil_el-Moumni; George Weigel, "Europe's Two Culture Wars," *Commentary*, May 2006, 29–36.

70. A summary of the Åke Green case is here: http://www.akegreen.org. The Dutch case is reported in "Putting the Fear of God into Holland."

71. Bruce Bawer, *While Europe Slept: How Radical Islam Is Destroying the West from Within* (New York: Doubleday, 2006).

72. "A Crucible for Secularism," *Chicago Tribune*, June 19, 2006.

73. Interview with Bernard Lewis, *Die Welt*, July 28, 2004, http://www.welt.de/data/2004/07/28/310913.html; Jenkins, *God's Continent*, 4.

74. Jenkins, *God's Continent*, 4.

75. George Weigel, *The Cube and the Cathedral* (New York: Basic Books, 2005), 20.

76. Ibid., 20–21.

77. Paul Johnson, *Modern Times, Revised Edition, From the Twenties to the Nineties* (New York: HarperCollins, 1991), 705.

78. Jenkins, *God's Continent*, 27–28.

79. John Morreall and Tamara Sonn, *The Religion Toolkit: A Complete Guide to Religious Studies* (New York: Wiley-Blackwell, 2011).

80. Kate Fox, *Watching the English* (London: Hodder and Stoughton, 2004), 354; "Church Seeks Spirituality of Youth . . . and Doesn't Like What It Finds," London *Times*, May 8, 2006; Niall Ferguson, "Heaven Knows How We'll Rekindle Our Religion, But I Believe We Must," *Daily Telegraph*, July 31, 2005; Steve Bruce, *Religion in Modern Britain* (New York: Oxford University Press, 1995), 33, 39–40.

81. Jenkins, *God's Continent*, 32.

82. Michael S. Rose, *Goodbye, Good Men: How Liberals Brought Corruption into the Catholic Church* (Washington, DC: Regnery, 2002), 11.

83. "As Scandal Keeps Growing, Church and Its Faithful Reel," *New York Times*, March 17, 2002; "Sex Scandal Stuns Austria's Catholics," *Los Angeles Times*, July 14, 2004; "Ampleforth Scandal: Silence and Secrecy at School Where Child Sex Abuse Went on for Decades," UK *Guardian*, November 18, 2005; Jenkins, *God's Continent*, 35.

84. Chris More, *Betrayal of Trust* (Dublin: Marino, 1995); Iseult O'Doherty, *Stolen Childhood* (Dublin: Poolberg, 1998); Tom Hundley, "How Catholicism Fell from Grace in Ireland," *Chicago Tribune*, July 9, 2006.

85. John Jay College of Criminal Justice, "The Nature and Scope of Sexual Abuse of Minors by Catholic Priests and Deacons in the United States 1950–2002," 2006 Supplementary Report (Washington: United States Conference of Catholic Bishops, 2006).

86. *National Catholic Register*, March 20, 1994; Thomas C. Reeves, *The Empty Church: The Suicide of Liberal Christianity* (New York: Free Press, 1996), 23.

87. Jason Berry, *Lead Us Not into Temptation: Catholic Priests and the Sexual Abuse of Children* (Urbana, IL: University of Illinois Press, 2000), xii.

88. Leon J. Podles, *Sacrilege: Sexual Abuse in the Catholic Church* (Baltimore: Crossland, 2008), 93; Walter Coville, Paul F. D'Arcy, Thomas N. McCarthy, and John J. Rooney, *Assessment of Candidates for the Religious Life: Basic Psychological Issues and Problems* (Washington, DC: Center for Applied Research in the Apostolate, 1968), 28; Eugene Kennedy and Victor J. Heckler, *The Catholic Priest in the United States: Psychological Investigations* (Washington, DC: United States Catholic Conference, 1972); William C. Bier, "A Comparative Study of a Seminary Group and Four Other Groups on the Minnesota Multiphasic Personality Inventory," *Studies in Psychology and Psychiatry* 7 (April 1948): 60–61; Vincent Herr, "Screening Seminarians," in Vincent V. Herr, Magda B. Arnold, Charles A. Weisberger, and Paul F. D'Arcy, *Screening Candidates for the Priesthood and Religious Life* (Chicago: Loyola University Press, 1964), 65–106.

89. Conrad Baars, *How to Treat and Prevent the Crisis in the Priesthood* (Chicago: Franciscan Herald Press, 1972), 10–11, 35.

90. Reprinted in Thomas P. Doyle, A. W. Richard Sipe, and Patrick J. Wall, *Sex, Priests, and Secret Codes: The Catholic Church's 2,000-Year Paper Trail of Sexual Abuse* (Los Angeles: Volt Press, 2002), 99–174.

91. Ibid., 8.

92. Ibid., 27.

93. Ibid., 50.

94. Dawn Fallik, "Ex-Seminarian's Charges Lead to Removal of Priest," *St. Louis Post-Dispatch*, March 8, 2002; Rose, *Goodbye, Good Men*, 23.

95. Peter McDonough and Eugene C. Bianchi, *Passionate Uncertainty: Inside the American Jesuits* (Berkeley: University of California Press, 2003); Berry, *Lead Us Not into Temptation*.

96. Berry, *Lead Us Not into Temptation*, 271–72; Rose, *Goodbye, Good Men*, passim.

97. Donald B. Cozzens, *The Changing Face of the Priesthood: A Reflection on the Priest's Crisis of Soul* (Collegeville, MN: The Liturgical Press, 2000), 18, 101.

98. Rose, *Goodbye, Good Men*, 56, 170.

99. Ibid., 59; Paul Likoudis, "Seminarians Were 'Fresh Meat' for Faculty," *The Wanderer*, May 9, 1996.

100. Norman Weslin, *The Gathering of the Lambs* (Boulder, CO: Weslin, 2000), 102.

101. Lesley Payne, "Salt for Their Wounds," *Catholic World Report*, February 1997.

102. Rose, *Goodbye, Good Men*, 23.

103. Pamela Schaeffer, "Court OKs Harassment Suit," *National Catholic Reporter*, December 17, 1999.

104. Mark D. Jordan, *The Silence of Sodom: Homosexuality in Modern Catholicism* (Chicago: University of Chicago Press, 2002).

105. J.H.H. Weiler, *Un 'Europa cristiana': Un saggio esplorativo* [Christian Europe: An Exploratory Essay], 2003, quoted in George Weigel, *The Cube and the Cathedral: Europe, America and Politics Without God* (New York: Basic Books, 2005), 72–74.

106. Jenkins, *God's Continent*, 88–89.

107. Andy Park, "What the Mega Church Can Teach You," *Christianity Magazine*, August 2006.

108. Stephen Hunt, *The Alpha Enterprise: Evangelism in a Post-Christian Era* (London: Ashgate, Publishing, 2004).

109. Jenkins, *God's Continent*, 84.

110. Hunt, *The Alpha Enterprise*, 9.

111. Jenkins, *God's Continent*, 93.

112. Ibid., 75.

113. Gordon Urquhart, *The Pope's Armada: Unlocking the Secrets of Mysterious and Powerful New Sects in the Church* (New York: Prometheus Books, 1999).

114. Jenkins, *God's Continent*, 68.

115. "Answering Prayers Poland Is Bucking the Europe-Wide Decline in Vocations, and Its Priests Are in Demand," UK *Guardian*, March 15, 2006; "Poland Digs In Against Tide Toward Secularism," *Chicago Tribune*, March 23, 2006; Jenkins, *God's Continent*, 57.

116. "Where Nothing Is Sacred," *Los Angeles Times*, July 14, 2003.

117. "The History of Christ for All Nations," http://us.cfan.org/History.aspx.

118. "Sharia-related Killings and Carnage in Kaduna Reenact Deadly Prologue to Nigeria-Biafra War of 1967," http://www.usafricaonline.com/shariashowdown_chido.html.

119. "The Book They Used to Burn Now Fires New Revolution of Faith in China," December 8, 2007, www.timesonline.co.uk/tol/comment/faith/article3019026.ece?pr.

120. Thomas F. O'Brien, *Making the Americas: The United States and Latin America in the Age of Revolutions to the Era of Globalization* (Albuquerque: University of New Mexico Press, 2007), 153.

121. Ibid., 193.

122. Ibid., 301.

123. Ibid., 276.

124. A similar trend was apparent in America. Laity in the United Church of Christ, for example, where membership was sinking, had "great difficulty" identifying anything distinctive about their denomination, according to a 1985 study. William M. Newman, "The Meanings of Merger: Denominational Identity in the United Church of Christ," in Jackson Car-

roll and Wade Clark Roof, eds., *Beyond Establishment: Protestant Identity in a Post-Protestant Age* (Louisville, KY: Westminster/John Knox Press, 1993), 296–307.

125. Reeves, *Empty Church*, 11; Kenneth L. Woodward, "Dead End for the Mainline?," *Newsweek*, August 9, 1993.

126. Dave Shiflett, *Exodus: Why Americans Are Fleeing Liberal Churches for Conservative Christianity* (New York: Sentinel, 2005), xiii–xiv.

127. Ibid., 55.

128. Robert Bezilla, ed., *Religion in America: 1992–1993* (Princeton, NJ: Princeton Religion Research Center, 1993), 10, 18, 22, 36, 55, 66.

129. *USA Today*, April 1, 1994.

130. Reeves, *Empty Church*, 52–53; George Barna, *Revolution* (Wheaton, IL: Tyndale House, 2005), 32.

131. George Gilder, "Breaking the Box," *National Review*, August 15, 1994, 40; *Wall Street Journal*, February 6, 1995; *Milwaukee Journal*, May 26, 1993.

132. Cindy Guier, "Christian Acts Make Strides in Otherwise Down Market," *Amusement Business*, September 10, 2001, http://www.allbusiness.com/services/amusement-recreation-services /4563496-1.html; Philip Rood, "Christian Music Sales Rise in 2006," January 5, 2007; http://www.rapzilla.com/rz/content/view/274/79/.

133. Julia Duin, *Quitting Church: Why the Faithful Are Fleeing and What to Do About It* (Grand Rapids, MI: Baker Books, 2008), 30.

134. Barna, *Revolution*, 31.

135. Ibid., 49.

136. See Bill Hybels's comments at the "Reveal" Conference, http://www.revealnow.com/story .asp?storyid=49.

137. Berlinski, *Menace in Europe*, 86.

138. Ibid., 87. Drabble presumably was referring to World War II, although she did not explain what part about Lend-Lease she thought unnecessary or which American troops the British did not need to invade France.

139. Ibid.

140. Siegfried quoted in Victoria de Grazia, *Irresistible Empire: America's Advance Through Twentieth-Century Europe* (Cambridge, MA: Belknap Press, 2005), 15.

141. Philippe Legrain, "Europe's Mighty Economy," *The New Republic*, June 16, 2003; Robert Samuelson, "The End of Europe," *Washington Post*, June 15, 2005; Fareed Zakaria, "The Decline and Fall of Europe," *Newsweek*, February 14, 2006; Mark Leonard, *Why Europe Will Run the 21st Century* (London: Fourth Estate, 2005); Charles Kupchan, *The End of the American Era* (New York: Knopf, 2002); Timothy Smith, *France in Crisis: Welfare, Inequality, and Globalization Since 1980* (Cambridge: Cambridge University Press, 2004).

142. Werner Sombart, *Why Is There No Socialism in the United States?* (White Plains, NY: M. E. Sharpe, 1976 [1906]), 109.

143. See, for example, claims by Simon Patten of the Wharton Business School (*The New Basis of Civilization* [New York: Macmillan, 1907]), 9; Daniel M. Fox, *The Discovery of Abundance: Simon N. Patten and the Transformation of Social Theory* (Ithaca, NY: Cornell University Press for the American Historical Association, 1967).

144. Thomas L Friedman, *The World Is Flat: A Brief History of the Twenty-First Century* (New York: Picador, 2007), 409.

145. Ibid., 410.

146. Ibid., 146.

147. Ibid., 418–19.

148. Ibid., 326–27.

149. Mira Kamdar, *Planet India: How the Fastest-Growing Democracy Is Transforming America and the World* (New York: Scribner, 2007), 9.

150. Ibid., 42.

151. Ibid., 10.

152. See the descriptions of Eric Weiner, *The Geography of Bliss: One Grump's Search for the Happiest Places in the World* (New York: 12 Books, 2008), 298.

153. Friedman, *The World Is Flat*, 478.

154. Kamdar, *Planet India*, 71.

155. Weiner, *Geography of Bliss*, 301.

156. Friedman, *The World Is Flat*, 539.

157. World Bank International Finance Corporation, *Doing Business 2004* (Washington, DC: International Bank for Reconstruction and Development, 2005), 12, 19, 28, 35.

158. Ibid., 35.

159. Ibid.

160. Ibid., 61–69.

161. Ibid., 44.

162. Friedman, *The World Is Flat*, 561.

163. Ibid., 562.

164. Ibid., 421.

165. Thomas Sowell, *Ethnic America* (New York: Basic Books, 1981), 153, and his *Economic Facts and Fallacies* (New York: Basic Books, 2008), 139–40. Also see his *Race and Culture: A World View* (New York: Basic Books, 1994).

166. Michael Slackman, "A City Where You Can't Hear Yourself Scream," *International Herald Tribune*, April 14, 2008.

167. Sharon LaFraniere, "Cellphones Catapult Rural Africa to 21st Century," *New York Times*, August 25, 2005.

168. William Easterly, *The White Man's Burden: Why the West's Efforts to Aid the Rest Have Done So Much Ill and So Little Good* (New York: Penguin Press, 2006), 103.

169. World Bank, *Doing Business*, 50.

170. Daniel McGinn, *House Lust: America's Obsession with Our Homes* (New York: Currency, 2008), 43.

171. Ibid., 149.

172. "Americans Are Far More Optimistic and Have Much Higher Life Satisfaction Than Europeans, Recent Surveys Show," May 21, 2003, http://www.harrisinteractive.com/news/allnewsbydate.asp?NewsID=624.

173. Weiner, *Geography of Bliss*, 45.

174. Charles E. McTiernan, "The ENIAC Patent," *IEEE Annals of Computing* 20 (1998).

175. Paul E. Ceruzzi, *A History of Modern Computing*, 2nd ed. (Cambridge, MA: MIT Press, 2003), 53.

176. Statistics on "most visited sites" are misleading, because almost all of the top ten most visited sites are gateway sites leading elsewhere—Google, Yahoo!, Bing, and so on. Nevertheless, studies by Ogie Ogas and Sai Gaddam (*A Billion Wicked Thoughts: What the Internet Tells Us About Sexual Relationships* [New York: Plume, 2012]) have calculated that only about 4 percent of all Web activity is pornography related ("How Much of the Internet Is Actually for Porn?" *Forbes*, September 7, 2011, http://www.forbes.com/sites/julieruvolo/2011/09/07/how-much-of-the-internet-is-actually-for-porn/.

177. Matthew Zook, *The Geography of the Internet Industry: Venture Capital, Dot-coms, and Local Knowledge* (London: Wiley-Blackwell, 2005).

178. For example, *The Matrix* (1999), *The Thirteenth Floor* (1999), or *The Net* (1995), while still others explored the tensions between increasingly capable computers and their ability to "become human" (*Bicentennial Man* [1999], *AI: Artificial Intelligence* [2001], *I, Robot* [2004]—all preceded by *2001: A Space Odyssey* and its creepy HAL computer [1968]). Standing in opposition to these threats are hackers who constituted either the sympathetic outlaws of the day (*Hackers* [1997]) or the rogue threats of living outside the structures of order (*Swordfish* [2001], *Live Free or Die Hard* [2007]).

179. Eric Gibson, et al., "Effect of Nonviable Infants on the Infant Mortality Rate in Philadel-

phia, 1992," *American Journal of Public Health* 90 (August 2000): 1303. For more on the measurement problems involved in infant mortality, see Journard, et al., "Health Status Determinants," 47–49; Kramer, et al., "Registration Artifacts in International Comparisons of Infant Mortality"; and H. E. Frech and Richard D. Miller Jr., *The Productivity of Health Care and Pharmaceuticals: An International Comparison* (Washington, DC: American Enterprise Institute, 1999), 28–29. In a comparison reported by Korbin Liu and Marilyn Moon, a small change in definition (combining infant mortality and stillbirths) moved the United States from eighteenth to fifteenth in infant mortality rate rankings and moved Japan from first to third. See Liu, et al., "International Infant Mortality Rankings,"109. While in the rich countries, life expectancy is probably better measured than infant mortality, this relationship reverses in poor countries. In those countries, life expectancy is generally derived from infant mortality applied to model life tables, not any actual count of age-specific mortality. See Lant Pritchett and Lawrence H. Summers, "Wealthier Is Healthier," *Journal of Human Resources* 31 (1996) 858–59. In a study of the major problems done by the Organization for Economic Development and Cooperation—especially the country-specific conclusions—a study of the major problems showed the country-specific conclusions to be unreliable. "Many external factors that influence health outcomes are either omitted or poorly measured. The net effect is to underweight the role that non–health care factors play in determining health. And since the United States scores relatively poorly on most of these external measures, omitting them or not adequately controlling for them increases the apparent relative inefficiency of the US health care system and probably biases the estimated productivity of health care as well." See H. E. Frech, Stephen T. Parente, and John Hoff, "US Health Care: A Reality Check on Cross-Country Comparisons," American Enterprise Institute, July 11, 2012, http://www.aei.org/outlook/health/global-health/us-health-care-a-reality-check-on-cross-country-comparisons/.

180. Brett Swanson and George Gilder, "Unleashing the 'Exaflood,'" *Wall Street Journal*, February 22, 2008.

181. George W. Bush and Mickey Herskowitz, *A Charge to Keep: My Journey to the White House* (New York: William Morrow, 2001); Paul Kengor, *God and George W. Bush* (New York: HarperPerennial, 2005).

182. Bill Sammon, *At Any Cost: How Al Gore Tried to Steal the Election* (Washington, DC: Regnery, 2001).

183. James V. Grimaldi and Soberto Suro, "Risky Bush Strategy Paid Off," *Washington Post*, December 17, 2000.

184. "Five Weeks of History," *USA Today*, December 14, 2000; *Bush v. Gore*, 531 U.S. 98 (2000).

185. "The Judicial View," http://judicialview.com/Court-Cases/Civil-Procedure/Democratic-National-Committee-v-Republican-National-Committee/10/201975.

186. See, for example, "Karl Rove Admits Mistake in Advising Bush on Iraq Invasion Response," *Huffington Post*, http://www.politicsdaily.com/2010/03/03/karl-rove-admits-mistake-in-advising-bush-on-iraq-invasion-respo/. Conservative radio host Rush Limbaugh repeatedly warned that the failure to respond to the torrent of attacks would cripple the Bush presidency.

187. Subsequently, a grand jury would find I. Lewis "Scooter" Libby guilty of perjury and obstruction of justice, for which he was sentenced to thirty months in prison. Armitage, the actual leaker, was never disciplined. See *United States of America v. I. Lewis Libby*, also known as "Scooter Libby" (Case No. 1:2005-cr-00394-RBW). See also Valerie Plame Wilson and Laura Rozen, *Fair Game: How a Top CIA Agent Was Betrayed by Her Own Government* (New York: Simon & Schuster, 2010). In fact, Plame's name had been in the public as an operative well before the date in question, and Bush's reference in a speech—that agents of Iraq were seeking to obtain "yellowcake" uranium from Niger—was proven true. See also Dick Cheney and Liz Cheney, *In My Time: A Personal and Political Memoir* (New York: Threshold, 2012).

188. Interview with Charles Calomiris, September 18, 2001.

189. Owen Moritz, "Chilling Tapes of Bravest in WTC," New York *Daily News*, November 16, 2002.

190. Lisa Beamer, *Let's Roll! Ordinary People, Extraordinary Courage* (Wheaton, IL: Tyndale House, 2002).

191. *Clear the Skies—9/11 Air Defense*, director Peter Molloy, 2005.

192. "America's Chaotic Road to War"; Nancy Gibbs, "Special Report: The Day of the Attack," *Time*, September 12, 2001, located at http://www.time.com/time/world/article/0,8599, 174655–1,00.html.

193. Ibid.

194. George Tenet, *At the Center of the Storm: My Years at the CIA* (New York: Harper, 2007), passim.

195. Ibid.

196. Posner, *Why America Slept*, 30; Richard Miniter, *Losing Bin Laden: How Bill Clinton's Failures Unleashed Global Terror* (Washington, DC: Regnery, 2003).

197. Bill Sammon, *Fighting Back* (Washington, DC: Regnery, 2002), 106, 131.

198. "The 9/11 Commission Report," June 22, 2004, http://www.9-11commission.gov/report/911Report.pdf.

199. "Bin Laden Determined to Strike in US," August 6, 2001, http://www.cnn.com/2004/images /04/10/whitehouse.pdf.

200. "The 9/11 Commission Report," chapter 6.

201. Peter Navarro and Aron Spencer, "September 11, 2001: Assessing the Costs of Terrorism," *Milken Institute Review*, Fourth Quarter, 2001, 17–31; Steven Brill, *After* (New York: Simon & Schuster, 2003).

202. George W. Bush, National Cathedral Speech, September 14, 2001, in Larry Schweikart, Dave Dougherty, and Michael Allen, eds., *The Patriot's History Reader* (New York: Sentinel, 2011), 408–9.

203. Nancy Gibbs, "Special Report: The Day of the Attack," *Time*, September 12, 2001. See also Donald Rumsfeld, *Known and Unknown: A Memoir* (New York: Sentinel, 2011).

204. Transcript of Hearing, 9/11 Commission, April 8, 2004, Testimony of Condoleezza Rice, http://www.9-11commission.gov/archive/hearing9/9-11Commission_Hearing_2004-04 -08.htm.

205. Karl Rove, *Courage and Consequence: My Life as a Conservative in the Fight* (New York: Threshold, 2010), 298.

206. David Martin, "9/11 Bombshell: New Evidence of Iraq-Al Qaeda Ties?" *CBS News*, October 1, 2002.

207. Larry Schweikart, *48 Liberal Lies About American History (That You Probably Learned in School)* (New York: Sentinel, 2009), 63–71.

208. George W. Bush, *Decision Points* (New York: Crown, 2010), 223–41.

209. Rove, *Courage and Consequence*, 342.

210. Gary J. Schmitt and Reuel Marc Gerecht, "France: Europe's Counterterrorist Powerhouse," American Enterprise Institute Online, November 1, 2007, http://www.aei.org/publications/filter.foreign,pubID.27057/pub_detail.asp.

211. Schmitt and Gerecht, "France: Europe's Counterterrorist Powerhouse."

212. Rumsfeld, *Known and Unknown*, 595.

213. Jenkins, *God's Continent*, 211.

214. Roy Licklider, "How Civil Wars End: Questions and Methods," in Licklider, ed., *Stopping the Killing: How Civil Wars End* (New York: New York University Press, 1993), 3–19.

215. Ibid., 14.

216. Roy Licklider, "Obstacles to Peace Settlements," in Chester A. Croker, Fen Osler Hampson, and Pamela Aall, *Turbulent Peace: The Challenges of Managing International Conflict* (Washington, DC: United States Institute of Peace Press, 2001), 697–718; Paul R. Pillar, *Negotiating Peace: War Termination as a Bargaining Process* (Princeton, NJ: Princeton University Press, 1993); Stephen John Stedman, *Peacemaking in Civil War: International Mediation in Zimbabwe, 1974–1980* (Boulder, CO: Lynne Rienner, 1991) and his "The End of the Zimbabwean Civil War," in Licklider, ed., *Stopping the Killing*, 125–63; Barbara F. Walter, "The Critical Barrier to Civil War Settlement," *International Organization* 51 335–64.

217. M. Nestle, "The Ironic Politics of Obesity," *Science* 269 (February 7, 2003): 781.

218. David Pimentel and Marcia Pimentel, "Sustainability of Meat-based and Plant-based Diets and the Environment," *American Journal of Clinical Nutrition* 78 (September 2003, supplement): 660S–663S.

219. Nathan Fiala, "How Meat Contributes to Global Warming," *Scientific American*, February 4, 2009.

220. Ibid.

221. Kelly Brownell and K. B. Horgan, *Food Fight: The Inside Story of the Food Industry, America's Obesity Crisis, and What We Can Do About It* (New York: McGraw-Hill, 2004), 8.

222. J. D. Wright, et al., "Trends in Intake of Energy and Macronutrients—United States, 1971–2000," *Morbidity and Mortality Weekly Reports* 53 (February 6, 2004): 80–82.

223. Gary Taubes, *Good Calories, Bad Calories: Challenging the Conventional Wisdom on Diet, Weight Control, and Disease* (New York: Alfred A. Knopf, 2007), 234.

224. "Taking Exercise to Heart," *New York Times*, March 27, 1977; "Passion to Keep Fit: 100 Million Americans Exercising," *Washington Post*, August 31, 1980.

225. Easterly, *The White Man's Burden*, 239.

226. Ibid., 243–44.

227. Ibid., 248.

228. Theo Smart, "Cultural Obstacles to Abstinence and Being Faithful Present Challenges for PEPFAR HIV Programmes," AIDsmap News, August 2, 2006, http://www.aidsmap.com/en/news/8EE84285-0656-4BD3-B206-3D1DF9BD78CD.asp.

229. Ibid.

230. Ibid.

231. Ibid.

232. Easterly, *White Man's Burden*, 252.

233. Jeffrey Sachs, *The End of Poverty: Economic Possibilities for Our Time* (New York: Penguin, 2006).

234. "Bono's 'Humbling' Realizations about Aid, Capitalism and Nerds," *Forbes*, October 22, 2012.

235. Jean-Claude Shanda Tonme, quoted in Easterly, *White Man's Burden*, 26.

236. Gregory A. Freeman, "Bug Chasers: The Men Who Long to Be HIV+," *Rolling Stone*, January 23, 2003, and since reproduced in its entirety here: http://www.freerepublic.com/focus/news/828217/posts. Also see D. A. Moskowitz and M. E. Roloff, "The Existence of a Bug Chasing Subculture," *Culture, Health & Sexuality* 9 (2007): 347–58.

237. Matt Butts, "Chasing the Bug," August 15, 2002, http://www.themindofmatt.com/creative-works/creative-writings/chasing-the-bug.

238. Michael Fumento, *The Myth of Heterosexual AIDS* (New York: New Republic, 1990).

239. Jeremy Laurence, "Threat of World AIDS Pandemic Among Heterosexuals Is Over, Report Admits," *The Independent* (UK), June 8, 2008.

240. Iain Murray, *The Really Inconvenient Truths* (New York: Regnery, 2008), 32.

241. Henry Miller, "Rachel Carson's Deadly Fantasies," *Forbes*, September 5, 2012, http://www.forbes.com/sites/henrymiller/2012/09/05/rachel-carsons-deadly-fantasies/2/.

242. John Higginson, "From Geographical Pathology to Environmental Carcinogenesis: A Historical Reminiscence," *Cancer Letters*, 117, 1997, 133–42, and his "Rethinking the Environmental Causation of Human Cancer," *Food and Cosmetics Toxicology* 19 (October 1981): 539–48.

243. Richard Doll and Richard Peto, "The Causes of Cancer: Quantitative Estimates of Avoidable Risks of Cancer in the United States Today," *Journal of the National Cancer Institute* 66 (1981): 1191–308 (esp. 1256–60).

244. John Higginson, "Developing Concepts on Environmental Cancer: The Role of Geographical Pathology," *Environmental Mutagenesis* 5 (1983) 929–40.

245. T. H. Maugh, "Cancer and Environment: Higginson Speaks Out," *Science*, September 28, 1979, 1363–66.

246. Ibid.

247. J. O. Hill and J. C. Peters, "Environmental Contributions to the Obesity Epidemic," *Science* 299 (February 7, 2003): 1371–74.

248. Michael A. Fletcher, "The Steel Industry Forges Ahead," *New York Sun*, May 29, 2008.

249. Michael S. Malone, "The Next American Frontier," *Wall Street Journal*, May 19, 2008.

250. "Pessimism for the Future," *California Bar Journal*, November 1994, http://www.jdunder ground.com/lawpractice/thread.php?threadId=26525.

251. Maryland Judicial Task Force on Professionalism, November 10, 2003, http://www.courts .state.md.us/publications/professionalism2003.pdf.

252. Dan Ariely, *Predictably Irrational: The Hidden Forces That Shape Our Decisions* (New York: HarperCollins, 2008), 210.

253. Ibid., 205–7.

254. "Reaching the Hip-Hop Generation," The MEE Symposium, New York, March 1–2, 1993, Final (Symposium Proceedings) Report, http://eric.ed.gov/ERICWebPortal/custom/portlets /recordDetails/detailmini.jsp?_nfpb=true&_&ERICExtSearch_SearchValue_0=ED3782 83&ERICExtSearch_SearchType_0=no&accno=ED378283.

255. David Brooks, *On Paradise Drive* (New York: Simon and Schuster, 2004), 137, 112.

256. Weiner, *Geography of Bliss*, 45, and the work of Ruut Vennhoven, who is a professor of "happiness" in Holland at the Erasmus University Rotterdam Faculty of Social Sciences, cited in subsequent notes.

257. Ruut Veenhoven and Michael Hagerty, "Rising Happiness in Nations, 1946–2004: A Reply to Easterlin," *Social Indicators Research* 79 (2006): 421–36 and Vennhoven's *Happiness in Nations: Subjective Appreciation of Life in 56 Nations, 1946–1992* (Rotterdam: Risbo, 1993).

258. Ariely, *Predictably Irrational*, 91.

259. "A Different Consensus," *Wall Street Journal*, June 7, 2008.

Chapter 9: Fastest to the Bottom

1. Francis Fukuyama, *The End of History and the Last Man* (New York: Free Press, 1992), stemming from his essay of the same year, "The End of History." http://www.wesjones.com/eoh. htm.

2. Ibid.

3. Benjamin R. Barber, *Jihad vs. McWorld: Terrorism's Challenge to Democracy* (New York: Crown, 1995) and his article in the *Atlantic Monthly*, March 1992, http://www.theatlantic .com/magazine/archive/1992/03/jihad-vs-mcworld/3882/. Fukuyama's tepid response was "they can only go so far," and radical Muslims have not taken over many states. But that missed the point that the very character of radical Islam is stateless, until its final evolution of a world under Sharia law. See Fukuyama, "They Can Only Go So Far," *Washington Post*, August 24, 2008.

4. Tom Standage, *An Edible History of Humanity* (New York: Walker & Company, 2009), 192; Amartya Sen, "Democracy as a Universal Value," *Journal of Democracy* 10 (1999): 3–17.

5. Ibid., 192.

6. Frances D'Souza, "Democracy as a Cure for Famine," *Journal of Peace Research* 31 (1994): 369–73 (quotation on 371).

7. "7,200 Israeli Millionaires Today, Up 13%," *Jerusalem Post*, June 28, 2007.

8. Standage, *An Edible History of Humanity*, 222–23.

9. Carroll Quigley, *Tragedy & Hope: A History of the World in Our Time* (New York: Macmillan, 1966), 181.

10. Waverly Root and Richard de Rochemont, *Eating in America: A History* (New York: Ecco Press, 1995), 462.

11. Steve H. Hanke and Alex K. F. Kwok, "On the Measurement of Zimbabwe's Hyperinflation," *The Cato Journal*, Spring/Summer 2009, 353–64. The Zimbabwean unemployment rate was triple that of Rwanda (http://www.indexmundi.com/zimbabwe/unemployment_ rate.html).

12. Deroy Murdock, "Rwanda's Economic Miracle," *National Review Online*, December 13, 2010.

13. Peter Doggett, *There's a Riot Going On: Revolutionaries, Rock Stars, and the Rise and Fall of the '60s* (New York: Canongate, 2007), 252.

14. Martin Meredith, *The Fate of Africa: A History of Fifty Years of Independence* (New York: Public Affairs, 2005), 468.

15. Jama Mohamed Ghalib, *The Cost of Dictatorship: The Somali Experience* (New York: Lilian Barber Press, 1995).

16. William Easterly, *The White Man's Burden: Why the West's Efforts to Aid the Rest Have Done So Much Ill and So Little Good* (New York: Penguin, 2007), 330. Easterly, a harsh critic of Western policies in general and of American, especially Republican, policies in particular, seems to ignore the profound and painful reality that *only* Western involvement in most of these countries provided any progress at all.

17. "South Africa's Apartheid Land Fix Withers in Fields," Reuters, April 24, 2012.

18. Victor Bulmer-Thomas, *The Economic History of Latin America Since Independence*, 2nd ed. (Cambridge: Cambridge University Press, 2003), 392.

19. Greg Gramdom, *Empire's Workshop: Latin America, the United States, and the Rise of the New Imperialism* (New York: Metropolitan Books, 2006), 58.

20. Ibid., 402.

21. Peter H. Smith, *Talons of the Eagle: Dynamics of U.S.–Latin American Relations* (New York: Oxford, 1996), 248–49.

22. Douglas E. Schoen and Michael Rowan, *The Threat Closer to Home: Hugo Chávez and the War Against America* (New York: Free Press, 2009), 1.

23. Ibid., 2.

24. Ibid., 6.

25. Ibid.

26. Bulmer-Thomas, *The Economic History of Latin America*, 282–85.

27. Ibid., 359.

28. C. Brundenius and A. Zimbalist, *The Cuban Economy: Measurement and Analysis of Socialist Performance* (Baltimore: Johns Hopkins University Press, 1989), 311.

29. "Raúl Castro pushes change for Cubans," CNN, April 26, 2008.

30. "Conversations with Chávez and Castro," *The Nation*, December 15, 2008.

31. Bulmer-Thomas, *The Economic History of Latin America*, 344.

32. Ibid., 336.

33. Larry Schweikart and Lynne Pierson Doti, *Banking in the American West from the Gold Rush to Deregulation* (Norman: University of Oklahoma Press, 1991), 209.

34. Thomas F. O'Brien, *Making the Americas: The United States and Latin America in the Age of Revolutions to the Era of Globalization* (Albuquerque: University of New Mexico Press, 2007), 302–3.

35. Easterly, *White Man's Burden*, 99.

36. "Mexico's Violence: a 12-Point Update for Travelers," August 11, 2010, http://travel.latimes.com/daily-deal-blog/index.php/mexicos-violence-a-1-7347/. Ironically, because of the massive expansion of police across the border, El Paso became one of America's safest cities by the fall of 2010, http://www.elpasotimes.com/news/ci_16675219.

37. http://www.immigrationcounters.com/.

38. John Rice, "An Old War Haunts a New Debate Between Mexico, United States," Associated Press, April 30, 2006. Several Hispanic scholars have picked up the *reconquista* motif: Rodolfo Acuña, at California State University, Northridge (*Occupied America: A History of Chicanos* [Englewood Cliffs, NJ: Prentice-Hall, 2010]), and Armando Navarro, University of California, Riverside (*The Mexicano Political Experience in Occupied Aztlán: Struggles and Change* [Lanham, MD: Alta Mira Press, 2005]).

39. Mark Krikorian, *The New Case Against Immigration: Both Legal and Illegal* (New York: Sentinel, 2008), 20.

40. Ibid., 43.

41. Ibid., 54.

42. Allan Wall, "Memo from Mexico: Spanish and the New Conquistadores," Vdare.com, February 21, 2002, http://www.vdare.com/awall/conquistadores.htm; Krikorian, *New Case Against Immigration*, 56.

43. "Liberals in Southern Arizona Seek to Form New State," Yahoo News, 5/10/2011; "A Tale of Two Counties," http://www.economist.com/node/18486323, March 31, 2011.

44. Robert E. Putnam, *"E Pluribus Unum:* Diversity and Community in the Twenty-first Century: The 2006 Johan Sytte Prize Lecture," *Scandinavian Political Studies* 30 (June 2007): 149–51, and his *Bowling Alone: The Collapse and Revival of American Community* (New York: Simon & Schuster, 2000). See also Gregory Robinson, "Mexican Americans Are Building No Walls," *Los Angeles Times*, February 29, 2004; John Lloyd, "Study Paints Bleak Picture of Ethnic Diversity," *Financial Times*, October 8, 2006.

45. Dora I. Costa and Matthew E. Kahn, "Civic Engagement and Community Heterogeneity: An Economist's Perspective," *Perspectives on Politics* 1 (March 2003): 104; Rene Boheim and Karin Mayr, "Immigration and Public Spending," IZA Discussion Paper no. 1834, November 2005; Arjun Appadurai, *Modernity at Large: Cultural Dimensions of Globalization* (Minneapolis: University of Minnesota Press, 1996), 171.

46. Pew Hispanic Center, "Survey of Mexican Migrants, Part Two: Attitudes About Voting in Mexican Elections and Ties to Mexico," March 14, 2005, http://pewhispanic.org/reports/report.php?ReportID=42.

47. Samuel Huntington, *Who Are We?* (New York: Simon & Schuster, 2004), 247–51.

48. Krikorian, *New Case Against Immigration*, 26–27.

49. Ibid., 5–6.

50. Ibid., 12.

51. Dennis Keegan and David West, *Reality Check: The Unreported Good News About America* (Washington, DC: Regnery, 2008), 160.

52. Ironically, liberal policies had contributed to a reversal of illegal immigration by 2012 in the United States as the economic malaise and fear of collapse dried up jobs ("Net Migration from Mexico Falls to Zero—and Perhaps Less," Pew Center, April 23, 2012, http://www.pewhispanic.org/2012/04/23/net-migration-from-mexico-falls-to-zero-and-perhaps-less/). The Pew Center found that since 1999, annual immigration from Mexico to the United States dropped steadily, by a fivefold factor over a decade.

53. "Obama: Health Care Reform Tied to Controlling Deficit," July 22, 2009, http://www.cbsnews.com/8301-503544_162-5181110-503544.html.

54. "Obama Underscores Need for Drastic Health Care Reform, Calls Status Quo 'Unsustainable,'" June 23, 2009, http://www.foxnews.com/politics/2009/06/23/obama-underscores-need-drastic-health-care-reform-calls-status-quo/.

55. "New Poll: The Supreme Court and the Health Care Law," June 7, 2012, http://thecaucus.blogs.nytimes.com/2012/06/07/new-poll-the-supreme-court-and-the-health-care-law/.

56. *National Federation of Independent Business et al. v. Sebelius, Secretary of Health and Human Services,* June 28, 2012, http://www.scribd.com/doc/98542275/Scotus-opinion.

57. Steven Rattner, "Beyond Obamacare," *New York Times*, September 16, 2012, http://www.nytimes.com/2012/09/17/opinion/health-care-reform-beyond-obamacare.html?_r=3&.

58. "Remarks by the President on Fiscal Policy," April 13, 2011, http://www.whitehouse.gov/the-press-office/2011/04/13/remarks-president-fiscal-policy.

59. Jay Bookman, "Why 'Death Panels' Are a Necessary Evil," *Atlanta Journal-Constitution*, April 20, 2011, http://blogs.ajc.com/jay-bookman-blog/2011/04/20/why-death-panels-are-a-necessary-evil/?cxntfid=blogs_jay_bookman_blog.

60. "Will Obamacare Bring Us Death Panels and Rationing?," *Life News*, December 7, 2012, http://www.lifenews.com/2012/12/07/will-obamacare-bring-us-death-panels-and-rationing/.

61. "Trends in End-of-Life Practices Before and After the Enactment of the Euthanasia Law in the Netherlands from 1990 to 2010; a Repeated Cross-Sectional Survey," *The Lancet*, July 11, 2010, http://dx.doi.org/10.1016/50140-6736(12)61032-4.

62. "Wrongful Life Case in Belgium," http://www.ieb-eib.org/fr/bulletins/bulletin-de-lieb-29-novembre-2010-41.html.

63. "Extreme Dieting Spreads in Asia," *USA Today*, March 30, 2010.

64. "Scientists' Elusive Goal: Reproducing Study Results," *Wall Street Journal*, December 2, 2011.

65. Ibid.

66. "Airport 'Pat-Downs' Cause Growing Passenger Backlash," *Washington Post*, November 13, 2010.

67. Ibid.

68. "Sources: U.S. Knew of Would-be Airliner Bomber's Terror Ties," Haaretz.com, December 26, 2009, http://www.haaretz.com/news/source-u-s-knew-of-would-be-airliner-bomber-s-terror-ties-1.1375.

69. Max Boot, *The Savage Wars of Peace: Small Wars and the Rise of American Power* (New York: Basic Books, 2002), 337.

70. Donald Rumsfeld, *Known and Unknown: A Memoir* (New York: Sentinel, 2011), passim.

71. "The New Way Forward in Iraq," White House, http://www.whitehouse.gov/news/releases/2007/01/20070110-3.html; Frederick Kagan, et al., "The New Way Forward," http://www.aei.org/events/eventID.1446/event_detail.asp.

72. Bill Roggio, "Anbar Rising," May 11, 2007, "The Long War Journal," http://www.longwarjournal.org/archives/2007/05/anbar_rising.php.

73. Peter Wehner, "Al-Qaeda Is Losing the War of Minds," *Financial Times*, March 4, 2008.

74. Ibid.

75. Ibid.

76. "US Soldier Suicides Outnumber Combat Deaths in 2012," *CBS News*, December 29, 2012.

77. Salma Samar Damluji, *The Architecture of the U.A.E.* (Reading, UK: 2006), quoted on wikipedia.org, http://en.wikipedia.org/wiki/Burj_Al_Arab.

78. Ibid., 37.

79. Ibid., 56.

80. Ibid., 259.

81. Clyde Prestowitz, *America's Technology Future at Risk: Broadband and Investment Strategies to Refine Innovation* (Washington, DC: Economic Strategy Institute, 2006).

82. Amar Bhidé, *The Venturesome Economy: How Innovation Sustains Prosperity in a More Connected World*(Princeton, NJ: Princeton University Press, 2008), 262.

83. Norges Bank, "Developments in Productivity Growth," *Monetary Policy Report 2/2007*, 44–47, http://www.norges-bank.no/Upload/62887/B4_developments_in_productivity_growth.pdf.

84. http://ec.europa.eu/grothandjobs/areas/ficheo5_en.htm.

85. Jeff Jacoby, "Made in the USA," Townhall.com, February 7, 2011.

86. Bhidé, *Venturesome Economy*, 288.

87. Eric von Hippel, *The Sources of Innovation* (New York: Oxford University Press, 1988) and his *Democratizing Innovation* (Cambridge, MA: MIT Press, 2005).

88. Jack D. Triplett and Barry Bosworth, *Productivity in the U.S. Services Sector: New Sources of Economic Growth* (Washington, DC: Brookings Institution Press, 2004).

89. Michael D. Bordo, Barry Eichengreen, and Douglas A. Irwin, "Is Globalization Today Really Different Than Globalization a Hundred Years Ago?," NBER Working Paper No. W7195, June 1999.

90. Anita Wolfl, "Productivity Growth in Service Industries: An Assessment of Recent Patterns and the Role of Measurement," STI Working Paper, 2003/7.

91. Bhidé, *Venturesome Economy*, 327.

92. Giovanni Peri, "Skill and Talent of Immigrants: A Comparison Between the European Union and the United States," Working Paper, July 2005, cited in Bhidé, *Venturesome Economy*, 373.

93. Niall Ferguson, *Colossus: The Rise and Fall of the American Empire* (London: Allan Lane, 2004), 19.

94. Lee Eisenberg, *Shoptimism: Why the American Consumer Will Keep on Buying No Matter What* (New York: Free Press, 2009), 27.

95. "Christmas 2012 Online Shopping Survey Report," Econsultancy, January 2013, http://econsultancy.com/us/reports/christmas-2012-online-shopping-survey-report.

96. "Middle Class Building China's Do-It-Yourself Market," *Dayton Daily News*, December 24, 2006.

97. "China's New Capitalism," *BusinessWeek*, September 27, http://www.businessweek.com/1999/99_39/b3648087.htm.

98. "Richest Village in China a Capitalist Commune," SeattlePI Asia, September 28, 2009, http://www.seattlepi.com/national/1104ap_as_china_rich_at_60.html.

99. Ted C. Fishman, *China, Inc.* (New York: Scribner, 2005), 11–12.

100. Ibid., 48.

101. Gordon G. Chang, *The Coming Collapse of China* (London: Arrow, 2002), 54–55.

102. "Move Over, Michigan, China Is the World's Next Rust Belt," *Forbes*, December 10, 2012.

103. Chang, *Coming Collapse of China*, 168.

104. Ibid., 113.

105. Helen Wang, "Myth of China's Manufacturing Prowess," March 2010, http://helenwang.net/2010/myth-of-manufacturing/.

106. Guy Sorman, *The Empire of Lies: The Truth About China in the Twenty-First Century* (New York: Encounter Books, 2008), 28–29.

107. Ibid., 30.

108. Ibid., 32.

109. Ibid., 44.

110. Ibid.

111. Ibid., 103.

112. Sorman, *Empire of Lies*, 107.

113. Fishman, *China, Inc.*, 74.

114. Keegan and West, *Reality Check*, 31–41.

115. "The Chinese Coal Monster—Running out of Puff," The Oil Drum, November 20, 2010, http://europe.theoildrum.com/node/7123.

116. Eric Fish, "China's 'Come to Jesus' Moment," *Foreign Policy* online, February 15, 2012.

117. Ibid.

118. Nanlai Cao, *Constructing China's Jerusalem: Christians, Power, and Place in Contemporary Wenzhou* (Palo Alto, CA: Stanford University Press, 2010).

119. Philip Yancey, "Discreet and Dynamic," *Christianity Today*, August 23, 2010; Alan Hirsch, *The Forgotten Ways: Reactivating the Missional Church* (Grand Rapids, MI: Brazos Press, 2006), 68–69; http://www.barna.org/FlexPage.aspx?Page=BarnaUpdateNarrowPreview&BarnaUpdateID=241.

120. "Church Attendance Has Bottomed Out: Research Shows that the Long Decline in Church Attendance Has Finally Stabilised," *Guardian UK*, September 11, 2010.

121. "Generation X More Loyal to Religion," *Science Daily*, August 26, 2010.

122. Karen L. Gushta, *The War on Children* (Fort Lauderdale, FL: Coral Ridge Ministries, 2009), 34.

123. "Puberty Too Soon: Girls Are Maturing Faster Than Ever, and Doctors Aren't Sure Why," *USA Today*, April 11, 2011.

124. CNN Money, October 14, 2010, "Boomerang Kids: 85% of College Grads Move Home."

125. "Japan Goes from Dynamic to Disheartened," *New York Times*, October 17, 2010.

126. Ibid.

127. "Lack of Babies Could Mean the Extinction of the Japanese People," Fox News, May 11, 2012, http://www.foxnews.com/world/2012/05/11/lack-babies-could-mean-extinction-japanese-people/.

128. "Shutting Themselves In," *New York Times*, January 15, 2006.

129. Ibid.

130. Thomas Sowell, *The Housing Boom and Bust* (New York: Basic Books, 2009), 10.

131. George W. Bush, *Decision Points* (New York: Crown, 2010), 458–59.

132. Ibid.

133. Bernard Goldberg, *A Slobbering Love Affair: The True (And Pathetic) Story of the Torrid Romance Between Barack Obama and the Mainstream Media* (Washington, DC: Regnery, 2009).

134. Barack Obama, "A World That Stands as One," July 24, 2008, http://www.spiegel.de/international/germany/obama-s-berlin-speech-a-world-that-stands-as-one-a-567920.html.

135. *Der Spiegel*, http://www.spiegel.de/international/world/0,1518,727235,00.html.

136. Dan Gainor, "Obama's Speeches—Obama Mentions Self Nearly 1,200 Times," FOXNews .com, September 23, 2009, http://foxnews.com/opinion/2009/09/23/dan-gainor-obama-speeches-ego/; David Limbaugh, *Crimes Against Liberty: An Indictment of President Barack Obama* (Washington, DC: Regnery, 2010), 17.

137. Limbaugh, *Crimes Against Liberty*, 17–19.

138. "The White House Canon," *Slate*, April 22, 2009, http://www.slate.com/articles/news_and_politics/politics/2009/04/the_white_house_canon.html.

139. Ibid., 23.

140. Jason Mattera, *Obama Zombies: How the Liberal Machine Brainwashed My Generation* (New York: Threshold Books, 2010), passim.

141. Vidya Rao, "Oprah Effect: Can Celebs Sway Voters?" MSNBC, October 25, 2008, http://www.msnbc.msn.com/id/27227264//; Mattera, *Obama Zombies*, 56–58.

142. "Youth Vote in 2008 Election Ranked Among the Highest Ever, Data Show," *The Chronicle of Higher Education*, April 29, 2009.

143. Limbaugh, *Crimes Against Liberty*, 296.

144. "Obamacare More Unpopular Now Than 2010," http://www.realclearpolitics.com/2012/10/30/obamacare_more_unpopular_now_than_2010_294571.html.

145. Matt Cover, "Obama's New Claim That 30 Million 'Cannot' Get Health Insurance Not Supported by Census Bureau," CNS News, September 22, 2009, http://www.cnsnews.com/news/article/54329; Philip Klein, "Obama Lies on Single-Payer, Disses Post Office," *The American Spectator*, August 11, 2009, http://spectator.org/blog/2009/08/11/obama-lies-on-single-payer-dis; and Limbaugh, *Crimes Against Liberty*, ch. 3, vs. Obama's claims in the State of the Union; Cato Editors, "State of the Union Fact Check," Cato Institute, January 28, 2010; http://blog.heritage.org/2010/01/28/state-of-the-union-fact-check/.

146. Bush, *Decision Points*, 468.

147. Limbaugh, *Crimes Against Liberty*, 258.

148. Peter Doggett, *There's a Riot Going On: Revolutionaries, Rock Stars, and the Rise and Fall of the '60s* (New York: Canongate, 2007), 256. Of course, actors and musicians often were clueless as to what constituted real fascism. The Who's Roger Daltrey once said, "You need a Hitler figure [today] to just say, 'This is what it is.' And Hitler was right for Germany at the time, they were really being shit on. He turned out mad at the end, but when he started . . . he just did marvellous things for the German people" (263).

149. Barack Obama, "Remarks at Cairo University," June 4, 2009, http://www.whitehouse.gov/the_press_office/Remarks-by-the-President-at-Cairo-University-6-04-09/.

150. Limbaugh, *Crimes Against Liberty*, 335; Fouad Ajami, "The Arabs Have Stopped Applauding Obama," *Wall Street Journal*, November 29, 2009.

151. Limbaugh, *Crimes Against Liberty*, 328.

152. Ibid., 329.

153. "Barack and Michelle Obama Decline Dinner with the Sarkozys," www.timesonline.uk/tol/news/world/europe/article6434141.ece.

154. "Sources Say Sarkozy Finds Obama's Iran Policy 'Arrogant,' Utterly Immature," ABC News Political Punch, October 28, 2008, http://blogs.abcnews.com/politicalpunch/2008/10/sources-say-sat.html.

155. "Arrogant Obama Alienates Friends," *The New Delhi Daily Pioneer*, April 11, 2010, http://www.daily-pioneer.com/248392/Arrogant-Obama-alienates-friends.html.

156. "Obama's Middle East Policy in Tatters," *USA Today*, March 3, 2013.

157. "America's Love Affair with Obama Is Over," November 5, 2011, http://politics.usnews
.com/opinion/mzuckerman/articles/2010/11/05/mort-zuckerman-americas-love-affair
-with-obama-is-over.html.

158. James W. Ceaser, "A Genealogy of Anti-Americanism," *The Public Interest*, Summer 2003,
3–18 (quotation on 4).

159. Ibid., 12.

160. Ibid., 13.

161. Kevin Mattson, *What the Heck Are You Up To, Mr. President?* (New York: Bloomsbury, 2009),
7. Carter contributed to the malaise: as his own pollster, Pat Caddell, showed, the number
of Americans he considered "long-term pessimists" *grew rapidly* during Carter's administration (22).

162. "Despite Frustrations, Americans Are Pretty Darned Happy," *Science Daily*, July 1, 2008;
Eric Weiner, *The Geography of Bliss: One Grump's Search for the Happiest Place in the World*
(New York: Twelve Books, 2008).

163. Peter H. Schuck and James Q. Wilson, *Understanding America: The Anatomy of an Exceptional
Nation* (New York: Public Affairs, 2008); "The Muslim West Facts Project," June 2008, www
.muslimwestfacts.com/nwf/108028/Young-Arabs-Poised-Maximize-Their-Potential
.aspx.

164. Mark Aguiar and Erik Hurst, "Measuring Trends in Leisure: The Allocation of Time over
Five Decades," Federal Reserve Bank of Boston Working Paper #06-2, January 2006.

165. Harold Evans with Gail Buckland and David Lefer, *They Made America: From the Steam
Engine to the Search Engine: Two Centuries of Innovators* (Boston: Little, Brown, 2004), 118–
25; William Russell Mead, *God and Gold: Britain, America, and the Making of the Modern
World* (New York: Knopf, 2007), 140.

166. Doggett, *There's a Riot Going On*, 9.

167. Barbara Julian, "Globish, Globish Everywhere: How English Became the World's Language," *The Ottawa Citizen*, August 1, 2010; Robert McCrum, *Globish: How the English Language Became the World's Language* (New York: Norton, 2011).

168. Samuel P. Huntington, "The Clash of Civilizations?," *Foreign Affairs* 72 (Summer 1993):
22–49.

169. Samuel P. Huntington, *The Clash of Civilizations and the Remaking of World Order* (New
York: Simon & Schuster, 1996), 20–21.

170. Ibid., 22.

171. Robin Wright, *Rockin' the Casbah: Rage and Rebellion Across the Islamic World* (New York: Simon & Schuster, 2011), 21.

172. "Egyptian Cleric Safwat Higazi Launches MB Candidate Muhamma Mursi's Campaign,"
May 1, 2012, MEMRI TV, http://www.memritv.org/clip/en/3431.htm.

173. "Egypt Constitutional Vote: 'Things Are Definitely Worse Than Under the Old Regime,'"
UK Telegraph, December 24, 2012.

174. "Christianity 'Close to Extinction' in Middle East," *UK Telegraph*, December 24, 2012; Rupert Shortt, *Christianophobia: A Faith Under Attack* (London: Rider Books, 2012).

175. See the Pew "Economic Mobility Project," 2007, 2011, http://www.pewstates.org/projects/
economic-mobility-project-328061.

176. Neill Howe and William Strauss, *Millennials Rising: The Next Generation* (New York: Vintage, 2000).

177. "Millennials Might Not Be So Special After All, Study Finds," *USA Today*, March 15, 2012.

178. "American Dream Fades for Generation Y Professionals," Bloomberg, December 12, 2012.

179. "Americans Express Historic Negativity Toward U.S. Government," Gallup Poll, September 26, 2011.

180. "Social Security Ran $47.8B Deficit in FY 2012; Disabled Workers Hit New Record in
December: 8,827,795," *CBS News*, December 27, 2012.

181. "What, Me Worry? Young Adults Get Self-Esteem from Debt," Ohio State University Research News, June 7, 2011.

182. "How College Students Think They Are More Special Than EVER: Study Reveals Rocketing Sense of Entitlement on U.S. Campuses," UK *Mail*, January 5, 2013.

183. "Columbine Documents," http://denver.rockymountainnews.com/pdf/900columbinedocs.pdf.

184. "Report of the Virginia Tech Review Panel," 2007, http://www.governor.virginia.gov/TempContent/techPanelReport.cfm.

185. "Opinion: The Rise and Decline of Mass Shootings," http://www.aolnews.com, December 20, 2012; Grant Duwe, *Mass Murder in the United States: A History* (Jefferson, NC: McFarland and Company, 2007).

186. Barack Obama, campaign speech, Roanoke, Virginia, July 13, 2012.

187. "White House Data Debunk Myth Bush Cuts Built Deficit," *Investor's Business Daily*, November 30, 2012.

188. "How Obama Won Reelection," *New York Times*, November 7, 2012, http://www.nytimes.com/interactive/2012/11/07/us/politics/obamas-diverse-base-of-support.html?_r=0.

189. "French Panel Overturns 75 Percent Tax on Ultrarich," Yahoo Finance, December 29, 2012, http://finance.yahoo.com/news/french-panel-overturns-75-percent-104219484.html.

190. Fotios Pasiouras, *Greek Banking: From the Pre-Euro Reforms to the Financial Crisis and Beyond* (London: Palgrave Macmillan, 2012).

191. "Merkel Makes Euro Indispensable Turning Crisis into Opportunity," *Bloomberg Businessweek*, December 9, 2011; "EU Risks Being Split Apart, Says Sarkozy," *Irish Times*, December 12, 2011.

192. "Spanish Commissioner Lashes Out at Core Eurozone States," September 9, 2011, http://euobserver.com/economic/113568.

193. "Unemployment in Euro Zone Rises to a New High," *New York Times*, November 20, 2012, http://www.nytimes.com/2012/12/01/business/global/daily-euro-zone-watch.html?pagewanted=2&_r=0.

194. "Analyst Makes Bombshell Prediction of $50 Oil, and More Production Than We Could Possibly Know What to Do With," *Business Insider*, December 27, 2012.

195. "Unemployed? Go to North Dakota," *USA Today*, August 27, 2011; Leonardo Maugeri, "Oil: The Next Revolution," Geopolitics of Energy Project, Harvard University, June 2012.

196. Maugeri, "Oil: The Next Revolution," 1.

197. Ibid., 6.

198. David Limbaugh, *The Great Destroyer* (Washington, DC: Regnery, 2012), 207.

199. Ibid., 208.

200. Ibid., 209.

201. Ibid., 220.

202. Ibid., 244.

203. Ibid., 247; "Solyndra Solar Company Fails After Getting Controversial Loan Guarantees," *Washington Post*, October 3, 2011.

204. Limbaugh, *Great Destroyer*, 252.

205. Brian Lee Crowley, Jason Clemens, and Niels Veldhuis, "The Canadian Beacon: What Washington Can Learn from Ottawa," *The Insider* (Heritage Foundation), Summer/Fall 2011, 4–8.

206. Milton and Rose Friedman, *The Tyranny of the Status Quo* (New York: Avon, 1985).

207. 2011 DuPage County Real Estate Tax Bill, Gwen Henry, County Collector, May 2012.

208. Kauffman Foundation (Robert Fairlie, author), "Entrepreneurial Activity," 2011, http://www.kauffman.org/uploadedfiles/kiea_2012_report.pdf.

209. It was completely consistent with Hollywood's view of itself—and entirely predictable—that *Argo*, a film about a phony movie company that had assistance from the Canadians to rescue Americans during the 1979 Iran hostage crisis, won the Academy Award for best picture. What could be more apropos than Hollywood riding to the rescue of Americans who were victims of a bad foreign policy that supported dictators?

Conclusion

1. Ayn Rand, *Atlas Shrugged* (New York: Random House, 1957).

2. Suzanne Collins, *The Hunger Games* (New York: Scholastic Press, 2008)

3. Francis Fukuyama, *The End of History and the Last Man* (New York: Free Press, 1992).

4. Todd Starnes, "Teacher Forced to Remove Reagan Quote, Bible Verses," Fox News, January 13, 2013, http://radio.foxnews.com/toddstarnes/top-stories/5332.html.

5. *The Economist* 406 (January 5–11, 2013).

INDEX